'I'm a geni... field... it comes to my profession. I know that I am a genius'

...is Students Jumping

...orsemanship

...aching's king...

...axes, bullies...

...lps class her...

GEORGE MORRIS, PRIX DES NATI...

EQUESTRIAN

New Canaan Boy Win... Trophy For Kindness In Handling Horses

Morris, a director of the U.S. Equestrian Team for... for American riders — forward seat, strong leg and... ...'s the style that has become stan... ...ct with the bit. Special to...

...s left his mark... on show jumping in U.S...

■ The former rider, 61, continues to have...

UNRELENTING

Also by George H. Morris

Hunter Seat Equitation

The American Jumping Style

Every Round Counts (with John Strassburger)

George H. Morris Teaches Beginners to Ride

Classical Riding with George H. Morris

Teaching and Training the American Way (DVD)

Dressage for Jumpers (DVD)

UNRELENTING

*The Real Story: Horses, Bright Lights,
and My Pursuit of Excellence*

George H. Morris

with Karen Robertson Terry

Foreword by Chris Kappler

TRAFALGAR SQUARE
North Pomfret, Vermont

First published in 2016 by
Trafalgar Square Books
North Pomfret, Vermont 05053

Disclaimer of Liability

The authors and publisher shall have neither liability nor responsibility to any person or entity with respect to any loss or damage caused or alleged to be caused directly or indirectly by the information contained in this book. While the book is as accurate as the authors can make it, there may be errors, omissions, and inaccuracies.

The authors and publisher have made every effort to obtain a release from photographers whose images appear in this book. In some cases, however, the photographers were not known or could not be contacted. Should additional photographers be identified, they will be credited in future editions of this book.

Trafalgar Square Books encourages the use of approved safety helmets in all equestrian sports and activities.

Library of Congress Cataloging-in-Publication Data

Names: Morris, George H., author. | Terry, Karen Robertson, author.

Title: Unrelenting : the real story : horses, bright lights, and my pursuit of excellence / George H Morris with Karen Robertson Terry.

Description: North Pomfret, Vermont : Trafalgar Square Books, 2016. | Includes index.

Identifiers: LCCN 2015031427 | ISBN 9781570767104 (hardback)

Subjects: LCSH: Morris, George H. | Horsemen and horsewomen—United States—Biography. | Horse trainers—United States—Biography. | Horse sports. | Horse-shows. | Horsemanship. | Horses—Training. | BISAC: BIOGRAPHY & AUTOBIOGRAPHY / Sports.

Classification: LCC SF284.52.M67 M67 2016 | DDC 798.2092—dc23 LC record available at http://lccn.loc.gov/2015031427

All photographs courtesy of George H. Morris unless otherwise noted.

Front cover main photograph by Alix Coleman. Background image and back cover photograph courtesy of George H. Morris.

Book design by DOQ
Cover design by RM Didier
Index by Andrea M. Jones (www.jonesliteraryservice.com)
Typefaces: Neutra, Bembo

Printed in China

10 9 8 7 6 5 4 3 2 1

This book is dedicated to all the worthy horsemen, students, and friends who are not mentioned herein. There simply weren't enough pages to tell all your stories, but all of them reside faithfully in my memory.

CONTENTS

FOREWORD

In 2005, George Morris took over the role of Chef d'Equipe of the U.S. Show Jumping Team. Shortly after, I received a call from a member of one of his first Nations Cup teams. "How did you do this?" the rider asked. "Chris, how did you work for George for twenty years?" As the new Chef, George was pushing limits in the pursuit of excellence. Commanding specific attitudes, turnout, and professionalism, he expected an extraordinary commitment from the riders, owners, trainers and support staff to do what it takes to dominate in international competition. I recognized immediately the intensity this rider was describing because I have felt it, in one form or another, for over thirty years. First as a junior competitor with George as my judge; then as his student, his employee and professional rider, his business partner, and ultimately his friend, I have experienced firsthand the zealous pursuit of excellence for which George is famous. "If you can take my pressure cooker," George would always say, "the Olympics will seem like nothing."

Over the years, I watched George teach hundreds of clinics, and in every one he masterfully orchestrated an atmosphere much like the one he created when he assumed the position of Chef d'Equipe. His mercilessly high expectations, daunting (sometimes fear-inducing) commentary, and willingness to play the riders off each other and off anyone who happened to be watching—whether educated auditor or innocent bystander—resulted in a highly intense, competitive environment where many a rider learned the meaning of "sink or swim." George was always a fierce competitor who believed in pushing himself and others to any manner of limits—his favorite T-shirt read, "Pain is just weakness leaving the body," and if you knew him long enough you'd come to accept that as not only true, but a desirable and achievable goal.

THE George H. Morris, as some might be inclined to describe him, is one of the last of the legendary horsemen still active—still out there, bridging the gap between the old and new worlds. He is one of the few remaining, working teachers with true, in-depth knowledge of the great figures of the past—Bert de Némethy, Captain Vladimir Littauer, Brigadier General Harry Chamberlin, Gordon Wright—as well as the rising stars of the equestrian world's future. He has taught two solid generations of our country's finest riders now; the young riders he guides today are the children of those he coached early in his career. I truly think of him as the Godfather of our sport, melding the techniques of the fine horsemen he admired through his own initial development with expertise painstakingly gained over a lifetime of study and a remarkable commitment to style and effectiveness.

George is the only person still riding and training and teaching who has been able to constantly, publicly evolve over such an extended period, not only as a horseman, but as an individual. When you really think about it, such sustained progress in the limelight and continual interest in effecting change in a single sport is an extraordinary accomplishment. Many of his contemporaries—other great riders who contributed during George's heyday as a competitor and trainer—aren't around anymore. The sport has changed significantly over time, from the genteel pageantry of its early days, when shows were formal social occasions, to today's common diet of near-constant showing with little time earmarked for schooling and horse-care fundamentals. And with this new reality in mind, I can't think of anything as valuable to our future as George's continued contributions and commitment.

George not only still wants to teach, he brings tremendous enthusiasm to it. I've watched countless times as, after hours of back-to-back lessons or when a clinic is wrapping up for the day, a rider asks for help or expresses interest in trying to get something right—and George will always drop everything to stay back, answer questions, and further instruct. If you really want to learn, he is absolutely willing to educate you.

This book, George's story as he has finally chosen to tell it, gives us a look "behind the curtain," exposing his many faces. There is the General-George-Patton-like leader with a sharp interest in history and an army-like precision in identifying targets and moving forward toward them, as well as a dedication to methodical, mechanical process. Then, there is the maniacal mentality that

George is notorious for—a compulsion for control coupled with a tendency to go berserk or become irate for seemingly no reason (I might say there is always a reason) and sudden, volatile, temperamental behavior. And, some will find it surprising to meet George as a fast-living playboy, who, in a time when it was not accepted by many to adopt or pursue a gay lifestyle, came out in a way that allowed him to abide by the strict boundaries of his professional life while still exploring his creative, tempestuous, spontaneous self. Not an easy balance, as is evidenced in many of the stories you'll find in the pages ahead. Finally, there is the master operative: a deft handler with an uncanny ability to measure and read people, always coming up with exactly what is needed at the right time— whether a pat on the back or a sharp setdown. His "feel" for dealing with people and situations, his insight into others' mindsets, is simply unmatched.

I've known George and all his faces since 1984. He has been like a second father to me, guiding me from a green junior to an Olympic champion to a successful professional—a constant in my life that both instigated growth and preserved principles. Looking back, I can't imagine navigating the path I've chosen without his tutelage or his friendship. I value both to no end. His influence has inspired in me a desire to carry on his legacy: to be correct, to do it better, and to always continue learning and striving for a better understanding of horses and horsemanship—as he always has.

I think that deep down, if George wanted to be known and remembered for only one thing, he would be happiest knowing that he had done more for the horse than anyone else before him. When we look at the impact the widespread system of riding he created and helped proliferate has had, and when we consider the meticulous methods of horse care and handling that have filtered out of his barn, his clinics, and his teachings, we might indeed be awed by the extent of his influence. While there are many of us who have writhed in the throes of one of his tantrums or withered in the face of a scathing remark, there is one who ultimately benefits from his perfectionism, attention to detail, and desire to get it right.

And, indeed, that is the horse.

Chris Kappler

Individual Silver and Team Gold Medalist, Athens Olympics, 2004
Winner of Over 100 International Grands Prix

PREFACE

Horses have been, and continue to be, the single most powerful grounding force in my life, and I never tire of teaching or training. I've been riding for over seventy years and teaching for sixty of them, and I still get excited in the moment a perfectly orchestrated connection occurs between horse and rider. As riders, each of us seeks to create and sustain such a connection, which brings us back to the ring again and again. I've had the privilege of teaching so many gifted riders during my career and love that even after all these years, I can still be awestruck by the raw talent of a great young rider. My life's work of teaching generations of riders, many of whom became teachers or professional riders, marches on today as committed as ever before. I still teach over forty clinics a year and have several dedicated clients whom I accompany to the ring. As long as I'm able, I will continue to learn all I can and pass it on, for we are all perpetual students—of riding and of life.

The organization of this biography revealed itself quite readily. Nearly perfectly aligned with the arrival of each decade was a shift in the direction of my life or my work as a horseman. Therefore, the sections of this book are arranged by decade, representing my coming of age and evolution as a young man, including growth from a student into a rider, a teacher, and a leader.

Across these pages is printed the truth, with very few details of my journey omitted. For an intensely private person like me, it wasn't an easy choice to publish such intimate details of my life. But any tale worth telling shines with the honesty of the entire human experience. Even a fortunate life such as mine has had its moments of searching for direction, of aching vulnerability, pain, and loss.

Many thanks to the generous individuals who provided their thoughtful interviews and comments; they were an integral part of our research and added invaluable color and depth to the book. Interviewees included: Cara Anthony, Gina Arechiga, Julian Arechiga, Sue Ashe, Peggy Augustus, Sue Bauer Pinckney, Ronnie Beard, Ludger Beerbaum, Marty Baumann, Bill Berman, Georgina Bloomberg, Carlene Blunt, Ashlee Bond, Nina Bonnie, Kenneth Braddick, Buck Brannaman, David Broome, Buddy Brown, Gincy Self Bucklin, Tom Bunn, Bobby Burke, Jane Burr, Diane Carney, Maria Cassone, Missy Clark, Noel Clark, Lizzy Chesson, Brigid Colvin, Victoria Colvin, Mac Cone, Jeff Cook, Norman Dello Joio, Charlie Dennehy, Wilson Dennehy, Glenna de Rham, Lisa Deslauriers, Robert Dover, Diane Dubuc, Pamela Erdmann, Kent Farrington, Rich Fellers, Shelley Fellers, Bert Firestone, Kevin Freeman, Thomas Fuchs, Nona Garson, Tom Gayford, Karen Golding, Allan Glaser, Winifred Gray, Dianne Grod, Cornelia Guest, J. Michael Halbleib, Jen Hamilton, Cynthia Hankins, Hap Hansen, Debbie Haimowitz, Whitney Ann Harvey, Jimmy Hatcher, Arthur Hawkins, Karen Healey, Patty Heuckeroth, David Hopper, Lauren Hough, Linda Hough, Leslie Burr Howard, Deedee Drake Howard, Susie Hutchison, Marion Hulick, Tab Hunter, Sally Ike, Lisa Jacquin, Bonnie Jenkins, Martha Jolicoeur, Chris Kappler, Julie Kellam, Harriet Kennaby, Reed Kessler, Tyler Klees, Laura Kraut, Anne Kursinski, Nancy Kissinger, Kathy Kusner, Joan Laarakkers, Eric Lamaze, Jimmy Lee, Armand Leone, Peter Leone, Lynne Little, Marilyn Little, Eric Louradour, Andrew Lustig, Beezie Madden, Frank Madden, John Madden, Dan Marks DVM, Michael Matz, Meredith McLaughlin, Meredith Michaels-Beerbaum, Ian Millar, Holly Mitten, Elaine Moffat, Luca Moneta, Kathy Moore, Michaela Murphy Hoag, Tania Nagro, Jan Neuharth, Matthew Neville, Peter Neville, Kathy Newman, Clea Newman-Soderlund, Betty Oare, Timothy Ober DVM, Betsee Parker, Mason Phelps, Ludo Philippaerts, Mark Phillips, Katie Prudent, Andrew Ramsay, Jessica Ransehousen, Judy Richter, Robert Ridland, Bill Robertson, Brody Robertson, Alison Robitaille, Paul Schockemöhle, Susie Schoellkopf, Sara Cavanagh Schwartz, Amy Serridge, Anne Savino, Will Simpson, Betty Beryl Schenk, Dudley Smith, Fran Steinwedell, Francie Steinwedell-Carvin, Debbie Stephens, Kristine Stephenson, Patty Stovel, John Strassburger, Melanie Smith Taylor, Chrystine Tauber, Geoff Teall, Jan Tops, Bernie Traurig, Kiki Umla, McLain Ward, Jeffery Welles, Kenny Wheeler, John Whitaker, Louise Whitcomb, Anna Jane White-Mullin, and Jimmy Wofford.

My sincere thanks to those individuals who have kept and continue to keep my daily life at home and on the road running smoothly: Bob Gutowitz, Lisa Cole, Stan Segal, Angie Massa, and Laurie Ucello. Thanks also to my three sisters in mischief Poppe, Coca, and Tina.

I'd like to express my gratitude to Trafalgar Square Books and in particular Martha Cook, Rebecca Didier, and Caroline Robbins, who served as the impetus for this project and provided encouraging guidance at all of the critical moments.

Thanks also to the United States Equestrian Federation and to *The Chronicle of the Horse*, as each served as valuable resources during our research and fact-checking. Thank you to the photographers who graciously allowed their images to appear in this book. We have wherever possible credited photographers for their work. Most of the photos are from my personal collection. Any oversight in photo credits discovered after publication will be updated in future editions.

Most of all, I want to thank Karen Robertson Terry for working with me for over two years on this labor of love, my autobiography. This book was a tremendous effort and she has done a magnificent job. At the beginning of it all, when Martha Cook at Trafalgar Square Books suggested that they send a writer to my house in Wellington for five days, I was dreading being stuck with some schoolmarm for a week! I'm a very free spirit and don't like having an albatross around my neck. But when I opened the door and this drop-dead gorgeous girl walked in and talked about her interesting life and adventures in New York City, it took about thirty seconds for her to connect with all the complex layers of my own personality. Karen and I are both disciplined types of people in our working life who also have a wild side. The connection we established in those early days led to a friendship and, subsequently, to my sharing more intimate details of my life with her than anyone ever before—even members of my family or significant others.

As a bonus, being seen out with Karen enhanced my reputation! The Wellington social set that we ran into raised their eyebrows, thinking we were an item. Well, I certainly didn't deny it, and we both had fun giving people something to whisper about. I can't thank Karen enough because there are very few people in the world who could have written it like she has done. Her writing mimics my own voice as much as anyone's writing could. This book simply wouldn't have been possible without Karen, and I want to acknowledge how much I appreciate her efforts.

WARNING:

This book is a candid portrayal of my life. Innocents
and those faint of heart or closed of mind may wish
to proceed no further!

CHAPTER ONE: THE 1940s

MY GOOD FORTUNE

I. THE FOUNDATION

My childhood's privileges and peculiarities set the stage for my story's telling, and therefore we have no logical option but to start at the beginning. I admit: in telling my story, it's difficult not to leap directly to sitting at the in-gate at Madison Square Garden, or to the first time I saw Bert de Némethy train a horse, or to my wild playboy years in the 1960s, or to the golden era of horse showing in the 1970s when the depth of Hunterdon's success was unparalleled. As my mind shuffles through vivid memories of the truly great horses, of my personal struggles and triumphs, and of the most breathtaking rounds in the ring, it's easy to lose a sense of order. To properly piece those moments together, let's perform a proper half-halt and start where life always begins…at the beginning.

I might never have started down my life's path if it weren't for the good fortune of my early beginnings. No matter how hard you work to achieve your goals, it can't be denied that affluence and geographical advantages can give you a leg-up in certain pursuits. It doesn't mean you can't be an Olympian someday without those advantages; you certainly can, as many athletes have shown! It simply means you might not have the same opportunities. My family's roots and my upbringing were pivotal in my success in the horse world. Without the influences of those people and places of my youth, I know with certainty that my life would have begun quite differently. However, privilege is only half the story. It was also the difficulties I encountered as a boy that steered the direction of my life.

Although my mother was originally from New York City, I grew up on the peaceful dirt roads of New Canaan, Connecticut, in my grandmother's family farmhouse on twenty-six acres. New Canaan was and still is an affluent New York City suburb populated with families successful in early American industry. My family was no different. My mother's family was from Brooklyn Heights, a lovely, prominent borough of Manhattan that was quite gentrified in the early twentieth century.

My great-grandfather William Van Anden's brother Isaac was co-founder of the *Brooklyn Daily Eagle*, the most popular daily newspaper in the world at that time. Due to the Van Andens' connections to the local and national news community, my maternal grandmother Louise (Van Anden) Frank grew up in a very progressive and intellectual environment. Jimmy Walker, Mayor of New York in the late 1920s and early 1930s was a close friend of my grandparents. Walt Whitman (the most famous editor of the *Brooklyn Daily Eagle*) and Hans Kaltenborn, the famous radio commentator, along with his wife Olga, were in my grandparents' wedding.

My grandfather, George S. Frank (Yale of 1895), had an insurance company in Brooklyn (Frank & DuBois), and he also rode horses in Prospect Park regularly. My grandparents were social riders, as was the fashion of the time for well-to-do families. I was named for my grandfather George, which of course endeared me to my grandmother, who was extremely influential in my life (photo 1).

When the Brooklyn Bridge was built in 1883 by Washington Roebling, Isaac Van Anden was on the Board of Directors for the building of the bridge. There was controversy about the bridge, with some opposing its construction. However, with Van Anden behind the desk of the *Brooklyn Daily Eagle*, the paper helped sway public opinon. With their role in promoting the project, my grandmother (at age nine or ten) was chosen as the first individual to walk across the Brooklyn Bridge at the opening ceremony. Watched by thousands on either side, she walked across the bridge in a dress that had silk streamers sewn into it, which were flowing about her in the wind. As the story goes, when she walked across, my grandmother was afraid of getting paint from the bridge on her dress.

My father, Harry H. Morris, Jr., grew up in Augusta, Georgia, and was part of a very important line of Morrises. The Morris family is very prominent in Augusta and Morris Communications grew to be a substantial media company there. Alice Kuhlke Morris, my father's mother who we affectionately called "Dearie," divorced Harry Morris, Sr. As the tale was told, he was a bit of a gad-about and apparently she'd had quite enough of it, because she left him and moved to Kew Gardens, Long Island (photo 2). Her three children went with her and my father was among them. Harry Jr. came of age in New York and eventually went to Cornell University.

My father, once settled in New York, worked on Wall Street for high profile New York-based enterprises. As a result, he knew all the heavy hitters and old guard of the rich in New York, which provided many of the connections I was to take advantage of as a young rider. He was also a member of Squadron A, an historic cavalry unit of New York City's Upper East Side formed by a group of wealthy young gentlemen with interest in equestrian sports who were inspired by the cavalry spirit and military discipline as well as the DTA (Downtown Association). These families were all part of the inner circle of the New York area, and they're the same families that ran the United States Equestrian Team (USET), the American Horse Shows Association (AHSA), and the National Horse Show.

Working in Buffalo after attending Cornell, my father became acquainted with my mother, Alice Van Anden Frank Mitchell, through business and New York social connections. At the time, my mother was already married to Elliot Whitney Mitchell, with whom she had three children. When the children were still very young, Elliot was tragically killed in an automobile accident and left my mother a widow. My poor mother, distraught and facing a difficult path ahead, moved back to Brooklyn to reside with my grandparents. There, she reconnected with my father and after a romantic relationship emerged, they were married in 1936. I was born two years later, in '38, at the Doctor's Hospital on the Upper East Side of Manhattan (photos 3, 4). The Mitchell children—Joan, Whitney, and Louise, from my mother's previous marriage—became my half-siblings.

One thing I can tell you without hesitation is that I had a magnetic attraction to horses from a very young age. As early as two years old, I have distinct memories of Dearie taking me up Oenoke Ridge to Dr. Benson Cannon's stable to see his big, beautiful foxhunting horses. My sister Louise, eight years my senior, was often stuck babysitting me as a child, and I owe her for my early exposure to riding. The youngest of my three older step-siblings, Louise was definitely the "horsey" one in the family when I came along. She would pick me up and put me on the back of neighborhood ponies and her own horse (photo 6). She didn't compete in big shows but loved to ride cross-country and was daring and brave on a horse. Louise's neighborhood friend Jane Cassky had two ponies living in a little run-in shed with an adjoining paddock, and Louise would take me with her to play with them. She'd get me up on the small black Shetland pony and lead me around, to my absolute joy.

Louise (Mitchell) Whitcomb

When George was quite young, he got a pair of skis. We had a little hill outside near the house. George put on the skis and, of course, immediately fell down. "These don't work," he said and took the skis right off! Thinking he might like riding instead, I started putting him up on my horse Apache Gold, with him sitting on the saddle in front of me. After that, I took him up to the neighbors to ride their ponies, which he loved. Where we lived in New Canaan, and just a mile up the road, there were hills, stone walls, and trails down behind our house. It was a wonderful place to learn to ride.

George was eight years younger than me and by the time he became really serious about the sport and took professional instruction, I was away at boarding school and missed a lot. One thing is certain: George was very bright and pursued every endeavor to perfection.

Like many children, I remember having dozens of stuffed animals in my bedroom. An early horsey memory was when my great aunt Grace Smith, a lovely, classy lady and horse enthusiast married to Paul Revere Smith, came to visit us in New Canaan. At seven years old, I was told Aunt Grace was coming out from Staten Island to bring me some sort of surprise! Scampering around the house in the days leading up to her visit, I caught wind of a rumor that she was bringing me a pony, which set my imagination afire. I knew that it must be a stuffed pony—but in my heart of hearts, I hoped and dreamed that when she arrived it would be a real pony. Like any child with that love of horses, I dreamed of having a living, breathing pony to call my own.

Perhaps horses had an attraction to me as well; one of Louise's favorite stories from my early years involved her first horse, Apache Gold. Apache Gold was chestnut with a lot of white—and a complete rogue! My father bought him from Sonny Brooks, a top African-American rider (a rare thing in those times), and we kept the big chestnut in a small barn at home (photo 8). One day as a toddler, I was sitting on the grass near the paddock fence when Apache Gold reached over, picked me up by the shirt, and pulled me right over the fence!

It was fortunate Louise was a bold, fearless girl because Apache Gold was green and would bite, kick, and crib in addition to being wild under saddle. Louise tried to break him of his rearing with the old trick of breaking an egg over his head to scare him into thinking it was his own blood, but he never settled down. One day, my father rode him up Turtle Back Hill behind our house where Louise would jump the stone walls from time to time. Well, Apache

Gold started anticipating some galloping and jumping up on that hill, and my father started to fight with him. Eventually, he reared over backward and my father fell off. That was the end of our time with Apache Gold. My father sent him to Otto Heuckeroth over at the Ox Ridge Hunt Club to get rid of him!

Horses and ponies were simply a part of life in New Canaan in the 1940s and there were farms and stables everywhere. Kids would ride ponies from one town to another, and it wasn't unusual for a child to ride for miles to a gymkhana show and back home again at the end of the day. During those war years, you would see neighbors hitching up horses to carts to budget their rationed gasoline. An early neighbor of ours was Barbara Lamb, who was close with my parents and whose son eventually became the famous actor Christopher Reeve. I remember I saw Christopher at a celebrity horse show decades later and he told me his mother had told him to "tell 'Georgie' Morris hello"!

Truthfully, I was not born with a talent for riding. Some riders have innate ability and are an instant genius on a horse; I was certainly not one of them. When I first began as a rider, I was stiff and uncoordinated. Growing up in the right circumstances was the key to my beginnings with horses. I needed a good riding education to develop my style on a horse and fortunately I received just that, from a combination of geographic advantages and familial circumstances that exposed me to horses and to a progressive riding education.

All the children in my family attended the New Canaan Country Day School, which is still a very good school today. Nearby was the New Canaan Mounted Troop, a riding club that originated as part of the war effort. Being in the Troop meant wearing uniforms and riding and marching in figures. As a seven-year-old in 1945, I was certain about wanting to ride horses and started at the Troop as soon as my parents allowed it. On Wednesdays, after a half day of school, we took a paper-bag lunch to Mrs. Margaret Cabell Self's house. Troop founder, Mrs. Self was a veritable Dr. Doolittle and shared her home with the creatures—chickens and other animals walked right through the kitchen. Even at that young age, I remember eating my brown-bag lunch very tentatively at the kitchen table. It's amusing to remember that even as a little boy, I was completely anally retentive about cleanliness!

Gincy Self Bucklin

Up until World War II, all of the advanced horse knowledge was in the cavalry—in the military. In Germany, they had state schools where they taught riding and students went on to be in the cavalry. When the cavalry was done away with, much of that knowledge was lost. My mother, Margaret Cabell Self, founded the New Canaan Mounted Troop in 1939 (and published over forty books on horses as well). The point of the Troop was to work with and around horses to teach children life skills. A child who wasn't necessarily a good rider still could become a responsible officer and leader to teach other children, so there were opportunities to excel. George rode with my mother at the Troop for a while but his allergy to stable dust and horse dander made it difficult for him and that's when he began riding at the Ox Ridge Hunt Club.

George and I both became horse trainers and teachers, but we went down different paths within that career. We would see each other periodically at horse shows—this was any time from the 1960s to the 1990s—and George always took time to say hello and see how I was doing. There was never any hint of arrogance in him, despite the fact that I had chosen to teach and train on a local scale while he was teaching on the national and international circuit.

The Troop first taught me how to groom and care for horses, which was part of the valuable horsemanship basics I learned in my early years. However, the Troop was not only riding, but lots of drilling and marching in uniforms. After many days with great ponies had been sadly cut short by hours of marching, I went huffing to my parents. With a hand on my hip, I tartly complained there wasn't enough riding at the Troop. They relented! In late 1946, I began riding with more purpose at the Ox Ridge Hunt Club.

New York and the surrounding area in Connecticut was a very unique hot spot for good riding and teaching in the late '40s and early '50s. The Ox Ridge Hunt Club in Darien, Connecticut, which is still a riding club and horse show grounds today, was founded in 1914 on the property of a former opera singer, John McCormack. In my childhood, it was not only a place for adults and children to ride, but also a social club for area families. Its close proximity to New York City provided a leisure escape for city families as well as a gathering place for locals living in the surrounding towns. Otto Heuckeroth arrived at the Ox Ridge Hunt Club in 1929 and managed it for over forty years. Miss V. Felicia Townsend, an English horsewoman who had been head teacher for two years when Otto arrived, continued on and they combined their training efforts (photos 12, 13).

Emerson Burr ran the nearby Fairfield Hunt Club and he and Otto were very much aligned in their horsemanship approach. All of the Burrs were excellent horsemen, but they didn't have quite the level of formalized schooling that Otto Heuckeroth brought to the riding education we received at the Ox

Ridge Hunt Club. Both clubs were two of the premiere clubs in the country with highly respected members (as was Flintridge out in Pasadena, California), but Fairfield had more of the Westport, Connecticut, area's artistic influences while the Ox Ridge Hunt Club was more conservative and formal.

Fairfield horse people tended to be more hands-on with their horses, but they also had a lively social scene there, hosting wonderful dinner parties. I chased after many beautiful girls from the Fairfield Hunt Club as a teenager! I would finish riding at the Ox Ridge Hunt Club at noon and drive up to the Fairfield Hunt Club. One of my best friends Rosalind LaRoche lived in a beautiful house near the Club. It had a pool and poolhouse with a porch that had a living room with a bar, like a bungalow. Rosalind was named after her aunt Rosalind Russell, the Auntie Mame and huge film and stage star, and their pool house became famous for its parties. As teenagers we got into all sorts of trouble over at the LaRoche pool house!

I was extremely timid as a child rider. When I began riding at the Ox Ridge Hunt Club, Miss Townsend was the instructor who put early mileage on the beginners. Mitsy and Mittens, school horses of "the living dead" variety, were two of the school horses used for young riders just starting out. Both horses were bombproof and voice-trained to go from a slow trot to a slow canter whenever Miss T. commanded it in her high trilled English accent. Despite the saintly school horses, every time Miss T. took me off the lead line, I would scream in terrified protest! Most children stayed on the lead line for just a month or two, but I was on it for my entire first winter. Eventually, she pawned me off on a young assistant named Nancy Moran who patiently led me day after day until I overcame my initial fears.

After I had gained a bit of confidence on a horse and the protests had ceased when they took me off the lead line, I began riding out and about at the Ox Ridge Hunt Club under the tutelage of Miss Townsend. We didn't have lessons like we have them today: almost all our riding was out of the ring and through the woods and fields together across Darien and New Canaan. If we were confined to the ring, it was only for a jumping lesson or to stay out of the snow and bitter cold in the wintertime.

Like any good riding stable, there was a string of school horses, and young riders would graduate from one to the next as they improved. One of my early memories is of riding Gaylark, a little gray mare that would often try to buck when we rode out of the woods and into an open field. One particular day as we rode into a clearing, Gaylark started to try her tricks! After I successfully wrestled her head up and kept her from bucking, Miss T. turned back to me and called, "George, I think you'll make it after all!" That was the first time I had solved a serious problem with a horse, and I was very proud to have worked my way through it.

Winifred Gray

The Morris family was our next-door neighbor, and George would come over to my house when I was a girl to play with my older brother, John. We had a barn with a stage and theatrical curtains, and we would put on little performances together. When George discovered that I loved horses, he and I became good friends. He'd invite me over to his house and some of my earliest memories are of playing with his dog Pooch, a beautiful English setter who could jump really high—four feet high! After school, we'd have little hunter and jumper shows with our dogs, running next to them, holding the leashes. We built a course ourselves for the dogs, and we'd reenact the big classes at Madison Square Garden and score "touch and out" and "knockdown and out." In the field across from his house we built a small jumping course with a log jump, a brush jump, an Aiken fence, and an in-and-out.

George was often given horses to ride in the summertime and he'd let me ride them sometimes, too. One summer, when George was about twelve and I was about ten years old, he was riding a Shetland pony stallion named Calico. Calico was piebald with a mane that came down to his knees and we'd ride him bareback with a Western bridle. He was truly the Thelwell pony come to life! And he was a complete demon to ride. George would stand in the middle of the field under the shade of a big maple tree raising up a crop in his hand. As I was steaming around the field on Calico and completely out of control, George would very calmly be calling out, "LEG!.... STICK!.... PACE!" I usually ended up landing in the tall grass! But it was a sign of things to come. Later on, George shared that teaching me in that field all those years ago had given him confidence to be an instructor.

I was a boy surrounded by very strong and adoring women all through childhood, with my mother, grandmothers, and sisters doting on me. Perhaps the most influential of all of the women in my family was my grandmother Louise Van Anden Frank, my mother's mother. She not only grew up in a smart, shrewd, and connected newspaper family, but was a Vassar graduate and a women's suffragette. I was in the right place at the right time to benefit from her attention, and I loved and admired her greatly. My mother and father were very social, country club types and would drink quite a bit. In contrast, my grandmother was just the opposite—a Quaker teetotaler and an intellectual with unshakable opinions. This formidable force that was my grandmother eventually became, in essence, my sponsor when it came to riding. Without her, I can't say what would've become of me. Even more than my parents, she recognized my need for horses as an anchor to stabilize my life and in turn, did all she could to encourage my riding.

My father was well-loved in social circles as a very outgoing, friendly man. He loved me, as I was his only child, but we were like a dog and cat: two different creatures. I was very much like my mother—high strung and emotional—and although my father and I admired each other, we were plainly cut from different cloth. He was very close to my half-brother and the two of them had interests in common like hunting and fishing. With my father constantly busy with business and social events, I found myself most often in the company of my mother and grandmother. My grandmother in particular took an interest in my education outside of my riding as well, and took me on trips to see other parts of the country—and of the world. It was she who took me to the West Coast for the first time, to Pasadena, California, in 1948 to visit my father's sister, and she also took me to Canada, to Toronto, that same year by way of my first airline flight.

As a result of the distance from my father and the closeness with the women in my family, by the time I was nine years old I found myself feeling insecure about playing ball sports at school with the other boys. In an effort to encourage my skills in sports, my parents sent me to Viking Camp on Cape Cod that summer—a boys' camp. It was a nightmare for me to be thrust into an environment where these insecurities about sports were suddenly highlighted! I was mortified on a daily basis and found myself lying in my bunk fretting about the coming day, which was sure to bring more embarrassment. After enduring many days of fumbling on the field and feeling out of place, my mother telephoned to say she and my father were coming to the camp for a visit. Instantly stricken with nerves at the thought of my parents witnessing my lack of prowess on the ball field, I became very ill. My seemingly physical illness was completely psychological. My mother, and others in her family, had experienced such reactions and nervous breakdowns during stressful times and it seemed I was destined for a similar malady.

When I got home from Viking Camp, the intense anxiety I felt didn't subside but instead carried over into the start of the fourth grade. I remember being so beside myself with nerves that I would worry myself sick on the school bus and the school nurse would send me home again. Handling the pressure of school became impossible. As I realized later in life when I knew myself better, I was absolutely having a nervous breakdown. My parents took me out of school to go to Silver Hill Hospital in New Canaan for outpatient psychological counseling as a nine-year-old boy. I missed the entire fourth grade recovering. My parents hired an older boy of college age to mentor me and help get me back on track, since my older brother was away at school and my father was busy working much of the time. My grandmother, being such an intuitive woman, had seen the way I loved horses and told my parents to encourage my riding as a way to help me recover from this nervousness. I'm not sure, to this day, how she knew it was just what I needed.

II. HORSES AS SALVATION

My nervous constitution as a boy undoubtedly influenced the direction of my career as a horseman. From that moment on, horses became my grounding influence and pulled me up from the depths during difficult times in my life. Riding became my salvation!

I remember in the late forties, someone in Darien owned a little 11.1-hand spotted pony stallion named Calico that we made arrangements to temporarily keep for them at our house. To transport this pony to my house, I simply rode him bareback with a halter and two lead shanks the six miles from Darien to New Canaan. It's hard to believe, but at the time it wasn't all that remarkable. Of course nowadays, an eleven-year-old riding a pony stallion by himself six miles home is unthinkable! Calico was at our house for a whole summer and I rode him around the neighborhood, often with Cookie van Beck (who later worked for Frank Chapot). Cookie had a very hot black horse named King, and she'd ride King to my house so we could ride together. In those days, we had total freedom and constructed homemade courses with chairs and branches in the Perkin's field across the street. We pretended that field was our Grand Prix of Aachen and had hours upon hours of fun playing and riding.

Cookie and I also got into mischief together! While playing with the horses in the field across the street, I'd saunter into the Perkin's yard and say hello to Winnie Perkin, who was younger and a perfect victim for our teasing. In a flash, I would kidnap her and then Cookie and I would put poor Winnie up on a bridleless King and smack him hard on the rump. King would bolt out of the field and gallop all the way up Oenoke Ridge to Cookie's house. When he got to his little barn, he would run into his stall, slam on the brakes, and catapult poor Winnie right off his back. That poor child! But that's how we grew up—horses were part of our play with other children. We were left to our own devices, to learn our lessons at the hand of whatever ponies or horses were available, often times learning with each fall to the ground or bitten finger.

Toward the end of 1947, I began riding a 15-hand mare named Peanuts. She was a lovely, soft ride and the first horse I ever jumped. At the Ox Ridge Hunt Club in those days, the first fence you learned to jump was a single rail—a vertical about six inches off the ground. At that age, I rode in little jodhpurs and cowboy boots. Miss Townsend would always teach us to push our heels down so that our toe was just ahead of our knee. I remember her yelling out, "Jumping position!" ahead of each jump. As an easily frightened rider, I would obey immediately, squat down, lean forward, and reach my hands generously up Peanuts' neck. Of course, this is still my philosophy today—to free the horse's back and mouth over a fence. Some things never change!

In the 1930s and early '40s, the forward seat hadn't yet become the predominant style over fences so you might assume that the jumping position I learned from Miss Townsend was the traditional, British-born, hunt-field position that had been in fashion since the turn of the century. On the contrary, Miss Townsend taught me the progressive forward seat, which was considered very avant-garde. Frannie Pryor Hawes, a beautiful rider who rode with Teddy Wahl in Greenwich, Connecticut, was a great example of the style popular in the early twentieth century. In the late forties while I was learning the newly developed forward seat, Frannie was a champion in the equitation ring with her beautiful English hunting seat: an open hip angle and straighter upper body, and her foot home in the stirrup. By the early fifties, the style Frannie was so successful with at Madison Square Garden was fading out of fashion. By teaching me the progressive forward seat in the forties, Miss Townsend was clearly ahead of her time. I learned the style that would eventually be admired around the world—what we all call the classic American forward seat.

Once a month, the Ox Ridge Hunt Club held a club horse show with both gymkhana and traditional horse show classes. Miss Townsend would create extremely difficult courses in the jumping classes. I was not the only future horseman to start showing at those club shows: Ronnie Mutch and Victor Hugo-Vidal were also there and the three of us became friends. Riding in my first Ox Ridge Hunt Club Show in March of 1948, in my first jumping class, Peanuts and I jumped a course of little two-foot jumps and we won! Perhaps winning my very first jumping class was a sign of things to come, but my success always seemed due more to destiny than my ability.

Those Ox Ridge Hunt Club Shows gave young riders a fantastic start with jumping, especially given that they were more challenging than the typical standard at the time, which was jumping twice around the outside lines. Miss Townsend's courses took the outside lines and added three fences across the diagonal and skinny jumps built with half a brush. Those courses required more memorization and strategic planning, and all of the students relished the challenge. As it turned out, showing over those creative courses made all the difference as we progressed. I witnessed the older children from the Ox Ridge Hunt Club showing at Madison Square Garden year after year and not only holding their own, but winning the ASPCA Maclay and AHSA Medal Finals due to the foundation and education they received.

My grandmother felt I should have a horse to lease for the following summer so I could ride a horse that was all my own. At the time, even well-to-do families didn't rush out and buy expensive horses for children. It was fairly commonplace to lease a horse from another family for a short time. The horse chosen for my first lease was named Robin, a pretty little pinto mare (photo 14).

In early June, just before my lease was about to begin, there was a club show, and I was sick and stayed home. Later in the day, we got a call with bad news. Poor Robin had been jumping into the sun at the last fence on the outside course and had fallen. She had somersaulted over the jump, broken her neck, and died. I was so stunned and horrified by the news that I became hysterically upset. My lovely Robin dead—the first horse that was meant to be mine alone and she was gone! Inconsolable, I cried and cried. With the history of nerves in the family, our trusty Dr. Wadsworth, a country lady doctor, came to the house and gave me a shot to calm me down. The truth is that for every nice story about a horse, there are many tragic ones. Life is fragile; life is especially delicate when it comes to horses. I learned this lesson well at a very young age.

My strong-willed grandmother, alarmed at my emotional state after the death of Robin, decreed that I must have my own horse. The next day, I was brought down to the Ox Ridge Hunt Club and Otto led out two horses for me to consider. The first was a pretty Appaloosa named Candy and the second a chunky Quarter Horse named Shorty. Candy was very pretty and moved well but hung his legs a little over the jumps. Shorty wasn't as attractive and fancy looking, but he jumped very well (photo 15). They told me to pick and I chose Shorty; I suppose even then the jumping was my focus!

As a student of Otto Heuckeroth, I learned to ride outside of the ring with no fences by my side as a security blanket. Shorty and I got to know one another and I started riding him in small local shows (photo 16). All of the children would hack together on our ponies and horses ten to twelve miles from the Ox Ridge Hunt Club to North Stamford for a show. There, we'd show in eight or so various types of classes, like egg and spoon, bareback riding, and of course jumping. Then we'd hack all the way back home afterward. I even recall riding all the way to the Fairfield Hunt Club together, which is close to fifteen miles! What a complete joy to grow up like that! I cherish the memories and wish that children nowadays had that experience.

Patty Heuckeroth

My father Otto Heuckeroth, who taught me to ride and gave me a wonderful foundation for riding, was not one to mince words. He had these sayings to tell you exactly how he felt while he was teaching you. Some of my favorites were, "It would be easier to teach a bear to dance!" and "Your hands are like my feet!"

My father had a great expression. He had a lot of horses for sale and of course we'd ride them and school them before potential buyers came to try them. In most cases, the horse would go very well and they would buy it and take it home. Sometimes, a couple of months later, they would call up my father and say, "Otto, this horse is not going like the day we bought it." And he would simply say, "The pilot doesn't come with the plane!" I can remember my father talking about finding a horse for George. He would say, "This is the right horse for George...for a year or two." It's a good lesson for everybody. If you buy a perfect horse for the moment, it won't stay perfect for you forever.

I remember when all the young riders were getting ready for the Medal and the Maclay and George would have lessons on Friday nights to practice for the Finals. One night after their lesson was over, George pointed toward the exercise he had finished and asked, "Patty, why don't you do this exercise?" He had built an exercise with sheep hurdles and made a chute that you rode through to jump a narrow fence. Afterward, you turned sharply around and jumped across over the sheep hurdles that were set as an oxer with parallel rails, which at the time, was a fairly new and daring type of fence. I can even remember my father saying, "Don't jump those parallel rails! The horse can't see the back rail—it's a bear trap!"

My horse was a little spooky and I told George, "I've never jumped parallel rails before and I'm not sure my horse will go between the sheep hurdles because he's so spooky." "Just give it a try," George replied. So off I went and my horse bravely galloped between the sheep hurdles and around the turn, but looked hard at the oxer and stopped—well, off I went and hit the dirt. George, who normally doesn't show much concern about anyone falling off, rushed over to me, crying "Patty, Patty, are you all right?" I told him I was all right, and then he said, "Oh my God, Patty, your father's going to kill me!"

I loved Shorty, but he had one fatal flaw which meant our partnership wasn't long-lived. That little Quarter Horse would not, under any circumstances, back up. In under-saddle classes at shows, the judge would ask the riders to line up in the center then ask everyone to back their horses up. You can imagine a plucky line of children and their horses and all of them backing up except for one pair: Shorty and me. We tried everything to teach him to back up, including setting up elaborate blockades between two cars where his only option was to back up, but it was useless. He simply would not go in reverse! With a competitive spirit even at that young age, my frustration grew. My mother, always one to speak very little but get her meaning across plain as day, gave Otto a baleful look after another failure to back up in a class. It wasn't long after that I traded up to my next horse.

Flying Banners, a 16.1-hand, three-quarter-bred, brown mare with a white star, became mine in the end of 1949. She wasn't particularly fancy to look at, but what a wonderful jumper! I began learning to jump bigger fences on her and get a feel for timing. Otto Heuckeroth would take us out in a group on long cross-country rides over fences, some of them incredibly lasting four hours or more. One of these cross-country rides earned the ominous nickname "The Terrible Three and the Gory Four"! I can still recall the steep uphill jumps and downhill drops over stone walls, jumping four- to four-foot-three in height—it took guts! Flying Banners made me brave because she was an absolute jumping machine (photo 17).

It's hard to imagine now, but at only eleven years old, Otto encouraged me to jump quite big fences and even show in the Open Working Hunter Division. Flying Banners somehow carried me as a boy over those four- to four-foot-six courses. For a timid boy with shaky nerves, it was playing with fire and as the summer continued, a few mistakes led to me losing confidence little by little. The jumps were more and more imposing. I felt so fearful at times that I wanted to quit riding altogether. One of Gordon Wright's twelve commandments for a teacher says, *Prevent physical fear, since it is impossible to learn with it.*

He was right. I had stopped learning and been consumed with fear of getting hurt over those big jumps.

A few of the older kids I knew from the Ox Ridge Hunt Club, like Glenna Lee Maduro (later: de Rham) and Victor Hugo-Vidal, rode with Gordon Wright at his Secor Farms which was about half an hour down the road in White Plains, New York. Gordon had developed a reputation as a teacher for serious young riders. Glenna's mother, a very good horsewoman herself who likely witnessed my deflating confidence over fences, took my mother aside and suggested that she take me down to ride with Gordon Wright at Secor Farms.

Jimmy Wofford

My father was a cavalry officer and graduated from West Point in 1920. Between wars, he performed the duties of a typical cavalry officer, including participation in the Olympic Games in 1932. Subsequently, he was posted as the Master of the Sword at West Point, which is the head of the Physical Education department at West Point. The young cadets at that time underwent riding instruction as part of their physical education program. Gordon Wright talked my father into giving him riding lessons. He became entranced with jumping over fences and the English style of riding. My father was his first instructor. His instruction would have been straight out of Colonel Harry Chamberlin, the preeminent horseman and equestrian theorist between 1920 and 1950. Chamberlin laid down precepts that George Morris and I still follow today. I absorbed them by osmosis, but George absorbed them directly from Gordon Wright, who promoted Chamberlin's teachings with the reach that only clinics could achieve.

In essence, Gordon invented the concept of the riding clinic and not only that, but he made it an honorable and successful practice. When President Truman mechanized the cavalry in 1949, these superb riders and instructors considered themselves officers and gentlemen. As such, they were never paid for their riding and teaching. We had to create an entirely new generation of professional horsemen. That's where Gordon came in, along with Captain Vladimir Littauer. They bridged this horrible gap that was created by the removal of the equestrian knowledge from the general fabric of the horse world in the United States. A professional's path was opened up, and especially in the hunter/jumper sport, the role of a professional trainer and horseman was created. Prior to the 1930s, professional horsemen were typically skilled stable managers with an eighth-grade education and a lifelong experience with horses.

They were the ones with the knowledge, and their work complemented
the more highly educated military officers/gentlemen who focused on
the riding and sporting theory.

Gordon Wright was a brilliant instructor with a gift for communication and
an understanding of the psychology of the horse–rider relationship. He grew up
on a ranch in Utah, skilled at riding anything he could throw his leg over, including broncs and bulls. As a young man, Gordon secured work with rodeos and
carnivals with his early specialty of riding two horses standing up on their backs.
He later joined the Army cavalry in the early 1920s, and while on leave from
the Army in 1927, he entered a competition at Madison Square Garden in Fred
Bebee's World Series Rodeo. Dazzling the crowd, Gordon won a $600 prize!
Weighing the limitations and danger of rodeo riding next to the potential for a
successful riding stable in the New York area, he took a risk and used his prize
money to finance the purchase of a stable in Bronxville, New York (photo 18).

Gordon quickly became known as the well-loved, premiere New York area
riding instructor in the 1930s and moved his business to a new stable called
Secor Farms in White Plains. Being a Jewish cowboy from out West, there was
some bias against Gordon because he wasn't what the social elite called "our
class, Dear," but he was so gregarious that few could resist his charms. Women
competed for his affections and men crowded around to play cards and drink
with him.

When World War II began, Gordon returned to the cavalry and served at
Fort Riley, Kansas, where he received the most sophisticated jumping training
available in the country at the time, through the methodology developed by
Colonel Chamberlin. As a second lieutenant, Gordon soon began riding for
the United States in international competition. After the cavalry disbanded in
1948, there was no representation in international competition by an official
U.S. Team. However, Bob Henry and his wife Betty Jane, who rode at Secor
Farms, worked with Gordon to incorporate the United States Equestrian Team.
Gordon rode on the USET in 1949 and held training sessions for team candidates. People had a love/hate relationship with Gordon: he was rough around
the edges with stable management and wasn't as polished as others would've
liked. Later, the leadership of the USET was taken over by some who felt Gordon wasn't the right choice.

By the time my mother began driving me to White Plains for lessons,
Secor Farms was already very well established. We used to joke around and call
it "Sucker Farms" because while the Ox Ridge Hunt Club charged only three

dollars for a riding lesson, it was a whole ten dollars a lesson with Gordon! The stable itself had three levels stacked one upon the other, with the top floor housing the well-cared-for, glossy, show horses. Even as a boy, I noticed how the standards fell off on the lower floors of the barn. After Otto Heuckeroth's top horsemanship and care at the Ox Ridge Hunt Club, I could see that some of Secor's horses suffered from a level of neglect.

Upon arriving at Secor Farms for my first lesson, I was instructed to get on an old school horse Silver King. He had probably foundered and wasn't good for much more than slow gaits and tiny fences, but it was the perfect way for me to relax and start at the beginning, learning Gordon's methods. He started me from scratch, literally from a standstill on Silver King, and taught me basics like keeping my eyes up and focused ahead. His very methodical and technical approach rebuilt my riding and my confidence.

Gordon talked my father into sending Flying Banners to Secor Farms for me to ride, but not long afterward she succumbed to the poor care and got botulism from moldy hay. My poor mare was sick for months and nearly died. All the ladies at Secor felt so sorry for me that my horse was sick and smothered me with their attention. As soon as she was well enough to travel, we sent Flying Banners immediately back to the Ox Ridge Hunt Club and Otto Heuckeroth's excellent care. Otto resurrected her, and I continued to ride her there, even as I was taking lessons down in White Plains with Gordon.

In the early days riding at Secor Farms, Gordon had a student named Mrs. Thomas Manville, the wife of a businessman who ran the H.W. Johns Manville Company, a famous chemical manufacturer. Mr. Manville's British (and much younger) wife Georgie was paired up with me to ride in semi-private lessons with Gordon. Even though she was much older than I was, Georgie and I became close friends. As he taught us in the ring, Gordon would call her "Big George" and me "Little George." Over time, I could tell that Gordon had grown fond of Georgie, and they had a twinkle in their eye for one another. Months later, we were at the Boulder Brook Horse Show and heard terrible news: Georgie was in her car on the way to the show and had somehow opened her car door accidentally at a traffic light, slipped out of her seat, and was run over by her own car. I still remember how Gordon was very shaken up by the news that she had died.

Squadron A had a big April horse show, and I planned to show Flying Banners. My father, being a member of this prestigious gentlemen's club, couldn't wait for me to ride and jump in the Open Working Hunters like I had back at the Ox Ridge Hunt Club shows the previous year. He no doubt had visions of watching me jump those huge fences while he looked on proudly, surrounded by his friends. As the show was approaching, Gordon fell ill from malaria and was in bed recovering for weeks afterward. When Gordon heard that I was going to ride in the show, he sent strict orders to my father from his hospital bed that I was not, under any circumstances, to jump higher than three-foot courses. That's just one example of the strength of Gordon's care and attention to detail that his pupils benefited from, and I was very fortunate to call him a mentor.

Nancy Kissinger

Gordon Wright was a wonderful teacher and had great patience along with a gregarious pep that was infectious. As young people, we had great fun riding at Secor Farms. Thinking back now, I don't know why we weren't killed! Gordon would take our stirrups away and knot our reins and we would be jumping four-foot fences. When I started with Gordon, he felt my position needed work because my legs were too far forward. One afternoon he took me up to The Hill where there were a number of stone walls, and he rode right next to me, keeping his leg right up against mine so I could feel exactly where my leg was supposed to be. We rode like that, side by side, legs touching, galloping over stone walls in tandem, and after that day, my leg was always in the right place. That was Gordon! It's incredible to think of him actually teaching like that, but it happened. It seems like it would be physically impossible, but I remember it like it was just yesterday.

Gordon never asked anyone to do anything he didn't think they could do, and I think George also thinks like that and pays attention to a student's limits. George is a wonderful horseman and a dear man. While I am no expert, I must say that George was the quietest rider I have ever seen. He simply imposed his will on a horse—done beautifully. Absolutely superb. He was always so friendly, lots of fun to be with, and such a gentleman with the best manners.

Dogs have always been part of my family and there have been special dogs that have been by my side throughout most of my lifetime. If you're a dog person, you'll know that there are good dogs and sweet, dumb dogs and then occasionally there are truly great dogs. Big Boy, our Irish Setter, was the first great dog in my life, although as a family dog he was not mine alone. When Big Boy died, we got a new family dog, an English setter named Pooch, who was sweet but not the brightest dog. When I was getting into riding at the Ox

Ridge Hunt Club, I was also really into dog jumping. I would jump Pooch endlessly over fences in the backyard.

Miss Townsend had several Shetland sheepdogs at her cottage and would have litters from time to time. The first dog that was my very own was named Kiltie, a Shetland sheepdog from Miss Townsend's. She was truly a great dog. I would jump her outside on the croquet lawn over courses made of lawn furniture and things I pulled from the woods and fields. Winnie Perkin, Pamela Erdmann, and other friends would bring their dogs over and we would jump those poor dogs to exhaustion! Apparently, I was a driller when it came to both horses and dogs. Every Tuesday night at the Ox Ridge Hunt Club, they would have dog obedience training in the indoor ring and I would take Kiltie. I also showed her in half-a-dozen dog shows, and she always won her obedience class.

When I first began riding at Secor Farms in 1950 with Gordon Wright, he was heavily involved with the USET, since he'd helped it get founded originally. At the beginning, Gordon trained the team himself and would hold USET training sessions in White Plains. I was only twelve but I remember I saw a girl unloading a horse off a trailer for one of the team training sessions and it was Franny Blunt (later: Steinwedell) from Chicago. She and her sister Carlene were top young riders, and they have been in and out of my life—and a big part of the horse show world—for decades. Carlene was even one of the girls I dated!

Fran Steinwedell

I first met George when Charlie "Denny" Dennehy and I went East to take lessons from Gordon Wright. George was twelve years old at the time. Years later, he also came out West and taught clinics and judged at Flintridge Riding Club, where my daughter Francie and I rode with Jimmy Williams. The East Coast social set in horse showing were very polished and educated and George was no exception. Jimmy wasn't from a conservative, conventional horse background like George, but we could all see how much respect they had for each other.

When Francie wanted to go East and show as a junior, riding with George was a great opportunity for her. Through the years, we got to know George better and all became good friends. One funny memory was on one of George's birthdays when we decorated the barn aisle at the show and waited to surprise him. We all stood and watched as he drove in, saw the decorations, and then turned right around and drove away! That was the moment I learned George didn't like birthdays.

Carlene Blunt

George and I go way back. I think he agrees that the courses back in the 1950s were so different from what you see at the horse shows today. The hunter courses had galloping distances between the fences and few jumps were set under three-foot-six. You rode off your eye. The Ox Ridge Hunt Club Show had a big, challenging outside course as did the Bloomfield Hills Horse Show, which had permanent obstacles. I remember the beautiful solid birch rails—the in-and-out was permanent too. The Harrisburg Horse Show was very impressive as the hunter courses were over four feet—your hunters really needed to be good jumpers.

I think the Hunter Derbies today are a good addition and encourage some galloping and challenging courses. George certainly helped make them happen.

I eventually taught Fran's daughter Francie Steinwedell (later: Steinwedell-Carvin) in the 1970s. Back in 1950, Franny was an older girl being groomed for the USET. Gordon's step-daughter Elaine Moore (later: Moffat) was a fearless rider, jumping five-foot jumps like they were nothing. She won the Maclay Finals in 1946. Those girls were my idols! Incidentally, Elaine's younger sister Pamela Moore penned the very well-known and somewhat controversial novel *Chocolates for Breakfast,* which made her the "American Françoise Sagan" at age eighteen.

The first Broadway production I ever saw was *South Pacific* in 1950. To my delight, my parents took me backstage after the show to see Mary Martin who played the role of Nellie Forbush. Mary was a friend of my parents through her brother-in-law who lived in New Canaan. She herself lived in Norwalk, Connecticut, and I remember she would commute into Manhattan daily, driven in a limousine followed closely by a second limousine just in case the first one broke down. Mary would come over to our house for dinner parties, and I still remember her singing and having a great sense of humor. She dubbed our house, an old 1750s revolutionary-era farmhouse with many bathrooms and powder rooms, "The House of the Johns"!

I n the era of my childhood, horses and dogs were part of our country lifestyle. The worlds of city people and horses were still intertwined, with riding being a common leisure activity for any family, whether in New York or out in the country. In the setting of suburban, rural, New Canaan, life with horses was casual and communal, and I was fortunate to absorb my basics of horsemanship in a very natural way (photo 19).

Today, in most parts of the country, learning to ride and handle horses is done in a structured, formal way. Although my relationship with horses was very basic in the forties, I learned horsemanship as a way of life. At the Ox Ridge Hunt Club, I handled horses and ponies and learned the basics on the school horses there. Riding was a leisurely and social pursuit; it wasn't yet a technical or formal era. I didn't learn how to be an expert groom, but I had enough to absorb a correct basis of horsemanship as a natural part of life. It was a basic start, with heels down, sit up, jumping position, and so on. I dealt with my first riding "problems" riding out in the fields and on the trails and had a great beginning to my horsemanship while learning from encouraging, disciplined, correct teachers. It's not uncommon for children to have a crisis of confidence as I did from jumping so high so early. I was fortunate that my mother took me to Secor Farms to ride with Gordon Wright, who rebuilt my confidence from the ground up.

Despite the fact that I was fortunate to be born and raised with every advantage of the social upper class, childhood was difficult. I was surrounded by adults, in my mother's family in particular, who were intelligent but high strung with fearful, nervous constitutions. It was a stressful environment some-times where I'd witness heated arguments fueled by alcohol. My older brother and sisters were away at boarding school, so I bore the brunt of it alone. Grow-ing up sensitive to the highly charged emotions of my parents set the stage for my boyhood insecurities and put pressure on my own nervousness. Those early factors absolutely played a big role in my decisions and desires, and paved the path as I tried to discover my place in the world in the 1950s and beyond.

CHAPTER TWO: THE 1950s

ASCENDANCY

I. MADISON SQUARE GARDEN

The century's halfway point marked a watershed moment in my life. By the late 1940s, I had a solid base of natural horsemanship and basic riding principles, but in the fifties I learned how to be a technician in the tack. Not having an innate feel and with fears and insecurities to overcome, I had no choice but to become a made rider. Lucky for me, riding with Gordon Wright was the beginning of my technical riding education. With Gordon's methodical, intuitive teaching I began to understand not just how proper riding should feel but also the mechanics of a horse and rider. My other interests began to fall away and my inquisitiveness about the art of riding took root.

Following on the heels of my increased focus were, naturally, more consistent results and more success in the show ring. Flying Banners and I were placing well even at the bigger, recognized shows. My eyes began to focus on the ASPCA Maclay Finals and riding at the venue that stood unmatched for the American junior rider: the National Horse Show at Madison Square Garden. Since its inception in 1933, the ASPCA Maclay Finals has been a symbol of not only skilled riding but also compassionate and responsible horsemanship.

When I was a young rider, the National Horse Show was in its heyday and the prospect of showing there was simply incredible. Historically, young riders who win either the ASPCA Maclay Finals or the AHSA Hunt Seat Medal Finals have often gone on to become successful professional riders and trainers. Regardless of ribbon color, any rider privileged to show at the Garden through the years is lucky to have simply had the chance to be an exhibitor there.

Nowadays Lexington, Kentucky, is a good home for the Maclay Finals—and Harrisburg, Pennsylvania, for the Medal Finals—but it must be said that the old Madison Square Garden was something to behold! It was a magical time in horse sports, where the shows were woven into the social fabric of New York City. The who's who of the entire country came to rub elbows and watch the fanfare. America's most famous horse show was, for decades, intimately connected to society in New York and the East Coast; in fact, in 1887 the directory for the National Horse Show served as the beginning of Louis Keller's first New York Social Register (photo 20).

With my sights on showing at Madison Square Garden, it became clear to my mother and father that the private schools my brother and sisters had attended for their high school years wouldn't work for me. Leaving school every afternoon to ride many miles away was simply not feasible in private school, and I would've been limited to riding only on the Wednesday early-release day and on weekends. That simply was not enough riding! Instead, I began attending the New Canaan Public High School in close proximity to the Ox Ridge Hunt Club and Secor Farms, and continued to enjoy the freedom to ride every day.

The public schools in New Canaan were very good and my education was top notch. After school my mother picked me up and took me to the Ox Ridge Hunt Club to ride. Once a week, she took me instead to White Plains for my lesson with Gordon Wright. Many of my friends from New Canaan Country Day had moved on with me to the public high school, and several of us also rode together, which made for lasting friendships. As it happens, the 1960s decathlon icon Bill Toomey was in my high school class.

I wasn't trying to qualify for the AHSA Medal Finals that year. With the Medal being a more difficult class and my young age, Gordon Wright didn't think I was quite ready for it yet, so I just focused on the Maclay. I needed one blue ribbon in a Maclay qualifying class to show at Madison Square Garden. There weren't nearly as many shows in those days, so it wasn't as if you could drive up and down the East Coast every weekend for months trying to get qualified. You really had to make it count. Jack Spratt, a friend of Otto Heuckeroth's, was judging at the Bethlehem, Connecticut, show that year. I put in a good round on my lovely mare Flying Banners and to my great surprise, I won! I was thrilled, but to this day I still remember beating an older boy from a local family named Llewelyn Ross in that class. It was his last year to qualify for the Garden, and I felt terrible for having any part in his missed chance.

Consequently, 1950 was the first year that a Medal Finals class was held at Madison Square Garden; prior to that, the AHSA Medal was awarded on accumulated points from the show season. In the coming weeks it started to sink in that I was going to ride at Madison Square Garden in the city. I can recall the anticipation I felt in the days leading up to it—the autumn leaves starting to fall and the chill coming into the air. The change of season meant the biggest show of the year was around the corner. Finally, it would be my chance to ride in that beautiful arena.

The National Horse Show at Madison Square Garden was, of course, the high point of the horse show circuit each autumn, and I was twelve years old when I first rode into that ring, the first of many times over the years. The tremendous building, on Fiftieth Street and Eighth Avenue in Manhattan, was the pinnacle of class. With my young eyes wide, I took in all the beautiful horses and the elegant spectators. The "hoi polloi" came out to watch the show and it was quite a spectacle. And year after year, elite families all over the country came to New York for it. All the men wore tuxedos and the women donned their jeweled gowns and hats. Even farriers and vets would be dressed to the nines and in their very best formal wear. These well-to-dos took turns walking around the promenade that encircled the ring at the old Garden. The elite would sit in the boxes right at the edge of the walkway and everyone would get a glimpse of the rich and famous as they strolled along and mingled. You would see Hollywood and Broadway stars, from Pavarotti to Andy Warhol. It was irreplaceable and a wonderful scene, with social events weaved through the fabric of the horse show. Spectators would go back and forth between the Garden and the Waldorf Astoria for luncheons and cocktail parties each day between the big classes.

Gordon Wright was a master at coordinating all of his students and their horses with the very limited room for stabling at the Garden. If the allotted stalls couldn't fit one trainer's group of clients' horses, typically some were relegated to the Squadron A stabling, which was far uptown. During the week the professional classes were held, and children's classes were on the weekends. Gordon would take the professionals' horses back to Secor Farms to free up stalls for the junior riders' horses so we wouldn't have to worry about transporting back and forth from Squadron A. All we had to do was warm up our horses by trotting up and down the ramp from the ring to the stabling area, and we were ready to go without hassle and stress. Gordon's method was head and shoulders above what other trainers did, and even at a young age I could appreciate the efficiency of his show management.

Elaine Moffat

My mother married Gordon Wright in 1947 and he was amazing; all the women fell in love with him, despite the fact that he was bald and heavy and not a particularly handsome man. My younger sister was often introduced by my mother as the genius in the family, and of course, this gave me quite a complex. I was determined to prove myself and became very competitive both in swimming and riding. With Gordon as my teacher, I learned to ride and jump on all of his horses. I remember once, in 1946, I was riding with Gordon on an old estate in White Plains in a fenced-in ring. I'd been riding for about an hour and the horse, named Lark Alley, had jumped quite a bit. Gordon told me for the last exercise he wanted me to jump him into the ring from outside. Well, the fence, which was about four feet high or so, was set up on much higher ground because the footing had become worn down on both sides and was quite hard in late summer. It was very imposing to jump, probably close to six feet, because of the ground being lower on both sides. Lark Alley was nervous, very green, and on top of that windy with bad breathing.

Now let me tell you, you never talked back to Gordon in a lesson, but I told him I didn't think the horse had it in him. "Well now," said Gordon, "you have a yellow stripe down your back a mile long, don't you?" This was the way he talked to us! I said, "Well, all right then," and I picked up a good gallop and rode up to the fence, and that poor horse tried but just couldn't get over it. It was a solid fence, too, and didn't give way. He flipped over and went down and launched me face-first into the ground. We just wore hunt caps in those days, with no strap whatsoever, so as soon as the bill of the cap hit the ground the cap flung off. I was unconscious for nearly an hour and by that time, they had carried me across the street into the club house and put me onto a cot. I had pieces of gravel lodged in the skin on my face; my whole face was scarred from that fall. When Gordon took me home, my mother was furious, yelling, "What on earth did you do to her now?" I remember I missed the next show, but when I got back to riding a couple weeks later, people didn't recognize me because of my face still healing.

George and I were showing together at the Boulder Brook Horse Show in 1954 and we each had a horse in the Open Jumpers. George was about sixteen, riding The Gigolo, and I was twenty-four and riding Royal Guard. The jumps were absolutely huge, up to six feet high! We each made some big mistake in the first class and got completely chewed out by Gordon. Afterward, while walking our horses nearby before the next class, we had a meeting of the minds. George and I said to one another,

"All right, no more goofs! We can't have any more of this nonsense!" And it was so funny because in every jumper class for the rest of the show, I won and George was second in all the classes. Royal Guard was a fabulous horse and would clear the rails by an eighth of an inch, no matter how large they became.

George is a strong teacher but he's always been very humble about what Gordon gave to him. What George did was take all of the knowledge that Gordon had absorbed at Fort Riley and from Captain Littauer and packaged it up for students like no one had ever done before. He presented it in an organized way that made more sense to people learning to ride.

Ronnie Mutch, my friend from the Ox Ridge Hunt Club, won the AHSA Hunt Seat Medal Finals that year. I was so proud my friend had won! The next day was the Maclay Finals and it was my turn to ride; I was overwhelmed when I saw that I was up against more than 100 riders. Awestruck at just stepping into the big arena, Flying Banners and I did marginally well, but of course I was too green to have any chance of placing. It was quite an opportunity to simply be able to ride at the Garden at such a young age and it was a natural progression. Growing up so close to New York meant riding at the Garden was much more easily accessible for me than it was for children in other parts of the country.

In late 1950 my mother recognized that it was time for me to trade up to a better horse and our family's connections came into play, matching me with an iconic horse. Mrs. John J. Farrell, a close friend of my mother's and the wife of Mr. John J. Farrell (the owner of Farrell Steamships) had a top hunter stable in Darien, Connecticut. The Farrell family (members of the Ox Ridge Hunt Club) stabled their horses at home but took them over to ride in the indoor ring during the wintertime. They were also known as erstwhile benefactors of the Club, having kept the Club afloat during the Depression era.

The Farrells had a Pennsylvania-bred six-year-old light chestnut horse with a big white blaze and three white socks named Game Cock. His movement was beautiful—what we called a "daisy-cutter" because of the way he glided effortlessly across the ground. Game Cock also had manners to burn, as we used to say in those days, which was likely due to the fact that he had been bred by General Charles Lyman at Maui Meadows Farm near West Chester, Pennsylvania. General Lyman was a Fort Riley-trained horseman whose wife and son were also skilled riders. He initially sold Game Cock to Jack and Kate Melville (famous judges), and then the horse ended up with the Farrell family a couple of years later. The young chestnut was green but dog quiet and displayed his great training and handling by both the Lymans and the Melvilles. When the Farrells discovered Game Cock wasn't going to cut it jumping fences over four feet, they were disappointed. Otto Heuckeroth suggested the Farrells pass the horse to me, since I was showing at three-foot-six. Everyone agreed and the lovely chestnut was mine!

Game Cock and I were a perfect match. He fit me beautifully and I absolutely loved him. He shone like a copper penny in the sun and was put together flawlessly. In those days the conformation hunters were so spectacular that despite his great conformation, Game Cock was simply considered a quality junior horse. Today, he would be without a doubt a Conformation Model winner. A fabulous mover, my new horse was a brave three-foot-six jumper with a quiet, sensible mind. At that height he won everything, but go up a hole on the jump standards and he started to fall apart. Our partnership was incredibly promising, but I was still only thirteen and showing age twelve, so we learned together. My new horse was also very trainable and we worked hard together to be more consistent in 1951, which was our introductory year (photo 21).

In our first year together, Game Cock and I met with modest success in the show ring. A typical Equitation Over Fences course in those days was jumping twice around the outside lines. After that, the judges would line up their favorites on the center line and test them by switching horses and jumping twice around the outside once again. Betty Haight, a top equitation contender that year, also had a chestnut with a blaze named Guard Hill. Game Cock and Guard Hill looked so much alike and yet they couldn't have been more opposite to ride. Judges would often have us switch horses and when I rode Betty's hot pistol of a horse, I couldn't stop him! Guard Hill would gallop three whole times around the course with me bracing in my irons, hauling back on his mouth, and doing all I could to stop. When it was Betty's turn, she couldn't even get Game Cock out of the line! He needed a lot of leg and Betty, being so accustomed to a hot horse and with short legs, would kick and flail to no avail. Everyone laughed at the two of us struggling with the other's horse. The judges must have loved to watch each of us flounder hopelessly.

Harriet Kennaby

George is one of my oldest friends. I have ridden with him and hosted him for years when he taught at Ox Ridge Hunt Club clinics and in Camden, South Carolina. Over the years there have always been antics at his clinics, whether it was George putting a rider in his or her place or a horse. I remember a clinic where some girls were wearing Christmas sweaters and one girl in particular was talking to her friend and showing off her sweater and not paying attention to George as he was talking. He told her to get off the horse and made her roll in the dirt in the ring for a few minutes. Then he told her to get back on, because now she'd have nothing to talk about! At another clinic, a girl's horse was misbehaving so badly that George got on the horse for her. He galloped the rogue out of the ring, across the sand driveway, up the grassy hill, around the horse show office, then back down the hill and into the ring. Everyone's jaw dropped, speechless. What he did on the other side of that building, we'll never know.

A lot of people thought that in George's world it was "my way or the highway," but that wasn't true. He believed his students should learn from any source they could. The Leone boys showed up one day at Hunterdon and started loading their horses up. They explained to George that they were going to ride elsewhere and try something different. George accepted it, wishing them good luck and a good summer, assuring them he was not cross. October rolled round, and in came the Leones' van. They said, "We're back, George!" and that was that. George said, in the end, it was good for them to try something else out.

Years later, I rode with George or others at Hunterdon various times. He just poured confidence right into you as a rider. If George had told me to pick up a gallop and ride across the field and jump over the barn, I would have thought I could do it. I recall one particular Sunday lesson when I'd just begun preparing for the Amateur Owner three-foot-six division. The day before I had a lesson with some younger riders and it had been a good confidence builder. But that day, I went out and saw I was riding with two veteran Amateur Owner riders, which made me think I might have trouble. As all three of us rode through an exercise, I didn't realize George was putting the jumps up in a very sly way. Suddenly, I noticed the horse jumping in front of me was really making an effort and as I approached next, George yelled, "Reach for her ears!" And what a jump! It was marvelous. I was walking on air for weeks afterward, thinking about those jumps that day. George has that gift of getting the best out of you, and it doesn't matter what age you are, what your background is, or how advanced you or your horse might be. At the end of that lesson, we were galloping uphill in the field to a triple combination! I jumped some fences that day I didn't see again for a year. It was such a thrill.

I became very close friends with Victor Hugo-Vidal and Ronnie Mutch, who like me were products of that wonderful riding community. We were a triumvirate of horse boys, all having grown up at the Ox Ridge Hunt Club together. I was the youngest; Ronnie and Victor were three-and-a-half and four years older. The three of us were always friends but also very fierce competitors, first as junior riders and, in the years to follow, as teachers and professionals (photo 22).

Both Ronnie and Victor became mentors to me and each of them had great influence on my young riding life. My mother even made poor Victor drive me all over God's green earth to give her a break from taxiing me around. My two friends, both riders whom I would watch and emulate, were different in the way they approached riding. Each of them rode beautifully in his own right, but Ronnie was a complete natural and rode from the gut. Victor on the other hand was quite the opposite—a made rider whose intellect and desire to succeed drove his improvement.

After mentoring me, Victor went on to mentor J. Michael Plumb, who of course became a major success. After winning the Maclay Finals in '57, Mike foxhunted, rode racehorses, and show jumpers, then rode in eight Olympic Games in three-day eventing, which is still the record for the most Olympic Games competed in by any Olympian.

Like the prior year, I was focused on the Maclay and wasn't trying to qualify for the Medal yet since I was still only thirteen. I had proudly witnessed Ronnie win the AHSA Medal Finals at the Garden that past fall, but 1951 was Victor's last junior year and he had his eyes on the prize. He was determined to go to the Medal Finals on his mare Touraine, a bay equitation mare that jumped fairly flat but could be very good. Occasionally, Touraine would have the odd stop at a fence the first time around a course. Victor hatched a plan: he asked me to ride Touraine in the Medal before him (since in those days two riders could ride the same horse). When Touraine stopped at a spooky fence her first trip around, I got after her with my stick and finished the course. The idea was that Victor would have a flawless round and win the class. It was fine with me because I wasn't seriously trying for Medal qualification and at the same time it was a fun way to get experience showing another horse.

In those days, a hopeful Medal qualifier needed to win three Medal classes to earn their spot at Madison Square Garden. At one small show in Connecticut that summer, Victor's plan backfired and Touraine didn't stop when I rode her in the Medal for her first look at the course. I ended up beating Victor and winning the class! I was pretty proud of myself, being four years Victor's junior and looking up to him as I did. We had a good laugh about my foiling his plans.

I was in many ways Victor's protégé and he was a very big influence on my life, both as a horseman and on a personal level. Victor was a bright student with a desire to learn and always seemed to have his ear to the ground. Naturally it was through my friendship with him that I was first introduced to a master of riding and training who had emigrated from Hungary. One day Victor told me he'd heard of a man from Europe training horses down at the Rockefeller's barn in Westchester County and took me down there to watch him. Peering into the schooling ring, I immediately noticed the foreign horseman's class and sophistication; he wore gloves and longed horses in side reins. He worked horses in snaffle bits doing basic dressage and gymnastic work over cavalletti. It was a different kind of horse training than we'd ever seen before. Victor and I would sit by the hour and watch him work horses. It was Bertalan de Némethy. Victor was so impressed with his methods that he sent his prized young horse Nemo to Bert for training before anyone had even heard of him. This was right after Bert de Némethy appeared in the United States and years before his eventual involvement with the United States Equestrian Team.

Another European horseman new to the East Coast horse show scene in the early 1950s was Gabor Foltenyi. He, like Bert de Némethy, was a great influence on me. Gabor also exuded a gentlemanly image of European aristocracy: the way he dressed and the gloves he wore were reminiscent of the military cavalry. Both men presented themselves in a way that demonstrated a respect for their craft and for themselves, which impressed me greatly. I recall Gabor training horses at the Ox Ridge Hunt Club, longeing horses over cavalletti and working on extensive softening and balancing flatwork in snaffle bridles.

The jumper riders of the time that I'd watched at the shows, prior to the influence of Bert and Gabor, were the epitome of rough and ready. By and large, the horses were "rang-a-tangs" in huge, harsh bits, and their riders galloped over fences in the ring as if it were the hunt field. The artful approach of Bert's new style, by working on balance and collection and accuracy, appealed to Victor and to our shared intellectual, detailed nature. He was way ahead of the game in recognizing the skill of these new horsemen; after all, a lesser young man might have poked fun or felt biased, as riders often do when they see a new or unusual method. Lucky for me, Victor led the way with his inquisitiveness and I went along for the ride and saw the value in being open-minded. In the sport and art of riding, it's important to remember that there are countless approaches worth learning. Nearly all of them carry something, however minor, worth applying to the classic approach.

I was curious and interested in the methods of Bert de Némethy and Gabor Foltenyi, but there was a moment of clarity that I can clearly recall when I suddenly *felt* the value of those training methods. Victor had gone away to his first year of college in the fall of 1951 and was coming home on the weekends to ride Nemo. During the week, he asked me to ride him, which I was honored to do—it was one of my first experiences riding someone else's horse at their request. After Nemo had been ridden by Bert all summer, I could feel a level of training in Nemo that I'd never felt before on any horse. He moved beautifully forward and laterally, was light and collected, and soft in my hand. I didn't want to ask much of Nemo while riding him, afraid I would undo the magic that Bert had conjured! I was instantly a convert to his philosophy of training and determined to learn how to produce that lightness and balance on my own.

The horse show circuit, both in the United States and in Europe, was quite different than it is today. Like now, there were small local and regional shows, then larger national and international shows. There were certainly many fewer shows held overall though, with more time off in between for training and learning. But what seems the starkest difference to me was the social scene that surrounded the sport when I was young. Hunt Clubs like the Ox Ridge and Fairfield Hunt Clubs weren't just about the riding, they brought together entire families in a community. The social events were just as much a part of life—and one's day at a horse show—as the riding. There were hunt balls and picnics, parades, committees, and connections to town and city politics. Results of the regional horse shows were published regularly in all the New York papers and there were journalists and newspaper photographers assigned to cover the horse shows throughout the year. Imagine reading an article about your blue ribbon at a summer show in *The New York Times* and all of your parents' friends remarking on it to one another at the weekend social events. That's the way horse showing was in those days; it went hand in hand with the New York social life.

Jane Burr

My husband Emerson ran the Fairfield Hunt Club, which was close to the Ox Ridge Hunt Club in Darien. Fairfield was definitely a fun place to be in those days. Emerson ran the Club for sixty years and was always at shows. Together, we watched George as he grew up and got famous. I was happy to see him get to the top. George was just a kid to me, always well dressed with wonderful manners and a very good rider. He went to some of the parties at the Fairfield Hunt Club and I think he really enjoyed them. When Georgie was young, the horse shows would end around five in the afternoon and someone would say, "Let's go into New York!" and we'd all go in and go out together as a group and have fun. Nowadays, the shows run so late and the days are so long that everyone is too tired for the socializing. There was glamour to it then and it attracted more than just the people riding and working. It was pretty wild, I'll tell you that! Someone would hire the orchestra playing at the Hunt Club for the show and bring it back to their house and everyone would meet there to celebrate. Georgie's eyes sure did open up wide being at those parties with the adults; he saw a lot! And he took it all in, being the youngest one who got in on those parties.

Game Cock and I had qualified for the ASPCA Maclay Finals that summer and I went to Madison Square Garden for my second time that fall of 1951. I was a little older, a little wiser, and had a wonderful horse. However, I was only thirteen years old—and twelve horse-show age—and still learning to handle competing at that level. My standout memory from being at the Garden that year was seeing nineteen-year-old Elizabeth Taylor in one of the spectator boxes in a floor-length, white chinchilla coat bedecked in emeralds. I'll never forget how beautiful she looked; I was dazzled!

The Hunt Team competition kicked off the Junior classes and I rode on a hunt team with Joan Parker and Glenna Lee Maduro (photo 24). Even with Elizabeth Taylor's emeralds and the rest of the glitz and glamour distracting us, we kept our wits about us and won!

When it was time for the first round of the Maclay Finals on Sunday morning, Game Cock and I warmed up on the ramp and waited our turn. We walked in, picked up a gallop, and had an excellent round. I walked Game Cock down the ramp grinning ear to ear, feeling like we had a good chance for a ribbon later that afternoon. The Maclay didn't have a flat phase in those days, but the judges called back the top fifteen riders for the second round in the afternoon. However, when the rider numbers were posted, I was dismayed: even with the great trip we'd had in the morning, Game Cock and I weren't called back. Everyone seemed as surprised as me and I felt bitterly sorry about it. I had a friend from the Ox Ridge Hunt Club named Nini de Jurenev who was a very pretty rider but was only riding a school horse, and even *she* was called back in the second round.

I was certainly disappointed about this, but what I recall most vividly about it was my mother's reaction. She rubbed in my failure for days afterward, poking fun and mockingly recounting how Nini was called back on a plain school horse and I hadn't made the cut on beautiful Game Cock. Her harsh ridicule dealt my sensitive nature a hard blow. Typically the apple of my mother's eye, I was doted on by my parents and grandmother and spoiled by their attention. Perhaps that made me a bit sensitive to criticism, but my mother had moments when she could be cruel. Most of those times, I came to notice, were inextricably linked with drinking.

My parents drank quite a bit socially, which was typical for those days, but my mother in particular had a habit for it. Her mood would darken considerably after enough drinks, and I learned to navigate those waters as I grew accustomed to it. I remember she'd wait out in the car for me to come out from school and I could tell she'd been drinking; one day I even found a bottle of liquor stashed away under the seat. Later in life, I would call my mother on the telephone and could easily interpret how many drinks she'd had just from the tone of her voice. She did eventually seek help with her alcoholism, in Alcoholics Anonymous. Drinking was part of the social fabric in the forties and fifties and there certainly wasn't the level of awareness then that we have today about the dangers of habitual drinking. I'm sure my mother's drinking began innocently enough in a social context, but perhaps the death of her first husband was so difficult to bear that it helped the habit take root.

That 1951 National Horse Show was the only time in my life when I felt utter grief after a show. Victor, who had worked so hard all show season, had a brilliant trip on Touraine in the Medal and when all was said and done, he'd won. Watching my good friend Victor win the biggest junior national class of the year plus the disappointment of not being called back in the Maclay, lit the fuse of my competitive desire. My ambition to win had been kindled fiercely, and I was determined that I would return to the Garden and ride better.

II. MAKING HISTORY

Glenna de Rham

George and I used to get our dogs together and build jumps and make my little Fox terrier Trixie and his sheltie named Kiltie jump the courses. We had such fun! We both took lessons at the Ox Ridge Hunt Club, but knowing I needed advanced instruction, my mother took me down to White Plains to ride with Gordon Wright. She recommended to George's mother that he ride with Gordon as well, and then George started driving down to White Plains with us for lessons.

George's mother would say to mine, "Now Lillian, you know George has asthma and you must take these pills with you in the car and give them to him if he has an asthma attack." My mother would humor her and take the pills, but I remember one day George came running up and said, "Mrs. Maduro, I think I'm going to have an asthma attack!" and she replied, "No you're not going to have an attack; get on that horse and keep riding!" He was so much younger than his half-siblings and his parents were a bit older and more prone to being concerned with his health. I think my mother influenced George in a positive way. One time, she was sitting watching us ride and George's horse stumbled on a fence and was halfway over the jump. George was pulling on the reins, hanging on for dear life, and my mother called out, "Let go! Let go!" and he did, and the horse untangled and George escaped any harm. Those kind of moments helped George feel more confident. I was always the one who would jump anything and be the first to try anything, and I remember George being a bit more timid. George was always the hard worker though—he used to stand on a step and push and push to train his heels to go down.

My good friend Glenna Lee Maduro from the Ox Ridge Hunt Club had become my main competition in the area for top junior rider. A year older than me, Glenna was a naturally talented rider and 1952 was meant to be her year for a chance at the year-end trophy. Glenna's mother Mrs. Lillian Maduro was a knowledgeable horsewoman and very encouraging to both of us. She would sit in the bleachers and push Glenna to properly school her mare, Teacher's Hope, a beautiful 15.3-hand chestnut Thoroughbred and the top junior hunter of the time. Teacher's Hope moved beautifully, would win the hacks, and was very hard to beat with Glenna in the tack.

In the beginning of the 1950s, the classic forward seat style was coming almost exclusively from Gordon Wright and a few others in the New York area. As I've mentioned, Glenna and I won the Hunt Team class at Madison Square Garden together and she won the Maclay Finals in 1953. Cynthia Stone, who won the AHSA Medal Finals in 1953, was another local rider with the classic forward seat style and position. Lou Raganetti trained Cynthia and also taught the same formal style of riding as Gordon Wright. The new style hadn't spread down into New Jersey or Virginia or even to Long Island yet in those years, where the style remained primarily a foxhunting-derived seat. However, as the decade progressed, the forward seat began to creep outward geographically at a rapid pace. In fact, most of the winners of the Medal and the Maclay during the fifties and early sixties were taught the same forward riding style I had learned. They were either students of Gordon Wright or other New York area teachers, of Jimmy Williams in California, or of similarly minded teachers from the Midwest.

The spring show season started as expected, with Glenna and me going toe to toe in the equitation classes. She had a definite edge over me, but little did we know fate was about to deal a blow that would change everything! On the short trip home from a one-day recognized show at Secor Farms, there was a horrible van accident and poor Teacher's Hope broke her neck in the trailer. Glenna called me with the tragic news, and I couldn't believe her beautiful horse had been killed, just like that. We were all desperately sad about it, but none more than poor Glenna, who lost her beautiful mare and partner, not to mention her best shot at winning at the Medal Finals that year. Life is fragile and no one, however blessed with fortune, can avoid tragedy in one's life.

Although there wasn't anything I wouldn't have done to give Glenna her beloved Teacher's Hope back if I had the ability, I found my own chances that year immensely improved by that turn of events. In essence, it eliminated my toughest competition. Glenna tried to establish successful partnerships with other horses, such as Step On. Step On was quite hot and although the horse was a fair replacement in the equitation, by no means was he equal to Teacher's Hope. As with any new horse and rider combination, Glenna wasn't as consistent in the ring, and I found that Game Cock and I were now bringing home top ribbons more often.

Greenwich, Ox Ridge, and Fairfield Hunt Club Shows were the biggest local shows on the circuit, and when they began I found that Game Cock and I had really hit our stride. Our partnership had become so strong; when I rode him, we were of one mind. He was an equitation machine who aimed to please. He was in fact so trainable and phlegmatic that I even somehow trained him to do tempi changes! Game Cock learned all sorts of tricks on command, and everyone at the horse shows grew to recognize and love him.

Riding the trails and fields at the Ox Ridge Hunt Club and lessons with Gordon with their intellectual focus gave me confidence on Game Cock, which resulted in consistency in the show ring and more blue ribbons. At Fairfield that year, we won eight classes and were second in one other. I must have truly sat on Game Cock's head at a fence to get second—that's how dominating we were that year. At the Litchfield, Connecticut, show we won every class.

The judges loved us. Of course, I was a boy and that helped give me an edge. Just like today, being a boy among so many girls helped me to stand out. "Penis power" simply cannot be denied!

I was a rider who subscribed to the "when in doubt, leave it out" maxim, and if I made a mistake in those days, it was a hard chip with me flouncing up the horse's neck. There weren't as many nuances to the jumping classes: counter-cantering wasn't penalized and attention wasn't paid to leads and making all the distances match throughout a trip. It was very much about style and being bold to the fences. Game Cock and I always rode in boldly and jumped around with confidence. As the summer waned, I found myself qualified not only for the ASPCA Maclay but also for the AHSA Medal Finals.

In early October, I heard the news that three good friends of my mother's—Hope Scott, Mrs. MacDonald, and Ivy Madison Wilson—were judging the Maclay and the Medal Finals that autumn. I was gleeful at my good fortune, for they knew and liked me. A couple of years prior, I wouldn't have dreamed of using this as an advantage. In previous years, my parents offered to say hello to judges they were acquainted with at the shows, and I teased them, calling their ethics into question. Clearly my own standards had over time become a bit muddy, because by that '52 season, things had changed. I'd nudge my mother over to the coffee stand to say hello to a judge, or I'd send my father over to rub elbows and talk business. The subjectivity of judging was no secret and, intent on putting my best foot forward, I had learned to play the game!

Once again, fate was creeping in from the wings to deal a blow. I was out on the trails in early October enjoying a beautiful fall day, me on my trusty Game Cock and my friend riding a school horse named Vanilla. Vanilla was a roguish albino polo pony mare with a roached mane who bit, kicked, and had a dirty stop at the jumps. As we made our way from the trail into a field, I opened a gate for us to ride through and the two of us navigated through close together on our horses. Suddenly, Vanilla squealed and kicked out, hitting me square in the left knee. Oh and did it hurt! I limped straight home and to the doctor's office. I hadn't broken my knee, but I was told to stay in bed for three whole weeks with my leg propped up, and of course, they were the three weeks leading up to the Finals at the Garden! There I was, with the sun, moon, and stars lined up, and I was injured right before my big chance at the National Horse Show. I was beside myself, but there was nothing to be done but abide by the doctor's orders.

The week before the National Horse Show arrived, and finally, I was allowed to ride again. My friend Kathy Taft had been riding Game Cock on the flat for me every day while I was lying in bed going stir-crazy. I leaped out of bed and drove down for two lessons at Secor Farms with Gordon Wright. Gordon's goal was to sharpen me for the Finals and prepare me for being called back to test. As a result of those three weeks off from jumping, Game Cock was dead sound and dead fresh. We practiced canter-to-trot transitions, and Gordon taught me a strategy for the age-old test of cantering the first jump in a line and trotting out over the second. He taught me how to angle very slightly into the wall to shift the horse's eye and get the trot transition more easily before the second jump. In future years I would teach that same preparation to my students many, many times.

It was finally time for the National Horse Show. With the horses prepared and my show clothes cleaned and pressed, my parents and I traveled into New York City, soaking up the familiar electricity. Madison Square Garden was alive with pomp and circumstance and as usual, the weekdays began with the professional classes and the various exhibition events. The first night of riding for the juniors was the Hunt Team on Friday night, a very popular class and a favorite for the crowd. I rode on a team with Cynthia Stone and Glenna Lee Maduro and we all rode well and won the class, giving us a wonderful start to the weekend (photo 27).

The following day was the Junior Hunter Under Saddle class and all the riders hacked together. Hope Scott, one of the judges, stood at the in-gate as I tried to enter a ring so packed with horses that it was hard to even find a chance to step into the crowd; there must have been close to 80 horses. As I walked by Hope Scott, she asked, "Georgie, what's your number?" and I jokingly replied, "80!" and she laughed. I was the darling of those horse show ladies!

Game Cock's ears were pricked forward as I rode him into the ring, feeling how fresh he was. He floated over the ground, gleaming with rest and care, and when we lined up with the others spanned out across the length of that big ring, I was eager to hear the announcer read the numbers. Out of all the dozens of junior hunters, Game Cock was pinned first! I was so proud to have such a spectacular partner and to feel the result of all of our training and hard work. All the girls at the horse show came up to pet Game Cock and kiss the white snip on his nose. He got so many kisses that he had red lipstick smudges on his muzzle, which I rubbed off to save him the embarrassment!

Sunday was the big day at Madison Square Garden, with both the ASPCA Maclay and AHSA Medal classes. The crowd sparkled—full of beautiful people in their Sunday best. The first round of the Maclay was held in the morning, with around 100 entries vying for fifteen spots for the second round. Game

Cock and I put in a solid round in the Maclay once again. I was a little nervous about a repeat of the prior year's surprising disappointment, but was very excited to see that I made the list for the afternoon round. My friends Ronnie Mutch and Glenna Lee Maduro were also among those called back, and we were all smiles, excited to be in it together. Although Ronnie had won the Medal two years prior, he was still trying for a win in the Maclay, and I knew he'd be hard to beat.

The Medal Finals had fewer riders, approximately fifty, that had qualified, but the difficulty level rose. The Medal course was quite technical for those days, with an end jump and both straight and diagonal lines. The jumps themselves were very simple hunter fences with plain white rails. Gordon Wright gave me a few words of advice and I rode into the ring on Game Cock, picking up our bold, galloping stride. We had another consistent, forward round, and it felt great! I was thrilled to hear we were called back to test, along with five other riders.

For the Medal test, which was immediately after the initial round was completed, the judges asked us to switch horses. To my excitement, I was switched with Glenna. She was on a horse named Shady Pete from Secor Farms, a classy looking, dark brown horse that I had ridden before. With a nice, soft mouth and a great stride, Shady Pete was a total pleasure to ride; he never stopped and he purred around like a Rolls Royce. I had a beautiful round on Shady Pete and watched the other riders also ride well. As we waited for the judges to decide, I tried to stay calm. Then they made the announcement—I had won! Despite all the other wonderful riders and horses, the judges gave me the top spot. I had won the Medal Finals!

After the Medal awards ceremony, there was a lunch reception at the Waldorf Astoria and all our friends from the area hunt clubs were there. I beamed from ear to ear, trying to be modest and gentlemanly in my formal attire, but doing cartwheels of celebration on the inside. I couldn't wait to get back in the ring on Game Cock for the second round of the Maclay that afternoon. We sat at a big table all together and my mother, who rarely spoke a word at these occasions, asked Gordon Wright, "Well, how's George going to do this afternoon?" to which Gordon replied, "Well, Mrs. Morris, he'll have to fall off to lose it!"

My personal superstitions about competing, some of which I've had my entire life, had already begun in those early years. My lucky number at the Ox Ridge Hunt Club schooling shows was 22 and when I registered at other shows, I could often request that number. I was given number 62 at the Garden that year, which still felt like a good number. Later, when I rode in the 1960 Olympics I was given the number 44, which felt very lucky because it was double 22.

In those days, I was also superstitious about going into the ring first. There wasn't a set order—riders would line up outside the in-gate and ride in as soon as each was ready to go. Over lunch at the Waldorf Astoria, my home-town friends had hatched a plan to try to change my luck. Knowing I wanted to go first in the second round of the Maclay, Ronnie and Glenna sat by the in-gate on their horses long before the class began in order to block me from going into the ring first. I saw what they were up to! I warmed up Game Cock quickly on the ramp and stood right up behind them at the in-gate.

Just as the class began and the gate was starting to open, Ronnie made his move to walk into the ring as the first to go. It was then I gave Game Cock a signal—one we'd practiced back at home—and put my hand on his croup. He leaped forward, doing a massive capriole and sailing clear over the in-gate and right past Glenna and Ronnie, kicking out behind him! Riders and horses scattered and we trotted into the ring first once again. To this day, I still don't know how I taught Game Cock those tricks. Our partnership was special, and he was one of the most trainable horses I've ever ridden.

I put in a quality second round in the Maclay and again was among six rid-ers called back to test. For the test, just like the Medal, the judges asked riders to swap horses and jump the course again. I was instructed to swap with Jill Diner, one of two Diner sisters I knew from the local shows. Incredibly, Jill was riding none other than Victor's former equitation horse Touraine. I knew Touraine very well, of course, from helping Victor get her kinks out at the shows. With Touraine having jumped the course already under Jill and settled into her job, we had an absolutely brilliant round for the test. The crowd cheered and I saw the smiles on my parents' faces as they announced the judges' decision. Incredibly, I had won the Maclay Finals, too! It was surreal after the previous year's disappointment, not to mention unprecedented for a fourteen-year-old to have won both in the same year (photo 28).

Winifred Gray

When George rode in the Medal and the Maclay in '52, I was twelve, and even though George invited me to the city to watch him, my parents wouldn't allow me to go because I was so young and still in school. I remember waking up the morning after he won the Maclay and see-ing his picture in *The New York Times*. Then just as I was finishing the article, the phone rang and it was George calling from New York. He said, "I won!" I told him I knew it and that I'd just read all about it in the paper. And he replied, "Oh I haven't seen the papers yet...." and after a pause, "Winnie, look at the picture carefully for me." "Yes?" I said. And completely serious, George asked, "Are my heels down?" "Yes," I replied earnestly. "Yes, George, your heels are down."

Winning those two classes at age fourteen was a life-altering accomplishment that is not lost on me, but neither is the way in which I won. Certainly, I had good rounds on Game Cock and consistently rode well on the other horses in the tests. However, Glenna's loss of Teacher's Hope eliminated my main competition that year and riding Shady Pete and Touraine in the tests was an advantage that helped me clinch the wins. The judges must have known that I was familiar with those two horses! Judging bias is a part of horse showing and it would be folly to deny it exists to some extent, even if it's not altogether a conscious bias.

With the social environment so intertwined with showing and the technical aspects judged in jumping classes less complex in the 1950s, the potential for bias was likely even stronger than it is today. When I became a judge, I recognized my own desire to see those riders do well whom I had already developed a respect for over time. Certainly, a fantastic performance in the ring by a newcomer should always be justly scored, but familiarity undoubtedly breeds a tinge of bias for any judge.

It was, regardless, an incredible feat: from elimination in the first round of the Maclay in 1951 to winning both the Maclay and the Medal Finals a year later. As the first to win both in the same year and at such a young age, I suddenly became the most talked about junior rider in the country. I had captured the attention of many, including older horsemen in the jumpers who would invest their time mentoring me in years to come. I was catapulted to an enviable position, yet at the same time the wins limited me to what classes I could show in for the rest of my junior years. There was an unwritten rule: winning both Finals meant it would be frowned upon to compete in other junior equitation divisions.

To set my sights on a new goal, Gordon Wright suggested to my father that I begin riding at Joe Vanorio's place and train for the Good Hands equitation medal in saddle seat. That was a common thing to do in those days—to try for ribbons in both disciplines' junior finals. Victor Hugo-Vidal had done it, and I would have been willing to try it as well, but it was not what my father had envisioned for my riding life. He was incredulous in his reply to Gordon; I believe his actual words were, "Over my dead body is he riding with those sissies on those saddle horses!"

When I won the Finals in '52, I had a girlfriend named Barbara who was one of the most beautiful girls at school. She lived in town and not up on one of the Ridges, so was considered a "townie." When I got back from Madison Square Garden that year I saw Barbara hanging out instead with a jock—a nice fellow named Vince. I realized that she'd dropped me like a hot potato because I was away riding all the time on the weekends. It really bothered me, and I was upset for a while afterward. My mother, who was never a fan of the girls I dated (but always took to the boys), would go out of her way to drive me by Barbara's house on the way home from the Ox Ridge Hunt Club and lecture me about how a 'townie' wasn't good enough for me anyway.

Through the following year, I continued riding with Gordon Wright and learning to jump bigger fences. At Secor Farms, I tried to watch and learn from the fabulous group of jumper riders there, including Elaine Moore (later: Moffat), her sister Pamela Moore, Nancy Maginnes (later: Kissinger), and Ethel Skakel (later: Kennedy). I also had a training project in a small, 14.3-hand horse named Bubble Gum; some clients of Gordon's sent him up and I had a hand in making him.

I set my sights on the Henry Bergh trophy (named for the man who founded the ASPCA in 1866) a year-end championship like the Maclay given on the basis of points earned at unrecognized shows. Every two weeks, Gordon hosted an unrecognized show at Secor Farms—it was like a schooling show— and every two weeks I rode in the Henry Bergh class to try for this third sort of championship.

By that time, Victor Hugo-Vidal had picked up two high-profile young students, Marshall Field's daughters Phyllis and Fiona. After Victor and Phyllis became an item, I ended up dating Fiona Field and we'd double date with the two sisters. Victor and I went out together to Huntington, Long Island, to visit the girls and stay at Marshall Field's estate called Caumsett (now a state park). When we drove into the estate, I looked at the immense house and said to Victor, "Wow, what a place!" to which he replied, "Oh George, that's just the stable!" My eyes widened as we drove up the long lane to the actual residence, a gargantuan mansion sitting on a steep cliff overlooking Long Island Sound like a king on his throne. I was stunned at the level of luxury and structured service at the Field's…it was a whole new stratum of society. A valet unpacked my suitcase for me!

In the Henry Bergh equitation classes I rode regularly against Phyllis, Victor's protégé and girlfriend, who by then was riding my little project horse Bubble Gum. I rode Pomperius, a drop-dead-gorgeous gray working hunter of Gordon's. Pomperius had a major flaw in that he was just too smart. If he had jumped a course once at a show, and he was asked to do it again, he would pass the in-gate, stop, and rear straight up! Nothing you could do would get that horse to go a second time. Gordon would take him to the Garden just to win the hack class and then take him back home again. Well, I rode this horse against Phyllis on Bubble Gum in the Henry Bergh class where the top two would get called back in to switch horses in the test. I'd gotten Pomperius around the course the one time already, and poor Phyllis had to be the one trying to convince him to go again! His big flaw gave me an advantage, and she never got him past the in-gate. Every two weeks this would happen, and that's how I won the Henry Bergh trophy that year. Interestingly, Phyllis Field later ended up being the patron of Nuno Oliveira, an iconic and famous dressage rider and trainer.

In 1953, I turned my focus to retiring the equitation championship trophies at the Greenwich, Ox Ridge, and Fairfield Hunt Club Shows. Judging one particular equitation championship that year was Mrs. Celeste Harper, a lady judge with whom I was quite friendly. I didn't have a great round in the class, and after dinner, the judge called us in to test and asked us to dismount while they decided which horses to switch us onto. After a while, Mrs. Harper said, "Gentlemen and ladies, instead of switching, please get back on your own horses, ride down the center line and show changes of lead." Well, the other riders did a couple of changes, some simple and others flying, while Game Cock did perfect tempi changes all the way down the center line. It was yet another trick we'd mastered at home and Mrs. Harper was so impressed she gave us the blue ribbon, despite our subpar round on the course.

My success with Game Cock continued, but some weren't happy with me taking the ribbons from other riders who were still trying to win the Medal and Maclay. Some older horsemen made it clear I was ruffling feathers by riding in the equitation divisions and breaking that unwritten rule. As happens with boys who get a lot of blue ribbons, I grew to be quite cocky; in fact, looking back I was probably unbearable! One day Victor Hugo-Vidal and I were playing croquet together and he scoffed at me, "Now I suppose you want to ride in the Olympics!" And quite seriously I replied that yes, of course I did (photo 29).

At the Greenwich Hunt Club Show that year, they took the equitation championship out onto the outside course. Ned Hancock, a friend of Victor

Hugo-Vidal's, had a successful equitation career but like Victor was older and no longer showing in the junior classes. Victor and Ned were at the Greenwich show that day and a rare rule of engagement was instituted for the equitation championship: for the test, a strange horse could be supplied by the committee to be brought in cold turkey and everyone would ride their test on this new horse.

Victor and Ned cooked up a plan before the show to get Savage Lover, Ned's very hot horse, as the new horse to be supplied for the test. Victor told me to be careful not to get run away with when riding Savage Lover over the wide open outside course. In the test, I rode first and galloped to the first fence, a stout three-foot-six brush jump, without much leg on him, thinking that such a hot horse should go well with a light ride. Right at the last stride before the brush, Savage Lover stopped dead! Glenna won the challenge trophy that day, and Ned and Victor succeeded in taking me down a peg with their scheme.

I remember feeling quite determined the following weekend at the Ox Ridge Hunt Club and winning nearly every class. Then, upon arriving at the Fairfield Club Show, we discovered Game Cock wasn't sound. Otto Heuckeroth looked at him and declared Game Cock needed a few months off to heal. He recommended I trade up to my next horse rather than wait around for him to be sound again, although later I realized Game Cock just had corns. We weren't as sophisticated in those days in knowing the nuances of the causes behind lameness; all Game Cock needed was his shoes pulled, the corns trimmed off, and his feet soaked for a week or two. Otto may have talked me into a new horse partly because he had his eye on rehabbing Game Cock for his daughter Patty to ride, because that's exactly what happened. Game Cock was such a wonderful horse; together at times we felt simply invincible.

Wilson Dennehy

I met George in 1952 and we were both just kids. I won a Maclay qualifying class that year in June, and that's the year George won both the Medal Finals. I beat George in the Junior Hunter class at the Garden even though he'd been champion all over the East Coast, which was a great feather in my cap. Afterward, he had to find out who this no-name kid from the Midwest was who had beaten him! Once we started talking, we became fast friends and visited one another every summer for a few years afterward. When I visited George I took lessons with Gordon Wright and that was a huge benefit to me, as I was otherwise only self-taught. Gordon was a wonderful teacher! In 1955 I came into my own, winning the Medal, the Maclay, and the USET Finals. I'm still the only rider to win all three in the same year. George is a wonderful friend and we've stayed in touch all these years, visiting together when he comes to Colorado to teach clinics.

After the Dennehys and my family met at Madison Square Garden in 1952 and became friends, Wilson and I would travel to each other's homes to visit. We were the same age and became great friends, especially because we were both totally horse crazy. That first summer, in 1953, I stayed with my aunt in Highland Park, Illinois, for a couple of weeks, and Wilson and I rode and spent time together. The Dennehys lived in Lake Forest and had a joint stable with Fran and Carlene Blunt, who I grew to know better in those summers.

Csaba Vedlik, another classy and well-respected Hungarian horseman, ran the Dennehy's stable. Liz Colby (later: McGuinn) who, along with her husband, now makes beautiful tack-room trunks and fixtures in Fort Lauderdale, was also a student of Csaba's in those days. After Csaba had finished up for the day, Wilson and I would have fun setting five- and six-foot fences for Liz to jump. When Csaba found out what we'd been up to, he was really livid. Remembering those days, I know it wasn't just for kicks; we were both cutting our teeth on teaching. Wilson went on to have a very successful career as a horseman and teacher.

While I was visiting, the Dennehys brought me to a local show and I rode in a few classes on a little gray horse called Ricochet. The legendary and colorful Jayne family was there: Si Jayne was a larger than life Chicago-area stable owner, and his wife Dorothy McLeod was one of the best riders in the country, male or female.

My reputation for winning the Finals had followed me to the Midwest and people at the show watched curiously as I rode into the ring on Ricochet. I had a tough round, missed to a fence and chipped badly. As I walked out of the ring, Si commented loudly, "Well now, that boy doesn't know how to ride!" and he was right! When I won a jumper class a few years later at Madison Square Garden, as I came out of the ring Si said to me, "Kid, you've learned to ride!"

I'd become friends with my aunt's oldest daughter Jocelyn Carey while visiting the Chicago area. One of Wilson's friends was Lynn Belknap, a beautiful, red-headed, local girl who was a very good rider and eventually married Bert Firestone. I can still see her riding Borealis, her gorgeous chestnut, at Harrisburg that fall in the amateur classes for Bobby and Sallie Motch. (After Bobby died,

Sallie married Kenny Wheeler.) Lynn threw a party at her house and my cousin Jocelyn and I went together. Everybody got very drunk as the night went on, especially my little fourteen-year-old cousin Jocelyn. I couldn't believe how drunk she was! And I absolutely couldn't take her home to her family. We tried to figure out which was worse: taking her home sober the next morning or not taking her home at all. It was one of my early partying memories! We all paid the price and were grounded, of course. Bobby Motch, incidentally, was also one of the characters who I later observed having another life outside of the horse world like my own. I'd run into him from time to time at watering holes.

III. ROAD TO THE JUMPERS

Discussions about my riding future continued between me and my parents and grandmother. Mrs. Farrell, who had sold us Game Cock, warned my mother that I should not be allowed to ride in jumper classes because those jumper riders were "the wrong element!" Jumper riders in the late forties and early fifties were considered to be from the wrong side of the tracks and a rough, low-class crowd. That's the main reason I'd continued to show Game Cock in the junior classes after winning the Finals. It wasn't until 1954 that my parents agreed to let me show in jumper classes. In that year, the image of jumper riders evolved and became more respectable. It had everything to do with the arrival of Bertalan de Némethy and Gabor Foltenyi. They legitimized the jumper scene with their class, style, and intellect.

My next horse was an excellent jumper that tucked his knees up tight and had a very quiet mind. He was a five-year-old, seven-eighths-bred, and I named him Holy Smoke. We paid about $2,500 for him, which was a fair price for a nice horse at the time. Game Cock had cost $3,500. It's hard to imagine such low prices nowadays with horses going for millions of dollars. I began showing Holy Smoke in the jumpers, and the other riders took me under their wing and called me "Georgie."

I also showed Holy Smoke in some Green Hunter and Working Hunter classes to develop our partnership and we began to have some modest success. Like today, the hunters segued into the jumper division, which we began showing in the following year. Ronnie Mutch offered to help me at my first jumper show in Greenwich, and in my warm-up, he told me to jump a triple bar backward. As my mother was driving into the show, Holy Smoke got hung up on that triple bar and flipped over, the standards toppling and poles scattering. Ronnie slapped me on the back, got me back in the saddle, and sent me into the show ring. We went clear and won the class because Holy Smoke was jumping over the tops of the standards!

Despite the jumpers having earned some class, it was still a faster world, and I started to grow up very quickly. Even though I was technically a junior rider, winning the Finals somehow had aged me morally, and I was hanging out more often with the professionals. I was shown the backside of the horse world both in and out of the ring—the more advanced schooling tactics, like poling, as well as the partying and drinking after hours.

My success the prior year catapulted me into notoriety among those in the horse show social scene, and I found myself venturing farther afield with the older riders at Madison Square Garden. By the end of that season, I went from fourteen to *twenty-five* years old, instead of fifteen. I would stay up late carousing with my friends. My eyes had opened to the adult world and it fascinated me. One particular moment of clarity was at Harrisburg that year when I sat behind two ladies who were being very affectionate, whispering sweet nothings in each other's ears. That was the first time I realized the existence of lesbians. I didn't know who those ladies were at the time, but later I found out they were Sallie Jones Sexton and Jane Dunscombe. When I grew up, they became very good friends of mine. Sallie was a famous horsewoman and very involved in the AHSA, and Jane was a wonderful theater person. The horse show world has always been at least a couple of steps ahead of the general populace when it comes to social revolution.

I followed Sallie and a group of professionals over to the fleabag Belvedere Hotel across the street from the Garden where she was drumming up support to break away from the American Horse Shows Association. Sallie had gotten all these professional riders riled up and held meetings there to talk it over. They called themselves the Hunter Jumper Exhibitors Association. To me at the time, I didn't grasp all the details but it felt like the Russian revolution.

From a young age, I was very much into flirting and chasing girls. Having spent so much time with my sisters, mother, and grandmother, I was at ease around women and girls and found it easy to win their affection. Once my hormones kicked in, I was definitely up for some fooling around and would take girls to the New Canaan Movie House where awkward adolescent couples would go to the farthest reaches of the balcony. Barbara Pease, a beautiful and popular older girl, took me across the Hudson River to attend the Devon

Horse Show with her. Barbara had won the ASHA Medal in 1948 and was definitely the attractive, older girl. I don't know what my parents were thinking, but for a fifteen-year-old boy to go to Devon with Barbara Pease in her early twenties was quite something!

Bobby Burke

In 1953, I remember running into a young George Morris at the Devon Horse Show. George had just won the Medal and the Maclay and was with Barbara Pease, who was quite a good rider. I had one of those plaid show jackets that had just come into fashion. And here comes George with the same jacket, trying to copy me! I had a good laugh over it that day. George is a great friend and I've always admired him as a teacher and as a horseman. What he has meant to the sport is unparalleled, but even after all of his achievements I still can picture him at age fifteen strutting around Devon in my jacket.

Even in those early days, I remember feeling the subtle leanings of strong attraction toward older boys I knew. I was stirred in both directions in my adolescence—toward both girls and boys—and began to be aware of those feelings. I had crushes on men in Hollywood films, like Tab Hunter (the Brad Pitt of that era), and occasionally, I would get the sense another boy was attracted to me in that way, although I never felt particularly certain about it. On a couple of occasions, I did have some fledgling encounters of a sexual nature with older boys in my life, despite the fact that my general focus was definitely on chasing girls. Then, in 1954, there was a strong hurricane that crossed Long Island, and my close friend and mentor Victor Hugo-Vidal and I were marooned in a motel for three days waiting out the storm. It wasn't just that Victor influenced me intellectually and in my riding—he also influenced some of my early forays into experimenting with my attraction to other guys.

That summer, I came down with a bad fever and a cough, and the family doctor said I had "undulant fever." Weeks later, a family friend who was also a doctor was over for a cocktail party. He took one look at me and told my parents that I had pneumonia and to get me to the Stamford Hospital. Those raucous teenaged years were the first of many times in my life when I burned the candle at both ends and paid the price for it.

My grandmother was still a wonderful force in my life and it was through my travels with her that I gained perspective about the world and other cultures. Late that summer, before school began again, I took a cruise to Buenos

Aires with her and rested after my bout with pneumonia. I had a girlfriend on that trip who was a couple of years older, and I still remember the two of us necking away in the prow of the boat, saying to each other that we would show those South Americans something!

Gordon Wright had quite a system worked out at Secor Farms and Victor and I became regular players in his training program on multiple levels. Gordon had a sharp mind for business, and he created a system that both he and his clients enjoyed within that wonderful, social atmosphere of riding and showing in the fifties. On Saturdays, I rode in a lesson with Gordon at eleven, then afterward we'd lesson on a client's green horse. The client would pay Gordon to have the young horse ridden by one of us in the lesson while he or she paid a second time to ride in the same lesson on an older, more experienced horse. After the morning lessons Gordon would head up into the clubhouse, flanked by his circle of admirers like the Pied Piper. The clients would buy Gordon lunch and a few rounds of drinks, which would surely evolve into an afternoon playing cards and drinking at the clubhouse bar. Meanwhile, Victor and I schooled more clients' young horses, for which they'd be charged.

Gordon also would take me along to school horses for his Westchester and Long Island clientele, and I learned a lot from watching him socialize and conduct his business in addition to his training decisions with their horses. In essence, I followed directly in Gordon's footsteps in the way I lived my life and ran my business as a professional. There was a lifestyle interwoven with the horse business in those years (which continued until the 1970s) that involved pool parties, cocktail parties, elegant black-tie dinners, and rubbing elbows with the clients. The only real difference between Gordon and myself was that he was always crazy about women while I eventually chased men!

In 1955 I turned seventeen and started doing the big Open Jumper classes with Holy Smoke and with Gordon's terrific horse Royal Guard. A typically fickle teenager, I renamed Holy Smoke and started calling him The Gigolo, much to the consternation of my mother. I thought it was a much cooler name. Royal Guard was a top mount for the jumpers but could be a tricky ride in that he would rear and not go in the in-gate if he felt he was boss. Gordon would sometimes get on him and straighten him out for me, then I would get on and jump around. I showed him several times in the spring, including at the Boulder Brook Horse Show in Scarsdale, and found I was gaining more confidence in the bigger jumper classes (photo 30).

The Fairfield Hunt Club Ball was in June, and I had a lovely date named Deidre Hannah. Everything was going great until I got so drunk that I threw up all over poor Deidre in the car out in the parking lot! The next day, after the jumper stake class in which I rode well, Gordon took me off Royal Guard. I lost the ride on that wonderful jumper of his because of my behavior at the Ball. It was a bitter pill to swallow but a valuable lesson. Gordon put Victor on Royal Guard instead, and I was steamed about it the rest of the summer. Despite that setback, I was jumper champion on The Gigolo at the end of the summer at the Westchester Country Club Show, which was a very big show just before the fall indoors (photo 32).

I felt I was proving that I could hold my own in a field of good jumper riders, many of whom were in their mid-twenties and thirties. During that same Westchester show, I gained a little swagger in my step when Patty Arcuni, who I had a little fling with, made a man out of me in her Bronx apartment. Patty, incidentally, was nicknamed "The Green Machine" by all the Virginia horsemen for her seasoned working hunter reputation even in her green years!

My goals for riding continued to get more serious. Now heavily involved with the jumper circuit, I naturally began to develop the goal of riding for the United States Equestrian Team. In the winter of 1955-56, in order for my education to endure missing six weeks of school to show at the indoors, I left my senior year of public high school and instead attended the Searing Tutoring School, which I could complete on my own flexible schedule.

The national jumper classes in those days were mostly "rub" or "touch" classes where faults were incurred when the horse merely ticked the rails of the fences. The jumps were very high, but not particularly broad, and there wasn't any limit to the time spent on course. What resulted from that class format were riders cantering collected horses to the base of the fences to achieve the highest arc possible over the fence in order to avoid a rub. If a horse ticked a rail up front, it was one fault, and if he ticked it behind, it was half a fault. The riders who made the USET got there because they could jump that great height cleanly. At the biggest shows, like Madison Square Garden or Harrisburg at the Pennsylvania National Horse Show, if you ticked any fence at all, there was virtually no chance of a good ribbon.

With the particular difficulty of rub classes and the lack of policing in those years when it came to using tricks to get an edge, I saw how virtually all the riders incorporated backside tricks to get an edge at some time or another. Poling or using tack poles was a common practice, but there were other strategies as well. One of the tricks of the time was when a horse was fatigued—sometimes I'd see this in Toronto at the end of the arduous fall circuit—riders would give their horses a little bit of "Bells." They were B.E.L.L Drops, an old colic treatment (still sold for that purpose today, although not commonly used). When you put a drop on a horse's tongue, his eyes would dilate and he would become hyper-alert, jumping out of his skin in the show ring. In the 1960s, everything changed, of course, and there were strict rules put in place. In fact, Sallie Sexton was instrumental in garnering support for the first drug testing (and penalties for drug presence) in horse showing. All competitors, in any sport, try to enhance performance, and it's often a fine line between what is appropriate and what is not. But right or wrong, in the 1950s before enforcement caught up with everyone's tricks, it was a veritable free-for-all.

At Harrisburg that year, I stabled with Dave Kelley, a legendary horseman and stable manager who I had gotten to know at the Ox Ridge Hunt Club. Whenever I saw any of the international teams ride out to school their horses, I would get on The Gigolo and tag along with them to see what I could learn. That poor horse was worked multiple times a day, every day at Harrisburg. I was always a driller at heart. All the practice started paying off. After Harrisburg, we moved on to Madison Square Garden, and I won a big jumper class called The Pen. I was thrilled that I was proving I could go up against the big riders of the jumper world with The Gigolo (photo 33).

During that indoor circuit, I managed to pull a fast one on Gordon Wright. I had apparently learned from the master himself how to be a shrewd businessman because I bought a fabulous new horse right out from under him. Gordon had a client named Corky Craig who owned a beautiful Thoroughbred mare, a granddaughter of Man o' War called War Bride. War Bride had been hunter champion of the country as a three- and four-year-old, but then became windy. As with any horse that starts to breathe like that, it meant she was finished showing as a hunter but was a great open jumper prospect. Gordon knew I was interested in the mare, but he wanted War Bride for himself.

The Dennehys had a top junior hunter named Alcis and Corky Craig had a couple of little boys who rode in the hunter classes. We had heard that Corky had gotten very sick and was admitted to New York Presbyterian Hospital during the Harrisburg show. Wilson, Charlie, and I concocted a scheme. Charlie would visit Corky in the hospital and while there, he would propose to swap Alcis for War Bride, dead even across the board. That way, her boys would still have a horse to show in the junior hunter classes. Charlie would then own War Bride, and I would pay him $2,500 for her. Charlie left for the hospital and when he returned, he had great news. Corky fell for it hook, line, and sinker and signed the papers lying in her hospital bed! Gordon must have been steamed when he found out, but I'm sure he also respected our craftiness.

War Bride became an absolutely pivotal horse for my early riding career; she had that Man O'War heart running through her bloodlines.

IV. THE 1956 OLYMPIC TRIALS

As high school was winding down, I took the college preparatory SAT exams in Stamford where all students in the area went to take the exams. I bumped into a good friend in the English exam and another good friend in the math exam. Although I was strictly ethical and never cheated in school, I found myself getting a bit of aid from these friends of mine!

My mother promised me I could take several weeks off after the SATs and travel to Mexico to train with my idol, General Humberto Mariles Cortez (photo 34). At that time I was most smitten with his training methods. He had led his team to double Olympic gold medals—both team and individual gold—in the 1948 London Olympics. He also won a bronze medal at the same Olympics for three-day eventing, which to my knowledge is a feat that has never been repeated. There was an enormous wall in the show-jumping course in London and General Mariles was the only rider to successfully clear that wall. He did so by purposefully asking his horse to step into the water and incurring faults in exchange for ensuring he had a balanced horse able to fit the strides to clear the wall just beyond. As a seventeen- and eighteen-year-old, I emulated the Mariles style and the Mexican team's tough training exercises. They rode in Pelham bits and incorporated hill work to strengthen the horse's hindquarters and back. But just before the trip, my mother heard a rumor about Mexico being a dangerous place and canceled our plans. When I heard, I freaked out and was so upset that she gave in and we went as planned. Once in Mexico City, my mother and I stayed at the Hotel Bamer. General Mariles's nearby riding club, the Club Hipico Frances, was under the racetrack, and expatriate horsemen from all over Europe rode there.

General Mariles himself acted as my host and picked me up at six every morning. The first morning I froze, staring at the revolver lying in the car between our seats. I could see the General was a very serious man! Upon arrival at the riding club, we would get on small, cat-like, school horses and ride full tilt cross-country for an hour, sliding down into ravines and jumping everything in our path. Breakfast after the early ride was dried beans, tortillas, and eggs. After that, I rode in longe-line lessons with the General's wife or his assistants then had flatwork lessons. Eventually, the lessons increased in difficulty, and we were jumping through the most terrifying gymnastics I'd ever seen. All of Mariles's gymnastic grids were fixed, cemented-in telephone poles with deep trenches underneath them. The height ranged from three to four-foot-six, with a bounce, one, or two strides between the poles. Mariles taught me to sit deeper and go forward boldly. It was a great experience to just be part of the intense training program at the club and get exposure to riders from all over the world.

One evening while at Mariles's club, my mother and I were watching a horse show and a young rider was killed after a rotational fall over a large roll top. That was it for my mother; she hailed a rented limo and a driver and we left Mexico City immediately, driving to Tasco, then Acapulco. We settled in at a hotel there, then later that night after dinner, I went out to see what adventure I could find. As usual, adventure found me! I drank tequila all night, made new friends, and when I got back into the room later I watched the pictures on the walls spin as I tried to fall asleep.

The next morning dawned and I was sick as a dog from all the tequila. My mother had arranged a deep-sea fishing expedition and woke me early that morning, picnic lunches in hand. I somehow pulled myself together and staggered down to the dock with her, but it soon became apparent that I was in no shape to brave the open water. Out beyond the reef, with the swells rocking the boat, I became so sick that I couldn't even stay on my feet. Knowing the source of my illness was excessive tequila, my mother became wildly angry. She ordered the captain to take us back to the dock and fuming, she promptly kicked me off the boat. Sitting on the dock were some poor villagers, and as she ordered me back to the hotel with a shout, she turned and invited them out for my day on the water and the picnic lunches. Oh, was my mother mad! But I supposed I earned it.

In the wonderful horse community of Tryon, North Carolina, the trials for the Stockholm Olympics were held, and I was chomping at the bit to try for the USET. William Joshua Barney, Walter Devereux, and Whitney Stone were the leaders of the United States Equestrian Team then. Tryon had become a USET nucleus, and the team trained there together with Bert de Némethy for periods of time each year when not competing. Gladstone, the eventual home and training center of the USET, had not yet been established. For decades even after this association with the USET, Tryon has remained relatively unknown. However, it has had a recent resurgence with the opening of the Tryon International Equestrian Center presided over by Mark and

Katherine Bellissimo, and Roger and Jennifer Smith. In a way, Tryon has come full circle since I was a young rider and is now once again at the center of the sport.

Betty Oare

I grew up in Tryon and my father, J. Arthur Reynolds, had a horse business there. Much of my knowledge of what makes a good hunter goes back to my dad, a wonderful huntsman in Tryon who took us foxhunting and cross-country. Of course, I was also influenced by Gordon Wright, in particular, when it came to hunt seat equitation. Gordon Wright started coming to Tryon in the fifties, and he and my dad became good friends. When Bucky and I were children, we saw Gordon teach for the first time. Gordon gave lessons to professionals as a courtesy and as we watched, I remember asking my mother, "Why is he so mean?" We found out later that Gordon was tough on the ones with talent. He was such a great teacher and my father was an excellent horseman; when together they played off one another. We all benefited from their partnership. Bucky and I had a chance to lesson with Gordon when he visited, and as a result, our base is very similar to George's. Bucky and I are both judges now and have been for a long time. I remember the first year I judged at Madison Square Garden and I don't know what I was more nervous about: judging such a big horse show or being under the scrutiny of Gordon Wright, sitting up in his box seat, not missing a thing.

In 1956, the USET trained and held the Olympic trials in my home town. All the riders with sights on the Olympic Team gathered with Bert de Némethy. The town has a lot of horse activity, so the whole community was wrapped up in the Show Jumping and Three-Day Eventing Team trials. Of course, George was one of the riders trying out for the team that year. He was about eighteen years old and I was fifteen. All of us there were so privileged to watch the team train and school. Frank Chapot and Hugh Wiley were there and, of course, Billy Steinkraus. I got to know George and we became friends. All the riders stayed at the Pine Crest Inn; the gentleman that owned and ran the Inn was a great horseman. We would go there to hear stories and updates about how the trials were going and talk to the riders.

George has always been so particular about doing things right, whether it was how you rode or how you took care of your horse. He never believed in taking any shortcuts. He teaches so much like Gordon, but he has also added a lot of knowledge and experience to it. Riders "ride up" when they ride with George. He knows what a good hunter is supposed to go like and as someone who specializes in judging hunters, I really appreciate that. I love that George is still trying to give back and impact the riders of this nation. You can't find a horse show in this country that hasn't somehow been impacted by George or by a program that he began. He has devoted his life and his wisdom to the sport. I know he's done and won everything that could be, but to me I just think of him as a true friend.

My ambition and early jumper-world success had been noticed: Mrs. Barney, the stylish wife of Mr. William Joshua Barney and head of the Olympic Team Committee, had taken an interest in me and offered me a couple of her horses to show at the Olympic trials. She had an old jumper named Magnify and also had recently brought a big, 17.1-hand, six-year-old, Thoroughbred timber horse called Master William back from the West Coast. As hard as it was to say it to the gorgeous and impeccably dressed Mrs. Barney, I told her honestly that I thought Master William was too green to go to the Olympic trials. Despite her dignified appearance, she was known to curse like a sailor. Making good on that reputation, she unleashed a string of obscenities in apparent disagreement with my observation about the horse! Pointing out the window to her riding ring, Mrs. Barney said, "George, I'm going to build a fence in that ring and you're going to see that he's ready to go to Tryon!" True to her word, Mrs. Barney marched outside and built a giant Puissance fence with every piece of spare material she could find. And she was right, Master William was raw but boy could he jump! Having jumped over timber, the horse was spectacular over big, natural, outside courses.

I shipped down to Tryon about six weeks before the trials began with War Bride, The Gigolo, Magnify, and Master William (photos 35, 36). My groom Mike, a fabulous Irish groom from the Ox Ridge Hunt Club, accompanied me. Otto Heuckeroth made it very clear that I must stop at the Warrenton show grounds and rest the horses. Otto always said you should never trailer horses more than twelve hours without letting them rest and put their heads down. Even as Chef d'Equipe of the United States Show Jumping Team decades later, I remembered Otto's advice. Horses must be well cared for during long days of travel, and it is foolhardy to rush and risk the health of top horses. I haven't forgotten the basics that Otto taught me; they are right and true horsemanship methods.

The stabling for the trials was at Harmon Field, and I lodged at the Pine Crest Inn, a lovely little place where all the horse people were staying together.

The Cotton Patch was a large outdoor grass ring with beautifully crafted fences where the trials themselves were held. Even though I was riding in the Olympic trials that year and trying to make the USET, I was still an outsider and not part of Bert de Némethy's fold. When I saw Bert de Némethy training nearby, I simply watched and trained on my own. For the first time at Tryon, there was an opportunity for me to get to know William Steinkraus and Frank Chapot. I had watched Bill Steinkraus in the mid-1950s showing Mrs. Farrell's horses at Madison Square Garden and was so impressed with his skill and style. At the Cotton Patch, I carefully watched how they handled the horses. Bill rode a slightly deeper, taller seat than I did, but he had such elegance! Raymond Burr, Emerson's brother, and Bill were each great stylists of the time.

Tom Bunn

I met George in the spring of 1956 in Tryon, North Carolina, when I rode with him in the Olympic trials. I went out about a week early, and I remember eating at the lodge with Bill Steinkraus, and he would play his violin after dinner. Being from out West, it was quite an experience to come East and ride with the team. Three or four days before the trials, I met George. He was the equitation champion; I was impressed by that. I liked him from the moment we met. George's position, when I met him, reminded me a lot of General Humberto Mariles. He told me he had trained in Mexico with him before the trials and you could see that because he had mastered Mariles style.

The fellow that came out from California to help me was Charlie Wheeler, a horseman and a fun guy a little older than me. I was stabled two or three barns away from the jumping field and George was right next to it, so I would ride by his barn each time I took horses back and forth. One day, I noticed a jump pole sticking out of a long, narrow pile of straw and shavings in the manure pile near George's barn. I mentioned it to Charlie and we decided to have a look. It was a normal length, show fence pole with hexagonal-like cuts on the edges. For a width of about four inches down the entire length of the pole were dozens of nails that had been hammered in and snipped down very short, perhaps a thirty-second of an inch high. It was a tack pole—and a very substantial one at that. I couldn't believe it! Here was the equitation champion of America, the nation's golden boy, with a tack pole hiding in his manure pile. A day or so later, I went out very early in the morning to school my horse. George wasn't at his barn yet, and Charlie and I pulled George's tack pole out from under the straw and set it up on a schooling fence. I jumped it three or four times. My horse rubbed it once or twice and after that, he wasn't going to get near it. I dismounted, and we tucked it back away in its hiding place. I don't think I ever told George about that—until now!

The following day, people were coming to shoot film footage of the riders and horses jumping around. I wasn't going to participate, but I walked over to watch. One of the cameramen needed to change his film case and was looking around for a place to put down the camera while he went for fresh film. So I offered to hold it for him. Standing out there with no film in the camera, I hollered to George to jump a few and I'd film him. Well, he loved the camera so much he jumped ten or twelve fences for me. I would've had some great shots if there was any film in the camera! I enjoyed the heck out of it and walked away chuckling. The next day during the trials, The Gigolo stopped out at a fence for the first time in his life, and I started to wonder if those fences I'd told George to jump had worn him down just a hair. Meanwhile my horse jumped brilliantly because we'd schooled over George's tack pole.

The Thoroughbred horses I brought with me to Tryon all did well over the large fences on the Cotton Patch. There weren't related distances between the fences, but I just galloped boldly and jumped, doing my best to support each horse with leg, seat, and hand. My parents and grandmother came to watch and much to our collective delight, after all was said and done, the point totals determined that I had placed second in the trials behind Bill Steinkraus. At the young age of eighteen, I had taken the trials by storm! Certain I had made the Olympic Team with this excellent result, my family and I returned to the Pine Crest Inn. A meeting was to be held wherein the committee would announce who had made the team.

The committee had a difficult decision to make, and knowing what I know now, they made the right call. It was a very tough pill to swallow at the time, and I was stunned at first to learn they had decided to leave me off the Olympic Team. I had never been to a show in Europe and was very green in terms of international competition. Things like this still happen every time there's a selection process for an international championship. When I was Chef d'Equipe, I delivered that kind of disappointing news many times; it helped that I'd been on the receiving end and knew how difficult it is to hear.

Of course I was bitterly disappointed because I had clearly earned a spot and begun excitedly imagining being an Olympian at Stockholm. But at the Pine Crest Inn that day, the ultimate sticking point was this: what brave soul would break the news to my fierce grandmother? Mrs. MacDonald, one of the lady judges our family knew and an old friend of my grandmother's, stepped up and delivered the news. My grandmother wasn't happy—none of us were—but we tried to enjoy the good results of the trials nonetheless. Experiencing that success in Tryon among all the top riders in the country, regardless of the outcome, made me even more determined to get on the USET.

My personal appetite for mischief continued and I had a romantic fling with an older woman named Jo Vandenburg while I was in Tryon. After the trials, Jo wanted to keep in touch and even mailed me a sweater that she knitted. My family stole me down to Boca Grande Island in Florida to distract me both from the disappointment of not making the USET and also from my dalliance with Jo, which they loved to tease me about—especially about the sweater. On the island there were nightly dinner parties and cocktail parties, and I experienced a new kind of nightlife that had grown-up class. Even though I was still young, I began establishing a pattern of being a social creature like my parents before me. Through all the fun distraction, my family successfully extracted me from Jo's attentions.

I sold The Gigolo after the trials in Tryon because I felt we had stopped clicking together. He went to a woman in Ohio and a very good home. I focused my attention on my partnership with War Bride. In 1956, I took a young guy from the Ox Ridge Hunt Club named Benny O'Meara to groom for me at the Devon Horse Show. I hadn't yet seen him ride except for some trick riding where he'd stand on horses' backs and jump them. My father gave him a $40 tip after the show ended, and later Benny told me that the tip went toward his very first horse. Benny became a legendary American rider with a unique style before his untimely death in a plane crash at twenty-seven years old.

V. THE UNIVERSITY OF VIRGINIA

Bonne Nuit was a freak Thoroughbred stallion who produced incredible jumpers; Gem Twist is a great example of a horse from the Bonne Nuit line that carried those wonderful athletic traits. The summer of 1956, I saw an ad in *The Chronicle of the Horse* for a mare that was by Bonne Nuit and immediately drove to Middleburg to look at her. The mare was very hot and a temperamental 15.2 hands at best, with a narrow body—she was like riding on a ruler! I had to jerk my stirrups up six holes just to stay in the middle of her back, but boy could she jump. She was like an eel and careful as a cat. With her body type, I thought the mare only suitable for a small lady rider, but she would buck, kick, bite, and was difficult to load. I still wanted her; with her Bonne Nuit lines, I told my father we were buying her because she was bound to amount to something. I named her Night Arrest.

My SAT scores came back and I had done so well (with some help!) that I could get into any school I desired. I chose the University of Virginia. It was in a horsey area and my friend and mentor Ronnie Mutch had gone there and encouraged me to follow. A couple of big future horsemen were freshman that year at UVA along with me, including Walter James "Jimmy" Lee and my friend from the trials in Tryon, Tommy Bunn.

My father drove me down to UVA in the fall and the closer we got to campus, the more anxiety I felt about it. Despite my success in the horse world, I was still very insecure about hanging with the guys and being part of a non-horsey crowd. As I watched my father drive away from the dormitory, I panicked. "I can't do this," I thought. "I can't stay here. I just know I'm not up for it." I took a nap in my bare dorm room and woke up still feeling forlorn and displaced. Restless, I left the dorm and took a walk down on the main street in Charlottesville. A total mess and not knowing what else to do with myself, I went into Carroll's Tea Room to have a beer. After I drank a beer, I suddenly felt okay. The friendly atmosphere in that iconic bar turned me around completely!

After my beers at Carroll's, I went back to my dorm room. As luck would have it, Tommy Bunn from California was my roommate, and he had brought four open jumpers with him to stable with Jack Payne. I drew a chalk line through the center of the room, which I still do sometimes with friends that I travel with because I'm so particular about my space being clean and orderly. He had his side and the upper bunk, and I had my side and the lower bunk, and it worked fine for both of us. Jimmy Lee, Tommy, and I became a close-knit crew and made other good friends, too. Most of my college friends were also horse people.

Jimmy Lee

At UVA, we had a crowd of fun horse people that we spent time with. We all had horses and rode but also went to school and socialized together. We did quite a lot of partying in those days, but there was a serious side to it, too. George's work ethic and passion for the sport is unlike anyone I've ever known. Even in our college days, when we were partying and going to shows, he was very, very focused. He's always been passionate about his riding or teaching, for his entire life. I think that's a little extra thing besides talent and beyond the work ethic even; having that supreme passion is a special thing. To this day, he's excited about wherever he's been or wherever he's going.

A few years ago, the USET honored George in Wellington along with Jessica Ransehousen for doing all the amazing things they'd done in their careers. He told me he was reading this book called *Tug of War*, and he kept talking about how I must read it. I asked him what it was about, and he said it was a dressage book written by German veterinarian Dr. Gerd Heuschmann about the extreme things that dressage competition requires from horses on a physical level and how some of the things riders do to get an edge aren't always in the best interests of horses' health. It struck me that George, who has won everything and taught so many riders who have won everything (let's face it, there isn't a lot left that he hasn't done and conquered when it comes to being a horseman), was reading a book about horse training. Right at this moment, it's wintertime and the Wellington, Ocala, and Thermal circuits are ongoing, and I'll bet there aren't five trainers at all of those horse shows combined who are reading a book about training horses.

After settling into our college classes and getting to know the campus, Tommy, Jimmy, and I started venturing off campus with friends to ride. Jimmy and I boarded our horses at Mrs. Drake's stable outside of Charlottesville, and I kept War Bride and Night Arrest, the little Bonne Nuit mare, there. Mrs. Drake had a flat field with a river bottom nearby, and the ground stayed quite elastic, which we liked because the Virginia soil had a clay component and typically became very hard in the warmer months. In the spirit of General Mariles, I built fixed telephone-pole gymnastics to school over in the field at Mrs. Drake's.

Virginia has always been the bastion of the hunter industry. The horse show scene there has always been—and still is—wonderful. Jack Payne, Bobby and Sue Burke, Paul Fout, Sallie and Bobby Motch, Kenny Wheeler—they were the center of the horse world. Being at the University of Virginia and having an opportunity to get to know all of the horse people in the state was even more important than I realized at the time. Kenny Wheeler, a legendary American horseman, managed Peggy Augustus's business and ran her stable when I first visited with Jimmy Lee. Peggy was a champion at Madison Square Garden in every division as an amateur riding against professionals at the four-foot level.

Old Keswick, her family's estate nestled between Charlottesville and Orange, was an absolutely gorgeous place.

In my life, if there was one property I could not help drooling over, it was Old Keswick. Peggy's place was heaven on earth, and my favorite of all time. The house, stables, riding ring, fields, and swimming pool were all perfectly constructed and maintained. In addition to going out there to ride, Old Keswick became a big social scene. Peggy hosted weekly parties that would start Thursday after class and continue through the weekend horse shows. Virginia horse people and fun friends of the Augustus's would all gather there week after week. One time we arrived just in time for a party, and Peggy opened the door with an absolutely wild outfit on—it was a white pantsuit with a bright orange hand print design right over the crotch! We couldn't believe it—but it was just a sign of the more adventurous times to come in the 1960s.

There was a lot of fun and mischief on those weekends of showing and partying; then we'd roll back to campus on Sunday night. The first year at UVA, freshmen weren't allowed to have a car on campus. There was a no-tolerance policy, which I'm sure was meant for our own safety and that of others. If you were caught driving a car, you were expelled from the University. I had a black-and-red Nash Rambler station wagon, and I wanted to use it badly and have the freedom to drive out to Peggy's place. Pam Erdmann, an old New Canaan friend, married Peter Thomas who was in graduate school that year at UVA; they had rented a house within walking distance of the dorms. I parked my car at their place on the sly and walked back and forth to town. Luckily, I never got caught.

I remember I was schooling a green horse out at the Keswick Hunt Club one day, with a sharp rowel spur in the Mariles way. I was trying to look cool and dismounted by throwing my right leg over the crest of the mare's neck to slide off the saddle front-ways. Instead of looking like a smooth operator, my spur brushed her crest, she spooked, and I went over backward! What was even more memorable was that while I lay there stricken with a concussion, Jimmy and Tommy stood over me arguing about which of them would drive me to the campus medical center. They were both afraid of getting kicked out for driving the station wagon!

Pamela Erdmann

George and I were both the youngest in our families with much older siblings. George's grandmother and my grandmother were friends, and our parents were both older when we were born. We were quite literally in the playpen together as babies. I always played with him; we were together so often growing up. He's like another beloved sibling. One of my earliest memories was at the beach club at Saugatuck Shores in Norwalk, Connecticut. One day there was a storm warning and the two of us were playing in the sand when the wind started really blowing. Suddenly I looked up and it looks like a tsunami coming across the sand right at us: a swirling of wind and water and sand. I remember suddenly the wind just picked George right up off the ground and away he went. It was like something out of Mary Poppins! I jumped up and grabbed him by the collar and we fought our way around the back of the house until one of our mothers ran up to get us. It was terrifying! I always wanted to tell the world I saved George Morris for bigger and better things. We laughed so much and were very mischievous together. Our parents hired teachers to show us how to play bridge, and we were so awful and spent so much time laughing that the teachers all gave up and walked out.

I was fifty weeks older than George and because I got my license first, I drove him down for his lessons with Gordon Wright many times. I also got to watch William Steinkraus ride. Gordon Wright was a fabulous teacher and it was such a great experience to go and simply watch. On one occasion down at Secor Farms, I walked into the clubhouse and went into what I thought was a bathroom and it was actually a small bedroom. There was Gordon, humping one of the many ladies who sought his attention! I ran outside and said, "George, you'll never guess what I just saw!" and we laughed and laughed. It was such an education spending time down at Secor Farms. We used to marvel that if our parents knew what we saw there, they'd be horrified.

In those days, jumpers with the greatest ability were often donated to the USET by wealthy owners who wanted to help the home team succeed in international competition. Typically, Bert de Némethy would pair up horses with the riders best suited for them. After my success on the big timber horse at the trials, Mrs. Barney sent Master William to Bert and he matched him up with Hugh Wiley. Miss Elio Sears, a famous Boston sportswoman who owned a lot of horses used for the USET, asked me to ride her horses on the indoor circuit that autumn. Miss Sears had seen the success I'd had on The Gigolo the previous year and wanted to give me the opportunity to show her string of three hunters and two jumpers. It was an incredible offer from Elio Sears to ride her horses and I wanted nothing more than to drop everything and say yes, but it was in direct conflict with my school schedule at UVA. I purposefully wasn't showing so I could concentrate on school, so I told Miss Sears that I simply couldn't make it work. I drove up to Harrisburg once or twice to watch, which simply served to kindle my desire to get back in the ring. Ironically, even with the lack of showing, I was so distracted by riding and partying that my grades eventually suffered.

As fall turned into winter, I learned that Bert de Némethy was going to spend the early part of winter in Charlottesville at Whitney Stone's Morven Stud, a large racehorse stable (and since 2001, part of the UVA land holdings when it was donated to the University Foundation). I perked up being in such close proximity to the temporary home of the USET, for even though Bert hadn't chosen me for Stockholm, I felt I could be next in line for a chance. Not long after, my hope was realized when Bert called and asked me to bring War Bride over to Morven so he could work with her.

Before Bert started working with her, War Bride was a hot, upside-down ride and never went round. Afterward, when I went out to ride her, she was so engaged, supple, and round from the day before that I was afraid to even touch her mouth. I didn't even canter her! I only trotted all weekend, trying to keep that softness and roundness. It was a complete epiphany and even more impactful than when I'd ridden Victor's horse Nemo. Ultimately, what feeling Bert's results taught me was that I really knew nothing. I had so much yet to learn!

Tommy Bunn, Jimmy Lee, and I were the Three Musketeers and had become good friends. In the spring, we developed a habit of stopping in Middleburg to visit Cappy Smith who lived there (and had a succession of wives, most of whom were named Betty). Cappy was Bill Steinkraus's mentor and was a great horseman and rider (photo 37). With movie star looks, he was hugely popular and larger than life. We dropped by to visit right around lunchtime on a Sunday and, being the gracious hosts the Smiths were, we would be invited in to eat.

On the second or third such Sunday, while imposing upon them yet again, Cappy took me by the scruff of the neck and dragged me outside. He was a big, gruff man, and I quaked in my boots as he had me in his clutches and told me, rather pointedly, "I have two three-year-olds out in that field and *you're going to buy one of them.* After you choose your new horse, then we'll have lunch." With knees a bit weak, I walked out into the field and clucked to the two horses to take a look at their movement. One of them was a daisy cutter and the other one was an egg beater. I bought the nice mover, a bay mare, for $1,500. I don't know where on earth I got the money, but I wrote him a check and probably figured it out afterward. He wasn't going to take no for an answer. After that Sunday lunch at Cappy's, I found that I now owned three horses.

Tom Bunn

We said we'd meet at the University of Virginia, and we became good friends there. George always had a great sense of humor. He used to treat me like I was from the pioneer country and wasn't up on modern life, since I was from out West. Even Bert de Némethy called me "the cowboy"! I took it in stride. I remember I visited George's home in New Canaan once and he said, "Now Tom, watch, I will push this switch—and see!—the lights come on! This is what we call electricity. I know you don't have this back where you live." He was always giving me grief like that; I enjoyed it but would also wait to get an edge on him. When I first got to UVA, he demanded the lower bunk in our dorm room and then in the course of conversation about riding and grooming, he told me he was allergic to horses. In our room my head was next to the closet and his head was down at the other end of the bed. When he irritated me about something, I'd reach over in the dark and pull out my riding coat and hang it under my bed. He didn't realize he had a dirty riding coat hanging just over his head. Every time it would only take a few minutes and I'd hear George say, with his nose all congested, "Tom, what is wrong with this room? I can't breathe!" I would tell him I had no idea, and I'd reach down and move the coat back into the closet, since I knew he'd be getting up to wash his face and air out the room.

Jimmy Lee had an older working hunter named Front Page, and he asked me to show the horse from time to time because he was self-conscious about his height. There weren't a lot of tall riders in those days, and he was six-foot-two and talked about feeling too big on a horse. I took Front Page to local horse shows in the spring of 1957 a few times. At one of the shows I happened to notice a red-headed boy who rode a little gray named Playboy. The boy was beating all the older kids in the junior classes and everyone called him a child prodigy. It was Rodney Jenkins at twelve years old, winning all over the Virginia show circuit!

I rode that year at the Devon Horse Show, and one of Gordon's more colorful and good-looking customers, Robbie Schmid, introduced me to J.J. Smith, a horseman from Hollywood. I was completely taken with J.J., who didn't have a shy bone in his body and seemed to be at the social center of the horse show world. He knew everyone in horses and in Hollywood and was also an actor and stunt man. J.J. instantly gravitated to me, and I felt like I could be myself with him in a way I never had with anyone before. It felt great to be with someone who wasn't afraid of what anyone thought of him; he lived life unabashedly and without fear.

One might think for J.J. that being in that Hollywood atmosphere made things slightly more open and accepting, but it was still the 1950s and alternative lifestyles were extremely hush-hush, even in the most liberal-minded circles. It was a big turning point in my life, because my experience with J.J. that summer helped me understand myself in a completely new way. I was 18 and exploring my own sexual identity as a young man. Whether it was the Jo Vandenburg fling in Tryon, a tryst with a new friend on campus at UVA, or partying with J.J.'s bohemian friends who lived in Greenwich and Fairfield, I found myself interested in exploring every direction. I still had girlfriends on and off throughout the 1950s, but when I met J.J. that year and saw how he lived his life so freely, I gave myself permission to also explore that other side of myself.

Bert de Némethy asked me to travel with the USET during the summer of 1957, which meant I would show with them at the Fairfield and Ox Ridge Hunt Club Shows, and eventually at Piping Rock. It was a first step to bringing me in, but it was also a trial of sorts; I hadn't been invited to join the team yet.

Deciding to lighten my personal stable, I sold the young bay mare from Cappy's place in June to a member of the Ox Ridge Hunt Club and made a little profit on her. I kept Night Arrest, as she was just getting into the green jumper division and becoming more consistent. Training with Bert and riding with Bill Steinkraus, Hugh Wiley, and Frank Chapot was an excellent developmental experience for me as a rider. I also observed how Bert managed the team and the team's horses, which of course had its differences from Gordon Wright's business management. Being able to focus on the horses again, with my college classes over, renewed my motivation to show Bert I was capable of handling the international stage (photo 38).

I became embedded with the team that summer and lifelong friendships were formed, in particular with Frank Chapot. I continued getting to know Hugh and Billy and also became very close with Sally Sears from the Boston area. I had a little romantic fling with Sally even though she was quite a bit older than me. She was irresistible, with a dramatic theater personality as a torch singer. She'd go to New York and lie on a piano and sing songs to the crowd, and she often got up to entertain at parties among the horsey set.

At the North Shore Show, I rode in a class against Harry de Leyer who was riding a bay hunter. The horse wasn't particularly hunter-like but he had an incredible jump, jumping over the top of the standards. I immediately loved the bay—named Sinjon—and approached Harry to try to buy his horse. To my surprise, Harry offered to *give* him to me to ride but only after he had a chance to ride him in the early, lower jumper classes at Madison Square Garden that autumn. As I readily agreed, thanked Harry, and went on my way, it was hard to believe my good fortune. Had I heard him correctly? As the National Horse Show of 1957 approached, I kept hoping it was true!

The Belvedere Hotel, a lowly hotel directly across from the old Madison Square Garden, was the hot hangout spot for all the professional riders. The classy Waldorf Astoria was where we were supposed to hang out, but the Belvedere was where all the real fun was had. We'd sneak over there after the morning classes to socialize over lunch and cocktails for several hours, and then we'd stumble back across the street to the Garden to ride in the late classes. Back in those days, all of the riders drank like fish as part of the daily routine. I enjoyed myself quite a lot over at the Belvedere and learned pretty quickly how much was too much. I distinctly recall one evening when the groom had to get me up on War Bride's back, lead me into the ring for the first evening class, turn us left, and cluck to get me cantering to the first fence. Somehow I stayed on and made it around the course.

A great friend of mine from Long Island, Eric Atterbury, who was a very prominent judge and ran the Garden for a few years, said to me on the second day of the show, "George, I have a friend coming tomorrow from California to watch the show, but he doesn't know anybody. Would you be kind enough to sit and talk to him and make him feel welcome?" I said of course, that I would be happy to. The next day, I rode in a class or two in the morning, then went across town to the Waldorf for lunch. When I came back, Eric told me his friend was there. The afternoon tended to be quiet there without as many spectators, and I could see that this friend of his sat in the stands by himself. "Oh, and by the way," said Eric. "It's Tab Hunter—you know, the movie star." I froze in my tracks. "Tab Hunter? THE Tab Hunter?" I couldn't believe my ears. Not only would I get to meet this massive Hollywood film star who I'd had a crush on for years, but it was my job to keep him company at the show!

Eric brought me across the Garden and into the stands and introduced me to Tab. I was completely starstruck! Not only was Tab a huge talent on screen and one of the best-looking men in the world, but it turned out he was fabulous company. Tab's outgoing nature and enthusiasm for life was totally infectious (and still is today), and the fact that he's a total horse lover meant we just clicked. He had, as it turned out, been plucked out of a stable by a Hollywood agent years before, and they chose his screen name because he rode and cared for hunters. We had so much to talk about and got along instantly. At dinner together that evening, I found Tab to be the quintessential New York City companion because he knew all of the best restaurants and lovely little spots in the city. Tab's love of adventure and carefree, West Coast personality were such a breath of fresh air for me at that age. I was nineteen years old, he was twenty-six, and the two of us had instant chemistry and friendship.

The horse show community has always been a little more liberal than the general public and even then, in the fifties, when American mainstream was extremely conservative, horse show people were quite savvy. Tab and I hanging out together the rest of the week certainly would not have gone unnoticed by everyone at the show. That's why, on that evening during the 1957 National Horse Show, I was forced to make a choice. I knew I wanted to spend more time with Tab—we were hitting it off—and I knew if I did spend as much time with him as I desired, people would notice. The road was diverging and there were two paths: either create distance between myself and Tab or throw caution to the wind and do exactly as I wished.

Well, of course I chose the latter. I made a conscious choice to let others think or say what they would and not concern myself with it. Although a few years before I had accepted my preferences in my own mind, I still felt very cautious about my public persona. With Tab, it was more of a public coming out because it was very obvious that we were together all the time. Looking back on that choice, it was a groundbreaking and sharply defining moment in my life. Choosing to let others notice my companionship with a man and not hide or pretend was a very big deal, especially in 1957.

Since that first night with Tab, I have never shied away from anyone I wish to have a relationship with. Choosing that definite path at such a young age served me well for all the years to follow. As a result of that unapologetic stance, I never—not even once—had a problem with others judging my lifestyle choices. Being gay was personal and not something that I wore on my sleeve all the time, but just the same, I didn't try to pretend I was straight. It never affected my business or career as a horseman negatively, and I've never experienced any prejudiced treatment because of it. I'm sure there were whispers behind my back but that never bothered me. My certainty about it encouraged those around me to accept me for who I was. That choice in New York at nineteen years old changed my life forever.

Tab Hunter

I met George at the old Madison Square Garden National Horse Show when he was just a young man. He was showing his wonderful mare, War Bride, and had just been selected to represent the United States Equestrian Team. George was thrilled. He was looking forward to working with Bert de Némethy and being a part of that great American team of incredible riders like Billy Steinkraus and Frank Chapot.

While out riding one day, we discussed the world of acting and the making of motion pictures. I realized that George was a no-nonsense individual who shot from the hip and I liked that. What you saw is what you got. Today, there are too many wimps around who can't make decisions or be responsible for their actions. It's important for serious young riders to be subjected to George's kind of discipline and leadership. I worked with a wonderful director, years ago, by the name of Sidney Lumet. I was doing a scene and he said, "Tab, you're playing it safe. If you're going to play it safe, you might as well stay in bed all day long. It's the safest place to be, but it's also the most boring." I've never forgotten that. Let's be decisive. Let's maintain proper forward motion—just like riding!

The show schedule in those years had a couple of days of hunter and jumper classes for the professionals after the long weekend of junior classes. I remember how proud I was that I got to stick around for those last couple of days and be part of that elite crowd after all the kids left. It really felt like I had arrived. I continued to watch Harry de Leyer ride his fabulous jumper Sinjon in the four-foot-three classes. Bert de Némethy, Bill Steinkraus, Cappy Smith—everyone was drooling over Sinjon and I kept thinking, "Harry must have been pulling my leg, there is no way I am going home with that horse!" After Harry jumped Sinjon in his last class, I walked down to the in-gate to wait for him. Harry hopped off Sinjon, threw his reins at me and said, "Where do you want me to put this horse?" And somewhat in disbelief, I showed him over to the Ox Ridge Hunt Club stalls. Incredibly, Harry loaned me Sinjon to ride—absolutely an altruistic gesture. However, Mr. and Mrs. Dineen, who owned Sinjon, also probably realized it was a mutually beneficial arrangement. They knew I was next in line to ride on the USET, and Sinjon needed some seasoning and international exposure.

VI. WEARING THE JACKET

Sara Cavanagh Schwartz

Showing at the Garden was absolutely wonderful; it was terrific! George and I often sat together during classes and analyzed other riders, trying to figure out how we could get better ourselves. We had met Tab Hunter that year, and I invited George and Tab to come out to Long Island to ride cross-country. I put George on a wonderful little mare named Night Lily and I rode my Zee King, who I took out to ride in the trials in Colorado in 1958 when they thought girls would be allowed on the USET. They were both terrific horses. In those days on Long Island, it was estate after estate, one after another, with huge open fields divided by three-foot-six to four-foot, post-and-rail fences, and you could gallop along and jump for three or four miles continuously, which was grand. I told George before we set off that we were going to go very, very fast and to just hang on and the mare would take good care of him. We took off and went flying along. Tab had never done anything but jumper classes in the ring, and he was back there pulling and going slowly, but George was just as game as can be, galloping flat out the whole time. When we pulled up at the end, breathless and flushed, he said what a marvelous time it had been. It was great fun!

After the incredible opportunity I'd been given to travel and show with the USET during the summer and fall of 1957, I knew I needed to respond and show my commitment. I decided not to return to the University of Virginia but instead to focus all of my energy on riding. After the Garden, we stabled for a while at the Ox Ridge Hunt Club and my new horse Sinjon came along. It was wonderful because it meant I could be home for the holidays in New Canaan with the horses stabled close by. Otto Heuckeroth didn't like Sinjon initially because he wasn't the one who sold him to me, and his opinion didn't improve much when he learned the horse was a weaver. The stalls were all built facing the indoor, and Otto was worried Sinjon would teach the other horses to weave. Despite his concern, I don't think we were there long enough for Sinjon to teach his stablemates.

Tab Hunter came out to New Canaan to visit just after the indoor shows were finished, and we rode out on the trails together. That chilly November day was my first time ever riding Sinjon. Tab and I trotted and cantered our horses for a while and on the way back, came upon the outside course. It was set at maximum height, but with my eagerness to jump Sinjon, I couldn't wait any longer. I turned to my friend, "Tab, watch this horse jump," and picked up a canter. There wasn't a cross-rail or gymnastic to warm up over, so I just galloped down to the first big brush fence. Sinjon sailed over it effortlessly, and I continued galloping, jumping the whole outside course of four-foot-three to four-foot-six fences flawlessly. The horse was incredible!

That winter, Bert de Némethy told me I needed to "learn how to sit" and sent me to ride with the legendary icon of German dressage, Richard Wätjen (photo 39). A bit puzzled, I wasn't sure what Bert meant; I was already quite successful at the shows, and I didn't quite know what was deficient with my seat. It didn't take long for me to understand. I took War Bride to Mr. Wätjen's stable in Bedford, New York, for two months and trained with him. In pre-war Germany, Richard Wätjen was revered above all others as a god among horsemen because of his incredible seat and position on a horse. The German school is, of course, very focused on the development of the seat. I worked with Mr. Wätjen on and off a longe line, usually without stirrups, and worked War Bride nearly the entire winter with side-reins to get her to soften and be less high-headed.

Many decades have passed since I outgrew riding with draw- or side-reins, but at that time in my riding education, it was a good experience to work on my seat, connection, and feel. Mrs. Wätjen, a traditional German lady who was very protective and possessive of her husband, would stand in the corner of the ring looking on fiercely. I was so afraid of her that I remember I would freeze up when I rode by the corner because she would be standing there like a statue barking at me or at Mr. Wätjen. As usual, Bert had been right and my time there was an integral part of my education. Exposure to the German school of riding was invaluable.

I found myself magnetically drawn to helping others with their riding even as a very young man. Bert was nervous about me teaching students because of the amateur rule: professionals were not allowed to compete in the Olympics and if you were caught earning money as a teacher, you would be disqualified. Gordon Wright was a teacher's teacher, and I had learned much from him about the structure and mechanics of correct riding. Since I hadn't been a natural rider and had to learn step by step to build my proficiency, an inherent respect and admiration of good teaching naturally followed. Victor Hugo-Vidal was also a great teacher because he was a "taught" rider. Taught riders often make better teachers than instinctual riders.

My oldest sister Joan and I had very similar natures and always got along well together. Eventually, she and her husband had five children and she was interested in them learning to ride. Joan bought a Shetland pony and stopped on her way north with the family to their summer place in North Conway, New Hampshire, to have me take a look at the pony. To my delight, the pony was darling and a great mover; knowing he'd be wonderful at the shows, I told Joan we had to get my eldest nephew Eddie riding. It was on my nephews and nieces that I cut my teeth teaching and there was little risk to my amateur status because they were family and I didn't get paid to teach them.

Joan gave me free rein to mold them into riders at a very young age and it was on Eddie, Whitney Ann, Peter, Matthew, and Cathy that I experimented with my own ideas about methods of teaching beginners. As each of them became old enough to begin riding, they rode constantly, and I taught them as often as possible. All of them did well in the show ring, but Eddie and Whitney Ann rode with me for the most years and had the most success (photo 40).

Whitney Ann Harvey

George Morris is my mother's brother. We lived near Uncle George in New Canaan so my mother and George decided that we Nevilles, five of us, should learn to ride. I was six years old and my older brother, Eddie, was seven when we began taking lessons from George at the Ox Ridge Hunt Club in Darien. My younger three siblings joined our lessons several years later. We had no idea what we were getting into! For the next seven years or so, we rode seven days a week, including holidays. If we had after-school activities, we would ride the following morning at five o'clock before school.

The riding lessons were terrifying. One exercise stands out as my least favorite. George would tie the reins at the withers of our ponies, remove our stirrups, and blindfold us. He would then lead each pony to the side of the ring where three fences were set up. He would hit the pony with a crop and we would jump the fences we could not see! If we didn't do it perfectly, we would have to repeat the exercise over again. Years later I broke my arm during this exercise when my horse went one way and I the other!

We competed in a number of horse shows over the years. We started the show season in the spring at local shows to prepare for the big Class A shows, such as Madison Square Garden, Devon, and Harrisburg. It was very important to George that we did well at the early local shows. I remember one show in particular in Connecticut when I was nine and Eddie was ten years old. It was an outdoor show with several large show rings. There were hundreds of trailers lined up in rows in a parking area. I remember, after competing in a variety of classes in the morning, we were having our lunch on a blanket beside the trailer, and George told Eddie that his fourth place, white ribbons were not acceptable. He should be winning first place every time! He said, "Eddie, your horse is tired. Follow me!" Eddie and I jumped up and trotted after George as he strode away across the grounds. He walked past rows and rows of trailers, looking into each one as we went by. Eventually he stopped at one, saying: "This horse will do!" He led a beautiful bay horse off the trailer, found the tack in the trailer and saddled him up. He told Eddie to get on the horse. I just stared in silence. I then followed Eddie who was riding the bay horse and George walking beside them to the ring. George told Eddie to enter the ring and ride in the very next class. I found my mother standing at the ringside. I ran to her, heart pounding, and whispered urgently, "Mom! George just stole a horse out of a trailer! Eddie is on the horse and he's going to ride in this class!"

My mother replied sternly, "Be quiet, Whitney Ann." It didn't seem to faze her. I started imagining sirens blaring as the police would soon come to arrest Eddie for horse theft. It wasn't his fault! I was shaking with fright. Again I implored my mother, "Mom, someone is going to find out it is not Eddie's horse!" She quieted me again. Fortunately, the next class happened to be on the flat. Who knew if the horse could jump? The horse could be blind for all we knew. The judges had the riders walk, trot, canter their horses and change direction. Then, what I feared most happened. A woman nearby started yelling at a man, most likely her husband: "Harry, that looks like my horse in the ring! It *is* my horse, Serendipity! Go to the trailer and find out if he is there!" I whispered to my mother, "Mom, did you hear that woman? She knows!"

"Be quiet, Whitney Ann," she scolded again.

A large crowd was beginning to form around this woman who was clearly upset. Harry returned and reported that Serendipity was not in the trailer. The woman shrieked, "That thief! That boy has stolen my Serendipity!" I was so afraid for Eddie. How was he going to get out of this? I thought that Eddie would be arrested and I would never see my brother again. At this point, the horses were lined up in the ring and the winners were announced. Eddie won fourth place, another white ribbon. I ran to the out gate where the woman in the hat and a huge crowd were gathering. When Eddie exited the ring on Serendipity, the woman started yelling at him, "You thief! You stole my horse right out of the trailer!"

George suddenly appeared, taking hold of the horse's reins. "Is this your horse?" he asked.

The woman replied, "Yes, it is my horse and this boy has stolen him."

George responded, "Your horse is a nag, a *naaaag!* Eddie, get off this loser immediately!" Eddie jumped off the horse and George handed the woman the reins. Eddie and George walked off, leaving the woman, her husband and the crowd behind. It was astonishing.

George was unpredictable and a perfectionist. He was also by far and away the best riding instructor anyone could ever wish for. We won many blue ribbons and enjoyed being a part of the horse world for a number of years. I now have the pleasure of seeing George on a more relaxed basis.

Sue White (later: Ashe) was another early student of mine. Officially, her trainer was Otto Heuckeroth, but I taught her quite a bit. She and her sister Judy were close friends; we all played together as children. I even remember that the Whites had a coat closet by their front door and a big group of us used to play spin the bottle and take turns kissing in there! When we were older, I offered to help her out when she was riding at the Ox Ridge Hunt Club, and Sue had a lot of success that following show season. When she won the Medal Finals in 1958, I was a little disappointed that I didn't coach her at Madison Square Garden myself, but it would've been risky with my USET associations. Even being so young, I remember feeling that satisfaction of helping another rider succeed.

Sue Ashe

We all grew up in New Canaan together and my older sister Judy was George's age. I remember we all had to go to this Miss Johnson's dancing school—it was mandatory. We'd have to wear white gloves and show our manners and different families would host dinners beforehand. My mother used to tell stories about how little Georgie would be flinging the peas all over the dining room. George picked me out of the crowd at the Ox Ridge Hunt Club. I kept my horses at home but rode at the club, and he saw some kind of potential and started helping me. At Fairfield, Ivy Wilson, who was one of the judges when he won the Maclay and the Medal, was judging. I remember he led me through the in-gate to be sure she knew I was riding with him! From the beginning, George knew how to help a student be successful.

At the end of 1957, I began my tradition of heading to California in the wintertime to see friends and teach clinics. While there visiting a couple of friends from the Devon area and Tab Hunter, as well, I met Mary Mairs (who eventually married Frank Chapot) and of course Marcia "Mousie" and Jimmy Williams. It felt like a different life out there! They were serious horse people but also very removed from the East Coast culture, which was refreshing. The mix of horse showing and show business made for a fun atmosphere. Tab had a ranchette in the Valley and a house in the Hollywood Hills, and he showed me all the West Coast had to offer (photo 41).

No one can dispute that Jimmy Williams was a legendary horseman, and I was eager to have him as a contact. Although we were rivals in some ways as the years progressed, we were also friends and both wholly believed in a foundation in classical riding. Jimmy had a background in Western riding, which meant he brought in the Western-influenced balanced riding principles, like correct flying lead changes, into English riding. Jimmy mentored dozens of riders who went on to be professionals and ride on the USET. When I introduced the crest release, Jimmy disagreed with its utility, and we wrote dueling articles arguing our points in horse magazines. It was a lively, constructive relationship fueled by mutual respect and the spirit of a natural coast-to-coast rivalry (photo 42).

After my California trip, I shipped Sinjon and War Bride down to Tryon for the rest of the winter for the USET training camp. I knew Bert de Némethy would likely choose the final four riders for the team before flying across the pond for a European tour later that year. It was my chance to transition formally onto the USET if I was invited, but I also knew there were five riders and only four spots. Charlie Dennehy, who was a couple of years older than I and had spent more time training with Bert had a better shot, but I still had hope! When I got to Tryon, Charlie wasn't there and I trained day after day in the cold weather with Bill Steinkraus, Hugh Wiley, and Frank Chapot.

In mid-February, Bert received a call from Charlie, who told him he couldn't go to Europe because he was marrying Daphne Bedford. Daphne's family was very highly respected with roots in New York City and went back three generations with my mother's family. Bert came to me, told me about Charlie's news and said, "George, looks like you're on the team." I was elated! Even when you predict such a wonderful thing might be in your future, there's still nothing like the moment when it really comes. I called my mother and father to share the news and started dreaming of what it would be like to represent the United States overseas.

During those weeks at the training camp in Tryon, I officially became Bert de Némethy's student and was indoctrinated with Bert's methodology.

Although Gordon Wright had introduced many technical aspects of riding to me already, it was my first experience with that level of technical and sophisticated flatwork. We drilled over cavalletti and gymnastics, and I learned the nuances of advanced dressage. In sensing that light, round, supple feel, I realized it was what I had been searching for since I'd felt that soft roundness in my horses after Bert had ridden them. Bert's patient, detailed regimen of strengthening the horses and building them up steadily each week was a revelation.

With Frank being six years older, Billy thirteen years older, and Hugh somewhere in between, I was clearly the rookie, the new kid on the block, and at times the whipping post. I didn't mind; I was so happy to be on the team. While in Tryon, I spent time with the Reynolds family and rode with Betty Reynolds (later: Oare) and her brother Bucky, both of whom would lead prodigious careers in horses. Friendships with each of my USET teammates were formed, each a little different. Frank Chapot and I became very good friends and also drinking buddies. For beer halls and house parties, Frank was my sidekick! Hugh reveled in social life and was great fun while traveling abroad because he loved the royal families and aristocracy we met there. He knew all sorts of interesting things about European royalty and high society.

In Tryon, I had two different crowds to spend time with: my straight-laced riding friends and more Bohemian, artist types. For the most part, the time spent with each was separate, which created a feeling of parallel lives. I enjoyed both worlds and loved spending time with different kinds of people. I had boyfriends and girlfriends both and was just enjoying being open-minded and living life to its fullest.

Frank and I were bored one day and had an idea to go down to the local hack stable and pretend we wanted to learn how to ride horses. We went down in jeans and the friendly stable owner agreed and started teaching us how to pull down our stirrups and mount and we played along with it all. Here we were, ready to go overseas to ride for the USET, and he was giving us a beginner lesson. Frank and I shot each other amused glances as we started riding the school horses. The guy's eyes start bugging out of his head! By the end of this hour lesson, he had us hopping the horses in and out of the ring over the sizeable fence and thought he'd discovered a couple of riding prodigies. We managed to hold it together until we drove away and then burst out laughing!

In April, we brought the horses north to show as a warm-up before our trip to Europe. The USET often based at the Ox Ridge Hunt Club or Boulder Brook because it didn't yet have Gladstone as a home base. Generous stable owners or hunt clubs offered their stables to the team in those days, and we would school at various East Coast riding clubs. For those club owners and trainers, it was a source of pride to host the USET.

Altogether, we had about a dozen horses and were preparing to go to Europe in early May. Occasionally, show organizers would hold USET benefit shows to raise money in support of the team. We went to a show once or twice at Gus Long's out in Cincinnati, Ohio. He was a wealthy supporter of the team and Bert thought so highly of his contribution that he shipped us out there to compete with a horse or two. No one handled owners and dealt with people with more tact and respect than Bert; he was all class. As an impressionable young man, I learned a lot by watching him.

VII. MY FIRST EUROPEAN TOUR

Tom Gayford

George and I competed against each other, but he was a little bit younger than I was. I started on the Canadian team in 1949 while my father was on it, after the war ended. Jimmy Elder started on the team, too, and we were both still pretty young, but we pulled together who-ever we could get to make a team. Riding family horses and coaching ourselves, we often put together teams just a couple of weeks before a show! We were friends with the Americans and our two teams were very close. When we were showing then, it wasn't as cutthroat as it is now; we had a lot of fun. In those early years of our friendship, George was still quite young and very outgoing. He was very friendly to our team, always, and we would rib each other. Once upon a time we were known as those "good Canadians who can't ride"! We still enjoy ribbing each other pretty hard today.

Whenever George teaches a clinic up here, my daughter, who is a professional rider, and I always attend. His vocabulary and description is part of what makes him so successful as a teacher. Whether he uses sarcasm (which is part of his charisma!) or some other method, George has a way of knowing how a lesson learned will stick with a rider. He absorbed all of Bert de Némethy's technique and philosophy and pol-ished it quite a bit.

In early May of 1958, we shipped over to Europe; Bert de Némethy had planned a leisurely tour that lasted from May to August, which is much longer

1. My grandfather and namesake, George S. Frank.

2. "Dearie," my paternal grandmother, Alice Kuhlke Morris.

3. Mother: Mrs. Alice Van Anden Frank Morris.

4. Father: Harry Hasson Morris, Jr.

5. *My father and mother with me in New Canaan, Connecticut.*

6. *When I was very little, my older sister Louise would put me in front of the saddle.*

7. With my family (left to right): Louise, Father, Mother, Whitney, and Joan.

8. Grandmother and Louise driving the rogue Apache Gold and saving gas during the war years.

9. *With Mother in 1941, Delray Beach, Florida, where the family vacationed every winter.*

10. *Basking after a swim in Florida.*

11. *An indication of things to come—1940!*

12. Otto Heuckeroth, who managed the Ox Ridge Hunt Club for over 40 years, with daughter Patty.
Courtesy of Patty Heuckeroth.

13. Miss Townsend ("Miss T.") on far right at the Ox Ridge Hunt Club.

14. Birgit Nielsen riding Robin, a mare that died from a fall over a jump just as she was about to be leased for me.

15. *My very own first horse, Shorty, at the Ox Ridge Hunt Club, 1948.*

16. Riding Shorty in Wilton, Connecticut, 1949.

17. Bareback jumping on Flying Banners, 1949.

18. Gordon Wright riding Sonny, 1930s.

19. The Morris family home, New Canaan, 1950s.

20. Madison Square Garden, 1950s.

21. *Riding Game Cock over the snake fence on the Ox Ridge Hunt Club outside course.*

22. *The 1952 Testimonial Dinner. Standing left to right: Julie Kellam, Victor Hugo-Vidal, GHM, Ronnie Mutch, Kathy Taft. Sitting: Linda Fitz Randolph, Barbara Kellam, Patricia Kelley, Glenna Lee Maduro.*

23. *Riding a borrowed horse at a camp show in North Conway, New Hampshire, 1952.*

24. *With Joan Parker and Glenna Lee Maduro, the winning Hunt Team at Madison Square Garden, 1951.*

25. *They called me "Bedroom Eyes"!*

26. *The powers that be at the National Horse Show: Whitney Stone, Walter Devereaux, Tubby Tuckerman, and Andrew Montgomery.*

27. *With Gordon Wright, Glenna Lee Maduro, and Cynthia Stone: Hunt Team winners in 1952.* © Budd

28. *With Game Cock: the youngest rider to ever win both the AHSA Hunt Seat Medal and ASPCA Maclay Finals, 1952.*

29. *Riding Game Cock in a Junior Olympic Jumper Class.*

30. *Boulder Brook, riding Holy Smoke, 1955.*

31. *Riding Royal Guard—a wonderful jumper—at Fairfield, 1955. I lost the ride on this horse after getting drunk at the Hunt Club Ball.* © *Budd*

32. *Riding The Gigolo at Madison Square Garden, 1955.* © Budd

33. *With The Gigolo, winners of The Pen at Madison Square Garden, 1955.* © Budd

34. *My idol, General Humberto Mariles, whom I trained with in Mexico, 1956.*

35. *Riding War Bride at Harmon Field, Tryon, North Carolina, 1956.*

36. *Riding Master William at the Cotton Patch at the 1956 Olympic Trials in Tryon.*

37. *Cappy Smith showing three-year-old Silver Comet at Upperville, Virginia, 1952.*

38. *With Bert de Némethy and Frank Chapot, schooling at the Untermeyer's in Greenwich, Connecticut, 1958.*

than the circuits you see for American riders today in Europe. The early fifties was the beginning of flying horses overseas on airliners, and our horses were split that year between traveling by air and by sea. One of our best horses—a really lovely jumper Rip Miller—actually died of pleurisy from the difficult journey by ship that year. We tried to save him once he arrived in Europe, but sadly he never recovered. It's very stressful shipping horses by boat because you must plan and purposefully get them unfit so they can tolerate standing still for days on end (photo 43).

While in Europe we based in Aachen, Germany, a town with not only a storied horse show but many fabulous stables and beautiful countryside. It was my first time ever in Europe and I took it all in. Bert knew nearly everyone in the horse business there personally, which of course helped our team tremendously. He had ridden at the Military Riding Institute as an officer in Hannover, Germany, and at several prestigious riding schools, so he had a lot of German connections, in particular. The team stayed in the little family-owned Hotel Lousberg that is still open and owned by the Knecht family.

Bob Freels, an excellent horseman, toured with us and managed the team. I knew Bob as a top rider and stable manager back at home, in particular with the hunters. He was an old-fashioned mid-Atlantic hunter man at the horse shows and a top trainer and teacher in Virginia and Tennessee. Jack Kettering and Louie Rittendale were there with us as grooms and Jack in particular groomed for Hugh Wiley. Jack became a great friend to me while on the European tours. Even after meeting Tab Hunter and making the choice not to hide my own personal preferences, I was still in the process of discovering how private to keep my personal life and my friendships. In those years, I wore different hats with different people. After becoming close friends and realizing we were both open-minded, Jack and I knew we could be ourselves around one another. Being so far away from home, it was good to have a friend like Jack.

I was very apprehensive at first about competing in Europe because it was all so new to me. The team trained in Aachen just as we did at home, using cavalletti and gymnastics. Bert set lots of airy jumps with thin, natural brown poles to keep the horses concentrating. Wiesbaden was the first show of the tour, but we went simply to watch and not ride. When we arrived and made our way into the stands, a class had already begun, and as I sat down and surveyed the course, my eyes widened. The jumps were condominiums! Every single jump looked like a Puissance fence. That particular class had timed, successive jump-offs, and I watched in horror as they shortened the course and made the jumps higher and wider for the jump-off. I elbowed Frank Chapot and hissed, "I gotta get out of here and go home, there's no way I can do this!"

The class format was completely different from the jumper classes at home. Rubs no longer counted for faults. Instead of trying to just clear the fences without a rub, the goal in the European classes was to be fast and keep rails from falling. On top of that, I came to find out that each European country had different kinds of class formats and rules, with courses and jump styles varying greatly from country to country: Germany had huge, solid fences to test scope and France was all about speed. England and Italy were very technical with their cattily designed courses, while Switzerland had courses with a lot of natural fences and banks.

The first show I was actually supposed to compete in, Norten-Hardenberg, loomed like the Grim Reaper. The week beforehand at the Aachen show grounds, the course was being prepared for their upcoming show and we caught glimpses of the fences as they went up. The jumps were so heavy and massive that I started having an anxiety attack just looking at them. There were triple bars made of three Puissance stone walls, and oxers made out of two solid gates with six-foot spreads! Condominium after condominium, each new fence was larger than the last and my knees kept getting weaker.

My grandmother and mother sent their close friend Una Mickle to Europe to act as a sort of invisible chaperone to me throughout the European tour. No one told me about it, but everywhere I went she would turn up, and I started to realize my grandmother must have paid her to keep an eye on me. I told her, "Mrs. Mickle, look at these jumps, there's no way I can do it!" She would say, "Oh George, you'll be fine! You can do it—no problem." I was never a very gutsy rider and would fret and fret until I walked into the ring. Once in the ring, I settled right down. Gordon Wright used to say that my stage fright worked for me. For some riders, it works against them. It can prove a big advantage learning to use your nerves to make you sharper and more alert, rather than letting them paralyze you.

We went to Norten-Hardenberg and I never saw a horse show so grand! The hotel at the show sat right on the short side of the ring, and you could look out of the window of your room right into the ring. The ancient castle of Norten-Hardenberg was visible atop a big hill in the distance and at night they launched huge fireworks. For my first class, I rode Sinjon and the jumps were about 1.40m. I went as fast as I could possibly go and was clean, but placed fifteenth. I started to think winning a class would be impossible.

I told Frank, "That's as good as I can do. I simply can't jump clean and go any faster!" In reply, he gave me a mental kick in the pants and told me to listen up. "Now George," he said, "you have to go as fast to the first fence as you go to the last fence." I started getting little tips from Frank and Bill Steinkraus on strategy in the ring. It was around that time that Billy gave me Night Owl to ride, a big, bay, 17-hand Thoroughbred gelding by Bonne Nuit. Billy had sold him to an Australian business man who moved to San Francisco named John Galvin. Mr. Galvin owned half the USET horses at that time, including eventing and dressage horses.

Night Owl was hot, quirky, and very different from The Gigolo, but he was exactly what I needed. The big bay had enormous scope, more so than Sinjon or War Bride. There wasn't a jump in the world that Night Owl couldn't hand canter, which gave me great confidence over those solid European condominiums. He was always entered in the Puissance class, which was of course the ultimate test of jumping height. In those days, most of the big Grand Prix horses did the Puissance as a warm up for the big classes. It wasn't like today where the best horses are kept out of that class for fear of risk or injury. I had never been in a Puissance before, but on Night Owl I was brave enough to try it. It's interesting what you can learn under pressure. My German language education rapidly commenced when I rode in the Puissance. When they would say, *"zwei meters, zwei meters zehn!"* I began to understand the measurements, since my very well-being depended on it!

Bert de Némethy was such a master conditioner of horses, and I had been learning, by then for months, about his cumulative training methods. In January, we were doing flatwork and dressage. In early February, cavalletti. In mid-February, cavalletti, and then a jump. Bert knew how to bring riders and horses along step by step to make them strong and confident, while also keeping horses sound. He also planned the shows in a progressive way. Wiesbaden, where we went to simply be spectators, would have been too difficult a show to begin with if we'd gone to compete. Norten-Hardenberg was a friendly, three-day show. It wasn't a coincidence that it was a great show for me to get my feet wet. Later in life, when I took students on tours in Europe, I tried to plan our shows with the same kind of care as Bert.

Back at our home base in Aachen, the course had really taken shape and now I was truly getting nervous about it, because it was our next show and a big step up from Norten-Hardenberg. Aachen was an eight-day show including two weekends, with the Monday in between as a day off. The jumps were so big and so solid that it took eight men working together to move one. The jump crews were small armies during the classes, with six men assigned to every fence. As the week began, the low 1.30m speed classes were dominated by a horse named Nico with Anna Clement riding; nobody could beat her and she won the speed classes year after year (photo 44). They called her "Schnelle Anna"! Frank would often be second to Anna, but try as he might, when the jumps were smaller, he couldn't catch her and her compact pony-like horse that could turn on a dime. When the jumps went up, Frank started to get revenge and win the bigger speed classes.

I started getting friendly with riders who were around my age from other countries and we would have great fun together. My comrades were Alwin Schockemöhle, Hermann Schridde, Fritz Thiedemann, David Broome, Harvey Smith, Hans Günter Winkler, and David Barker. I also got to know the d'Inzeo brothers from Italy, who were idols of mine and more of Bill Steinkraus's generation. We got especially friendly with the Germans because they all spoke excellent English and were very welcoming as hosts of our home base for the summer. The Germans were also excellent stable managers. Everything in their stable was uniformly tidy and well kept. However, our American team quickly became noteworthy to all of the Europeans because of how our horses gleamed with good care. I credit Bob Freels, a Southern horseman of the highest class. I remember the Germans would take photos of our barn, our horses, and their braids. The notoriety of the American method had begun to take root and eventually, the world began adopting our style both in horse management and in training and riding.

The American jumping style was startling to see in Europe in those days and even an uneducated spectator noticed the difference. At that time, there was no opportunity to watch show jumping on television and the crowds at the shows were often seeing an American ride for the first time. The typical European rider rode with a straight back and deep seat, pulling on the reins with sometimes hard hands in an effort to get deep to the base of the fence. As the horse left the ground, a rider would often throw his body and kick his lower leg back with a huge, visible effort. Imagine watching a dozen or more riders with that rough style, then watching a rider entering the ring, picking up a gallop with a softness of hand and seat, and seemingly floating around the course like water streaming over stones in a riverbed. Those watching were inevitably struck by the beauty of that flowing, soft style with the rider positioned quietly forward and the horse freed to make his best effort. Not only was it beautiful, our American style was effective, and we gave the Europeans a run for their money.

David Broome

I first met George Morris when I was nineteen years old. My father got to know George very well and had tremendous respect for him in every way, especially his wonderful understanding of horses. I very much appreciated the deep respect my dad held for him. There is one particular story that holds a special place in my memory book and one I have recalled and told many times over the years. It was in the seventies and George was at the Windsor Horse Show with his American team. We were all walking the course and I was following George with his riders. By the third fence George was explaining that the distance was either ten hard strides or eleven soft strides. Moving on, I caught up with George and I remarked to him: "This is such a long way, why don't you tell the riders to just open their eyes and pick up their stride?" George's reply was a classic: "For your advice," he smiled, "they [the pupils] give you nothing. But for mine, they give me hundreds of dollars!" I remember this incident with great affection every time George Morris's name is mentioned. But I will also remember George for his outstanding contribution to the equestrian world, and I am proud to be able to call him friend.

There was a speed class on Sunday morning, which was a German version of a "Last Chance" class, meaning to enter you had to be a rider who hadn't won a class at that level yet. As I was eligible on Sinjon and War Bride, I rode them both. On Sinjon, I was clear and fast but sat up a little bit through the timers. I learned a big lesson that day. When I came out of the ring, Bert read me the riot act up and down for pulling up early and adding seconds to my time. Consider, this man was in the Hungarian cavalry for the Third Reich; he was all about discipline. When you made a mistake, you heard about it. I've described Bert in the past as having an iron fist in a velvet glove, but when he was really after you for something, that iron fist felt more like an AK-47! He had two sides, but in that era, it was par for the course—it wasn't like it is now—and you expected teachers to be tough on you.

I went into the ring next on War Bride fired up after being verbally flayed by Bert. I went to the stick around the entire course, around every corner, and through the timers—again and again to the stick. Well, I won the class. But I had upset War Bride and she never got over how I rode her that day. Remember, she's a hotter version of Man o' War. She didn't need that heavy hand. After that day, no matter how soft I tried to be with her, she was always quicker and jumped flatter and was less careful because she was racing on course. I had learned yet another lesson from that day. Never ride angry and never use more discipline on a horse than necessary, for not only is it cruel, but it works against your cause.

That afternoon, I rode Night Owl in the Grand Prix of Aachen and it was my first of three times riding in that historic class during my career. The grandstands were filled to the brim with a roaring German crowd; I'd never seen such fanfare, not even at Madison Square Garden! The course was big but I felt bold on Night Owl and we had a fabulous round. When all was said and done, I was thrilled to place third—an excellent result against all the top European riders and their horses. I started to feel like perhaps I belonged in the ring with them after all (photo 50).

Julie Kellam

George and I were at a show and Otto Heuckeroth had me ride Patty's horse (and George's former horse) Game Cock in the Junior Division. Patty wasn't experienced enough at that point to jump him at the shows, so she rode in the flat classes and I rode in the jumping. We were tied with another horse going into the last event, a jumper class. Otto asked George to take me over to a schooling fence to practice. George said, "Julie, walk him over that fence. Let him hit it so he'll jump well in the ring." So that's what I did. Game Cock crashed through the fence and I fell off. George ran to Otto and said, "It's all my fault!" I can't remember how we did in the class!

My little sister who was quite petite and a good little rider, rode for George and learned so much riding his nephew and nieces' ponies, Jet and Weathervane. What a wonderful teacher he was even back then. They went to numerous shows together, training those ponies for Whitney Ann and Eddie. I remember Whitney Ann, at a very young age, being longed on Jet with no reins and stirrups, screaming her head off. I told George that the child would never want to ride again if he didn't ease up with her. And he did ease up, thank goodness.

One day, George was at our house in New Canaan when we were in our early teens, and my older sister Barbara and he were down in the lower paddock trying to catch Dad's Arabian named Kuffi. Barbara was frustrated that he wouldn't let her catch him. She went to Dad and said, "Dad, you don't know how to catch him!" Well, my dad went down and caught him right away, came back and asked George, "Son, do you ever think your father doesn't know anything?" and he said, "Mr. Kellam, my father really *doesn't* know anything!"

In 1957, Glenna Lee Maduro and I went to Harrisburg to watch George ride. There were parties everywhere, and I'll just say there were two guys and two gals in a hotel room and George was snooping and got pushed right through the transom at the top of the doorway into the room. Whether he had his hunt cap on, I don't remember, but it was pretty funny. It's a wonder he came out alive—for snooping and for the fall!

The next stop for the team was the International Horse Show at the White City Stadium in London, England. While in London, we were guests at the Hyde Park Hotel, and it was the first time I had ever experienced that level of luxury living, with butlers and high tea. We wore tuxedos for dinner every night and we even dressed up in sport coats to travel back and forth to the show. We kept our riding clothes in the locker room at White City and each of us had a valet in the locker room who polished our boots and cleaned our breeches and jackets each day. After showing, we'd change back into our sport coats and travel back to the hotel. The fences at White City were big, delicate verticals with no massive spreads like Aachen. Each night for the week of the show, a different member of royalty would attend. As I've mentioned, Hugh Wiley was fascinated with European and British royalty, so it was great fun to travel with him to White City (photos 51, 52).

With the shared language, I made a lot of British friends and painted the town, going out to the pubs and having some late nights with new friends. From White City we traveled to Dublin, and it was there that I started thinking I might have a problem—the kind of problem you pick up from being a little fresh with new friends! I showed Frank, who was often my roommate on the trips, and he agreed that I should definitely see a doctor. I went right away and returned with a bottle of big red penicillin pills. The very next day, I won the first speed class I entered with War Bride. After that, I won one of the big Table A classes with Sinjon. And then to top it off, I won the Grand Prix of Dublin on Night Owl. With my sudden winning streak, Frank became convinced that it was the big red pills making the difference. Not only was I improving, but I was winning nearly every class. Years later, Frank and I would still laugh about those magic pills.

We finished the tour in Rotterdam, which was very similar to Aachen with its massive fences; it also had a remarkably big water jump. All in all, my first European tour had been wonderful. It was a thrill to experience the new cities and horse shows, make new friends, and even win some top ribbons in big classes. I took home great memories and an eagerness to return to Europe a veteran of their show circuit.

Back in the United States in August, the USET continued showing on that year's national show circuit. One of the biggest shows of the season was Piping Rock out in Locust Valley, Long Island, which was just before the indoor shows. Bert would show off the team and we'd put on an exhibition of sorts in the rub classes. The Blitz tested riders with very large vertical fences and faults accumulating over three days' worth of classes, with huge prize money (for those days!) of several thousand dollars. The indoor circuit followed, with the team showing first at Harrisburg, Madison Square Garden ten days later, then spending two weeks in Toronto. Even though the Washington Horse Show began in '58, it wasn't added to the USET schedule until '59, when it was slid into the schedule between Harrisburg and the Garden.

In November, I went West to visit friends in California like J.J. Smith, Tab Hunter, and Jimmy Williams. I rode with friends and judged a show at the Flintridge Riding Club, Jimmy William's place. J.J. called me and said, "George, I have a palomino over here that is exactly like Nautical!" Despite Nautical's interesting story as Disney's *Horse with the Flying Tail* and his wonderful jumping ability, he was known as a very hot horse and ran away with everyone. Still if there was a horse just like him, he was probably worth seeing.

Bert de Némethy had also come West to Santa Barbara to visit the USET owner John Galvin, so I suggested to Bert that we go together to take a look at this supposed Nautical twin. A day or two later, Bert and I climbed into J.J.'s car and to be polite, I gave Bert the front passenger seat and got into the back seat. Bert had never met J.J. and when he did, it was instant *rigor mortis*! Bert was as conservative as they come and next to him sat perhaps the most colorful, flamboyant man in the horse business. There couldn't have been two men cut from more different cloth! There I was in the back seat, watching a dog and a cat sitting in front of me. To add to the discomfort, there was bumper-to-bumper traffic all the way down and it took us hours to get there. As J.J. talked and showed more of his colors, Bert got increasingly uncomfortable. Bert was no saint himself and a total ladies' man, but he was still a straight-laced European. We finally arrived and J.J. got on the palomino, who turned out to be a complete maniac. I got on him too and jumped a few fences—the horse was a lunatic and hung its legs. Bert, in his militaristic way yelled, "Off! This horse is life-dangerous!" It had been a total wasted trip. We piled back into the car and it was the same horrible torture all the way back up!

During that same trip, I stayed for a while with Sandy Swayne, a friend of mine who rode at the Flintridge Riding Club (in Pasadena, California) and had a nice, classy family. Mr. Galvin, the big sponsor of the USET, asked me to ride a horse to see if it might work as a team horse, so Sandy and I drove up to Santa Barbara to see Tally Ho, a useful half-bred Irish horse. I rode him and he was quite good. Late that afternoon, Sandy and I began the drive home and the traffic was so terrible that we decided to stop for dinner to let the roads open up. After a leisurely couple of hours at a restaurant and getting back on the road, the traffic was still horrendous. It took ages to get back to her house and we finally rolled in at eleven at night.

Apparently, Sandy's father had called Mr. Galvin and asked where his daughter was. Not only did Mr. Galvin say we'd left his place at five o'clock, he editorialized that he was sure we'd gone to some motel and that I was up to no good with his daughter. Upon arrival late that night Sandy's father charged me with taking advantage of Sandy. We of course denied it up and down, because it certainly wasn't true. No matter what I promised him, Mr. Galvin would never shake my hand again after that—he was convinced I had shacked up with that nice girl!

The year 1959 settled into a familiar rhythm, with the horses given a bit of a break after the last indoor show of the year in Toronto. Then the cycle of winter reconditioning began with flatwork and cavalletti down at Boulder Brook. Team riders like me, who had learned from Gordon Wright and grown up with a technical riding foundation, settled very comfortably into Bert de Némethy's program. On the team in those days, Bert's Hungarian background of very correct riding and horse management merged with our American style of horse care led by Bob Freels. Sometimes others who joined the team didn't fall into Bert's system as well, but those of us who had ridden with Gordon felt right at home.

Bert was a great mentor for me in terms of learning how to manage an entire operation, including the schedules for riders and care of the horses, management of the stable, the hierarchy of the staff and grooms, and even how to store equipment and fences. Bert and Bob Freels were a winning combination and no detail was forgotten, which taught me how much success grows from attention to detail. It wasn't a coincidence that we had such a consistent record during Bert's tenure as Chef d'Equipe; the standards he set were a significant factor in that record.

During Bert's time, the team certainly didn't get gold medals across the board, but they were consistently in the top spots in Nations Cups and Olympic Games. Even on bad days, the team would finish with a decent result. When Bert's influence on the USET, which continued for several years even after his retirement, began to fade, the consistency was lost. Not to say the team hasn't had some great successes in recent decades—we absolutely have—but we've had some very disappointing periods as well. The high of our highs and the low of our lows fell farther apart. That's the difference. That's what happens when you lower your standards. It's hard for me to see riders today—at every level—and their lack of attention to detail. If you have the power to create a first-class operation, and you recognize how setting the highest standards with your horse care and training is a key to success, why wouldn't you strive for it with all of your might?

At Boulder Brook, there was a horse dealer and professional named Joe Green who was a self-made success from Pennsylvania. He had a very old-fashioned, rough-and-ready riding style and was a great rider and horseman. Joe would watch Bert in the ring, as he was teaching someone the rhythmic-stride approach method to a jump. Bert would pound his fist into his other hand, and sternly call out, "da–da–dum, da–da–dum, da–da–dum, NOW!" as you approached a fence and left the ground. Joe poked fun at Bert while jumping around a course in his own style: sitting in the back of the saddle with his hands way up and his stirrups home on his feet. Watching Joe, I was amazed at the contrast and clash in riding styles that winter at Boulder Brook. It was representative of the evolution of the American jumping style that was beginning at that time.

In March of 1959 we shipped to Rome, and because Bill Steinkraus and I had asthma, Whitney Stone booked us first-class beds on Scandinavian Airlines, which flew the Polar route. The first year, I had been so asthmatic and sick shipping with the horses that I'd had to sit up in the cockpit with the pilots so I could breathe. We never heard the end of it from Frank and Hugh because we got those first-class beds all the way to Europe that year. The tour that summer was in many of the same cities: Rome, Wiesbaden, Norten-Hardenberg, Aachen, White City, Dublin, and Rotterdam, and we returned to the States at the end of August in time for the indoor shows. My great friend from UVA Jimmy Lee traveled with the USET that year and studied riding across Europe. He was always very dedicated to the sport and we had a great time together in Rome. My father gave me $500 beer money for the whole four months; that's how cheap it was!

One of the new shows for me that year, the Rome International Horse Show, was held in the famous Piazza di Siena. Bert de Némethy used to say that the USET rode with a mixed Italo-German style, with seventy-five percent Italian and twenty-five percent German. We stabled at Passo Corese, Piero d'Inzeo's base, and would drive every day from the Flora Hotel at the top of the Via Veneto down to the stable. The Flora was a first-class hotel; in those days the USET always went first class. It was meant to be a luxury trip while enjoying the sport at a leisurely pace. It wasn't a business then, it was a pursuit at the top of its game!

I noticed the good looking concierge at the Flora Hotel almost immediately and since we stayed there for six weeks, I had quite a chance to get to know him. He was a sociable Italian guy who knew the city, and we had a sort of casual friendship during our stay. He would knock on my door at odd hours of the day and night when he got off his work shift. I'm not sure if anyone ever caught onto us, but as it didn't interfere with my riding obligations, it carried on right under Bert's nose.

Bert brought us to Rome on purpose because the Olympics were there the following year and he wanted us to have a chance to get comfortable there. The course builder was notoriously diabolical, and he was also going to build the Olympic course in 1960. The fences were very big but unlike Aachen, the rails were thin and the course had tough turns and trappy distances. It was really difficult and very few riders had clear rounds. His combinations were ridiculous! One particular combination was a massive triple bar, twenty-six feet (a one stride) to a stone wall, then thirty-one-and-a-half feet to a six-foot-wide square oxer. You virtually didn't know until you got there and felt how well you jumped into the combination whether it was going to be one or two strides between the wall and the oxer. It was extremely difficult and these days would also be considered unacceptably dangerous.

My grandmother, ever a supportive and thoughtful presence in my life, happened to come to the show in Rome to watch me ride, which was quite a rare occurrence. She had such stature. Bert would stop all goings-on and talk to her because her sheer intellectual power commanded such respect. One particular jump-off course in a class included that nearly unrideable combination I described above, and as a result, twenty horses had falls and one horse even had to be put down. I knew ahead of time that it was going to be a bloodbath with that combination and told my grandmother to stay in her hotel and rest. I had a premonition that I might fall myself riding Night Owl through the combination and that's exactly what happened. Thankfully my grandmother was spared the show!

While in Munich with my grandmother that summer, she took me to see the world-famous *Passion Play*, a dramatic rendition that depicts the Passion of Jesus Christ and is a traditional part of Lent for some Christians. To my knowledge, no other American has attended that special theater presentation as frequently as my grandmother. That year, Hugh Wiley and his girlfriend both planned to go along with us. However, when we got to the theater we found there weren't enough tickets for all of us. We ended up playing musical chairs, taking turns with the tickets. Then all three of us had to sleep in the same bed!

That summer was the very first time I remember learning about phenylbutazone—or bute, as it's known casually—being given to horses. It was of course a legal drug in those days but a fairly new medication. Bob Freels and our grooms went out drinking with the Italian grooms and they were complaining about their horses having some minor issues with soreness. Bob recommended bute to the Italian team to help, which it must have done because in the Nation's Cup in Rome that year we jumped off against the Italians. The crowds at that show were unbelievable. The spectators all lit their programs on fire like torches during the jump-off and it looked like the stadium was on fire! We beat the Italians that year, but just barely.

In White City on the tour that year, a girlfriend of mine from Virginia named Jane Bryant came to London to cheer me on with her upstanding family. She was a very sweet girl and was so supportive, as was her family, who bought me horses to ride and had a gorgeous farm in Virginia. Tab Hunter kept telling me I must marry her so that he could have a place to go foxhunting! When we had gone together to visit Jane at her family farm, I would put the poor girl on her horse, take her stirrups off her saddle, and tell her to work on the flat until I came back from lunch! My relationship with Jane Bryant was a touch sadistic on my part, but she was a wonderful girl and we had great times all together (photo 53).

Tab Hunter

I remember going down to Virginia to foxhunt with George and the Bryants. Jane and her family were such lovely people with a gorgeous stable. I'll never forget talking with George as we were driving over the Chesapeake Bay Bridge. We were talking about how amazing Jane was and after hinting at marriage, I turned to him and said, "Yes, but George, one important question: do you love her?" He looked at me and said, "Tab, I think I'd kill myself!" and we burst out laughing. I told him, "Well, do me a favor and let me out of this car before you drive off the bridge!"

George Masters, the Hollywood hair and makeup magician who famously worked with Marilyn Monroe, also happened to be in London. I'd met George Masters back in California and he brought Venetia Stevenson, the Hollywood starlet, to watch me ride at White City. After the show, I saw Venetia and George, wearing a black mesh shirt, getting on the Tube and we chatted and they started coaxing me to come and party with them. Meanwhile, down the Tube platform Jane Bryant and our families were beckoning to me to catch up with them. Jane had planned an evening back at Claridge's with cocktails, dinner, and dancing. Talk about a crossroads! Two choices lay at my feet: an inevitable *ménage á trois* at Venetia's father's penthouse apartment with two beautiful Hollywood personalities or an upstanding, classy evening with Jane and our families? The clock ticked as I turned, looking back and forth between them. I was never very good with temptation—so of course I took the path of mischief!

Let me be perfectly honest—I was active for many, many years when it came to being game for casual sex, starting in the fifties and then certainly also in the sixties and seventies. Remember, this was before the AIDS epidemic and it was a time when both men and women, straight and gay, were shedding the puritanical inhibitions of the 1950s. Perhaps I was helping lead the charge. In those decades and since, I have had…well, let's say 10,000 and counting!

I spent that whole next week in London partying all night, every night with George and Venetia. I would show up each day to ride at White City then rejoin my Hollywood rock stars for more partying. By the Nation's Cup at the end of the show, I had partied so hard there was nothing left of me. I was so out of it that, deliriously, I told my mother the course was just like at Madison Square Garden and all I had to do was ride two times around the outside. Then I rode in and promptly went off course! It was a new level of exhaustion. My mother stormed out of the show and abandoned me there because she was so angry. Bert de Némethy raised his eyebrows a little bit, but as long as I was there on time and ready to ride, he didn't mind a little carousing. He was no saint himself, after all!

A few weeks later, in Dublin, we all dressed for an evening and dinner at McKee Barracks, which was a men's military club. Dublin was still a pretty conservative city in those days: women were riding on national equestrian teams but they were still excluded at men's dinner clubs like McKee Barracks. I had brought three different colored tuxedo jackets with me to Europe: white, black, and powder blue. I dressed in my powder blue jacket with black trousers and walked down the spiral staircase to meet the others. Bert, standing in the lobby in black tie, took one look at me, pointed his finger up the stairs and simply said, "Up!" I said nothing, did a turn on the haunches, and headed back up to change into my black jacket.

In late July, we traveled home from Europe for the Pan American Games in Chicago at Soldier Field. Bert had taken such a liking to my nephew Eddie that he said I could bring him with us to Chicago. Eddie stayed with friends of my sister's in Chicago and became sort of a mascot of our team. It was August and very, very hot. Those Pan Am Games really turned me against three-day eventing as a young man because I was horrified to see that several horses died from the extreme heat in the cross-country phase. Now, of course, it's different, and I like to be involved and have on occasion helped out our U.S. Three-Day Teams. But back then, precautions taken in the hot weather weren't like today and it was a cruel business. Mr. Galvin's daughter Patricia won the gold medal in the dressage that year, which was wonderful. At that time, dressage looked like a completely different sport—it was more riding with the horses "up and out" and not nearly so manufactured and precise as it is today.

The show jumping was on the infield of the track at Soldier Field and in those days, the Nations Cup portion was a team competition with no individual rounds. As usual, Bert had me ride first. I jumped a clear round and with sweat running down my face, pulled up in the intense heat. As I walked out of the ring, I jumped off the horse to get a Coke at a stand and the judges eliminated me! I was through the timers, out of the ring, and out of the infield, but they still interpreted that I had dismounted while still in the arena. Perhaps those judges from other countries were looking for a way to take the Americans down a peg. Bert and my teammates were all wildly angry that I was eliminated and lunch that day was very chilly indeed, despite the heat. Fortunately we won regardless of the elimination.

Harry de Leyer and the Dineens owned Sinjon, and it was shortly after the Pan American Games that they told Bert they wanted Sinjon back for their daughter Ellen to ride. There was nothing to be done but agree, since it was through their generosity that I'd had the chance to ride him at all. Wondering if Sinjon might be too much horse for Ellen, I told him, "Absolutely Mr. Dineen, you take him back and I'd be happy to come down to your place and give Ellen some help getting to know him." Ellen could ride but she was an amateur rider and certainly no Kathy Kusner! In the end, Sinjon was so hot to handle that Ellen couldn't get past the trot on him. There were no tranquilizers in those days and many of our Thoroughbred jumpers were very, very hot.

I loved riding Night Owl, but he wasn't a great indoor horse. He was a wonderful first horse to ride on the team because his pure power and scope gave me confidence over those large European courses. But when it came to the smaller rings and trappy courses at the indoor shows, he struggled a little bit with the quick thinking required. That's why Bill Steinkraus had passed him to me (as the team rookie) initially, because Night Owl wasn't always careful enough. I rode him a little bit differently than Billy: I would drop his head and ride him deep in front of the jumps, which made him carry himself up and over the fences. But I recall we had a rather mediocre Harrisburg that year, partly because the small ring and careful courses weren't Night Owl's best stage.

Mrs. A.C. Randolph, a wonderful supporter of the team, had by then given me High Noon to ride, a big palomino jumper who was starting to settle in and be a competitor. I sold War Bride at the end of 1959 because I had, in essence, outgrown her. She was a very useful jumper but didn't really have Olympic scope. Who began to ride War Bride but a talented young boy riding with Jimmy Williams named Robert Ridland. War Bride helped put Robert on the map in the jumpers. I even remember talking to Robert on the telephone when he was about eleven years old from my mother's house in the late 1950s.

Robert Ridland

George and I have a lot of history. I remember riding War Bride, the hot Thoroughbred mare that George rode internationally. In the later years of her career when she was a junior jumper, my mother bought her from George, and then I ended up showing her in my junior years. There was a large group of us who grew up on the West Coast and Jimmy Williams was the feeder system to so many great careers. Jimmy and George had great respect for one another and Jimmy trained me on War Bride. Because she was a hot mare, it really taught me a lot about being able to ride that type, which was valuable since I rode a lot of other hot Thoroughbred horses later on and was able to adapt. War Bride influenced my style of riding in a way that impacted my whole career.

Bert de Némethy approached me just after the Grand Prix at Harrisburg and said, with a grin on his face, "George, I have a new horse for you to show at Washington." He walked me down to where the horses were stabled and there's Sinjon's pink nose sticking out over the stall door! It was my old pal! Walter Devereux, one of the biggest sponsors of the USET, practically with a gun to his head, paid $25,000 for him, which was a monumental price for the time. I think what the Dineens may have planned for all along was that Sinjon would become so instrumental for the team that they would get to name their price. Or perhaps it was a Plan B when he was too much horse for Ellen. Either way, it was wonderful to have my favorite back. The team showed at Washington for the first time that year, and together Sinjon and I won the President's Cup like we hadn't missed a beat.

Kevin Freeman

I was from Oregon and ended up going to Cornell University in '59; I'd ridden in the AHSA Medal class at the Garden that year and knew who George was. A lady I'd ridden for, Ellie Smith, up in Washington was a riding instructor at the Ox Ridge Hunt Club, and she said she could talk George Morris into giving me riding lessons. So that's what happened. That was fifty-five years ago! George would work with me every day—this was before he turned professional—and I hung on every word he said. He would take me over to Boulder Brook afterward, and I would watch the team riders school their horses. George and the others were getting ready to go to Europe for the Rome Olympics. It was a great experience and I vowed somehow to fulfill my dream to get on the team, which I eventually did—the Three-Day Eventing Team from 1962 to 1975.

When I was first on the team, we all wanted to ride with what we called "Team Style" and George and Bill Steinkraus were two of the first to embody it. Nobody talks about that now, because everybody rides that way. And not only that, but European riders ride differently too, having evolved over time in similar ways. In those days, everyone wanted to ride like Billy Steinkraus; not to take anything away from Billy, but he didn't do what George did, which was to bring the wisdom to the hinterlands and teach it to the whole world.

Over the years he's helped me out a lot. I remember riding in a clinic where he said if you don't have a strong enough bit on a horse, you teach kids to have bad hands. At the time I remember thinking it didn't make sense, because you don't want a kid to catch a horse in the mouth with a strong bit. But I soon found that he was right. I can think of a whole list of those types of lessons he's taught me over the years. I remember he said when you come around to a jump, don't bend your horse. Because we did dressage in three-day, we always thought we had to bend our horses around the turn to a fence. He said, no, if you bend your horse to the inside, he will fall to the outside. And if you bend him to the outside, he falls to the inside. Even young riders know that now, but we didn't always think like that! It shows you how far the sport has come through the years that a concept that Olympians didn't grasp then is now common knowledge.

ow lucky could I be? After my elementary foundation at the Ox Ridge Hunt Club from Otto Heuckeroth and Miss Townsend, riding with Gordon Wright provided more technical, high school-like years of my riding education. Then, my years with Bert de Némethy and the USET were clearly my college and graduate education as a horseman. Varied in their roots, those phases of learning exposed me to several different schools of thought. Gordon Wright's school was very French- and Italian-based and gave me a forward-seat style, but in the mix was the wonderful ingredient of English and Irish horsemanship. Jimmy Williams did the same in taking the natural Anglo-Saxon horsemanship principles from the Irish and English and adding the French/Italian school, the Fort Riley principles, and the strong German seat. It was a wonderful recipe that molded me, a timid, unnatural young rider, into someone able to win the Medal and Maclay Finals at a very young age. I would never have been able to jump around in the big jumper divisions at Madison Square Garden without the solid base that Gordon Wright helped me develop.

From a professional standpoint, during the fifties I learned the classical tenants of riding and horsemanship that I held onto for the rest of my life, from learning over cross-rails to riding on the USET as the decade came to a close. It was my technical era, and I learned the fundamentals of riding from top to bottom. Bert de Némethy's Hungarian influence was indebted to the Caprilli school of light, forward-seat riders. However, Bert's long stint at the cavalry school in Hannover also came into play. He taught us cavalletti and gymnastics exercises to create strength and advanced flatwork concepts like impulsion from the inside leg to the outside rein. There were similar concepts to the French school but vocalized in a different way. Bert's school was a light version of the German school, but he made sure I had proper German influence by sending me to Richard Wätjen, the dressage master. I don't believe anyone could've planned better beginnings than my serendipitous start as a horseman.

Naturally, I have elaborated on all of that learning through the course of my career, but the base of my horsemanship originated in the 1950s. In later years, I solidified my education by watching, teaching, and reading, and naturally my knowledge became more sophisticated. My development during the fifties from a personal and professional standpoint set up the path my life would take.

I came of age as a young man, growing from a timid child into a bold young man. It was true that I thrived in the setting of my family's social advantages, but in reaching my young adulthood, I found myself also constrained by the straight-edged expectations of the sportsman's life on the USET. The decade to come, the 1960s, started a new chapter in exploring self-expression and proved to be pivotal in determining the path of my career.

MY PATH OF DISCOVERY

I. WHEN IN ROME

The highlight of my third year on the USET was of course the 1960 Rome Olympic Games, but that summer was full of wonderful experiences at several shows in Europe, leading up to Rome. I rode Night Owl, Sinjon, and my newer speed horse, Mrs. A.C. Randolph's palomino High Noon (photo 56).

Our base that summer was in Munich, where we stabled about fifteen minutes outside of the city at Reitakademie bei Riem. It's still a top-notch Olympic-level facility today and has hosted riders for many decades. During World War II, the Reitakademie served as the Bavarian SS headquarters, and I started noticing little historical details leftover from wartime around the building. There were even chandeliers hanging in the indoor arena with little SS hooks on them and the Third Reich insignia. Sitting in the lounge one day, a bartender pulled magazines from under the bar that were saved from the 1930s, containing Nazi-related news and propaganda. A fire damaged the facility and many of the historical nuances perished in the blaze, but it is still magnificent. Many years later, I took Meredith Michaels (later: Michaels-Beerbaum), Ray Texel, Jen Emmitt, Anne Kursinski, and Vinton Karrasch there during a European tour. It was Meredith's first European show, as a matter of fact.

Prince Georg of Hannover ran the Reitakademie and was married to Princess Sophie of Greece and Denmark, elder sister of Prince Philip, Duke of Edinburgh. Prince Philip visited while the USET was stabled there to lunch with Princess Sophie. We were privileged to meet him; I still recall him walking through the stables and going from stall to stall, looking at the horses in the barn. Prince Philip pointed to a particular horse and said he'd like to see it out in the yard. The horse he picked, Pike's Peak, happened to be the Conformation Champion that year at Madison Square Garden. Bert de Némethy had brought him for Frank to give him some mileage in the speed classes. It was clear to me at that moment that Prince Philip knew what he was looking at when it came to horses (photo 57).

In early August, we showed once again in London at White City. As before, each day a different member of the royal family attended the show, and one particular evening, Queen Elizabeth II was in attendance. Sinjon and I had a fantastic round in the Horse and Hound Cup and won it! As part of the trophy presentation, I dismounted and walked up the steps to the Queen's Royal Box to receive the Horse and Hound Cup. I was so nervous walking toward the Queen and tried to keep my wits about me and act properly (photo 58). For the rest of the White City show, the crowd picked me to win because earning the Horse and Hound Cup was considered lucky.

Winifred Gray

I was in London in 1960 and George was riding on the team that year. I went with friends to watch the White City Horse Show and we happened to be seated in a box just underneath the Royal Box where Queen Elizabeth was seated. We were all so excited and just being at the show was incredible. George rode Sinjon and won the Horse and Hound Cup, and I was cheering like wild. At the end of the class, when they presented the Cup, George dismounted and walked up a red carpet to the Royal Box where the Queen presented the Cup to him. George didn't even know I was there that day, and he walked up the red carpet right alongside our box seats. He was so close I could touch him. It was such a thrill to see him receive the trophy from the beautiful Queen. I still remember what she was wearing: an ice-blue, satin dress with a light-beige, mink stole. She was probably in her mid-thirties then and George was only twenty-two. I was so proud of him. I idolized him! He was such a good friend and I knew early on there was something very special about him. He had told me when we were kids that he wanted to ride in the Olympics. And sure enough, he did.

I heard that when George had Zara Phillips (the Queen's granddaughter) training with him years later, someone asked him, "How do you like having a princess in the barn?" to which George replied, "There's only one princess in this barn and that's me!"

After White City, we showed at Ostend in Belgium. Ostend is a very elegant city on the water. I could look out into the show ring from my hotel window. The ring was so close, in fact, that you could wait until you were 10 trips away from showing, hop out of bed, and go ride, if you were so inclined! I rode Sinjon in the first class and Miss Elio Sears, the generous sponsor of the USET from Boston, was there that day to watch us compete. Bill Steinkraus and I were the only two clean rounds in the Grand Prix, and we faced off against one another in the jump-off.

Bert de Némethy, who admired Miss Sears and wanted badly for her to be pleased with our performance, asked me not to go all-out in the jump-off because Billy was riding one of Elio's horses. When he asked it of me, I was taken aback and bothered. My family happened to be at Ostend to watch as well and for both my own sake and theirs, riding half-heartedly didn't feel right. I went into the ring and although I didn't go absolutely full tilt, I still beat Billy. When I told my father about what Bert had asked me to do, it really bothered him, too. My father was a very principled man and honest to a fault, which made him admirable, even if less successful in business. There were a couple of moments between me and Bert that eventually influenced my decision to leave the USET and explore different directions for my life, and that day was one of them.

Back in Germany, our successful tour continued. Even with all our success, we each had rough days in the ring too. Like any rider, I made my share of mistakes (photo 59). Showing for the third time at historic Aachen was wonderful! The pomp and circumstance was unequalled; I felt that I was riding in the birthplace of show jumping. Night Owl and I were clean and fast in the Grand Prix of Aachen and, incredibly, against all of the best in the world, I won! Winning the historic class was one of the highlights of my entire riding career (photos 60, 61). There is simply no Grand Prix class in the world that has the history, fanfare, and level of difficulty as the Grand Prix of Aachen. When I took my students to ride in it themselves many years later, I learned to appreciate even more what I achieved as a twenty-two-year-old young man back in 1960.

My oldest sister Joan Mitchell Neville was married to a Harvard graduate, and they were both well connected. A friend of theirs in Darien, Connecticut, named Ann Cutler, whom I'd met before leaving for Europe that year, insisted I contact a friend of theirs and fellow Harvard grad when I stayed in Germany on the tour. His name was Ernst Hanfstaengl, but everyone called him Putzi. Mr. Hanfstaengl invited me to dinner at his penthouse in Munich, which was a fun evening since he was eccentric and entertaining to talk with. Many years later, while reading a book on World War II history, I discovered my gracious host Putzi Hanfstaengl was a fascinating character.

After many years as an intimate friend and associate of Adolf Hitler's during the 1930s, during which time Putzi helped Hitler deal in art and gain favor in higher society, he found himself falling out of favor with the Führer. As the situation became strained, Putzi was put on a plane with sealed instructions to parachute into Spanish Nationalist territory to conduct negotiations with Francisco Franco on Hitler's behalf. By becoming friendly with the pilot en route, he discovered that his negotiation mission was actually an elaborate prank Hitler and his associate Joseph Goebbels had devised as retribution for unfavorable comments Putzi had made about the Reich. The pilot had been instructed to drop Putzi behind Communist lines, which would have meant certain death. Instead, he talked the pilot into feigning engine trouble and landing at a small airport, where Putzi began his defection, moving to Switzerland to ride out the war. During the war, however, he was imprisoned for his past associations and eventually handed off to the Americans, whereupon he provided valuable intelligence on Hitler and 200 other Nazi leaders as part of President Franklin D. Roosevelt's "S-Project." To think, my innocent dinner with my brother-in-law's college friend was actually a night with the man who helped win the war!

After showing in several cities, the USET traveled to Rome for the Olympic Games. The individual competition was in the Villa Borghese, in the Piazza di Siena. It's still a gorgeous venue today. Once we arrived in Rome, my nerves started acting up and I had major doubts about my ability to ride well. It was one thing to ride for the United States Team around Europe at big shows, but it was an entirely different matter to have the entire world watching while you are alone on course at the Olympics. The competition was fierce, especially at a time when the team wasn't considered as premiere a team as the Europeans.

It was my first Olympic Games of many and one thing I learned was that everyone pays attention when it comes to the host team trying to take a home-field advantage. Frank Chapot told me that he saw exactly the same course as the Olympic course set up forty-five minutes outside of Rome at a training stable. Perhaps the Italians had a little bit more time to train over the Olympic course than the rest of us! It's hard to say for sure, but I learned over time that there are always politics and funny business at the Olympics.

At my hotel with my family before the show jumping events began, I became increasingly anxious. The night before the individual class, I didn't sleep for even a minute! I paced and fretted all night in the living-room area of the hotel, wearing down a pathway in the carpet. The first horse was slated to go at seven in the morning. There was no qualifying in those days, which meant every rider from every country rode in the individual competition. I finally gave up completely on sleep and before dawn got dressed and walked down to the Piazza di Siena.

I walked into the Piazza as dawn broke over the stadium, which was lined by tall thin cedar trees and thick grass soaked through from the morning dew. I stood at the in-gate and looked out over the course for the individual show jumping event. The size of the fences was absolutely staggering. In those days, Olympic jumping courses were significantly bigger than even the largest Grand Prix courses, even the Grand Prix at Aachen. The course, to me, looked positively unjumpable. I thought there was no way I would get around. My order in the class was very early, and I knew the turf would be slippery still from the dew and the sun would be coming up over the hills right into our eyes. But there was nothing to do but try my best, even if it was an impossible task. A feeling of dread followed me as I prepared and warmed up Sinjon, convinced the day would be a disaster.

Daniel Marks, DVM

I was told that a single fence coming out of an almost impossible combination in the Rome Olympics resulted in nineteen broken rails (see William Steinkraus's important book *Reflections on Riding and Jumping*). For example, in the mid and late 1900s when we went to Aachen and other major continental shows, we needed to rest the horses for two or three weeks so they could recover. It was a serious test to jump those massive fences with their heavy rails. Nowadays, it's about technical jumping and delicate fences. Today, there is a large pool of very good riders, while in the late twentieth century there were only a dozen really competitive riders at any one time. The fiftieth best rider in contemporary Grand Prix jumping is light years ahead of the fiftieth best rider half a century ago. It's hard to measure rider ability from era to era, because the game changes. However, the greatest riders and many of the best horses of the last century would also be very good today.

The crowd was so enormous that I couldn't even make a guess at how large it was. Fields of faces extended infinitely in every direction from the edges of the arena and the roar of crowd noise was a constant hum. Terrified but having no choice but to focus on the enormous jumps, I walked in the ring and picked up my gallop. Sinjon pricked up his little ears and gave me confidence.

We made it over the first fence and then I heard a rail fall, and then another rail fell at the next fence. Toward the end of the course, the crowd was cheering for me and I thought how odd it was to hear with all the rails we had down.

Having miraculously made it around in one piece, Sinjon and I walked out of the ring to thunderous applause—with twelve faults! When I saw Bert, I gave him a bewildered look. What he told me was stunning: I had been the first one on course to jump around with fewer than forty faults. Raimondo d'Inzeo, the ace of Italy, won it all with a total of twelve faults after the two rounds. To top off the family pride, his brother Piero won the silver medal. I had twelve in each, for twenty-four faults total and for a time, I was sitting in third place. David Broome from England had yet to go in the second round with his horse Sunsalve. When they had finished their round, they landed a total of twenty-three faults and just barely nudged me off the medal podium, earning themselves the bronze medal. David was a great friend of mine and I was very happy for him.

Sarah Cavanagh Schwartz

I had the good luck—or perhaps misfortune!—of sitting next to George's father Harry during the individual competition at the Rome Olympics. The fences were gigantic and so imposing. George rode brilliantly. Harry would get so excited that every time George jumped a fence, he would slam his fist down onto my knee! I could hardly walk when we left the stadium. He was so close to getting the bronze medal, and we were so proud of him.

The Nations Cup, the team jumping event, was inside the main Track and Field Stadium after all the other Olympic events had finished. That has often been the case at the Olympic Games; it allows for a bigger crowd and since the track and field events have by then finished up, they can dig up the footing. The stadium held about 100,000 spectators and there was a ramp leading down into the ring. I was even more nervous than I had been for the individual event, knowing it was going to be such a difficult course once again and in front of an even bigger crowd.

I got on Sinjon and walked toward the ramp entrance with my throat parched, gripping the reins. Bert de Némethy, who had a sweet side to him and knew about my terrible butterflies, walked up and took Sinjon's bridle, leading me down the ramp to the ring. I don't remember how many faults I had in that round, but it was good enough in the end when we put all the US scores together! Our team won the silver medal, and it was an incredible moment up on the podium with the American flag flying (photos 63, 64).

Jessica Ransehousen

The USET in those days was surrounded by an aura, where we all dreamed of being able to "make the team." It's because the USET was the backbone of our teams. This was before the USET merged with the United States Equestrian Federation (USEF) in 2003. It was absolutely the most solidifying and uplifting experience to have the USET so completely in tune with what we needed and what we wanted to do when it came to oversight of the Olympic equestrian disciplines. That was lost a little when the USET became part of the USEF, because the Federation's governance is much broader than just the Olympic disciplines and can't invest as much attention as the USET had previously done.

In the early days, George and I were on two different paths, with me riding dressage and George riding the jumpers. Regardless, by the time we both went to Rome we were good friends and the two youngest riders on the 1960 Olympic Team, so we stuck together (photo 65). Before the Olympics, we were both showing in Aachen, Germany, where the jumper riders were having a bit of a problem. George came over to me and, frustrated, he told me, "I've had it!" I asked him what the matter was and he said, "Well, when your coach is telling you that you can't go in the ring to win, what's that?" I couldn't believe my ears! He said, "Bert doesn't want us stressing ourselves before the Olympic rounds, so we're to go in the ring and take it easy! All of us are pretty steamed about it."

I considered this for a moment and said, "Well George, can't you just pick one of your classes where you go for it and ride the other classes more conservatively?" So from what I understand, the jumping team got together and made a plan to be strategic about how each of them would choose a class to go all out, giving our Team a legitimate shot in each of the classes. Those moments on the team were so intense, but they created that absolute passion to do the right thing and ride as well as you could. It was a marvelous time filled with such passion and determination!

The World Championships in 1960 were held in Venice, believe it or not, only two weeks after the Olympics. Today, the World Equestrian Games (WEG) as the championships are now called, are held only every four years in between each Olympic Games. It's hard to believe that the horses were recovered enough to show at that level again, but they had received the best care and as much rest as we could possibly give them. The World Championships followed a similar format to today's WEG even before the name changed. Just like today, the final four top riders switched horses with each of the other three to ride the course and the final score decided the winner. Bill Steinkraus was in the lead at the final four stage, but had a fall on Broome's horse at the water jump and broke his collarbone. I finished tenth overall, which I was quite happy with.

II. THE OTHER FISH

After that summer tour and winning the silver medal at the Olympics, I went home with a thirst for something new. It had been an amazing few years riding for the USET and I appreciated all I'd experienced, both in traveling abroad and showing internationally. Having learned so much from Bert de Némethy and my teammates, I had become the rising young star of the show jumping world. Perhaps I should've been feeling on top of the world and ready for more.

However, sitting in Aachen or at the show in Ostend that summer, watching horses hour after hour, I found myself wishing I were somewhere else. Of course I enjoyed the thrill of riding on the big international stage. Life on the USET was grand! But the structure and expectations of it forced me to neglect another side of myself. What was expected of me—having the right kind of public persona, saying all the right things for the sake of my family, leading a square, vanilla life, and marrying a classy girl—it just wasn't something I could stomach.

In my mind, I knew who I was and what else I wanted. There was a side of me that needed to be explored and I didn't want to hide it anymore. The angst I was feeling told me I simply couldn't ride on the USET and be true to who I really was. I'd had a taste of the city life and I was drawn to it like a moth to flame. Deep down what I wanted, more than anything, was to be an actor and a movie star like Tab Hunter. Oh, the irony of it since Tab had told me his dream was to ride on the USET! I pined for the life I knew my colorful, artistic, wild friends were living in the city.

This realization that I wanted more was the moment I walked away from the horses and from Bert and my teammates. I gave up my spot on the USET and set aside all that I had learned to go in a completely different direction. It was a huge risk to walk away from everything I had gained. But I knew it was right, because it was easy to let it go.

My leaving the USET opened up a place on the team for a phenomenal rider who became a lifelong friend: Kathy Kusner. Kathy was a jumping genius with guts of steel, and she also had a very curious brain for other worlds. Once I took her to a little avant-garde restaurant in London, and we went to see *Rhinoceros*, Ionesco's famous play. Our friendship has always been filled with wonderful adventures through the years.

Kathy Kusner

In the beginning, I was working at the shows doing anything I could do— mostly braiding, grooming, and sometimes I got a "catch ride" on a horse to compete on. I became great friends with the regular professional grooms; it was all a lot of fun! With many, many chapters in between, this adventure led me to eventually ride on the United States Equestrian Team. Along the way, I showed a lot of hunters and jumpers, most of the jumpers were for dealers. Luckily for me, I ended up riding for Joe Green, who had been a good rider and now was one of the best dealers in the country. He could really prepare horses to jump and to win; that was one of the best parts of my education. The best was yet to come. I became connected to Benny O'Meara, and no one, but NO ONE, could ride any better and "deliver the goods with jumpers" as well as Benny! When George left the USET at the end of 1960, there were only three riders left, so I, then Mary Mairs, became the next riders for the team.

From when I was just a "hayseed," George and I were friends and it was nice; he was an important person in the picture. We would have some adventures together. And, we would talk.

When I first rode on the team, I could not believe my lucky stars. I had admired it in every way—constantly! I was friends with George's groom, Louie Rittendale, and (George never knew this) during this time of my progression, every day at the Royal Winter Fair in Toronto, I cleaned and shined his boots and braided his best horse, Sinjon. Later, when I first got on the team, Bert de Némethy assigned Sinjon for me to ride. Bert told me everything to do, every step of the way, when jumping this horse. Holy Cow! I wanted to do everything Bert told me to do as "perfectly as possible" but the result was I didn't do anything but "stink" on George's best horse that he had ridden beautifully. But, Sinjon was saved! Billy Steinkraus became his rider, and that, like when George rode him, was perfect.

Bert de Némethy was a totally honest and good person—and a totally thorough and hard worker (photo 68). He wanted the best for his riders. I could not really apply his way of jumping, but he taught me many other very good things. We became wonderful friends. He is very missed by me—and not only by me.

As Kathy stepped into my place on the team, I made a break for New York City. There was a lady at the Ox Ridge Hunt Club named Miss Edith Van Cleve, a sweet but frumpy looking lady with an aged, three-gaited saddle horse stabled there. Miss Edie was a little bit of an oddity riding a saddle horse, but I befriended her. I didn't realize who she was at first but then discovered she was an agent at Music Corporation of America on Madison Avenue. Her top three clients in the theater were Montgomery Clift, Grace Kelly, and Marlon Brando! All the heavy hitters knew Miss Edie; she was a powerhouse in theater and film. We went out for dinner in the city together sometimes and everywhere we went, people would stand up and greet her with respect.

Edie brought me one day along with her to visit Talullah Bankhead, a very famous actress on the stage and screen. Walking into her apartment, her larger-than-life persona struck me with that undeniable star quality. Talullah was smoking when we arrived and then I noticed her take out a new cigarette. Being a gentleman and a smoker myself at the time, I pulled out a match and offered her a light. She looked at me and said, "Oh DARLING, you don't have to bother doing that—soon you'll see why." And I did. In short order I noticed that she lit a cigarette, took one puff, and then put it out into the huge ashtray on the coffee table in front of her before immediately lighting a fresh cigarette. She repeated the cycle for our entire visit!

That fall, even while the USET was still showing at the fall indoor shows, I told Miss Edie I wanted very badly to try theater. She tried to talk me out of it and told me I was too talented with horses and needed to keep riding, but I eventually wore her down and she agreed to make a call on my behalf to Rita Morgenthau, founder of the Neighborhood Playhouse School of Theatre on East Fifty-Fourth Street. I was granted admission without any meeting or audition. They even allowed me to start the school year late, around Thanksgiving.

After being named Leading Rider at Madison Square Garden and for the entire North American circuit, I raced home in anticipation of going to the Neighborhood Playhouse School. I found an apartment sublet through MCA, and it turned out Joan Crawford's daughter Christina was my new landlord. Christina had to move quickly to California so I moved in and stayed there for two years. Christina left behind cardboard boxes in a closet that contained letters from her mother and incidentally, I'm certain they held some of the turmoil evident in Christina's famous memoir *Mommy Dearest*.

With heightened anticipation, I arrived at the Neighborhood Playhouse on my first day of theater school (photos 69, 70, 71). My first instruction was to change into a leotard, as it was the unfortunate uniform of theater schools. I went into the changing area and held it in my hands. Peering at that tiny thing, for a moment I simply couldn't bring myself to put it on. After all, riders' bodies and dancers' bodies are not created equal! I took a deep breath, swallowed my pride, put my leotard on, and walked out onto the stage where all the other students had gathered. Immediately I noticed a friendly face—an expressive, pretty girl in an electric blue leotard. She winked at me and gestured me to come sit with her. My new friend's name was Janice Wylie.

Actors and theater people are the most humble and accepting people I've ever known; they are simply wonderful. Janice Wylie was the daughter of advertising executive Max Wylie and niece of the well-known novelist Philip Wylie, who wrote *Generation of Vipers*. She was a wonderfully free spirit and we had a close, almost sibling-like friendship. Janice and I would rehearse roles together and share all our most intimate stories with one another. It was so refreshing to have a friend who knew nothing at all of horses or riding. She was simply an outgoing, caring friend who appreciated me for who I was outside of horses. Oddly, in our early years of friendship, Janice always seemed to have a premonition of being in danger. One night she came to my apartment and was completely spooked, with a feeling of having been followed there. I always teased her about being paranoid, but years later I had to wonder if all along she had some precognition of future events.

Theater school was a totally new life for me. We had dance class, acting class, improvisation, and voice lessons. We also took fencing, worked on costumes, props, and sets, and learned about the technical running of a stage production. The Playhouse was a very comprehensive school. Some of my classmates regularly worked out at the gym and I started to do the same after school. Since then I've always been someone who makes fitness a priority; I still go to the gym regularly today.

The legendary Martha Graham taught our dance class once in a while, although usually we were taught by one of her assistants, top dancers Bertram Ross or Richard Kuch, with Louis Horst accompanying on the piano. When Martha Graham did grace us with her presence, it was always a big deal. Standing about four-foot-ten feet tall, she was absolutely the scariest lady I've ever met in my life. She terrified everyone! I remember Martha called Janice "Blue

Bird" because of her bright blue leotard. Later in the same class, she stood up and remarked, "I don't know any of your names, and I don't want to. You bore me. The one thing I hate is to be bored!" And she got up and left the room.

Even as wrapped up as I was in my city life, I still drove up the Merritt Parkway to New Canaan on the weekends to keep a lifeline with the horses. I rode a little and taught my niece and nephews. I also started judging one-day shows out on Long Island and that was when I first noticed Bernie Traurig. Judging him, I noticed what a great, talented young rider he was. Once, when judging Bernie in a Medal class, I called back four riders and left Bernie out of the four even though he'd clearly won the class. I just loved to surprise him and pin him first after the test! He won both the Medal and the Maclay Finals that year as a student of Captain Vladimir Littauer.

Matthew Neville

I began riding lessons with my Uncle George when I was five years old. George did all of these crazy things when he taught us, and I was too young to understand them. Why place a crop behind your back and through the crook of your elbows while you jumped? Why jump without stirrups and reins? I thought he was nuts! But George also loved us and was concerned for our safety. I was riding our pony Jet one day and my mother had sent me to my lesson in cowboy boots. I was bounced off after a jump and one of my feet was caught in the stirrup. Jet was dragging me around the ring. Thankfully, George caught Jet quickly. I got up, he asked me if I was okay, and then he turned to my mother and growled, "I told you to get him proper riding boots! I don't want to see him in this ring without proper riding boots. He could have been killed!"

Another day, I was riding Jet again at the Ox Ridge Hunt Club. As we rode around the corner by the gate, a new rider entered the ring by opening the gate all the way. Jet made his move and scooted right out of the open gate. I fell off as Jet galloped to his stall. I lay on the ground listening to George yelling at the man who had opened the gate. He stuck up for me even though I was doing a terrible job controlling the pony! Uncle George was always serious about taking precautions and being safe around horses.

Years later I took my daughters (who are both riders) to audit a clinic George was teaching. I wanted them to see who my trainer was when I was a child. We listened to him speak all day and I was blown away. Because it was a clinic for trainers, I heard him explain many of the methods he had used when we were kids. After forty years, I finally understood why he had us do all of those crazy things on our ponies. I have always known that Uncle George is an amazing horseman, but on that day I learned that he is also an exceptional teacher and communicator.

Peter Neville

I remember George teaching me one day—unusual in that I was alone with him in the ring—the difference between looking and seeing. He told me when I was showing I should always know where the judge was sitting and whether he or she was watching me, but that I should never look directly at the judge. Instead I must learn to use my peripheral vision. In the lesson that day, George set up a line of fences to jump on my pony. He told me to jump through the line as he stood to the side and to yell out what time was showing on his wrist watch as he held it up without looking directly at the watch. I cantered through the jumps as he instructed. "What time did the watch say, Peter?" he asked. I told him the big hand was on the two and the little hand was on the five. "Don't you know how to tell time, Peter?" I replied that no, I didn't know how to read a watch yet. George turned to my mother, who was some distance from the ring. "JOAN!" he hollered. "How is it that Peter has NOT yet learned to tell time?"

New York City has always been a vibrant center of opportunity for all who venture there. There was no denying how happy I was at the Playhouse in the city that year. I had a lifestyle around art, theater, and culture and the side of myself that had been neglected was now being cultivated. I could take risks and express myself in new ways on stage. Nobody cared where I came from, as long as I showed passion for theater craft. I've always been torn between the horse world and the artistic, bohemian world because I feel totally at home in both. Although it might have been tempting with the city's nightlife calling my name, attending the Playhouse was a lot of work and we didn't do much partying. I went out with friends on the weekends, but during the week I was completely committed: I went to the gym, walked twenty blocks to the Playhouse, and rehearsed for twelve hours a day.

In the theater in those days, even though it was an artist's world, it was pretty straight-laced when it came to alternative lifestyles. People outside of the arts tend to think the theater world is very open and accepting of gay actors, but the reality is that it wasn't accepted then and still isn't today! To be successful in Hollywood, any gay actors must keep their personal life hidden to avoid being limited in the roles they're offered. It's still not widely accepted: Look at

Hollywood now—there are still many famous actors about whom rumors are always swirling.

Two fantastic horsewomen I got to know about that time were Carol and Judy Hofmann, daughters of Philip Hofmann who was then president of Johnson & Johnson. Judy, who later married Max Richter, has been in the horse business for over 40 years in Bedford, New York. Judy and Max were married at that time and living in New York while I was attending the Neighborhood Playhouse. Judy was also a very good friend of Janice's older sister Pamela Wylie, who was also an actress, so we'd socialize from time to time. It was a fun link between the city life and the horse world.

Judy Richter

One evening our friends in the apartment downstairs called to invite us for a beer as they had a surprise for us. After we met my friend Pamela's little sister Janice, we settled onto their couch, beer in hand, and exchanged pleasantries. George, who had been hiding in the bathroom, charged into the room and leaped onto the coffee table, shouting, "I am Orestes!" and quoted several lines from the Greek tragedy they were rehearsing that week. I couldn't believe it was George and we all laughed. He was full of enthusiasm about the theater but, not being one to mince words, I told him, "George, forget Orestes! You will always be George. You ride so well. Orestes, Orestes, go back to the horses!" He did, and ever since he has dominated the horse world and made it his own stage.

For the summer, Miss Edie got me a job in Cooperstown, New York, at the Duke's Oak Theatre. I had a Brentwood, California, friend at the Neighborhood Playhouse named Anne Schlumberger, and she was like our very own Judy Garland. Anne sang "Somewhere Over the Rainbow" in a showcase at the Playhouse and had a spectacular voice. I was a rookie at Summer Stock and just before I left the city I heard the girl with the ingénue role had dropped out. I instantly called Anne and told her she had to come with us to Cooperstown. She wasn't the most confident performer and was hit with an instant case of nerves. She said, "No, no, George I can't do it, I'm not good enough!" and tried to hide herself away in her apartment. I showed up at her apartment in my station wagon, "kidnapped" her, and took her to Cooperstown with me. I knew what it was like to suffer from nerves and need someone to give you that little push!

The Duke's Oak was run by Dorothy Shea and her partner Joanne Miller, an openly lesbian couple (a rare thing in those days). There was a wonderful cast

39. *An icon of German dressage, Richard Watjen, displaying the perfect seat.*

From Tug of War *by Dr. Gerd Heuschmann and used by permission of the publisher.*

40. *Teaching my niece, Whitney Ann Neville, 1956.*

41. *The California equestrian life was a refreshing change from the conservative East Coast!*

42. The legendary Jimmy Williams.

43. Europe-bound (left to right): Jack Kettering, Bert de Némethy, Hugh Wiley, Bill Steinkraus, Frank Chapot, GHM.

44. In Aachen, 1958, with "Schnelle Anna" Clement, the speed queen!

45. *The U.S. Team in Dublin, 1958 (left to right): Bill Steinkraus (Ksar d' Esprit), Frank Chapot (Diamant), GHM (Night Owl), and Hugh Wiley (Master William).*

46. *Riding War Bride in Weisbaden, 1959.*

47. *Riding War Bride in Dublin.*

48. *Schooling Night Owl in Greenwich, 1959.*

EUROPE BOUND

49. *At the Greenwich training quarters before a trip to Europe (left to right): Frank Chapot, Bill Steinkraus, Bert de Némethy, Hugh Wiley, and GHM.*

50. *Riding Night Owl at Aachen, 1959.*

51. *Riding at White City in London (left to right): Wiley (Nautical), GHM (Night Owl), Chapot (Diamant), and Steinkraus (Ksar d' Esprit).*

52. *On Night Owl at White City, 1959.*
© *Kit Houghton*

53. With Tab Hunter and Jane Bryant, whom I nearly married!

54. Sinjon leaping over the huge, 15-foot water jump at Aachen, 1959. Note the enormous crowd.

55. At Delray Beach with my father.

56. *High Noon jumping the water in Lucerne, Switzerland, 1960.*

57. *Left to right: Hugh Wiley, Frank Chapot, Bill Steinkraus, GHM with High Noon, Prince Georg von Hannover, and Bert de Némethy at the Reitakademie bei Riem in Munich.*

58. *Accepting the Horse and Hound Cup from Queen Elizabeth II.*

59. *NOT the horse's fault! They called me "Big Move Morris" for always trying for the long spot.*

60. *Night Owl had scope!*

61. *Winning the Grand Prix of Aachen on Night Owl, 1960.*

62. *Frank Chapot, Bill Steinkraus, and Bert de Némethy.*

63. *The crowd was enormous at the Rome Olympic Games. I'm riding Sinjon.*

64. *My Olympic silver medal for Team Show Jumping. Rome, 1960.*

65. *Jessica Newberry Ransehousen, an American dressage goddess, riding Forstrat.*

66. *Night Owl in Aachen, 1960.*

67. *The USET was all class!*

68. *Bertalan de Némethy, USET show jumping coach and my mentor.*

69. *With Beverly "Boobs" Rubin on stage at the Neighborhood Playhouse.*

70. *On stage at the Neighborhood Playhouse.*

71. Taking center stage at the Neighborhood Playhouse with Joanna Pettet to my left.

72. Uncle George with Eddie and Whitney Ann Neville.

73. One of my best dogs, the Doberman Baron (1961–1968).

Painting by Molly Hanford Northrop

74. Showing dressage at the Ox Ridge Hunt Club on Colprin, 1963.

75. *Big Line "hid" his knees.*

76. *With Grandmother (to my left) on the Australian cruise, 1963.*

77. Always game for a good time...

78. ...and, always a party animal!

79. Hans V. Kaltenborn, the legendary wartime newscaster and friend of the family.

of characters at Summer Stock. In theater, it's all inclusive—there are beautiful and not so beautiful actors; there are skinny and fat actors; there are old and young actors. After all, to fill a cast for a theater company, you need all kinds! I found the variety and passion in that group of actors a wonderful thing to be a part of. We all worked extremely hard and bonded quickly through what we did together. Each day was a marathon. I rehearsed for a new show during the day and performed in a different show in the evening that I'd learned the previous week. I built sets, gathered costumes, and sold tickets. The entire cast and crew pitched in to do everything needed to put on the performances week after week.

As a teacher, my voice has always been a central part of my identity and livelihood and people tell me it's my voice that sets me apart at any horse show. But you might be surprised to know that my voice has also been the cause of massive stress and anxiety at times in my life. As a teenager, I was teased about my high-pitched, boyish voice and I retrained myself to speak with a deeper, more masculine voice as I grew up. Also as a young man I experienced terrible anxiety about public speaking. Bill Steinkraus would take me with him to benefit dinners; I was paralyzed about speaking in public on behalf of the USET; when the time came, I couldn't say a word at all!

Being trained in the theater, I further developed my voice and learned how to enunciate and project my voice from my diaphragm, which is part of where my teaching voice comes from. I also fully conquered any remnants of stage fright by working hard within the safe environment of theater school and at Summer Stock. I achieved a level of comfort by taking risks in singing, acting, and dancing on a daily basis. Facing those insecurities head on and thriving in the theater world was a wonderful personal experience. What it taught me is that people don't realize what they are truly capable of—being pushed beyond their perceived limits is not only a way for them to grow, it's a way to succeed. Human nature tells us to play it safe, but pushing the boundaries has amazing results, whether on stage or in the show ring.

That summer up in Cooperstown, I had many big roles and often in musicals with a singing part. All of a sudden, one day, there was a line in a play that started with an "h" sound and when I went to speak, no voice came from my throat, just empty breath—the sound completely stuck in my throat. No matter what I tried, I couldn't recover. I panicked because I thought I couldn't speak at all for a time. That night, and in the days following, the problem worsened and became a downward spiral. My anxiety about my voice made it exponentially worse—it was a vicious cycle of fretting about it and being even more affected when on stage. At that time, I didn't realize that this same speech issue would become a major challenge and point of insecurity for me throughout my life. Much later, I discovered there was a physical reason for it, a tiny gap in my vocal chords, and I learned that fatigue caused it to crop up, then anxiety caused it to worsen. Unfortunately, I didn't know this for decades to come.

The following year, I was invited back to the Neighborhood Playhouse, which was quite an honor. My second year at the Playhouse was still enjoyable, but my confidence was damaged as a result of my speech problem over the summer. Most days, I would be all right and my voice would seem fine. When it wasn't fine, it was terrible and I couldn't relax and enjoy performing. Obviously, such an unpredictable issue made a performing life filled with worry. Even though I wasn't as sure of myself, I still loved the theater school environment and my city friends.

On a personal level, I formed a crew of wonderful friends that year and started exploring the nightlife scene with other men with whom I could truly be myself. The group of guys I went out to the discos with were called "the A-list" because they were good looking, straight-acting, classy, successful professionals. I was comfortable around them because we didn't typecast ourselves; there was no flamboyance or struggling for an identity as gay men. But all the same, it was the first time ever in my life that I could go out on the town and feel completely at home with those around me.

As I said, I didn't party a lot while I was a student at the Playhouse because we were always working and rehearsing, but I certainly had a few adventures. For one thing, I discovered Fire Island. I had been to the island (on the south shore of Long Island) as a child with my family on beach trips to Point of Woods. That was the family-oriented side and the polar opposite of the nightlife side, called Cherry Grove and The Pines. The eastern half of the island was so unbelievably over the top—I had never seen anything like it!

In the sixties, the Beatles played out of loudspeakers over the long wooden boardwalk streets from the bars and clubs on Fire Island. That place was drugs, sex, and debauchery twenty-four hours a day, seven days a week. It's the Sodom and Gomorrah of the world, and in my whole life, having traveled and partied all over the world, Fire Island is still the most decadent place I've ever been. The first time I went out there with my friend Terry Soldwedel, we didn't have a hotel room and ended up sleeping in boxy wooden tabletops that housed the fire hydrants on the street.

I continued to go out to the Ox Ridge Hunt Club to ride and teach on weekends, and I met a boy while I was out there one particular day; he came up to me and said, "Mr. Morris, I want to be on the Olympic Team." He was a great young rider from the Midwest, and I told him, "Okay kid, I'll get you to the Olympic Team." It was Bill Robertson. I started giving him lessons, helping him at shows, and I also took him down to Boulder Brook where Bert de Némethy schooled horses. The first couple of times Billy came with me just to watch Bert train. The third or fourth time I brought him, Bert led a horse over to Billy and said, in his accent, "Just I let you this time, you are walking this horse around to cool him out, then off!" After that, he told Billy to get on a horse and trot once around and, "then off!" The next time he said, "Okay, Billy, now just take that horse and trot through those cavalletti." And so on. That's how Bill Robertson got on the USET. Billy was a good rider and had a wonderful, outgoing personality.

Bill Robertson

In the spring of 1960, I bought a French horse that was very Thoroughbred-like and had been shown by Dave Kelley in the hunter division. He was a little sulky, had an occasional stop, and didn't like the dressage someone had brought him over from France to do, but he was a beautiful mover and jumper. Le Bon Chat is what I named him. I rode him a while and got a little handle on the stopping, but he'd stopped a couple of times at the last horse show before Devon, and we had a pretty dirty one. It was the week before Devon and George told me to bring the horse over to the Ox Ridge Hunt Club. He set up a big vertical and said not to warm the horse up, but just canter him around and point him at the jump. I did, and the horse took full advantage and stopped. We made stopping an unpleasant experience for him and offered a better alternative. I walked around the ring for a few minutes giving him a chance to catch some air. With a fresh step in his stride and a feel that he was definitely in front of my seat and leg, I asked him to jump the vertical. The feel of that ride on the approach to the jump was so positive and simple. He simply felt GREAT! That was the last school I did with the horse before Devon, and he jumped great there and never stopped. There was a USET Jumper Stake class and it was the first class televised on the *ABC Wide World of Sports*—Billy Steinkraus did the color commentary for it. And I won the class! Nobody knew who the heck I was, I was just some kid from Indiana. After fifty-plus years, I still thank George every day that I ride for the opportunities he gave me and his continuing help along the way.

Billy was first and second at Devon and it put him on the map. I watched it on television from New York. Between Bert de Némethy's familiarity with Billy and his high profile win at Devon, it catapulted him to Gladstone. It was in 1961 that Gladstone, New Jersey, became the home of the USET. For many years, it's where all hopefuls and team riders went to train and prepare together year-round.

III. BACK TO THE HORSES

Jimmy Hatcher

Betty Beryl ("B.B.") Schenk was the greatest lady hunter catch rider on the East Coast, and she was the regular rider for the great horse Duke of Paeonian. B.B. and I are a few years older than George and we were all friends. Tab Hunter came to New York, as he often did, to the National Horse Show during the time George was in theater school. B.B. took Tab down to the stabling to see the Duke and a herd of little girls followed after them down the ramp, since Tab was quite the Hollywood heartthrob. Tab ducked into the Duke's stall and B.B. shooed away his admirers. Then, in the course of their conversation, B.B. asked how it was going for George as an actor and Tab replied (as pertaining to Bert de Némethy), "Well as long as roles for Hungarian riding masters keep coming up, he'll do just fine!"

After acting in Summer Stock again after my second year at the Neighborhood Playhouse, I started to look ahead to what was next and was scratching my head a little bit. I was twenty-four years old and good-looking enough, but I wasn't a genius on the stage. I think back to some of the actors who were at the Playhouse with me—amazing performers who at the time I felt sure would become huge stars—and not one of them ever hit it big in Hollywood.

My desire to become a Hollywood star like my friend Tab had not diminished, but the reality was that the industry was going through a strange transition. Television had come in and taken the film industry by storm. The big movie studios would hold actors under exclusive contracts for extended periods of time but were taking fewer risks in spending money to make feature films. It was a real possibility that a big studio could hold my life hostage, in a sense, and keep me from working at all. I knew actors under studio contracts who sat around doing absolutely nothing but weren't free to work outside the studio, either. Similar to Tab's experience, it was difficult to be "owned" by a studio in those years. I started to realize what a risk it could be to follow him to California. Always in the back of my mind—and discouraging me from reaching for stardom on stage—was the voice issue. Adversity in your life is often a blessing in disguise.

With Miss Edie and others encouraging me to go back to horses, I decided to follow their advice, but I hadn't yet worked out how. As my mind was sorting through my reentry into the horse world, out of the blue I saw Mrs. Newberry, Jessica's mother, at the Washington Horse Show. When I told her that I was planning to get back into horses, she invited me to come up to Au Sable Forks in Upstate New York to their new farm. C.T. Newberry, Jessica's stepfather (of the Newberry Department Stores and founder of the Washington Horse Show), had left Tarrytown to get out of the rat race and built a beautiful horse property with cabins near Lake Placid.

Jessica Newberry (later: Ransehousen) and I, of course, had grown up together and gotten very close on the USET and went to the Rome Olympics together. I even called her my girlfriend for a short time in our youth, since we dated a little bit. I remember watching her dressage exhibitions on her Lipizzaner when she was only seventeen years old; what a talent! It was a wonderful opportunity to follow her up to Au Sable Forks to her family's farm and begin riding again. When the indoor shows ended, I packed my station wagon, and with Baron my beloved Doberman as co-pilot, followed Jessica up the thruway with the city fading in the distance behind me (photo 73).

Jessica was training for the Pan American Games in São Paolo, Brazil, and was away from the farm a good bit when I first moved up there, which was fine because there were plenty of others who kept me busy. Victor Hugo-Vidal had a student named Lex Anderson who was aspiring but didn't have very deep pockets. Lex decided to follow me up to Jessica's to be a working student, and it worked well because he and I both had the hunter/jumper background. Stig Rasmussen had a cute Thoroughbred mare, and so I had both him and Lex to teach. Michael Kirkegaard was also a student of mine for jumping lessons, although he was primarily a student of Gunnar Andersen's. Gunnar Andersen was also at the Newberrys', which presented an amazing opportunity to learn from a master of classical dressage. I very much enjoyed training with him and learning on some wonderfully talented high-level dressage horses. It was my last true moment as a student and a fabulous experience. The Newberrys' was a true cross-training stable with open jumpers, hunters, and top-level dressage horses. It was the perfect place to get my mind and body tuned back in as a horseman and a professional.

In some ways, 1963 was my best year with horses, as it was a rebuilding year that found me rediscovering my love for the sport. I realized how fortunate I was to be passionate about horses and have talent and my unique background. My epiphany was that horses simply had to be my profession. After that, never again did I think of leaving the horse business. Those two years in the theater taught me that horses were where I belonged.

Having been out of the horse world and therefore without a horse of my own, I started to keep my eyes open for one. I attended a Hunt Ball in the fall of '62 down in Pennsylvania, and Jean Spaulding had a beautiful Thorough-bred she was trying to sell. Jean told me she would never even consider selling him but that he jigged when out hunting. He was a glossy chestnut with four white legs, an exotic-looking dished face, and gorgeous conformation. With a docked tail from an infection he contracted while shipping, he looked as if he'd stepped out of a nineteenth-century painting. I loved his look and he had lovely gaits, so I trotted him over a cross-rail. He was so hot he bounced four feet over it like a trampoline! My mother bought him for me to get me back into the business, and I took him back up to Jessica's so we could get to know one another. His name was Big Line (photo 75).

I had an odd relationship with the USET after having left them to go to New York to attend the Neighborhood Playhouse. Being the hottest young rider in the country in 1960 after winning the Grand Prix of Aachen and part of the silver medal-winning team in the Olympic Games, you can bet I earned some criticism for kissing it all goodbye. I didn't do anything legally or ethically wrong by leaving, however, my relationship with Gladstone was understandably awkward even a few years later.

Taking a risk and going to the Neighborhood Playhouse was a personal choice and something I felt deep down that I needed to do. I was a Pisces—two fish swimming in opposite directions. I had needed to feed that other fish, which was the side of me that loved the arts and the city life with all its adventure and diversity. I sympathized with those like Bert de Némethy and Billy Steinkraus who had mentored me and invested their time and energy in my riding career on the team. They had good reason to be miffed that I had walked away.

Many of my horse friends even came to watch me on stage in Summer Stock. Then, when I left the city and started riding and teaching, I think there was a feeling on all sides that I would probably go back to the USET. When I was at Jessica Newberry's, I briefly discussed riding with the team again with

Bert, and I'm sure he told me that it wouldn't be easy; he couldn't simply give me back those high-level horses to ride. I understood, but I also couldn't very well ask my family to continue supporting me while I waited, keeping my amateur status, for the invitation back to the team. I felt strongly that I had to do *something* to earn a living, whether that was work in the theater or go into business or some kind of profession.

I was still in regular contact with my team friends and soon after I bought Big Line, Hugh Wiley and I were both invited to a party we couldn't wait to attend. Back in my team days, Hugh was chummy with some of the English aristocracy, and at the White City Horse Show in London we'd both become friendly with the daughters of the 16th Duke of Norfolk. Mary, Jane, and Sarah Fitzalan-Howard lived with their father at Arundel Castle in Sussex. They were wonderful girls and horsey people, very classy and down to earth. When Hugh and I received invitations to a party at Arundel Castle, we jumped at the chance to visit our friends.

The largest castle in England, Arundel was just as you would expect an historic, grand, 400-year-old seat of the Norfolk family to be. However, castles do not have modern heating so instead, there were large fireplaces in every possible room, including bathrooms. It was a very damp, cold, English winter night with freezing rain falling, and we mingled about the rooms of the castle, moving from friendly fireplace to friendly fireplace. As the night wore on, we even played a little hide and seek, which was no easy task in such a vast place.

One of the guests at the party was Anneli Drummond-Hay, a high-profile Olympic lady rider in eventing and show jumping who won the first-ever Burghley Horse Trials in 1961. At the time, Anneli had an incredible horse called Merely a Monarch. He was the horse of the century, capable of Olympic-level, Grand Prix dressage, show jumping, or three-day eventing. At the party at Arundel Castle, I sat with Anneli on a settee and we talked horses—how wonderful Merely a Monarch was and how excited I was about Big Line.

Gordon Wright told me and my family on several occasions that if I aspired to be a professional horseman, I must learn to teach. What goes hand in hand with buying, training, and selling horses is teaching others to ride. Gordon was the creator of the riding clinic, and when I got in touch with him to tell him I was back in the game, he took me along with him to clinics. The first one I attended was in Alpharetta, Georgia, at a stable called Rockridge Farm owned by George Montgomery, vice-president of the Atlanta Coca-Cola Company.

My father happened to be in Georgia on business and came out to visit during the clinic. Gordon taught from nine until eleven in the morning, and

I would teach with him. After lunch I continued teaching private lessons through the afternoon, until eight that evening. Gordon played a lot of cards with friends in the afternoon and would often walk away with his pockets full of winnings. I wasn't getting paid much more than a token amount—and much less than Gordon—and seeing the disparity between the work put in by Gordon and myself, my father considered it very unfair and raised the roof with him about it. From then on, at the end of any clinic, Gordon would split the paycheck with me down the middle.

I had promised my grandmother, now almost ninety years old but still sharp as a tack, that I would take an extensive three-month cruise to Australia with her. After Christmas that year, we embarked on the trip. It was my first time to that part of the world and the beginning of many winters spent in Australia and New Zealand. The cruise stopped in port after port and a sort of daily agenda was established. In each port, my grandmother and I would sightsee together and visit every little church you could possibly imagine (photos 76, 77, 78).

In the evenings, I would put my grandmother to bed around eight and my real day would begin. There was a very colorful café society on the cruise. I would party late into the night and carouse with everyone on board. At the beginning of the trip I was with those on the top deck and by the end of the trip I was down on the bottom deck, partying with the Scandinavian staff! At one point, nearing our arrival back in New York, my grandmother couldn't find me and literally had a heart attack because she feared I had fallen overboard. Of course, I was simply below decks and between the sheets with some handsome Viking. When they finally found me, we were pulling into the harbor, and I helped get my poor grandmother to the Stamford Hospital. Thankfully, she recovered and lived to be ninety-three.

Jessica Newberry was very generous and we had a wonderful friendship. I was also close with Gunnar Andersen and his wife. They had dressage classes at the Ox Ridge and Fairfield Hunt Club shows in those years and we each showed in each other's divisions for fun. Jessica had several top dressage horses and some other prospects that we turned into jumpers. I got her a third-rate hunter and I taught her to jump in three weeks; she saw the jumps right from the get-go! Three weeks later she was jumping the three-foot-six outside course at Fairfield with total ease. With her being one of the top dressage riders in the world, it was no surprise that she was able to do it. That was the only time I showed dressage. I remember winning some classes, but keep in mind I was getting the best dressage training and riding the wonderful horses from Jessica's barn. I mean, it's not like I beat Isabell Werth and Anky van Grunsven or anything!

Jessica Ransehousen

After George came back from his years in New York City at the theater, we had such a wonderful time. We had a jumper together and he rode my dressage horse, Colprin. I also had a little hunter horse to ride as well. I had never really considered jumping, but because of our friendship it suddenly seemed like the sensible thing to do. We had an absolute blast! In one day, we could be doing a dressage class, a hunter course, and some jumpers, as well. All in one day. Your weekend was busy with preparing for all three, with George riding a dressage test or me fumbling my way around the outside hunter course. It was really fun and quite different. We had the classical side and the fun side, both of them. Things have become so heavy duty and serious now. It has lost a little of the fun factor that we had then, with the outside courses and all the disciplines riding together.

It's been a wonderful, long friendship between myself and George. I so appreciate everything he has stood for all these years and continues to stand for because they are the same things I hold important and dear in my life. It's so fun to think that we were on the team together in our first Olympic Games, and we then had so many other points in our lives when we came together. I miss him now, because Athens was my last year "chef'ing" with him. He said to me, "I want you to extend your Chef d'Equipe role for four more years so we can retire together," and I said, "No way!" So I retired before he did. I was ready!

While at Jessica's, I occasionally drove down to New York to see my city friends, find out the latest happenings in the theater, and get a taste of the nightlife. One of those times, when I was driving down the West Side Highway having just arrived in the city, I heard on the radio that two young girls were murdered. I got the strangest feeling in my gut that somehow I had a connection to these murders. When I arrived at my hotel that night, I dropped my bag and ran down the street to get an evening paper. Horrified, I read that one of the girls killed was my dear friend Janice Wylie. Janice had been working as an actress and also as a researcher for *Newsweek*. She and her roommate Emily Hoffert were murdered in their apartment in what the media dubbed the "Career Girls Murders." Poor Janice was only twenty-one years old and after all my teasing about her premonitions of danger, I couldn't believe her fears had come true.

Janice's murder was a very high-profile case, both because of her family's notoriety and the controversial case against the man accused, which in part led to the Supreme Court's institution of the Miranda rights warning. Three years after the crime, they did charge the real killer, Richard Robles. One of the details surrounding the case was a very bizarre coincidence that always makes the hair on the back of my neck stand up. Joanna Pettet, a beautiful blonde from Toronto who Janice and I were friends with at the Playhouse, had met Janice for dinner the night before her murder. Joanna had a short but successful film career and starred in the movie about Vassar called *The Group*. Not only did she have dinner with Janice just before she was killed, she also happened to have lunch at Sharon Tate's home on the same day that Sharon was murdered by the Manson Family. It's hard to fathom how things like this occur or how she must have felt to have brushed so close with two terrible crimes in her life.

That summer I was back on the horse show scene at North Shore and Piping Rock. Jessica stayed home because there was no dressage there, but she sent me with the jumpers. I brought Big Line and Rigoletto, another green jumper. During the show, I stayed at my grandmother's friend's house right across the slip from the North Shore Show Grounds. It was the house of Hans V. and Olga Kaltenborn, the legendary wartime newscaster in the thirties, forties, and fifties. They had old ties with my grandmother through the *Brooklyn Daily Eagle*, as did the Ward Melville family who owned the North Shore Show Grounds (photo 79).

Living with Leonard Bernstein at the time was a young Greek protégé named Nikki Nikephoros whom I'd met and hooked up with while attending the Neighborhood Playhouse. I would go out and paint the town red with them, all over New York City. While at those shows on Long Island, I rode all day, drove across Long Island, and then took the ferry to Fire Island to be out all night long. I would get back to the Kaltenborns' house with barely enough time to shower, get back into my riding clothes, and head to the horse show at seven the next morning. There was hardly any sleep! That was my life.

The next show was Piping Rock. Big Line was beginning to be quite competitive in the jumper division. Just like at the Fairfield Hunt Club, there were warm-up jumps set up in the woods around the Piping Rock horse show. I went clean in a knock-down-and-out class and went back into the woods before the jump-off to warm up again. Walking on the trail, I noticed someone had strung up a wire across one of the warm-up jumps. Now, I knew all about devices used to sharpen horses up and I'd seen a lot of that used both in the United States and Europe. There was, for many years, no enforcement of rules about such things. Regardless, I should've known better than to try it. I figured it was relatively harmless—after all, I hadn't devised this plan. It was just one jump tempting me in the woods that day! I thought I'd jump Big Line over the fence one time, let him brush across that wire, and it would surprise him a bit and sharpen him for the jump-off.

The outhouses were also in the woods and one happened to be sitting near the jump. Just as I was sailing in midair over that fence, Walter Devereux, one of the directors of the USET, AHSA, and National Horse Show, popped out of the outhouse! He said, "Morris, I caught you!" He had indeed caught me. I had to go to an AHSA hearing and answer for my actions. Of course, nowadays it would be a very big deal to be caught doing something like that, but everyone I spoke with after it happened predicted I would get a harmless slap on the wrist. In those days, everyone tapped horses' legs in the warm-up ring. Instead, I was suspended for three months! I had planned to show dressage at Washington that year and also judge at Madison Square Garden. I missed the rest of the season and learned a tough lesson: just one moment of weakness can be your downfall. And be wary of directors peeing in outhouses!

IV. GOING IT ALONE

The 1960s marked revolutionary changes to the sport of showing and it was in those early years that some of the aspects of jumping courses that we all take for granted today started to come into play—specifically, flying changes and counting strides. It's hard now to imagine a modern young pony rider not learning to change her leads in the corner and count her strides down the lines. But then, the judges didn't expect to see you change to the correct lead in the corners because the hunters showed over wide-open, outside courses to simulate foxhunting. As long as the horse was balanced, it didn't matter what lead you were on! Forwardness, brilliance, and talent were the focus. If a horse cross-cantered or even stayed on the wrong lead through a turn, it wasn't penalized as long as forwardness was maintained. Everyone rode off his or her eye and there weren't related distances between fences, so unlike today, you didn't plan ahead for how many strides you'd get.

The suspension I'd received for jumping the wire in the woods at Piping Rock wasn't the end of the world, but I went stir-crazy not being able to show for three months. I had an itch that told me it was time for me to go out and be a professional on my own. The Newberry family had been incredibly generous and done backward cartwheels to make me welcome and help me back on my feet. It was difficult for me to tell them I wanted to go out on my own, but I had to do what was right for me. The Newberrys thankfully took my decision in stride.

Dave Kelley, an iconic professional of that era, had a place in Armonk, New York, but was leaving to go elsewhere. Dave offered his place to rent, so I moved myself there with Big Line, a nice hunter prospect named Tomintoul, and my school horse, Big Lift. It was an old, historic barn with a courtyard in the middle and an old house adjacent to the stable. It wasn't ever meant to be a riding stable because the geography was rocky and the ground uneven. But the front sand ring and the cross-country field were lovely. There wasn't an indoor, but that wasn't unusual in those days. It was a brand new concept for me to have my own stable.

I have unfortunately always had terrible asthma and am quite allergic to horses, straw, and mold. Many people who ride are allergic and learn to cope with it as I did. At the Ox Ridge Hunt Club, grooms helped get members' horses ready, which worked well to avoid asthma attacks when I was a boy. When I became busy teaching and riding, I started hiring my own stable managers and grooms. That's one of the reasons stable management is my least proficient area of being a horseman—it's my weak link. I know how to manage a stable, but because I never gathered the experience over many years of hands-on committed horse care, I would certainly not consider myself an expert. There were, however, a couple of times in my life when I was solely responsible for my horses and took care of everything by myself.

That time in Armonk was one time in my life when, for several months, I cared for the horses completely on my own. I fed, mucked stalls, cleaned the barn, turned out, tacked up, and worked the horses by myself. I had no help whatsoever. Right across the valley was my old friend from my USET days Bob Freels at his Harkaway Farms. At the beginning, I called him three times a day on the phone to get his advice: "Bob, what do I do now?" I would ask him. "George," Bob would reply, "Give them hay and water and don't forget to feed them breakfast and muck out their stalls." It was time for me to learn everything I'd missed out on!

I can recall perfectly every detail of my barn and tack room in February of 1964. I mucked and swept and groomed to the sound of the radio and settled into the soothing rhythm of caring for the horses each day. I can still hear the radio playing in my mind, announcing that the Beatles were coming to play in the States.

That was the time I really stepped out as a teacher with my own philosophy based on forward-seat jumping with full-seat dressage flatwork to complement the jumping. My philosophy had been imprinted on me by Gordon Wright and Bert de Némethy, but Gunnar Andersen was my last official teacher at the Newberrys' and he had influenced my methods, as well. Horsemanship methodology derived mainly from Germany, France, Italy, and other European countries tended to be a product of one or two of those three influences. For instance, Gunnar Andersen was from Denmark and a product of the Swedish school of riding, which was a combination of the German and French schools. The Spanish and Portuguese schools were the product of the French method. The Russian school was also heavily influenced by the French. The two schools of dressage, French and German, are very, very different in approach, but in essence they arrive at the same destination.

By 1964, I had been influenced by the French, Italian, and German schools by the various combined approaches of my teachers. Added to that recipe was the natural American style of forwardness that evolved in the middle of the twentieth century to best suit the American Thoroughbred. Deep-seat dressage and light-seat jumping are very amiable partners and they married to make my system. The correct and rigorous horsemanship that I had learned from Otto Heuckeroth, combined with Bert de Némethy and Bob Freel's American stable management and training/schooling regimen, gave me a very solid foundation upon which to design an effective program. There were very few in the early 1960s who received this varied training from so many different pure sources.

My goal was to combine *practical* horsemanship and *classical* horsemanship. I was very hot at that time on Gunnar Andersen's dressage methods, where he used only fat snaffle bits and slow flatwork in a smaller dressage ring. Admittedly, I was a bit too beholden to the fat, hollow-mouth snaffle for a few years afterward! That bit simply doesn't work for horses galloping over country when their blood gets up. That's why the Europeans still have problems trying to use such bits. Gordon Wright taught me that the use of Pelhams or double-twisted wire snaffles and running martingales are made for the jumper ring.

Similar to Gordon Wright, I had a relationship with Otto Heuckeroth and the Ox Ridge Hunt Club. However, I made sure not to fall into the trap that Gordon did with letting the stable management become subpar. Superb stable management became a high priority, perhaps even more so because I knew it was my weak link. There was a very competitive top show stable outside Philadelphia run by a horseman named Milton Kulp, Jr., who everyone called "Junie." Junie taught the elite Philadelphia clients and he was not only a great teacher and rider, but also a wonderful caretaker. I noticed that Junie's horses were always turned out the most beautifully at the shows. Great students of his were influenced to be great caretakers, too. I remember thinking I may have had an edge on Junie with my teaching or my riding, but my horses didn't shine like Junie's. That triggered a desire to raise the level of care for my horses and my client's horses to the highest level possible.

After casually teaching some of the young students at the Ox Ridge Hunt Club as an amateur in previous years—like my niece, nephews, David Lackey, and Sue White—I now took on other students based there as a professional. Sue Bauer (later: Pinckney) and her brother Freddy were students I taught Tuesday nights in the early sixties and they officially became my clients while I was based in Armonk, even though they kept their horses at the Ox Ridge Hunt Club.

Sue Bauer Pinckney

I remember in mid-1962, I mentioned to George that I had these horses to show at the Garden and I had no one to help me. He immediately offered and I loved riding with him. I can still remember individual lessons I had with George, and that's saying something, since I can't remember what I had for lunch yesterday! One time, when we were riding in a small area behind the indoor ring at the Ox Ridge Hunt Club, George told me I was on the wrong diagonal. I glanced down and said, "No, I'm not." And he said,"Yes you are, change your diagonal." I looked at him and said, "No, I'm not!" And he just gave a curt nod. He was just testing me to see if I had the courage of my convictions. He challenged us to contradict him, when it was the right moment.

In '62, leading up to my first time riding in the Medal Finals, his lessons really paid off. George would school us in the indoor at the Ox Ridge Hunt Club over such difficult courses that when we went to show at the Garden all the other kids were intimidated, but for us, it was a walk in the park. When we were riding with George, he would send us to horse shows by ourselves. Nobody does that anymore! He wanted us to be independent and self-sufficient. Nowadays, they'll hold a ring for a long time to wait for a trainer to come over from another ring. In those days, you just went in on your own and used the knowledge you had from your lessons at home.

For me, as a girl, George knew I was an overachiever. I wasn't the most natural rider and made plenty of mistakes, but he never ranted and raved with me. He knew I couldn't take it! My parents didn't have a lot of money to spend on horses and I was lucky to have the chance to ride with George. In later years, wealthy families would have to apply for their kids to have that chance. In the beginning, it was really special. I'm not sure any of us knew how special it was.

My first official new customer at Armonk was a girl named Kathy Doyle (later: Newman). Kathy's uncle funded her riding and was tough as hell. He read every book on horse care and riding. He brought top-quality, three-year-old conformation hunters from Virginia up to Armonk for her to ride. Oftentimes, I took students out to ride a nearby cross-country course through the woods and fields with fixed fences. It was all blood and guts out there, and we had a great time. Kathy was one of those first students to go out with me and those beautiful conformation horses would be ridden hard—I admit on occasion they may have come back a bit scratched up with the occasional splint; Kathy's uncle would have a fit. But I must say, I really taught those early students how to ride. Look at Kathy! She's been an excellent horsewoman her whole life and has ridden, shown, and judged for many, many years.

Kathy Newman

In the beginning it was really fun, because it was no holds barred—you were going to learn how to ride. We did a lot with the horses that you'd never think to do with a show horse today. Now people are so boxed in by the cost of the horse and vet bills and the litigious culture. We were riding before safety was invented, so we had the best times. No one ever said you couldn't do something. Of course you could. You just did it! George allowed you to do things on your own, too. I remember at the Ox Ridge Hunt Club show one year I told him I could warm myself up without him, and he was fine with that. He didn't have to be there watching me every second and that gave me more confidence and independence as a rider.

It was so exciting riding with George then because we were on the cutting edge of a new system. George actually is the one who started teaching us to do lead changes consistently in the ring. No one had thought we had control over whether the horse changed his lead or didn't as you went through a turn—he either did or he didn't. He was teaching us other technical flatwork as well—shoulder-ins and turns-on-the-haunches. I remember being so impressed that I was learning how to ask my horse to do a flying change. He might as well have been teaching us Grand Prix dressage for how new and technical this was at the time.

I also remember when counting strides came into the picture. The first year I rode at Devon with George, my uncle had bought me this wonderful working hunter. I can remember standing with George at the in-gate while he was coaching me to go up the first line in a nice forward stride, but then to sit up a little bit coming home in the next line. That's generally what you were thinking about: either moving up and riding forward, or sitting up and balancing. But no one counted the strides, because at that point, the fewer strides you did the better, in general.

Now what's happened is that kids learn so much to focus on the counting that they forget to trust their instinct. I just remember George would watch others jump the course and then he'd tell us how many strides to plan for. I don't remember consciously thinking that we were doing things differently than before. I think that's because we still rode off our eye so much. They never had the numbers up on the board for the hunter classes. The course designers weren't consciously designing courses with a stride in mind.

Unfortunately, what we're seeing is that a lot of the younger trainers don't know what we experienced in the earlier days. They never saw the hunters back when brilliance mattered more than perfection. Admittedly, they're trying to change that now in judges' clinics and reward a horse's expression and not penalize a little freshness, especially in the pre-greens and professional divisions. When the hunters get to be expressive and bold, it's much more exciting to watch! I always fondly remember the wonderful hunter classics we held in Upperville in these huge fields with four-foot-six fences. As part of the course, there was a bank and a ditch, and you'd jump out of the ring, circle round and come back in! The crowd would be ten spectators deep on the rail all the way around. It was an exciting class to watch and people turned out for it.

Another excellent rider from that time was Jen Marsden (later: Hamilton) who I began teaching while I was still at Jessica's place. Ronnie Mutch sent her up to me before he became a professional, when he still worked in advertising in the city. Jen was short and stocky but an excellent, strong rider; she was the Beezie Madden of the 1960s! Jen followed me to Armonk with her little chestnut hunter mare named Winter Fair and a big open jumper named Wee Geordie. Believe it or not, Jen showed in the Puissance and against the professionals in the big jumper classes at Madison Square Garden—at sixteen years old. Then after all that, she would show her hunter in the Medal and Maclay Finals over the weekend.

One day in 1964, I thought about the related distances that Bert de Némethy had taught us for training the jumpers and decided to try it in the hunter ring. It was one of the first shows I took Jen Marsden to and she was riding her cute, but average little chestnut mare. Winter Fair was not a particularly great mover or jumper, but Jen was a great rider. We talked about the distance between the jumps and I taught Jen to ride the numbers. What happened when she counted strides was that the distances to each of the jumps matched and the judges appreciated the fluid, consistent stride. At that show, and the others that followed, Jen won much more often than she would have on just her horse's hunter suitability. The culture of precision was coming into play and the sport was becoming a science! In the late sixties and seventies, precision and perfection became an obsession in the hunters and equitation, for better or for worse.

Jen Hamilton

The back of *The Chronicle of the Horse* in the fall of 1963 had a full-page ad for George Morris becoming a professional. It had a picture of him jumping Sinjon. I saw that ad and I told my parents that all I wanted for Christmas was a lesson with George Morris. I was fifteen and living in Schenectady, New York, where there was almost no one to ride with. We went to the Boulder Brook Horse Show over Thanksgiving weekend. I was showing a junior hunter and George was there, so my father went up to him and said I wanted to ride with him. George watched me ride in a big class and wasn't I lucky, because I actually won, and George said he would take me on. George was very theatrical as a teacher and enunciated every single word and syllable like he was on stage. At my first lesson, my father wrote out a check to him dated December 11, 1963—to the tune of fifteen dollars! My father, who questioned everything, taught George perhaps one of the most important lessons he ever learned: all riders should be orphans with large trust funds! People talk of surviving a clinic with George and he's known nowadays for tough criticism in clinics, as well as occasional theatrics. But that isn't George to me. He was always compassionate, telling me what I did right when I came out of the ring before he told me what we were going to work on. And that's how I teach my students now.

I had a jumper named Wee Geordie who was 17 hands and I'm pretty short. George had me put him in a fat snaffle and a running martingale. At Farmington, I did great in the speed class because he was running away with me the whole time! My father told George enough was enough and that he was going to get me killed. George would say, "If I can hold him, she can hold him!" Then Bob Freels piped up and said sixteen-year-old girls were not as strong as grown men—and that's when Geordie was put in a Kimberwick and a standing martingale!

Business started to pick up and as much as I wanted to do everything myself, I realized I needed some help. I called Frank Chapot, who I had remained close friends with from our days on the team. He sent Bob Mickyl up to be my assistant. Bob was with me a year or so and he taught me a very important lesson: I couldn't be a one-armed paper hanger! If I was to survive as a professional, I would have to delegate responsibility to others. I was giving a lot of lessons and riding a lot of horses, and that meant I couldn't be hands-on in the barn. Someone like John Madden, who started as a groom, is a hands-on guy with every part of the business. He can do anything and everything with his own two hands—and I take my hat off to him. But there's a trade-off. If you're going to be riding and teaching all day, you just can't be as hands-on with those aspects of the day-to-day operations. Through my career, I established a network of the best grooms, managers, vets, and farriers that I could find. Right from the get-go, I realized the importance of trusting a great staff and delegating responsibilities to them.

My first, and in some ways my last, working student was David Hopper who rode and worked with me in Armonk. David had a nice jumper, The Actor, and did a great job in the stable. He's a top professional rider and horse dealer today, and we've been friends for many years (photo 80). I learned that the working student relationship is an inherently dissatisfying arrangement because the student nearly always feels he is not getting enough riding time and the trainer feels like the student is not getting enough work done! Often it's better to simply keep someone as a student or hire him outright. That's not to say that I didn't have certain arrangements with students in future years, but I wasn't a professional with a revolving door of working students.

David Hopper

That was a fun summer at Armonk, because George's nephew Eddie Neville was working there; he was fifteen at the time and I was twenty and a junior in college. We used to go out drinking with Bob the barn manager, roll in at two or three in the morning, then be up mucking stalls at five. We had a great time! George was twenty-six at the time so we became good pals. He was particular even then about the care of the horses, but he didn't have the confidence or bravado that he exhibits now. I had this wonderful jumper that had a little bit of a stop in him, which is why I could afford to buy him. When he stopped, I'd really get after him. I remember George saying, "David, there are eight degrees of punishment. Why do you go directly to the eighth degree?"

V. A PROFESSIONAL REPUTATION

Making connections in the horse business is so important, as is keeping good relationships with horse people throughout your career. Many times, students would come to me by way of a friend. Carol Altman was a student at Secor Farms who won the Maclay and the Medal Finals in '62 and then married Jimmy Fallon, a horseman who also ran Bennett College. Jimmy called me in Armonk to say he'd just judged the old Indio show out in California, and he'd seen an outstanding rider named Jimmy Kohn. He and his sister both rode well and were very ambitious. Jimmy Fallon told me he'd heard they wanted to move to the East, so Mrs. Carolyn Kohn telephoned and asked if her children could ride with me.

In early July, the Kohns arrived, and that week I happened to be giving a clinic in Texas. My assistant Bob Mickyl got the Kohns settled in and gave them lessons, but Carolyn Kohn was not happy. She was a strong, opinionated woman, and I'm sure she was thinking that they had not come 3,000 miles to get lessons from my assistant. Back from Texas the following Monday, I went directly from the airport over to a barbeque Carolyn was hosting at their new place in Armonk. When I got there, I saw evidence the Kohns were about to pack up their luggage and leave to go somewhere else! Thank god I'd gotten there just in time to turn the tables. Jimmy and I became instant friends, and he told me that evening that he really wanted to stay and ride with me. He was a lovable, sweet guy and a talented rider who soaked up his riding education like a sponge. His sister Edie was adorable and very supportive of her big brother. I turned on the charm for their mother and talked about our plans for the show season. By the end of the evening, the crisis had been averted!

Jimmy had a big gray equitation horse named Stonehenge and a jumper named On Cruise. His sister Edie bought a lovely mare soon after they came East named Silk n' Satin from Clarence Nagro. Silk n' Satin eventually went back to California and was a top working hunter on the West Coast. As a student, Jimmy was a quick fix. I gave him a few lessons and the following weekend he was Equitation Champion! Even being the new kid in town, he was a force to be reckoned with and it felt great to have him under my banner (photo 81).

With the Kohn kids joining Sue Bauer, Kathy Doyle, and Jen Marsden, I found myself with a team of great young riders. Rather quickly I'd built a powerful stable and began facing off against my friend and mentor Victor Hugo-Vidal and his bevy of students. My close ties and friendship with Victor continued as we rode on parallel tracks in our lives once again. Soon, Ronnie Mutch was right on our heels, and the triumvirate of horse boys became fiercely competitive in business. Victor's farm was a top stable in the early sixties called Cedar Lodge, a beautiful estate owned by the Cullman family (of Philip Morris). Antique and beautiful, the farm had a rustic, woodsy, camp feel. Since it was only a short drive away from Armonk, I went over to socialize with Victor and his clients regularly. Students would come in and out, sometimes staying at Cedar Lodge for extended periods of time, making for a fun atmosphere (photo 82).

Victor's latest protégé and project was a modest, unassuming student named Larry Kert. Larry was also the original "Tony" and star of *West Side Story* on Broadway (the original production) and was performing in the show at that time. I became good friends with Larry, and it was a sensitive issue because Victor and I were always competing over the same things. Admiring his success in the theater and his ambition to ride, I was instantly drawn to Larry and went into New York to watch the show. It's something I'll never forget, sitting in the back row watching Larry perform, singing *West Side Story* directly to me. We were very close for months, but in the end, Larry was too nice for me. I have a devious side and eventually, I get bored in relationships that don't have a little bit of an edge.

I was starting to compromise on my fat-hollow-snaffles-only philosophy and bitting horses more strongly—and more appropriately. But not before I took one last stand: Jimmy rode Stonehenge in the North Shore Show in a fat snaffle over the outside course and afterward he was whining that he couldn't hold Stonehenge in that bit. I decided to show him that there was nothing to be afraid of so I pulled the horse out of his stall, hopped on bareback with the fat snaffle, picked up the canter and jumped around the course myself. It was a little bit of a tricky thing I did, to pull the horse out of his stall cold and go jump around like that, because Stonehenge wasn't awake yet—he was just warming up when I was finished. It wasn't quite fair of me to do that. Even though I'd put on exactly the show I'd intended to for Jimmy, it wasn't long after that I put the horse in a double-twisted wire.

That year at the North Shore Horse Show, I saw Triplicate for the first time. A young pro from northern New York named Chucky Graham rode her—a beautiful chestnut mare. It was like *déjà vu*: she reminded me so much of my Olympic horse Sinjon. Triplicate jumped a foot or two over all the top rails with beautiful technique; I loved her and decided I had to have her! Toward the end of my time at Armonk, I bought her from Chucky and brought her home (photo 83).

Patty Heuckeroth

Once you get to really know George, he has such a great sense of humor. If you can hold your own, you'll get along great. I remember once he tried to get me to ride in one of his clinics and I told him no, and he asked, "Well, why not?" and I said, "George, if I were to ride in any clinic, I would feel obligated to do what the clinician asked me to do. I just don't want to put myself in that position!"

George came to my farm to visit many times between Christmas and New Year's, and one year I told him, "George, I have a surprise for you—a record album of you teaching a lesson." Someone I knew had given me a few records and one was a recording of "George Morris Teaches." I didn't even know something like that had been made, and as it turned out, neither did George. I suggested we listen to it, since I hadn't played it yet, and he agreed. I put the record on and he didn't recognize his own voice—he was convinced it wasn't his. I told him of course it was him. He said, "Well why don't I sound like me?" And I said, "George, you were younger then and your voice is deeper now. That was from before you went to acting school and started talking funny!" We listened for a while, and then he turned to me and said, "Patty, this is really boring." I laughed out loud and said it must get better after the flatwork, on the flip side, and he said, "No, I don't think so!" We both cracked up.

One time, before George came for a clinic, one of my clients told me that she'd read about how George had broken some girl's ankle in a clinic. I was incredulous; how could that have happened? I figured I had to ask him about it when he came, which is exactly what I did. He said, "Oh, that was a mistake!" I said, "Oh, okay, so you didn't really break her ankle and it was a misprint?" He replied, "Well, I didn't mean to, but the girl's heel wouldn't go down—it goes down now!"

At the indoor shows in 1964 I met Johnny MacGuire from Long Island. He reminded me of J.J. Smith a little bit, as both men were great horsemen and caretakers with outgoing personalities. Johnny, in particular, was a wonderful stable manager, and he joined the staff in Armonk. We became very close friends—he was my sidekick and roommate for a time. He would work himself to death for me! A total perfectionist to his own detriment, Johnny even got pneumonia at Harrisburg because he worked himself to the bare bones. We'd also go out partying together in the city. One night we went to the Blue Bunny, a really crazy sixties disco. The lighting inside was pitch black except for tiny iridescent blue lights blinking all over the walls and ceilings. Everybody would dance and scope each other out in the dim lighting. That's where Johnny and I discovered "group therapy"!

Earlier that summer, Jimmy Kohn's mother Carolyn had a visit from her friend Sally Kennefick who wrote for a magazine out in California called *Horses,* which was owned by Judy Spreckles, the sugar heiress. Every trainer worth his salt took out a full page ad in *Horses,* and it was filled with in-gate gossip and lots of pictures from the shows. In those days, just like today, there was a lot of showmanship, publicity, and advertising. Sally and Carolyn came to the Branchville show and after Jimmy Kohn jumped a nice round, Sally and Carolyn started whooping for him. No one had ever heard whooping on the East Coast before that! It caught my ear and I loved it, so I adopted it and started whooping for great rounds from the in-gate. Now my voice is so weak and strained that I can't do it like I used to. But I started the massive trend of whooping at the in-gate that year, 1964, after I'd picked it up from these California ladies. I was the King of the Whoopers! I would start whooping just as the horse was in the air over the last fence. Come to think of it, one time I started whooping too early, when the horse was still leaving the ground at the last fence; the horse hung a leg and knocked over a wall and the wall came rolling along as I was whooping. Beware of the premature whoop...!

Jimmy Kohn and I became inseparable brothers in arms, traveling to shows together all season long. Sometimes Carolyn was very protective and possessive about Jimmy, and other times she gave up and let us run wild. On one such trip, she let me drive her trailer. We went to a one-day show on Long Island and then the next day to a one-day show in New Jersey to get Jimmy qualified for the Medal and the Maclay Finals. After the Saturday show on Long Island, we drove to Greenwich Village, parked the horse trailer on the street with the horses inside, and both went out drinking! I went on my circuit of favorite watering holes and Jimmy, preferring to chase girls, went his own way. The horses sat snoozing on Greenwich Avenue overnight while we were out partying. We picked a time to meet back at the trailer, but I went back at three in the morning and left a note for Jimmy saying it was too early and to meet me instead at five. Then I'd get back at five and there would be a note from him saying he'd be back at five-thirty!

At Madison Square Garden, Jimmy and I stayed together in the hotel, and we always went out. We were kindred spirits! I was twenty-six and he was eighteen, and we were so similar in many ways—we rode alike and thought alike. That year at the Garden, at least I kept Jimmy inside the night before the Medal Finals, but it wasn't easy. It was his turn to take his shot at the Finals, and it was his last junior year, so we were both determined to make it count. Everybody watched the Finals; winning meant instant notoriety and possibly a trip to the USET. Mary Mairs (later: Chapot) and Chrystine Jones (later: Tauber) were both invited to Gladstone after winning the equitation Finals.

That year Judy White, Sue Ashe's sister, was judging at Madison Square Garden, along with Cora Cavanagh Cushny, a family friend of ours. One of the highlights from that year was an amazing girl who rode a little horse that positively flew around the ring because of its short stride. Despite her speed, she ended up sixth that year in the Medal—incredibly, at only nine years old! It was Katie Monahan (later: Prudent). For years to follow, I'd see her at the Garden and ask, "Miss Monahan, are you really still a junior?" And she'd smile at me and say, "Why yes, Mr. Morris, I'm only twelve this year!"

In the Medal course that Saturday, there was a brush fence near the in-gate on the diagonal. You jumped the brush, then rode to a stone wall perpendicular to it on the other diagonal. Most riders rode it on a big loop in six strides, but Jimmy did it direct in three strides. The direct line was very difficult because of the sharp angles of the jumps, which is why most people didn't consider it a viable option. Even though Jimmy was a relatively unknown rider and Victor's top girl Susie Wallace was the favorite, there was no contest and Jimmy won. The bold strategy paid off! I was so proud (photo 84).

The next day in the Maclay Finals, Lane Shultz had the round of the day in the morning. Gordon Wright's last year coaching at the Finals was in '62 when his student Carol Altman won both of them. Lane was from Secor too, but a student of Frank and Wayne Carroll, who picked up where Gordon left off. Jimmy had a different type of round with a more formal style, while Lane's trip was more of a hunter round. They were both great rounds, just different. Lane and Jimmy were called back in the test to do a figure of eight on the flat. Lane did her figure facing the short end of the ring, giving herself more space and her horse played a little bit and wasn't bent around her inside leg. Jimmy rode across the center of the ring for his figure of eight, which was harder and gave the judges more of a vantage point on his straightness. Stonehenge went beautifully and was bent nicely. Despite it, they pinned Lane first! I was surprised; Jimmy clearly rode the better test. When I talked to Cora Cavanagh Cushny about it she said, "George, we made a mistake, didn't we?" and I replied honestly that yes, I thought they had.

I was never a patsy when it came to hunter or equitation judges. I was very involved with trying to educate judges, as was Rodney Jenkins' father Ennis— his focus was good conformation and jumping style. It's the responsibility of the experts in the field to guide judges, whether it's through clinics or at shows. Speaking up to judges when you don't agree in an important situation is part of educating them. It's not as if Judy or Cora were dishonest at all; I believe they were absolutely trying to judge fairly. However, a good judge should acknowledge that facing the middle on a figure of eight is much more difficult than facing the wall, not to mention the difference between how each horse went. Lane had a wonderful first round in the morning and they gravitated to taste rather than excellence, perhaps. I never held a grudge and many of my students did well in future classes they judged. However, Jimmy and I will both always feel the sting of disappointment from him not winning that Maclay class.

Jimmy Kohn winning the Medal catapulted me into a strong position as a trainer for juniors aiming to win the equitation finals, giving Victor and Jimmy Williams a run for their money. It was very soon after that Bert de Némethy telephoned me to scoop up Jimmy for the USET. I was ecstatic that he had the opportunity. Admittedly, I also felt a bit heartbroken that he was leaving my place—I worried I'd never have another superstar like him.

Unfortunately, once Jimmy got to Gladstone, he and Bert were like oil and water. Jimmy was a very sensitive and independent type of person, and I had allowed him a lot of freedom. We shared the satisfaction of the "work hard, play hard" lifestyle. Bert's system must have simply been too structured for Jimmy, because it only took six weeks for them to decide it wasn't going to work. Bill Steinkraus told me his attitude was a problem, and Jimmy said he couldn't get along with Bert. It surprised me at the time, because for me it was effortless to get along with all of them. I suppose their personalities were simply at odds. Jimmy went on to a great career nonetheless, and other students of mine had a great experience with the USET.

That year, I went out to San Francisco to celebrate Christmas with the Kohn family. While I was there, I met Lorraine, Linda, and Maggie Lorimer —wonderful horse people and good friends of theirs. Linda Lorimer (who Jimmy and I dragged out on the town for some mischief) eventually became

Lauren Hough's mother. I like to tease Lauren and ask her why on earth her grandparents let her mother and Aunt Maggie gallivant all over San Francisco for the weekend with us!

Linda Hough

I met George when I was about twenty-one years old at Jimmy Kohn's mother's apartment in San Francisco, and we became instant friends. We all went out on the town and didn't get back until late the next morning! I've never been to so many different bars in my life and still able to walk! We laughed and laughed—but my mother didn't think it was so funny because my little sister (who was dating Jimmy at the time) was a lot younger. My mother teased George about that night for the rest of her life.

Even though I was a Californian and George was from the East Coast, we stayed friends through the years, and he's been a really gracious friend to me, as well as a mentor. We've had a lot of fun together, too. Lauren really broke into the top of the sport with his guidance, being on the Olympic Team in Sydney and the World Equestrian Games in Kentucky. Even when she was riding ponies my ex-husband would take her to ride summers with George. His guidance was instrumental for what Lauren has achieved. To this day they are still confidants, and I'm so grateful that George has been in our lives. You can count on him being a friend in good times and bad. He's still the only person I know who hand-writes notes and letters; he wrote me a beautiful note when my mother died. He's so gracious to those people he loves, and I feel lucky to be one of them.

My grandmother by then was ninety-two, and I'd promised that I'd accompany her on a Mediterranean cruise during the off season for horse showing (photos 86, 87). It was cloudy, cold, and rainy—a horrible time of year for such a trip. How could I refuse her, though? Grandmother was my guardian angel, and I had to try and make her happy while I still could. With the lousy winter weather, the sea was rough, and the cruise ship was rocking in the wind and rain. But that didn't mean I couldn't have a little fun on the trip!

Despite her age, my grandmother was still a domineering personality; I was the only person in the world who could tell her what to do. As we docked in Nice, France, I asked her for $500 to tip all the staff on the boat. She gave me the money, even though it was a ludicrous amount to use just for tips. Then I told her, "Now grandmother, walking around on the ship in this rough weather is too dangerous, you must stay in your cabin—it's simply not safe!" Then while she rested, I left the ship, flew to Paris, and had an all-nighter, partying with several new friends. The next morning I flew to Rome and stayed up all night again, partying with a fabulous crew of Australians and Italians. On the third day I met the cruise ship in Naples and boarded it with the tip money spent and a grin on my face. My sweet grandmother was still in bed, waiting for me to return, none the wiser. As far as she ever knew, I was a straightlaced, responsible young man!

With my stable in Armonk not having an indoor ring, my ears perked up when I heard that some area horsemen (who were also policemen) were planning to build a beautiful new equestrian facility in North Salem, New York. I jumped at the chance to move my growing stable there, and we all agreed to it. Johnny MacGuire organized the entire move while I was on the cruise with my grandmother. When I got back, my entire stable was in its new location and it was beautiful! With a great new facility, my business had even more legitimacy and opportunity for growth. It was perfect timing because several great young riders were about to arrive.

VI. PRODIGY

Bringing my students to the Medal and Maclay Finals became a big focus for me as a teacher. Only two equitation finals were held in those days so they were even more critical then to achieving the goal of riding on the USET. In the fall of 1964, with Jimmy having moved on, Jen Marsden aged out, and only Sue Bauer left in the juniors, I was feeling a bit light on equitation riders. While teaching clinics, I sometimes discovered students with such talent and ambition that I offered to support their riding, with the goal of getting them to Madison Square Garden.

At Alameda Stables in Texas back in '62, I'd heard about a boy in Houston who people claimed was a child prodigy. The boy rode with Charlie and Ginny Zimmerman, top horse people down in Houston who had, like Gordon Wright, emerged from the Fort Riley school of riding and training. The boy was only ten the year I'd first heard about him and too green to ride in my clinic, but they told me he jumped all their working hunters around four-foot-six courses. In '64 when I returned, the boy, Conrad Homfeld, rode in my clinic. I hadn't met him yet, but as the riders were warming up, I noticed him immediately.

Conrad rode a very attractive, spotted large pony named Melody. He trotted past me and I noticed he was short and gripped with his knee. Even without the most correct position, there was something about the boy that was simply ethereal on a horse. You could just see something special in the way he sat and rode. Much like I did with Jimmy, I showed Conrad how to put his lower leg on his pony and after three days of teaching him, I saw marked progress. After the clinic, I marched out of the ring, right up to Conrad's father Ken Homfeld, and told him we had to talk. I knew Doris and Ken had six children and thus did not have endlessly deep pockets, so I made them a deal. I would take Conrad up to train with me that summer. Not only that, but I *guaranteed* the boy would win both Finals and that he'd someday be on the Olympic Team!

How could I possibly guarantee such a thing to the father of a twelve-year-old boy? I never said anything like that again to a parent. And lucky for me, my prediction about Conrad's potential for greatness was right on the money! Ken Homfeld was a straightforward guy and after we'd talked about the horses Conrad would need, he said, "Okay, George. I'll pay for the horses and all expenses for one year. After that, you guys are on your own." I shook his hand and we had a deal (photo 88).

Once Conrad got out of school, he came up to ride for the summer and brought the spotted pony Melody and a little junior jumper named Mr. Z, who had a nasty stop in him. Every week Mr. Z would stop out at the triple combination, so we started a habit where I would get on Mr. Z and school him at home over a triple, then Conrad would get back on and he'd be good. It wasn't Conrad's riding style to ride hard and get after a horse with stick and spur; it wasn't his nature! He was a sensitive, finessed rider and great on the hot horses.

The same policemen who built Salem View owned some nice horses and one was called Hobo, a brown Thoroughbred equitation horse with a great mouth. Conrad showed Hobo at a one-day show on Long Island; he looked like a little pea on Hobo, but his position and riding were impeccable. Michael Page was judging and in the first Open Equitation class, Conrad was second, which was an incredible result for a thirteen-year-old! Michael came up afterward to ask me who the kid was. That would often happen, because Conrad had a noticeable quality on a horse. At the Ox Ridge Hunt Club Show later in the summer, Conrad indisputably won the Equitation 14 and Under.

At one show in Newburyport, Massachusetts, Conrad showed his horses over an outside course that was set in a little sand spit right on the beach. Somehow I got the idea to teach the entire weekend in a bikini—a little black string bikini! I don't know what I was thinking, especially since the mosquitos were always terrible there, but I didn't have any horses to ride, so I figured why not? I would get a tan and have some laughs. Conrad was totally mortified and didn't want to admit to anyone that I was his trainer—and rightfully so! What can I say? It was the Fire-Island-theater-guy in me crossing over into the horse world. That was definitely one of the very few times I truly "outed" myself!

Sunday after Sunday, Sue Bauer and Conrad would be asked to switch horses for the test in equitation classes. It usually ended up making the judge's job harder, because they both rode so well. Sue had a very difficult, hot six-year-old and Conrad would get on him and ride him beautifully. Sue would get on Conrad's spotted pony Melody and ride him just as wonderfully.

Melody was a great pony, but Conrad needed a horse for the equitation so that when we went to Madison Square Garden he could get down the galloping lines. Hobo was no longer an option, but since he'd proved he could finesse a hot horse, I let Conrad ride Big Line in the equitation a few times—but what I learned was that it was a delicate balancing act. Big Line had a jumper mindset and was too hot by nature, but if I medicated him and he got too quiet, that didn't work out so well either. Failing to find the middle ground with Big Line, I knew we needed to find a consistent equitation horse for Conrad.

Up to that point, I'd shown Triplicate in the Green Jumper Division, which was right in her range at about four-foot-three to -six. I had discovered that she wasn't going to be an Olympic-level jumper, but she was very careful and correct. Of course, it's quite different now, but in those days tapping your horse's legs with a light pole, sometimes bamboo, once or twice in the warm-up ring was accepted as a smart strategy with jumpers. It was meant to be done gently, so of course, there was no injury to the horse. It simply planted the notion in the horse's mind to put even more effort in to clear the rails. Now it's completely against the rules to pole horses, which is an improvement on the sport in my opinion. Once they outlawed poling, riders and trainers could no longer rely on it as part of the strategy, meaning the strategy focused back on good riding and a good relationship between horse and rider.

Gordon Wright taught me never to pole horses for the first class because they were fresh then, and at their best. It was smarter to wait until they got a bit tired then tap them when they needed a little wake-up call. On the Thursday of North Shore, I remember Rodney Jenkins was riding a wonderful and careful green jumper entry—they would be hard to beat. In the first course of that day, I didn't tap Triplicate but Rodney tapped his horse. We both went clean. I tapped Triplicate for the second class that afternoon, got an edge on him, and we won!

Since I was scratching my head trying to decide who to put Conrad on for the equitation, I figured I would see how it went on Triplicate. After I showed her in the green jumpers at North Shore and Piping Rock and she won nearly every class, Conrad began riding her in the equitation and did quite well. After he had success with her, I thought we were on to something with Triplicate (photo 89).

The indoor shows were upon us and I took my little group of juniors to Madison Square Garden. That was a year of learning a few lessons myself as a trainer. The judges that year loved Conrad, Sue Bauer, and Chrystine Jones. After deciding on Triplicate as Conrad's best option for the equitation Finals, I made a mistake by putting her in a big fat snaffle. Conrad had a great round, but he couldn't hold her, and she ran right past the last fence.

Sue Bauer, on the other hand, was the victim of bad advice from me. I'd been working with her on having a strong start to the first fence; for riders that tend to begin their course a little off the pace, it's important to practice this. Unfortunately, any change in pace can risk becoming an over-correction. I reminded her to start boldly, and Sue let her horse go so forward to the first fence that he ran right through it and knocked the jump down. I felt badly that I'd pressed hard upon her to go so forward. The rest of her round was so good that the judges told me they still considered calling her back for the next round. In the Maclay, Sue rode wonderfully and was second to Chrystine. She could've been the winner, but second place was nothing to sneeze at.

The next day, Conrad was fourth with a rubber Pelham in the Maclay. Fourth place was a fabulous ribbon for a thirteen-year-old, but he never let me forget the fat snaffle incident! That was a great second year for me at the Garden as a professional. I continued to use what Gordon Wright had taught me about strategy while also learning a lot from seeing how trends had changed since the fifties.

Where there are horse show people, there are always adventures to be had! J.J. Smith had moved to California and taken a job with Betty Kern Miller, Jerome Kern's daughter. J.J. worked for her at a lovely place overlooking the Pacific Ocean in La Jolla and that was where I taught my first clinic out West. While J.J. was back East showing that following winter with Betty at Secor Farms, we decided to drive up to my cottage in Katonah, New York, to have some fun after the show ended.

It was the dead of winter and there was deep snow with an icy crust over the top. Once we got up to the cottage, we had to make our way down a dark, steep snow-covered path from the parking lot to the cottage. Johnny MacGuire was with us, along with J.J., Betty, and her husband, Lee. Betty, who along with Lee, had so many cocktails at the show she was practically pickled, had on a dress and little slip-on booties. Every step she took in the deep snow, she broke through the layer of icy crust and scraped her legs. She was squealing and we were all talking and laughing as we made our way down the hill through the snow. I don't think Betty was feeling any pain, but when we got to the cottage we saw her poor legs were completely cut up and bleeding. There was nothing we could do but patch her up and pour another round! We all drank our way to happiness and when it was time to go back up through the snow to the parking lot we all carried Betty up the hill, laughing the whole way.

Soon afterward, I inherited a young rider, Kristine Pfister (later: Stephenson), from a Westchester pro named Ann Grenci. I first noticed Kristine at Secor Farms because she rode with a cerise-colored hunt cap. A talented young rider, I welcomed her when she wanted to come and ride with me—the hunt cap had to go, but the rider could absolutely stay! We went horse shopping in Maryland and found a big, powerful, 16.2-hand Thoroughbred timber horse. Kristine called him Highclere. Although she was a small girl, she was strong and a great rider (photo 90). She rode Highclere beautifully but he had a hitch in his gait behind; he wasn't unsound but I worried he might get thrown out of a jog at the show just for his natural way of going. Judges were very particular in the jogs then so it was a concern. At the time, my vets were from the Delaware Equine Center, a top practice in Unionville, Pennsylvania. Their advice was to give Highclere 5 cc of Azium (dexamethasone) the night before the show to help reduce any inflammation, and thereby, perhaps reduce the appearance of his hitch in the hind end.

I'm not a fan of medicating horses, as a rule; it's not the way I solve problems. I never used medications across the board with all my show horses like many trainers do nowadays. Phenylbutazone is a horse-friendly miracle drug and my opinion is that it should never have been banned completely. "Bute" makes horses sound and feel great, too. The only drawback is that it brightens up a horse and can make him buck or play and get strong in the mouth. One must remember that in many cases, a bucket of ice does the job as well as bute. However, with the occasional horse, just like a human athlete, therapeutic drug use is called for because it makes that horse happier and more comfortable doing his job. Bute is also a preventive drug.

I followed the vet's instructions and gave Highclere a little Azium the night before the show and the first day he was good and Kristine got decent ribbons. The second day, Highclere was even softer, went very well, and she got even better ribbons. The vet had really predicted the benefit, because his hitch had all but disappeared and he went beautifully. To my amazement, Kristine started totally dominating in the hunter ring. Thirty years later, we all realize, of course, that whatever else Azium does, it also mellows a horse! We didn't know that then. It wasn't until many years later that I heard trainers used Azium to quiet their horses. Due in part, however small, to his Azium regimen, Highclere settled into his job with a solid focus. He became a perfect equitation horse and one of the best junior hunters in the country for years. Kristine was one of the best riders I've ever had on a hunter, and she and Highclere really made their mark. They would even beat Rodney Jenkins frequently in the Working Hunter division! At Harrisburg that year, Hugh Wiley pinned Kristine with the blue in all three Junior Hunter Over Fences classes on Highclere. Suddenly, I found myself one of the leading junior hunter trainers.

Kristine Stephenson

When you send a kid in the ring as a teacher, you have to be positive in your system to believe that the kid can get the job done. That's what George was all about: "Do what I ask and I will show you that my system works." And if something didn't work, then it didn't work—but you had to be bold and try! I tell others who plan to ride with him, "If you try to do what he tells you to do—not what you think is right or wrong—and if you believe in him enough to do what he tells you, you will never disappoint him. You may not succeed, but if you're trying and working at it and not making excuses, you'll be fine."

George had just started out at Salem View when I began riding with him at age fourteen. I was from a small barn where we weren't that concerned with being very traditional, and I showed up wearing a bright red hunt cap! He said, "The girl can stay but the red hunt cap must go." I know George gets criticized for having been very tough on students back in those days, but there was no resistance from me. I was a big ball of clay, and I was quite willing to be molded into whatever shape George wanted! My father loved him and the feeling was reciprocated; we were no-name people and happy for the guidance. I was young and wanted to do well so badly.

In the sixties, we were still trying to simulate foxhunting, galloping through the countryside. One year at Devon, I had a horse with a huge stride and George said to me, "If you gallop well into the line, go for the two strides instead of the three," and I did! The numbers weren't so set and expected. The lead changes were also less of a mistake because you were on a hunt course and staying on the wrong lead was accepted. The changes were necessary in the equitation classes, because you had to show tight turns and proper balance in small rings. In 1968, I was riding in the Medal Finals and Judy Richter was judging. The horse I used for equitation had gotten hurt, so I rode my hunter who wasn't good at lead changes. I got called back in the Medal to test and missed the lead change after a trot jump. That mistake moved me from first to sixth, so lead changes were really becoming necessary to win.

VII. MOVING ON TO MILLBROOK

The owners of Salem View found themselves in some financial hardship, and it became clear they were in serious trouble. David Wright of M.J. Knoud (the old saddler in New York) told my father that they couldn't pay their bills and to get me out of there. It was time to make another change of venue for my home stable. As it happened, my friend Amory Winthrop Ripley wanted to build a riding facility. Amory, daughter of Mrs. A. C. Randolph and sister to Nina Winthrop Bonnie, had become a good friend. My friend Louie Rittendale who groomed for the USET in the fifties had introduced me to Amory. Amory was a good student with great ambition despite the fact that she was tall and a bit awkward on a horse. Like a duck in water, she loved training alongside my junior equitation riders. The Ripleys had a beautiful home and stable in Millbrook, New York, called Winley; it was across the street from Winley that Amory built a new facility with an indoor ring and a lovely barn. It was decided I would move my business to her new place when it was completed at the end of 1965 (photo 91).

Nina Bonnie

My mother, Mrs A.C. Randolph, a noted horsewoman, was both opinionated and outspoken. At first, she lumped George in with the types of riders who went out foxhunting in a snaffle and couldn't hold their horses. That was certainly not George, but I can still hear her saying, "those dreadful drop nosebands and snaffles!" For quite a long time she was very dismissive of George (she tended to be somewhat critical) until she went to Ireland to the Dublin Horse Show with my sister Amory, a close friend of George's. George won the biggest class of the show for the U.S. Team, and from then on, he was in her highest graces!

Amory was just an intermediate rider when she became George's student. My mother had been hard on all of her daughters, in particular Amory. George did such a wonderful job of teaching her so that at Devon, on her talented mare Singin' the Blues, she won a major Open Jumper class, beating one of my mother's horses piloted by the greatest rider of that era, Rodney Jenkins. Though not particularly close growing up, we stayed in touch. After I married and moved to Kentucky, Amory called and suggested I host a clinic for George. What an eye-opener! I realized as a rider who grew up with next to no formal training, I knew very little about the basics of horsemanship. After that awakening, I rode with George whenever I had a chance. I had a pretty successful run making and showing hunters over a lot of years, and I give George the credit for that. His fierceness in those days was legendary and at that first clinic, he turned to me and said, "Your sister has a dozen pairs of dark glasses—and she needs every pair!" I taught Pony Club for many years, and George would come and do clinics on his way back from Florida. What great memories. My husband Ned and I not only respect George as a great teacher but also consider him a great friend.

I traveled to St. Louis that year for a clinic with August "Gussie" Anheuser Busch, Jr., which became on additional stop on my clinic tours in Georgia and Texas. Some of Gordon Wright's customers rode there, and he connected me with a clinic at B & B Farm, which was the commercial riding stable adjacent to the Busch's enormous Grant's Farm. I had known Gussie Busch since my days of riding at Secor Farms in the fifties, and he and I had remained friends. St. Louis turned out to be a very heavy party town. Even being in the prime of my youth and game for a party, I could barely keep up! We'd have wonderful dinners at the Busch residence, which was like walking through time to Bavaria. I still remember that Gussy would get upset if you asked for a beer at his home. I learned fast that when you asked for a beer, you had to do it by name: Bud, Michelob, or Busch!

Dave Rose, Gordon's assistant back in the fifties, and his wife Maida, were from Houston, Texas, but traveled to St. Louis for the clinic. Dave was a good rider and a good teacher who eventually went out on his own. Gordon once warned me against hiring male assistants who might steal my customers. It's good advice to be careful who you hire as an assistant, but I've been fortunate to have wonderful male assistants through the years: Bill Cooney, Frank Madden, Jeff Cook, and Chris Kappler. Maida Rose had brought a horse up with her for the St. Louis clinic: a plain, raw-bone Texas Thoroughbred horse that could really jump. He was unusual looking, with lop ears and two little bumps on his head like horns. Maida, who I'd known at Secor Farms, was simply not up for riding him anymore and told me he was for sale. To try him out, I jumped him cross-country on a group outing and boy, could he jump! Amory and I decided to buy him for $3,500, and we shipped him home to Millbrook.

The Danish stable manager from Jessica Newberry's, Knut Rasmussen, had followed me to work in the Millbrook stable, and his son Stig rode with me. I put Stig, a junior rider, on the new Texas horse at the Boulder Brook show. He wasn't flashy-looking or a great mover but he was an excellent jumper and the judges loved him. After Stig placed well on him, I told Kristine Pfister she had to sit on him and try him. She rode him beautifully and ended up buying him for $7,500. Amory was annoyed that we didn't keep the horse because in the end, he was a hunter superstar worth much, much more. Kristine called him Valhalla after the town she grew up in New York.

Valhalla went into the history books as a legendary hunter. The ideal show hunter picture continued to evolve in response to the compact courses and the focus on accuracy, consistent pace, and style. It's interesting how decades later, the style we see in the hunter ring today evolved from superstars in the sixties like Valhalla, Highclere, and Amory's lovely gray mare Singin' the Blues (by Blue Murmur, out of the Bonne Nuit line). In any time and place, truly great hunters become the standard that all others try to emulate.

While I was out of the business and doing theater, Benny O'Meara had catapulted to the top of the jumper divisions. He was a great friend of Dick Keller's and he became a famous, legendary horseman. Benny went to Devon as my groom in 1956; ten years on, he was a total phenomenon! Benny had his own style—he carried his hands high and rode in the back seat with his legs in front of him. He was a horse-training machine: he got horses off the track or at auction and in a matter of days they would be at the horse shows and winning in the open jumpers. We called a horse like that a "ninety-day special." If a horse survived Benny's training, which was a hard test, he was quite a good horse. Benny taught his horses how to fend for themselves, to be quick in front and good behind, to get very round, and above all to concentrate on the fences. He took scruff horses you didn't look twice at and made them into champions (photo 92).

Benny had teamed up with Kathy Kusner, the legendary USET Olympic rider and one of the first women, along with Mary (Mairs) Chapot, to consistently challenge the top male riders. After Kathy grew up a natural, gutsy rider, just as I did, she experienced the dressage flatwork training with Bert de

Némethy while on the team. Although the flatwork was a good education, in some ways it clashed with Kathy's instinctual, natural riding over fences. When she and Benny partnered up, he had a wonderful influence on her. Kathy was Benny's alter ego. They won at every top show in the country, trading champion and reserve champion places back and forth between them (photo 93).

Back at home in Millbrook, I can still picture the moment when I picked up the telephone in the barn and heard the news. Conrad, just back up from Texas to ride with me for the second summer, was sweeping the aisle. It was Kathy Doyle (who had moved to Virginia), and she told me Benny had just been killed in a crash. He loved flying and was in a vintage World War II plane that was difficult to pilot. Benny's death was a devastating blow to the sport; he was a total legend and irreplaceable.

Conrad's father stopped supporting his riding after his initial year, and instead my parents, other clients, and I all came together to ensure he had opportunities. He was such a talent that we all wanted to see him be successful and shared the cost of his horses and his entries. Conrad and I decided to try Triplicate in some hunter classes that year. She had started as a hunter, after all, but she didn't move particularly well on the flat. We took her to a show up in Millbrook and to our delight, Chris Wadsworth pinned her first in all the hunter classes. With Conrad in the saddle, she was especially soft and her jump was so fabulous. I usually showed Triplicate in the jumpers but decided to let Conrad use her in the Working Hunter division.

Bernie Traurig, a very respected rider and teacher, had by then established a top hunter barn in New Hope, Pennsylvania. Bernie was winning all the Second Year Green classes at Fairfield on a big, dark-brown horse with a skinny blaze on his face that caught my eye. I wanted to buy that horse for Conrad and bring him along, since he was still green. He'd been priced at $12,000 for potential buyer Marvin Van Rappoport, a restaurateur from New York City with connections to the city and theater scene. I priced the horse for Mrs. Ripley at $15,000 with my commission on top of his price—but people looked differently on commissions in those days. When Mrs. Ripley heard about my raising the price, she didn't want any part of it! Conrad loved the horse, but it just didn't work out; in the end we missed our chance to buy a legend named Idle Dice. That's the horse business! Rodney Jenkins had unbelievable success with Idle Dice in the jumpers after Bernie started him in the hunter ring.

In 1966, the AHSA Medal Finals was moved from Madison Square Garden to the Washington International Horse Show. Conrad rode a horse named Triple Crown that year and had a top round in the Medal. Gordon Wright judged and called two groups back to test. In the first group, he called four riders back to test over fences. For the second group (including Conrad), Gordon called back five riders to work on the flat. In the end, Conrad was fifth. Even with a decent result, I was disappointed because he'd had such a great round.

The Maclay Finals course was diabolically difficult that year at the Garden. It was built by Dr. Henry Chase, secretary of the horse show who later rode with me as an amateur. Henry was a devoted horseman, patron of the arts, and a well-liked New York bachelor. Due to the challenging courses he built, many riders had stops and run-outs and several were eliminated. Conrad had a good round on Triple Crown, and the judges called back four riders, including Conrad, to change horses with other riders in the test.

Debbie Wilson (later: Wilson Jenkins) from Michigan had a horse called In My Cap, an easy open jumper they used in the equitation. In contrast, Triple Crown was trickier to ride and very sensitive; he was long and heavy and cut corners badly. When the judge told Conrad and Debbie to swap, I remember thinking Conrad was a shoo-in for the win. I couldn't see Debbie being able to control Triple Crown, and I couldn't imagine Conrad missing with In My Cap. As it often goes when you think something is in the bag, I was wrong! Debbie rode in and had a beautiful round on Triple Crown. Conrad, on the other hand, galloped up to the first fence a little weak, saw a long distance to the roll top, and chipped hard. Debbie won and Conrad dropped to third.

That Thanksgiving of 1966, my grandmother died. It wasn't out of the blue, but it marked the end of an era. Despite her death not being a shock, I felt the loss deeply. The matriarch of our family was a hugely influential figure in my life. Experiencing the world by traveling with her and witnessing her endless strength and dedication to intellectual pursuits has always inspired me. In my home today, I still possess dozens of her travel journals, with her observations and drawings from her journeys around the world.

Johnny MacGuire, who had managed my stable for years, moved down to Coconut Grove in southern Florida. Once he was settled there and had his own business started, he organized clinics for me to teach at his new place. Consequently, I first met Margie Goldstein (later: Goldstein-Engel) when she rode in one of those Florida clinics as a young talent. On my way to Florida that year to teach, I got snowed in at LaGuardia Airport for twenty-four hours, and it was there that I decided to write a book. *Hunter Seat Equitation* was written over the course of many months, but the idea was conceived the night I was stranded at LaGuardia.

Business was booming by 1967. In addition to Conrad Homfeld, I had other wonderful and talented young riders in my stable that year. Matt Collins was very promising and he and Conrad became great friends. Matt eventually bought Singin' the Blues from Amory and showed very successfully in both the hunters and jumpers. Kip Rosenthal also began riding with me after leaving Victor's tutelage, and she brought with her a wonderful dapple gray horse named Good Boy Dee. At fourteen years old, Kip told me she felt overly criticized by Victor and that her riding suffered as a result. I told her I didn't think she'd done too badly that previous year, given the fact that she was second in the country! Debbie Wilson Jenkins sold Kip a horse called Rome Dome who stopped at the jumps with everyone but Kip! She rode just a tad behind a horse, and as a result, insecure horses had great confidence in her.

Patty Heuckeroth

At Piping Rock, Kip was riding in the equitation on her horse Rome Dome and it came down to the last two fences. She either had to do a steady three or a flying two, and George told her to do the three. Rome Dome was a very scopey horse and when Kip jumped in a little strongly to the first fence, it became apparent to her that she wasn't going to fit three strides in. She made a quick decision and lengthened and did it in two. She just bent over and went with her horse and it worked out. She finished her course and George clapped and whooped. Then he turned to me and asked me what I thought of that. Well, I knew she hadn't ridden to his instructions, but as I told George, I didn't think she had any choice because of the way she jumped in. He said, "Yes, but I told her to do the three and she didn't. What do you really think? Quick—here she comes! I need to know whether to be mad or not." And I said again that I didn't think she had any choice but to do the two. So he turned to Kip and said, "Good job, Kip, very good!"

Back in New York for a visit, I hung out in the city with a very good friend who I had a brief dalliance with named Rich Stange. Lying in bed one night, I was restless and told Rich I had to go meet some friends uptown and would be back. Off I went with my alibi in place, ready to prowl—how wicked of me! Out at a watering hole, I saw a guy wearing a reddish plaid sports coat, about five-foot-nine and devilishly handsome. It was one of those moments in life where you meet a complete stranger and feel instantly attracted and comfortable with him. Both being the prowling sort, we fed each other's wildness when we were together; it was like riding on a live wire all the time. His name was Bob Smith. After we met that night, we gallivanted all over the city together for about twenty-four hours straight. Afterward, I finally called poor Rich to tell him I was still alive! Bob and I continued to see one another, and he became in some ways the love of my life. I was obsessed with him, which happened sometimes when I met someone who I really clicked with. My addictive personality kept me crazed and distracted all day long thinking about him while I was trying to teach and ride.

My new relationship with Bob triggered some inner turmoil. By the end of '66 my business in Millbrook was very successful, but I felt strongly that I needed to be closer to the city. With customers at the Ox Ridge Hunt Club, it was an awkward business when it came to the logistics of driving all over creation to teach my students. Millbrook is a beautiful pocket of horsey living, but it was just a little isolated. Two hours' drive was too far from the city; I had a circle of friends who I wanted to see more often. I found myself feeling lonely and restless being so far away from the action and it wasn't good for me. My mood began to darken.

The Ripleys were great personal friends of mine and I learned a lot about running a business from both of them. It was difficult for them in some ways to manage a facility that hosted public clients. Always fastidious business managers, they had to deal with people and families milling around the property; a place inevitably wears down more quickly with public use. It was also expensive for them to maintain. In addition, Amory, whose family I essentially worked for, was competitive against my other students, which had become a point of tension in our friendship. Between my restlessness to be closer to New York and the discontent of the Ripleys, I knew it was time for me to once again take my students and horses and find a new home base. In early June, I left Millbrook with the understanding that I was going to freelance.

VIII. BURNING THE CANDLE AT BOTH ENDS

Anne Savino

I was lucky. I studied with George earlier in his career when he gave so much time to students like me who weren't on the USET fast track. I was simply an aspiring rider and he mentored me in my formative years. It was always tough love with George. My heart would start to pound when I heard his voice. I had to be on my best behavior every second.

The moment I hit the horse show grounds, I knew exactly where he was and where I was supposed to be. As much as we wanted to be rebellious and suggest that maybe he was being too hard on us, we knew that he was making us so much better than we would have been otherwise. He never pandered to anyone. He would tell you exactly what he believed and never held back. He never compromised no matter what; he would rather sacrifice his relationship with someone than compromise his craft. George recognized that demonstrating any lack of ambition, even down to the smallest detail, holds a rider back and meant they won't succeed. If you can't polish your boots to come to a lesson, how can you have the level of focus necessary to walk into the ring and ride a difficult course? When I rode with him, we were prepared and turned out properly, and not only was that a sign of respect for him, but he taught us it was also a sign of respect for ourselves.

One of the other things he taught us was that at all costs, we must keep going. In the course of many clinic sessions, and on various occasions, he would run out in front of us when we were on our approach to a jump. He would run right out in front of us and demand that we run him over. We got used to this after a while, believe it or not. It is how I learned to keep riding and continue going forward no matter what happened.

One day, we were at the Washington Horse Show schooling before the show, and it was pandemonium in the warm-up ring. There were dozens of us warming up and jumping jumps all at the same time. I was riding my regular working hunter and galloped down to a big fence. I didn't realize it at first, but Frank Chapot, who was warming up for the jumper classes, was riding down the diagonal line coming toward this same jump. We didn't see each other until the last minute. He crossed my path on the landing side of the jump and at the same moment left the ground jumping the fence in the opposite direction. It happened so fast that it didn't faze me. We both landed and galloped off. When I left the ring, George looked at me incredulously and asked, "Do you know what you just did?"

All that preparation—having learned to keep going and keep riding no matter what—had saved my skin in that warm-up ring. And on a few occasions when I've been behind the wheel of a car, I have avoided accidents because this trained instinct kicks in to keep going and get out of the path of another vehicle. I'm able to mentally focus and continue, even in a fearful situation. George had an enormous impact on my life and did more than just shape my riding career. He had so much to do with giving me strength of character in my personal and business life. I owe a tremendous amount to him. He took someone who wasn't very brave and allowed me to do things I never would have been able to do, and have success doing it.

A pattern emerged in my life, going back even to riding for Bert de Némethy: I have never really worked for someone else in a harmonious way, for any meaningful length of time. Happy to be free from obligations to any one client, I rented a great apartment on Sixty-Ninth Street in the city—one of five apartments I had in New York through the years. It was small but very lovely with a little garden. My friend David Holman, the nephew of Libby Holman the iconic torch singer and stage actress in the twenties and thirties, decorated the apartment for me. Today I still have many pieces in my home that David bought for that apartment.

Coincidentally, my childhood big sister from Secor Farms, Nancy Maginnes, lived in the building next to me. Nancy was a wonderful, intelligent, and attractive young woman and worked as a research assistant to Nelson Rockefeller. I would occasionally spy her through my window stepping out of limousines in her mink coat at odd hours. Nancy eventually married Henry Kissinger and became part of American history, but I always knew she was destined for great things.

I loved being back in the city after years out in the rural towns, and I felt alive with a wonderful nightlife and cultural energy back in my life. My group of friends in the city was dynamic—they loved the nightlife as I did, but they also had interesting careers and great minds. My finger was back on the pulse of the city! Bob Smith and I roamed around it having adventures together. Little did I know that this endless attraction to Bob and the city would cause my entire life to unravel.

With my new apartment as a home base, I began a grueling schedule as a freelancing trainer and teacher. Most of my students stabled their horses in Lagrangeville, New York, at Carl Knee's place. Carl was a great professional and caretaker for the horses and our partnership worked very well. On Mondays, I taught at Amory and Carl's barns up in Millbrook. On Tuesday, I taught at the Ox Ridge Hunt Club and stayed overnight at my parent's house in New Canaan. At the crack of dawn on Wednesday, I drove out to Old Mill Farm on Long Island and taught there all day. Wednesday nights I'd spend at my apartment in the city, then teach out in New Jersey at Clarence and Tania Forman Nagro's place on Thursday.

After that Monday through Thursday schedule, all the clients would come together for horse shows on Fridays, Saturdays, and Sundays. Sunday night was always my free night out, just like most horse people. I would go out and carouse with my friends in the city on Sunday nights, then I would get up Monday and start all over again. As you can imagine, this traveling dog-and-pony show was very tiring. Eventually, this impossible schedule and the very intense relationship with Bob wore me down completely. Once you added clinics and judging to the pile, my schedule was filled to the brim and overflowing.

Clarence and Tania became very supportive of me during the 1960s. He was a top New Jersey professional and a horseman's horseman. He foxhunted, was a successful horse dealer, and an old-fashioned, tough-as-nails horse-man. Their daughter Sandra Nagro Lobell is still in the horse business today. Tania's family was a wealthy upper-class family from Russia that immigrat-ed to the States. She and I became friends showing together at Madison Square Garden in the fifties, and when Tania married Clarence, it was a wonderful partnership. Tania rode with me as an amateur rider in the sixties and seventies.

In the spring of '67, I judged a big horse show in California at Del Mar. Horse shows were a wonderful social scene in those days and still carried glamour of the fifties. I wore a tuxedo and there were champagne dinners in the judges' box. I loved seeing my West Coast friends as always and had some adventures that year. Wendy Mairs, Mary's sister, came to the show one day and slipped a bag of pot in my pocket, which I'd never tried before. She said to take it back to the hotel and that I must try it! Being the curious and adventurous sort, I did just as she recommended and smoked it at the hotel. High as a kite by myself in my room, I realized the entire place reeked of smoke. Suddenly I had visions of being led away in handcuffs and opened the windows trying to clear the room. I started freaking out. I would be arrested! I would go to jail for life! Soon enough I became so paranoid I flushed the entire bag of pot down the toilet. Pot has never been my drug of choice—it makes me cough and choke and I never liked it. But it's a funny memory of that time. Wendy also took me to a bizarre house party at a huge mansion where there wasn't a single light on. It was a party in total darkness. What a trip! The late sixties were about exper-imentation, there's no doubt about that.

A Long Island show had come onto the scene called C.W. Post; that sum-mer there was a hurricane with torrential rains during the show. I thought for sure they would cancel it since it was outdoors, but they decided to go for-ward. When many of my students were trying to earn points toward qualifying for the indoors or earning year-end awards, they didn't want to miss a single chance at points. So off we went in the wind and rain, but I was very irritated at the organizers for not canceling.

As a show of protest at having to show in a hurricane, I made Kip Rosenthal ride over the outside course holding an umbrella. It was quite a sight, her jumping with the umbrella held aloft like Mary Poppins! They caught a strong gust of wind at one point and, nearly pulling Kip out of the saddle, the umbrella stopped the horse just by sheer force of the wind right in front of a fence. Kip's father was irate and read me the riot act, because the stop meant she was only Reserve Champion. The next day, though, Kip's photograph—jumping with the umbrella aloft—was on the front page of *The New York Times*! Kip's father's friends saw that picture and suddenly he was calling and telling me what a genius I was to have called attention to the fact that they should've canceled the show.

That summer, I went down to judge a show at Francis Newbill Rowe's place in Virginia. Conrad Homfeld, by then about fifteen years old, came along with me. That's where Joe Fargis befriended Conrad and it was the beginning of a very long partnership that has lasted, incredibly, almost fifty years. Around that time I bought Conrad an inexpensive rogue called Ariba, who was a hell of a jumper but the type to get stuck in the corners. Ariba would put his head on his shoulder like a bird and you had to ride him hard to get him out of the corner. I bought him because Conrad had never ridden a cold, balking horse like him before. After Ariba, he could ride anything—hot or cold.

The 1967 Medal and Maclay Finals were fast approaching. Conrad was riding many different green horses, so the question of who he'd ride in the Finals was raised once again. To our great fortune, Francis Rowe stepped up and loaned Conrad a little bay horse for the Medal. The two weren't necessarily the perfect picture, but it was a fine horse for the job. That was the first year they moved the Medal Finals out of New York—to Bloomfield Hills, Michigan, at the Hunt Club near Detroit. When I flew to Detroit for the show, I felt suddenly very sick. My eyes ached badly and I thought I had the flu. My solution to being ill was, unwisely, a daily regimen of gin and tonics. Not surprisingly, I felt worse and worse as the week wore on.

The judges were Cora Cavanagh Cushny along with a great horseman from Fort Riley, General Franklin "Fuddy" Wing, Jr. They had nothing but love for Conrad! The last fence in the first course was a single fence on the far end, riding away from the judges on the centerline. Conrad had a beautiful trip but then missed badly to the last fence and the horse patted the ground. As all good riders do, Conrad made the best of a bad distance and held his position. It was a bad chip, but from the judges' perspective—a direct view from the back—it didn't look nearly as bad. I told Conrad he'd likely be called back at the bottom of the list of fifteen for the second round and that's exactly what happened. Then Conrad had, without a doubt, the best round of the day in the afternoon. He was then called back fourth out of four to test and the judges asked riders to switch horses. Again, Conrad had undisputedly the best round of the four—and he won! There was great consternation about his chip in the first round. Did Cora subconsciously remember her mistake with Jimmy Kohn and give Conrad just a bit of a break on that chip? It's hard to say, but I had to wonder. Regardless, I was so happy for Conrad—he was a brilliant rider and had worked hard—he deserved to win (photo 98).

I was so sick on Sunday night after the Medal Finals that as we boarded the plane in Detroit, I called ahead and asked my family to meet me at the airport with an ambulance to take me directly to the Norwalk Hospital. After looking me over, Dr. Resnick informed me I had acute hepatitis A and checked me into intensive care. I wasn't out of the woods for an entire week and was on bed rest for weeks at home afterward. The gin and tonics definitely hadn't helped!

Getting sick was the result of being physically and emotionally run down for six months. There was no medicine to take; I simply had to rest and the doctors prescribed sugar. Barbara Massey, my first "Girl Friday" who did my bookkeeping and horse-show entries, made the best chocolate chip cookies on earth (photo 99). I stayed in bed in New Canaan in the company of my sweet Doberman Baron and ate a few dozen of her cookies every day to fulfill the doctor's sugar recommendation. Carl Knee handled all my clients while I was sick, and I was barely out of bed when it was time for the Maclay at the Garden. I still couldn't train or ride; all I could manage was to sit in the stands to watch and then go back to my apartment and fall into bed exhausted.

Conrad had another horse named Golden Alibi, a wonderful hot hunter, that he rode in the Maclay Finals that year. He had a fabulous round and was called back on top. Being a hot horse, Golden Alibi didn't usually go well in flat classes so I was worried about Conrad staying on top in the flat phase. Visiting me up in the stands, Conrad told me not to worry about it and that he'd hack just fine. As he promised, Golden Alibi went beautifully, he stayed on top, and he won the Maclay. Conrad was the second youngest at age fifteen to win both the Finals—second only to me. He might have beaten my record if I hadn't put him in that fat snaffle on Triplicate the year before!

There were very few who ever told me what to do with a horse, but as Conrad grew up, he was more and more intuitive about horses. He was one of the few students I had who would sometimes give me advice that turned out better than my own plan. If I were an artist and my students were works of art, then Conrad Homfeld was my Sistine Chapel. Of course, he was a prodigy and I was lucky to have him as my student. No doubt he would've been great no matter what teacher he rode with. But he was a sponge and absorbed everything I taught him in such an intelligent way. Conrad had such a depth of understanding and feel on a horse. Witnessing his success over time was a great experience as a teacher, and I was honored to have shaped some of his younger years.

After the indoor shows ended, I packed up my things. Johnny MacGuire and I drove my car down to Florida together with Baron in the back seat. I had my own room at Johnny's house that winter and continued recuperating. In those years, the winter horse shows weren't a circuit like today, but instead a series of beach-club horse shows in Tampa, Ocala, Jacksonville, Palmetto, Winterhaven, Bradenton, West Palm Beach, and Wellington. Despite being close to Miami, a huge city for nightlife, I didn't drink for a solid year after my bout with hepatitis. I used my sick time to continue writing *Hunter Seat Equitation* and took the now iconic pictures for the book with my Pentax camera. Karen Harnden (a friend of Margie Goldstein) and Anna Jane White (later: White-Mullin) were my photography models, both of whom had beautiful positions.

The following spring, I felt I'd recovered but knew I still had to be very careful. Back in New York, I continued freelancing until 1970 but was much more measured about how busy I let my schedule get. The Yohai family's Old Mill Farm on Long Island became a home base for a couple of days each week, which provided some stability. I went to the Ox Ridge Hunt Club to teach a little and my Millbrook clients shipped down to Long Island sometimes for lessons. Anne Yohai (later: Savino) was a very gifted young rider with a beautiful Appaloosa jumper named Appy Leo and a small but wonderful working hunter that I picked up in St. Louis named First N' Ten. Anne was one of my biggest students and her parents had a lovely place out there. One unfortunate downside was the horrible traffic, which of course is still a nightmare today.

During those years I became closer friends with Marion and Hank Hulick, who I had known for a long time. They were top professionals based up in Massachusetts. Victor taught the Hulick children then, but because they were all very close friends I started to gather that it was becoming complicated. Hank rode in the jumpers and they had two talented children coming along, Gail and James. The Hulicks, Victor, and I decided to go together to the 1968 Olympics in Mexico as spectators.

When we arrived in our rented room we realized the sleeping arrangements were a bit on the awkward side. There was only one bed for all of us! Hank, Marion, James, Victor, and myself all stood there trying to decide how it would work. In the end, Hank slept on the floor (and the rest of us in the bed) but his main concern was that Victor and I must not sleep next to either his wife or his son! Despite the sleeping situation, we all had a wonderful time. The restaurants were some of the best in the world with unbelievably sophisticated menus and relatively inexpensive prices. I did learn a lesson there when paying for a taxi at the end of the ride. I had got out and handed about the equivalent of fifty dollars to the driver through the window. Instead of passing me back change, he simply drove away and left me feeling like a fool.

The fences at the Mexico Olympics were the largest ever seen in any international competition, before or since. The jumps were six feet in height and over seven feet in width. It wasn't a question of whether you would catch a rail and have it down; it was a question of pure physical ability for your horse to clear the fences. The cross-country phase of eventing was a bloodbath once again due to heavy rain and lots of mud. Two horses died, which increased my bias against three-day eventing. The show jumping, being so difficult with those huge solid fences, was a race to the fewest faults. Bill Steinkraus won the individual gold medal, which was a wonderful win for the United States Team. The Canadians—with both of my friends Jimmy Elder and Tom Gayford on the team—won the Nations Cup with the least number of faults, which were something like ninety-nine total faults!

Ronnie Mutch had now come onto the scene as a professional and he joined Victor and me as a top trainer in the area. I was fortunate to have wonderful, hard-working students who continued to be successful. Brooke Hodgson was a very beautiful rider who began riding with me—she was the Lillie Keenan of that time. With a wonderfully empathetic feel on a horse, Brooke was an elegant stylist with a lot of class; judges simply couldn't resist her! Her equitation horse, Advanced Ticket, was fabulous and on him she won both the Medal and the Maclay Finals in '68. That was the first year the Medal was in Harrisburg so Brooke was the first Harrisburg winner. After those two amazing years with Conrad and Brooke's double wins, I was really on a roll in the equitation (photo 100).

For the first time in my life, I had extra cash in my pocket—it helped to be a professional with virtually no overhead. Victor Hugo-Vidal and I hatched a plan to go to Africa together, a place we both had always wanted to see. It was an amazing trip and such a wonderful departure from life at home. We traveled with a group of people from all over, and one of the men on the trip was particularly interested in birds. It turned out he was Roger Tory Peterson, the preeminent bird expert and author of many books.

As I have said before, Victor and I had a friendship with a lot of admiration but we were also extremely competitive in business. On the trip, I discovered Victor was worried I was going to steal the Hulicks away from him, since we were all so friendly with one another. One night we got into an argument about it and it escalated into a bit of a scrap! It was all over by morning, but after that things remained a little bit strained between us.

Even though our travels continued on amiably, two funny things happened with Victor after our fight that made me wonder. One day we were on a secluded beach on the West Coast of Africa with beautiful surf. Victor remarked it was a perfect beach for swimming so I went running down to the beach in my trunks, ready to cool off and enjoy the water. Suddenly, a local man started waving me off and I slowed to a stop, quite confused. He ran up, yelling at me that it was not safe to go into the water. As it turned out, the undertow was so dangerous that nobody was allowed to swim. As I made my way back over to Victor, I was suddenly a bit suspicious of my longtime friend. "What are you trying to do, get me killed?!" I asked him. He just laughed at me.

We flew from camp to camp on a wing safari and one camp was at Lake Rudolph in northern Kenya, where the second funny thing happened. I went out of the base camp to swim in the lake, which Victor had encouraged me to do. As soon as I got my toes in the water, I realized it was crawling with crocodiles! Victor insisted he was not trying to get rid of me, but I still watched my back the rest of the trip in case Victor tried any more of his pranks!

While still in northern Kenya, we went out on a long hike that involved crossing a river in a rubber raft then riding through some big game areas in a Land Rover. Joining the two of us were two bachelors from New York and a young guide named Jane. After driving two or three miles, the Land Rover sputtered and quit running. It was hot and we were stranded very far from anywhere. This was before cell phones and satellite phones, of course. Commenting on the wild dogs she heard howling in the distance, Jane told us the only option was for someone to walk back, cross the river, and call for help from the nearest checkpoint. Jane and I drew the short straws so we had to walk back together to get help. The bachelors and Victor stayed in the Range Rover. As we're walking back, Jane and I saw all sorts of wildlife, including lions and wild dogs. Having survived that experience, it's easy to look back and appreciate the chance to see all the animals. However, I wouldn't recommend getting out of your Land Rover if you ever find yourself in a similar situation.

After the safari and my multiple brushes with mortal danger, Victor went home. I continued on alone to Ethiopia, Madagascar, and eventually ended up in South Africa where I discovered an insulated horse community of English and Dutch backgrounds. I also had a friend named Gonda Butters (later: Betrix) whom I'd ridden with in Europe so looked her up. She had this wonderful little horse named Oorskiet that jumped against all the big horses in White City and Rotterdam.

While hunting her down and other contacts I knew from Europe, I stumbled onto a horse show in progress. Before long, I was recognized and began to get some attention and make friends. The American style was very sought after then and everyone seemed very interested in watching me ride firsthand. I didn't have any riding clothes with me, but after a suggestion was made that I ride, people at the show started loaning me things to wear—a hunt cap here and a pair of chaps there—and before long, they sent me into the ring. It was great fun! After this very nice visit, my new friends invited me back to teach, so in 1969 and 1970, I returned and gave several clinics, both in South Africa and Rhodesia (now Zimbabwe) hosted by Mickey Lowe and Gonda Butters (photo 102).

When I was a very little boy and visited Florida with my grandparents, racial segregation was still in effect, and I remember the separate white and black restrooms. I saw that with my own eyes at home in America in the forties in the South. Due to the existence of apartheid and also because of African horse sickness, all South African athletes couldn't compete in the Olympics in 1968. Seeing the segregated culture in South Africa was like going back in time, to somewhere stuck in the past. When I was there, they segregated three racial categories: black, white, and non-white, to account for those of Asian descent. The irony there was that the white stable owners all had black grooms that acted as trainers. The families I visited were all very close to their trainers and other staff in the stables, and I witnessed a mutual respect between them, but I'm sure it wasn't always that way. Nelson Mandela, an incredibly insightful figure, changed all of that.

While on that long trip in Africa, I received a call that my beloved Baron had died of a heart attack; it was devastating news. It's so difficult to lose a dog. They're truly members of the family. Baron had been with me during my theater days and through the years establishing my business as a professional. He was one of the truly great dogs in my life. I don't believe we ever stop missing the great ones.

As it turned out, Victor wasn't wrong to be worried about the Hulicks switching teams. Later that year, they asked me to start teaching James and Gail. It's just part of the business and I lost my share of students to Victor through the years, too. I happily took on James and Gail, as both children were very good riders.

In the summer of '69 I judged the Oak Brook Show in Chicago and there was a girl that was constantly at the top of the pile—a child prodigy named Katie Monahan. It was the same little girl I'd seen year after year at the Garden riding in the Medal and Maclay Finals while being several years younger than most of the others. Katie was then riding with John Slaughter and Bill Queen. The top junior in the country at that time, I was convinced Katie was going to win the Finals that year; there was no way to beat her! Her Milltown had a short choppy gait but was a wonderful jumper. Having collected good ribbons in the Medal and Maclay Finals but still striving for the tricolor, Katie Monahan came to ride with me in 1969. Her father, with perhaps some guidance from Sallie Sexton, thought she would have a better chance at winning the Finals if I brought her to the in-gate. True or not, I was thrilled to have the opportunity to teach Katie and welcomed her. That was the start of a twelve-year relationship with Katie, teaching and mentoring her riding until she started her own business in 1982. Admittedly, she took over my focus a little from Conrad. C.Z. Guest, who was the queen of American society, had become friendly with Katie and Chrystine Jones. When Katie came East to ride, she moved in with the Guests out on Long Island, which worked well since it was close to Old Mill. Eventually Katie also taught C.Z.'s young daughter Cornelia, to whom I also gave lessons from time to time.

Cornelia Guest

When I was a little girl, George would come out to teach me how to ride my pony. I would sit all ready for my lesson, holding my pony, on the bench in front of the house, eagerly waiting for George. The New York horse show world was so wonderful then and a dream to grow up around. I'll never forget the horse show at the Garden—wonderful artists and celebrities would be there and all my parents' friends would come. It was so grand! Also in Manhattan was M.J. Knoud's Saddlery; we called the owner, Dave Wright, either Mr. Knoud or "the millionaire of Madison

Avenue." The shop made all the wonderful tack, boots, riding clothes, and carriage brass—everything you could think of—and when I was little, we would go there and pick things out for riding. It's gone now, but it was a sign of that wonderful time. I've had my jodhpur boots from Knoud's since I was sixteen and Hank Vogel measured me for them. I've had them almost my entire life, and any time I wear them people remark on how beautiful they are.

Bobby Burke trained and rode horses for our family for many years and was an especially dear friend of my mother's. We also had an incredible groom named Johnny Leach. He would go out in the woods and collect clay and moss for packing hooves and poulticing legs. When George had a special horse with a need for the best care, he used to come out and get Johnny to give him his "magic" treatment.

George sent Katie Monahan to be my teacher and quite simply, she changed my life. I wouldn't be who I am if it wasn't for Katie. She taught me so much about life, not just about horses and riding. When I was young, George would step in and take me to the ring at the shows sometimes, if Katie was busy. He's a dear, dear man and a total gentleman. When my mom and dad each died, George was there for me in such a supportive way.

When I began teaching Katie, I was amazed at how good she was already. She was like Victoria Colvin; you have to hunt down things to criticize. Milltown was a trick horse and they had such a close collaboration; however, that doesn't mean I told her how wonderful she was! All young riders need encouragement to ride better, no matter how good they are. Otherwise they'll get bored or complacent and lose the edge on their greatness. I remember in a lesson I asked her to go from a trot to a halt and, of course, Milltown stopped on a dime with his head on his chest. I told her that it was not a good halt at all, because he was clearly behind the leg!

Katie did very well all that show season and when the indoors came along, I had a big group of talented young riders showing. Katie had an excellent round at Harrisburg in the Medal Finals, but Milltown had to run down the lines just a little to make up for being a bit light on scope. Fred Bauer, Sue's younger brother, had been my student initially but went to ride with Ronnie Mutch once Sue and Ronnie married. Fred was a beautiful picture on his horse Birch Bark and they had a great trip with an easy gallop. Fred won and Katie was third; I remember being irritated because her round had been quite good, and her father was also a bit huffed.

At the Maclay Finals, after a great first round Katie was called back to flat. After the flat phase, the judges moved her up to the top spot. Her parents attributed her improvement on the flat to my teaching, because she had never gotten a bump up after the flat class at previous shows. Then, Katie put the nail in the coffin in the afternoon with a stellar trip and won the Maclay Finals! I give her and all her previous teachers the credit, still today. It wasn't just politics of having me at the in-gate (photo 103).

While teaching a clinic in Knoxville, Tennessee, at the end of 1968 at the farm of Sue Ashe, I was approached by a stocky, older girl from Memphis with a strong opinionated mother. I took note that she was a good rider, but because she was nineteen and riding a not-so-flashy horse, they didn't strike me particularly. After the clinic, her mother asked me if her daughter could ride with me outside of the clinics. By that time I had set some firm boundaries for what clients I would accept, so I gently explained that they didn't have the horseflesh and that they likely couldn't afford to buy the right horse. The following year the mother and her daughter, Melanie Smith (later: Smith Taylor), were back at Sue's and I recognized them. They were good country horse people and Mrs. Smith approached me again after the clinic, "George, you gotta take Melanie!" she said. I protested again, explained how Melanie was out of the juniors and that they couldn't afford the horses…but she was persistent! She wore me down and I reluctantly agreed that they could meet me down in Florida.

In the late sixties, I began teaching the crest release. Up until then, the automatic release with a following hand from elbow to bit was the only type of release taught. What I had found was that less experienced riders were more effective if they used the crest as a balance point for their hands. They were less likely to commit the cardinal sin of catching the horse in the mouth. Today, as I have written about many times in past years, the crest release is overused and the automatic release not embraced enough by advanced riders who are clearly capable of the more advanced feel.

Off I went after indoors on another whirlwind trip to far-flung countries—Hawaii, Japan, Hong Kong, and Nepal to name just a few. In Kathmandu, I met an extremely good-looking guy at my hotel and it turned out he worked at the American Embassy in Bangkok. We chatted a bit and as fellow Americans in a foreign land, he invited me to dinner, which I gladly accepted. First, though, he said he had to go and pick up his Christmas presents for some friends and invited me along.

It turned out the present my new friend picked up was a pumpkin-sized ball of hashish, which we sampled before leaving the little shop. I'd never even had hashish before and as we walked through the colorful little lanes and paths in Kathmandu, I began positively flying. I floated along in a dream, with the chaotic, crowded, medieval–like streets flowing around me like a rushing river. It felt like a hallucinogenic trip. Back at the hotel, in the very formal and proper Chinese restaurant, we were so ridiculously high that we laughed endlessly, tears running down our faces. The staff and Chinese orchestra glared at us for being so inappropriate, which just made us laugh harder. We spent all night together—this great guy, and a lot of hashish. The next morning, I'd booked a tourist trip to Mount Everest and we decided to go together. To this day when I hear Mount Everest mentioned, it takes me back to that crazy trip on that Nepalese hashish.

Back at home I based in Tampa, Florida, for the winter circuit at a stable where I'd taught regular clinics for a trainer there named Peggy Touchstone. She taught a girl named Anne Keenan. Anne would later teach Laura Kraut, before she came to ride with me. My clients came down and joined me in Florida, including Amory, Tania Nagro, Kip Rosenthal, and Ann Yohai. I wasn't sure whether they would find their way South but sure enough, the Memphis girl Melanie Smith also joined me down in Florida for the four or so shows. She had a couple of Thoroughbreds: the first was a hot, handsome horse off the track for the hunter classes called Bootlegger; the second was a horse named The Irishman meant for the jumper divisions. Melanie's mom had found them by traveling around to auctions searching for prospects—she was a really good horsewoman. Years later, I taught a clinic at her farm in Tennessee and it was like Old MacDonald's with farm animals everywhere; I had to chase chickens out of the ring during the clinic!

Melanie Smith Taylor

When I first rode with George I'd only had lessons with my mother and through Pony Club. My mother had heard from a friend that a man named George Morris was teaching something new over fences called the "crest release." So we hitched up our purple station wagon to our matching two-horse trailer and drove eight hours on two-lane roads to Knoxville from Germantown, Tennessee, for a clinic with him. When I met George I was completely mesmerized! He was so handsome. He was fresh out of acting school and had those steely blue eyes. I was very shy but my mother was not. Mother, a strong character just wanting the best for her daughter, asked George if I could ride with him. He replied that there really wasn't a place for me as I was no longer a junior and

the Amateur Owner division was still in its infancy. George added that
my horse didn't impress him. I could understand that as George tested
me and my horse, The Irishman, after the clinic, and he did hang his legs
a few times.

We weren't discouraged, though. We waited a whole year and went
back in '69 and I rode in the clinic once again with the same horse. When
this clinic ended, my mother approached George once more about my
riding with him. George asked my mother what she wanted her daughter
to do. She replied: "Well, how about the Olympic Team?" By this time I
was so embarrassed I was sitting on the ground cringing. George finally agreed and suggested we meet him in Florida the following winter. I
know to this day that George figured these two country bumpkins would
never even find their way out of Tennessee, much less to Florida! George
didn't like "pushy mothers" but he told me in later years that he liked my
mother because she was strong, not pushy, as well as a great horsewoman. He loved her personality and determination.

That next March, we loaded up the purple horse trailer with my two
horses and headed down to the first show in Winterhaven, Florida. I got
my horse ready for the first Amateur Owner jumper class and George
was nowhere to be found. I'm sure he was so embarrassed at how "country" we were that he was probably watching from a hiding spot behind
a tree. So I went on up to the ring and jumped around clean in the first
round, and I looked for someone at the gate on my way out, but there
was no one. At home, I had competed in hunter and equitation classes so
was unfamiliar with jumpers, but George had told us what to enter. The
announcer said I was qualified for the jump-off but I didn't even know
what a jump-off was! You see, I knew how to ride and care for horses and
all of that, but I didn't know all the fancy names for things or how the big
horse shows worked. I had to ask a stranger what to do in a jump-off and
she told me to go as fast as I could. So I did! And I won! Well, after that,
George came out from behind that tree and was always there to school
me. My little country horse and I ended up Circuit Champions, and at
the end of the Florida circuit, George asked me to come and be his su-
pervising instructor. What that ended up being was a working student,
more or less, because I cleaned stalls, braided, and exercised horses for
my lessons. But I'll tell you this: I never paid for a lesson with George
ever, my entire life. He was so good to me. He knew we couldn't afford
it and that I would work for everything. I spent that first year riding with
George on Long Island where he was based. I'll never forget going with
him when he first looked at the property that became Hunterdon. It was

nothing but a farmhouse and little ramshackle barn, but he had a great vision of what it could become.

In 1972, Katie Monahan and I began the Florida circuit in the Preliminary Jumpers and finished in the Tampa stadium competing in the American Gold Cup. Katie had a working hunter named Hallelujah and I had a part Tennessee Walker named Chapo. Chapo was owned by one of our boarders in Germantown who had shown him no higher than three-foot-six. George had given a clinic at our pony farm in the fall of 1971 and decided to "test" me on Chapo. I don't believe I have ever jumped higher fences than I jumped that day in our little dirt riding area on top of a hill. The jumps were barrels and pieces of plywood leaning against standards with poles hung high in the air above them. Afterward, George announced, "Bring this one to Florida next year. He's going to be your first Grand Prix horse." And he was right! I won the Gold Cup Qualifier against the best of that era and ended up fifth and Leading Lady Rider in the actual Gold Cup—my first Grand Prix. It was said afterward that the Gold Cup course was the biggest course ever built in America up until that time. It was to prepare the horses and riders who were headed to Munich for the 1972 Olympic Games. I remember walking the course with Katie, our knees wobbling, as we said to each other, "Does George really expect us to jump this?" But George had prepared me months before on that sacred piece of ground where I grew up riding. He always gave me the confidence that I could jump any course anywhere. I think back on those days with a chuckle, for ignorance is bliss when you are young.

Fresh off her Maclay win, Katie Monahan also came to Florida with her jumper, a big chestnut, seven-eighths-bred horse called Hallelujah who could jump over the standards. Later, Rodney Jenkins ended up with that horse and called him Katmandu. Melanie rode Chapo, a twisty jumper who would break to a half-pace, half-trot before slithering over the fence. Katie and Melanie both did excellently on the circuit. These two girls rode in the Green Jumper divisions and did so well they both ended up qualifying for the Tampa Invitational Grand Prix. European riders started calling me trying to buy the horses out from under them. That winter, both Melanie and Katie started riding in the Open Jumper classes and setting their sights on the USET and the Olympic Games.

Mrs. John Graham, who owned Katie's chestnut working-hunter-turned-jumper, Hallelujah, eventually sent him to Rodney Jenkins because she thought Katie was too young to make the most of him. But for that winter, showing those horses gave those two girls a leg up and some genuine notoriety in the jumper divisions.

The following spring, Melanie came to work for me on Long Island and just kept on winning. In June she'd been champion already at Saratoga, Syracuse, and Farmington. We were at the Ox Ridge Hunt Club Show and I said to Melanie, "Look at the points you have for Horse of the Year!" to which she replied, "What's Horse of the Year?" All the color drained from my face. It turned out she had never even registered her horses! I almost had a stroke! Melanie was a country girl from Memphis and didn't know about the AHSA and registering her horses. Even without Florida or any of those spring shows, after she did register them, she won so much that in the end it didn't matter; she was still high score and riding the Horse of the Year!

For my first twenty years of riding, nobody ever taught me about how to see distances, but I must have had some kind of eye because I won the Grand Prix of Aachen. From Secor Farms to the Olympic Games and into my professional career, I never had a technique to find distances to jumps. It's not something anyone talked about, the concept of finding the jumps—they would just describe it as "timing." Either riders had timing or they didn't. Glenna de Rham always had great timing, as did Ronnie Mutch. At the horse shows, we would stand at the rail, watch, and be envious of a rider who always met the jumps well. When I started riding hunters professionally, I was very mediocre. For me, it was hit or miss with the distances and they really started to matter. If the distance angels were there I would do well, but if they weren't, I didn't. It was some mystery! Then, in 1968, Carl Knee taught me a simple exercise to predictably place a horse to a jump and after that I figured it out and improved my eye more and more. What he told me was to ease off in the turn and measure the jump in the approach—to "let go" and the distance will appear. It worked!

Pete Bostwick was an iconic sportsman, gentleman, and businessman of the twentieth century. He was particularly known for his prowess in equestrian sports including polo, racing, foxhunting, and showing. Pete lived out on Long Island as part of an established American aristocratic family. One day, after knowing of him but never meeting him face to face, he called me at Old Mill and asked if he could ride in a lesson with me. I agreed and he insisted that he ride in my advanced lesson group. At that time he was well into his late fifties, but I knew he was a horseman's horseman so I was sure he'd be fine. On the day of his lesson, Pete arrived with his wife Dolly who sat nervously watching at ringside. I put Pete into the advanced lesson with my Maclay and Medal riders who I often had ride and jump without stirrups. Well, we carried on as usual and, in the course of the lesson, Pete pulled his groin muscle. This would be like pulling the groin muscle of the King of England! Dolly, who was very protective of her husband, had a fit about it. Pete was not happy with me, either. What could I say? After all, he had insisted on riding with my advanced group.

In recent years, I've become friendly with Pete Bostwick's daughter Sissy Armstrong and her daughter Henrietta of the King Ranch family. I met them through my very close friend Susie Humes who is a member of the Whitney Vanderbilt family of Long Island. I can still remember the day Susie told me she was engaged to Paul Humes and I nearly choked. I had seen a lot of Paul in the past, who had been a major player at Mason Phelps' inner-circle house party in Newport, Rhode Island, when he ran the Hunter Derby there.

⁊☙

T he sixties established me as a professional teacher and a hunter rider. I had my last moments as a true student when I rode with Gunnar Andersen at the Newberrys' but I continued learning from my peers for the rest of my career. For nearly twenty years afterward—until 1983—I was hunter- and equitation-focused with my teaching and primarily rode in the hunter divisions, with some green jumpers occasionally. As soon as I had a student who needed a horse, I gave them my green jumpers to ride. The bulk of most professionals' business then was the hunter division and mine was divided approximately forty percent hunters, thirty-five percent equitation, and twenty-five percent jumpers. I was never as excellent in the hunter ring as Rodney Jenkins or Bernie Traurig, but I won a lot and rode many wonderful horses. I was right there with the best of them.

The decade also marked a shift in how I approached life in that I became more bold both in my personal and professional life. I stopped letting the influences around me contain who I was as a young man and took more risks. The decision to attend the Neighborhood Playhouse and stretch myself physically and mentally on stage—in a leotard!—was a personal risk, but one I knew I had to make. I had to satisfy the other fish, swim in the opposite direction, and explore that side of myself.

It's no mistake that I have been known for my characteristic voice, because that voice was developed in the theater. When I went back to horses I applied the lessons I learned on stage to that other world. Teaching students how to present themselves and make an instant impression when they walk into the ring is another crossover from skills I learned in performing. Leaving the theater was a choice I made in part because of my voice problems, and I consider it a blessing in disguise. It led me back to where I needed to be—with horses.

Perhaps more than any of those little things, I knew that pushing people beyond their comfort zone and giving them license to stretch within themselves was the way to guide them to personal success. This is true in any sport or profession. To accomplish ambitious dreams even in the face of fear, they must be impressed upon and pushed by the positive forces around them. For six decades after my time in the theater, I sought to be that positive guide to my students, to help them break free of their limitations so they might achieve their lofty dreams.

In my twenties, I explored living both in the city and in rural areas and hosted my business at various places, honing in on my own preferences. Those years also allowed me to establish my interpretation of an alternative lifestyle while still being a successful horseman, but on my own terms. For the rest of my life, I had to walk a balance between my professional horse life and my personal city life after the sun went down. Never fully comfortable in the straight, family-oriented horse world and just as out of place in an alternative subculture with a stereotypical identity crisis, I learned in the sixties to seek my own circle of friends. It hasn't always been easy, living two very delineated lives and bouncing from one to the other. But as the world has become more modern and accepting, the gray area in the middle has become more comfortable, and for that, I'm grateful.

THE GOLDEN DECADE

I. A TRANSITION YEAR

It was a thrilling time for the horse show world in America; the depth of quality horses and talented young riders began to impact the advanced levels of national Grand Prix and international show jumping. There was something particularly special about being a young rider in the seventies in America because even though there were fewer teachers than today, they taught with a stronger, less diluted background. Bertalan de Némethy and Gordon Wright had planted the seeds in the fifties and sixties and laid the foundation of horsemanship and classical riding and passed it to the next generation of teachers.

The horse show schedule wasn't as grueling as it is today, with more time for learning and working with horses at home. When we did show, it was extremely competitive with hardly any beginner classes. Hunters still galloped over big, outside courses with fixed, natural obstacles. That training was combined with the technical advancements seen in the sixties—riders were expected to be more proficient with dressage flatwork and to relate distances and demonstrate flying lead changes on course. This combination created riders with great ability, skill, and fortitude. Young riders across the country were being developed into a deeper pool of talent, and successful juniors from the sixties had progressed into jumper riders trying to earn a spot on the United States Equestrian Team.

For me, 1970 began with a difficult personal challenge. The same voice problem that I'd encountered at the Neighborhood Playhouse School of Theatre, which had receded into the background for eight years, suddenly returned. The problem came back after I'd been spending a lot of time at Harry's Back East, a New York City watering hole with a classy crowd and the perfect atmosphere for unwinding with friends. I was often staying out too late and stretching my-self a little thin. Then, when I went out to teach at Old Mill Farm one summer Monday, I found I couldn't speak. My voice wouldn't work normally. Certain breathy consonant sounds were impossible to form and pronounce. It wasn't just difficult to speak—it was impossible. It was a hundred times worse than my trouble on stage in the theater and it really put a scare into me.

As a teacher who couldn't speak properly, I had massive levels of anxiety. The physical loss of my vocal ability triggered a mental reaction of insecurity and of feeling out of control. I had no choice but to find a way to keep going, for my career depended on it. I assumed that it was triggered by combining too much work with too much play and as a result, becoming exhausted. So I rested. I eased up on the nightlife and got more sleep. I tried everything I could to get my voice back. And when I saw no improvement, I had a major nervous breakdown. I had lost control of my voice completely.

Marion Hulick

One year George was scheduled to teach a clinic in Framingham, Mass-achusetts, and he hadn't arrived. It really concerned me that I couldn't reach him at his New York City apartment and as time went by, we grew more and more worried. I had to see what I could do from afar. I called the mother of a little girl who rode with us, and asked if her elderly mother, who lived in the city near George, could look in on him. She went and knocked on his door, and when he looked through the peephole, this grandmother in her eighties was there to check on him. It was a relief that he was all right then, and in the end, he was fine. George has worked very hard through some difficult times like that. He's taught himself how to persevere, which I consider a testament to his personal strength. George even came and stayed with us in Massachusetts for a short time. He was a wonderful teacher for both our children, Gail and James. Gail won many championships on her wonderful horse Good Boy Dee, and James met with great success in both the equitation and the jumpers, winning Grand Prix classes with George's coaching. James's ailing health from multiple sclerosis eventually prevented him from con-tinuing his riding.

Marion and Hank Hulick were my closest friends. It meant so much that Marion, who really understood me on a personal level, sent a friend to knock on my door to check on me. I was a complete mess and needed help; I couldn't even go out to the grocery store. Most people never knew about it, but for nearly a year, I was really haunted psychologically about my voice. Somehow, I slogged through it and tried to function as best I could. I've learned that one cannot give up when life presents these personal challenges. What would I have become if I had given in to my nerves and shut myself away and quit teaching? You must remember to take the offered hand of those around you whom you trust. Kathy Kusner gave me a little handbook called *Recovery, Inc.* It's not for substance abuse or addiction; it's for people with nervous constitutions. I read it and it resonated with me so completely that I fully embraced it. I followed the advice diligently and it taught me how to deal with my nerves in a healthy way. This little handbook is like my bible and it resides on my bedside table to this very day.

I saw a number of doctors about my vocal problems but no one could seem to figure out anything physical that was causing them. I even saw a psychiatrist, the famed Dr. Wardell Pomeroy in New York, who after examination told me, "Your only problem is that you need to stop chasing boys and start reading books!" And in a way, he was right! It had been my wild lifestyle and stressing myself physically that had contributed to my problem with my voice.

That following autumn, I came to terms with my voice problem in a new way while teaching clinics. I was determined that, as difficult as it was, I could bear it. Ever since then, I've had periods of time when it comes back—if I'm tired or under the weather and am teaching a lot, it will rear its ugly head. To be quite honest, I've been dealing with vocal issues my entire life. That's why I'm so particular nowadays about having a microphone when I teach. If I strain my voice, I risk losing it altogether for a period of time. I have to manage my voice very carefully and be regimented about getting enough rest. It was only a few years ago now that I went to see a New York specialist and learned there was a physical reason for the problem: there's a gap in my vocal chords and it worsens under stress. It was an immense relief to receive a diagnosis for this problem of mine and to know, after all those years, it wasn't due solely to emotional stress or strain.

In early September of that year, I met Jeremy Wind. I was at Harry's Back East, saw him across the bar, and felt an instant psychological connection and a sort of magnetic heat. He was very attractive with reddish-brown hair and simply reeked of class. I met him and discovered that he was a musician and very involved in the arts, which of course I've always loved. At the time, I was just getting my feet back underneath me after my nervous breakdown and he came in on the ground floor. To some extent, our friendship helped me recover my confidence. Jeremy was intellectual, talented, and fun, and he inspired me with his brilliance. As we became good friends, I found that he helped me balance my fast-paced horse life with my love of the city and the arts (photo 104).

Despite my difficult start to the decade with my voice issues, my students didn't miss a beat and continued to be successful at the equitation Finals. At Harrisburg, for the 1970 Medal Finals, James Hulick had to switch horses in the test with a girl named Ellen Raidt, who eventually became an assistant to Bert de Némethy. Ellen had a high-headed, rather tense, hot, little chestnut horse. James had a hot horse, too, but he rode him very well. When they switched horses, I did a very simple thing to Ellen's horse: I shortened the horse's martingale six holes! I'm not one for overuse of martingales, but in the context of a big horse show like this it was the right move to tie that horse's head down. It worked well because the horse went beautifully and James won. At Madison Square Garden, for the Maclay Finals, James traded horses with Freddy Bauer and Freddy beat him. Freddy was a wonderful rider whom I also spent some time teaching. James was second in the Maclay in both '70 and '71, but that Medal Finals win in '70 was a wonderful thing for the son of my very great friends (photo 105).

Back at Old Mill Farm where I was based, I was starting to wear out my welcome with Mr. Yohai. He was a wonderful guy but like me, he had a slow burn. Those kinds of business partnerships with clients always had an expiration date for me. He and I had a petty disagreement about which side to face the barn at the Tampa show and I thought, "Screw it, I'm ready to get my own place!" It was time to leave Old Mill, but I always took care in those situations not to burn bridges. I left the Yohais on good terms and continued our relationship. Keeping clients and friends even when a partnership ends is a tricky business, but the best professionals find a way to preserve the good side of the relationship.

During my visit to Australia, Rhodesia, and South Africa to teach clinics, I experienced a moment of clarity. I had brought Conrad with me to be a demonstration rider for him to have a good experience, and we visited friends in Rhodesia—Elsa and Nick van Heerdan. Nick was a tough, practical, street-smart guy. We had a talk one evening and Nick mused, "George, you can only push the boat off the dock so many times." Suddenly, I understood. This was my life and I couldn't live it in fear of my voice problem. When I got back to New York, I went over to Jeremy's apartment, leaned against his grand piano, and pitched the idea of forming a partnership in business. I wanted to get my own place, and he seemed like the right man to partner with to do it right. He agreed to be a silent partner in my business venture, and I was thrilled to launch a new beginning.

With my desire to be in close proximity to New York, the question in my mind was where my business should be based. Frank Chapot had moved from northwest New Jersey to Neshanic Station, and when I went down to try a horse there, I noticed the rural and open country. New Jersey wasn't as woodsy as Connecticut, but it was in the same close radius from the city and it was gorgeous country. Bernie Traurig's place, Bloodstock Farm, was in New Hope, Pennsylvania. In the seventies, New Hope was a very hippie, artsy area and I considered it very charming. After seeing Bloodstock Farm and Frank's place in Neshanic Station, I started looking at real estate around Gladstone and Chester, New Jersey. Although I went to Florida to teach at a show or two that winter, I spent more time up North looking for the right property. Chee Chee Delker, the realtor, was a horsewoman and became a great friend.

Jeremy and I searched all over Hunterdon County and near New Hope and looked at dozens of properties. By March, I was tired of kicking tires and wanted to make a decision and get things started. We'd seen a beautiful twenty-five-acre property with some old barns and a big, centuries-old house that needed a complete renovation. It had a huge chicken barn that I had a good feeling about because it sat on the high point of a wide-open, fifteen-acre field on a slight grade. Otto Heuckeroth told me that one should always build a barn at the top of the hill because of drainage. I bought the property for $67,500 and it became Hunterdon.

II. THE RISE OF HUNTERDON

Ronnie Beard

In 1972, I was working for a good friend of George, Jimmy Lee. Jimmy sent me to take a job that he didn't take himself—for a man on the Eastern Shore of Maryland who had a daughter who needed a private trainer. The man turned out to be a once-in-a-lifetime client who gave me free rein to build the best stable and training facility money could buy. That's how Winterplace Farm came to be. It seemed only natural that George be involved as a mentor for me on a professional level. In the very beginning, George thought, "Here's this kid (me) and he's got all the best horses and riders and a big purse of his owner's money to spend. These kind of people are a flash in the pan; they never last!" My job was to prove him wrong.

We had several volatile moments in those early years. Katie Mona-han was riding this wonderful horse for me named Old Dominion. The horse had been champion at most of the shows that year and we really wanted that icing on the cake with a championship at Madison Square Garden. Things were very tense that particular day and George became frustrated and hollered at Katie and then turned upon me, "...and YOU!" he snarled. "You're the worst. You're the worst there ever was!" And I re-plied, "George, I never want to speak to you ever again." Two days later, I was standing at the in-gate at the Garden and George walked up and stood beside me, watching the horse go. I didn't say a word or acknowl-edge him. After a few moments, he turned to me slowly and said, "Ronnie, you didn't mean that." After that, we never fought again. Through those Winterplace years, George helped me and taught me so much. I always wanted to be a part of the international show jumping scene and he opened those doors for me.

Then, on the other hand, there is my long friendship with George. We have been close for so many years. One of my favorite stories about him is when we went out on the town one night. We hopped from place to place and it was getting quite late as we left one watering hole to walk to yet another. George looked at me as we were walking and el-bowed me in the side. He had this way of jabbing me to get my attention for what he was about to say. So after he'd got my attention, he said, "Ronnie, this next place is ten blocks away—let's race!" Incredulous, I said, "Are you out of your mind?" and he said, "Yes! We're going to race!" and he took off running and I took off after him! We raced all the way up Columbus Avenue to the other bar. Well, little did he know, I can run fast! I beat him to the bar and he came running up and stopped, panting, his eyes flashing. "You know what Ronnie? You...are very...fast." To this day, when we tell the story over dinner, he'll point to me and say to the others, "You may not realize it, but Ronnie is very, very fast."

I kept the horses at Frank Chapot's stable that spring while Hunterdon was being readied. While I waited, Vince Dugan sold me a horse named Abu Simbel, a green, seven-eighths-bred horse with just a little spook in him. I took my new horse to Devon and stabled with the Chapots, but I was on my own there and did all the work myself. I arrived early every morning and fed, braided, turned out, tacked up, and walked the courses. It was my proudest show because I did everything myself! It's a good experience for all profes-sionals, no matter how big an operation they have, to know enough about their horses to do everything. Abu Simbel won the Second Year Green and the Open Handy on the same day, which was an excellent result for such a green horse.

In July 1971, Hunterdon was born. It was in the town of Pittstown, New Jersey, but Hunterdon—the name of the county—just seemed to fit. Jeremy and I christened it and fixed up the old house on the property. Most of the antiques I decorated the house with were picked out with the help of Emily de Némethy, who had a high-class antique business. I also had the wonderful things that David Holman had helped me choose for my New York City apartment and eventually, the old house was positively stuffed with beautiful furniture, décor, and works of art. Our first group of customers included Buddy Brown, Leslie Burr (later: Burr Howard), Cynthia Hankins, Debra Baldi, Stevie Stockowitz, Teddi and Sunny Ismond (who later married Kelly Klein's father, whom I know well).

Jimmy Kohn and I had remained friends and through him, I met a woman named Jan Smith at the West Coast shows—she and I just clicked. Jan's daughter Julie was a successful junior rider in California on her little horse Periwinkle. Jan was a real business-minded sort and suggested we work together to organize clinics, which began in Westlake Village. An executive genius, she would stalk through mud, sleet, and manure in a miniskirt with not a single hair out of place! Jan was wonderfully accepting of alternative lifestyles and one of those special, caring friends who was a catalyst for success. We ran clinics all over the West Coast together until she was killed in a car accident in 1989. I was heartbroken when she died, but I'll never forget what a bright, smart, lovely person she was in my life.

Jeremy Wind, my new partner in business and closest confidant behind closed doors, was a very talented musician but also an all-around dilettante. Life was just too easy for him! Learning new things appeared effortless. I taught him to ride in approximately five minutes. He learned to jump and saw the jumps immediately. Jeremy excelled at everything, was well-liked, and seemed to brighten the world around him just by being present. He was also good for the occasional surprise.

At one show that spring in Saratoga, Jeremy came to help me out. I told him, "Jeremy, when I'm in the ring jogging the First Year Green horse, get on Abu Simbel and trot around the outside course so he can take a look at the jumps." As I stood in the ring, jogging the First Year horse for the judge, I saw Jeremy out on the outside course as I'd asked. Then, to my astonishment, Jeremy picked up a gallop and rode right up to the big brush fence and saw the jump perfectly. I was aghast—it's not kosher to jump the course during the show on your own! The judge noticed where I was looking and turned to watch. With our jaws in the dirt, we watched Jeremy jump around the entire outside course. He was a complete natural! Abu Simbel went like a finely tuned machine once I got on him and we won the class. It was classic Jeremy. If he'd had the ambition to really commit to riding, who knows—he might have been another Rodney Jenkins.

Even though he rode a little, Jeremy never got into showing. He might have gone to one or two shows in the early days, but it was almost too easy for him to develop the desire. But if you asked him to throw a dinner party or charm the birds out of the trees, he would do it better and more effortlessly than you imagined anyone could. Jeremy was my partner at Hunterdon through the seventies and his stamp of style and taste was all over the place. He established the beauty and elegance of Hunterdon from the beginning.

Being part of a new local horse community near Hunterdon was wonderful. Jeremy became great friends with Karen Golding, an iconic steward and groom, who worked for Bernie Traurig in New Hope and later worked for Michael Matz (who was a working student at Bernie's in those days). Karen still helps me today as the stable management expert at the USEF Horsemastership clinic. The New Hope area was a very artsy and avant-garde but was also a very high-profile horse town. If you could win a hunter or equitation class with a client at the local shows, you could win at Madison Square Garden. With so many top trainers and riders nearby, you couldn't help but let the geography raise your game.

Bernie Traurig

That area was inundated with talented riders and horses. There were some little, one-day, winter, schooling shows in an indoor near New Hope in New Jersey at Four Seasons Farm. We called it "The Snowflake Series." We all looked forward to those for something to do in the dead of winter and would work off the van, without stabling and with literally no warm-up place. Just go in and compete. We mostly competed with our young horses that needed mileage or were for sale. Frank Chapot, whose stable was quite close, often showed up with his horses. Well, it might as well have been the Olympics! Frank was just as competitive there as he was in any international championship.

George has been a longtime friend and his impact on the sport is unparalleled. George's contribution to the younger generation today is so important for the future of our sport and country. Depth is the key to sustained success. His passion for education and his extensive back-ground, combined with his philosophy and clarity on classical riding, is to be admired.

Back at Hunterdon, I built a Grand Prix field fashioned after the wonderful courses at Aachen and Hickstead. The field was enormous and had a slight grade that kept you on your toes when you jumped the course. I didn't want an outdoor fenced-in ring, which simply made horses sour and riders weak with outside aids. We schooled and taught in the field every day, unless inclement weather forced us into the indoor arena. The main barn was a pole building with twenty-two stalls and had an adjacent office and tack room with a little apartment up above. There was also an older lower barn with three stalls and hay storage, where I initially kept my own horses. Over the years, all the name plates from all the horses that lived at Hunterdon were mounted in there and it has become quite a legendary sight to see (photo 108).

Once in a while, a horse comes into your life that teaches you something and changes the way you ride. Usually, it's a horse that's a complicated ride but worth the extra effort, and as a result you improve your feel. Early in the spring one year in the late sixties, Clarence Nagro spotted a green horse in Virginia he liked and bought him for his wife, Tania. I remember when I first laid eyes on that horse, named Flying Along, at the Boulder Brook Horse Show. If there were a thousand horses at the show, Flying Along was the most beautiful horse of them all; he was simply stunning. The dapple gray had a dish face and gorgeous head and he graced the cover of the first edition of *Hunter Seat Equitation*. Flying Along wasn't the best mover of them all, but he was still quite good and excellent over jumps. He was truly a flashy, sexy horse.

It was love at first sight, but Flying Along was Tania's horse. She had brought him to Boulder Brook and it turned out he was a complex, sensitive ride. Tania rode him in the First Year Green Hunters and he stopped at a few jumps and was being inconsistent. Meanwhile, as one of the best hunter riders in the country by then, I was dying to try him. I coached Tania the best I could on him, but even a few weeks later at Farmington, their troubles continued. In the first class, he stopped out again. Tania came off the outside course, jumped off and threw me the reins. She said, "George, I can't ride this horse! He's your horse now."

I rode him into the ring for the second trip, cracked him with the whip over a couple of the fences, and he won every class for the rest of the show. He wasn't perfect, but he was simply a beautiful show horse. I had to protect his front end a little and carry him a bit, and he was a little chicken about certain sorts of jumps. If you blatantly missed a distance, he was too insecure to just get over it. You'd pay for a missed distance for the rest of the day. However, if you could get him to the jumps right and keep his confidence up, he was unbeatable. Riding Flying Along taught me how to fine-tune accuracy to the jumps and how that accuracy makes or breaks the way the horse carries himself around the rest of the course. Tania rode him again later and showed him to great success. Tania is still today one of my inner circle of oldest and best friends.

Tania Nagro

My husband Clarence was a professional horseman and would coach me, but I would sometimes go to the shows on my own while he was home running the business. I would see George coaching Tina Pfister and others and I said, "That's who I need to ride with!" He's always been the best, and he understands that the basics are the foundation of good riding. George can make riders do things they never thought they were capable of. You never think you couldn't or wouldn't do something. He would always find a way to help you do it.

George had Abu Simbel at Hunterdon and thought he would be the perfect horse for me. He was right—I loved him and he became my favorite horse of all time. When I wanted to buy him, Clarence came to see him and he approved. George asked if we wanted to have the vet take a look at him before we bought him and Clarence replied to George, "You know the horse, you say he's okay, the horse is right here, and I can see him! What do I need a vet for?" It was so funny! George couldn't believe his ears and we always laugh at that memory.

My other horse, Flying Along, was such a beauty that people would gasp and ask about him, even at such shows as Madison Square Garden. George and that horse got along like two peas in a pod! Flying Along was very difficult to ride but George knew just how to finesse him. We would have to humor him sometimes, too: down in Florida in the sand warm-up ring, Flying Along would balk at the ruts in the footing that the other horses had created by jumping back and forth over the warm-up jumps. When he saw the ruts and the spiky cactus plants on the sides of the ring, he refused to even get near a jump. He was so sensitive that we couldn't get on his case about it; if we did, he would throw a fit and wouldn't perform well in the ring. Instead, George would hack him a half-mile down the road to another ring to warm him up. Now that horse was a prima donna!

There were great judges at Harrisburg that year: Robert Egan from Michigan and Zander Powers from Minneapolis. I thought Katie Monahan couldn't lose on Milltown. She had to go very early in the order and I recall that there was a line early in the course down to a wall at a little bit of an angle. I told her it was seven strides, but we didn't have a chance to watch enough horses go before us, and neither of us realized how long the seven strides would be for Milltown. He didn't have a lot of step, as I've mentioned before, although Katie loved him and he was her pet. She galloped in to the line well, but she chipped out and didn't make the seven. It was a massive chip; she might have even knocked it down. There was nothing to be done about it and no question that she was out of the running.

I have had fifty or so dogs throughout my life but four of them were truly great dogs. At Harrisburg, Larry Aspen, who worked for Junie Kulp, and later, for Rodney Jenkins, came up with a tiny dachshund puppy in his hands. She was so cute I couldn't resist her, so I bought her right then and there and named her Wiggle. She became an epic dog of Hunterdon and I loved her so much that I would worry about her constantly. After Kiltie and Baron, Wiggle the dachshund was the next great dog of my life and the mistress of Hunterdon throughout the seventies. Jeremy loved Wiggle, too; she became part of the family.

Anna Jane White had been my student for years after I first saw her riding in a clinic I taught with Gordon Wright. She was young but had a wonderful position, and I developed her through the years (photo 109). I sold her a green horse named Rivet in the late sixties and they were a lovely pair. In the early seventies, she decided to leave and ride with Ronnie Mutch because she felt I already had James Hulick and Katie Monahan to soak up my attention. At the time I was very upset she had chosen to leave, but perhaps it was a wise move on her part because she won the Maclay Finals in 1971. It's just another example of the competitiveness between Ronnie, Victor, and me. We were the three games in town on the East Coast when it came to the junior riders. Clients would sometimes hop from one to another and it was simply part of the game.

Anna Jane White-Mullin

I first met George just before my eleventh birthday. After I rode with him in a group clinic, he asked me to ride again for him that night. There had been an ice storm in Atlanta, and as the temperature rose, the icicles on the covered arena began to fall on the railings of the ring, spooking my horse and making my audition much more difficult. He had set up an eight-sided pen in the middle of the arena and worked me through every possible exercise, then declared to my parents, "I must have her." After fifty years, he's still got me!

Throughout our relationship, I've always found George to be a charitable man. One year, a clinic was scheduled shortly after Red Frazier's Rockridge Farm burned to the ground in Marietta, Georgia. When the clinic was over, George said to my father, "Don't worry about paying me this time. Just give the money to Red." On another occasion, after my father purchased a horse that ended up not working out, George realized we were in a financial crunch. He spotted a horse that he thought might work, and when he saw that my father couldn't make that happen on the spot, he offered to buy the horse. We didn't end up accepting his extraordinary offer, but the memory of his kindness stays with me to this day.

I rode with George for seven years and credit him with all of my technical knowledge. He teaches a system of riding that will always be successful because it is based on the way a horse thinks and feels. This is acutely evident when he gets on another person's horse during clinics and, in only a few minutes, transforms it into an obedient animal. Horses submit to him, not out of fear, but out of understanding of what they're being asked to do. No one comprehends what is going through a horse's head better than George Morris.

Finally, on a very personal note, in my last year as a junior rider, I decided to switch to another coach—Ronnie Mutch, who had coached the previous year's winner of the Maclay Finals. This was a tactical move based on the fact that my two greatest competitors, Katie Monahan and James Hulick had decided to train with George, too. I thought it was important to have a coach singularly committed to my success in that crucial year. Also, I felt so close to George after the many years we had been together that I found myself bearing the extra pressure of wanting to win for him. It's one thing to feel disappointed in yourself if you don't succeed, but quite another to feel that you've let someone down whom you love and admire. This sudden turn of events was very shocking to George, but he never treated me any differently than he had before. In fact, the first show I was with another coach was the Ox Ridge Hunt Club Show in Darien, Connecticut, followed shortly by the Fairfield show. I had a date for the Fairfield Ball, but at the last minute, my date became ill and couldn't attend. "Who would have a tux and could fill in?" I thought. It occurred to me that George would, so I asked him to go and he generously agreed. To me, this said more about his character than anything.

III. HITTING THE SWEET SPOT

Katie's last chance to win the Medal Finals was in 1972 and Milltown's inability to get the seven strides in that line the previous year had pushed me to look for a different horse for her to ride. Katie wanted to ride Milltown again, but Chrystine Jones offered her horse Acca, a beautiful but more difficult horse. Katie could ride Acca well and in the end, she agreed. We had great judges again, including Frances Rowe, who built a scopey course. The lines were set very long and I was so relieved Katie was riding Acca when we walked the course.

Katie had a gorgeous round, was called back on top and stayed on top, to my great delight. At the bitter end, in a quarter of the ring area, Frances asked a group of ten riders to work on the flat in a small circle at a counter-canter. Acca was very tense and had exploded in the past being asked to flat like this, so I watched from the in-gate nervously. Katie held Acca together beautifully and they won! After all those years of Katie riding at the Finals, back to when she was just a little girl, it took her very last junior year to get top prize in the Medal despite all of her talent. Katie's experience proves how everything has to come together perfectly, even for great riders to win at the big indoor finals— not only the things you can control, like preparation and focus, but also a little bit of luck (photo 112).

That year, my old friend Kathy Kusner was having some trouble with time faults in the jumper ring, and we talked about it at the Washington Horse Show. We often worked together and helped each other as friends. At the Garden that year, she was riding a wonderful mare named Fru in a Table A class against the clock. There was a three-fence line down the center of the ring—a seven or eight stride to an in-and-out. Wanting her to be fast, I told her, "Kathy, go in there and get six strides," and always a game and gutsy rider, she grinned and said, "Well, okay, why not!" Kathy galloped into the ring and went for the six, but of course there was no six! A stretch would've been the seven strides. Fru gamely left the ground and tried, but the distance was so long she hit the back rail and somersaulted into the in-and-out. Because it was a combination, she went end over end into the second jump. Poor Kathy was underneath Fru with a badly broken leg. I felt terrible!

I went to visit Kathy at the New York Presbyterian Hospital just a couple of days later and I told her, "Kathy, we have to get you out of this bed. Get up and show me you can make it to the end of the hall!" I forced her to get out of bed with her broken leg and crutch down the length of the hallway, which was so far that it practically ended in the Hudson River. Kathy was tough and not a complainer ever. I practically killed her twice, first by telling her to get the six and then by making her go down the hall and back.

Kathy Kusner

After I went "end over end" in the combination, I saw George and he said, "Oh no, Kathy, the six was too long!" We still giggle about it. He did make me crutch down the length of the hallway at the Presbyterian Hospital and when I did it, my back was hurting like crazy. I mentioned it to a doctor afterward. An X-ray showed I'd also broken two vertebral processes in my spine.

A friend of Melanie Smith's from Tennessee came to Hunterdon and his name was Mac Cone. He was a fierce competitor and later rode for both the USET and the Canadian Team. Like Melanie, Mac is a tough, seat-of-the-pants rider, and he brought two Quarter Horses to Hunterdon named Bomber and Rootin' Tootin' who weren't big but they were great jumpers. They could even jump Grand Prix height! In six months they put Mac on the map and he had some terrific wins, including one of two clear rounds in the massive Grand Prix up in Montreal at the show they called "Man and His World."

Mac Cone

I rode with George at a clinic in Atlanta the summer after high school and that was my first exposure to his teaching. The Germantown, Tennessee, horse world was a big community, but the training wasn't on par with George. After one year at university, I told my mother I was through with school and the only thing that came out of her mouth after that was, "Mac, you have to get a job." Unlike many of the young riders we see now, I knew I wouldn't get much financial support from my family. I had one horse and a two-horse trailer, but it was going to be up to me beyond that. I was looking through *The Chronicle of the Horse* one day and saw an ad that said, "GEORGE H. MORRIS, HUNTERDON: I have a job for the right person." That was all it said! I called George and, much to my surprise, he remembered me from the clinic the prior year and hired me on the spot. He knew my background. He knew I was a country boy who could drive a tractor and build a barn, in addition to being able to ride.

On the way up to Hunterdon, I met George on the road at North Shore and he got me a job with Roger Young (Gary Young's father), and I mucked stalls and groomed for him, since George didn't have work for me there. I also showed my horse there, but these horse shows were a different world from where I'd come from. My part Quarter Horses didn't have the big strides that the horses have today. We'd also grown up in small rings, some of which were rings meant for gaited or walking horses. It was the school of hard knocks for those early months riding with George. I spent more time on the ground than I did on the horse! You had to be tough; the rails were heavy and solid, with no breakaway cups. You learned to jump no matter what, because if you didn't, you could really get hurt. It was in many ways a different sport then.

George became a father figure to me, because I left home at nineteen and never went back there to live. He realized after I'd been working for him a while that I didn't have any financial backing and the only way I was going to be able to do this sport was to become a professional. That was the only way; no trust fund to use for buying horses. He began to set up opportunities for me to learn beyond the work I was doing for him, because he knew it would benefit my career as a horseman. He sent me over to Jack Gordon's sales barn in New Jersey, and I rode his sales horses and learned about buying and selling horses. The next winter in Florida, on another Quarter Horse named Bomber, I won the Grand Prix of Florida at age twenty under George's guidance. We beat Rodney and Idle Dice, among others. That was really something special, to get that win. As that year continued and we got back into the fall and the indoor season, George told me he'd arranged for me to ride with Bert de Némethy on the USET. I was in complete disbelief. It was a dream come true.

The jumper courses became more technical in the early seventies than they had been previously. The American jumper class format had undergone major shifts since my youth. In the early days with the rub classes, we jumped each jump as carefully as possible, pulling up between fences (practically trotting!) and getting to the base of the jump, to launch and clear the huge fences. In the sixties and seventies, the Europeans taught us we had to ride in a more forward galloping style to avoid time faults and get around the new style of courses with longer lines. If you tried to pull up and add a stride before the fence in those days, you'd get in trouble with time faults.

Mac, a great addition to Hunterdon, faced this kind of a difficult technical question in a line that Bob Rost, a great course designer, set at a horse show.

Bob loved to set a particular challenging line: a vertical to a nearly six-foot-wide oxer with the distance between them measuring fifty feet. Today, they're very reluctant to exceed a spread of five feet. Mac jumped into the line and tried to fit four short strides, but he didn't have enough impulsion to make it over the huge oxer spread. After going ass over tea kettle at the second fence multiple times, Mac got it: he had to go forward and gallop the line in three strides to have the impulsion to make it. With lines like that, there was simply no place for that outdated, slow-to-the-base ride. You had to gallop like you were out on a big outside hunter course! Pam Carruthers was another course designer who made things very technical in those years. Nowadays, with tight time limits on course, the main challenge course designers present to riders is being obedient enough to add a stride while also maintaining the needed impulsion.

There was a small army of staff that helped make our success at Hunterdon possible in those early years. Barbara Massey did the books, and Sue Engelhard and Betty Douglas helped keep the business running smoothly. An assistant of mine at the time, Gary Baker, helped me find good horses down in Virginia; Gary was a prominent show manager until his recent passing. Sally Dohner, a friend of Patty Heuckeroth's from Harrisburg, sent me a bright young girl named Karen Healey to be a stable manager. At Hunterdon, Karen was my first direct assistant, and like Johnny MacGuire in the sixties, she was a one-armed paper hanger! She taught lessons, ran the barn, groomed at the shows, and drove the trailer. Karen was a wonderful caretaker when it came to the horses, and she would, like Johnny, work herself into ill health because she was such an overachiever. A godsend to me in those early days of Hunterdon, she was one of the most brilliant people in my life, and she's had a very successful career as a teacher and professional. To put it bluntly, she saved my ass for the four years she worked for me.

Karen Healey

I grew up in Harrisburg and had ridden in George's clinics, but then I went off to college because I really loved school. In terms of horsemanship I was very influenced by Junie Kulp, who was the first one who really turned out show horses the way we do today—he started the trend of sixty small braids down the neck and the real spit and polish. In the winter of 1971, I went to work for George as a groom in Florida, and I remember in the back of my mind I was dreaming I'd be discovered. When I got down to Florida, the horses were all still going in the ring with knot braids, egg-butt snaffles, and big flat nosebands. So, with the habits I'd learned from Junie, I changed all that and George welcomed it. I was a decent rider, but by the end of the Florida circuit I was pretty much managing the barn! I followed George back home to Hunterdon, and after a while, I rode in some lessons and even started teaching a little. Over time, George recognized my work ethic and I assumed more responsibility.

In essence, it was easy to work for George; you had a list and if it took you twelve hours to get it all done, it was a good day! If it took you eighteen hours instead, well, that's just the way it was. I did everything he needed me to do, and eventually, I discovered I had a knack for teaching. I was not a natural rider; I had to really learn how to ride well from an intellectual perspective. George was much the same way so I took his system and swallowed it hook, line, and sinker. It's hooked in my belly still to this day and I've never wavered from it. I believe in it one-thousand percent! If it happens overnight, you're doing it wrong. I don't use draw reins, and we do everything at my place as correctly as possible. There's not a day that goes by, when I'm riding or teaching, when George's voice doesn't go through my head. I consider my time with George like a college education. It was a ton of work but I learned so much; I treasure every part of it.

George never ever yelled at me, even though he had a right to yell a couple of times. We had a fancy hunter mare named Isle of Erin and at Lake Placid she'd gotten cut pretty deeply right above her pastern while jumping on the outside course. She was under my care and I had been religiously icing and changing the dressings for weeks at Hunterdon. One day, I hand-walked her out to the field where George was teaching to show him how good she looked. All of the sudden, she spooked and ripped the lead shank out of my hand, cutting my hand open. As I watched in complete horror, she went galloping off across the cornfield. I took off running after her; I don't think I've ever run faster in my life! I finally caught her and thank God she hadn't hurt herself or made the injury worse. But as I led her back to the barn, I was literally quaking with fear—I was sure that I was fired or at least that George was going to read me the riot act. When I faced him, he was completely calm. He said he knew I was excited, but that I needed to remember to be careful. He knew I was being harder on myself than he could ever be.

Leslie Burr came to ride with me during those early Hunterdon years; she was always a beautiful rider with great empathy for her horse. Her mother, Billie Burr, was quite a stage mother at the horse shows, which made sense because she was in top theater circles. Billie performed in *South Pacific* in London and counted Doris Whitehead and Celeste Holm among her friends. Like her mother, Leslie was kind, ambitious, tough, and a deadly competitor. She had a quality in her riding that went beyond a successful equitation rider. Empathy combined with a high level of intelligence and physical bravery made her great.

Back in her junior days, the equitation was so easy for Leslie, but I had to stay on her case about her position! Thumbs up and heels down and so on, because she was a loose, natural rider. I still remember Leslie rode over to Hunterdon one day to have a lesson on her green horse when she was about fifteen years old. She was trotting around the circle during the lesson, chattering away, telling me how she thought she should ride the horse and not doing much listening to her teacher. I kept my mouth shut and let her prattle on, biding my time.

I had bought an inexpensive, black, three-quarter-bred horse named Fast Talker for Jeremy to ride but decided to give Leslie a lesson on him. As a side note, that horse really fit the old saying, "black of color equals black of heart." However well he jumped, he was a biter, a kicker, and a brutally mean horse. That same black horse stopped at a jump once with Jeremy who was thrown over his head. Jeremy got up, never touched the reins, and punched that horse square in the nose and stalked off to the house. The horse had a really hard time shortening his stride, so I set up a gymnastic for Leslie in her next lesson that was physically impossible for Fast Talker to jump through comfortably. It wasn't high, but he tripped and mangled his way through the gymnastic again and again, tripping and falling, and Leslie ended up in the dirt once or twice. I figured I had taught her a lesson and brought her back down to earth—both literally and figuratively.

In the '72 Equitation Finals, Leslie rode Suzette, and at Harrisburg, she had to really run down the lines because her little horse had such a short stride. You might have argued that she had the best round of the day on Suzette, but it was so fast by necessity that it couldn't compare to the relaxed effortless look of Acca and Katie. People took note of Leslie's great trip though, and it teed her up for success in the Maclay Finals.

Leslie was called back in the Maclay, sitting in fifth after the morning trip and the flat phase. The afternoon rounds began and Suzette was standing there tacked up and ready. Unfortunately, Leslie was nowhere to be found! Everyone was running around looking for her everywhere when she wandered nonchalantly up the ramp to the ring with a friend she was having lunch with. I grabbed her and we stood up on the steps together, where I taught her the course in just a few seconds. There wasn't even time to talk about striding in the lines or strategy for the course. She was forced just to eyeball it, but even so, she had a fabulous round. There was a test with simple changes that she rode beautifully and in the end, she was the clear winner. In true Leslie style, she pulled it off! She was only fifteen and won the Maclay (photo 115).

Leslie Burr Howard

There are two people who have influenced my life and contributed to my career more than anyone: My mother and George. Both my parents were in the New York and London theater and George, having done some acting himself (both on and off stage!), got along with them beautifully from the beginning. George adores my mother but along the way there were also some knock-down, drag-out fights. My mother is a very strong lady and George, as we know, is no pushover!

I'll never forget one year at the National Horse Show when it was still at Madison Square Garden. I was sixteen and had this horse called Gala Performance who was a great jumper but a dreadful mover. George very generously gave me a client's horse named Castaway to ride, who was a gorgeous mover but not a great jumper. Both horses had gotten even scores over fences and it was going to come down to the Under Saddle or Hack class. George assumed I would ride Castaway in the Hack but, of course, my mother assumed I would be riding my own horse, Gala Performance. Fifteen minutes before the Hack class George says, "All right now, time to get on Castaway." And my mother says, "What do you mean? Time to get on Gala!" The disagreement escalated to one step shy of a fistfight and I was in tears of disbelief that this was all happening right at the in-gate at the Garden. In the end, my mother persevered, and I rode Gala Performance. I think it was the only time in George's career he was upstaged by a mother!

George has been such a great inspiration in my life. When I look back at what made my career, the credit indisputably goes to George. By example, George taught me a great work ethic. He always said it how it was. No coddling or mincing of words; you either were good enough or you had to work harder because you weren't good enough.

My parents couldn't afford to support me when it came to horses and showing. George was always very good to me in that respect. I remember I used to muck stalls in the morning to work off lessons, but George also gave me opportunities to ride and show horses both as a junior and afterward. He put me in the position where I could take the next step in my riding career. As a teacher, George has a great feel for what every student needs in terms of building up and, at times when called for, tearing down (and I don't mean that in a negative way). George can bolster your confidence more than anyone I know. However, after winning the ASPCA Maclay Finals I was a little too cocky, so George decided it was time for some humble pie. He put me on a green horse called Fast Talker who was slow and uncoordinated. George put up an eighteen-foot in-and-out, but unfortunately, Fast Talker was twenty feet long! The jump fell, the horse fell, and there I was at the bottom of the heap! George dusted me off, put me back on, and watched it all happen again. He has that ability, just when you thought you knew everything, to show you that you really know nothing.

The fast lane that I'd been living in got faster and faster, despite the fact that I'd moved out to the country. When I bought Hunterdon, I'd made a very clear decision that I was too old for the younger crowd out on Fire Island. I haven't been back to that meat market since 1969! I let my Sixty Ninth Street apartment go, and later, Jeremy and I rented a beautiful apartment in the heart of the Village on West Twelfth Street. That was the best New York apartment I ever had: it had a great view, two bedrooms, a foyer and a doorman downstairs. I heard Sharon Stone bought it years later, and she knocked down a wall to combine two apartments. Hunterdon wasn't too far out of New York for me and New Hope was a Bohemian town nearby that had a fun dose of night life.

Jerry Baker organized two big-money Grand Prix classes in Southern California in August of 1972, one in Santa Ana and the other in the Rose Bowl. Many East Coast riders shipped their horses out, like Rodney and Idle Dice, but we had decided it was too far to take our horses for just a couple of shows. However, a few riders from Hunterdon borrowed horses from our West Coast friends to ride in them. Jimmy Williams had a legion of excellent young riders entering the classes including Susie Hutchinson, Hap Hansen, and Anne Kursinski.

Linda Hough

I specialized in the hunters and hardly ever rode in the jumpers, but when I heard all the East Coast professionals were coming out for those big classes in the early seventies, I thought I would go give it a try with my black horse who was a good jumper. I was in way over my head—I almost had a heart attack when I saw the size of the fences. Not to mention going up against riders like Jimmy Kohn, Michael Matz, and Rodney Jenkins. There I was a mere hunter rider attempting courses that George said were Olympic standard. Let me tell you, that was the end of my jumper career! Despite it all, I managed to get around both courses and my horse showed special potential. In hindsight, having George on the ground with his expertise was part of the reason I got through it. I didn't even get worried about it until it was all over, then I thought, "Oh my God what did I just do?" It's something I'll never forget—quite an experience!

While we were there, I stayed with Mason Phelps who rode and worked for Jimmy Williams as a young professional. I dragged him and his housemate, Randy Redmer, out all over Hollywood, including on the night before the big Grand Prix he was riding in. Randy was a young man who had basically never gone out on the town before, and boy, did we open his eyes! We outed him and after that he never went back in! Mason, Randy, and I hopped from watering hole to watering hole and when the clock struck three, Mason left me behind at some den of ill repute. Wisely, he'd decided to go home and get some sleep because he had to be up early to school his horse. He didn't sleep long! A couple of hours later I called and woke him up, begging him to come pick me up since I had no idea how to get home. He dragged himself out of bed to collect me.

The next day dawned and the Grand Prix course Jerry Baker built was of Olympic proportions. It was nearly un-jumpable. Most of the riders were completely overfaced by the enormous fences, and many horse and rider teams were eliminated or had falls. Those classes set back those California riders fifteen years. Mason was riding in this impossible Grand Prix—the biggest class of his career thus far—and after our big night out, he missed his schooling session in the morning. Jimmy Williams was livid with him, and in the end he didn't quite get around the gigantic course—understandably. After all, he had nothing left! Most of us have been there once or twice in our careers. Those were definitely two interesting weeks in show jumping.

Mason Phelps

One year in the early seventies George was teaching a five-day marathon clinic in Southern California. There was a cocktail party get together a day or two before it began. I was planning to ride a horse in the clinic each day, as most of us were. George and I got to bantering at the party, and George was teasing me that I should ride in all three sessions all five days. He said, "I would break you, Mason! You'd never survive all five days." So that was a challenge I took! I had to borrow some horses that, literally, were three- or four-year-olds off the racetrack that had never seen a jump before. I did survive all five days! It was a marathon for sure. Afterward, that Sunday night when it was all over, I hosted a small party and cooked dinner for four of us in my apartment. I'd been strategizing how to get a little revenge for the clinic, when it suddenly came to me. In those days, we were young and a little bit foolish, so I slipped some acid in George's mashed potatoes. Payback's a bitch! Then we drove to Hollywood and I made George drive. After a while, the streetlights were spinning and the street itself was spinning, and he got wise to what I'd done. I ended up dropping him off at Studio One, the huge discotheque in Hollywood, and I immediately drove home while I still had the capacity. George didn't resurface until the next day!

The 1972 Munich Olympics were that September, just after the big California Grand Prix classes. Jeremy and I flew directly from California to Munich to watch the Games, and we were on the plane with Bill and Jerry Baker and a group of friends. We rented a big house all together in Munich with a pool and a courtyard and arrived eager to settle in and enjoy the nice house. As it turned out, instead of water in the pool there was a huge pile of old furniture! The pool was their dumpster, but we still had a great time. Every Olympics is wonderful to attend and has its quirks. There are always rumors of funny business about someone trying to get an advantage. There was a rumor in Munich that one of the teams was secretly training over the course in the locked stadium after hours and poling their horses illegally.

The course was about the same size as the California Grand Prix courses; I joked that I had already been to the Olympics! The United States Team won the silver medal and Neal Shapiro took home the bronze medal in the individual round. Billy Steinkraus, riding Main Spring, had to go clear to get the gold medal. Heartbreakingly, he rode way to the end of the ring and galloped as fast as he could in order to clear the water jump, but in the end he still hit the tape. Historically, the U.S. Teams have had repeated issues with the water jump: some of the greatest show jumpers have struggled with the water. I think it's psychological—or becomes so, eventually. Europeans treat the water like another jump, like a cross-rail. The Europeans' young horses are always jumping the water and it's not a big deal. When Americans look at a course, the water jump is always a standout and giving it reverence makes it a bigger challenge.

Diane Dubuc

I met George when he was in Montreal for the "Man and His World" show in the seventies. He was always my dream trainer, but I met him for the first time when he approached me after the show finished late on Sunday evening. In those years, it was difficult to get horses over the border to the United States on the Monday of a holiday weekend, but George needed to find a way to get across. He came to me because he heard I might be able to help, and sure enough I had a friend who could work out all the necessary papers, and we made it happen. George was grateful and since he had seen me ride at the show, he invited me to go ride as his guest at Hunterdon. I was so honored to be invited but needed to raise money to be able to afford to go down.

When I was ready, I took a hunter and jumper to Hunterdon for two months to ride with George. He treated me so well, and it was a dream to ride there. I schooled with George often while I was there, and one day in a lesson, I broke a jump pole. He told me, "Diane, you must go and repair that pole!" I thought, "Well, that's impossible! You can't fix a broken jump rail." He was just having fun with me, but he had me wondering if I *could* fix the pole for a minute! He has a great sense of humor. I had a fantastic two months there and even assisted him at the indoor shows. It was a wonderful experience, which had a huge influence on me. As a professional, I have since taught George's system. With the knowledge George gave me, I taught Eric Lamaze as a child and junior rider. Eric lived with me for several years and every single day I taught him lessons on multiple horses. Then when I took the kids to Florida to show, George noticed him immediately and was very impressed by his ability. Now, Eric is an Olympic champion!

Back at home, we went up to the "Man and His World" show in Montreal (the very same one where Mac Cone had a great result in the huge Grand Prix). While watching a class, a woman came up and hugged me from behind like a bear! It was an old New Canaan friend named Jackie (Monroe) Morold. Jackie rode horses when we were kids but could never afford to own her own horse; she just had lessons on school horses at the Ox Ridge Hunt Club. As we caught up with one another, she told me that she was now an heiress to the Coors beer fortune and was starting a big stable near Ottawa called Dwyer Hill Farm. She asked me to be the director of her new place, but of course I wasn't in a position to help given my new business at Hunterdon. Then she mentioned she had a young man working for her named Randy Roy. I knew Randy; he was a young friend of Karen Healey's. I'd heard that Randy had a desire to work for me, so I made a deal with Jackie: Randy could work at Hunterdon for a year. He would ride with me and learn how we manage the business so when he returned to Dwyer Hill, he'd be a better trainer and manager for Jackie.

Peter Stoeckl was the professional and teacher at her place at that time, and his father Kurt was the superintendent of her property. Peter was a great stylist on a horse. Since I liked working with him and knew Jackie and Randy, I started going up to Dwyer Hill four times a year to teach Peter and some others. A few months later, with Jackie's relationship with the Stoeckls became strained, she was on the hunt for an established professional and asked me to help her find someone. Tommy Gayford and Jimmy Elder, the icons of the Canadian Team, told me to give Ian Millar a chance at it. Back then, Ian was an effective rider but not a particularly polished one, and I told them I didn't think Ian was right for the job—he was already twenty-five years old and too rough around the edges with his style. However, a few months later when I was back at Dwyer Hill, Ian was suggested again and I reconsidered. The first time I taught a clinic up there with Ian around, Ian didn't ride in it; he didn't even come and audit. Ian is a very sharp guy! He and his wife Lynn watched from the road, observing my teaching from a distance. The next time I went up to teach, he rode with me and I told Jackie I could only smooth him out by working with him on some nice hunters. Jackie, Ian, and I went down to Gene Cunningham's in Virginia and bought two or three top young hunters. Working together, I helped craft Ian's wonderful style and position that he still rides with today. Showing in Florida that following winter, Ian rode beautifully! He gave Rodney Jenkins a run for his money that year and racked up a lot of championships.

Ian Millar

Prior to meeting George Morris, I was already competing at the Grand Prix level and had ridden on the Canadian team at the 1972 Munich Olympics. However, support from an owner was lacking and difficult to come by. When I was contacted by Jackie Morold of Dwyer Hill Farm regarding a riding opportunity, it was with the understanding that George Morris would be the overall coach. I certainly had no problem with this and moreover viewed an association with George as a tremendous opportunity. George, however, had his reservations, but thanks to a strong endorsement from the great Canadian Team rider Jim Elder, I was hired! Randy Roy, now a respected hunter and equitation judge and author of several very well respected books on the sport, was already working at Dwyer Hill and had previously worked for George Morris at his Hunterdon training establishment. Randy knew the Morris system very well and advised me to read *Hunter Seat Equitation* to learn and practice the various techniques and skills that he knew George would expect. By the time I rode in my first clinic with George at Dwyer Hill, I was already on the job! George and I got along fantastically, and I enjoyed and treasured his training. The structure and clarity of his teaching made learning very achievable. I style my own clinics to my personality, but I incorporate a great deal from my George Morris training. George is an extraordinary motivator. Whether it is teaching a clinic or training at a competition or leading the United States Show Jumping Team, there is an incomparable focus and energy brought to bear. George has an incredible sense of humor. He comes across strict and stern, but at the same time is very kind and generous. His insight on people and horses is remarkable. What he innately senses, most people totally miss.

Tommy Dembinski was a tall, superstar junior rider who had been very successful riding with Ronnie Mutch. As often happens with riders, he got restless and decided to move over to me to try to end his junior years with a win in the Medal or Maclay Finals. I eagerly took him on, but it turned out there was a catch! He had a close friend named Norman Dello Joio who hoped to ride Tommy's coattails into Hunterdon. Norman was a nice rider but didn't have Tommy's talent or resources, and I turned him down. After I had taken Tommy but turned down Norman, his mother Grace Dello Joio called me several mornings in a row at six in the morning. My phone would ring at that early hour and Grace would ask me please to take her son as a student. In response to her first couple of calls I held my ground. But she wore me down eventually and I grudgingly relented. Just like Ian Millar and Melanie Smith, I had no idea what a total superstar he would become. It's interesting that I had what I thought was Olympic caliber potential in Tommy Dembinski, but it was Norman who persevered and won an Olympic medal and the World Cup Finals!

Norman did, incidentally, have a very famous father (also named Norman) who was an iconic musician and composer and won a Pulitzer in 1957. Being a musician himself, Bill Steinkraus heard I was teaching the son of the famous composer and was so excited that he called me up to ask if Norman was ready to ride for the USET. I told Billy, "No, not yet! He's only sixteen, Billy. He's still doing the Medal/Maclay!" Billy kept calling me year after year hoping to bring Norman to Gladstone.

Tommy didn't win either of the Medal/Maclay Finals in '74 but he got very good ribbons. Robin Ann Rost won the Medal that year. Like the Hulicks, the Rosts were a top family in the business, with Robin's parents Joan and Bob both very good riders and teachers. I gave Robin lessons a great deal on the side, but her parents coached her at Harrisburg. Bob Rost went on to become one of the most innovative, modern course designers in the sport.

Bob Penney, my great veterinarian friend from the Northwest, had a breeding program at his farm in Yakima, Washington, and he helped me hunt down some nice prospects. Don Munger had a stallion called Kaneohe Bay, a Thoroughbred off the track with a great reputation on the West Coast for producing jumpers. Bob and I went to Don's place in 1974 to see what young horses they had, and it turned out he had a horse about to turn three and another about to turn four out in the field. I clucked to them and they both moved well, so we built a chute in his shed row and had each of them pop over a bale of straw. They were brave and jumped the straw bales with their knees up to their eyeballs. One of them also had Man o' War blood, which could be a bonus since he produced some great jumpers. I bought both of them and brought them back to Hunterdon. The younger of the two horses turned out to be, at least to start, a cold-backed bronc that Karen Healey took on as a project, to work him through some quirks. We named him Dillon (photo 117).

Karen Healey

Dillon was an absolute rogue. He was the most cold-backed horse I've ever dealt with in my life. George gave him to me as a project. He was used to being manhandled, and he was very spooky. We'd be home for a couple weeks at a time between shows. I'd put him out in a paddock with a saddle on his back and the stirrups hanging down banging on his sides, and he would just bronc and buck. Then I'd move him to the longeing paddock and longe him with the stirrups banging on him. Anytime you'd tighten the girth, he would just bronc. I would then get on him in the longeing paddock, and if I felt confident I'd ride him in the paddock next door. One day, I'd spent three or four hours on this gradual process, and he felt really good when I got on, so I popped over a few jumps in the field. Well, he bronced me all the way back to the barn like a rag doll, throwing me backward and forward. We had to handle Dillon just the right way but he was a wonderful horse. I remember I was in his stall at Boulder Brook braiding him, and I made the mistake of unbuckling the front of the sheet and hadn't undone the surcingles—it slipped back an inch. He freaked out and destroyed the flimsy wooden horse show stall;

he kicked the whole stall down! Regardless, that year I got top call at Devon in First Year Green and top call in every Green Conformation class before the jog.

Dillon became an iconic hunter; he was Grand Champion at Madison Square Garden and later carried Michael Sasso to a huge win in the Maclay Finals. The older of the two horses I got from Don Munger's place was a nice hunter mare. Though I misspelled her name when registering her, I called her Halekalani after the iconic Hotel Halekulani in Hawaii I had stayed in with my grandmother on Waikiki Beach in Honolulu. She ended up Horse of the Year and High Score Junior Hunter. You see, part of the magic of those early years of Hunterdon was that we took horses that had issues and developed them into champions through regimented training and care. These days, a lot of riders miss out on that joy of working through issues because they only know how to ride a made horse. Too many teachers only teach for the show ring and not how to train. Seeing through horses' problems, helping them reach their potential, and getting a top ribbon is the ultimate way to win. Transforming a horse like Dillon from a completely green, cold-backed rogue into Grand Champion at Madison Square Garden gave all of us such a sense of complete success.

Alex Dunaif, a rider of Judy Richter's, won the Maclay Finals in 1974 with a hell of a trip. Norman Dello Joio had what I considered to be the best round of the day on his horse Narcissus, but somehow he didn't even make the cut. I was furious! Narcissus was a plain bay horse and wasn't showy, but Norman was effective and correct and had a beautiful round. In the end, perhaps the judges just missed him because they weren't familiar with him and he didn't have the reputation. He absolutely deserved to at least be called back, and I was very frustrated. Understandably, Norman soured on the equitation, but he also rode Narcissus in the Open Jumper division at Madison Square Garden. Eventually, Narcissus became his Grand Prix horse. Today you can't even imagine a horse going in both sorts of classes, but in those days, it wasn't uncommon. Norman is just one example of a rider who, regardless of not winning an equitation final, became one of the most famous riders in American history and a critical member of the USET. There are many other examples like him: Anne Kursinski, Melanie Smith Taylor, Michael Matz, Beezie Madden, McLain Ward, Laura Kraut, Lauren Hough, Reed Kessler, and Rich Fellers, to name several. Norman went on to dominate in the early eighties, winning the World Cup in 1983 and nearly repeating the win in '84.

Hunterdon was a booming business and my clients were winning in every division, from the pony divisions to equitation, junior hunters and jumpers to green and working hunters, and also in the Grand Prix jumpers. Something was really working because we witnessed consistent success up and down the horse show schedule. Hunterdon didn't specialize in any one discipline; we did everything and had great range. I had a great large pony named Wait Up who cleaned up in the pony divisions. He looked like a little horse and would win the Model and jumped well for Doug and Greg Scher. The Schers were great clients with several horses who lived nearby in New Jersey.

While judging at the Oak Brook Horse Show in Illinois, I heard about a new working hunter that was not yet well known. She was a beautiful, flashy Thoroughbred mare and one of the best movers of all time, but she hadn't yet been shown on the East Coast. Her name was Isle of Erin. I had a client from California, Luann Beach, who I knew would be a good fit with the mare. Luann had won the saddle seat and stock seat equitation medals but had never won the hunter seat medals. I tried Isle of Erin, loved her, and immediately bought her with the help of Luann Beach.

It's always a little bit dicey when you have a new horse and you bring it right to a show. Isle of Erin was fresh off the trailer at Hunterdon with perhaps a few days there before we shipped her to a big Philadelphia stadium horse show reminiscent of The Forum out on the West Coast. When I got on her in the warm-up ring, my new mare was hot as a pistol! On the approach to the jumps, she scooted left and right, and no matter what I did to try to focus and calm her, she wouldn't settle down. I worried that buying her had been a huge mistake and figured she'd been tranquilized for the shows and when I tried her in Chicago. With a horrible feeling of dread and Isle of Erin a live wire under me, I walked her into the first class. Much to my surprise, she looked at the bigger jumps set at four-foot-six for the working hunters and absolutely transformed. She suddenly had respect for the situation, backing off tremendously and jumping beautifully. We were second! After walking into the ring regretting my decision to buy her, coming out second at that huge national show was a total shock. The judges loved her and it was a sign of things to come. She began collecting working hunter championships with considerable regularity. In the hack classes, she was either pinned first or not at all because she blew up from being too fresh (photo 118).

Isle of Erin was one of the great hunters of the decade; she required a very specific training program to prepare her for the ring. I had to really work on all the basic technical flatwork with her—transitions, lateral work, shoulder-in, haunches-in, on the bit, long and low, collection. That mare was a Stradivarius violin and needed to be tuned just right. At home, we turned her out all the time and never schooled her over fences. We wanted to keep her fresh and happy. At the horse show, I would get on and flat her—not a hack, but the best quality dressage flatwork possible for a half hour or more every morning. If for some reason I couldn't ride her, she would be carefully longed like Bert de Némethy used to do, in a balanced workmanlike way—not galloped off her feet at the end of the line until she was tired.

Luann Beach was a good friend of mine and a great client. She was a very emotional type of person and wore dark glasses at the shows because she was always crying! If she won, she cried. If she missed or stopped or fell off, she cried. Luann would sit way up in the stands by herself watching me ride her mare, and if I got third or fourth place in a class, she cried because I didn't win. If I won, she cried with happiness! She had some success on the mare herself, but overall there were ups and downs. Isle of Erin was a gorgeous hunter and she was one of the horses that established me as one of the top hunter riders in that era.

Another great hunter client was Nancy Easton Townsend, who had a handsome bay horse called Bonnie Castle. Loved by the Townsends, he was a showy horse and a beautiful mover. Over fences, though, Bonnie Castle had a weak front end that bordered on hanging. His first year at Winter Haven, he was seventh out of seven in the Model class. The second year we had him, we shipped him to Florida and on the way he developed a cough. To treat the cough we gave him Azimycin, a combination antibiotic drug that unfortunately caused him to founder. This was my first experience with the allergy risks associated for some horses with dexamethasone (Azimycin contains small amounts). Not only did Bonnie Castle never get ridden in Florida, we were worried he would never show again. To be extra cautious, we gave him the whole year off.

The following year, we brought him back, and lo and behold, he was even prettier! He moved better, he jumped better, and he started winning the Conformation Model classes. For whatever reason, the horse matured and had lost some of his coarseness. I also had learned how to ride him better by protecting his front end and getting to distances that kept him away from the base of the jump and gave him room to jump well. Bonnie Castle was Horse of the Year after foundering. He was not only Circuit Champion of the Green Conformation Hunter Division on the Florida circuit, but also Champion at Madison Square Garden in 1978. It was a Cinderella story, that Bonnie Castle horse (photo 119).

In the early years of Hunterdon a young girl was brought to me to teach. She had been taught her riding basics by Junie Kulp and had such a lovely position on a large pony that it was impossible not to admire it. I was very rough on her and made her cry in her first lesson with me, but she was a tough kid and survived it. She went on to be an excellent rider. Her name was Cynthia Hankins and she won the Medal Finals in 1975. Cynthia was a beautiful equitation rider; she's still a judge, a clinician, a Grand-Prix-level rider, and a very dear friend to me (photo 120).

Cynthia Hankins

I've known George for nearly forty-five years and the relationship has evolved from clinic student to full-time student, from working student to assistant trainer, and from Chef d'Equipe assistant to friend. He loves that when riding in my first clinic with him, when I was barely twelve and on a pony (he wasn't fond of ponies, especially "evergreens"), he had me in tears— silent tears, but tears nonetheless. My mother and her friend Sieta Platten, who also had a daughter several years older than me in the clinic, were sitting quietly beside the ring (as one must do when auditing one of George's clinics), when we were called to a halt and I stopped alongside them. I was nervous and rigidly serious and they encouraged me to loosen up and smile. I grinned in reaction and somehow The Master, with eyes in the back of his head, spun around and asked, "What do you find so amusing, young lady?" I barely whispered, "Nothing." Big, fat tears rolled down my face. I was shy and hugely embarrassed for something clearly not my fault. I hid in the trailer after my session finished and had no desire to return for the afternoon group, but my mother had paid for that clinic, and she insisted that I was going to ride! Evidently the afternoon went much better, because soon after we were driving up to Long Island after cutting out of my last class in grade school to ride in back-to-back lessons on school horses at Old Mill Farm.

Today, George comes to visit me from time to time now that I'm living in France and recently did so. He wanted to ride the two mornings he was here. No problem. "Nothing quirky" was his only request, which is fine because we don't do quirky. He rode two horses each day. I told him I'd put some cavalletti around if he wanted to play. After getting on, he remarked, "The jumps look big." I explained that to keep things running efficiently in the stable, there were a few small jumps, then we just go right to the 1.15-meter square oxer and do parts of the course—oxer to the pair of Liverpool verticals, combination, triple bar with water under it, and so on. George did a nice warm-up on the flat: lateral work, counter-canter, flying changes on the straight line. While walking, he put his stirrups up a hole (feet never leaving the irons, of course). He did a cavalletti or two, the high cross-rail, then cantered right to the square oxer. I only held my breath for that one jump. He asked to have the triple combination lowered the first time, then back up it went. He was fabulous and jumped around all the jumps up to 1.20 or 1.30 meters with a relaxed arm, softened at the base, out of the tack just enough, with the motion, and his eye was dead on.

Afterward, George asked me, "How was I? I teach the American System because I believe in it so much, but do I still ride the American System?" I looked at him. "George, I'm not flattering you just to be nice while you're on vacation, but you rode great. As well as, or better, than you rode twenty years ago!" It was inspirational watching him ride. He said he hadn't jumped in months and I know he had the time of his life.

Katharine Burdsall (later: Heller) was another giant junior rider talent who came to me and was destined to ride on the USET. She first rode with Huey Kerrigan in Hartford, Connecticut, and was a stylist in the equitation ring on her horse Old Salt. Today Katharine still teaches and helps riders. As a junior, she was very much like Katie Prudent or Beezie Madden, with huge talent and great empathy for the horse.

The Maclay course in 1975 was interesting; there was a three-fence line with a fifty-one-foot distance to a forty-two-foot distance. It was a little bit of a long three stride from the first fence to the second, then either an extremely long two or a very tight three strides to the third fence. The challenge was to make a big adjustment look invisible, whichever choice you made. I had half of my kids continue galloping out of the line, doing the three to the two. In the second half of the class, I had my other kids do the three to the three, which was a hand ride. Jimmy Lee was watching; he commented that I had put the judges in an interesting predicament by splitting my strategy and having my kids ride each option. Katharine Burdsall did the three to the short three and nailed the test, a turn-on-the-haunches. She came out on top! It was her day to win the Maclay (photo 121).

IV. THE HUNTERDON DREAM TEAM

As Hunterdon settled into the business of horse showing in the mid-1970s, I remember hearing about Frank Chapot's bronze medal at the 1974 World Championships in Hickstead. Of course I was thrilled because Frank is such a great friend of mine, but I also felt a prickle of desire to be back in Europe myself and get more involved in the big international jumper scene from a teaching perspective. I had for ten years been ensconced in the hunters and equitation, but I started to feel like the jumpers were on my horizon.

When it comes to the equitation, it should be ridden on a horse that is somewhat fresh and not the living dead. In those days, we couldn't drill the equitation horses and longe them until they were positively docile because the same horses needed to jump well and be fresh in the hunter classes. We sometimes had equitation horses that didn't do the hunters, but most of the time they did both, which helped naturally settle them. Now, equitation horses have to be spiritless robots and can't toss their heads or hop up and down.

Francie Steinwedell-Carvin

In the early 1970s, my mother, Fran Steinwedell, was smart enough to recognize that—at the age of thirteen—it was time for me to go back East to spread my wings at some pretty big shows. Before leaving, Jimmy Williams, my trainer at that time, definitely tried to keep "us kids" humble. He told us it was a new playing field and to lower our expectations and not expect to do as well as we had in California. We won a lot in California! Jimmy told me if I was to win an eighth-place ribbon to treat it like a blue one. Period! That was not that difficult to do as I did not have that much confidence in myself anyway.

Being the underdog was my most comfortable position to ride in. My first time was showing in Lake Placid in 1974 with Kathy Moore training me, and I rode in the 17 and Under Equitation over Fences. I had no worries about winning the class, as I'd been told that I could not, but I received a score of 95 from the three judges and ended up winning by a large margin! I was really happy but not allowed to show much excitement because I might be labeled as a poor sport. A few years later this mindset of not expecting to win really got me in trouble.

Jimmy and Mousie Williams' Flintridge Riding Club produced legions of top riders and professionals. California still misses Jimmy Williams; he kept that coast together and maintained their high standards. Kathy Moore was Jimmy's "Girl Friday" and when I first met Kathy, we just clicked right from the start and became great friends. Kathy taught some of Jimmy's top clients like Theodora "Teddy" Gaston's daughter Gigi. When they came East to show at Lake Placid, Kathy was helping Gigi Gaston and Francie Steinwedell who were very competitive in the equitation, hunters, and jumpers.

Meanwhile at Hunterdon, Karen Healey had moved on in her career. She came to me at some point in those mid-seventies and insisted that Howard "H" LaBove, who she was very close with, come to manage Hunterdon. I didn't agree that he was right for the job, and she and I decided to part ways, although under very amicable terms. That's when Karen started her own business, which is still very successful today, and I still teach clinics regularly out at her current place in California. After Karen and H. LaBove parted ways as well a few years later, he was killed in a big Virginia horsey-set scandal. H. was caught in bed with Monique "Mo" Dana by one of his friends (and Mo's estranged husband) Theodore Gregory and shot dead on the spot. The case went to trial and the jury let Gregory off with a $1,000 fine!

Another big change in the Hunterdon team happened around that time, because I'd come to realize that conflicts between Jeremy and my office manager Barbara Massey were not going to improve—the two of them were like a cat and a dog! Jeremy went back and forth to the city to avoid Barbara, making life at home pretty strained. When Jeremy and I heard Kathy Moore was interested in staying East, Jeremy jumped at the chance to replace Barbara. It was a delicate situation because Kathy worked for Jimmy Williams, but we tried our best to handle it right. Kathy coming to Hunterdon was the beginning of an eighteen-year relationship. Having come from a very good family with old-school values and discipline, Kathy knew how to structure a business and manage people. She, in essence, ran my life for almost two decades.

Hunterdon simply could not have been as successful a business without Kathy. She was as hard-working and resourceful as you can imagine anyone being in that role. Kathy could do everything—teach, take riders to the ring, ride anything, handle new clients and parents, keep the books and payroll, as well as deal with horse show and travel planning and set up. She was an extraordinary type of executive secretary, because she knew everyone in the business, managed staff, ran international team tours, and kept my life organized. Kathy also didn't play favorites when it came to the clients and was straightforward and fair, with the patience of a saint. If something needed to be done "by tomorrow," she would stay up all night to be sure it was done. In the early days of personal computers, Kathy used them for tracking billing and printing invoices. She was a marvel of productivity and organization, and I could count on her to uphold my standards for the business in every last detail.

Nina Bonnie

I remember later on in the seventies, one year I got to Harrisburg and saw Kathy Moore, who ran George's barn at that point. She was in a full-length mink coat sweeping the barn aisle! I couldn't get over that. It was so fabulous!

After her fabulous performance in the Maclay Finals the prior year, Katharine Burdsall was the odds-on favorite to win the Medal Finals at Harrisburg in 1976. I'd noticed her horse Old Salt was a little body-sore the day before and in trying to ease his soreness I instead made a big mistake…I gave him a little bute. The bute made Old Salt overly fresh and bright, and they had some hiccups because of it. That year was Katharine's last junior year and if Old Salt had been his usual self, she probably would have won.

When Kathy Moore joined Hunterdon, she brought a wonderful junior rider with her—Francie Steinwedell. Francie is the daughter of my longtime friend Fran Steinwedell whom I knew from the fifties, and she had a classic, soft style as a rider—clearly a product of Jimmy's excellent teaching—and came from a very well respected family, as well. Judges couldn't resist Francie! Leading up to Harrisburg in 1976, Francie's horse Hot Soup went lame and she didn't have a horse. Gigi Gaston, Francie's friend from the West Coast, had two—Opening Night and Emerald Bay. Since Gigi was riding her hunter Opening Night in the Finals, she generously loaned Francie Emerald Bay, her junior jumper.

Emerald Bay was a jumper, not an equitation horse, so I paid particular attention to getting on him to school at three in the morning on the day of the Finals. He was very tractable, but he didn't have the look of an equitation horse and carried his head high, so I wanted to make him soft for Francie. I worked him on the flat until he was relaxed and engaged, making flying changes on a straight line. Unfortunately for Gigi, Opening Night cross-cantered in the initial round and just like that, it dropped her out. For Francie, Emerald Bay purred around the ring, dropping his head and masquerading like an equitation horse! Francie was called back second for the test and one of my junior protégés at the time, Michael Hart, was called back on top. I'd discovered Michael while teaching clinics in Minneapolis; he was a great talent and came to ride at Hunterdon. Laurie Pitts and Betsee Parker, who is now an integral part of the business, grew up riding with Michael, and all three of those teenagers were very close friends. We all used to go out from time to time and drink and dance, sometimes to Studio 54—I can still picture Betsee in her wild outfits, wearing roller skates with her hair in long braids.

Betsee Parker

In the seventies we did have fun and partied together as most young people do. Michael Hart was such a talented rider and even looked like he had Olympic potential, but as George used to say, he loved the bright lights a little too much. Michael was one of those people who struggled with drawing the line between real life and the nightlife, while George— in my mind—has always been one of those people who is good at knowing when to pull back on the throttle.

I rode in clinics with George and training with him is one of the central reasons that I got into Harvard. He taught me so much about focus, attention to detail, dedicating myself to an effort, and pressing forward. You had to work hard and he never took no for an answer. Even when you failed you had to get up again. I learned so much about diligence and the proper way to study from George—more so than from any teacher I had in school. I was sharper, quicker, and able to think on my feet because of George. He helped people train their intellect, not just train horses. He pushed so that either you broke or you broke through to a higher level. I needed help learning to be diligent; George could see that and he was hard on me about my effort. Even while we were terrified of George in those days, we also adored him! He was a kind of a god to us—you didn't challenge him; you simply tried to absorb his concepts and use them. And if you didn't get them, you just kept working until you did. Some people thrive on that tremendous pressure, and I was one of those people. He also helps you understand that repetition—to the point of monotony—is part of good training, and it's only through perseverance that you'll get results.

When readying riders for the equitation Finals, naturally part of the preparation is for potential tests that might be asked for by the judges. Back at home prior to Finals, I'd challenged my students to make up their own equitation test, and Michael had chosen the practice test of flying changes on a straight line. Night Club was a sensitive Thoroughbred type and when Michael had drilled him on tempi changes to get ready for this test challenge, the horse got frustrated. Afterward, anytime Michael asked for tempi changes, Night Club would get tense and Michael's temper would flare, causing that horse to melt down.

At the in-gate that day with Michael called back on top and Francie second, we awaited the judges' chosen test. Kathy Moore was coaching Francie and I was helping Michael. I told Michael if he asked Night Club for lead changes they were going to be in big trouble, and if that was the test, to do simple changes. Well, fate came into play and the judges asked for exactly that: changes of lead down the centerline every four strides. Michael's one weakness on Night Club was their downfall, and Francie won the Medal (photo 122)!

Francie Steinwedell-Carvin

They called us back and Michael was on top. At the end, they said changes of lead every four strides from the in-gate to the out-gate. Always wanting clarity on details, I turned to Kathy and asked nervously, "Flying or simple?" She said we could choose which one, so we went to the warm-up ring and I jumped my two jumps and practiced a lead change or two. I told Kathy I would do flying changes and that we'd be fine. I didn't know at the time that Michael was having problems with his flying changes on Night Club. Kathy knew it, but I didn't. I rode in and did flying changes and Michael did simple. Michael probably made the right choice to do simple changes given what might have happened. When I came out of the ring, I heard George's whooping, but as I walked down the long, dark aisle toward the in-gate, all I could think about was how I'd done changes every five strides instead of every four. But I was always a little off about strides because out in California, when we counted strides in a line, we counted the jumping-in stride too, so when we landed we counted "one-two-three," not "land-one-two-three." Thank goodness for Kathy Moore because she'd really worked with me on changing from "counts" to "strides." When I told Kathy I thought I'd done five strides between changes she told me that no, I'd done them every four so I believed her. It was the first time in my life I got really excited that I had won! Juniors from the West Coast could be in the Top Ten, but someone from California hadn't won in decades. I did it!

We moved on to Madison Square Garden with the promise of another battle. Francie needed a horse to ride; she couldn't borrow Emerald Bay again for the Maclay, given that the Gastons had come up short, in part because of their generosity. Gayle Everhart, another client of mine, had a wonderful junior hunter horse named Tiberius, and she loaned him to Francie for the Maclay. I thought Francie had a heck of a good chance in the Maclay, too.

I was (and still am!) a good-time Charlie and went out Saturday night after the show at the Garden with a group of friends. We usually ended up at Studio 54 or some other nightclub in New York. That time, the night before the Maclay Finals of '76, I sauntered into the club and who do I spy? Well, none other than Francie! She was only sixteen or seventeen years old and out partying with Pierre Jolicoeur, a good-looking French Canadian kid who is still in the horse business today. I'm not sure who was more surprised to see whom—after all, it was two in the morning the day of the Maclay. Granted, I was partying too—but at least I was an adult!

Several hours later, the warm-up began at the horse show and Francie hadn't arrived yet. Tiberius needed to be ridden that morning, but I simply couldn't ride him like I had done with Emerald Bay in the Medal; it was impossible. I had twenty-five or so entries in the Maclay and warm-up times in the Garden's tiny area were very tight. Each rider had their allotted time to ride and there was nowhere else to go, other than in the ring. The Garden isn't like Harrisburg when you can start at three in the morning and ride outside anytime you want. Plus, I had too many clients to coach and couldn't show her that favoritism, it simply wouldn't be fair. Tiberius might have gotten hand-walked but that was it. He was a Thoroughbred and wasn't very hot, but he was still a horse that came out feeling good and needed to be worked.

Francie rushed in after oversleeping—the victim of no wake-up call at the hotel—and when she rode Tiberius in the first round, she had an excellent trip despite the lack of a warm-up and was called back in first. It was the flat phase that undid them! Tiberius was high as a kite, and he bucked her right out of the ribbons. Francie was always on top in the flat classes, and she might have won the Maclay if she'd got to the show on time. It was a very tough lesson for her to learn, but you can bet she was in bed early the night before every big class after that.

That day was Collette Lozins' time to shine! Collette came to ride with me from Ricky Harris in Chicago earlier that year for her last junior year. She was one of those riders who *willed* herself to win the Maclay. Her horse Sandman was half-brother to Sandsablaze, an epic horse ridden by Buddy Brown and the subjects of Kimberley Gatto's recently published book. The two horses looked alike, but Sandman never had the big Olympic-level scope like Sandsablaze. Collette herself was an equitation specialist, similar to Anna Jane White-Mullin and Fred Bauer, with a lovely position, style, and talent. Collette orchestrated her own Maclay win that day, and there was no way in hell she was going to make a mistake. She knew exactly what her plan was every step of the way and had the self-discipline to execute that plan (photo 123).

There was a young man named Bill Cooney who was, in my estimation, the best up-and-coming teacher in America in the mid-seventies. Bill had partnered up with another young man named Frank Madden, a friend of the Hulicks with a wonderful horse-care background. I hired Bill after the indoors in 1976 to come work at Hunterdon, and Frank rode in on his coattails shortly thereafter; they both fit in beautifully! Pancho Lopez, who was a superb horseman and had worked with Jimmy Kohn and Kathy Moore on the West Coast, also joined the staff along with Katie Mellgard, Danny Marks, and Seamus Brady. Kathy, Pancho, Bill, Frank, Danny, Katie, and Seamus formed an incredible Hunterdon team. Our business was a powerhouse with an all-star staff; we lived and breathed excellence in every facet of the organization.

In the late seventies, more and more Latin Americans were immigrating to the United States, and it changed the face of the workforce in the horse industry. In the fifties and sixties, the labor force at stables was comprised mostly of Irish and African-American men. A noticeable shift took place in the seventies when Latinos began filling the roles of grooms and caretakers, and that has, for decades, been the norm across America.

Frank Madden

We were down in Florida in the winter of 1978. George decided we should go to a show in Jacksonville, but we got our entries in late and they didn't have any stalls left for us. The show organizers really wanted us to come anyway, so they put up another tent for us on the show grounds. The only place they had room for the new tent was on a lower ground area on the property. We set up with about forty horses and the whole crew was there, including several grooms. Due to Kathy Moore and Pancho's California connections, we were one of the first show stables to have Mexican grooms. We showed for a day or two, then when I came into work on Friday morning at five, it was pouring down rain and the stalls were completely flooded. Even more shocking was the fact that there were no grooms to be found anywhere.

I slogged around in the muck trying to figure out where all the grooms had gone—some of the guys usually stayed in cots in an extra stall or two, but everyone had vanished. Unbeknownst to me, immigration authorities had come in during the night and taken all the grooms. Every last one of them was gone! And we had forty horses standing in eight to ten inches of mud and the only people left to help were George, Pancho, Kathy, Bill, Katie, and me. We couldn't even muck out the stalls with all the mud; it was a complete nightmare! Pancho and I devised the only plan we could think of—we treated it like a riding school and tacked up every horse at once. All the horses were standing tacked up and ready to go. George and Bill stayed up at the ring, and we just shuttled horses back and forth to the ring all day long. It was a horrible situation, but we got through it. We had no choice! It was those times together, along with our respect and admiration for George, that made us such a close-knit team.

Armand, Peter, and Mark Leone didn't live far from me in New Jersey and their father called me, wanting to send all his boys to ride at Hunterdon. He told me that since he wasn't enlisting them in the Army they were coming to me instead! He insisted that it had to be fair all around for the three brothers. If Peter got a hunter, all of them needed a hunter. If Mark had an equitation horse, they all needed to have equitation horses. The three Leone boys each have unique personalities but all of them are excellent horsemen. I taught them from the mid-seventies until the early eighties, and I still help them from time to time (photo 124).

V. A RETURN TO EUROPE

The 1976 Olympic Games were based in Bromont, Quebec, but the Olympic stadium for the Nations Cup was in Montreal. Kathy Moore and the Leones traveled north with me to be spectators. What we noticed immediately when we laid eyes on the course for the individual jumping was that it was all about scope again, like Mexico. The courses were gigantic! They were so big that I'd say only a small number of horses were even physically capable of jumping the course clear. It wasn't until Los Angeles when Bert de Némethy revolutionized Olympic show jumping that the design of the courses changed from massive tests of sheer power and scope to technically complex. It was a different level of physical scope back then. The fences were so much bigger than Grand Prix classes that it was a huge challenge for the United States riders and horses.

Buddy Brown rode on the team that year, and it was the first time I had a student riding in the Olympics. What a very proud moment for me, watching

Buddy ride at that level! How incredible, too, that Sandsablaze, a horse I once considered to be simply a three-foot-six equitation horse, ended up being an Olympic jumper. If a horse has try and heart, you never can tell what he might be capable of. With a wonderful touch on a horse, Buddy had an incredible connection with Sandsablaze. I always admired his ability and also his friendly but confident demeanor. Buddy won the Medal Finals on Sandsablaze in 1973. In his last junior year, he could've had one last chance to win the Maclay Finals, but instead he sacrificed that chance and accepted an invitation to ride with Bert de Némethy and the USET. After he rode as an Olympian in 1976, I always had at least two riders on every American Olympic Show Jumping Team who were my students (photo 125).

Buddy Brown

I had been riding exclusively in the hunters, and when I went to George at age sixteen, I was most interested in the jumpers. George asked me who my equitation horse was, and I told him I didn't want to do the equitation. He insisted that I do it as part of his training program. That's how Sandsablaze got thrown into the mix; he was green but he was the only one that I could say probably wouldn't blow up on the flat or be spooky at the jumps. My hunter at the time was an unpredictable type, so Sandsablaze drew the short straw and became my equitation horse. I had done so little equitation that in 1972 I was still eligible for Limit Equitation and won my way out of Limit by winning the AHSA Medal at Devon.

In hindsight, as much as I dug my heels in and resisted doing the equitation, it was good for me. That experience rounded me out and improved my thought process on the flat and between the jumps. Especially in those early days, riding with George and earning his praise meant a lot for my self-esteem. He pushed us, for sure. He pushed us to a level that I probably wouldn't have got to on my own. I think we were more afraid of making a mistake because of his reaction than we were actually worried about making the mistake itself! But accomplishing what I did riding with George made me wonder what else I could accomplish if I worked that hard.

What I took away from my time riding with George was learning to handle the pressure of being a favorite and still being able to pull it off. In the seventies, at every horse show and not just the Finals, it was very competitive. We were always switching horses and being tested in those equitation classes. I've had kids riding with me who didn't want to do the equitation, and I encourage them to, just like George did for me. I was

80. *David Hopper, here on the Actor in 1963, was my first—and in some ways, last—working student.* © *Budd*

81. *Jimmy Kohn showing PERFECT form on Stonehenge, 1964.* © *Budd*

82. *With my very close friend and mentor, Victor Hugo-Vidal, Jr.* © Gloria Axt

83. *Triplicate showing her immense ability over fences.*

84. *With Jimmy Kohn, 1964 AHSA Hunt Seat Medal Finals Champion, at Madison Square Garden.*

85. *With Margot Graham and Victor Hugo-Vidal, Jr. at a year-end celebration.*

86. *Living it up on the Mediterranean cruise, 1964.*

SS INDEPENDENCE　　MADEIRA, PORTUGAL, 1964

87. *With Grandmother on Madeira Island.*

88. *Conrad Homfeld, age twelve, riding his pony, Melody.*

89. *Conrad Homfeld riding Triplicate, 1966.*

90. *Kristine Pfister riding the legendary hunter, Highclere.*

91. *Amory Ripley, a true soul mate.*

92. *Benny O'Meara showing his own style on Jacks O' Better.*

93. *The legendary Kathy Kusner riding Untouchable.*

94. *Teaching a clinic in Alpharetta, Georgia, 1968.*

95. *I could turn on the charm when I needed to!*

96. *Out West with Tiffany Traurig, Tab Hunter, J.J. Smith, with Dianne Grod riding.*

97. *Judging, here in California, was a part of being a horseman I always enjoyed. Fellow judge, Carroll Curran, and I confer during a class.* © George Axt

98. *With Conrad Homfeld, 1967 ASPCA Maclay Finals Champion, at Madison Square Garden.*

99. With my first professional "Girl Friday", Barbara Massey.

100. Brooke Hodgson, a class act and 1968 AHSA Medal Finals champion at Harrisburg.

101. Walking a course with students in Chagrin Falls, Ohio, 1968.

102. With my friend Mickey Lowe in South Africa.

103. Katie Monahan and Milltown, 1969 ASPCA Maclay Finals Champion.

104. *Jeremy Wind was a Peter Pan.*

105. *James Hulick on Tiny's Thoughts, 1970 AHSA Hunt Seat Medal Finals Champion.*

106. *Teaching at Devon in 1969.*

107. *Coaching Teddi Ismond.* © *Robert A. Heinhold*

108. *Hunterdon, a bird's eye view.*

109. *A great technician, Anna Jane White-Mullin and Rivet, 1971 ASPCA Maclay Finals Champion.*

110. *Walking the course at Madison Square Garden, 1971.*

111. *The course walk for the ASPCA Maclay Medal Finals at Madison Square Garden, 1977. Left to right: Francie Steinwedell, Steve Weiss, Debra Baldi, GHM, Martha Wachtel, Bill Cooney, Kathy Moore, Elizabeth Sheehan, Mark Leone, Peter Leone, and other riders in the background.*

112. *Katie Monahan with Abu Simbel.*

113. *Teaching a clinic in the 1970s.* © Carl Leck

114. *The Hunterdon tack room at a horse show, with Baron's likeness to greet friends.*

115. *Madison Square Garden, 1972: I'm with Leslie Burr who, age 15, rode to win the ASPCA Maclay Finals on Suzette.* © Budd

116. *Judging in Warrenton, Virginia.*

117. *I'm riding the iconic hunter Dillon who transformed from cold-backed rogue to Grand Champion.*

118. *On Isle of Erin in the early 1970s. She was hot as a pistol.*

Courtesy of Lorna Drake,
Freudy Photos Archives, LLC

119. *With Hunter Champion Bonnie Castle and Sheila Lenehan.* © Walsh

120. *Cynthia Hankins on Nissen, the 1975 AHSA Hunt Seat Medal Finals Champion.* © Stacey Holmes

121. *A horseman's horsewoman: Katharine Burdsall, 1975 ASPCA Maclay Finals Champion.* © Tarrance

such a sponge at that age and there were great horsemen and teachers all around me to learn from during those years. We were presented at the USET Screening Trials in 1973 and got exposure to Bert de Némethy. The whole process of going from George to Bert was like going from college to graduate school. Still, when I'm teaching sometimes, I hear George's words coming out of my mouth. And when I ride I hear Bert's voice talking about rhythm.

As always, I watched the dressage at the Olympic Games and Dorothy Morkis had a brilliant gray horse named Monaco. Sitting at the gorgeous facility, I watched her warm up in a field nearby and she rode up to me after to say hello. We had a little talk and she was feeling nervous that she or Monaco might not be good enough for the world stage. I gave her some encouragement that day, and she ended up having great success. Ever since then we've been friends.

Team jumping was in Montreal at the track stadium because, as usual, it was the last Olympic event. Next to the bloodbath at the individual competition, the team course didn't look nearly as big. I didn't have accreditation to be down in the ring, but as I sat on the sidelines, Buddy walked over to me and said, "George, this is a four-foot-six junior jumper course. There's nothing to it!" He was right; it did look small. As it turned out, it was a footing issue. Many times at Olympic Games when the track stadium is prepped for the team jumping at the very end of the Games, the footing isn't prepared well. I heard that it happened in Tokyo in 1964 and in Montreal it happened once again. The surface was very deep and saturated, so horses were slipping and getting bogged down. They were forced to make a much greater effort to get up and over each fence. It looked like a four-foot-six course but everyone said it rode like a six-foot course!

At the Olympics I saw a horse that I absolutely loved named Gai Luron, that François Mathy won a bronze medal riding. A few months after the Games, I asked Dr. Leone if we could go over to Europe and try Gai Luron. Even though we decided not to buy the horse, the Leones met François Mathy and formed a connection that became a decades-long partnership.

Back at home, it was far from just a horse life! As hard as we worked, it was never all work and no play. Together with Bernie and Tiffany Traurig (later: Teeter) based nearby in New Hope, we had a lot of interesting local friends. Doris Whitehead was a newspaper editor and an "Auntie Mame" of sorts. Living in a big old frame house, Doris would have us over all the time, and she always had beautiful, classy, interesting people staying with her. Airline stewards and stewardesses would float in and out of her place. She also had a young European model working for her named Norbert Thomas. Interestingly enough, Norbert eventually bought a little farm on the Neshanic River nearby. Eventually, Ken Berkley bought it and dubbed it River's Edge Farm, now a huge operation run by Ken and Scott Stewart.

Jeremy loved Doris for her bright, open-mindedness, and avant-garde life-style. Fascinating people came into our lives via her house constantly. She was the social glue for Hunterdon in that era and contributed to a wonderful mix of influences from New York and Europe. Celeste Holm, the Academy-Award-winning actress and her husband were friends of ours. We'd host holiday dinners and country barbecues with our eclectic crowd of local and city friends. It was a cosmopolitan life we led, which is rare when you run a stable.

Matt Collins rode with me for a while and then went to work for Rodney Jenkins in Virginia, but now and then Matt would show up and have horses for sale. One year at Madison Square Garden, Matt met Doris's model friend; Norbert took one look at Matt's handsome face and dragged him over to meet Wil-helmina Cooper, founder of the Wilhelmina Agency in New York. Wilhelmina instantly signed Matt to a modeling contract, and he became a world-renowned male model in the seventies and even posed with the popular models of the day, such as Cheryl Tiegs and actress-to-be Rene Russo. Matt eventually returned to the horse world, but he had a huge career in modeling for four years.

Arthur Hawkins

Teachers like Wayne Carroll, Emerson Burr, or Gordon Wright—they all had a desire to get an edge. When they asked questions of the judge in that time, it was a way for them to learn what was being looked at so they could better prepare their students. George was also an active commu-nicator when it came to discussion with judges. I can remember instances where his rider had a wonderful first round but then had a miss in the work-off and was moved down in the ribbon order. George would come up to me and say, "Arty, c'mon, they were so great in the first round!" and I'd reply, "But George, if they call for a work-off, I have no choice but to take the work-off into consideration." He would agree with that and per-haps we'd disagree on how much the work-off should impact initial results. It was all part of a learning process, in talking through things.

A lot of the younger trainers, when they got out of the equitation, wanted to see what the judges would put a lot of emphasis on. They would try to understand what was counted. I was a stickler in the equita-tion ring about a rider turning to look at the next jump while they were still in the air over the top of the fence. I told that to George once and he thought for a second and said, "You know, you're right. I'm so close to the teaching that I never thought about that before." Such a small detail wasn't going to mean a rider was counted out, but I would absolutely use that kind of a detail to help break a tie between two very good riders. At that high level, you need to pay attention to those kinds of details to differentiate between the near perfect rounds.

With operations running smoothly at Hunterdon and an excellent staff of teachers and managers, I found myself gaining a little more freedom. I was eager to return to Europe for the first time since the 1960 Olympic Games, in particular, because riders whom I had taught and coached as juniors were reaching the level of international competition. Melanie Smith had acquired powerful owners, Pam Duffy and Neil Eustace. They liked her and hired her to be their rider. Melanie was still an amateur by necessity, but there were associations between owners and riders like her. I found an interesting horse for her to ride for the Duffys down at the Radnor Hunt Club. He was a bay Thoroughbred horse, about six years old, and I called him Radnor II because I'd gotten Big Line there sixteen years earlier.

One of Melanie's first shows on Radnor II was in Jacksonville, Florida, in the winter of '77. The jumper-ring footing was firm and solid but the schooling area on the racetrack had deep sand. Radnor definitely remembered what a racetrack was all about and as soon as he stepped into the schooling area his eyes started rolling around in his head. He was the type of horse to jump with his head held a little low, and as confident as Melanie was as a competitor, she also had a cautious side. She hadn't yet learned to trust that horse. With him being so wild-eyed, Radnor got deep to a fence and Melanie didn't leg him off the ground. He fell down in the deep sand and pitched her off. I'd had enough of her riding so conservatively and I ran up while the horse was still on the ground and jumped into the saddle. I kicked him up, galloped him straight into the show ring myself, and we jumped around clean. I didn't even do it with any forethought! I was purely led by my emotions and after all was said and done, it was exactly what Melanie needed to see. After that day, she had great confidence in Radnor II. With their success together all year, he was Horse of the Year and an excellent Grand Prix horse of that era.

Melanie went to Europe that summer along with Michael Matz to show in Aachen and La Baule, France. I met them at Aachen and coached Melanie, which was my first time as a teacher on an international tour. It was exhilarating to be back at the big show grounds in Aachen. Karen Golding was with the team working for Michael, and I was so excited to be in Europe again that I told her, "Karen, we're going out—bring your passport!" She had no idea what she was in for. We did three countries in one night: Germany, Belgium, and Holland. It was her "coming-out" tour!

Jimmy Wofford

Our younger daughter Jennifer was getting married at our farm, and George, who is an old and dear friend, called the Saturday morning of the wedding, asking if he could stay overnight on Sunday evening. The "English Woffords" had arrived in force and the "inn" was pretty full, but we told George we'd make something work. The party included my sister-in-law, Dawn Palethorpe Wofford, who had been a close friend and competitor of George's in the fifties, along with her daughter Valerie, who had an eerie resemblance to her Aunt Jill (another competitor from the same era). Quite a reunion ensued, so we sat out under the reception tent at the rented tables and had ourselves a fairly raucous night-after party with the wedding leftovers. We all fell into bed late, tipsy and tired. The next morning, my wife Gail's parents had an early flight out; however, in trying to leave they found that they were blocked in by George's car. My older daughter, Hillary, who was nursing an infant at the time, walked upstairs with her baby and knocked on George's door at about six in the morning. Thinking she heard, "Come in" from George, she opened the door. To her surprise, there was George stepping out of the bathroom wearing nothing but a pair of Calvin Klein briefs. Hillary screeched, jumping back out into the hallway as George leaped back into the bathroom. After a quick explanation through the bedroom door, George reached through a crack in the door and relinquished his keys. When George came downstairs a few minutes later, we all had a good laugh. I told him, "George, you have to stop bringing those Calvin Klein models over to my house!" George replied, "Trust me, the guys I bring home aren't as classy as Calvin Klein models."

At Aachen, I reconnected with two men from my younger days. One was Harry Gilhuys, a Dutchman who had worked at the Ox Ridge Hunt Club in the mid-fifties teaching dressage back in the time when it was rare. The second was Nick Pawlenko, international dressage judge and trainer Natalie Lamping's father. Harry and Nick were both great horsemen who were ahead of the curve in their generation—they knew how to do piaffe, passage, and to properly get a horse on the bit. Nick had a horse named Isgilde, a top dressage horse that then became a Grand Prix jumper. I remember he would tie his nine-year-old daughter Natalie's feet to the stirrups—she would jump Grand Prix courses tied to the horse! Isgilde eventually went down to Kenny and Sallie Wheeler's place and became the top working hunter in the country. What a horse—she did it all!

While at Aachen, Harry Gilhuys told me he had a horse for me to see. In those days it was still unusual to import horses from Europe and there was still somewhat of a bias against them, with Americans still favoring our lighter Thoroughbreds. Melanie and I went over to Harry's wonderful stable and socialized for a while in the lounge over a few heavy Dutch beers. Afterward, we went out to see the horse, a little, 15.2-hand, chestnut stallion with a great expression. He looked like a big pony and jumped like a rubber ball, not coming close to touching a fence. I was drunk enough by then, with another beer in hand, and suddenly buying that horse was the best idea I ever had. I declared, "Melanie, we are buying this horse!" I have no idea whether that horse cost five and he sold him to us for fifty, but either way he's a clever horse dealer!

When we brought the horse from Harry's place back to Connecticut, I was pretty nervous because I could hardly even remember what he looked like. Thankfully, he turned out to be wonderful. Melanie called him Vivaldi; his limit was four-foot-six, but Melanie had great success on him, and he was the top speed horse in the country. With his bouncy pony style, the horse show crowds recognized him and everyone loved him. Vivaldi's popularity helped spur the coming tsunami of imported horses from Europe in the years to come.

VI. THE JONES BOY

Back in 1975, my old friend Kathy Kusner steered me in the right direction. Living in Maryland, Kathy had gotten a jockey's license and was trying her hand at racetrack life. She and Danny Marks' friend Vivianne Rawls had a big, rangy, six-year-old, bay Thoroughbred off the track. Kathy had a great eye for talented jumpers and saw him jump a couple of fences; she called me and said I had to see the horse. At about 17 hands but light and with immense scope, The Jones Boy could really jump. I loved him and bought him on the spot for $7,500.

After I'd worked with The Jones Boy a while, we started with a little one-day show in Jacksonville, Florida. First, I trotted all the fences in the Pre-Green class. Next, I trotted in and cantered out of all the lines in the three-foot-six First Year Green Hunter class. After that, I rode him in the Working Hunters and cantered all the lines. Then I rode him in the Mini Prix at the end of the day. The Jones Boy was a quick study, which was not uncommon for those big, athletic Thoroughbreds with so much heart. Nowadays, with these slowly maturing Warmbloods it would take four years to teach what I taught The Jones Boy in four days!

I entered The Jones Boy in the Preliminary Jumper division in 1976 after we had a little mileage under our belts. Boy, was he a head-turner! He had that big Olympic horse look with immense scope and stride, and started getting legitimate attention. He wasn't the most careful horse ever, but he could trot a five-foot-high fence. At Lake Placid that year in a Preliminary class, we jumped around clean, but when I walked out of the ring Katie Monahan was glaring at me. "George, get off him! You're using too much leg and you're going to ruin him!" I obediently dismounted and handed her the reins. (She was one of the only people who could ever tell me what to do!)

Katie was a legendary rider. She was like Beezie Madden in the sense that she did as little as possible but just as much as necessary. That's how you would describe her on a hunter, a jumper, or an equitation horse. Katie got on The Jones Boy and rode him in the jump-off and they won the class. That's the only time before or since that I have seen one rider jump in the class and another ride the same horse in the jump-off. I'm sure it's against some rules that they have written nowadays but no one seemed to blink an eye about it then! After that day, Katie never got off The Jones Boy. He wasn't mine anymore—he was all hers (photo 127).

Katie Prudent

I feel so fortunate to have known and gotten tutelage from George in those early years. He was fresh off the team and still riding jumpers, but he'd been influenced by Gordon Wright and wanted to be the best trainer in the equitation, too. One of the greatest things about those times was that everything he taught us in the equitation had form with meaningful function. Your straight back was for strength, and your heels were your anchor. Everything he taught us made so much sense and that knowledge transferred from the equitation to the jumpers.

We had Thoroughbreds and never tranquilized them; we had to fig-ure out how to ride difficult horses. Trainers and parents weren't like they are today. They didn't pull a child off a horse that was bucking and fresh, and get rid of it. In today's world, there's hardly a horse that goes into the ring without ear plugs—it's such bad horsemanship. George taught great horsemanship and understanding of the animal. Nowadays, it's form without function.

The Jones Boy wasn't the most careful horse but he had the most unbelievable, huge jump. Being so young and hot-blooded, I was prob-ably way too excited in my ride on the horse, knowing what I know now. George took us all over the place to show, and I thought we would get better and better, but at one point, George was disappointed with The Jones Boy because he didn't have consistently clear rounds. Soon after, he let me take him to Upperville to show by myself. I was determined to be more consistent, so I did absolutely everything I could think of to set the horse up well. We went for trail rides and I rode him around the show grounds just to relax him. I schooled him very carefully and at the end of the show, the time I'd spent paid off—we were second in the Grand Prix. I was thrilled that my recipe had worked and knew important progress had been made with him. It was the very next show that someone came up and tried to buy him from George.

We arrived at the 1977 Ox Ridge Hunt Club show and everyone was staring at Katie on The Jones Boy. The horse simply had a presence about him. My old friend Jimmy Kohn was by then a very successful horse dealer, buying up horses for $10,000 and selling them six months later for $100,000 because he was such a good rider and could sharpen them up and train them so quickly. At the Ox Ridge Hunt Club, Jimmy Kohn came up to me with a briefcase in hand. In it was $100,000 for The Jones Boy. I was so shocked and impressed with the huge sum he offered me that I agreed, shook his hand, and took the briefcase. I immediately went looking for Katie and when I found her, I broke the news that I'd sold the horse. She looked at me in shock and then positively melted down. I led her out to sit in the car with me and we got in and turned on the air conditioning. Katie sobbed so hard and was so hysterically upset that it completely broke my heart. I realized suddenly how much he meant to her. What had I done? I had to fix it.

I ran to find Jimmy, his briefcase in my hand. "Jimmy, I know I shook your hand," I implored him, "but I can't sell you the horse. I have to give the money back to you." Jimmy was irritated, but we had an old friendship, and he was a gentleman, so he agreed. I had helped him a time or two, so even though he wasn't happy, he accepted it. Katie had her horse back and suddenly, I knew in my gut that he could be her ticket to the Olympic Games.

Thankfully, Jimmy forgave me for going back on my word. Jimmy was my close friend until the day he died, when I sat with him in the hospital. I'll never forget our wild days together when I was just starting out as a professional and we parked the horses in Greenwich Village between horse shows!

Ronnie's son Hugh Mutch was heavily favored to win the 1977 Medal Finals. Elizabeth Sheehan, who rode with me and was a beautiful picture on a horse, upset the apple cart and won instead with the horse show of a lifetime (photo 128). Admittedly Liz, who rode Michael Hart's former horse Night Club, also had a bit of clever coaching on her side. The judges wanted badly to pin Liz second and Hugh Mutch first, because he was an excellent rider with a great reputation as Ronnie's son. They tested the top riders with the age-old challenge of "canter fence one, trot fence two" in a line.

Just as Gordon Wright had taught me, I had prepared Liz for this test. She angled her horse's path subtly to the outside and the trick worked brilliantly, with a very clear trot to the second fence. Liz nailed it and Hugh's transition was a bit shuffled and not as clean. The judges still weren't getting what they wanted and they asked Liz and Hugh to change horses and repeat the test. Liz got on Hugh's horse, cantered fence one, trotted fence two, and nailed it again! On Night Club, Hugh's test was tense and choppy. At that point, the judges had no choice; Liz had clearly earned the win! Not surprisingly (since she had only gotten better and more comfortable showing on the East Coast since her last trip to the Garden) Francie Steinwedell won the Maclay Finals that year on her horse Hot Soup. It was sweet redemption for her missing her warm-up the year before.

Of all these fabulous young riders, both the equitation specialists and the natural talents bound for the international arena, Katie Monahan was the best equitation rider I ever witnessed. She didn't have the perfect build or the textbook look like Conrad or Cynthia. She didn't need it. Katie had the ability, the style, the form, the nerves, but most of all the showmanship. If they said halt, she'd halt on the exact spot and be a statue for a half an hour! If they said turn, it would be on a dime every time. If they said trot a fence, she would trot so slowly and accurately to the base and jump beautifully every time. Katie not only mastered the precision that dominated in the equitation ring, but she also had the scope of talent to make history at the highest levels of international show jumping. Katie was the best equitation rider in history, in my opinion, despite the fact that she didn't have that tall, thin build that is the most striking look in the ring. That long and lean appearance always looks great on a horse, but the look is only a small piece of what matters in the show ring.

Business was booming and in addition to the equitation, I continued to seek out great young hunters for some top clients. Union Blue was a beautiful gray that was Green Working Hunter Champion at Washington that year. I also matched up Bonnie Jenkins with Gozzi, an iconic show hunter. That winter Tiffany Traurig and I went horse shopping in South America together. We'd seen some talented horses originating from Argentina and Brazil and decided to check it out ourselves. I hadn't been there since I went with my grandmother in 1953, when Eva Peron had just died and the place was covered in gloom. What a different place it had become! Liberal, colorful, and fun, both countries were wonderful. I officially discovered my love of Brazil and it's still one of my absolute favorite places to vacation and enjoy nightlife. We had a lot of fun dinners and nights on the town.

One night, I went out in Rio de Janeiro and met all sorts of fun Brazilians, two of whom came back with me to my hotel to continue the party. It was all fun and games until morning came when they wouldn't leave! In a stroke of genius, I called Tiffany over in her room on the sly and proposed that she come to my room and pretend to be my irate wife. Let me tell you, Tiffany did not disappoint! She came over and put on an Academy-Award-worthy performance, chasing them into the locked bathroom and eventually beating the two guys out the door with pillows! She really saved me that day—although I usually preach "safety in numbers," it's not always advisable. The rest of the trip went wonderfully. I bought a few horses in Argentina for the Leone brothers and a big chestnut horse for Katie to try. We made great contacts in Buenos Aires, which is a fabulous city. Tiffany and I found a few nice horses there on a couple of different trips.

Later that year, I judged The Forum out in California with Patty Heuckeroth and some Hollywood stars were in attendance. Alan Balch, who ran the show, told me to come up to the sky box after judging and meet Mae West. I walked in the door and Mae had six huge bodyguards with her. She looked up and said, "Baby, here comes the judge!" She was such an icon and I was smitten! Unlike those times when you find yourself disappointed in the real thing, meeting Mae West was exactly like I'd hoped it might be. As we chatted, bantering back and forth, she told me, "George, when I'm good, I'm good—but when I'm bad, I'm better."

Dianne Grod, an iconic jumper rider and horsewoman who has seen and done just about everything in the horse world, had a horse called Pretentious for her student Julie Taylor. Pretentious was a beautiful Thoroughbred mare that jumped like Triplicate but with enough scope that she won two or three of the biggest Grand Prix classes in France. I liked the horse when I saw her jump at The Forum and considered her a possibility for Armand Leone, but I thought she was a little overpriced. I told Armand that we wouldn't forget about her, but that we'd go look in Europe at some horses first.

I continued traveling to California to teach clinics, see J.J. Smith and other friends, and make contacts with good customers and students out West. That year, I decided to go a bit farther and teach a clinic in Hawaii after Franny Pryor Hawes, an old New York and Connecticut friend, invited me. The people were colorful, the weather was beautiful, and the equestrian community really growing. Two great young students, Brendan Damon and Valerie Monnett, became my clients and had some success.

Brendan Damon, who was a gorgeous young woman and a talented rider, became a very close friend and eventually my girlfriend as we had a brief romance. She was really the last woman I ever really went out with. One night during the wintertime, Brendan, Valerie, and I went out with Bernie Traurig and his girlfriend at the time, a fashion model named Michael Cody (Bernie had been recently divorced from his wife, Tiffany). We ended up at a wild gay dance club and late into the night, Michael busted Bernie getting friendly with Brendan in a dark corner of the club. Michael took one look at Brendan with her boyfriend and grabbed fistfuls of her waist-long hair, dragging her out the door of the club and into a snow drift outside. What drama! Both Valerie and Brendan were probably a little young for that club scene, and it wasn't long after that Valerie was scooped up by her parents and shipped home from Hunterdon, which they felt was a place of ill repute!

When it came to choosing good young horses, I wasn't always making the right choices. The South American horses I had bought earlier that year were mostly a disappointment. With horses, it's never a guarantee—sometimes they're better suited for a different job than the one you have in mind for them. Other times, there are surprise health issues. I bought this wonderful little brown horse for Betsie Bolger (later: Day) down in Brazil and when we got him to Miami, it turned out he had piroplasmosis, a tick-borne infectious disease that requires complete isolation in quarantine. They have a test for it now and it's very rare, but back then customs wouldn't even let him through quarantine in Miami. I had the option of putting the horse down or sending him back to the sellers for no refund, so I sent him back. We never got a penny of the $60,000 back that we'd spent on him. It's "buyer beware" when it comes to horse shopping!

After sending that poor sick horse back to the seller, I was desperate because the Bolgers needed a horse to replace it. Silver Exchange was a Working Hunter out West being ridden by Ronnie Freeman; he'd won everything in California. Like War Bride, I heard that his wind had started to make a whistle and I knew his hunter career was over. It was split-second timing. Perhaps there was a three-week window between his hunter career ending and the beginning of his jumper career. Ronnie gave me a fairly decent price for the horse, and it was out of my own pocket, so I gave him to the Bolgers. Silver Exchange went on to be ridden on the 1980 Olympic Team and was second in the Hickstead and Dublin Grand Prix with Katie Monahan.

VII. BACK TO THE JUMPERS

Martha Jolicoeur

We all learned how to ride from George and had wonderful riding careers but more than that, George taught us how to be successful in life. Recently, a dinner reunion was planned for a group of us that rode with George in the late seventies. I realized every one of us had accomplished so much in our lives after we grew up riding at Hunterdon.

George spent so much time with us. We would get on our horses at six-thirty in the morning and practice, practice, practice. On a horse show day, we would be preparing, studying, caring for the horses, and riding the entire day until late. We never wanted anyone to think we weren't doing something to improve ourselves—whether it was taking care of our horses or sitting by the ring analyzing other people's rides on a course. All of us rode in a system with George and we were consistent. He told us to go home and write down our mistakes so we would be less likely to repeat them. I kept a journal that I still have. In it, I wrote down all of the things I learned day to day at Hunterdon and at the shows. And not just about riding. The grooms were wonderful and taught us about our horses and about managing their health and happiness.

There weren't thoughts like, "Oh I didn't win the Medal Finals. I only came in third that one year." We were always proud of everything we accomplished. We wanted to win, but it was the judge's decision. I don't remember ever wanting to beat this or that other rider. We were always happy for one another. We would stand and watch other riders with George and we never heard, "He does that better than you." It was, "Look how beautiful he or she did that. See if you can do that, too." George had us all sized up. He used to tell me that I'm a worrier and he was right! I used to get really nervous in the ring when I was about fifteen years old, and he made me go around the ring, reciting out loud, "I know I'm going to see a distance. It might be a little short or a little long, but I know I'm going to see something." I would have to say it out loud over and over again on course, and everyone standing around the ring at the shows could hear me. It was all part of the learning process, and he tailored it for everyone a little differently.

By 1978, I had refamiliarized myself with Europe and took my up-and-coming riders Armand Leone, Betsie Bolger, and Debby Malloy (who later married Hans Günter Winkler) on a tour in France. It wasn't affiliated with the USET—it was a private tour run out of Hunterdon. After riding so many hunters through the sixties and seventies and handing home-grown jumper prospects to my students, I was eager to get back in the jumper ring myself and brought along a green jumper to show on the tour.

Debby was a very talented rider and, like Meredith Michaels, who married Markus Beerbaum, she stayed overseas for nearly her entire career after she got a taste of it. Betsie brought her wonderful hunter-turned-jumper named Silver Exchange. France is a wonderful place to introduce young riders to European showing because the experience is very elegant and not as serious as Germany. It's important not to let riders get in over their heads starting out in Europe; I had learned that from Bert de Némethy's management of the USET. Adding to the experience in France are the beautiful hotels, show grounds, and great restaurants.

Nelson Pessoa and his wife Regina are both very good friends of mine and our friendship began many years ago. Regina was a bit of an artist, a Bohemian type, and very sympathetic to alternative lifestyles, so she and I got along swimmingly. Regina had a Parisian friend named Philippe Jouy and he had a beautiful gray horse named L'Arc de Ciel that he brought to the States to show in the early seventies. Philippe was the Bob Penney of France, in a way, because he was very classy, a great horseman, and a beautiful rider. He and I were birds of a feather, and he was very helpful as a contact for planning that European tour. Philippe was a fun friend to hit the town with as well, since he knew all the great watering holes.

We began in Fontainebleau and then went on to Royan, Agnac (near Cognac), and Dinard. Despite the refinement of the French shows, the competition was very difficult, especially in speed classes. One thing the French and most of Europe hadn't yet picked up was riding the related distances between fences by counting the strides. The Americans were all counting strides and as a result, we had advanced significantly in our ability to compete. It was no longer the days when American riders were struggling to keep up with the time allowed in European jumper class format. By the late seventies, we were technically more advanced than most of the Europeans. It wasn't just the related distances. The classical flatwork that Bert de Némethy had imported, educating riders with concepts like bending, collection, rhythm, and striding, was giving us an edge. Not only were we keeping up, but we were winning more and more often.

On that same tour, John Madden came along as my groom. By that time, he and Johnny Black had begun helping me with stable management at Hunterdon, and John was always a meticulous groom. The green jumper I'd brought to show was one I'd bought from Bob MacDonald in Southern California when I was teaching there the previous winter. I called him Santa Ana. He was part Thoroughbred and part Quarter Horse—brave but still very green. Starting him a few months earlier, I rode him in the hunters to get him comfortable, but he was a very good jumper with nice scope. By the time we got to Europe, I was trying to get Santa Ana more seasoned in the jumper ring and rode him in the speed classes. John would bring that horse up to the ring looking completely spotless and beautiful, without a single hair out of place! I started to feel badly for John though, because he turned that horse out like a superstar but we would only get a few ribbons here or there and nothing special.

That tour was John Madden's first trip to Europe, and he made some great contacts in the business, including Johan Heins who became his long-standing partner in Holland. Making those contacts in the business all around the world launched John's career. Very soon after that tour, he moved on to work with Katie Monahan down in Middleburg, Virginia. There, John met and later married Beezie Patton as Beezie was riding with Katie then. I always take great pleasure in how fantastically well John and Beezie have done.

John Madden

I've known George since very early in my career, and he shaped it a lot, especially in the early years. When I got to Hunterdon, the business was focused on hunters and equitation, which is the direction my brother Frank went in as he was much more advanced than I was. I got the opportunity to focus on the jumpers and the international showing, which gave me the ties to Europe while Frank stayed on the national circuit. The exposure that I got in those early years with George was incredible. I saw how big the world was! To a couple kids from Massachusetts, Frank and I couldn't imagine anything bigger than the Finals at the Garden in New York. That exposure to Europe and the rest of the world was crucial to my business and career. John Madden Sales was completely based on finding horses in Europe for American owners and riders. George helped me, and probably many others, understand how to go from being where you were at that moment to where you wanted to be. Seeing those French shows, meeting Johan Hein—it broadened my view so much. The people I met there had never even heard of the Maclay Finals!

George helped me understand that there's a process to getting to a higher level. You have to know what you don't know, ask the right questions, then make a plan to get there. Whether they are his principles or my principles, he wants you to be consistent. Even in his clinics, he tells people, "You don't have to do it my way forever; just do it my way for this clinic." That's how he's helped so many people. No matter what your endeavor might be, George fuels you to commit and keep high standards and be a winner. The biggest compliment he ever gave me is that I'm a "plodder." You can talk about putting the horse first, or you can talk about good equitation, but the "why" is what's important. George helped me understand that being at the top and achieving those big goals are possible by being committed to, following, and sticking to basic fundamentals that never change.

At the first show in Fontainebleau, to get Santa Ana around the course, I had to go to the stick a few times to get him over the ditches, banks, and water. Alwin Schockemöhle, Paul's gold-medal-winning older brother, was there promoting his horse show in Germany and watching the class. I ended up fourth out of a field of about eighty horses and Alwin said to me, "Georgie, you still have it!" He thought I was trying to be competitive by going to the stick with Santa Ana, when really I was just trying to get around! I told him, "Alwin, I was just trying to get around!" but he shook his head and said, "No, no, Georgie, you still have it!" Our finish wasn't too shabby, especially for a dead green horse.

After Fontainebleau, we went to nearby Paris for a day or two and stayed at the Meurice Hotel. In those days, everything was much more affordable in Europe than it is today. That hotel was as good as you get in Paris, it was even the headquarters of the German command during World War II. We all stayed there and the concierge would even take care of Kathy's dog and feed it in the dining room! It was a different era in the seventies and very, very good fun over in Europe. After a couple of days at the Meurice, I headed out to Marseilles on my own, which is a very long drive from Paris. Having that old itch I needed to scratch, I went on a partying tear in Marseilles! Being out and about electrified me, and I blew off some necessary steam after the long, busy horse show days. All I had to do was get back to the show by Wednesday, but it took me two whole days to get there because I felt worse than death, paying the costly consequences of my all-nighter in Marseilles. I drove myself through the tortuously windy mountain roads, stopping to rest and get my head to stop spinning. It was terrible! I'll never forget that drive to Royan.

The late seventies marked the start of the Europe horse-shopping bonanza and after the tour with our young jumper riders, we stayed behind to look at a few horses. The same horse dealers in France who were driving 200 kilometers per hour while negotiating prices of top horses on their car phones had picked up on the fact that Americans needed good sport horses. Their breeding program was so much further developed than ours at home and connections started to be made. At the beginning, the price conversion wasn't exactly fair. If a horse had been priced at 100,000 Deutschmarks, they would simply say it was a $100,000 horse, which was quadruple the value!

I traveled to François Mathy's place to look at horses with Armand Leone, Kathy Moore, and my good friend Bob Penney (who would vet a horse for us on the spot, which was a great thing to have on hand). François didn't have any horses we liked enough to buy, but he was at that time partnered with Paul Schockemöhle. We went over to Paul's to look at a horse, which marked the beginning of a long relationship with Paul helping me find good horses. Paul showed us Wallenstein, a fabulous German jumper who was a little cold and needed a strong rider. The horse looked difficult but he sure could jump, so we brought him home.

Paul Schockemöhle then sent us down to southern Germany to look at some horses formally ridden by Hartwig Steenken. Hartwig was the reigning World Champion (Hickstead 1974) jumper rider who had been in a terrible car accident in July of 1977. He was still alive but in a coma with little hope for recovery, so three of his horses were up for sale in Mannheim. François drove us down there at about 230 kilometers per hour—literally well over 125 miles per hour on the Autobahn. It was terrifying! I stopped driving with some of those guys after fearing for my life enough times. Of the three horses, two were unremarkable, but the third was a small, 16-hand, dark brown Thoroughbred type with a beautiful, scopey jump. The only thing was that he slapped the verticals on the way up, which was odd because he would make your mouth water with his Olympic-sized scope over the oxers. I told Armand, "I really like this horse, but I can't ask your father to pay $125,000 for a horse that slaps every vertical out of the cups." I told them we had to pass.

That horse we passed on was Deister, destined to become an iconic championship jumper in the hands of Paul Schockemöhle. With me, Deister never would've been as great as he was with Paul. He was very hot and not the most careful horse, but made into a champion with Paul's excellent riding and management. Eventually, after the European shopping expedition, we bought the beautiful chestnut mare of Dianne Grod's that we'd seen in California. We called her Encore and she and Armand were superstars together.

Paul Schockemöhle

In the beginning, Deister was very difficult. I myself had to learn how to ride him. And he had to learn how to jump. He always had scope, but he was so quick in his mind that he often had a fence down. He was super honest and had the desire to learn; he was a fighter, too, all of which eventually led to his success. I decided I simply couldn't sell him.

I was eight years younger than my brother Alwin, and I tried to start a business very young to earn money because the family inheritance was to go to my brother as the eldest son. I was even in the chicken business before the horse business! I would see George at the shows along with my brother when we were all very young men. I admired the entire American team led by Bert de Némethy and everyone was very interested in the Americans' style of riding. There was always a big fight between the Europeans and the Americans. Bert's best pupil was George Morris who was a fantastic competitor. I saw him riding many times. George was one of the first to introduce the European sport horse to American riders.

In America they had fantastic Thoroughbred and Standardbred breeding, and when Americans first came to Europe to do show jumping, the whole American team rode only Thoroughbreds. They were all different kinds of Thoroughbreds, and they were very successful. The European sport horses are a result of breeding for jumping and rideability, versus the Thoroughbred horses being bred for speed. In my opinion, the American jumping style was a direct result of those Thoroughbred horses. In order to ride them, you need a lot of feeling and lightness. These skills in riding helped American riders succeed on European horses as well with a sensitive light feel. Even today, if you're watching unfamiliar riders at a show, you can usually tell just from watching them ride whether they are American or European.

After we passed on buying Deister, it was quite late and a very cold, stormy evening. François Mathy had hired a private plane to fly us back to Brussels. I was in favor of avoiding the three-hour drive, but when we arrived at the airport and I saw the pilot cracking ice and pushing snow off the wings of the small plane, I got a little nervous. Bob Penney sat up with the pilot, who was an older German guy. François was sitting next to Kathy Moore (of course he was, to better flirt with her, as she was quite a dish!), and Armand and I were in the back seat together. We took off into the storm and it was very rough going, with terrible, icy snow and wind conditions. After a while, I heard something change with the sound of the motor, a shift in the rumble of it, and then I really started to worry.

That night I learned that pilots around the world all speak in English on the radio. My ears picked up the English as our pilot radioed to Frankfurt, saying we were ten miles out. To my horror, I heard air traffic control respond in kind, "Do you think you can make it?" Not good. Not good at all. Armand, normally a stoic young man, had sweat pouring down his face next to me. Ahead of us, François figured this was the time to go for broke and made his move on Kathy. I couldn't see Bob up in the front seat, but I was sure he was freaking out because he was a cautious-minded type like me. The bumps and dips continued during our descent but the pilot somehow managed to land the plane. We climbed out, exhausted and weak-kneed from the stress. I could see that the wings were completely iced over and felt lucky to be on solid ground. It was late and we were all hungry, so we went into the small terminal and sat down to eat sandwiches and the pilot joined us. As it turned out, our pilot had been in the Luftwaffe, the air force branch of the German Wehrmacht during World War II. He told me, "Even if we had no engines at all, I know how to do it! I crash landed three times in the war and it was fine." Lucky for us, if there was any pilot to have in that situation, he was our man.

I had a fabulous time riding in the jumper ring again that year, not to mention seeing old friends and establishing new European contacts. Armand Leone swept France, winning several Grand Prix, and was the talk of the circuit. That French tour really got me thinking about shifting my focus back on the jumpers. Hunterdon had a great staff to keep things running, giving me more time to ride—and to be perfectly honest, I was losing a little interest in the equitation and hunter divisions.

VIII. ERROR IN JUDGMENT

In the early sixties, horse tranquilizers came into the sport for the very first time with the appearance of acepromezine. Reserpine (Serpasil) came into play in the late 1970s. Since then, the horse show world has been associated with such drugs used to quiet horses in the show ring. Personally, my love of classical riding deterred me from using drugs, and I felt it was better to avoid using them. I was never the first or the biggest user of drugs. I like bute and Banamine and Azium (dexamethasone) as options for occasional use when it's called for.

I don't remember horses going lame very often in the early days; accidents and injuries happened, of course, but you didn't see the prevalence of tendon and joint injuries that are so commonplace now. In addition, with the emphasis on pace, the judges didn't care about a horse being fresh and playing in the hunters or the equitation. It wasn't until the technical side of horse showing evolved and precision became such a primary focus that things changed. With perfection the ultimate goal, it was impossible to take a horse that was too fresh into the ring and be successful. At first, we relied on schooling and longeing horses to work the freshness out of them, but the level of competitiveness around precision emerged with such a vengeance in the seventies that tranquilizers became a trend at the highest levels.

Susie Hutchison

There was a time when acepromezine was legal and was sparingly used as a tool to quiet hotter horses in the show ring in a way that didn't endanger a horse's health. A horse that was fourteen or fifteen, for example, who started out a bit fresh but was too old to go on a longe line for thirty minutes every morning, would give an older amateur adult rider a lovely ride around the ring on a little bit of ace. As a result, that older horse was healthier and experienced more longevity as a show horse. Often in those days, if a horse was for sale, the seller would communicate openly that it showed best on one cc of ace. However, as with any drug substance, there will always be people who misuse or overuse it—and misuse is indeed a risk to a horse's health. In some cases, unfortunately, the banning of one safer type of drug will lead to the use of other, more dangerous drugs—drugs that are far less regulated and about which much less is known as regards to their safety.

In the late seventies, reserpine became popular and it wasn't a drug that was detectable with a test. I started to be able to identify its use when observing a horse, because he went differently—he purred in the way he breathed and had a wooden look, with a stiff tail that was held out a bit. If you were horse show savvy, you could see the signs, but it was nothing a judge could criticize. I like to work horses and longe them a little bit to get them quiet and focused, so I had no desire to use reserpine at first. Admittedly however, when the competition was halting at X and standing like a statue, trotting a jump quietly in the middle of a course, and never shaking its head or playing, trying reserpine on one particular horse for the very first time was a temptation hard to resist. There's a lot of pressure to be successful as a trainer and when you know others are getting an edge like that, there's a natural desire to take action and level the playing field. It's easy to be drawn into a trend for the sake of pleasing clients and staying sharp at shows.

After the incident with Bonnie Castle's foundering, I had never used any drug containing dexamethasone to quiet a horse—the possibility of another adverse reaction was simply too much risk. I had many hot Thoroughbreds showing who never received a single tranquilizer. But I did fall into the use of reserpine for a short time. Until a drug is officially banned and a test is developed to enforce the rule, it will be used by some if it's effective. As with any sport, the regulation and testing is always behind the use of a new drug and there's a period of time when it needs to catch up.

One day, I got a heads-up from a good friend that a test had been developed for reserpine by the AHSA. I presumed it would be several weeks before the test would be sprung on competitors at a show, but to be careful, I administered it to a few horses a week prior to the next show. I figured that if I gave a horse a little on Monday, it would be out of his system by the show over the weekend. Well, I was very careless. At a little weekend show in Massachusetts to get points for

Devon, they tested one of our iconic, wonderful hunters and the test came back positive. I was truly caught red-handed, and I wasn't the only one; many other professionals around the country who used reserpine were caught that week.

For me on a personal level, it was an awful thing to face suspension by the United States Equestrian Federation as a respected horseman, especially given that I was a member of the AHSA Drugs and Medication Committee. At the time I feared it would permanently stain my life and career. As I got older and was in the business over the decades, I learned that these things happen to horse trainers, even ones at the top of the sport. If you keep your chin up and continue to be successful, eventually those rare infractions are forgotten.

The Federation suspended other riders just three weeks before the World Championships in Aachen, which absolutely pulled the rug out from under our United States Show Jumping Team's chance. Thankfully, upon my request the Federation allowed me to postpone my suspension until after the French tour we had planned. However, I traded the postponement for a longer suspension period in the fall, and I was forced to miss all of the indoor shows in 1978. It was all deserved, but looking back I wish they had let the others' suspensions fall after the World Championships so that our team could have had a better shot at a gold medal. Other countries might have done it for the good of the national team, but on the other hand, the actions by the USEF showed the world that the United States had high standards.

Despite the loss, Michael Matz rode brilliantly with Jet Run at the World Championships and won an individual bronze medal. Conrad Homfeld, Buddy Brown, and Dennis Murphy joined Michael in winning the Team bronze medal, which was a great result. I was there to watch and Bert de Némethy was so nervous when Michael made it to the final round of four that he approached me and asked, "George, do you have a 'little yellow one'?" And by that, he meant Valium! I said "Yes Bert, I have one," and gave it to him. As the ride-off proceeded, he was so wound up that he came back and said, "George, I need another one!" Two little yellow ones!

Seeing Conrad represent the country alongside Buddy was a wonderful experience for me, especially since I'd helped develop them both in their junior years. The year 1978 was actually the last time I ever had Conrad as a pupil when he came to Hunterdon for five days to school horses with me. Conrad was a light rider and once in a while he needed a hand in reestablishing his more aggressive aids—he called it his "whipping lesson"!

After getting back from the European tour, I sat down and took my reserpine suspension during the indoor circuit. All the riders rode with Kathy,

Melanie, and Katie under a different stable name because of my suspension, and that meant all the tack trunks and show set-up pieces had to be re-painted. I taught clinics while Kathy kept me updated from Harrisburg, Washington, and New York on how things were going. I won't deny that it felt devastating at the time to miss it, but those girls were perfectly capable and the clients supportive, so we didn't miss a beat.

Kathy Moore

In the spirit of Charlie's Angels, which was at the height of its popularity then, Roger Young affectionately dubbed us girls (Katie, Melanie, and me) "George's Angels." The moniker stuck with us for the next four weeks while we tried to pretend everything was normal in the absence of both George and Bill. George, in his brilliance, had divided up all the riders and assigned them between the three of us. Once we fumbled a little at Harrisburg, we were humbled, got even more serious, and delivered after that. We practically won every ribbon and championship at Washington and the Garden, including the Maclay Finals.

Everyone knew Kathy's riders were from Hunterdon, but there was a lot of sympathy for her managing the entire operation by herself and it was a great solution to keep things moving. After losing to Elizabeth Sheehan the year before, Hugh Mutch won the Medal in 1978; he was very much a chip off the old block and a very talented rider like his father Ronnie (photo 130). His mother Patti Paterno was also a top horsewoman from Westchester County, daughter of the Master of Hounds at Golden's Bridge. Another top junior Steve Weiss was second to Hugh Mutch at Harrisburg. Hunterdon horses won a number of hunter championships at all of the indoor shows. Michael Sasso, a boy from Delaware (whose mother was from the Du Pont family) had bought Dillon, who had since his cold-backed rogue years become a champion hunter. That fall while I was suspended, Michael and Dillon were 1978 Maclay Finals champions (photo 131).

Hunterdon buzzed with top hunters, equitation, and Grand Prix jumpers. By the time we rang in 1979 in Florida, everyone in the horse community was off the hook for reserpine-related infractions, and it was good to get back to business. An amateur named Gayle Everhart from Sanford, Florida, started riding with me. I had about forty acres at Hunterdon and there was a sixty-acre property bordering ours. Tom Everhart, Gayle's ambitious father, decided to build a property right next door for Gayle. It was more of a show barn than mine. They called it Emeralda and we rented some stalls from them to give us more space. We had thirty stalls at our barn and there were twenty-five more next door at the Everharts' place. Gayle watched a show at Aachen, and she and her father had their eyes on the Olympics, but they never made it quite that far. She was a lovely girl and had great success in the hunters and low jumpers.

A few years later, once the bloom was off the rose, they wanted to move on and sell Emeralda. Tom told me, "George, it would be a shame to see another professional right next to you up on this hill," and he was right! It would have been a sexy property for some other professional, and I wouldn't have liked someone else moving into a newer facility than mine right next door. Although it stretched me financially and may not have been the wisest move, I purchased Emeralda and Hunterdon grew to a dead even 100 acres. The place became even more beautiful. With fifty-five stalls, a fifteen-acre Grand Prix field, and extensive turnout, horses loved it up there. It had a special magic about it. Horses took a deep breath and got fat at Hunterdon.

I didn't organize a tour to Europe in '79, but I went to the European Championships in Rotterdam where I saw Paul Schockemöhle earn a silver medal on his wily and talented horse Deister. I also looked at some jumper prospects, taught some clinics and saw friends. Gerhard Etter from Switzerland, another important friend I came to know then, became a big horse dealer in Europe and collaborated with me on buying horses many times in years to come.

I had taught clinics in various countries, including Switzerland. Those had begun one year in the late '70s when the Swiss team was showing at Madison Square Garden, and they had a young rider named Thomas Fuchs on the team. Thomas and I became friends and while at the Garden, he was having trouble with a big gray jumper that was a little chicken jumping through the combinations. If Thomas legged him in the combinations, he would get too quick and flat, but without the leg, he lost confidence. I suggested, "Thomas, how about you just try a little cluck?" It worked! A well-timed cluck gave the horse confidence but kept him from getting too quick and having a rail. The cluck is a good riding aid when used correctly. The collaboration at the Garden led to an invitation from Thomas Fuchs to teach clinics in Switzerland, which I began in '79 and continued two or three times a year through the 1980s.

Thomas Fuchs

Once I was competing at the Garden in New York, and I trained a bit with George and took some lessons before the jumper classes. He had taught me to cluck my tongue if I got deep to a fence. The whole Swiss team hadn't got a placing for the entire week thus far. Then in Table C class, I had a fault at a triple bar because I got too deep. Afterward, I came out to the grandstand and George was sitting with Melanie Smith. I sat down next to Melanie, and on the other side of her George leaned over and said, "Jesus Christ, Thomas! Why didn't you cluck your tongue?" and I said, "Listen, because I got so drunk yesterday, my mouth was so dry I *couldn't* cluck my tongue!" Melanie leaned back and shrunk down in her seat, preparing for the worst, but even George had to laugh. When George left to go help the next student, Melanie admitted no one there would ever dare tell George something like that!

At one of the early clinics in Switzerland, they stopped it because they had discovered I didn't have a teacher's certificate. In Switzerland, even then, you had to be a licensed teacher to teach riding. We had a big discussion about it, and people were panicking and running around frantically. In the end, we got it figured out—I think they wrote up some interim license on a piece of paper. After teaching for twenty-five years, it was my first time being stopped about a license! I also taught a lot of clinics to Belgian riders during the eighties and nineties. On both the Swiss and Belgian Olympic Teams, you can still see the stamp of my style on the riders as it has filtered down to the younger generations.

While I was abroad, my then seventy-six-year-old mother called me from her home in Delray Beach, Florida, and she complained of bad back pain. Still hopelessly devoted to her (and the only person who could ever tell her what to do), I told her she needed to swim, stretch, and get more exercise. A week or two later, I called her to ask how she was and the pain hadn't lessened. Soon after, she was diagnosed with late-stage lung cancer—a devastating blow. A product of the 1920s generation, my mother had been a heavy smoker and drinker for most of her life.

Frank Madden

It was a totally different era then—the sport has changed so much in the last forty years. In the seventies and early eighties it was quite an acceptable thing for alcohol to be around more in the sport. As time went on, George began to rely more and more on his staff, and it gave me an opportunity to be involved with his coaching at the major horse shows. We were at the Devon Horse Show and it was a Thursday evening, which was the night of the traditional Grand Prix. It was pretty much a mandatory thing that at five every day, somebody would get George either a

Heineken or a red wine. That was industry standard back then. On that particular night, one or two Heinekens turned into more than his standard allotment before the Grand Prix. George certainly wasn't drunk, but he was a little loose! I was helping him get Melanie Smith and Leslie Burr warmed up for the Grand Prix. We were in the Gold Ring schooling them over some fences before the class and George was having them finish over a very airy gate that had been left in the ring from the day's earlier classes. Well, George wanted to put the gate up a little higher and the standards didn't have holes for the cups that went higher, so we took the ends of the gate out of the cups and rested them on the tip-top of the standard posts themselves. George said to them, "OK, come gallop down to this," and Melanie turned and called out to George, "I'm not jumping that—you're drunk!"

In 1979, the Pan American Games were in Puerto Rico and Melanie Smith rode a French horse we'd bought for her named Val de la Loire. The horse had come in second in the Grand Prix of Aachen in 1977 with Luis Álvarez de Cervera. When Melanie first bought him, he had the odd stop in him, and she tried to ride him the way his European riders had. Val de la Loire would drag her past the distance because he was used to a stronger, male rider, and I told her that she wasn't going to be successful just adapting to his style, she would need to find a way to make him go for *her*. She spent a lot of time doing flat-work and schooling and it worked! When they started showing again, he was listening and being more patient to the jumps; they started winning everything. Val was Horse of the Year in 1978 and Melanie was Rider of the Year and Lady Rider of the Year.

After the third round of the Pan Am Games, Melanie was eight or twelve faults ahead in the individual scoring and Mrs. Smith and Melanie's owners, Mr. and Mrs. Neil Eustace, planned a celebration before it was all said and done. I'm still not certain why, but Bert de Némethy forbade me to ride Val de la Loire in the mornings in Puerto Rico, which I had always done before to keep him electric to the leg, since he was a cold European type. Perhaps they jinxed Melanie with that early celebration, but after she was the shoo-in they had a bad stop at a simple vertical and she was thrown off. In those days you could get back on after a fall and she ended up fifth. Still, it was a disappointing slide for Melanie and we were fortunate the team still came out on top. Michael Matz won the gold on Jet Run and the team won gold as well, with Buddy Brown on Sandsablaze and Norman Dello Joio on Allegro rounding it out.

Mark, the youngest of the three Leone brothers, won the Medal Finals at Harrisburg on Bridegroom and was third in the Maclay. While his older brothers had a stronger work ethic, Mark was the youngest and the most naturally talented of the three. Mark and I had a system where I would ride and set up his horses and would literally put him on the horse at the in-gate and send him into the ring. He was better with no warm-up at all. It's interesting what works for different students. Mark had to put in his work just like all my kids, but at the shows he was brilliant riding cold.

I was also helping Roger and Judy Young's son Gary in the equitation. The Youngs often sent me horses from the Genesee Valley, New York, when I was starting out in the fifties, in partnership with Otto Heuckeroth. A very solid rider with a fabulous foundation, Gary won the Maclay Finals that year, which was extra special because I knew his parents so well. Gary has been in the horse business his whole life and we're still good friends (photo 132).

That autumn, I flew back and forth from the indoor shows to Delray Beach to visit my mother during her treatment for lung cancer. After the show at Madison Square Garden came to a close, I taught a clinic in the Bahamas, then raced back to see my mother who by then was in an assisted-living facility with an oxygen tank as her constant companion. Sitting with my mother, I remember her telling me she wished she could come and watch me teach. But the reality was that she was simply not strong enough.

My clinic tour marched onward that fall. Teaching in Kansas City with Todd Karn assisting me and acting as a demonstration rider, my phone rang during the lunch break on Sunday. It was my father calling to tell me that my mother had died. As expected as the news may have been with her terminal illness, it still struck me with such force that I floundered emotionally. Like the day my father dropped me off at University of Virginia, I didn't think I was going to make it through the rest of the clinic. Somehow I pulled myself together and taught the afternoon session. When the last session ended, I had a complete meltdown. My mother and I were so close and so much alike; it felt like I lost a part of me when she died.

My next clinic was in California. I decided in the spirit of carrying on in the face of hardship, as I had been taught growing up, I had to keep moving forward despite my sorrow. Actually, I decided to take it a step further and went wild partying with J.J. Smith. Deep down it was a very sad time for me, but my reaction to adversity has always been to take the bit in my teeth and rush forward into distraction. When I need to escape from something difficult, I find solace in moving forward instead of standing still. I flew back to Florida the night before the funeral service. At the service, the minister looked at me in my sunglasses and said, "People with dark glasses have something to hide." I'll never forget him saying that, it startled me. I think he smelled a bad actor!

After my mother passed away, I began to have strange spells of illness that would come and go, lasting a day or two. On a Saturday during some of my clinics, I would have pain in my chest and be convinced I was having a heart attack. All night I would lie awake, staring at the ceiling in the darkness, with a dreadful feeling that death was staring me in the face. These awful spells would come and go for many years, but it seemed to mostly occur the Saturday of a clinic. The episodes were completely unpredictable; while something small would trigger them some days, other days I would fly all night on overseas flights and be under intense stress and feel completely fine. Not many people knew I was having any problems; Kathy Moore was one of the only ones I shared it with. No doctor ever had a definitive answer for me, but eventually, I was diagnosed with a mitral valve prolapse by doctors at the Mayo Clinic. From that time on, I had a way of immediately reaching the Mayo Clinic if there was an emergency. Thankfully the attacks have dissipated over time, but like my vocal issues, they plagued me for years.

After buying the little speed horse Vivaldi and reestablishing a friendship with Harry Gilhuys, I got a tip on another horse through Harry. Melanie Smith's owner Neil Eustace was over in Europe buying antiques. He called me while I was giving a teacher's clinic in Louisville, Kentucky, at Nina Bonnie's farm; Melanie happened to be demonstrating for me at the clinic. Harry approached Neil in Holland and told him about a horse he thought might work for Melanie. The horse was a five-year-old and by Lucky Boy, who was a Thoroughbred stallion with a great record of producing jumpers. Neil isn't exactly an expert horseman, but he looked at the horse in his stall, loved his cute pony face, and immediately wanted to buy him. I advised Melanie to hop on a plane to go try the horse before Neil made a big mistake, which she did. Well, it turned out she loved him even more than Neil! He was a little bit of a pony type and about 15.3 hands with a light jump and a nice quality about him. His name was Calypso.

I liked Calypso. He was careful at the jumps and light off the ground, but I had a few reservations. He was a horse in a pony's body and a little bit loose in front when we schooled him at home. Melanie, with her typical genius, worked to develop his front end by training him over a lot of gymnastics. Once he settled into an effective style, his front end was always tight. We headed to the Florida circuit and discovered that Calypso was a ring horse: he woke up and jumped fantastically at the shows! He was careful, fast, and could turn on a dime. Melanie rode him wonderfully; she has a way of holding a horse together in front. You could see that Calypso was a winner; with his big heart he wanted to win as badly as Melanie. In my opinion, much more significantly than Vivaldi before him, Calypso's notoriety opened the floodgates to the desire for top European horses. He had such a wonderful look to him and everyone recognized him and saw his greatness. That one horse turned on the whole of North America!

Jeremy, who was also my silent business partner for many years, was drawn back into the arts and music in the city, and he eased out of life at Hunterdon. Although our partnership ended, it was amicable and we continued to be friends and share our rented apartment on West Twelfth Street. We were still very friendly and there was no longer a business relationship, which relieved some of the issues we'd faced. In the early eighties, after sharing the apartment for a few more years with Jeremy, the owner of the building offered us $76,000 to let him take the entire apartment and all its contents, and I agreed. It seemed like a great deal at the time, reimbursing all the rent I'd ever spent on it plus all the furnishings. Now, of course, that apartment is worth ten or twenty times that amount!

I still made time for city life and nightlife and my typical haunts were either in Greenwich Village or on the Upper East Side. At a watering hole on Christopher Street called Ty's, I bumped into a gregarious, athletic, outgoing guy named Mark Frederick. I liked him immediately because he had an infectious energy and was a high-class drifter type of guy. He was a little bit like Bob Smith in his adventurous personality. We had a great time together. The next day, we went together to get his car, which turned out to be a complete wreck that, against all conceivable odds from its appearance, was still driveable. He followed me out to Hunterdon where I convinced him to dump the car at the junkyard nearby.

Kathy Moore told me later that when Mark Frederick walked into Hunterdon that day, her red flags went up and alarm bells rang. At the time, though, I was hooked on him! When we went to Florida that year, he came along and we rented a house in Wellington. A group of us all lived together—Kathy, Mark, Jeff Cook, and me. Jeff Cook, still today one of my closest friends, came out to teach and work at Hunterdon as a young professional after growing up riding in the Pacific Northwest. Not surprisingly, Mark was a complete distraction in Florida. He'd try to drag me out in Palm Beach to party and would cruise up and down the turnpike looking for trouble. Restless and dying to be on the move, Mark constantly tried to talk me into road trips and crazy adventures. At the horse shows, he was an unhealthy distraction for me and others. Thankfully, regardless of Mark's influence, the show circuit went well for Hunterdon.

IX. THE WORLD CUP FINALS BEGIN

Jan Tops

George is one of the most dedicated horsemen that exist. He has worldwide respect as a great trainer because he produced many top riders. George has a real passion for the sport, which is one of the reasons why he is so successful. He was himself a very competitive and successful rider and fortunately he has passed on his knowledge to many riders all over the world. I'm sure that I can say that almost every rider has learned something from George—that, in itself, says a lot about a great horseman.

The year 1979 marked the first ever World Cup Finals in Gothenburg, Sweden, and the course was huge but simple, in the older style of European courses. We had a great group of riders and horses for the team, including Katie Monahan on The Jones Boy, Melanie Smith on Calypso, and Norman Dello Joio on Allegro. Unusually private for stabling at an international event, our horses were housed in a separate barn above the warm-up ring for quarantine purposes. There was only one door in and out of the big open aisle with the attached warm-up ring. Kathy Moore stood by the door in her mink coat, smoking cigarettes and serving as our lookout while we warmed up each day.

I didn't have any responsibility for coaching, but The Jones Boy was my horse, and I was there supporting the team. During the show, I was almost completely missing in action due to the influence of Mark Frederick, but I showed up just in time to see our trips into the ring. We went out in groups and explored the night life, staying out in Gothenburg all night. Jerry Baker, who Michael Matz first worked for, ran the tour for the American team. He hired a young Swedish man as our taxi driver to take us from bar to bar all night long in his taxi. We made that poor guy wait for us outside each bar, and by the end of the night, Jerry owed the driver $300 (and he never even got what he was hoping for)! We had such a wild time there. One night I got in a fistfight with a Russian guy, and the next night we thawed the Cold War with the same hot Russian! It was all in the name of foreign diplomacy....

In the show ring, the American team took Europe by storm at the first World Cup. Katie was second in the first leg, first in the last leg, and ended up tied in points with Hugo Simon riding Gladstone for Austria. Katie had jumped off late in the order on The Jones Boy in that final leg to tie it up with Hugo, and then immediately had to jump-off again against Hugo for the tie-breaker. It was so much to ask of The Jones Boy because he was tired and still recovering from the first jump-off. They were so close, but Katie had one rail down and they were second to Hugo and Gladstone, another terrific horse. Norman Dello Joio tied for third and the others on the team were also in the top ten. This fabulous finish for the Americans was a huge feather in our caps for the first World Cup.

The Mark Frederick era was one time when my personal life certainly impacted my professional life. In fact, I had come to realize on that World Cup Final trip that Mark's impact was not exactly positive, despite the fun we had. On the way home, we stopped in Copenhagen, and I decided it was time to create some space between us. I convinced him to fly to London without me to explore the city, in order to take advantage of being in Europe. I bought him a ticket and saw him off, telling him we'd catch up back home. He stayed in London for a few weeks and afterward we grew apart. I saw Mark from time to time in the years to come, but I managed to keep him at arm's length from then on. I think it probably saved me! He would've driven me to my death, or at least to a life committed to debauchery.

Jerry Baker had plans to leave Gothenburg with the horses at three in the morning following the end of the World Cup Finals. The Jones Boy had jumped off twice and was exhausted; in my gut I felt it was a bad choice to leave that quickly. Air travel is stressful on horses and they were already very tired and stressed, in particular my horse. Jerry was an experienced horseman and it was his choice, so I didn't say anything. As it turned out, my instinct was right. After we got home it was clear The Jones Boy had a touch of shipping fever. About three weeks later, I was teaching a clinic with Gordon Wright in Nashville, Tennessee. The great veteran USET horseman Tommy Veile called me and said The Jones Boy had a fat hock. It was odd that he would bother me with such a minor issue so I told him to quit bothering me and just cold hose the hock. That night, our regular vet Pete Bousum called me to say that The Jones Boy's head was swelling up right in front of his eyes.

The Jones Boy had contracted, as a secondary infection from the shipping fever, *purpura hemorrhagica*, a very serious illness that causes painful swelling from inflammation of the blood vessels. A horse's legs become tender and sore because circulation is impaired. Horses that develop this condition are either infected with strangles and progress to the *purpura* stage or were previously exposed to the strangles virus without developing an infection, but later fall vulnerable to it. We were all stricken about The Jones Boy being so ill. Not only was he incredibly talented and well-loved by Katie Monahan, but he was extremely valuable. As the hottest new face in show jumping, one of the biggest European horse owners of the time had offered a half-million dollars for him.

I sent The Jones Boy to the University of Pennsylvania for treatment. Danny Marks and Matthew Mackay-Smith at the Delaware Equine Center cared for him through the terrible infection and recovery for nearly two years. With round-the-clock nursing, he had to have extensive plastic surgery to repair blood vessels. His recovery became a famous case study for the treatment of *purpura hemorrhagica*. The Delaware Equine Center, Danny Marks, and Matthew Mackay-Smith had groundbreaking treatments for windy horses with breathing issues and also for founder.

Daniel Marks, DVM

I think The Jones Boy was the best horse George ever owned. A very talented Thoroughbred jumper, who as a relatively green horse, and fortunately ridden by Katie Monahan, was individual second in the World Cup jumping finals in Sweden. When returning home, he developed a life-threatening immune disease called *purpura hemorrhagica*. Without very committed and expensive treatment, The Jones Boy would have died. George could have collected on the insurance policy, but instead he elected to try to save "Jonesy." This required extensive skin grafting of his hind legs where large amounts of skin died and fell off. He lived at our clinic for almost a year. During one stage of healing, at the suggestion of a consulting human plastic surgeon, we bandaged him with human placenta that his groom, Tommy Veile, picked up each morning from the local hospital. Months later, as The Jones Boy was almost ready to go back to George, I did some easy flatwork on him to start getting his strength back up. There was a small jump set up, maybe two-feet-six-inches high, and on a whim I cantered down to it. He exploded! He burst the breastplate and felt like he jumped seven feet in the air, with me hanging on for dear life! The Jones Boy was a wonderful horse, and I was proud to have helped save him. But even though he won his first Grand Prix with Katie after his recovery, he was never quite as good as before. He changed in other ways. Prior to getting sick, he was not that interested in people; he was not antagonistic, just indifferent. During his treatment, he became quite affectionate and liked people; this continued.

The 1970s were a golden decade in the horse world. A crossroads where old and new horsemanship congealed, it was an absolutely wonderful time to be a horseman. We experienced the best of both worlds: the classic tradition of the old days was alive and well while at the same time, the technical aspects of riding that had been so new in the sixties had become accepted and expected. We were still galloping big fences on beautiful, outside courses but advanced concepts like striding, related distances, flatwork, and position had raised the level of complexity. Madison Square Garden and the indoor circuit were in full bloom and the Florida circuit had gained traction, but the old traditional summer shows had maintained their fanfare, guts, and glamour.

A ship in many ports as a professional horseman throughout the 1960s, I sunk my anchor in the seventies and established a permanent base of operations for the very first time. Purchasing Hunterdon was a big transition from the nomadic previous years of freelancing. My life hadn't been anchored to a home base since I lived in New Canaan, and Hunterdon was my own business with my own property. While I had great success in the sixties with the equitation, establishing Hunterdon solidified that success in a totally new way. My team at Hunterdon crafted a powerhouse stable across the hunter, jumper, and equitation divisions. The purity of the training methods at Hunterdon turned young horses into champions again and again. I so rarely bought made, known horses in those years, and there was a wonderful satisfaction in manufacturing legendary show horses with traditional, patient horsemanship. Evolving further, we produced Grand Prix level riders like Buddy Brown, Katie Monahan, Melanie Smith, Leslie Burr, Norman Dello Joio, and the Leone brothers. Molding those riders into international superstars simply wouldn't have been possible without having Hunterdon as a base. The 1970s truly were the pinnacle of American horsemanship and set the stage for the United States show jumping domination in the eighties at the top levels.

Despite the fact that the decade was still a free-wheeling, wild era of party-ing, those years marked my first long-term, live-in relationship: my partnership with Jeremy Wind. We were together for the entire decade, and his style and taste were stamped on Hunterdon as a business. With Jeremy comfortable mix-ing with the horse show social scene, I found my professional and personal lives coexisting harmoniously. The New Jersey and New Hope, Pennsylvania, horse community's close ties with the avant-garde, artsy city lifestyle felt seamless, and I felt personally fulfilled because of it. Life in the horse show scene was full of style and class. We were young and full of energy and passion. It was the best of all worlds.

122. *Francie Steinwedell, 1976 AHSA Hunt Seat Medal Finals Champion, displaying her beautiful style and elegance.*

123. *Collette Lozins made it happen on Sandman, ASPCA Maclay Finals Champion, 1976.*

124. *The Leone brothers in the 1980s.* © Dr. Armand Leone

125. *Buddy Brown, 1973 AHSA Medal Champion, schooling over cavalletti with Bert de Némethy in Gladstone.*

126. *Coaching Melanie Smith.*

127. *Katie Monahan and The Jones Boy at Lake Placid, 1977.*   © Budd

128. *Elizabeth Sheehan, 1977 AHSA Hunt Seat Medal Finals Champion, on her Medal horse Night Club in Chagrin Falls, Ohio.*
Courtesy of Elizabeth Sheehan

129. *Our first private European tour (run out of Hunterdon) in 1978: with Armand Leone, Betsie Bolger, Debbie Malloy.*

130. *Ronnie Mutch (left) and his son Hugh, a chip off the ol' block.* © *Budd*

131. *Michael Sasso and Dillon, 1978 ASPCA Maclay Finals Champions.* © *Budd*

132. *Gary Young and Ivory Coast, 1979 Maclay Finals Champions.*

133. *It's always good horsemanship to experience other disciplines first hand, as I am here, working cattle at my childhood friend Glenna Maduro de Rham's ranch in Montana.*

134. *With Patrick Guerrand-Hermès, sponsor of the Junior World Championship, and Chrystine Jones Tauber.*

135. *With Joan Scharffenberger, who had guts and style on any horse.*

136. *Riding Fortuna, a lovely mare, at Varsity Stadium in Toronto, Canada.* © Mark Rein

137. *With the late, great Bill Cooney.*

138. *J. Michael Halbleib—the quickest study I ever taught.*

139. *Melanie Smith and Calypso beating them all at the World Cup in Gothenburg, 1982.* © *Findlay Davidson*

140. Planting a kiss on the first woman to win the World Cup Finals, 1982.

141. Coaching Lisa Jacquin in France with Kathy Moore.

142. *Nations Cup, 1982: with Anne Kursinski, Donald Cheska, Norman Dello Joio, and Melanie Smith.*

143. *Norman Dello Joio accepting congratulations from Prince Philip at the 1983 World Cup Finals.* Courtesy of Max Ammann/The Volvo World Cup

144. *Anne Kursinski, Pan American Games gold medalist, sharing the podium with Michael Matz and Jimmy Elder, 1983.*

145. *Winning the Wellington Grand Prix on Brussels, one of my favorite horses ever, in 1983.*

Courtesy of Pennington Galleries Archive Collection/PenningtonGalleries.com

146. *Chatting with Robert Hoskins, with Joanne Woodward looking on. Clea, Joanne's daughter with Paul Newman, was a student of mine. Robert, who grew up in Tennessee with Melanie Smith, was a very successful Long Island trainer in the seventies and eighties.*

147. *Paul Newman with Clea at Madison Square Garden.*

148. Coaching with Frank Madden and Bill Cooney.

149. Rio, the most complicated horse, hot and sensitive, needed quality flatwork every morning and a sophisticated ride.

150. *My father, Harry, died suddenly in 1984.*

151. *Joe Fargis and Touch of Class at the 1984 Olympic Games in Los Angeles.*   © *Tish Quirk*

152. *Conrad Homfeld and Abdullah at the 1984 Olympic Games.* © *Tish Quirk*

153. *Melanie Smith Taylor and Calypso at the 1984 Olympic Games.* © *Tish Quirk*

154. *Leslie Burr Howard and Albany at the 1984 Olympic Games.* © *Tish Quirk*

155. *The gold medal team in 1984 was the best United States Show Jumping Olympic Team we ever fielded: Joe, Leslie, Conrad, Melanie.* © *Tish Quirk*

156. *Gordon Wright out in the hunt field in the 1980s, still surrounded by admiring women, riding with impeccable positions.*

157. *Melanie Smith and Calypso.*

CHAPTER FIVE: THE 1980s

JUMPER RENAISSANCE

I. A RENEWED FOCUS

In 1980 I was coming off an immensely successful decade in which Hunterdon built a national reputation for producing winners in hunters, equitation, and jumpers. Our riders under the Hunterdon banner had, for several years, taken home the majority of Top Ten ribbons at both the AHSA Medal and the ASPCA Maclay Finals. Despite all that success, I wasn't sure I wanted to be an equitation specialist anymore. My recent experiences in Europe and the advancement of a number of my students to the Grand Prix had refocused my attention on international show jumping.

In the early eighties, a high-profile junior came onto the East Coast scene. She was Jimmy Williams's professional-level junior rider. The girl could ride the good ones, the bad ones, and everything in between! She had her own look in the saddle, with a parallel foot (not toe out) and a soft back from riding a lot of green horses, but her style reeked of elegance. She was an equitation winner, in addition to being a winner in the hunters and jumpers. Her name was Anne Kursinski.

Kathy Kusner moved out to Los Angeles in the seventies and she befriended Anne, becoming a mentor. They were both independent, strong women and just clicked. In those days, everyone wanted to ride with Bert de Némethy at Gladstone with the USET. If you were serious and had potential, the USET was the ultimate goal and for those talented riders on the West Coast, coming East was a smart move because it increased your visibility. Anne had seen Francie Steinwedell and Kathy Moore move East and up the ante, and she followed suit. I had gotten to know Anne on my visits to teach and judge out West, and we discovered the two of us even had some distant ancestry in common. She contacted me in 1981, and I welcomed her at Hunterdon. She didn't even bring a horse with her—just her saddle, boots, and hat, ready to ride anything!

Anne Kursinski

I always had childhood dreams of going to the Olympics someday, but I didn't talk about it much because when I was young, you didn't see riders from California on the USET. I had a little voice inside nudging me to just go for it. Kathy was the bridge between Jimmy Williams and George; it was tough for us to leave Jimmy—we were all like one big family. But I had to try riding on the international stage and Hunterdon was definitely the place to go. With George's encouragement, along with influence from Melanie Smith, Bill Steinkraus, Kathy Kusner, and Kathy Moore, I made it.

At the beginning, I briefly stabled in the upper barn at Hunterdon, then afterward, I rented stalls in the lower barn. In those years, I rode with George day in and day out, schooling with him and watching him ride and teach some of his best students like Melanie and Conrad Homfeld. He always said he never wanted to take away the great base that Jimmy Williams had given me but that he would add on to that base, and that's just what happened. All I did back in California was ride, ride, ride! With Jimmy I learned to ride anything—good, bad, stopper, leg-hanger. Jimmy and George had similarities in philosophies and also differences—both had a military kind of style—but George added a more practical, disciplined focus to my riding when it came to top horses. The way George and Kathy Moore created a formula with diet, nutrition, care, and working with the vet and farrier all combined was so good, I still use it for managing horses.

When I got great ribbons in World Cup qualifiers with Third Man that first summer on the East Coast, I knew riding at that level was what I wanted to do with my life. George also found Livius and we just clicked. Everything fell into place when a wonderful group of contacts back in California together bought Livius for me to ride. It was a great way to stay connected with the West Coast.

Not long after, I found myself on a team at the Pan American Games winning a double gold medal, and at the Olympic Games the very next year. Horsemanship and what it took to have an Olympic level horse was George's passion and it was contagious! George had vision and made it all happen; he took us all with him. It was an amazing time. George helped you figure out how to be your absolute best. For him, there is no other way to be in life.

Tom Everhart had sold me his Hunterdon-adjacent property and taken his daughter Gayle to Rodney Jenkins. Tom and Gayle had bought a big, gray, hot Thoroughbred Grand Prix prospect named Third Man. The horse had a hard drift to the jumps, which led to a bad fall for Rodney, so he sent him to Conrad and Joe down at their stable in Petersburg, Virginia. Conrad, who has a quiet riding style like Rodney, felt similarly mismatched with Third Man and he called me to see what ideas I might have about what to do with him. Apparently, the horse had sat on some oxers and wrecked some jumps down in Virginia, too. Anne needed projects so I suggested she take on Third Man. Everhart's new barn had become the Hunterdon "lower barn" and Anne stabled there independently with her own grooms. I never once gave Anne a lesson, but we rode together as colleagues and schooled together for eighteen years. I was a mentor to her at times and with similar classical riding backgrounds, we coexisted wonderfully for many years.

Impressively, Anne rode the socks off Third Man! She wasn't afraid to drive him with her stick and spurs, and she gave him his confidence back. He was scopey, careful, and brave when Anne rode him and together, they were very successful. In her first year being based on the East Coast, Third Man put Anne on the map. His Grand Prix career was unfortunately cut short from an infection he contracted from some minor splinters during a Puissance class in Toronto, but he had a great run with Anne in the saddle.

Bonnie Jenkins

After riding for many years, I went to Hunterdon to ride with George in 1977 and just driving into the driveway was an experience. Every pebble was in its place and each blade of grass was perfectly mowed. The barn was impeccable. Every detail was perfect—the place was a gorgeous place to ride. It exuded class and set the standard for everything George represents. If you're going to do it, do it right, and pay attention to details. At the end of the day, it's all basics. Nothing is difficult to understand, but if you pay attention and work hard, you will succeed! I rode with George for my last two junior years and they were totally transformational and life-changing for me. I had a lot of success and certainly owe that to the experience of riding with George. He teaches mental and physical toughness along with the horsemanship.

George matched me up with one of the best hunters this country has ever seen—a horse named Gozzi. I have no idea to this day why he chose me; we were looking to buy a horse and maybe it was just good timing. I remember trying Gozzi early one morning at the Washington International Horse Show. Just getting on his back was incredible; I loved him instantly. The price was astronomical and my family did well but weren't in the league of many in the sport. George told my father what the horse cost and said, "It's a foolish price, Mr. Blake—a foolish price!" So my dad told him he'd think about it. A couple of days later, he called George and said, "Well, George, I'm going to be foolish," and George replied, "It's fun to be foolish, Mr. Blake." My last junior year riding that horse was in 1978. It put my name on the map and we had a fabulous year.

In terms of my professional career, that success mattered. I started working for the American Horse Shows Association after college and worked my way up there. I can attribute much of my success to the work ethic I learned from George. You didn't have to be the smartest one in the room, but you had to want to be the hardest-working and make goals. I never would have thought I would be the Executive Director of the USET Foundation, but here I am. I was a good rider, but I was probably never going to be good enough to ride on the United States Team internationally. Instead, I had a chance to be part of the team in a different way.

The second-ever World Cup Finals were held in Baltimore, Maryland. The World Cup was still very new and exciting because it brought the Americans and the Europeans together once a year for a showdown. Bert de Némethy built marvelous but very difficult courses in the indoor stadium. The course was so technical that riders and coaches stood on the rail many hours before the start of a class, analyzing the course, and developing a strategy. Bert built a big water jump and a pair of Liverpools—no one had ever seen that indoors before. In many ways, it felt like an indoor Olympics and, as it turned out, it was a preview of coming attractions. The organizers used a very difficult scoring system (which has since been revised), and at the end of the Final round, nobody in the stands was certain who had won. Everyone waited and when they announced Conrad Homfeld and Balbuco had come out on top—the crowd erupted! The Americans put on a hell of a show and our success reaffirmed how our technical proficiency had edged us ahead of the Europeans.

My tradition of teaching clinics out West in December had long since been established, but I added an annual clinic at the stable of my old friend and assistant Karen Healey. At the clinic that year at the Will Rogers Park in Los Angeles, Hans Günter Winkler stopped by to watch since he was visiting friends with his wife Astrid. Karen had a little girl riding that year who was about eleven years old and had learned to ride at the Foxfield Riding School. I remember the girl's mother kept their horse at home and they trailered in for the clinic. Karen was really excited about the little girl's talent and focus—and that was the first time I met and taught Meredith Michaels.

Joan Laarakkers

I grew up in California, at first riding Western on my pony—I used to jump him bareback because I didn't have an English saddle. When my mother realized I was pretty serious about wanting to jump and ride "English," she sent me to my first trainer, Judy Martin, who helped me find a more suitable jumping horse. I started riding competitively at age seven in California and did my first clinic with George when I was twelve. It was so amazing—I'll never forget it! He was so hard on me but the last day asked how old I was and complimented me on my perseverance. From that day on I dreamed of riding with George but knew that I would need a lot more experience before I would be ready. The logistics of moving my horses all the way to New Jersey and switching schools wasn't easy, and convincing my father was another barrier. Now, being a mother myself, I look back on this time and realize how amazing my mother was in orchestrating this huge step in my life. I lived in a small motel the first year, riding at first with Judy Richter for six months who mentally prepared me for showing on the East Coast. Finally, with two junior years left, I was ready for George and moved on to Hunterdon. I rode a young jumper named Classified I bought from Judy Richter and her sister Carol Thompson. With my father convinced that the USET— and the Olympics—was the only worthy goal in horse showing, we sold my hunter and concentrated on finding a suitable equitation horse, one that could help me win the Finals. The horse was called Constant Comment, a chestnut with lots of white and an amazing trot that caught the judge's eye the moment I entered the ring. He wasn't easy to ride and didn't like other people to ride him, which worked well for changing horses in Medal class work-offs.

I was trained mainly by George and Kathy for the jumpers and Frank and Bill for the equitation and hunters. It was definitely a team effort! I look back on my idyllic days spent at Hunterdon galloping around that enormous grass field set on a hill. It was the greatest place on earth— heaven for horses. I doubled up on classes in high school my junior year and was able to graduate a semester early, enabling me to spend long days at Hunterdon and extra days at the shows, including staying in Florida without any commute. I helped ride and even show some of the other juniors' horses while they were back home in school. I was Circuit Champion and Champion Junior Jumper at Devon in 1980 and because of my catch rides on all these wonderful hunters and my wins on Classified, I was best child rider at the Devon and Ox Ridge Hunt Club horse shows.

In the summer of 1980, George took a junior team to France comprised of top junior jumper riders around the country. We started at the international show in Biarritz, then went on to the junior world championships in Saumur sponsored by the Hermès family. George arranged for me to ride Silver Exchange, who was then for sale and already in Europe with Katie Monahan. We had an unbelievable time on the tour; it was so eye-opening for us. We were served wine at lunchtime and Hermès made some calls and got a disco opened up for all of us on Monday night. We danced with the French team boys and our tag line from the trip became, "More wine!" Of course, the other teams didn't have to wake up early and have team meetings and schooling sessions at dawn like we did. When we got back to the States and went to the equitation Finals, it was hard to get our heads in the game—the jumper classes in Europe really felt like the "big time" in comparison. This new perspective actually helped me win the Medal Finals at Harrisburg that fall because I realized the equitation was not an end in itself, but a means to becoming a world-class show jumping rider.

Along with several other countries and athletes from around the world, the United States boycotted the Moscow Olympics in 1980 because of the Soviet invasion of Afghanistan. The designated substitute Olympics for show jumping was in Rotterdam, Holland. Bert de Némethy took the U.S. Team, but I didn't attend because I was occupied with teaching Hunterdon clients. The team that year was Melanie Smith on Calypso, Terry Rudd on Semi Tough, Norman Dello Joio on Allegro, and Katie Monahan on Silver Exchange. The Canadian team won the gold medal in a traditional Nations Cup format in Rotterdam, although their medal isn't officially recognized.

Even though I didn't make it over to Rotterdam, I did take a young-rider team to the European Junior Nations Cup in France, which was a great experience. The team was Louis Jacobs, Joan Scharffenberger (later: Laarakkers), Cara Forstmann (later: Anthony), Lisa Jacquin, and Chrissy Bushkin. Cara was the youngest of the group and didn't have the same mileage as the others but she'd just come on board with guts and a great horse. Lisa had a wonderful horse called Four Corners that I owned, and Joan rode Silver Exchange after the Bolgers sold him to the Scharffenbergers. Cara had a wonderful little chestnut Appendix Quarter Horse named Johnny Rotten. It was a very good junior team and they did very well, cutting a swath through France! Louis Jacobs was the only one who hadn't ridden with me before, but he rode with Geoff Teall who came along as an assistant trainer. At the time it was unusual for riders on a tour to bring their own trainers (unlike today!) but Geoff has always been one of my disciples and a wonderful horseman, so it was great to have him along.

Continuing with Hunterdon's success in the equitation, Joan Scharffenberger won the Medal Finals in 1980 under my banner. She was another one of those beautiful, brave riders who went on from the equitation to ride in the jumpers (photo 135).

Cara Anthony

One of my favorite memories of riding with George was participating in the Junior Nations Cup class in France. I grew up in Idaho and was sixteen years old, and it was incredible for me to be showing in Europe. Fourteen countries had junior teams representing them, and we all stayed together in dormitories, which added so much to the experience. Now, when you go to international Young Rider competitions everyone stays in hotels and there isn't the same social setting. Junior teams from Russia were hardly ever seen riding outside of the country during the Cold War, so it was interesting that the Russian team had shown up to ride there, too.

George ran the team as Chef d'Equipe. He prepared us and gave us coaching and got us to the ring. Kathy Moore organized the tour and made sure we were all where we needed to be and were ready to ride. In Biarritz, they had this crazy bank where you had to run up to a five-foot drop, gallop two strides, then jump back up onto the bank and run off. We never saw those kinds of things in the junior classes at home, but I loved them and just went for it! I had done crazy things back in Idaho, like get on my horse in the middle of the night and jump from pasture to pasture with the full moon reflecting off the snow. I had no fear. I think that's why I did well in France over those crazy bank jumps. I was sixth, which was the highest placing American rider in the Junior Nations Cup class.

I remember standing next to George one day listening as he was talking to the Portuguese Chef d'Equipe. At one point I piped in with some brazen sixteen-year-old comment, like, "That bank jump wasn't that hard!" I was clearly talking out of turn. George stopped and turned, slowly, looking at me. He pointed at the ground, at a speck of dirt, and said, "You see that? That's you." And he put the toe of his boot down on it and twisted, stamping it down like he was putting out a cigarette. "You know *nothing*." Stunned, I just stood there, frozen. I was incensed at first and felt I hadn't deserved what I'd got. But that moment stuck with me;

I learned a very important lesson. George was listening very carefully to that Chef d'Equipe from Portugal for any piece of information that might be helpful to our team and I interrupted. From that moment on, I knew what it was to be a good student. A good student doesn't talk; she listens. I will say this about George: he was very clear about what was expected of us and told us when we did something wrong. Teenagers need that level of clarity sometimes for a lesson to sink in. There were so many others: don't take short cuts, work ethic is everything, and if nothing else, be gutsy. My children grew up learning those same lessons, and they're having successful beginnings to their riding careers, as well.

The Americans continued to show they could dominate on non–American soil when Michael Matz won the 1981 World Cup on Jet Run in Birmingham, England. Donald Cheska was second on Southside at the young age of twenty-one and our riders earned multiple other ribbons. One standout memory from Birmingham for me was going out at night with the Austrian rider Thomas Frühmann, who really knew how to party. We drank until five in the morning and he ate his champagne glasses when they were empty. I personally chose not to eat my glasses, but otherwise I kept up with him!

Being back in Europe meant the opportunity for connections to be made once again. I began teaching clinics in England, and one of my best early British students was Robert Hoekstra, who much later became the very successful and popular Chef d'Equipe of the English team. The European Championships, which followed the World Cup later in the year, resulted in two fabulous opportunities with quality horses. Emile Hendricks from Holland was fourth on a lovely chestnut gelding called Livius and I loved him. I called Fran Steinwedell who was part of a group from Flintridge Riding Club supporting Anne Kursinski, and Anne immediately flew over to try Livius. The group from Flintridge all together bought Livius for Anne to ride. That helped bring Jimmy Williams and me closer together—we had Anne in common and both wanted to see her be successful.

Johan Heins had a difficult Selle Français stallion named Noren that I had tried at his farm earlier that year when Johan was having a hard time with Noren's mouth and asked me to ride him. I could feel the horse didn't adhere well to the deep seat and low hand of the German/Dutch system, being a French horse and used to a lighter ride. When we arrived at the European Championships that year, I had Katie Monahan try him, and the European riders stood around the ring watching. She rode completely differently—with her heels down, light in the saddle, and hands carried high—and the horse responded wonderfully. Noren jumped out of his skin, but the audience still snickered at the way she rode.

That would happen all the time to American riders in those days—we'd hear comments and see the looks from the Europeans when we schooled our horses. Naturally, both curious and biased feelings contributed because there were philosophical and methodological differences between our backgrounds. One thing was certain after Katie's schooling session: Noren had an amazing jump and I wanted nothing more than to snatch him up for the American team. We bought him and Katie dominated the jumpers with him in the following years. Noren earned the Horse of the Year title in 1983, and our ability to spot great talent in European horses was really starting to pay off.

Ludo Philippaerts

In the beginning, I met George through his student Jean-Claude Van Geenberghe. I learned so much from George about exercises to do with the horse and the importance of position for the basic things. At the big competitions when George was there it was always wonderful to learn from him. We've had a wonderful friendship now for many years. He is a super horseman and a very nice person. Even my children have ridden in clinics with George, and he is always welcome at my place to teach as often as he comes to Europe. He's a workaholic! I have such an appreciation for him and the work he has done in the United States and in Europe, with so many riders.

After being invited to teach some clinics in Switzerland and France, I met a girl named Catherine Bonnafous at a stable outside of Paris. Michel Pelissier, who bred Selle Français horses, produced a tremendously talented seven-year-old jumper named I Love You that Catherine rode in the clinic. A super jumper, I Love You was for sale but Catherine told me she would only sell him to an American, and not to a European, because she admired the American work ethic and their lighter style of riding. As a rule, the French are very emotional about their horses and consider them part of the family! I Love You was a horse worthy of a top rider on the USET, and I immediately thought of Norman Dello Joio, my former student who worked for George Lindemann and his family. I also knew the Lindemanns had the resources to buy I Love You, who was priced at 4.5 million francs (around a half-a-million dollars), an enormous sum for a horse in the early eighties. The pieces came together and they bought the horse for Norman, creating an historic partnership.

I found myself drawn deeper and deeper into the jumpers, drifting away from the hunters and equitation. Bill Cooney and Frank Madden kept their focus on that side of the business, which kept things moving at a high standard. That winter, Joan Scharffenberger came down with mononucleosis and couldn't come to Florida, so I showed her wonderful Dutch jumper Natal, who was a big, scopey, straightforward ride. When I rode him in the big division, I realized I could really ride at that level again! After thinking for so long that I'd never be back in a position to ride in the big classes, it was exciting to find myself there and great fun. For the first time in two decades, I started buying jumper prospects for myself instead of just for my clients. I picked up a couple of green jumper entries named Maxim and Fortuna (photo 136).

On a horse-scouting trip with the British rider Timmy Grubb in Europe, I bought Brussels, a hot, gray, seven-year-old mare from an old European line of sport horses. Very few people really would have wanted to ride her; she took a lot of horse sense. Brussels was virtually untrainable and to ride her, you had to be the kind of horseman who knew when *not* to train. A terribly precocious horse, there were times you simply went along for the ride, but she was beautiful and brilliant to the jumps. I showed Brussels first in Ohio in a Schooling Jumper class and while I interfered with her as little as possible, she never looked right or left. A few weeks later, she showed bravery and boldness over a bank, grob, and ditch in Mason Phelps's Speed Derby in Newport, Rhode Island, and we were fifth. The mare was so locked in that I rode her in the Intermediate Jumpers at Harrisburg that first year, which was incredible for such a green horse. Brussels was like Sinjon—she was never really green!

I had by then spent about $300,000 on The Jones Boy's treatment and recovery—which today would be about a million dollars. He came back to Hunterdon and we steadily brought him back to work, but he never had the same ability. On pure heart and against all the odds, he won the Grand Prix of Tampa in 1982 with Katie Monahan aboard and it was his last big win. Even with that, it took too much out of him, and I realized we should never have tried to get him to jump at that level after his illness. I did bring him back after we'd spent a lot of time reconditioning his legs and fitness later that year. The horse started to look so strong that I couldn't resist showing him a little myself. Although I had hoped he might return to his old form, he was never as sharp as he was at that very first World Cup in '79. I showed him at Harrisburg in the Open Jumpers over very big courses and although he tried gamely, I could feel the strain it placed upon him. After that, we eased up and didn't push him anymore. He lived at Hunterdon as a happy, retired horse for many years.

In 1981, judging at Jimmy Williams' Flintridge Show in La Cañada, California, I saw my old friend J.J. Smith and a young man from Texas working for J.J. named J. Michael Halbleib. Michael and I became good friends and totally hit it off. He'd never ridden English or jumped before, so while I was out West, Jimmy Williams let me borrow a school horse and I gave Michael a couple of lessons. After two or three lessons, I had Michael in a good position jumping low fences on the outside course at Flintridge. Like Jeremy Wind, Michael had an incredible eye from the instant he began jumping and innately knew where he was at the jumps. However, unlike Jeremy, Michael wanted nothing more than to immerse himself in a life with horses. I loved Michael's ambition and took him with me on my clinic tour, where he borrowed horses along the way to ride in the two-foot-six group. As a total beginner to jumping, I really threw him in the deep end, but before no time he was becoming a successful Grand Prix rider. Michael had the most accelerated riding education that I've ever witnessed (photo 138).

J. Michael Halbleib

To this day, I can't believe it myself. I actually lived it, but I wonder sometimes if it really happened. I was lucky to have someone like George Morris in my life. I grew up without a father and George taught me a great work ethic and about interpersonal skills. He's one of the tough disciplinarians in our sport, but he simply has a way of carrying himself that cannot be denied. I studied psychology in college, but working with George was like getting a master's degree. The thing about George is that his education is available for anyone who shows an interest. He'll allow you, through osmosis, to see his work ethic and witness the results. He always says talent was last on his list as important qualities for success.

I decided to move to Hunterdon to work and learn to ride in the winter of 1982, after getting to know George and Kathy Moore and taking a few lessons from them in California. It's true that I developed fast. I'd ridden before but had never sat in an English saddle. By that following season, I was showing in the Amateur Owner Hunter Division and we won Circuit Champion in West Palm Beach, Champion Amateur Owner Hunter at Devon, Grand Champion at The Hampton Classic, and Grand Champion at Old Salem Farm. It was an incredible experience and George helped to guide my career. I went on to ride in the Grand Prix for more than ten years.

The World Cup Finals that spring of 1982 were back in Gothenburg, Sweden. Melanie Smith was riding Calypso and I went to train and support her. A couple of German riders stonewalled us in the warm-up area, holding court at the only jump in the ring to keep Melanie and Calypso from being able to school before their round. Little did they know that "Lyps" didn't need schooling! He only needed one fence—and a good thing, too, because that's all we had time for. Melanie rode brilliantly and won, beating them all on little Calypso; I was thrilled! Paul Schockcmöhle and Hugo Simon were second and third but they couldn't catch Melanie and Calypso. That pair had a great run for a few years. Clearly, he was one of the greatest horses I ever had and Melanie rode him fabulously (photo 139).

Melanie Smith Taylor

George is brilliant at teaching his students the importance of long-term vision when it comes to preparing horses for Championships and Olympic Games. That is one of the most important things I learned from him: how to plan and prepare for your biggest goals. If I had to get back in the ring today, I would want George by my side. He's such a confidence-builder! I went out on my own and rode for other people, doing my own schooling and preparation, but George met me at the big shows. He was always there when it counted—for the big events—and I always rode better for it.

George taught me so very much that it is hard to say what was most significant. On the flat, he stressed the importance of riding from leg to hand. His flatwork is exceptional and I loved when he rode my horses and showed me things. We had a great system through the years. George would often ride my Grand Prix horses the morning before a big class and then I would win that afternoon. It was the carrot and the stick—George was the bad guy getting my horse more responsive to the aids, and I became the good guy able to navigate huge courses with ease.

George taught me two both technical and positional elements that stand out as critical to my success as a jumper rider. The first was the "give in the elbow" to follow the horse and easily find your distance. You can't have a soft hand without a soft arm. The second thing was how to use my back. Having strong legs and arms was all about how you used your seat and back as an auxiliary aid.

I remember George teaching me another great lesson with a Grand Prix horse, Radnor II, that I showed in the mid-seventies. Radnor was an ex-steeplechase horse that had trouble with flying changes, at first.

George used to yell out, "Melanie, you have to get his flap up," which meant to get after him and get him excited, so he'd be up in front of my leg. He'd say, "If you get his flap up, he'll relax through understanding what you want from him." I always remembered that. With a hot horse, you have to leg him through the excitement until you get what you want— then, through understanding, the horse will relax into it. But that is hard to do when he is already running away with you!

With Katie Monahan and me, George didn't try to change our style on a horse. He would make little adjustments to riders, but he didn't try to put everyone into a mold or force everyone into the same position. George makes riders stronger and softer, which sounds like a contradiction but it's true! He gives them what I call "soft strength." He teaches a classical foundation on the flat with clever and appropriate schooling exercises to prepare you and your horses for any challenge. More than anything, George knows how to win the biggest championships. He knows how to prepare horses and riders, how to pick the best team, and how to back off and taper at the right time. So many people make the mistake of overtuning and overpreparing a horse. There's no one I'd rather have by my side for a big championship because George always had that tremendous sense of what it takes to *win*.

II. WINNING WAYS

I n early 1982, I went to Europe to teach a few clinics and J. Michael Halbleib came along with me. My lifestyle was still primarily working, but on Sunday nights I routinely went out to a watering hole and got a little wild. I wasn't an alcoholic, but I did have a drink or two in the evenings and had those big Sunday nights where I occasionally drank to excess. I had learned early in the seventies that if I drank the night before a horse show, I didn't ride or see the jumps as well. When I started having success in the hunters, I made sure I didn't drink the night before. But when there wasn't a show and I had a night off, I really let loose. After my hard-working lifestyle with the responsibility of such a big business, having a night out was a major tension release for me. But when I drank, I was always on the muscle and on the prowl.

One night out in Paris with Michael, I was really in one of my wild moods and there wasn't a leash that could hold me. Apparently Michael had had enough of my drinking, because after witnessing my antics that night, he told me in the caring way only a close friend can that he thought I should stop drinking. Deep down I knew it wasn't a healthy lifestyle and with that one conversation, I didn't drink a drop for fourteen years. I have a very strong tendency to get obsessive and habitual about things I'm focused on at any given time, whether it is drilling horses and going to the gym, or less healthy pursuits like drinking and partying. I refocused the energy back onto horses, my riding, and getting into better shape through running.

I have, throughout my career, preached to my students about the importance of taking care of one's physical self. I work out regularly and have felt the great effects of such a regimen for decades. Staying healthy, lean, and fit not only makes you a stronger rider, but it's a sign of discipline and shows others that you respect yourself. Through the years, I've on occasion been tough on young riders who are overweight, but it's often a sign of issues with self-discipline. Of course, people can't help the shape they're born with, but I'm talking about what they can control. My comment about weight to a rider is no different from getting after riders about their position or their work ethic when they're in a clinic. People don't ride with me to be told everything they're doing is right! I'm honest and forthright about what might be holding riders back from reaching their potential, and my goal is to convince every individual to work harder and challenge themselves. Criticism from me has always intended to serve the same sort of influence as Michael's advice to me about my drinking that evening in Paris. It often takes a kick in the pants to lead to positive change.

Holly Hugo-Vidal, Victor's wife, called one day to tell me that Joel Bloch had died. Joel Bloch was an acquaintance of mine and both J.J. Smith and Victor knew him very well. After being sick for months, Joel had gone into the hospital in June of '82 and died days later of an unusually bad pneumonia. This was the first death I heard about that was eventually attributed to the AIDS virus. Nobody at the time had even heard of AIDS, but in the following months, people began to talk in hushed voices about a terrifying, mysterious disease.

That September, I went to visit Seattle to see my great friend and horseman Dr. Bob Penney. Our friendship was totally platonic but we'd always just been two peas in a pod. That fall we were planning to look at a couple of nice horses he'd found. Bob was always up for a night on the town together and would say to me, "George, let's go out and swing our tits!" But Bob shook his head and kept going to bed early every night, claiming he was too tired to go out. That was really not like Bob and I was instantly concerned. A couple of months later, he held his marvelous annual horseman's seminar in Yakama, Washington, with all the top vets in attendance, so I went out to see Bob again. It was clear that he wasn't well, and I knew in my gut it must be the awful mystery gay plague. Somehow, the following autumn he managed to bring some young horses up to Calgary but he was terribly sick. In his poor condition, I don't know how he did it—I'm sure it was his strength of character that kept him working, but he only hung on for a short time. Bob passed away before the Los Angeles Olympic Games and he was my first close friend to die of AIDS. Bob Penney was a true horseman and a man of class and character. I still miss my friend.

Native Surf was a Model Conformation Hunter in his first year; I'd bought him from Tommy Serio in Pennsylvania (a wonderful horseman now in Virginia who always had quality horses). He sadly popped a splint in his second year near the end of the Florida circuit. At Syracuse in April, Arty Hawkins was judging and he spotted the splint and penalized him in the Model. Knowing it would continue to hurt his chances at the shows, I had a vet take the splint off, but as a result of the operation Native Surf completely lost his four-foot scope. He was limited over three-foot-nine and could only solidly show at three-foot-six after the procedure. As with many horses' career paths, his job evolved and he became a beautiful equitation horse. In fact, Olympic medalist Peter Wylde won the Maclay Finals on Native Surf in 1982. Peter's trainers were Fran and Joe Dotoli; Fran was a student of Gordon Wright's, so you can see how so many quality riders originate from different branches on the same tree. Peter rides the forward seat just as it should be ridden, and he does it beautifully.

Leading up to that year's World Championships in Dublin, Ireland, American riders rode in a number of shows on a European tour. Although Bert was the figurehead Chef d'Equipe for the tour, he brought me in to be, in essence, the working Chef of that tour. I schooled my students Melanie Smith and Peter Leone. I also became very close to Chrystine Jones on that tour (she helped keep everything organized) and we've been fast friends ever since. Chrystine rode with Bert on the USET in the 1960s after I left the team and today, she's President of the United States Equestrian Federation. A wonderful leader in all equestrian sports, Chrystine has ferried the USEF through many years of issues and evolution.

Chrystine Tauber

In the sixties, the USET was known for its style of riding. It was world-renowned, and that was partially to do with our equitation division in the United States and also because of Bert de Némethy and George Morris.

What I observed over the next couple of decades, as George was teaching so many young riders in the hunters and equitation, was that the level of style was raised on a global scale. George started giving clinics all over the world, and it triggered a tremendous change in how people rode. George instilled form and technique in young riders who then applied it at the highest levels when riding big Olympic courses. You can definitely see which riders came out of his school just from their technique. Due to changes in course design through the years (with technical lines, flat jump cups, and lighter rails), the horses best suited to show jumping have evolved. The forward seat, American jumping style has proved very successful with those types of horses, just as it was originally with our homegrown Thoroughbreds.

One thing we used to laugh about was that if you survived a schooling session at Hunterdon, the horse show would be a piece of cake! I remember riding in the field at Hunterdon and George was teaching from a golf cart at the top of the hill with a megaphone. There was a triple combination at the bottom of the field, and the horse I was riding slammed on the brakes at the first jump, a plank fence with a metal strapping along the top. I flipped over the horse's head and landed on my back and ribs. I crumpled into a little pile on the ground, but managed to keep a hold of the reins. I laid there trying to breathe, having knocked the wind out of myself. From the megaphone comes George's voice, "Chrystine, you have two choices, my dear. You can either get back on and jump it or we call an ambulance! Which one is it?" So I got back on and I jumped through it, then later I went to the hospital for the hairline fractures in my ribs. That's the kind of grit he instilled in us as riders.

Many years later, I had a horse stabled with George that we were trying to sell for a client, and I was schooling him in the warm-up ring at the Old Salem Horse Show before a jumper class. I turned away early from an approach to a big oxer because the horse was sulky and behind my leg. Well, George started screaming at me in front of everyone, "Don't you ever do that with me! If you're going to do that, you can go ride with someone else!" I just kept riding, circled and jumped the jump, and rode in the class. Later, back at the barn, George said, "Oh Chrystine, do you think I was too tough on you?" I laughed and said, "George, if I thought you were being too tough on me I would've told you."

His point was valid. If you always take the easy way out and make a circle instead of fighting for it and making the distance work, you'll never learn how to fight your way through anything. If you end up with a missed distance or a messy rail down, you and the horse will learn from it.

You don't get to wimp out and circle. You have to make it work. And what a great life lesson: do not bail out when times get tough. George makes a lasting impression on you, even in a moment as simple as that. When he is hard on a student, he's trying to teach a lesson that will stick for a lifetime. He helps riders banish that little needle of doubt that creeps in and makes them hesitate. You can't be great without learning to be bold and always keep riding. He eliminates any doubt and his riders have 100 percent belief in making it happen. When you watch any great athletes, they have that in common and they make great things happen.

At the first show of the tour in '82, Joe Fargis broke his leg in a fall off Second Balcony at the first jump at Hickstead. The injury was a heartbreaker for Joe, but our American team had depth and took it in stride. We had a long list of riders with great horses: Bernie Traurig, Michael Matz, Conrad Homfeld, Leslie Burr, Melanie Smith, Peter Leone, Anne Kursinski, and Donald Cheska. The team chosen by Bert for the World Championships consisted of Peter on Ardennes, Melanie on Calypso, Michael on Jet Run, and Bernie on Eaden Vale.

Melanie Smith rode wonderfully in Dublin! Europe took home the top spots on the podium but the United States was fourth, so we were hot on their heels. By the time we got to Paris to a show at Longchamps on the racetrack, the team was on fire. Melanie and Calypso won the Grand Prix and Peter Leone proclaimed, "If we win the Nations Cup, I'm taking everybody to Tour d'Argent!" which at the time was the highest profile, most expensive restaurant in Paris. Well, the team won the Nations Cup and he had to make good on his promise! He almost choked to death when he saw the bill. There must have been over twenty people at that dinner and for what he paid, he could've bought a new horse.

That year marked Bert de Némethy's last year as Chef d'Equipe of the United States Show Jumping Team after almost thirty years. I considered that I might be next in line for the job since I had assisted Bert in Europe at the shows leading up to the World Championships that year. However, when Frank Chapot expressed interest I knew it made sense for him to take Bert's place. After all, Frank had ridden and worked with Bert for decades. The type of shared arrangement I had with Bert on the tour in '82 continued to some extent when Frank took the lead, which worked well given each of us had a business to run at home. In the following years, if Frank couldn't be present at a show here or there, he asked me to stand in as acting Chef d'Equipe. I was quite willing to step in and complement his leadership whenever I could.

In fact, when all was said and done, I served in some kind of Chef d'Equipe-type of capacity on international tours on and off from 1977 until 2012.

Pancho Lopez left to join Katie Monahan's business that year, but my guardian angel Julian Arechiga arrived afterwards to take on the fabulous care of Hunterdon. Julian single-handedly ran Hunterdon by working twenty-five hours a day, eight days a week. On many mornings, by six-thirty he had all the stalls mucked and the horses given hay. When the staff arrived, all they had to do was feed and sweep the aisles to start the day. Julian is *still* at Hunterdon today. Words can't express how important Julian was to my business and how much respect I have for him as a friend.

Julian Arechiga

I was working at a farm in California and my brother Robert was working at Hunterdon. Pancho asked me to come East, too, and join my brother because a groundskeeper was needed at Hunterdon. I left my family in California and moved to New Jersey. When I first arrived, George was in Europe and Pancho helped get me started. On one of those early days, I was out mowing in one of the fields and a tall man walked up to me and asked, "Who are you?" and I explained who I was and that I was Robert's brother. He asked me, "Who told you to cut this grass without consulting with me first?" and I replied, "Well, I decided to cut it. It was too long and needed to be cut." He said, "Since you've already begun, that's okay. Next time, I'm going to instruct you exactly how I want it, because it needs to be a certain length in inches and this isn't right, the way you're cutting it. We'll work on it for next time." George would look at the grass at different angles and tell me exactly how he wanted it. He was very particular. I was the groundskeeper at Hunterdon beginning in 1979—I still am today.

I would travel to the horse shows with George, too, set up the barn aisle, and set jumps for George. I had the honor of seeing George teach and also Anne Kursinski and Chris Kappler ride and train, and it was a wonderful experience to be part of that. I watched the history of the sport ride by me while I was standing there waiting for the moments when we put the jumps up, or back down, or move them.

Of all the bosses I have ever had, on a professional level, I have the highest regard for George. He would give me instruction on what he wanted and was very specific and detail-oriented, but once he trusted me, he never looked over my shoulder. He left me alone and presumed I would get the work done the right way—and his way. I think he and I are similar in that we're both perfectionists and straight shooters. We had an understanding: I knew what he wanted and he trusted me without reservations.

Our trust grew through the years and as it grew, our friendship grew. He would come over and my wife would cook for him because he loved Mexican food. Our family was the only family on the farm with children, and they grew up with George coming over for dinner whenever he had the opportunity and around the holidays. He would tell us stories of his travels, competitions, and comical encounters. It was a great time of fun and laughter. George would treat my children like he was their uncle and would offer them advice and bring them little gifts. My daughter Eujenia remembers as a young girl peeking into the indoor arena to watch George teach, and she would giggle when he yelled at his students for not following his instructions.

I slipped on ice about ten years ago and bad headaches afterward led to the discovery that I had a hematoma in my brain. I was rushed to the hospital, and they found I had a blood clot and needed surgery. Even though he was traveling and always busy, George checked on me every day and ensured I was receiving the best care. He was even more present than some of my own family. George will always be considered part of my family and a very dear, close friend.

The United States Equestrian Team had become a show-jumping powerhouse. We won the World Cup Finals for the fourth year in a row in 1983 when Norman Dello Joio beat the whole field riding I Love You. The following year he nearly won again but ended up second, and it showed American riders consistently succeeding against the world. Norman, if nothing else, is living evidence that hard work and dedication can make you a champion (photo 143).

Norman Dello Joio

I remember very clearly the early morning following the Maclay Finals at Madison Square Garden when I was a junior. I had a very good round but was called back rather low and in the end finished out of the Top Ten. I didn't have a lot of name recognition and had been working with George and trailering in for lessons for only a short while. I was quite disappointed in the result and perhaps a bit discouraged. George called me around seven the morning after what was an exhausting and very long and stressful show for him. I was surprised to hear from him and he proceeded to explain how little or of no importance that event would have in what was to become my career. He had really encouraging and motivating things to say that were normally rarely said by trainers back then—or even today. From that day, I never looked back and have always tried to keep my eye on the big picture for both myself and my students.

That moment defines the relationship George and I have had over the last forty years. Our friendship has been filled with a great deal of advice, honesty, and intelligent discussion, as we are both by nature keen students of the art of riding.

Anne Kursinski became the first female rider to win the Grand Prix of Rome and then at the 1983 Pan American Games in Caracas, Venezuela, she won the individual gold medal on her lovely gelding Livius and Michael Matz won the bronze medal on Chef. Then, the American team put the icing on the cake by winning the team gold medal, with Leslie Burr and Donald Cheska rounding out our fabulous team. It was a wonderful Pan Am Games for the Americans (photo 144).

By the end of the year, I felt comfortable riding the big courses again, which set the stage for easing out of the hunters and equitation. My jumper Brussels, who I owned in partnership with a friend and famous horseman in Holland, Daan Nanning, had matured into a very strong intermediate jumper after the Florida circuit. I decided to try her in the two Sunday Grand Prix classes at Lake Placid. In the first Grand Prix, Brussels was fabulous and only had one cheap fence down. The second week, she went clean and was second to Melanie Smith and Calypso in the jump-off! After the incredible finish at Lake Placid, we won the Cleveland Grand Prix and the Wellington Grand Prix at the old show grounds. Brussels really catapulted me back into the big division. I was hooked (photo 145).

Realizing what a special horse I had in Brussels, I was determined to be very cautious with her. With the ability she was demonstrating, she was getting more and more valuable. After Lake Placid, I bumped into my old friend Hugh Wiley at the Chagrin Valley, Ohio, horse show, and he told me he had an investor named Clyde Pitchford, Jr. who was part of The Rex Group. Together, he and Clyde wanted to invest in Grand Prix jumpers. It was perfect timing—to get things started, The Rex Group asked me to buy out Daan Nanning for his half of Brussels, so that they in turn could buy her from me as an investment. I sent Daan a check for $55,000 which, at the time was quite a sizable amount for half a horse! The Rex Group bought Brussels from me afterward and in a way, it was a relief to have her off my hands. As much as I loved the mare, once a horse becomes that successful—and, in turn, that valuable—the risk is that much greater. I had turned a decent profit in bringing her along and could still ride her myself, but now the risk was in the hands of a bigger player.

III. ADVENTURES IN HORSE SHOPPING

After selling Brussels, the money was burning a hole in my pocket. I was foaming at the mouth to find another jumper prospect as a backup for Grand Prix classes. I looked at a few horses with Gerhard Etter near Geneva, Switzerland. Afterward, Gerhard took me on a very long journey to see another horse he'd gotten a tip on. We drove for hundreds of miles across Switzerland, boarded a ferry to cross Lake Constance, and then drove hundreds of miles across Germany to the Czechoslovakian border, east of Munich. After traveling ten hours, we finally arrived.

The farm we had driven that enormous distance to reach was owned by the lovely family of Rupert Möll. Rare for Germany (where they seldom turn out horses), the horse we'd gone to see was in a stall with a run-out paddock, reminiscent of the family barns in New Canaan. I looked in the stall at the horse and immediately fell in love with him. The bay gelding was a son of the Bavarian stallion Rasso, who was by the famous jumper stallion Ramiro. Like an American Thoroughbred, he was tall and lean, with fine bone structure. The owner tacked him up and rode him an eighth of a mile to a jumping field. The horse trotted out with a huge, light stride and when he started jumping, I could see he was light off the ground, very careful, and scopey. I liked him. His jumping style was a little flat and he wasn't the tightest with his front end, but I still couldn't wait to get on him.

The owner dismounted and it was my turn to try the big bay. As soon as I had my feet in the stirrups and began sinking into the saddle, he completely freaked out! I barely had picked up the reins when he started panicking. My only option was to whirl him in tight circles and look for an opportunity to get off him. The horse was clearly mentally unstable—all I could think of was getting off, getting back in the car, and driving the ten hours back to Geneva! As we spun in circles, I began driving him forward with my leg and making him canter over poles on the ground in an attempt to distract him from his panic. Little by little, he started to settle down and accept me and I continued riding him. I kept him working and thinking, and he eventually relaxed. Despite the rocky start, in the end I had a great ride on him. We jumped a little and I liked him well enough that I thought it was worth trying him again the next day.

We slept overnight at Rupert Möll's home and in the morning, I went out and got back on the bay horse. He freaked out all over again when I got on him, but settled down faster than the previous day. I knew his tricks and had him figured out by then. We set up a gymnastic that I always use as a scope test when I try horses, a vertical-oxer-oxer line, and it went beautifully. He had so much scope and was so light and balanced with an excellent, soft mouth. He definitely had his own style and wasn't an orthodox jumper, but he was great nonetheless. I wrote out a check that day for $85,000. His name was Rio.

I took Rio to Harrisburg and Washington with me that year since I was there riding hunters and coaching equitation students. One day I jumped Rio in the schooling ring and after watching us, Kenny Wheeler agreed my new horse could really jump. I told him I'd make a deal with him and suggested he and his wife Sallie buy half of him and co-own him with me. Well, he turned me down without consulting with Sallie and for years afterward, Sallie teased Kenny that he'd missed out on a big opportunity!

Kenny Wheeler

George and I were both riding in the 1950s and '60s and he has always been such a beautiful rider. I'm from Virginia, but we'd go up to the Ox Ridge and Fairfield Hunt Clubs where George was always showing. When he went to the University of Virginia, I trained for Peggy Augustus and he used to come and ride; we got to be great buddies then. From the very beginning he was a natural, gifted teacher, too. We judged in Buffalo together, which I really enjoyed. Throughout his life, George has done so much for the horse show business. He has always been truly committed with his whole heart and soul in it—that's why he's so good. George is all class and couldn't be a better friend.

Running Hunterdon no longer interested me as much as it had before, but I still had my hand in that part of the business a little bit. I felt like the hunter and equitation divisions were tiring of me, just as I was tiring of them. There were other great professional hunter/equitation trainers and riders doing well like Paul Valliere and Ronnie Mutch. Hunterdon still had very good junior riders like Lisa Tarnopol (later: Deslauriers) and Paul Newman's daughter, Clea, who both just missed winning the equitation Finals in the early eighties.

Paul Newman and Joanne Woodward were wonderful clients—they were the easiest, nicest people and never got upset about anything. It helped that Clea was a good rider and always did very well, but her parents were so unassuming. I still remember before the Maclay Finals I went walking into the barn area early in the morning to work the horses and I saw a strange man pulling Clea Newman's (later: Newman-Soderlund) boots off. Now, she was a very high profile young girl, and I wasn't going to have some guy trying to get cozy with her! I yelled down the aisle, "Hey, leave that girl alone." The guy turned around—and it was the first time I met Paul Newman (photos 146, 147).

Shortly after Clea started riding with me, she had a terrible fall at Madison Square Garden at an in-and-out with solid log fences. She crashed so hard and was knocked unconscious for a long time; we were all terrified she had been killed. Thankfully, she was fine. The next year I invited the Newmans over for lunch and I had an old housekeeper named Mrs. Ronk who was helping serve. It was a simple lunch of soup and sandwiches, and while we sat out by the pool, Mrs. Ronk brought the lunch out on trays. As she walked across the patio, I noticed the soup trembling violently on the tray. The woman almost fainted she was so nervous about serving lunch to the Newmans! I painfully watched that soup slowly bobble all the way down to the table.

Clea Newman-Soderlund

I lived on both coasts when I was growing up. Luckily, George happened to be judging a horse show I was competing at in California and afterward he went up to my parents and invited me to ride with him when I came back East. I was so excited because he was known for being the best in the country, but I was also terrified. I wasn't sure I could rise to the occasion. Happily, George and I had a wonderful relationship and he taught me so much. Although he could be pretty tough, he really was very patient with me.

My last junior year was 1983. I was picked to ride first in the order in the Maclay Finals, which was a horrible draw. Bill Cooney and Frank Madden were so nervous and chatty as we were walking the course with George. Typically, I wasn't a worrier, but George told them that he and I were going to walk the course alone and it was just what I needed. I remember so clearly that the last line walked in between strides, where you could choose to add or leave one out. George looked at me and asked me what I wanted to do, and I said, "George, I think I want to leave it as an option." He was about to argue that I should make a decision ahead of time, but I told him, "If I hunt out of the last turn and have the distance coming in, I'll leave it out. If not, we'll add and make it look beautiful." Then he just smiled and nodded. It was so wonderful that he trusted me. I'll never forget that.

Bill and Frank were spinning around me at the in-gate and George said to them, "Let's leave Clea alone now," and then when I walked into the ring they all went up to the grandstand to watch. Everything worked out as I planned, and after I got off my horse, I walked up into the seats to see them. Every round you ever ride with George, he will always have noticed something you could have improved on. Even with a beautiful round, he'd see your heel slip up over the third fence or something like that. I'll never forget what George said to me that day. He said, "That was the most beautiful round—I'd give you a 100!" I ended up second in the Finals—they had me on top all day and kept testing me and testing me until I made a mistake. George was disappointed but I wasn't upset. I had such a great year with great horses and training. I learned so much from all of them.

At the end of 1983, I was ready to specialize in the jumpers on a more official basis so I gifted my hunter/equitation business to Frank Madden and Bill Cooney (photo 148). It was a million-dollar business with a deep pool of clients and, of course, a reputation for winning. They moved into the lower barn at Hunterdon and called it Beacon Hill Show Stables. After being at Hunterdon a couple of years, Bill and Frank moved out to Old Salem, New York, and then to Colts Neck, New Jersey. Eventually, they decided to split and run their own businesses and Frank continued his Beacon Hill business with Stacia Klein (later: Madden).

Jessica Springsteen was one of the many very skilled riders to come out of Beacon Hill in more recent years. Still teaching and showing jumpers from my Hunterdon base during the 1990s and early 2000s, I watched as Jessica grew up, seeing her ride and occasionally judging her at shows. I also had the pleasure of getting to know her parents, Bruce and Patti, when Jessica moved out of the equitation and into the jumpers. The Springsteens are some of the kindest people you could hope to meet. Jessica has really risen to the top ranks and I expect we'll continue to see her vying for U.S. Team spots for many years to come.

Frank and Bill immediately carried on successfully, winning Trainers of the Year at Madison Square Garden in 1984, and with students winning all three equitation Finals: the Medal, the Maclay, and the USET Finals. While Bill and Frank moved on with my former hunter and equitation clients, I continued on with Hunterdon as a jumper-focused training and teaching business. Michael Halbleib had made great strides as a horseman and started teaching, at first helping some clients based outside of the barn who rode in the amateur jumper classes. Eventually, he transitioned into coaching and riding as a professional, which he still does today at his own stable.

That was the year I first noticed a young rider named Chris Kappler. Mousie Williams and I were judging the Medal Finals together and we called him back on top; we both thought he sat a horse a lot like Conrad Homfeld. Chris didn't win the Finals but we really took notice of his talent and soon after, his mother called Hunterdon to see if Chris could ride with me, which I welcomed. Bill and Frank took him to the ring when it came to the equitation Finals, but I began teaching him as well.

Chris Kappler

I like to say that one jump changed my life, because when I was competing in the AHSA Medal Finals in 1984, my success came down to how I rode one particular line. George, as course designer and judge, had set up a fairly simple course of outside-diagonal-diagonal-outside-diagonal and the lines were set pretty long. One of the lines across the middle was either a balancing seven or a forward six. Everyone was trying to analyze what the judges would want to see and they thought probably doing the seven made more sense to show you can balance up after the previous forward riding lines. My trainer was Alex Jayne at the time and Alex said, "We're doing six," and I did it. At Harrisburg, they announce the riders on the standby list in reverse order of preference. The announcers rattled off the list of called-back riders' numbers and after so many had gone by without being mine, I started thinking, "Oh well, another year at Harrisburg gone by." And suddenly, don't you know it, they called out last the number: 184. It was mine! I virtually toppled over in the stands in shock. After the next round of thirty riders went, I was still on top and I rode in to test. When we switched horses for the final test, I didn't have quite as good a round on the other horse and ended up third overall.

What that led to, a couple of months down the road, was my mom getting up the nerve to call George out of the blue—we'd never even met him or had any particular excuse to reach out—and she talked to J. Michael Halbleib, who took the message. My mom didn't think she'd hear back, but within an hour, George called back! He called from California while teaching a clinic, and we made arrangements to bring my sister and me, along with four horses, out to Hunterdon. We spent the school break of Christmas to the New Year having lessons and learning about horse care and stable management on a whole new level. By the New Year, we'd made plans to go to Florida and show with George. The course of my life was forever altered by being bold and doing the six strides in that line at the Medal Finals.

My new horse Rio wasn't as precocious as Brussels but instead was the most complicated horse I'd ever ridden (photo 149). Hot and unbelievably sensitive, Rio would panic and bolt when anyone mounted or dismounted unless we were very careful where and how it was done. That winter I took Rio to Florida where by then the entire circuit was in Wellington. At the first pre-show of the circuit, I showed him in the Intermediate Division (four-foot-nine) and the Open Jumpers (five-foot-one to five-foot-three), in two classes a day for three or four days, and he went well.

On the first day of the real show circuit, I told my groom Sandy Atock, who was from a famous English horse family, that I didn't want to drill Rio too much and override him early in the day. I asked her to simply bring him to the ring for the class, so she brought him up ten or fifteen minutes before. In the ring, he was so fresh that he ran past the distances. I would see the distance and he sensed it and scooted up too close to the base of the jump, making for a very awkward effort for him. That's a good way to have a lot of rails down. I thought either Rio was having an off day or that I needed to rate his stride more carefully and not tip him off with my body when I saw the distance.

The second day, I had Rio brought up to the ring just before the class once again, and he was worse. We had several rails down and I was really discouraged. I started to think Rio was just too crazy in his head to be consistent. I considered giving him to Barney Ward to sell. Before I went down that road, though, I thought maybe I'd try something a little different the next day. I got up early the next morning and worked the hell out of Rio on the flat and over cavalletti. Then I put him away and Sandy brought him up when it was time to show. With his morning school fresh in his mind, Rio was utterly brilliant in the ring. With the key to consistency discovered, he went very, very well and was the talk of the show! From then on, just like the prodigious hunter Isle of Erin, Rio had the same routine for his entire career. He got worked on the flat in the morning to tune him into his job. Rio never ever was given a tranquilizer. He was a hot-blooded, sensitive horse and needed only proper riding to be good. Giving him drugs wouldn't have been an effective shortcut—it would've taken away his edge.

Rio was going so well that I started to enter him in Grand Prix classes. In hindsight, I probably rushed him into the big classes a little too soon. He was seven when I bought him and I should've given him mileage for perhaps a year in the Intermediate Jumpers, but I went straight to the Grand Prix. We had our ups and downs and it didn't ruin him, but he would occasionally have a green moment. In one big class that February there was a narrow, cut-out wall on the course and he wouldn't go near it! He took one look at it, stopped thirty strides out and no matter how hard I pushed him, he wouldn't get close to that jump. He had a few chicken moments like that and could be a drama queen, but by and large he was an incredible athlete and never stopped at the jumps.

The old cavalry books teach that the peak age for a horse jumping at the Olympic level is eight to twelve years old, but since those books were written, the length of time it takes to develop Grand-Prix-level horses has increased. While in previous decades some Grand Prix horses could be developed in a mere matter of months, it was a time with much simpler course design. It wasn't unheard of for horses to be pulled out of the hunting field and trained to do Grand Prix very quickly; in fact, The Jones Boy was one of the last horses I fast-tracked in that way. However, when courses became more technical with light jump rails and flat cups, years of experience was needed to develop the skills to be successful at that level. Today, the peak ages for a Grand Prix horse are more like nine to fifteen years old, with an eight- or nine-year-old still a very young horse for that level.

Both Brussels and Rio were going well at the Grand Prix level and needed sophisticated, complex rides. They were both hot horses and demanded a sensitive ride, but Brussels would come out of her stall much the same day to day, whereas Rio was more unpredictable. I loved to ride each of them; they were downright players in the ring! For several weeks we showed in Wellington and then went to Tampa for the last couple of weeks of the winter circuit.

That very night of the class where Rio threw a fit over that cut-out wall jump, my father died. Years before, after my mother's death, he'd met a younger woman in Delray Beach, Florida, and married her. I loved my father very dearly, despite the fact that we were like a cat and dog and so different, but distance grew between him and my siblings and me after his new marriage. I didn't see much of him in those years. He did, however, come to watch me ride in that Grand Prix, then he suddenly died soon afterward. I was told they found some pain pills and alcohol in the room with his body, but I never knew for sure if that's how he died. My father was a very sensitive man and I'm more like him than I ever realized (photo 150).

IV. AMERICAN DOMINATION

At the close of the Florida circuit, Bert de Némethy built the course for the Tampa Invitational, which had traditionally been the biggest jumper class in the nation. It was a big money class and very difficult. After the Americans had dominated the World Cup Finals several years running, Hermann Schridde and several members of the German Olympic committee came to Tampa to watch the Invitational. We were on another planet than the Europeans, and they were scratching their heads and thinking perhaps we knew something they didn't. They wanted to crack the code! It wasn't just show jumping, either. Jack Le Goff had taken the three-day eventers to a level that was unbeatable in the seventies and eighties. Hermann Schridde later told me the German group went back to Germany and said, "The Americans don't do anything differently than we do—they put their pants on one leg at a time!" While they were impressed, they didn't see anything very original about the way we rode, outside of a slightly more forward position and being freer with our hands. They still hadn't caught on, at that point, to the related distances and counting strides between jumps.

Despite all the wonderful success in my professional life, there was a dark cloud hanging over the eighties. I had an awful intestinal illness that went on and on around this time and it might have been *H. pylori* (the bacteria that cause ulcers) or it may have been stress-related. I never did find out, but I saw a dozen different doctors and no one could seem to figure out how to help me. It was debilitating and I wonder, thinking back, if it was in part the stress of being afraid of the AIDS virus and if I would somehow end up with it. At the World Cup Finals in 1984, a friend of mine told me he had a gastrointestinal specialist he knew in Geneva and offered to help get me an appointment. I agreed eagerly and that doctor gave me a couple of kinds of medication over the counter—within twenty-four hours, I was over it!

All through the eighties, between competing at shows, I taught many clinics to riders from France, Belgium, England, Switzerland, Sweden, Finland, and even a few in Germany and Holland. While teaching in Helsinki, I first met Kyra Kyrklund the dressage legend and we got along very well. Kyra and I have a similar philosophy and approach to teaching. Under my tutelage, Thomas Fuchs began to have great success and the Swiss team was beginning to do very well at the big shows. Their eyes were opening and they had adapted by combining the European foundation with the American technical aspects. As a result, they were beginning to rapidly rise in the ranks.

Thomas Fuchs

I first saw George in 1979 showing in America, and I remember seeing him schooling horses in the morning and he was always in the counter-canter. I thought, well he must know he's on the wrong lead and be doing it on purpose! We had a really hard time at the shows in New York, Washington, and Toronto that year. The Swiss team was always last in the Nations Cups. I talked to George a little bit and then organized a ten-day clinic in Switzerland that following year with all the best riders in our country. We became friends, and he came back to show a bit and teach for many years. What happened after was that people started laughing at us because we were counting strides and measuring distances on the courses and we rode with longer martingales, all because of George's teaching. In the early eighties nobody measured, so this was really new to us. Good German riders were laughing at us, but then we started to place better and better at the shows. We had quite a few good European Championship results.

We had other good instructors in Switzerland and ones who were very good on flatwork, but nobody was very technical with jumping a course. George had made the biggest influence on my riding and the Swiss show jumping team. He is a very tough teacher and some people can't cope with it. I organized a clinic in a big grass arena near an army base. That was probably the most difficult clinic we ever had. We were all riding very fresh Grand Prix jumpers and they were shooting nearby with tanks in some military exercise. George was yelling, "Jesus Christ, what is this, the Third World War?" He told us to take off our stirrups and we never put them back on again! We drilled on the flat and over cavalletti and the horses were bucking and running, and by the end of the warm-up session, we were all completely exhausted. Then we had to jump the big bank—and not the silly little one—the very big bank, with a big jump up, two strides on top with a big ditch in between, then down the steep hill—all without our stirrups! The next two days of the clinic our legs were really hurting. But we were young and tough and we learned so much. The Swiss team became very successful because of George's influence, and the laughing stopped when we rode into the ring. Today I teach young riders in Switzerland and that is definitely a result of what I learned in George's clinics.

The Los Angeles Olympic year was the best show-jumping Olympic year we've ever had as a nation. Hosting in the United States for the first time since 1952, it was a very big Olympic Games for all the sports. For American show jumping, it was hands down the best team we've ever fielded—and is likely to be the best team we will *ever* field. Training with Bert de Némethy, hard work, top horsemanship, and the American jumping style were the perfect recipe for success. The pinnacle of American show jumping was 1979–1988. Not to say that we haven't had very successful moments before or since; there have been short periods here or there when we dominated the show jumping landscape. However, there simply hasn't been that long a stretch of unquestionable superiority over all other nations as there was during the eighties. We were invincible!

Melanie Smith was an obvious choice for the team with the wins she had racked up in the years leading up the Olympics. Olympic trials were also held and Frank Chapot consulted various others to make his picks, resulting in the following team: Joe Fargis, Conrad Homfeld, Melanie Smith, Leslie Burr, and Anne Kursinski as the alternate. It was so difficult to relegate Anne to the alternate spot because she and Livius had been solid winners for years and it would've been so special for her to be an Olympian right in her hometown. But it was simply impossible—as you went down the list to choose whose place she would take, you couldn't make a switch. All of them had earned a spot. We could've easily fielded two, gold-medal Olympic Teams! Our twenty-first-century teams, in comparison, have been quite green, with either green riders or veterans riding green horses. Every one of the five horse-and-rider pairs on the '84 team could've won the Grand Prix of Aachen on any given day. We had amazing depth then! Consider who *didn't* make the team: Katie Monahan, Terry Rudd, Michael Matz, Norman Dello Joio, Rodney Jenkins, and others down the line.

Joe and Touch of Class were a great partnership and had been riding with Bert de Némethy for many years (photo 151). Even though Joe was never my student, he rode with the same philosophy. I had seen the mare Touch of Class as she was developed and the evolution of her career was astounding. In the late seventies, I taught a student named David Boley, a horseman who ran his own business in Pennsylvania. David rode with me as an outside client and would ship in for lessons. One particular autumn, David brought six different horses to Hunterdon—two at a time over a number of lessons—and, in part, my task was to help him choose the four he would take down to the Florida circuit that year. One day, David brought a little, hot, 15.3-hand Thoroughbred mare off the track, and he wanted to know if I thought she'd make a good hunter. After watching her go, I said, "David, this mare is very hot, cross-canters all the time, has no stride, and doesn't jump with a good style. No. She's not a hunter. But next week, bring her back and we'll test her scope and see if she's a jumper."

When David brought her back the next week, I set up an oxer in the middle of the ring and we jumped her back and forth up to about four-foot-three. Afterward, I shook my head and said, "David, this mare has no scope. Send her to Vince Dugan the horse dealer and let him do something with her. She's no hunter and she certainly doesn't have enough scope to be a jumper!"

Incredibly, that mare was Touch of Class. The next time I saw her, Leslie Burr was riding her in a Low Preliminary Jumper class and the mare was slithering between the cracks over the fences. But what I remember most was that the ring they rode in at Tampa had a little pond with ducks in it at the far end. For the entire show, Leslie couldn't get that mare to go down to the end of the ring because of the ducks! She'd jump around the top half of the ring and would never go down to the bottom. It's hard to believe it was the same mare that went to the Los Angeles Olympics!

Everyone else on the team had been a student of mine, and I remember the excitement I felt going to the Olympics to support these riders I had seen grow up and reach these great heights. Conrad Homfeld and the gray stallion Abdullah were a new partnership that year. When I had gone to the Rome show in May the year before, Debbie Shaffner was the leading rider at the show on Abdullah for Mrs. Sue Williams. Later that year, Sue telephoned me to say she and Debbie were parting ways and asked my advice on the $300,000 the Canadian team had offered her for Abdullah, for Jimmy Elder to ride. That was a huge sum at the time! The Williams family didn't have completely endless pockets, by the big owners' standards, so it would've been easy to defend them selling the horse to Canada. To her credit, Sue didn't want the horse to leave the United States. I told her that Conrad needed a top horse after selling Third Man because he didn't get along well with him. With her desire to be a USET Olympic horse owner, she was glad for the tip and gave the horse to Conrad to ride (photo 152).

Abdullah was a great jumper but did have a little chicken streak. He needed a lot of flatwork, which suited Conrad fine since he was an absolute maestro when it came to flatwork. However, Conrad only began riding Abdullah in late '83, and it takes time to really form the fine-tuned partnership needed for that level of competition. He threw Conrad off once or twice at the World Cup Finals in the spring, and while some would have been concerned, Conrad dug in and resurrected the situation. He put the fear of God in that horse and a month later, they won the Florida Olympic Trials with convincing consistency.

Leslie Burr's Olympic mount was Albany, a brown Thoroughbred that she'd sent me to look at for her a couple of years before in California. A student of Jimmy Kohn's was riding the horse in a Grand Prix at Griffith Park. Albany was fabulous and I called Leslie and told her to snatch him up immediately. Leslie and Albany were fantastic together at the Olympic Games, and her student Debbie Dolan also rode him to great success in later years. Mclanie Smith was of course riding Calypso in the Games and Anne Kursinski and Livius were ready to step in as very capable alternates (photos 153, 154).

With Frank Chapot as Chef d'Equipe of the team, I needed to secure accreditation so I could get into the stabling and ring areas at the Olympics to help when I was needed. Alan Balch was running the equestrian sports at the Games and he'd told me the winter before, at a dinner party at Kathy Moore's apartment, that he'd get my accreditation. When the time came, it didn't appear he could come through for me after all. It became a huge worry for me because my former students were counting on me being there. Chrystine Jones pulled some strings with Olympic committee members to get it done, thankfully!

Before the Los Angeles Games, Olympic show-jumping courses were diabolically large and a completely different sport than the courses at the Grand Prix level. It was a total bloodbath! The fences were a foot higher and two feet wider than any Grand Prix, even the Grand Prix of Aachen. When you see the fantastically beautiful jumping courses at today's Olympic Games, know that it was Bert de Némethy that delivered us into that world. When he designed the courses in Los Angeles, he flipped course designing on its head in one fell swoop. Always obsessed with the strategy of course building from basic gymnastics to Grand Prix, Bert was a genius in the creation of the most complete test of horse and rider. He knew how to challenge the scope, strength, and guts of a horse and rider while also testing intelligence and quick thinking when it came to precision, speed, turns, and judgment. Bert de Némethy singlehandedly took Olympic course building from the historically huge, solid, and dangerous to the extremely technical, varied courses we see in international championships today.

Since Bert had, in essence, trained American riders for nearly thirty years to face the kind of challenge he designed as the all-around test of a show jumper, the team rode brilliantly in Los Angeles. It was complete domination! It won the gold medal in the team competition, and in the individual event, Joe Fargis and Conrad Homfeld were the only riders to have zero faults, jumping off

158. *Retiring the Champion Hunter Dillon at the 1985 National Horse Show with Bill Cooney, Frank Madden, and Michael Sasso.*

Courtesy of Pennington Galleries Archive Collection/PenningtonGalleries.com

159. *Joan Scharffenberger riding Victor at Aachen, 1987.*

160. *A fabulous rider, Jean Claude Van Geenberghe is riding Quintus at the Beijing Olympics in 2008. Tragically, he died at 46 the following year from unknown causes.*

© Bob Langrish

161. *I'm with Katie Monahan and Melanie Smith at the Ox Ridge Hunt Club's June show.*

162. *Sometimes all you can do is laugh!*

163. *Leslie Burr Lenehan and McLain, winners of the 1986 World Cup Finals.*
Courtesy of Max Ammann/The Volvo World Cup

164. *I'm on crutches with (left to right) Joan Scharffenberger, Jeffery Welles, Lisa Tarnopol, Danny Marks, and George Lindemann at the Donaueschingen Nations Cup.* © Kathy Moore

165. *Left to right: George Lindemann, GHM, Joan Scharffenberger, Danny Marks, and Kathy Moore, ringside.*

166. *Eric Louradour and I had a wonderful friendship in the eighties and are still good friends today.*

Courtesy of Eric Louradour

167. Conrad Homfeld riding Rio in Aachen, 1986.

Courtesy of Pennington Galleries Archive Collection/PenningtonGalleries.com

168. *Walking a course with Peter Leone, Norman Dello Joio, and Mark Leone in 1986.*

169. *Celebrating with Anne Kursinski at The Gold Cup at Devon where she placed first and second on Dynamite and Eros.* © Alix Coleman Photography

170. *All-female Nations Cup winners at Hickstead, 1987 (left to right): Debbie Dolan, Katie Monahan, Joan Scharffenberger, and Anne Kursinski.*

171. *Leslie Burr Lenehan and Pressurized.*

172. *Rio wilting at the 1988 World Cup Finals in Gothenburg.*

173. *Ian Millar winning the 1988 World Cup Finals on Big Ben; he won in 1989 too!*

Courtesy of Max Ammann/The Volvo World Cup

174. *At Spruce Meadows Masters in 1988 with Katie Monahan Prudent, Joan Scharffenberger, Leslie (Burr) Howard, and Peter Leone.*

175. *Rio was one of the best jumpers I ever had, perhaps second only to Sinjon. I'm riding him to the win in the Grand Prix of Calgary, the du Maurier, 1988.*

176. *Accepting the trophy at Spruce Meadows in Calgary.*

177. *Greg Best and Gem Twist, silver medalists at the Olympics in Seoul, South Korea, 1988.* © PhelpsSports.com

178. *Anne Kursinski riding Starman in Seoul.* © Tish Quirk

179. *Greg Best, with his silver medal in Seoul.* © PhelpsSports.com

180. *With my old friend David Broome from Great Britain at the 1988 Olympic Games in Seoul.* © Bob Langrish

181. *Doris Duke looking on as I teach Imelda Marcos her first riding lesson in Honolulu.*

182. *Anne Kursinski riding Starman at the 1990 World Equestrian Games.* © PhelpsSports.com

183. *Yogi was the only jumper I ever showed in a rubber snaffle—he had a wonderfully soft mouth.* © PhelpsSports.com

184. *Zanzibar, a new jumper prospect but a little bit of a rogue.*

185. *Anne Kursinski planning her domination of the show jumping world with her win on Starman at the Grand Prix of Aachen, 1991.* © PhelpsSports.com

186. *Meredith Michaels-Beerbaum and Markus Beerbaum at their stables in Germany.* © Pascal Renauldon

187. *Zanzibar—I'm showing him here at Devon— mysteriously lost his scope for nearly three years.*

Courtesy of Pennington Galleries Archive Collection/PenningtonGalleries.com

188. *Anne Kursinski and Eros.*

© Peter Llewellyn

189. *Greg Hall.*

190. *Riding So Near across the top of the enormous bank at Hickstead, 1991.*

191. *My last jumper project, Yogi.* © *Brandy*

192. With Rodney Jenkins and Buck Brannaman, teaching a clinic relating natural horsemanship to universal flatwork and jumping concepts.

193. Anne Kursinski, inspiring Cannonball to jump a clear round at the 1992 Barcelona Olympic Games. © Kit Houghton

194. *Norman Dello Joio and Irish, Olympic bronze medalist in Barcelona.* © *Kit Houghton*

195. *Lisa Jacquin and For the Moment in Barcelona.* © *Kit Houghton*

against one another for the gold medal. Joe and the fabulous little mare Touch of Class won the gold medal and Conrad silver on Abdullah; how truly incredible! Conrad and Joe are the kind of lightning that could never strike twice: they met in 1966 and formed a personal and professional partnership. Then each became a superstar in his own right—and tied for first place in the Olympics. It speaks to their characters that they have had such success as partners in the horse business, where there is undoubtedly so much change through the years. In many relationships, there is only room for one superstar ego, but they have both been humble enough to share in each other's great success (photo 155).

Armand Leone

I was fortunate enough to go with George on one of his first trips back to Europe to show in the 1970s. Our team was Debby Malloy, Betsie Bolger, George, and myself. George was riding and coaching on the trip. Back then it was still the pioneer days of Americans going to show in Europe. I really learned how to make a good strategic competition and logistics plan by watching how George managed the horses and riders on that trip. George's particular brilliance is his work ethic. He has talent but that's not what has made him great. What's made him great is his power of analysis, his belief in the fundamentals, his perseverance, and keeping a goal-oriented vision.

George's biggest contribution, in my opinion, was how he developed so many great women riders. One of his greatest talents was helping riders overcome stage fright. George had to overcome it himself. It was very simple: you make a plan, you work on that plan and focus on it, then you don't have time to be nervous! He was able to address and understand both the psychological fear of making mistakes, which most everyone has, and the physical fear of being hurt. He was able to inspire riders to rise above their self-imposed limitations and insecurities. He pushed students out of their comfort zone and instilled a certain drive and aggressiveness, in women in particular, to enable them to become the world's greatest generation of riders—the Katie Prudents, the Leslie Burr Howards, and the Melanie Smith Taylors. When you think about it, George was very central to women excelling in the sport of show jumping during a time when women were still redefining their role in our country.

As Americans, we had planted seeds of success by starting with a great tradition of American horsemanship, which began with our Anglo-Saxon roots. From the beginning, we believed in natural horsemanship and caretaking, in turning horses out and not keeping them cooped up, and in making the most of the qualities of the horse by keeping his spirit intact rather than breaking it. The American Thoroughbred embodies that spirit and athleticism, which we cultivated in our early American history with foxhunting and racing. The cavalry at Fort Riley combined its military discipline and emphasis on a strong base of support with the cross-country, forward-seat style.

Those critical early American seeds that were planted produced tremendous growth when a group of incredible American horsemen took the Fort Riley method and applied it after World War II: Gordon Wright, Jimmy Williams, Cappy Smith, Raymond Burr, Bobby Burke, and Bill Steinkraus. These great horsemen brought it to the masses across the nation and joining them were others from Europe who brought us Caprilli's system of forward riding, like Vladimir Littauer. In classic American collaboration, the horsemen emigrating from Europe brought their own classical backgrounds in horsemanship, like Bert de Némethy, Gabor Foltenyi, Jack Le Goff, and Richard Wätjen. These men brought the European influences from Germany, France, and Italy and our home-grown system became more sophisticated and supported by dressage and full-seat methods. Wätjen brought excellent dressage flatwork and combined it skillfully with the forward-seat method.

Bert's dedicated leadership of the team was fed by a pipeline of disciplined, hardworking, talented young riders in the sixties and seventies who were a product of that winning recipe. The culmination of all of these influences fully bloomed during the eighties, when American technical riding prowess was finally realized. Los Angeles was the greatest Olympics we ever had and the few years that followed represented the absolute pinnacle of American show jumping. Even though Bert had retired as Chef d'Equipe, it was primarily he who had nurtured the growth of the USET with his regimented program. The Europeans, who once had laughed at us, were suddenly on their heels trying to catch up!

V. THRILLS AND SPILLS IN EUROPE

Debbie Haimowitz

I always knew I wanted to ride with George. In my early twenties, I called a friend who rode with him and asked how I could get a chance at it. She said, "Debbie, you have to want to do this more than anything else in the world." I told her I was all in! I remember calling his number, and he answered the phone, which for some reason caught me off guard. He wasn't available to teach then because he was traveling to Europe so much, but I rode with someone at his barn and kept going back. Then one day I went for a lesson and he was home, so he taught me and it was fantastic. You can see the gleam in George's eye when he works with a horse and when he teaches. His love of teaching comes through. I never minded when he was being tough or raising his voice because when you ride with him, his voice is like a vice that holds you up. He knows how to stretch and push you and also when to ease up. George doesn't baby anybody! He just tightens his grip to mold a winner.

My business at home was strictly jumpers by the middle of the decade, although I was invited to judge the hunters and equitation from time to time, which I really enjoyed. In 1986, I was asked to judge the Maclay Finals with Linda Allen at the Garden; we had a very interesting course that year. A bright-red chicken coop was placed off a short turn, then a right-hand turn to an in-and-out. To complicate things, there was a barrier made of flower boxes on the ground that riders were forced to stay inside, hampering the line from the coop to the in-and-out. Meredith Michaels, who grew up riding with Karen Healey out West, was in her second-to-last year as a junior. She was one of the heavy favorites that year, but when she faded out after jumping the coop and hopped over the flower boxes, she was eliminated. Incidentally, many years later, in 2008 in the Beijing Olympics, there was a low flower decoration in the individual show jumping final, and Beezie Madden beat Meredith in the jump-off by jumping through the flowers and saving time in the turn! Afterward, I told her, "Oh Meredith, it was those flowers—they got you again!"

Seeing consistent success in the jumper ring on Rio and Brussels, I felt like we had found our groove. That summer, Rio won the $100,000 Grand Prix at Culpepper, which was the first $100,000 class ever in the United States. We managed Rio very carefully, giving him time off to rest his suspensory ligaments, which would occasionally flare up and get irritated. Although I schooled him every morning on the flat at the horse shows, there was no need to drill him at home unnecessarily. Between shows, all we did with him was long trot work sessions to keep him loose and fit.

The Rex Group decided to send Brussels to Michael Matz to ride, and he did very well, winning The President's Cup on her that year. They felt Michael would have more success with her than I might. Although it was their prerogative as the owner to send her to Michael, it was devastating for me to lose her as my mount. Brussels was a great little mare with a fiery independent personality and I loved riding her! That's business, though, and I accepted their decision. After Michael rode Brussels for a while, they sent her to Joe and Conrad. I bought another horse named Rocco from Gerhard Etter and brought him along in Florida later that year. Trying to fill the gap left by Brussels, I pushed him into the big division too quickly. He had the scope for it, but he needed more time to develop. Unlike Rio, he never really became a superstar.

The Rex Group, witnessing the success Rio and I were having, wanted to buy him from me as well. I wasn't opposed to it, since like Brussels he'd grown too valuable to be in my hands alone. They drew up a purchase contract and we had banners, blankets, and name plates for Rio made with The Rex Group brand. However, even though we'd agreed in principle that they would own him, they never paid me for him. As the months went on with the purchase never actually transacted, I grew very nervous. Rio continued to win and his value increased even more. Something about The Rex Group had begun to smell funny; I could sense things were amiss. I tried to explain my predicament to Hugh Wiley, telling him I would be forced to sell Rio to someone else since they hadn't followed through and paid me. When still nothing materialized from The Rex Group, Frank Chapot gave me some friendly advice and I sold Rio to Jane Clark instead. Jane has been a wonderful, top team owner for many years.

That sense something was amiss with The Rex Group wasn't unfounded and a lawsuit was filed against me, wherein they claimed Rio was theirs because it had been their intention to buy him. Eventually, the case went into litigation, where I became suspicious of the apparent coziness between the local Richmond, Virginia, judge and Clyde Pitchford, Jr. The ruling was that Rio might have to go back up for auction, because the judge said the tack trunks and blankets showed the intention of The Rex Group to buy the horse. To keep Rio off the auction block, Jane had buy Rio all over again by buying him back from the court for the same price once again. It was a handsome price for a horse still coming up and not yet proven in the Olympics. Later that year Clyde Pitchford, Jr. was convicted and sentenced to twenty-five years in prison for embezzlement and loan fraud.

One night that year, Kathy Moore woke me up in the middle of the night to tell me J.J. Smith had been killed in a car accident. J.J. was a larger-than-life personality and such a wonderful, colorful part of the horse show world for decades. The great horseman Hermann Schridde was also sadly killed that year in a skydiving accident. It's always a shock to lose friends, especially when they are healthy and die so suddenly.

Lynne Little

Unlike many of his other students, I began riding with George after I had already established myself as a professional and was working within my own system—purchasing, developing, and marketing show jumpers. At that time I had two horses I was successful with—Mangrove Mattie and Csar—but George completely refocused my ambition regarding them and myself. Honestly, it is safe to say he changed my life. Previously, I had been intent on a beautifully produced sales horse. With George, I came to believe in myself as an athlete and a winning competitor and ran with it. George gave me a whole new direction. He taught me to want to win.

When I look back I realize that was the environment of excellence that my daughter Marilyn was raised in, and her fierce winning spirit, her unwavering commitment to a system of detail and discipline, is attributable to my years with George. George has a very consistent system. He imposes a real discipline and takes every rider he works with to the next level no matter what that level is. He always produces. And in my life that changed everything—for both me and my daughter, whose accomplishments astound me. And George was, and remains, a great and supportive friend.

Marilyn Little

As a horseman's and professional's daughter, I was luckily born with the same daredevil spirit, survival skills on a horse, and the desire to win that my mother Lynne had become known for. However, it was in my early teenage years that George became a serious part of my life. He took on the responsibility of imparting what he deemed the "fundamentals that must be added to the recipe," which, of course, were the importance of classical technique, attention to detail, the study of the sport, and the absolute discipline required not only to win, but to win consistently.

Looking back now, I can say that George's influence in my career has truly transcended disciplines and ridden with me through the Medal Finals and Grand Prix rings as a teenager, on U.S. Team Nations Cup Show Jumping Tours in Europe, into my first International Grand Prix wins in my early twenties, through each of my first four-star three-day events around tracks at Kentucky, Burghley, Luhmuhlen, and Pau in my late twenties and early thirties. And in 2015, it helped propel me onto the podium at the Pan American Games for the U.S. Eventing Team in Toronto at thirty-three. When our country's anthem was played at the Pan Am Medal Ceremony, I thought of the hundreds of thousands of hours required from so many to help a rider achieve a day such as that, and of course, George's words, time, and the "fundamental beliefs" he began to instill in me more than twenty years ago. Though I was far from my days as a thirteen-year-old in the back rings at the Wellington Hunterdon Ring in a "No-Stirrups Tuesday" lesson with George, when I stepped off the podium with two gold medals to get a leg back up onto my horse for the victory gallop, George was with me as I looked down at my boots and thought, "I probably could have polished them just one more time." That thought would have never come from my mother.

Hunterdon had become a jumper-focused business, and I was happy to host professionals there from time to time, like Peter Wylde and Jeffery Welles. Katie Monahan and Anne Kursinski were solidly independent and out on their own by that time, so my teaching focus turned toward the next wave of talented young adult riders. I had a strong stable of amateur jumper riders who aspired to the USET, including Joan Scharffenberger, Michaela "Mikey" Murphy (later: Murphy Hoag), Lisa Tarnopol, and George Lindemann, who was by then riding the fabulous I Love You. In 1985, we embarked on a European tour together. I rode as well, so the five of us made a team. We began in Sweden and then went on to Germany, Hickstead, Dublin, and Rotterdam.

Joan Laarakkers

George was a visionary in realizing that there must be another way to strengthen our base of team-level international jumper riders. In the years to follow (and with the great organizational skills of Kathy Moore) he took a group of us to Europe every summer. This was a great risk because there wasn't all that much support for sending teams over to gain experience in those years. Those first teams were a mixed bunch of young kids who, although lacking experience, had a good mixture of talent and guts to compete with the best senior teams in Europe. All funds of the USET were spent on sending Olympic or World Championship teams, so we had to foot most of the bill ourselves, but quickly it became apparent that showing in Europe could be no more expensive than at home. Prize money was good and entry fees were almost nonexistent. Most of the hotel expenses were paid by the shows in those days!

George had a great influence on my life growing up and not a day goes by that I don't think of something he said! My favorite thing is, "Under, over, or through!" which he would say when a rider was timid and allowed a horse to stop or run out, or if (God forbid) a rider would turn away from a jump. In other words, even if you are afraid, don't let your horse feel it by giving him a weak ride because this takes away all his confidence. This for me says it all—no matter what challenges you are faced with in life, always keep moving forward! Whether it's my horses, students, or kids this always rings true: make sure they know you believe in them so they have a chance to succeed. Never dwell on or mention the possibilities of things going wrong—but expect them to go well. Maybe the most important thing I learned from George is that life is a long process of learning—listen to what others have to say, be aware of what they do better, and try to emulate them.

At the show in Falsterbo, Sweden, that year, they put us in a quarantine stable way on the other side of the road away from the ring. On our side of the road there was a beach and some of the girls on the tour came up to me freaking out because it was a nude beach! Right there by the barn! It was very funny. In those days, the FEI shows didn't have the security they do today, with badges to get in and areas cordoned off with limited access for horses and riders.

Rio was a very spooky horse, so I would ride him around the grounds and rings and into the woods to get the spooks out of him. I rode him virtually everywhere possible so he could take a look at everything. As Chef d'Equipe of the tour, I always went first in a team class so afterward I could focus on coaching the rest of the team. In the Nations Cup, I was on my way to the second fence and heard the crowd snickering in the background about something. Rio was going so well that I didn't understand what the reaction was about. I wondered if they thought I was a hypocrite because I'd just published my book and here I was, ducking over the top of the fence! I finished the course and the crowd kept laughing at me, and I walked out of the ring puzzled. Then I realized I had a branch sticking out of my hunt cap like Robin Hood! Apparently I'd picked up a little foliage from riding Rio through the woods before the class. We ended up winning the Nations Cup, which was such wonderful fun to be a part of as a rider again. When I went double clear, David Broome said it was "vintage Morris"!

I had driven the previous year to Belgium to look at a horse of Jean-Claude Van Geenberghe's. A great professional horseman in Holland (and very good friend) Henk Nooren sent me to look at a horse named Sans Pardon that we eventually bought for George Lindemann. Henk was Jean-Claude's teacher and mentor and Jean-Claude was an up-and-coming Grand Prix rider from a wealthy Belgian family. I didn't meet Jean-Claude himself when I went to see the horse, but I met his young resident professional. It was a beautiful place in the Flemish part of Belgium called Moorsele, not too far from Brussels.

At Falsterbo that year, I finally met Jean-Claude Van Geenberghe in the flesh. He was a very ambitious young rider in his early twenties and while I walked the course with my team, he started following us around. I remember overhearing his young trainer scolding him for shadowing our team and he barked back at him, saying, "I want to hear what Mr. Morris has to say." After that, we talked and I became his coach for many years. He won the Grand Prix of Aachen twice, rode in the Seoul and Beijing Olympics, and was an equestrian icon in Europe for twenty years or more. In addition, Jean-Claude was involved in building the Zilveren Spoor, a grand equestrian complex and one of the best riding facilities in Europe, at which several international events are hosted annually today. He was married several times and eventually married a Ukrainian woman, moved to Ukraine, and started riding for his new home country in 2006 (photo 160).

Under very odd circumstances, Jean-Claude's life tragically ended after just a few years of living in Ukraine. After winning a big jumper class there, he suddenly collapsed during the awards ceremony and died. I heard rumors that he had told friends shortly beforehand that he believed he was going to die. Some suspect Jean-Claude was murdered by envious or crooked business associates, because the circumstances were so bizarre for a man in such great health. He didn't drink or smoke and was the picture of health at age forty-six. They didn't do a proper investigation into the cause of death but the media reported that it was related to a stroke or brain aneurism. His body was taken back to Moorsele and the funeral held there. I was devastated at the loss—he was like a son to me, as many of my students are, not to mention a fabulous rider who might have had a couple of decades of top riding yet to come.

Hickstead was a real horseman's horse show in those days; it brought the beautiful country into the show ring. The grounds held a big, shadowy ring with natural, elegant fences and the slope in the ring made it very pretty but also difficult to ride. The natural fences were substantial: deep ditches, water jumps, and huge banks. I think it was the most difficult place I have ever ridden, and even though it was so tough it's definitely one of my favorites. We all had a great time that year at Hickstead, as those wonderful jumps added a bit of adventure to the game!

Susie Schoellkopf

Many years ago, George was showing a couple of horses in the Working Hunter division at Madison Square Garden. Melanie Smith and I were sitting in the stands watching and George rode into the ring on the first horse. There was a two-stride across the middle of the ring and he turned the corner and started flying toward it. Melanie and I were wondering why he was going so forward, when the horse slammed on the brakes and rails went flying. He walked out of the ring. Then a while afterward, George came in on his second horse and did the exact same thing. We couldn't believe that horse stopped, too, and Melanie and I cracked up! We couldn't help it! It was inconceivable to us that it happened to such a perfectionist like George. As the horse was in the process of spinning around after his second refusal, I saw George's gaze browse the stands to see who was laughing. I instantly stopped laughing and wiped the smile off my face. Melanie didn't see it and was still howling—then as soon as she noticed I wasn't laughing, she turned to see George looking up at us. We were so scared that we got up, left the Garden and ran across the street back to the hotel! It was so funny. We tease George about it still and he likes to remind us what brats we were!

George used to complain that I taught his students to be trouble-makers. Susie Blaisdell and Pam Carmichael (Lillie Keenan's mom) were the only ones I ever knew who played pranks on George. They used to short-sheet his bed and put itching powder in his shorts!

I've hosted George Morris clinics for over forty years in Buffalo, New York. George has been so important for my career, our sport, and the country. He brings so much great teaching and so many horseman-ship and life values to our sport that are sorely needed. His clinics are unbelievable; they're beautifully done. In the early days we had some adventures: we did a foxhunting clinic in East Aurora one year and when the group got back, one girl was bleeding and one horse was bleeding. George walked up, got off the horse, handed someone the reins, and said to me, "I've ridden all over the world, over all sorts of country, but I've never seen anything like that."

That '85 tour put great European showing mileage on my amateur jumper riders. Conrad and Joe also ran a tour out of their stable and that American team won the Nations Cup at Aachen, which was wonderful to see. That spring of 1985, Conrad Homfeld won the World Cup on Abdullah, with his textbook beautiful style. Every year since the inception of the World Cup Finals, American riders had either won or placed second. We were a force to be reckoned with and the Europeans were reeling! They had never seen anything like it. It legitimately changed the world. Unfortunately, with success sometimes comes a reaction of bitterness and some of the European friends I had made back in the late fifties turned frosty about our dominance. A few German horsemen I know, as they age, have become very cynical and bitter. I'm always sorry for this and recall wistfully the friendships I cherished in our youth.

Conrad mentioned to me that he wanted to travel to Dinard, France, to watch the European Championships late that summer. It was a fantastic idea to observe our competition before the following year's World Championships, to be sure we stayed a step ahead. Jane Clark and I also went to Dinard to watch. Jane was becoming more and more involved as a big owner with Leslie Burr Lenehan. Paul Schockemöhle won on Deister—they continued to be a power-house pair on the world stage.

I recall a funny memory from Dinard about Conrad as a young man. While at a restaurant the first night on that northwest coast of France, I ordered mussels cooked in wine and loved them so much that I ordered them again the following night. Conrad had been a very picky eater when my mother looked after him in the sixties, and he never would've entertained eating such a thing. After wrinkling up his nose at the mussels at first, Conrad grudgingly agreed to try one after much urging and seemed to like it. Then on the third night, as we returned to the little village restaurant yet again, Conrad relented and said, "Well, I think I'll go ahead and order the mussels!" He grew out of that finicky youth. Chris Kappler was much the same way when he was young.

Brussels was fantastic to ride in big indoor classes because she was very brave and a quick thinker. Being such a hot mare, the big jumps in a smaller ring focused her and she jumped very well. In contrast, even though Rio was also hot, he became too backed off, thinking and reacting more slowly on course and having mistakes, so he wasn't fantastic indoors. To get ready for the Grand Prix at Washington, I decided to go into the Puissance with Rio and just jump the wall a few times to get his confidence up in the ring. The first time it was about five-foot-six and he jumped it well and I thought it might be good for him to go back at it again. I was first in the group and when I cantered down around the end of the ring for the second attempt, the announcer said the jump was six-foot-six and I thought, "Oh hell, what did I get myself into?" It was too late to back out now! After all, it wasn't as if I could trot all the way down waving to the crowd and leave the ring. I took a deep breath and Rio galloped down and jumped it, but in his effort to clear it he twisted so hard in the air that he almost twisted me right off his back!

Mikey Murphy Hoag

George instilled a set of discipline that no one else demanded. You needed to be careful of the way you looked when you entered the barn, how you composed yourself, and it was best never to show weakness. If you whined or were ill-prepared, George would smell blood and you would be destroyed publicly. I knew the standards and appreciated the level of expectation he demanded.

On our first trip to Europe, in the mid-eighties, George took six of us for some international experience. There were five Americans and one Canadian, Linda Southern. It was the first time that a group of young riders rode for the U.S. Team. We were truly so ill equipped to compete in the big league of international Grand Prix jumping. However, with George's guidance and Kathy Moore's handholding, we thankfully held our own. That summer and the next summer were like taking a graduate course in riding. The miles that we put under our belts were fantastic. There were so many memories from those trips, but my favorite ones of George were shopping for an additional Grand Prix horse. From the people I met to the horses he made me jump over the top of the standards—it was character building. Getting into a long car ride with George, there was nothing off limits in our conversations. I really admired the career and legacy he built in the horse show world and much appreciated the time with him as a coach.

The 1986 World Cup returned to Gothenberg, Sweden, and Leslie Burr Lenehan won the first leg on Corsair, her speed horse, which I missed seeing. Then once I arrived, I watched as she surprised everyone by winning it all on McLain over the big courses. I was so proud of her ability to hold up under the World Cup format and show the world what a fabulous rider she is! Conrad continued his winning ways and was third on Maybe, a very capable little horse. Our reign as superstars in North America continued (photo 163).

Lisa Deslauriers

I feel very fortunate to have had the amazing opportunity to ride with George for over ten years. I went to train with him when I was sixteen years old and rode in the equitation and hunters. It wasn't until I was out of the juniors that I sat on a jumper for the first time. There were definitely more talented riders than I, but I was a very good student: I was a good listener and observer, and I tried to incorporate whatever he was teaching. If you are a good student, you work well with George, and that was where our respect for each other began: me as the student and George as the teacher. The discipline he instills in his training was instrumental in much of the success I had in the ring—and in life.

George was responsible for finding great horses for me, in particular, Revlon Adam. Adam was for me to learn on and give me confidence—and that he did. We got Adam when he was six years old and I competed with him for ten years, which was a "fairy tale" length of time in show jumping. I had never even dreamed of jumping in Grand Prix, but here was a girl from New York City qualifying a few times for the World Cup Finals and becoming the reserve rider on the 1986 gold-medal World Championship Team.

When I started competing internationally, it was at the same time as George's return to the international arena. To go on this journey together (teacher and student) and compete on U.S. Teams together was an extraordinary experience.

The first time I qualified for the World Cup Finals, I was a senior at the University of Pennsylvania. The timing of the World Cup coincided with my having to study for final exams, which were the very next week. I remember arriving in Berlin, my first foray at an international show and feeling I was over my head. However, deep down, I knew if George thought I was ready, I was ready! He wouldn't let me go there unprepared. We had done our homework and once we were there, we did our normal school and I actually felt at ease. I finished twelfth that year in the finals, and it was fun!

As time has passed, I appreciate more and more what we were able to accomplish together. We had a great team, inside the barn and out. We jumped a lot of clear rounds at some of the biggest shows in the World (Aachen, Hickstead, Dublin, Calgary) with great horses and a great system. I am truly appreciative!

VI. UPS AND DOWNS

The darkest hour of the AIDS epidemic was 1986. It was frightening for everybody, but especially terrifying for people who were gay because nobody knew exactly what was making people sick. Rumors abounded and hysteria had by then taken over. Having any kind of sexual exploit or indiscretion while in a relationship became a very risky proposition. People were afraid to even shake hands or hug. It was a horrifying time, to fear a plague you didn't fully understand. It filled all of us with dread. For me personally, my abstaining from any sort of physical relationships felt demoralizing and depressing after several years.

After Los Angeles, the Olympic Committee eased up on the amateur rule for riding in the Olympics, which was confirmed by the Ted Stevens Olympian Amateur Sports Act of 1978. Unless you received payment for teaching Olympic-level riders in other countries, the committee considered you an amateur and you were able to compete. Suddenly, almost anyone could ride on the team, including professionals who taught nearly all levels of riders. Nowadays, everyone in the Olympics is a professional, but it was definitely an evolution. It's interesting to remember what a sensitive issue it was for so long, like Bert de Némethy's concern in 1960 about my teaching my niece and nephews at the Ox Ridge Hunt Club being a threat to my eligibility.

The World Championships were approaching and early spring trials were held at Valley Forge. Chris Kappler and his horse Concorde were a little young to be in the mix for the Championships but he was at Hunterdon continuing to gain experience. Great riders converged on Hunterdon to school together and prepare for the trials. It was a wonderful time we had together out on the Grand Prix field with Hap Hansen, Katie Prudent, Jeffery Welles, and Anne Kursinski.

Hap Hansen

George was the Chef d'Equipe for a California Nations Cup Team at Spruce Meadows. We had a great day, and at the end of the Nations Cup we were tied and had to jump-off. In those days, the whole team jumped off, and I was the last to go. John Whitaker from Britain had just gone on Milton and had been fast and clean, so they were ahead. The only way we were going to win was if I was clean and faster. George stood at the in-gate and as I walked into the ring, all he said to me was, "Fast." I was and we won the Nations Cup! He likes to tell me I did the impossible. He's always been such a fan and so supportive.

I went back East to ride for a couple of months and show in the team trials for the World Championships, and while there, I kept my horses at Hunterdon and went to some shows with George. When it came to getting ready for the trials, George held some organized schooling sessions in the big field at Hunterdon. George had set a big combination and went first on Rio, who went beautifully. They were done and walking out while George told me the course and gave me a few pointers. In the middle of the combination, my horse tripped and we had a spectacular crash, sending poles flying. I was lying on the ground and my horse was running all over the place. I was okay and just starting to get myself off the ground, but George was worried and wanted to help. He went to get off and swung his leg over the saddle and Rio took off. George tumbled off the back of the horse and fell right at my feet. Imagine how badly I felt! There he was lying on the ground and all he said was, "It's broken." By the time the rumors spread back to the West Coast, I had people asking me why I broke George's leg!

Rio was a lightning-fast bolter and it caught up with me when I was schooling with Hap Hansen in the Grand Prix field. Before I knew it, I was on the ground and I remember thinking, "Oh, that really stung," and I lay there a minute. Then I went to get up and I couldn't. I had never, in all my years of riding, had that experience of not being able to get up after having a fall. I knew something was terribly wrong. The vet Danny Marks and Kathy Moore were there helping both Hap and me, and they got me sitting up, but it was clear I needed an ambulance. I had broken my femur and it had splintered, making it a very serious situation. I had a comminuted fracture, which meant the bone broke unevenly in many places. My excellent physician, Dr. Stover, took care of me through an operation. They found that bone fragments had entered my blood stream and it was lucky that none of them did additional damage. I almost died that night.

The injury was a huge blow. I had finally been in a position to potentially qualify for an international championship team for the first time since I left the USET in 1960. I really hadn't thought I would ever get back to riding at a Grand Prix level, and to risk losing that ground I'd gained, both with my edge in the saddle and with the horses I had at my disposal to ride, was terribly disappointing. However, looking back it might have been a blessing in disguise that I didn't have the chance to go to the World Championships on Rio. Rio was going so well at that time and he could have qualified, but he wasn't a Championship horse. Rio probably didn't have the heart for it; he was too complicated a horse to hold up to that pressure of a World Championship.

The USET was heavily favored in Aachen and our team was Michael Matz, Katharine Burdsall, Katie Prudent, and Conrad Homfeld, with Lisa Tarnopol as the reserve. I attended the Championships in Aachen, but I was still recovering from the horrible broken femur and using a walker to get around. Everyone was very accommodating, and I rode around the show grounds in a golf cart.

The U.S. Team won the gold medal that year in a very impressive win over a huge, difficult course. Gail Greenough from Canada won the individual and she was the first North American, the first woman, and the first rider ever with zero faults to win the World Championships. It was Gail's day, no question about it. Conrad was second in the individual, continuing his incredible streak of great results on Abdullah.

While in Aachen, I saw a very good-looking blonde guy in the lobby of the Quellenhof Hotel and we started talking. His name was Don and he was Donatus Prince von Hessen, a first cousin of Queen Elizabeth. After becoming friends, I planned to contact him when I was back in Germany with a tour of young riders later that year. Making good on my word, a group of us went to visit Don's home in northern Germany. After driving across hours of flat farmland to get there, we arrived at the gates of his property in the little town called Panker and could see his gorgeous estate. As we were all admiring the house, we suddenly realized it was the stable we were looking at! This was clearly a very wealthy man. The house itself was a castle and the entire surrounding town laid out like a medieval village. Not only was Don incredibly wealthy, but he was a very welcoming host and blue-blooded to the core. We all had a great deal of fun spending time at his estate. Afterward, I invited Don to Hickstead and he came to the show.

Robert Ridland

Following the World Championships at Aachen in '86, I was selected for the Nations Cup team at Spruce Meadows about a month later. It happened to be an all-West-Coast team. All the other countries had the same team members at Spruce Meadows that they'd had for the World Championship, and we were a new, young team and were figured to come in last. When I look back on just that week, I still remember things that George said to me and the way he interacted with all four of us. I don't think any of us had ever ridden on a team with George before that week—I know I certainly hadn't. The way he interacted with us as Chef d'Equipe was something I'll never forget.

George couldn't get there in time for the draw (where they establish the order of go) because of a flight delay, so he asked me if I could sit in for him. So I went, but there was a problem. I remember Pamela Carruthers was doing the draw and being very theatrical and humorous about it. The American team was drawn to go second and France was drawn shortly after, but later in the draw she called France again—and we all stopped and said "Wait a minute, we already had France!" Our early order of go wasn't a very good spot and Britain was second to last or somewhere much better. So when we realized Pamela had called France twice, I went flying out of my seat to protest. I was sitting next to Ronnie Massarella (British Chef) and he was looking at me like, "Hey kid, shut up and just go ride your horse!" but I jumped up and down and demanded a redraw. Ronnie suggested they just redraw that one position, and I didn't think it was fair and said they should start from the beginning. After a debate, they eventually agreed with me and redrew the whole order. I figured there was a good chance we'd improve our position and be later in the order, but of course, there was always the possibility we'd get first position and it would be worse! Odds were in my favor. They put all the slips of paper back in the hat and redrew. We ended up fourth but the critical thing was that the British ended up right in front of us in third. We went from being in front of the Brits (who were originally second-to-last) to behind them. We didn't know it at the time of course, but we ended up in a jump-off with the British, so every one of us got to ride right behind one of the British riders based on that draw order.

I always liked going first. I told George I would ride anywhere he put me but that I wasn't sitting on the strongest horse and would probably be more useful going first since I didn't need to see anybody ride the course and felt comfortable going early in the draw. I also liked the fact that after my jump-off round, I could go help George and watch the rest of the team. After I did my second round, I was already on the clipboard with George and it became apparent mathematically that we might end up in a jump-off with the Brits. As soon as I figured that out I realized that obviously I'd be first of our riders in the jump-off. My horse was a little bit of a tough ride and you couldn't work him hard enough. Even before Hap had gone back in the ring for his second round, I was back on my horse working him and jumping him in the schooling area. One of the things I'll never forget was afterward, Hap said, "When I saw Robert warming up for the jump-off before my second round, I knew I had to go clean!"

It was incredibly exciting when we ended up in a jump-off with the British, and in those days, the entire team would jump off against one another. The rest of us just wanted to do the best we could to keep us in the game and give Hap a chance to bring us home. I remember George's advice to Hap at the in-gate. There wasn't much strategy to it! He said, "Basically, you have to ride as fast as you've ever ridden in your life and leave all the jumps up! That's the only way it's going to happen." Hap came through and jumped three clear rounds, cementing the win for our team. George instilled a passion in us. You follow your leader and we were just kids. We were all going to battle for him, and I'll never forget that feeling. In the grand scheme of things it wasn't all that important a win for our team, but it's a day we'll never forget, that's for sure.

When George was helping me learn the ropes of being Chef d'Equipe a few years ago, I always remembered that experience. That's what it's all about and why I so passionately love being the coach of teams. Back when I competed in Europe as a rider, I would always look forward to Nations Cup day more than Grand Prix day because of the team component. There are so many unique aspects to our sport but most of the time it feels like an individual sport, even though it's about the symbiotic relationship between the horse and rider, which in itself is a team. Competitively, ninety-nine percent of the time it's an individual sport. When we get those few chances to be teammates, it's very unique for us.

Despite my injury, it was a lovely summer. After trying to ride again in August but realizing it was way too early to attempt it, I took more time to heal. I was chomping at the bit to get back on Rio and into the jumper ring. I tried to distract myself by teaching clinics, judging, and heading another European tour in the lead up to the 1987 season. While teaching a clinic at Astrid Winkler's place in Germany, something a bit controversial happened. Astrid was at the time in partnership with Andre Sakakini of Italy and started running clinics for me. The American style was the envy of the world and even in Germany, in those years, my teaching was sought after. Astrid had two young students who rode there, one of whom was Ulrich (Uli) Kirchhoff, and I remember Uli watching the clinic that year. Nearly ten years later that boy won the gold medal at the Atlanta Olympics in 1996. In that clinic there was also a girl from Belgium named Evelyne Blaton riding a nice bay horse called Careful. I called Jeffery Welles who was in Europe looking at horses and he came over to try the horse. Uli was watching the clinic and watching Jeffery. A vet was called to come over and do a pre-purchase exam. As we were waiting, all of a sudden, Evelyne Blaton sold Careful to Uli Kirchhoff instead! I suppose there were no written rules against it, but our eyebrows went up and we were sorry to lose our chance with the horse.

Armand Leone married Susan Bond, a colorful young woman from a prominent family in Australia. Her father was famous for his businesses and great fortune. Susan rode with Ricky Eckhart who had worked for me at Salem View, but Armand hired me that summer to help them both. I was still on a walker but I would drive all over Germany with that thing. Teaching

Susan that summer in Germany spurred an invitation to teach in Australia and to this day, I still travel there on and off to teach clinics during the wintertime. Later that year, I taught a clinic in Bordeaux, France, around the holidays and by that time I was getting around with a cane. At one of the stables, a young Frenchman named Eric Louradour jumped up and asked if he could assist me during the clinic (since I was still on crutches!) and I agreed. He was a very attractive young guy and very ambitious when it came to riding.

After the clinic, Eric served as a guide and host while we were in Paris for the World Cup Finals in the spring of '87, and he and I became close friends. He lived in France, but I invited him to join me in Florida to ride a couple horses on the winter circuit. As Eric's career progressed, he became a very well-respected rider and horseman and has since published a couple of books on training and riding theory. Eric rode a gray mare of mine in the Preliminary Jumpers called Catania, and they were blindingly fast together in the jump-off. He had a wonderful win that winter in Florida, beating fellow Frenchman Henri Prudent who had married Katie Monahan. We ended up having a wonderful friendship, seeing each other here and there over a few years' time. He's still a very good friend.

Katharine Burdsall, my former student who happened to be riding the first million-dollar horse named The Natural, won that Paris World Cup. The Natural was the first drop of water in a wave of massively expensive prices for top jumping horses. Recently, a jumper sold for fifteen million dollars, so you can see how much these prices have compounded in only thirty years. Lisa Jacquin took home third place on For The Moment, another excellent result.

Eric Louradour

I met George during a clinic in Bordeaux and afterward we kept in touch. He came to my stable in eastern France to visit and teach several times. George recognized that I worked hard and was ambitious to be successful as a horseman. He pushed me to leave France with him and work and ride under his mentorship. I was young and spoke no English, but packed my luggage, took a risk, and went with George. It was a wonderful experience; I had the opportunity to help manage his stable in Florida and to be a demonstration rider for him at his clinics. I was so impressed with George because he was by that time world famous and buying the best horses in the world for the American team.

I was young and loved the American system where everything was so perfect and well organized in the care and training of horses. For example, the way the Americans managed the stable was impeccable down to the last detail. They would have everything packed neatly in one truck for each horse and have a groom for two or three horses maximum. They always had a stable manager and would spend so much time making sure the horse was well cared for. The horses would be turned out and hand-walked more as well. In Europe, it was impossible to do that. You'd see a groom for six to eight horses and it was completely different.

Also, the Americans gave a fantastic gift to all the sport: it changed so much in the seventies and eighties because their position and style and forward-seat system was so successful. Today, all over the world, the horses go out three times a day and are cared for in a certain way; in large part, it was the Americans who influenced that. George is a really unbelievable teacher; the best in the world. With his discipline, you don't have any struggles in your mind. You go forward and you can do anything. I am so grateful for all George taught me and did for my life and career. He has such strength and taught me strength as well, through hard work (photo 166).

That November, I traveled to Toronto to judge the annual Royal Horse Show at the Toronto Agricultural Winter Fair. Just after I had left, Kathy Moore called and said Jackie Kennedy Onassis wanted a riding lesson. Even though I would have loved to do the honor of teaching her myself, I had a contract to judge in Toronto and had no choice but to ask Anne Kursinski to teach her in my absence. With such an important student coming to Hunterdon, Anne and I conferred and agreed that she would give the lesson on a big, quiet horse we had named Bold Murmur (by the well-known hunter sire Blue Murmur). The day of her lesson, Mrs. Onassis—who was very kind, soft-spoken, and petite—rode Bold Murmur as planned in the indoor ring. Now, that horse never bucked, spooked, or got strong; he was always dead quiet. That same day, my angel of Hunterdon, Julian Arechiga, decided to paint the indoor ring. Julian started rolling the fresh paint onto the outside wall and for the first time in his life, Bold Murmur spooked. Off went Mrs. Onassis! It wasn't anyone's fault—certainly not Anne's or Julian's—but just an unfortunate accident. In the sport of horses, sometimes the sure thing backfires.

Because of my broken leg, others had to ride Rio and keep him sharp for me. Conrad rode him on the Florida circuit, and did a beautiful job (photo 167). He had such a light touch and ability to finesse his ride that it worked well with Rio who was such a sophisticated ride. Later that winter in Tampa, however, Conrad had a bad fall off Abdullah in the Tampa Grand Prix. Just as I had, he broke his left femur! It was an awful injury and although he continued riding, it turned out to be the last time Conrad ever seriously competed in the jumper ring. In essence, that fall ended his career on the USET after so many years of dominance. Because Conrad was supposed to ride Rio after Abdullah in that very same class, the Tampa Grand Prix, I had to scramble and come up with a Plan B. I asked Jeffery Welles to ride Rio—Jeffery is a very savvy, natural horseman and a fabulous rider. He had ridden horses for me sometimes, and I'd taught him a little bit and felt he could handle it, especially because he was young and willing!

Jeffery Welles

When Conrad had the bad fall on Abdullah and broke his leg during the class, George came to me and told me, "You're going to ride Rio." Today, I probably wouldn't hop on someone's horse spontaneously like that. But it was fine then, I was young and foolish and wanted to ride him. There were about seventy entries in the class but only seven or eight horses between my spot riding my horse Byron and Rio's spot. George told me, before I went in the ring on Byron, that as soon as I was done I had to run back to his barn and get on Rio back at the barn because I couldn't get on him in the schooling area. He didn't say what Rio would do, but I knew Rio could be difficult to get on. Byron went very well but we had a couple of rails—the course was enormous that day. Then I ran back to George's barn. When I got on Rio, he bolted down the barn aisle and knocked up against a trunk a little bit as I was getting him under control. I was thinking, "Whoa! This is going to be fun...." I got my stirrups organized and trotted him up to the schooling area. I remember as I started warming up over jumps he didn't feel very good. He was sort of scooting out from under me at the jumps. I think he sensed I was a different rider and was frazzled a little because of that and what had happened in the barn. Jane Clark stood there watching, and I told her it wasn't feeling too great and she said, "Well you know, you don't have to go." And I looked over at George thinking that I probably needed to make it work. As we kept jumping, Rio felt better and better over the bigger jumps, and I started to get used to his twisty style. The course was huge and there were only a couple of clear rounds in the whole class, but Rio went very well and we had a rail or two. He took very good care of me. I ended up showing Rio for the next couple of weeks and at the end, we had a clear round in the Invitational and ended up fifth. I was very honored and appreciative that George asked me to show Rio for him. Rio was a little bit quirky but a great jumper. I still remember one day schooling him with some coins in the pocket of my breeches—Rio heard them jingling and was spooking at the noise, but when I reached in my pocket to take them out he freaked out even more! I couldn't even take the change out of my pocket while on his back. So I just kept riding and remembered to empty my pockets before I got on him from then on!

VII. THE HICKSTEAD HEDGE

While I was getting back on my feet after my broken leg, Jane Clark loaned me some of her hunters to ride so I could get back in the show ring. Her horses were just wonderful—you thought, "Wait," and they waited, you thought, "Move up," and they moved up—I never knew horses could ever be that simple to ride. It was a great way to strengthen my body after my injuries.

I took an all-women team on a tour to Europe that summer, which was a combined private tour with Conrad Homfeld and Joe Fargis. Debbie Dolan rode Albany, Anne Kursinski had Starman (a wonderful horse from Germany), Joan Scharffenberger rode her favorite Victor, and Katie Prudent rode Make My Day and Special Envoy.

I also brought Rio on that summer's tour and decided to take my first crack at a Grand Prix in thirteen months at the Windsor show, a national-level show and a good one to get my feet wet again. Well, my plans to take it slow with an easier Grand Prix course were foiled. Thinking we'd feel right at home, Alan Ball built a huge course! He likely wanted to show his course-designing skill and get invited to build courses in America, and in particular at the Garden. I guess he didn't realize that I was hoping he'd go easy on us! That was also the show where we had two queens in attendance—Queen Elizabeth was on one side of the ring in her Royal Box seat, and Joanne Woodward the queen of American theater watched from her seat by the in-gate. Rio jumped around beautifully that week with me back in the tack. It felt like we hadn't missed a beat, despite the fences being so huge. I was on top of the world, being back in the Grand Prix ring.

The next week we showed at Hickstead. Between shows, I drove up to David and Lucinda Green's place. Lucinda is a famous Olympic event rider with a dozen medals from international championships and Olympic Games during the seventies and eighties. Mark Phillips of Britain, and Mark Todd and Andrew Nicholson, both from New Zealand, were also there, completing an A-list crew of world-class eventers. I taught a two-day clinic with them and not only did they ride hard, but I learned that eventers leave show jumpers in the dust when it comes to partying! They are all guts and gusto, living life to its absolute fullest whether in the saddle or celebrating afterward. We had a wonderful two days and I really enjoyed (as I always do) crossing over into that world.

Mark Phillips

I rode with George in England at a clinic with all the top eventers, and that was quite an experience. I remember he had us all line up and jump a line in four strides. Then he had us each jump it in five, then six, then seven, then eight, and even nine strides, where we were forced to put a huge bend in the line to fit that many strides in. Then after all that, he said, "Okay, now do the three." So I went down to the end of the field and had to really gallop to get the three strides! George is classical equitation through and through, everything he does and teaches is out of a classical textbook. For George, jumping is very simple. You come to the jump in the perfect canter, with the perfect balance, in the perfect rhythm, to the perfect spot, and it will always work out! Truly, George has much wisdom to offer and one would be daft to not listen to what he has to say. As well as help you through a riding moment, he also makes you think and work out the best way to solve the puzzle for your particular horse. You take away so much from his lessons.

At the Olympics in Athens and Beijing, I was coaching the three-day eventing team at the same time that George was coaching the jumpers, and George was always super supportive for the eventers. When we won the World Championships in Jerez in 2002, he walked the course with us and was a great help. He also has a great sense of humor that shows itself: one day he was helping my eventers and they kept leaving a massive gap, so maybe out of frustration he said, "You've got to learn to looooove that deep spot!"

After Windsor we moved on to Hickstead, and with the Bunn family as our hosts going back to the fifties, it always felt like a home away from home. On the first day at the show, the master of Hickstead, Dougie Bunn, suggested he and I go for a ride together. I thought that would be wonderful, as the Hickstead grounds were an old English countryside estate with beautiful trails and fields. I met up with Dougie and much to my surprise, followed him on Rio as he walked his horse into the main arena. Typically, you aren't allowed to ride in the arena before the horse show for obvious reasons. Douglas knew exactly what he was doing and I wasn't in a position to argue, so we hacked around in the main arena for forty-five minutes together. Of course, this was the perfect preparation for Rio, to have this chance to look around in the ring. As a result, the first day of the show went more smoothly that it likely would've otherwise.

The second afternoon at Hickstead, the course wasn't a scopey course but it was a very careful one with lots of verticals, planks, and flat jump cups. It was like a rub class, since even rubs would end up being faults. The second fence on course, the massive and historic Hickstead hedge, was set seven strides after the first fence and on a turn going away from the in-gate. The difficulty with a hedge like that one is that sometimes a horse misjudges it as a bank. The Hickstead hedge that day had been built with a wide oxer over it. I rode in the middle of the order and witnessed over a dozen horses struggle with the Hickstead hedge. Some paddled and knocked down the rails and others had bad falls or simply refused it. Paul Schockemöhle and Deister were among those who had trouble, nearly falling down. I didn't really worry about it much because the fences at Windsor were very big the prior week and Rio had a lot of scope when he was feeling confident. After that big hedge jump, the course required a delicate, careful approach, so my biggest concern was overriding the hedge and getting Rio so wound up that he'd be more likely to have a rub at the jumps afterward.

I rode Rio into the ring, jumped the first fence and galloped down the seven strides in a nice forward hunter stride to the Hickstead hedge. In the last couple of strides, I felt I might be getting there too soft and a bit early, without the torque to attack it appropriately. Rio had never been a horse to swim through a fence, but if he got to a fence awkwardly, he would simply *wilt*. When he did that, he felt like a tire with the air rushing out of it over the top of the jump. He would jump weak and upside-down, and I would have to whip him across the fence to give us a chance to make it to the other side. Rio jumped the giant hedge oxer, but he wilted as he did so, bringing rails down and catapulting me off his back.

I landed on the ground and was quite shook up. I saw lights behind my eyes and my fingers tingled. I lay there and got up slowly. Michael Rüping, a German rider and also a doctor, took me up to the jury room and examined me. After he was done poking around, he patted me on the back and said, "Georgie, I think you're all right. You go ahead and get on and ride in the speed class." As I walked back to the barn, my fingers were still tingling and my head and vision didn't feel quite right. Having been raised in a very cautious family when it came to health, I didn't think getting back on right away was a great idea. I figured it would be smarter to pop over to the nearby hospital and get checked out, and perhaps some radiographs taken.

Kathy Moore and Danny Marks drove me to the hospital. The X-rays were taken and after several hours of waiting and speaking with doctors, they gave me a clean bill of health. As we drove out of the parking lot, a doctor in a lab coat came sprinting up behind us and pounded on the trunk, hollering at us. Kathy slammed on the brakes and nurses came trotting out of the building with a gurney. Panting, the man informed me that I had a broken neck! As the story went, a radiologist was walking by the film viewing box, where my films still hung, and asked, "Where's the patient with the broken neck?" Not only was there a fracture, but it was unstable and could have caused paralysis. They put me on a stretcher with a neck brace, wheeled me back into the hospital, and drugged me up with sedatives. Consequently, after my injury and the falls of so many others at the hedge that year, Dougie Bunn decided to substantially cut it down!

Cooped up in the hospital for the weekend with a halo on to stabilize my neck, I tried my best to keep up with what was happening over at the show. Kathy kept things running and from my hospital bed, I watched on television as my all-women team won the Nations Cup! Even in current record books, this was one of the only instances when an all-female team won the Nations Cup at a five-star show. To end up on top of all those great teams from around the world on their home turf was a major accomplishment, and the Europeans were taken down another peg by stellar American riders (photo 170).

After only riding one entire show at the Grand Prix level, I found myself grounded once again. Frustrated, it helped I had two burly male nurses by my side as I floated all the way back to New Jersey, drugged to the hilt. I was so high I didn't need an airplane! Back in the States, the Hunterdon medical center welcomed me back for more treatment and thankfully, the recovery wasn't nearly as long as the broken leg. Still, I had to suffer through another few months out of the show ring.

Later that same summer, we organized a short, all-Hunterdon trip to Europe for some and Martha Wachtel (later: Jolicoeur) brought a couple of mares. I was supposed to have ridden myself at one particular German show but with my broken neck I couldn't. Instead, I sent Martha there with her second horse. Surrounded by German men hitting on her the entire week, Martha kept placing higher and higher against all of them with each day that went by!

Martha Jolicoeur

George told me I had to ride in his place at the smaller German show since we had accepted the invitation. I agreed, but I could only ride my second-string horse Servus, who was a mare by Lucky Boy (my other mare wasn't good in the mud and the weather had been very wet). I was really nervous about taking George's place, and when I first got there I felt a little out at sea. I didn't speak a word of German and I remember the German riders laughing at me and mocking me, especially because Servus didn't flex and they were all into their flatwork, of course. George arrived a day or two afterward and, day by day, as the show went on, we improved our results. I was sixth the first day, then second or third the next day.

At the end of the show, George came to meet me and watch—and I won the Grand Prix! I even won a Volkswagen. It was such a thrill! I hadn't seen George yet that week and after the victory gallop and presentation, I saw him working his way through the crowd to see me. He put a hand on my knee and said, "You know, Martha, you always whine and worry, but you're a winner. I forgot that about you, you always win!" and then he turned, without missing a beat and said, "But you can't take that car you just won, because you're driving me in the Mercedes back to Aachen." And I replied, "Of course, I'll drive you to Aachen, but not until tomorrow morning. Tonight, we celebrate!"

In 1987, the girl I'd seen on her way to becoming a huge talent in California, Meredith Michaels, came to Hunterdon. Karen Healey still coached Meredith in the equitation Finals that year, but otherwise she trained with me for the jumper ring. Meredith had something special from the beginning. When I traveled back to Aachen later that summer, I invited her to come along to give her exposure to the international scene. She also came with me to the Pan American Games later that year in Indianapolis. I wasn't in the habit of taking teenagers with me to Aachen or to the Pan Am Games, but she was so ambitious and bright with a wonderful work ethic. Nobody knew who she was yet, but people were very impressed when they met her, in particular William Steinkraus. Long before she became known as the famous rider she is today, I helped her get some important exposure to the top of the sport.

Meredith Michaels-Beerbaum

Riding with Karen Healey exposed me to George from the very beginning and I rode in clinics with him regularly from a young age. It was always a dream for me to go east and ride with him. I worked hard in school, got into Princeton University, and went to school in New Jersey. That meant I was very close to Hunterdon and could ride with George. It was such a dream come true to have that opportunity.

Later, George brought me with him as a student to Aachen and the Pan American Games in the late eighties, when he was Chef d'Equipe for the Belgium team. George also took me to Europe on a Young Riders team to give me exposure to competing in Europe. Those two trips opened my eyes to the international world. I badly wanted to compete for a gold medal and ride at Aachen. I was a good student in school and interested in a lot of potential career options. Before I went to Europe with George, I hadn't yet decided that horses were going to be my profession and my life. Taking me to Europe showed me the world stage and that's when I decided what I really wanted to do. So you see, George had a huge impact on the path of my entire life. Even more than the important lessons he taught me about riding and training, that exposure sparked a dream. When they all went home at the end of the Young Riders tour, I stayed in Europe and followed that dream.

To this day, Aachen remains my favorite show in the world. I later went on to win the Grand Prix there, which was an amazing experience. Throughout my career, despite staying in Europe and changing my nationality, George continued to resurface and be present during big moments in my life—like when I was nominated to be the first woman ever to ride on a championship team in Germany when we went double clear and won at Hickstead. He was there when I won three World Cup Finals, when I made the final four in the World Games with Shutterfly, and he was also there when I lost a bronze medal by a couple of tenths of a second. George was there again and again and again and always supportive of me. He's not just a mentor but a very, very close friend.

Our team for the Pan American Games in 1987 was Rodney Jenkins, Katharine Burdsall, Lisa Jacquin, and Greg Best. Ian Millar won individual gold on Big Ben and Rodney Jenkins silver on Czar, with Canada winning team gold and the USET silver. Canada impressively stood toe to toe with the American team, with Ian Millar leading the way. After three months recovering from my broken neck, I regained strength and started showing once again, rising quickly back up to the Grand Prix level. I went to Calgary that fall and to the indoor shows and Rio did very well, despite the fact that indoor courses weren't as comfortable as the outdoor ones. I continued helping younger riders, like Joan Scharffenberger and Lisa Tarnopol, and others in the jumper group out of Hunterdon.

Jeff Cook, a wonderful friend and excellent rider, horseman, and teacher, became a very important part of Hunterdon in those years. Jeff worked for me for periods of time on and off, and was always a fabulous fit for our operation. He's a phenomenal horseman, with the necessary attention to detail, intelligence, and personality that works excellently with students and clients. Working side by side with Chris Kappler, Jeff practically ran Hunterdon for many years in the late eighties and early nineties.

Jeff Cook

I grew up riding in clinics with George Morris at Don Kerron and Joan Curtin's farm in the early seventies. From a professional, etiquette, and commitment standpoint, I've learned so much from him. I saved my money to go back East to watch him teach when he still had the big hunter/equitation operation, with Bill Cooney and Frank Madden working for him. When I went to work for him the first time in 1986, George was in the upper barn doing the jumpers and he was still riding competitively then. Perhaps the biggest thing I took away from working for him was the day-in, day-out training of the horses. It was so meticulous, how much he flatted and jumped day to day. He also was creative in getting out of the ring. In Florida in the late eighties we would do a lot of trail riding, because Palm Beach wasn't very developed then like it is now. George would trot down the trails and we'd follow behind him.

Every detail matters to George. One of my favorite things was to sit with him and go through the list of clients and horses when he was in town. We would talk through each one and he would give us feedback on what direction he thought made sense for that rider or horse. I really cherish those moments, looking back. I learned so much from listening to his thought process.

George's string of hunters was unbelievable and many of them he spotted as very young unproven horses. It wasn't just George training top show horses for the Garden. He bought Dillon as a two-year-old at a training stable out West where they raised racing Thoroughbreds. He just jumped him over a couple of hay bales and saw his potential; that horse was a national champion year after year. That's something people don't realize about George, that ability to spot and bring along horses when they are very young. He has always had such an excellent eye.

I remember one day in particular: a hot summer Friday late afternoon. A young student and his mom pulled in with their two-horse trailer for his lesson. The boy was a fairly green rider with a pony and it had been a very long day, so I offered to teach the lesson for George. He said no, that he would teach him, and I so watched and help set jumps. The boy didn't jump more than cross-rails that day, but George gave him a careful and detailed hour-long lesson. That taught me something just as important as what I learned watching George get someone ready for the World Cup: that you have to put your all into it, no matter what.

The World Cup Finals in 1988 were back once again in Gothenberg, Sweden, which is the official home of that show although it does travel from city to city. I was thrilled to be competing that year on Rio, who was in peak form. The first leg is a Table A course under Table C rules, which is a speed class. Rio was clear and for him, he was very good. I didn't ask him to race around and be a speed demon because if I did that, he was liable to get scared and worried. We ended up fourteenth after the first class, which I was very happy with because of the way they used to score it. If you were in the top eighteen after the first round, you still had a chance to win it. Nowadays, with the current scoring system in the World Cup, you really need to be in the top five after the first round to end up on top.

The second night was the big Friday night jump-off and overnight the schooling ring had been completely flooded. It was a total aberration—I've never seen it before or since, but I believe a pipe broke at the facility overnight and caused the flood. Rio was completely undone by the footing, dancing and spooking and unable to focus. Warming up was a nightmare and with him so flustered, he went poorly in the class, wilting at the fences and not jumping confidently. It wasn't necessarily a surprise after his behavior in the warm-up ring, but I was so disappointed. I rode him in the big class on Sunday but his confidence had unraveled…it was the only time he stopped in his life. It wasn't a quick stop, it was one of those slow motion "giving-up" stops at the fourth fence and I knew he was just shaken up. His heart wasn't in it—so I tipped my hat and left the ring (photo 172).

Ian Millar won that World Cup Final with Big Ben, which I was very happy about, as it was yet another North American winner (photo 173). In fact, Ian won back-to-back World Cup Finals in 1988 and 1989, an incredible feat! Out of eleven consecutive World Cups, the score was: Europeans 1, North Americans 10. I'm not sure we'll ever have an era of dominance like that again. Of the winners during that era, most were either my students or my classmates, so to speak, under the tutelage of Bert de Némethy, like Michael Matz.

After Rio had lost his confidence in the sloppy warm-up ring at the World Cup Final, he needed to be rebuilt from the ground up. First, we did a lot of flatwork to relax him and then literally began by only jumping cross-rails, steadily raising his confidence. Rio's program was totally designed to build his confidence as solidly as possible, and by the time Spruce Meadows Masters rolled around, he was sharp and ready to go to Calgary. I just hoped we wouldn't run into any issues like the flooded footing at the World Cup Finals.

Nearly every year I was Chef d'Equipe for the American riders in Calgary, and it's a fabulous show with one of the best Grand Prix classes in North America. The du Maurier International was one of the richest Grand Prix in the world—these days it still is, but they call it the CN International. In the Friday night class, Rio went excellently and we were fifth. We would've been even faster in the jump-off if not for slipping in a turn from deep footing. Chris Kappler was the youngest rider on the team and placed eighth on his horse Concorde, which was an excellent result for him. Chris was really starting to show his ability in the big jumper ring, and he worked Concorde through some difficulty at Liverpools and the water jump.

The du Maurier format was the old fashioned Grand Prix approach with two full jumping rounds followed by a jump-off, if necessary. Rio felt great warming up and we went clear in the first round—then we went back in, rode ninth in the order and were clear in the second round too—the only ones to go double clear. I was thrilled! Only one rider was left to go after me, and I walked Rio down the backside of the stabling area, since I had to get off him near his stall. Katie Prudent came running down the road and yelled, "He had a fence down—*you've won!*"

Katie Prudent

George and I joke about that day, because I was trying to help school him in the warm-up ring before the second round of the du Maurier. I was talking through some of the lines on the course, and George was so focused on what he wanted to do in the ring that he barked back to me, "Stop it, I can't listen to this! I know what I'm going to do." And he was right. He was in the zone. The second round was a lot of pressure but he rode it beautifully. After he won, I told him he was just the absolute worst student, talking back to me like that!

At last, my wonderful and quirky Rio whom I loved so much had shown the world he was a winner! We finally had our day in the sun. The du Maurier was the richest class in the world then, with the purse of a half-million dollars. I never would've dreamed I was capable of that kind of world-class win after more than a decade out of the jumper ring. We had each overcome obstacles to earn the win—to have success on such a fragile, complex horse was quite a feat, especially after our difficulties at the World Cup and my rehabilitation after two injuries. It was of equal importance to winning the Grand Prix of Aachen in 1960, but it was particularly special to win with Rio, a horse I'd trained and developed myself. That day was one of the proudest moments I've ever had as a horseman, because it was truly when all my hard work and patience with Rio paid off. I was thrilled beyond words, and it was a great ending to that year of many ups and downs (photos 175, 176).

After we'd won the du Maurier International up in Calgary, I took Rio to Washington to show. As we were warming up in the schooling ring, he stopped at a cross-rail about six inches high—acting like he'd never seen a jump in his life! Caught so off guard—with Rio putting his head down and dropping his shoulder so suddenly—I slid right over his head, hit the ground, and separated my shoulder. I couldn't believe it. All my war wounds were from that horse!

By the Florida circuit in 1988, Rio was one of the best horses in the country. Down in Wellington and Tampa that winter, he was back at the top of his game and consistently in the ribbons. We were second in the Tampa Grand Prix to Joe Fargis riding Mill Pearl, an Irish TB mare that Joe took to the Olympics in Seoul. Both Joe and I went clear, but there was an inside turn to a fence that Rio simply couldn't make and so we ended up second. It was nothing to sneeze at, no doubt about that, and as a result of that great placing, I qualified for the World Cup Finals.

I heard from a friend that while a famous past Olympian looked out over the ring as Joe and I were getting our ribbons, he commented that the Americans had so many good riders for the Seoul Olympics that they could field a men's team, a women's team, and a gay team. I didn't hear him say it myself—I heard it secondhand so he may not have—but I'd like to think he did. To me, it was a sign of both our enormous depth of good riding in the United States at that time and that alternative lifestyles were becoming more accepted. Even though this guy allegedly made the remark in a very friendly way, I do remember feeling a tad bit sensitive hearing about it at first, simply because I was very private about my personal life. However, looking back I think it said a lot about the horse world in those years.

VIII. THE SEOUL OLYMPICS

Jeff Cook

I'm so thankful I had that opportunity to watch George and witness the way he trained the jumpers he was showing during those years. It's no surprise, knowing the way he teaches, that he trains like that with horses he is himself showing. But I was very fortunate to have witnessed that firsthand. Rio is a classic example of the meticulousness of how George trained. That horse was dicey to just get on and he could get set off at the drop of a hat. He had to be on, a very specific program in order to succeed; George may have been the only one capable of it. After George came back from Spruce Meadows I asked him how it went and he said nonchalantly, "Oh, pretty good...we won." Pretty good, indeed!

Before the Seoul, Korea, Olympic Games Kathy Moore, Eric Louradour, and I traveled to mainland China and did some sightseeing. We went to Shanghai, Beijing, and Hangzhao and had a wonderful time. We didn't do anything horsey but had a wonderful trip and simply experienced being in that part of the world.

Show jumping at the 1988 Olympic Games in Seoul is well remembered, and rightfully so, for Greg Best and Gem Twist's great success. Paul Schockemöhle was helping the German team and they had very strong riders that year. In my view, the German horses weren't as great as the American team horses at that Olympic Games. We had Gem Twist with Greg Best, For the Moment with Lisa Jacquin, Starman with Anne Kursinski, and Mill Pearl with Joe Fargis. Katharine Burdsall and The Natural were the alternates. On paper, ours was a gold-medal team, no question about it. Paul Schockemöhle brought four very good riders that year to face off against us: Ludger Beerbaum, Wolfgang Brinkmann, Dirk Hafemeister, and Franke Sloothaak. The team competition was very close, with Germany just barely edging us out in the end. Our team earned the silver medal, and then Greg Best and Gem Twist were brilliant and won the individual silver behind Pierre Durand, Jr. on the fabulous horse Jappeloup for France (photos 177–180).

Overall, it was a very good Olympics for American show jumping, but it certainly wasn't like Los Angeles. The European teams were very clever. I saw the handwriting on the wall as the days progressed in Seoul. The Germans beat us fair and square, but my antenna was up! I could sense the Europeans were catching up to us again. They knew the game now and they knew how to prepare their horses. Some poling devices were found at those Olympics and there were also rumors of switching horses around in their stalls so that any testing might be performed on a dummy horse instead of the competing horse. There's always hanky panky at every Olympic Games! But even outside of these things, which may have given our opponents an edge, I could see the European teams' technical skills had improved greatly since Los Angeles.

I helped Jean-Claude Van Geenberghe in Seoul, as well, since that was still during his time on the Belgian team and he was my student. I coached the Belgian team as their Chef d'Equipe on a couple of occasions in the late eighties and in 1989 I was the Chef d'Equipe for the Swiss team at the European Championships, which was the result of my relationship with Thomas Fuchs. My footprint as a professional in Europe had really been carved deeply and not only was I was giving clinics all over Europe, but I was also buying European horses, assisting Frank Chapot with coaching the USET, and leading private European tours out of Hunterdon with young jumper riders.

After each Olympic Games, the following year is more restful as the start to the next four-year cycle. We weren't preparing for a World Championship, Pan American Games, or Olympic Games in 1989 and simply had the World Cup in the spring and the standard show circuit. Those "off years" are times to build for the future and focus on business priorities. I was often involved with initiatives and committees that have an impact on changes in the sport and that year, new rules were discussed with the Federation Drugs and Medications Committee around drug use and testing at horse shows.

John Strassburger

I remember back in '89, before the AHSA's annual convention, the Drugs and Medications Committee had developed a proposal to establish quantitative limitations on NSAIDs—bute, Banamine, and Ketofen were the major ones—and this was a new world to allow therapeutic administration of NSAIDs that was not performance-enhancing. Marty Simensen, DVM, and John Lengel, DVM, worked out a very carefully orchestrated presentation to convince the members of the AHSA of this proposal's need and merits. After they'd made their presentation, a couple of people in the audience responded, mostly vaguely in favor, but some in opposition or doubt about certain technical or administrative aspects of the proposal. Then George stood up, and his presence raised the discussion to another level. He swayed the room, saying, "People, this is what we *must* do as members of this organization and as horsemen. There is no question that we must pass this rule."

I remember that we named John and Marty *The Chronicle of the Horse's* Overall Horsemen of the Year for what they had done, and they told me later they were so relieved to have George's support that evening. Now, more than twenty-five years later, it's the cornerstone of our Federation's governance. This rule was in historic contrast to the foolishness of the FEI rules, which treat horses not as the athletes they really are: the FEI rules don't leave any room for the fact that, as with human athletes, proper drug therapy can alleviate stress and add comfort to animals with the heart to perform at the high levels at which we ask them. A quarter-century later, the AHSA rules have stood the test of time.

The authority George demonstrated at that meeting epitomizes his stature and leadership in the sport. If he had stood up and denounced the proposal, it would've probably ended the discussion right there, and who knows what would have happened. But George wouldn't have ascended to that level of authority without being sensible and intelligent about the sport. Thankfully, George's innate belief is that, even though our horse sports have become a big business, the horses must always come first. Period.

Ray Texel became both a client and a working student for a few years at Hunterdon and joined my team of young jumper riders. Ray had won the AHSA Medal and ASPCA Maclay Equitation Finals in 1989 under the coaching of Michael Henaghan. He was the fair-haired boy of the country with a metric ton of potential. Robert Dover also came to lease out the lower barn for his horses and clients for some time and it was wonderful to train alongside a great horseman who was focused on dressage. From time to time I would have a chance to ride his wonderful Olympic-caliber dressage horses.

That summer, I took a tour again to Europe with Anne Kursinski, Joan Scharffenberger, Gary Young, and Ray Texel. We went to Stockholm, where they had a wonderful summer show, and also to Hickstead, Luxembourg, Aachen, and Dublin. The World Championships (which became the World Equestrian Games in 1990) were planned for Stockholm the following year and I took my team there as a preview, giving them experience and a comfort level with the show and the city.

Rio had squishy suspensory tendons and the first part of the '89 tour I couldn't show him because he had strained one of his suspensories. Meredith's sponsor Isaac Arguetty helped me buy a jumper to ride named Slinky, a mare ridden by a very good Australian friend Rod Brown. Rod had ridden her at the Seoul Olympics and did a super job with her, but Slinky never really had the scope or carefulness to fill Rio's shoes in the big classes. Slinky had a difficult mouth and would pull me past the distance and rob herself of scope over the fences. In Copenhagen, Gary Young suggested I try a double-jointed snaffle with a port on Slinky and it worked like a magic charm! Not that Slinky had huge scope, but it gave me a chance to help her across the oxers. That bit made that horse so much more rideable that we almost won the Grand Prix of Copenhagen and ended up fifth. After all was said and done, Slinky and I did all right, but I never duplicated Rod Brown's success in Seoul with her.

Ludger Beerbaum

I remember the first time I met George very well—it was the mid-eighties. He was Chef d'Equipe of the best riders in the world: Michael Matz, Conrad Homfeld, Katie Prudent, and Joe Fargis. For me, this first meeting was extremely impressive because of the outstanding professionalism in their performance. It's difficult for me to describe but from the first meetings up until today, there has always been a positive chemistry between George and me, and even though we've had our fights, there has always been an underlying mutual respect.

It was May 1989; we were competing at Hickstead. George was coaching the American team; I was riding on the German team. It had just been announced that I was leaving the Schockemöhle stables, meaning, at that time, I would lose all my horses. We met while walking the course, and I remember asking George what I should do without all those good horses, to which he replied, "Which good horses? You have never had one!" Three years later after I won the individual Olympic gold medal in Barcelona, he approached me with a smile, "Do you remember what I told you in Hickstead?"

At the close of the show season in Baltimore, I rode Rio out of the ring and Jane Clark told me she was ready to retire him. Jane was afraid Rio would break down in the ring with his squishy suspensory tendons. He was only thirteen, and I didn't think he was any more or less sound than ever, but he certainly did have soundness issues. Jane tends to be very definite with those kind of decisions with her horses so Rio was retired.

In 1989 the High Performance Committee established a rule that you couldn't be Chef d'Equipe and ride at the same show, so they asked Linda Allen to be Chef d'Equipe in Calgary that year instead of me. I'm still not exactly sure what triggered the change—I had certainly balanced my own riding with the support of the other American riders well enough. Perhaps I did too well!

Robert Dover

I kept my horses at Hunterdon for several years and rented out the lower barn. George and I love to talk about the technical aspects of riding. We used to sit, just talking and debating what worked with horses and why. We would talk about half-halts at length! The inquisitiveness is what we always shared and enjoyed about one another, which is of course a characteristic of all successful horsemen. In those first years at Hunterdon, I had a variety of clients—some who were quite driven and ambitious about the level of riding and showing they wanted to do and others who simply wanted to ride with me and enjoyed being part of my stable. I recall once that I was complaining to George about how I was working nonstop, early morning until late in the evening every single day, and that I had no time off and was always exhausted. He said, "Robert, you haven't learned! What you do is send a letter to all of them doubling your prices. Half of them will leave and the ones you are left with are the good ones who are serious competitors. You'll bring in the same amount of money for half the work!" And what really got through to me was that I had been undervaluing my work at that time; I had been charging the same as when I had first begun as a professional and had never raised my fees, even after riding in the Olympics, the World Cup, and WEG.

I put George on my Grand Prix dressage horse more than once. Even though he wasn't as practiced in a classical dressage seat because he was always riding hunt seat and the jumpers, within five minutes he could do the entire Grand Prix on my horse. It didn't matter if it was an easy horse or a hard horse. He'd ridden with top dressage people in his life, and he had such a strong feel that he was able to look very good. He delighted in the advanced movements: the piaffe, the passage, the pirouettes, the tempi changes—all thrilled him!

I rode up one day into the arena at Hunterdon. It was a very hot day and some riders were jumping inside to get out of the hot sun. There was a young guy setting jumps in the arena who caught my eye. I rode right past him and up to George and asked, "George I just have one question: who in the hell is *THAT*?" He said, "That's Robert Ross and he's here from California for a clinic." Later that evening, I promptly invited myself over to George's pool party the next day. And that was the beginning of a twenty-seven-year relationship with Robert Ross. Now we're married!

Childress "Chile" Rodgers was a great horsewoman and a fan of mine back in the 1950s. Chile brought up generation after generation of young riders at her riding school in Cincinnati, teaching them how to foxhunt and ride cross country. Chile was a friend of Doris Duke, the daughter of Duke University's founder and descendent of a very wealthy tobacco family. Doris had a big property in Somerville, New Jersey, which was a little closer to the city than Hunterdon. She was never into horses, but Doris's adopted daughter Chandi Heffner was a horse lover, and at Chile's suggestion, she sent some of her young horses to Hunterdon for training.

Jeff Cook helped Chandi find some horses, and they even flew him to Ireland on their private jet, which was snow white with the American flag on it. Inside the plane there were no seats but instead piles of mattresses and throw blankets, as a sort of homage to Middle Eastern style (they were both Hare Krishna devotees). They were very interesting, eccentric people, and after I returned from Europe I became friendly with them. Doris had a butler named Bernard who would rollerskate up and down the halls and aisles serving them. She also had a Newport, Rhode Island, mansion that was so enormous they brought camels right into the house!

Jeff Cook

Doris Duke sent some grooms to Hunterdon to talk to us about some horses she had. They didn't say who they worked for, but George was off in Europe on a tour, so I sat down with them to chat. Not that it would've mattered when they finally trusted me enough to say who they worked for; I was a country kid from Oregon and didn't even know who Doris Duke was! Well, I told them I would come look at the horses they had and ride a couple of them. I told Kathy Moore about the plan and she tried to impress upon me who the Duke family was, but I think it didn't completely sink in until I pulled up to the estate and saw the place. They had me trot the horses back and forth on the lawn in front of the mansion because it was the best footing! Bernard the butler was bringing out trays of drinks and so forth—it was surreal! Once George came home, of course, the Dukes wanted to meet him and we went for dinner there together. Those types of things made me nervous, but George was great at it. He and Doris hit it off immediately and ended up being quite good friends.

I visited Doris and Chandi in Oahu, Hawaii, at one of her five grand homes—a Moroccan palace. It was a nice stopover on the way home from Australia, and I taught a clinic and stayed with Doris. Sean Steffee, now a trainer and Grand Prix rider but then still in his early twenties, met me there to assist in the clinic. He'd ridden with me at a clinic in Chicago earlier that year and I'd been quite impressed with him. Imelda Marcos came over to visit for dinner at Doris's several times that week because Ferdinand Marcos was back in the Philippines, and she was lonely and wanted to see her friends. I found myself the contented audience of fabulous stories of how Mao Tse Tung would give her foot massages and Muammar Gaddafi had a crush on her. She had an arrestingly beautiful face.

Out of nowhere, Imelda decided she wanted to take a riding lesson with me (photo 181). Unfortunately, I was sick as a dog that week with the flu, but how could I refuse? Chandi and Doris had some horses at a nearby stable with a covered ring. Oddly enough, Imelda had both a hunt cap and a pair of paddock boots (among her hundreds of pairs of shoes) at her house even though she'd never been on a horse in her life! With the help of her beefy bodyguards pushing and pulling her, we got her into the saddle on a very quiet horse. I tried to take it easy but all she wanted to do was go faster and jump, and she was bouncing around in the saddle at just the trot! I walked her over a line in the sand, teaching her to get into two-point and grab mane. Then Doris, who was watching from the sidelines, decided she wanted a lesson, too!

❧

The decade of the eighties was my unexpected but happy renaissance in the Grand Prix jumpers after I began to specialize in the late seventies. I had realized that in the horse business, unless you're hands-on and focused on one division, you can't truly have success. You must specialize, whether it's hunters, equitation, ponies, jumpers, or Grand Prix. I'd had a great run in the equitation and hunters but I wanted to go back to my first love with riding, which was Olympic-level show jumping. I'd been there with Bert de Némethy and the team, won an Olympic silver medal and the Grand Prix of Aachen, and I knew it was the right direction. One of my favorite teaching roles—introducing young jumper riders to Europe—helped give our teams depth and instilled confidence in our riders who were new to the scene, helping create better teams for international championships.

Shifting to my focus on the jumpers, I started with my pupils going to Europe, then caught the bug myself, buying investment horses that ended up being quite talented. Brussels and Rio took me up though the Preliminary divisions and ultimately to a win in one of the biggest Grands Prix in the world. If you'd told me in 1979 that I would win the Grand Prix of Calgary in '88, I would have asked what you'd been smoking! In the seventies, I rode hunters and the odd green jumper over four-foot jumps—I never thought I'd jump the big jumps again.

From a personal perspective, the eighties were a decade of austerity. When I quit drinking in '82, my healthier lifestyle had a huge impact on my return to riding in the Grand Prix. If I hadn't stopped being wild during those years, I never would have been capable of the success I had in the jumper ring. In terms of relationships, I had some adventurous times but the AIDS epidemic caused a major half-halt in the free-wheeling, party atmosphere we'd all enjoyed in the seventies. The fear of the so-called "gay plague" caused the entire nightlife scene to shift, and while previously I had relied on going out as a way to let go of the pressure of running a business, all of that stopped for several years.

Today it's quite different in that being gay is very accepted, but the feeling of being stigmatized—being an aberration from the norm—never stops, no matter how respected you are in your field. Despite my unapologetic stance that I'd held onto since the late fifties, I've struggled through my entire life with not feeling entirely comfortable in either straight or gay society in America. Most often, I feel at home with certain special people in my life or groups of friends who seem to strike the balance between the two worlds with intelligence and open-mindedness.

CHAPTER SIX: THE 1990s

THE EVOLUTION OF A LEADER

I. THE FIRST WORLD EQUESTRIAN GAMES

The decade of the nineties began with a watershed year for the United States Equestrian Team. The World Championships held every four years was transformed into the World Equestrian Games, held in every even year between Olympic Summer Games. Under the previous World Championship format, each equestrian discipline had its own championship in a different geographic location. With the inception of the World Equestrian Games, all championships came together in one location with the exposure and international stature of a huge multi-disciplinary event. It's a wonderful idea and gives each discipline exposure to the others.

As Chef d'Equipe, Frank Chapot ultimately chose the team for the WEG that year, but consideration was given by a committee of selectors. Linda Allen was head of the High Performance Selection Committee and Katie Prudent, Conrad Homfeld, and I each served as selectors who gave Frank our opinions. I was also helping Anne Kursinski and Joan Scharffenberger with their preparation because I had a history with each of them as either a mentor or teacher. Debbie Dolan rode with Joe Fargis and Conrad Homfeld, so I wasn't the only one on the Selection Committee with a relationship with a rider under consideration for the team. In those days it wasn't squeaky clean in terms of separation between clients and administrative roles like being part of a committee.

The team for the WEG was to be selected based on the judgment of each horse and rider's readiness and consistency. To gauge sharpness, we all observed the riders at both U.S. and European Grand Prix classes. Joe Fargis and his wonderful horse Mill Pearl, and Greg Best on his iconic Gem Twist, were definite team picks. Joan Scharffenberger had been rock solid and consistent in her results with top ribbons throughout, so everyone unanimously thought she deserved a spot.

The question remained: who would get the fourth and the alternate spots on the team? Anne Kursinski had been a little inconsistent at U.S. shows but was leading rider in Europe on Starman, who looked very sharp (photo 182). Debbie Dolan had won at the Devon selection trial back home, but then had tough rounds at the European shows, incurring time and jumping faults and hitting the water in Luxembourg. Debbie had a wonderful horse in VIP but those who saw her ride in Europe could plainly see she'd lost some of the edge she'd had at the shows at home. It was common for even great riders to have difficulty on that big European stage.

In the end, Debbie and Anne were vying for the remaining spot and an alternate spot. Beezie Patton on Northern Magic, with loads of talent but less experience internationally, had already been slotted in as one of the two alternates.

The Selection Committee met after the Luxembourg show ended to choose the team for Stockholm. Our conference room was the schooling area at the show and our chairs were the jump rails! Frank gave particular weight to whom was having success in Europe on the basis that those horses and riders were likely to continue to be successful there. He nominated the choices of Greg Best, Joe Fargis, Anne Kursinski, and Joan Scharffenberger with Debbie Dolan and Beezie Patton as the alternates. Conrad, who is very strong-minded, was adamant that Debbie be on the team, not an alternate. He felt Anne shouldn't be on the team because Starman had been careless with some fences down at Devon, but it seemed he'd forgotten she'd won the Grand Prix at Old Salem. Starman wasn't known as the most careful horse, it was true, but he'd risen to the occasion in Europe, and they were in consistent peak form. Frank, Katie, and I all felt strongly that after Debbie's faults in the European classes, she wasn't performing at the same level as the other four. Linda Allen could see both sides and was wavering. We argued about it for about an hour and a half while some of the Europeans stood near the schooling ring watching; our meeting had turned into "the show after the show"!

Then, the situation became confusing. Linda, the chair of the committee, reached into her briefcase and took out a fax of a document that outlined criteria for selection of a team. She and Conrad had been communicating back and forth about the criteria and according to those rules, Debbie was on the team. There was even a threat of legal action if we didn't put Debbie on the team! Frank threw his hands up and said, "Okay, well that's it then, it's decided!" The rest of us couldn't dispute it—it was a fait accompli! We had no choice but to let Debbie onto the team.

I got into my car and sped back to my hotel room in Luxembourg City to call Bill Steinkraus and Vince Murphy. It was important that the USET Executive Committee understand how Debbie ended up on the team despite a majority of the selectors feeling she shouldn't have made it. Such a contentious selection needed to be communicated upward so that everyone was clear the decision was made under an air of disagreement. It was through these conversations with Executive Committee members that I came to understand that the faxed document Linda had produced was not actually the current rules! In fact, the rules they pointed to were simply a work in progress—they were recommendations developed by Linda and Conrad for what criteria they wanted to see put in place for the future. The rest of us had misunderstood!

The Executive Committee overturned the Selection Committee's decision and laid down an edict that Frank's originally proposed team—with Anne one of the four and Debbie as an alternate—was the team going to the WEG. Understandably, the Dolans were crushed by the news that Debbie wasn't one of the main four chosen to ride; they had considered her a shoo-in after her win at the Devon trials. I'm sure it was terrible to be celebrating and then afterward to hear that the decision had been overturned. Joe and Conrad were bitterly disappointed, too, since she was their student. In those days we didn't have the internet and the American public didn't have a chance to witness Debbie's rounds in Europe themselves. People were really upset that she didn't make the team and those in Debbie's court felt that there had been unfair bias in choosing my students (Anne and Joan) over Debbie. This debacle was the beginning of a civil war.

Every Chef d'Equipe of the United States Equestrian Team has tried to improve upon the selection system and, as a result of his efforts, has learned it's inevitable that some will have objections. In equestrian sports, where so many variables—both physical and mental—impact the performance of both horses and riders, being purely objective and using only class results to choose a team doesn't predict a winning team. The health and competitive edge of horses and their riders are delicately balanced. Using subjective judgment, which, in essence, means combining results of trials with observed sharpness and confidence of horse-and-rider pairs—results in the best team most often. However, with subjectivity at play, it's simply a matter of human nature that unavoidable or unconscious bias may also enter into the equation. Everyone is happy some of the time, but no one is happy all of the time! It's the nature of the beast and I know Bert de Némethy, Frank Chapot, I, and Robert Ridland have and shall continue to try to make the best choices for the success of the country.

After the drama, the team itself focused and rode very well at the WEG in Stockholm. The team was fourth in the team event and just out of the medals. The WEG format dictates that three separate classes over three days count toward the final round of the individual competition, where the top four riders square off. Each rider starts again with a zero score and jumps a course on his or her own horse. Then each rider switches mounts, riding the same course on each of the others' horses. The rider with the lowest combined faults on all four horses wins. Greg Best and Gem Twist were in first place going into the final round, but dropped to fourth after the faults Greg incurred riding the others' horses. Still, having representation on the final four and finishing fourth as a team was a great result.

Despite a good result for our American team, it was overshadowed by the hot debate over the relegation of Debbie Dolan to the alternate spot. The civil war just kept heating up as time went by and 1990-91 was the darkest time in the history of the USET. With top riders and powerful owners feeling that the selection of the WEG team had been unfair, controversy began to drive a wedge into the show-jumping community. If you tell parents the judge is crooked and their child was the victim of bias, parents, of course, believe you— they *want* to believe you! Soon, there was litigation by the Dolans, whose lawsuit charged the USET Selection Committee with conflict of interest in choosing riders we were personally connected with.

Many riders spoke out. Others cried foul about favoritism in the selection process and called for more objectivity in the choosing of championship teams. The legal action broke out a battle within the community with very strong feelings on each side of the issue. Joe Fargis, Conrad Homfeld, and Armand Leone led the rebellion with powerful owners and clients behind them, in addition to the Dolans. Many criticized the rebels for putting the USET and the American Horse Shows Association at risk of financial ruin with their attempted hostile proxy takeover. The debate proved extremely divisive with the unfortunate result of longtime friends discovering they were in opposite camps.

Politically, it was the worst thing I've ever experienced in the horse business. My friendships with Conrad Homfeld and Armand Leone became strained, with them firmly in the opposing camp. The legal proceedings lasted for years and almost resulted in a judicial order to replace the entire leadership of the AHSA and USET! By the skin of its teeth, the establishment won and maintained its leadership. In the end, I was relieved that the AHSA/USET maintained leadership, because we desperately needed to reestablish stability in the organization.

Leslie Burr Howard

During Bert de Némethy's era as Chef d'Equipe, the selection of the team was always subjective. This system worked because the pool of horses and riders who had the experience to compete at the international level was so small. This system continued when Frank Chapot took over. However, as the pool of riders grew so did the problems of selection.

Looking back, perhaps things did need to be shaken up a little bit—not necessarily how teams were selected, but just in transparency of the process. Everyone wants to have the best team they can but some people felt they were in the dark as to how decisions were being made. Of course, the lawsuit itself was a result of strong feelings that the decision was unfair, specifically for the Stockholm team. However, I think that reaction was partly due to a lack of understanding about how the decision was made and why.

The whole shake-up resulted in almost complete objectivity in the selection process for years afterward, to avoid the appearance or accusation of any unfairness. We had some very good teams in those years, but there were also instances where using objective scoring didn't produce the best possible team.

There are always factors that come into play over the months leading up to a big event. Today, we have a great system where there's objectivity to create long lists of candidates and some subjectivity as well in the final choices. It's all spelled out and there's excellent communication about the process. In the end, subjectivity can be used as long as its defined carefully how, when, and why it's being used.

The era of very expensive top horses was in full swing and horses like Rio had become either impossible to find or impossible to afford. One new jumper prospect was Yogi, a lovely Thoroughbred I bought from George Lindemann with a dainty mouth and fabulous speed. He's the only jumper I ever showed in a rubber snaffle! He had a wonderful, light mouth, and he was similar in type to Rio although didn't have the physical power and big scope to win at the Grand Prix. However, Yogi was a perfect 1.40-meter speed horse. I took him on some European tours as a third horse and also had some luck with him up in the Eastern Canada Grand Prix classes (photo 183).

That previous winter in California, Meredith Michaels started teaching a young student from the Arguetty family through a friend of hers. The girl's father, Isaac Arguetty, was a man of means and took a shine to Meredith, deciding to sponsor a few top horses for her to ride. Having support like that is such an important part of opening doors for Grand-Prix-level riders. Mr. Arguetty was also somewhat of a character; once, he told me he didn't mind paying for the horses and the shows, but that the monthly invoices with all the little charges were irritating to him! That following year, Mr. Arguetty moved to London for his business and worked out an arrangement to stable his horses with Paul Schockemöhle. The only thing that made sense for Meredith was to follow her horses to Germany; we made a plan for her to do just that.

The following year, the 1991 Pan American Games were in Havana, Cuba, and the team was picked solely on the basis of dollars won in prize money between September 1, 1989, and the deadline for choosing the team. The USET won the bronze medal in the team event, but no individual medals were won by American riders. I didn't attend that Pan Am Games because I had riders showing on a European tour.

With great style on a horse as well as talent and guts in the jumper ring, Ray Texel was my prodigy over a three-year period in the early nineties. Like Ray Texel, Vinton Karrasch came to ride with me and train for the jumper ring. Vinton was a great student and met with a fair bit of success despite having a limited junior career—he only started to ride at age fifteen. He looked at a nice young jumper prospect when he and Jeff Cook went to Chris Kappler's place, but the bay was young and a little bit of a rogue. They did eventually buy the horse, named Zanzibar, and afterward the Greenbergs, sponsors of mine, bought him from Vinton. I took Zanzibar and Yogi on the European tour that summer (photo 184). Jen Emmitt, also a fabulous young jumper rider, brought a wonderful horse named Freestyling.

Anne Kursinski, Vinton Karrasch, Jen Emmitt, Ray Texel, and Meredith Michaels made up my team for the European tour early that summer. Our first show, in Munich, was Meredith's first time competing in Europe, and she had a mix of schoolmasters and green horses we had brought along for her to ride at the Grand Prix level. One of them was a beautiful seven-year-old Isaac Arguetty bought from Will Simpson in California named Quick Star. Quick Star was a very fancy, well-bred horse for Meredith, but he was very difficult to ride.

Meredith was always deadly accurate and fast in any jump-off and that was one of her early strengths. She always had that fearless California-junior-jumper, belly-to-the-ground style, and it made her a fierce competitor if she went clear in the first round. Quick Star was an electric hot, careful, sophisticated ride and he never touched a jump. As is typical with careful horses, he had a little bit of a chicken side and would sometimes doubt his own ability and wilt in the air like Rio. He wasn't easy to ride by any means and Jeff Cook and Chris Kappler each spent time riding the horse to help Meredith get Quick Star dialed in.

Diane Carney

I grew up in Colorado, and in the early eighties, a fellow professional suggested I ride in a George Morris clinic. I agreed even though I didn't know who he was. I rode in the clinic and his lessons on the mechanics of the horse and rider made a lot of sense to me. I was a young professional at the time and had horses in training back home. When I returned, I took all the exercises from the first day of the three-day clinic with George and I did them with all the horses on Tuesday and Wednesday; on Thursday and Friday, I did the exercises from the second day of the clinic and moved on to the third day's exercises over the weekend.

I just kept repeating his sequence of exercises, which was, of course, very progressive. The marvelous effect across the board on fitness, soundness, and athletic ability of the horses became apparent over time. With George's program, my horses were getting stronger—and in particular, stronger behind. There was no question about it. I had one quality horse, McAllister, who was hot and hadn't been ridden with any leg before he came to me. George taught us that you always ride a horse with leg—hot or cold—and it really worked with McAllister. It got his confidence up and six months later at Good Year, which was the big Arizona winter show that later became known as Indio, I was Circuit Champion with him. By following the tenets and progressive exercises from George's clinic, my horses excelled. It had a huge impact on my career. What most of us don't have before we meet George is a system. Once we meet him, we do. Whether you apply it or not is a choice, but I found his system right for me as a professional.

George always says, "Never let the business get out ahead of the horse." I always go back to that concept to help lead my own ethical decisions. Every professional in this industry has made a mistake in their career and that's just part of the learning curve. "What's the right choice for the horse?" I ask myself. Horsemanship is first. If I do my job right, I protect the horse in that situation. I want to jump as high and go as fast as anyone! I'm not about saying no, but I want to say yes in a smart way.

Next was the Aachen show and, of course, the highlight was Anne Kursinski brilliantly winning the Grand Prix of Aachen on Starman. Winning perhaps the most famous Grand Prix in the world, in the heartland of show jumping's European roots, was a gigantic feather in Anne's cap and also very special for me to witness. It felt in a way like a rite of passage, since I had won that class myself in my youth. Seeing Anne get that win, beating out all those top riders in the biggest Grand Prix in the world made me so proud of our homegrown American talent (photo 185).

After the show at Aachen, it was time for Meredith's horses to head to Paul's place and Kathy Moore dropped her off there in the dead of night. I was terribly sad to see her leave my stable, but I was behind her decision 100 percent. Moving to Germany was absolutely the right move for her. It was a wonderful opportunity to be immersed in the European show-jumping community. Kathy told me some tears were shed as she left Meredith in the stark little staff apartments at Paul's huge stable. Meredith was only twenty-two years old, barely spoke five words of German, and had never lived that kind of working life before.

History tells us that Meredith survived Paul—or perhaps, Paul survived Meredith! The amazing thing is not only how she survived that challenge, but how she exceeded everyone's expectations. That five-foot-four blonde California "Valley Girl" conquered the most powerful equestrian country in the world! Meredith absorbed the European technique and style, blending it expertly with the base of her education from Karen Healey and myself. With the support and horses provided by Isaac Arguetty, she made the absolute most of her chance in Europe and put herself in a position to succeed with patience and hard work. As everyone knows, she then made Germany her home, eventually married Markus Beerbaum, and now rides for the German team. It's a testament to her fortitude, brains, and personal strength (photo 186).

Continuing on our tour, we arrived in Hickstead to show without a full deck. Anne had gone back to New Jersey to work with clients and Meredith had stayed behind at Paul Schockemöhle's. Ray Texel was doing fabulously riding a few horses including one of mine called Ike, but he was certainly no veteran, and Vinton Karrasch and Jen Emmitt were still getting their feet wet in the Grand Prix ring.

At Hickstead, we faced a big challenge. The FEI rules stated that if your team has three or more riders from the same country, you must compete in the Nations Cup. If you only have one or two, you can choose to ride as individuals. For my team at that show, it was a daunting prospect to compete in the Nation's Cup without enough horse power and mileage. After some serious consideration, I spoke to the organizers and we were granted a special dispensation to be excused from the Nations Cup. There are times when you must acknowledge your limitations and not put your team in a position to be overfaced. To ask green horses or riders to jump in a huge class they aren't prepared for can result in an experience that sets their confidence level back unnecessarily.

Back in Munich earlier in the tour, Zanzibar had jumped very well, but the footing there was very wet and deep. With the endless rain, they moved the Grand Prix indoors and we scratched and decided to head to our home base in Germany to train for two weeks and prepare for the next show. While there, it became clear that something was wrong with Zanzibar. The next time I schooled him over jumps it was like he'd lost his scope completely! He wasn't lame, but something wasn't right. This horse had jumped around in Florida at Grand Prix height easily the prior winter but his ability was now clearly hindered. I gave him a few days off and then tried again, but he still wasn't right. By the time we got to Dublin, we jumped perhaps five jumps in our first class and then I pulled up and left the ring. He simply wasn't able to get around (photo 187).

Even just two decades later, we have more advanced technology for pinpointing injuries, but we didn't have the same modern assessment tools in the early nineties. I could only assume that Zanzibar must have strained something in his back. On several occasions, he could barely get himself over a low two-foot oxer, where before he jumped six-foot spreads. I tried to limp along with him for the rest of the European tour, resting him for longer periods, then trying again, but he was very inconsistent. Where at one show he seemed to have regained his edge with a four-fault round, at the next, he couldn't get around the course. It took him two or three years to recover from that mysterious injury. It was a huge disappointment because I had just started to experience consistent success with Zanzibar.

II. THE FINE LINE BETWEEN CAREFUL AND CHICKEN

Brody Robertson

I would take a bullet for George. Equal to my father, George has been the other most influential person in my life, with and without horses. When I first started getting help from George, I was about twenty. I can vividly remember riding in a group flat lesson in an empty field, over in what is now Grand Prix Village, back in about 1991. He asked for shoulder-in, and I had to look around to see what everyone else was doing, because I had no idea what it was.

Although I got very good instruction and had wonderful examples to follow in both of my parents, George was the first to give me a system. He gave me my college education. During that time, I was blending a lot of riding ideas that I saw and liked. As it turned out, some of that wasn't so very good for me. As I was young and thinking I knew more than I did, I offered a bit of resistance to George. I may have even tried to persuade him to my thinking. And this is where I can't ever thank George enough, because he didn't cut me loose. Here I was a young, scrappy kid with no real money questioning his system, and George had a long list of people who were willing to pay anything for his help. Thankfully, he didn't pat me on the shoulder and tell me, "Goodbye and good luck, kid!" He stuck it out with me. In the years to follow, you could definitely say I drank the Kool Aid! After moving to St. Louis, I had George come and give a clinic every summer and those clinics were fantastic.

The first year he taught a clinic at my farm, George brought a friend from Brazil named Leon along with him. He asked if I might be able to get some girls to take Leon out on the town one night of the clinic. I picked up George and Leon at the airport and en route to the hotel, George asked how the clinic turnout was. I told him we were maxed out in each of the three groups, but some of the other "A" circuit barns weren't coming because they had heard how tough he was. George said, "That's ridiculous. I've simmered down a lot over the years. That was a long, long time ago." A few minutes later, George asked, "What sort of entertainment do we have for Leon?" I said Cher was in town the next night as part of her farewell concert tour. Leon, in the backseat flipping through a magazine, sprung forward and asked, "Did you say Cher? I love Cher!" and proceeded to pull out no fewer than four Cher CDs from his backpack. We all laughed and George said, "Normally I don't like to stay out late during a clinic, because they're so exhausting. But for Cher, I may have to make an exception. And about being tough—maybe I'll live up to my reputation after all!" I got us great seats to see Cher about twenty feet from the stage, and we all went and had a great time. The next morning, two young ladies made their way into the first group at the clinic about three minutes late. George said something to them about tardiness, and they giggled. With that, he lit into them and twenty seconds later they were both in tears. And so the legend grows...!

The business at Hunterdon continued to boom, and Chris Kappler had become a very talented and well-known teacher, trainer, and rider. A friend and horseman, Adam Wootten, came to Hunterdon from Australia in that summer to ride and show a nice five-year-old jumper prospect. Adam's young chestnut Thoroughbred jumped with an unusual, twisty sort of style, but had immense ability and could clear the standards. Adam rode him in the Low Preliminary Jumper classes, and after showing in eastern Canada, he traveled home and left the horse with me to sell. At Port Jervis, one of the big shows in September, several of the best professionals tried Adam's horse: George Lindemann, Tim Grubb, John Madden, Katie Prudent, and Beezie Patton, but for various reasons, nobody liked him enough to buy him.

Anne Kursinski still leased the lower barn at Hunterdon and carried on her own business. She had a horse named Cannonball who was very careful but a little bit of a chicken. Before Thanksgiving, as I was getting ready for a west coast trip through the holidays, I asked Anne Kursinski if she would ride Adam Wootten's horse while I was gone. She has a special way of getting the best out of a horse; it has everything to do with her flatwork. When it comes to dressage and working a horse on the flat, Anne is hands-down the best rider in America. She took that lovely chestnut horse down to her barn and off I went to California.

While in California, Anne called me and said she loved the horse and wanted to buy him, which was of course terrific news. The horse's name was Eros. Eros was one of those horses that needed an expert rider like Anne to bring him along just right and figure out his complex quirks. An amateur or a lesser rider never would've been able to have the success that an expert could. All those professionals who had tried Eros were really kicking themselves in the years to come, watching Anne win classes with him all over the world. Anne was fortunate to have a few very good horses in those years and Eros was one of them (photo 188).

Peter Leone

Detail, discipline, work ethic, a commitment to doing things right—all with a focus on the "good of the horse"—captures much of what George has imparted to me as a professional horseman. He identified and instilled in me the goal of achieving the Bert de Némethy/William Steinkraus U.S.-team style of riding, horsemanship, and success. This goal defined how George taught me to be a successful horseman, rider, and coach. The result was that the core "GHM-eration" of riders he taught brought riding, teaching, and horsemanship to a level the world had never seen before. George broke down the competitive horse-and-riding experience into several key areas: the management of the horse, the management of the rider, the actual training of the horse, the actual training of the rider, and most importantly how to "teach." The methods George taught me in terms of *how* to teach and *what* to teach were a monumental contribution to me as a professional. He incorporated passion, discipline, methodology, history, and planning for the future in his lessons, all in the context of the principles of traditional horsemanship, riding, and jumping. By recognizing what makes George the great horseman, rider, and father of the American riding system, I have been able to share with others what George taught me as a professional.

For many years, I had walked the straight and narrow path and steered clear of drinking and staying out late, while putting my complete physical focus into riding, training, and preparation. The effect of my sobriety was the ability to maintain a sharper mental and physical edge with my riding. Steering clear from alcohol had absolutely helped me rise—and return post-injury—again and again to the Grand Prix level. After the austere decade of the 1980s when the black cloud of the AIDS virus drove fear into everyone's minds, the social aspects of my life began to open up again in the mid-nineties. Science and education had caught up to the epidemic and the nightlife started to feel more comfortable and fun again. Having suppressed my urges for mischief and partying for many years, I started to let go a little bit, going into New York City on Sunday evenings for my one weekly night out, as was my tradition since the sixties. I was still magnetically attracted to the city and after being in fairly predictable relationships for so long, it was fun to go out and meet new people.

One Sunday evening at a classy watering hole called Rounds on Fifty-Third Street in Manhattan, which catered to younger, available men and their admirers of a more advanced age, I was chatting with people I knew at the bar, when I noticed someone I had met before but didn't recognize at first. He didn't recognize me either, but as we started talking, we both realized he'd set jumps for me at a clinic a few years before. His name was Greg Hall and after spending the evening talking, he came out to a show the following week at Old Salem Farm. His family lived in Millbrook, New York, and I gave Greg a couple of lessons on his horse named On My Roan, a green, attractive hunter that was stabled nearby at Primrose Farm (now Andre Dignelli's place called Heritage Farm). Having only taken up riding as an adult, Greg was a little stiff and nervous on a horse, but he looked fabulous in the saddle being very tall and lean. We hit it off and started spending a lot of time together.

As we became closer friends, Greg Hall brought On My Roan down to Hunterdon and moved into the house with me (photo 189). Kathy Moore lived in the big house at Hunterdon too, and had for many years, since my days with Jeremy. It was sometimes a hard transition for Kathy when I had someone new in my life, and although Greg and Kathy never got along very well, we all made the best of it. Greg settled into life at Hunterdon and became a part of my work and personal life, traveling with me to all of the shows. He showed On My Roan and also Jones Peak, a handsome gray Amateur Owner hunter type. Jones Peak was still green but the son of The Jones Boy's full sister off the track, who I'd bought and bred in hoping to reproduce the wonderful ability of The Jones Boy.

Debbie Stephens

When George goes to a show, he goes to be the winner. When he sees riders satisfied with anything less, he just doesn't understand that point of view. George has never lost what it takes to win. If it wasn't for him, I don't know where my career would've gone. He gave me my break. He asked me to come to Rome with his team in the early eighties. I had mediocre horses, but he believed in me right from day one and said I would make up for it with my hard work. His enthusiasm is infectious and it made all the difference for me.

In the eighties I began taking riders up to eastern Canada on a brief circuit as a stepping stone to competing in Europe. With FEI rules up there, it's a great way to get experience without the overseas trip. I continued to ride in jumper classes alongside my younger pupils, but with Rio now retired, my options were quite limited at the Grand Prix level. Yogi was a great speed horse but had limited scope and power and Zanzibar continued to struggle with the mysterious back injury from the muddy footing in Munich the prior year.

If you are forty-five or older and still competing at the Grand Prix level, it's a plain fact that you have to work much harder to keep up a very high level of fitness and strength. Riders who are successful at an advanced age tend also to specialize as professionals—they focus on riding and often don't teach students and run their business. Even more importantly, an older rider must have very good horses. What stops riders who have the expertise and capability to ride at that level is the quality of their horses. When you're still in your twenties, you can ride anything—horses with not quite enough scope, stoppers, or leg–hangers. You fall and get right back up! But who wants to do cartwheels through the jumps and get banged up at age fifty like they used to in their twenties? Owners who can buy the very expensive horses gravitate naturally to the younger up–and–coming riders and those who are more certain to make Olympic Teams. It's a fact of life that older riders need better horses to ride at that level and have more to prove when it comes to being selected for championship teams.

Holly Mitten

I ran across George Morris up in Canada at a show, and he encouraged me to come and train at Hunterdon. I switched over to showing my event horse because the longevity of the horses is so much better in show jumping and he was rehabbing from a ligament injury. Two years later, against all odds, that horse and I rode into the ring for a World Cup-qualifier class up in Ottawa. Afterward, somebody told me that when I walked into that ring, George crossed himself at the in-gate and said, "I hope they make it!" In the end, I only had one rail down. George has a way of making you believe you can jump a house as you walk into a ring.

When I spent time at Hunterdon in the nineties watching George teach, I learned so much about how to make a program successful for clients. I remember one instance when one of the young kids at Hunterdon had a little mare that I got on and flatted. I was using my solid background in quality flatwork and got her going really balanced and round and organized. George watched me and said, "Holly, that's useless, because that's not how the girl rides." Then I watched him get on and set up the horse for the girl. And the light bulb went on! When he trains, he looks at the rider and he rides the horse for that person, not for himself. Our job as trainers is to know the rider and set up the horse for that rider in that moment, not to set up the horse for ourselves. Realizing that was part of growing up as a professional. Ultimately, it has to work for the client.

One day at Hunterdon, a local trainer called to say some of her students were going to be late for a lesson with George. It was a terrible weather day, cold with heavy fog, and the riders were going to be an hour late—and it was already five in the evening. George and I sat in his office and chit-chatted together, waiting for them. George did not tolerate lateness or any sloppiness with students and when those kids finally showed up, they were in a total panic. George told them to settle down, and he asked me to go get some cones. I was thinking, "Cones? We never use cones," and I went out to look for them. On the way, I saw

Anne Kursinski and she asked me whether George was miserable about how late those kids were for the lesson, and I told her that he didn't seem too bothered by it. I found the cones and brought them up to the indoor ring. And to my surprise, that lesson, was like a party that night! George changed his teaching style to calm the kids down and get them in a learning mindset. He taught them until seven-thirty and did all sorts of fun exercises with the cones. The kids had a great time and learned so much. I had never seen George teach that way before, using those creative, beginner-rider tactics. As I was closing up the indoor and shutting down the lights, I remember shaking my head at the fact that George could still surprise me. It was a pretty incredible night with him, and I loved being there to witness it. It was brilliant.

George treats every level of rider and horse with equal importance. He doesn't diminish the care and attention if it's a green horse showing when the more advanced open-jumper horse is later on in the day. Every horse is treated as if he matters every day. Coaching at a show, George believes in the preparation that got you there. Sometimes at shows, you'll hear trainers teaching a lesson in the warm-up ring. When that happens, the rider gets in the ring and her head is spinning trying to change how she's riding. George just warms you up. He warms your eye up. He's not trying to get you to fix anything unless things are really going wrong. If he sees something that he wants you to change, he saves it for your next lesson.

With Zanzibar laid up, Yogi became my focus for showing. As I mentioned, we had success in the speed classes but weren't very competitive at the Grand Prix level (photo 191). At a show up in Canada that year, I rode Yogi in some of their Grand Prix classes, which at that time were not as big as Wellington or Calgary, but very nice courses. We had some luck and good ribbons, but at the last show I had a fall at a triple combination. I saw a mirage distance and we got to the first of two Liverpools too deep. I tried to drive him through the combination, but we couldn't get through it and I fell over backward off the horse.

After my fall, the travel back home to Hunterdon the next day was horrendous. I hadn't broken any bones, but for a week afterward I was a complete cripple. I felt like I'd broken every bone in my body! My doctor told me it was simply a fact of getting older. I was by then fifty-four years old and Greg, who was very supportive, started talking me out of jumping the big jumps. Falling into that more mature category myself by the nineties, I no longer had the luxury of being able to challenge a green or less scopey horse and deal with the consequences. I had several great students and my business at Hunterdon, so specializing only in my own riding wasn't a viable option. My personal renaissance in the Grand Prix ring began to wind down and my focus returned to helping my students reach their goals.

I continued to teach all over the country as well as overseas and made sure to carve out time for the clinic tour. Traveling to teach clinics is a great way to stay in touch with some of my oldest and closest friends, like my childhood riding companion Glenna Lee Maduro. She invited me out to teach at her ranch in Montana, which is beautiful country. I had been there many times before and had tried working cattle on a Western horse, which was great fun. This time, I struck up a friendship with Buck Brannaman.

Glenna de Rham

Buck Brannaman, a revered Western rider, trainer, and teacher, put thirty days on all my colts, and you could put a baby on any one of them. Buck is an incredible horseman with a sixth-sense intuition about a horse. I invited George to dinner with Buck and told him that Buck was going to show us his video of starting a colt. George reminded me how busy he was and that he had to leave soon. Well, I told him to sit right down and that he wasn't going anywhere, and we all sat down to watch. In twenty minutes, Buck was riding a wild mustang that had never laid eyes on him before. The mustang was standing quietly with his head turned around in Buck's lap. George was stunned at what he saw and said, "I don't say this very often, but you're quite a horseman." Then he proceeded to tell Buck that he was going to teach him to jump the next day. I told Buck he didn't have to, if he didn't want to. George said, "He has to and he wants to!" and they got together and George had Buck jumping immediately! They've done a couple of clinics together since then, too. Obviously, they're very different in some ways, but they have great respect for one another.

Buck Brannaman

A lot of people know George for his bark and they take him so seriously, but he has such a keen sense of humor and wit. Most people have never been around him like I have. I feel honored to have a friendship with him and be able to appreciate his unique point of view. What's interesting and unique about someone like George, who has spent his life as a horseman and is from that great generation, is that when we met,

I dressed and looked like a cowboy and he didn't judge me on that at all. He basically gave me the benefit of the doubt and formed his opinion on what I knew and what I was capable of doing. The humility with which George approaches life and others is one of the things I admire most about him. One of the first times I ever talked to George, he saw me playing polo on some Thoroughbreds in West Palm Beach. George walked over after a while and asked where I'd learned classical French riding. I told him, "Well I don't know, I haven't even met a Frenchman!" I told him I'd spent my life around Ray Hunt and devoted my life to doing what he and Tom Dorrance had taught me. He said, "Well you may not know it, but that's classical French style."

Everybody knows that in the jumping horse world, George is king, because he's reached the absolute pinnacle of respect in that world. I find it really admirable that he doesn't have an axe to grind; he's receptive to something that is new and different, or something he didn't grow up around, perhaps a different approach to something with horses. He's such a great horseman that he can see what works for the horse and what's good for the horse. That humility and eagerness to learn, even with all his experience and success, is something I find an interesting thing. He's still a student of the horse, even to this day. I wish people could take that example and be more that way.

I'll have people in the clinics I teach from all different types of riding—working ranch cowboys, backyard owners, hunter/jumper riders, and dressage riders. I find that there are an awful lot of people that could certainly use some help to make them better horsemen, but it's like some of them get to a certain level and the only thing they ever really master is being a snob. With these modern riders, it's almost like it's not even about the horse anymore—it's about them. It's about how the horse can make them look good. In George's generation, it was about what they could do to make the horse look good. They were coming from a different place. There's a lot more that George has to offer than just how to get your horse over a jump. Fine horsemanship goes way beyond that. The truth about the horse doesn't change—and hasn't for several lifetimes before we were here. What's true about horses today is the same as what was true about them hundreds of years ago. Horsemen like George, who have a logical approach and teach the basic fundamentals, will always be successful. He's right—there are no shortcuts. Good horsemanship will always prevail over the latest gimmick sold at your local tack shop. It doesn't matter what discipline of riding you're talking about.

The 1992 Barcelona Olympics arrived during a rough patch for show jumping, due to the suspicion around the selection process and leftover political tension. The atmosphere around the team took a few years to ease up and improve. Meanwhile, the selection process was handled with complete objectivity for Barcelona to avoid any risk of bias. The highest-placed horses and riders from the selection trial classes earned a spot on the Olympic Team. Gem Twist and Greg Best had continued to be a top American pair, but they had a bad round at one of the selection trials. Gem Twist stopped out at a Liverpool under the lights at Devon, and as a result, Greg didn't get a spot.

The Barcelona USET show jumping spots went to Anne Kursinski and Cannonball, Norman Dello Joio and Irish, Lisa Jacquin and For the Moment, and Michael Matz on Heisman. It was Anne's third Olympics in a row. The courses in Barcelona were very old fashioned and huge, clearly a throwback to the days before Bert de Némethy. They were stark, old school fences, designed plainly with big height and very wide spreads. I personally liked the courses, but they were difficult and there were certainly others who didn't share my view.

Lisa Jacquin

As a junior, I had a chance to ride with George, and it was my first encounter with riding on the East Coast. One of the turning points was the Junior Nations Cup tour George brought us on. He loaned me his horse Four Corners, and it was an incredible experience to have George show us the ropes on that kind of a tour. It really gave us confidence to ride in big classes, and it was a huge honor to be part of it.

As we all moved on in our careers and became young professionals, the one thing that has stood out is that George has always been there. Whether he's at in-gate or in the schooling area, or giving an opinion on a horse, he was always there for me, especially in my early career, and to this day, he is still there to support me. I feel so lucky that I've had him on my side all these years. George not only taught us horsemanship and discipline and proper etiquette he's a special human being in the way he continues to take care of all of us.

Truly great, careful jumpers are always ridden on a fine line between careful and chicken. That's why those kinds of horses can't be ridden by average amateurs, because they make mistakes, miss at a fence, and take the horse's confidence away. Cannonball was a typical light German horse and you had to be really careful with him because he could get chicken. In the first round of the Nations Cup, Cannonball had a light rub behind at a fence a few jumps into the course. I was instantly worried, and sure enough he stopped out at a spooky-looking vertical-oxer-oxer triple combination.

When Anne rode out of the ring, we walked to the warm-up area together and made a plan. It was one of those moments where I just knew what a horse needed to get his head right. The warm-up area at Barcelona was very unusual; rather than three or four plain verticals to warm up over, there were dozens of fences and they were just like those in the ring: a few colorful rails, some walls, and other decorations. We set up a course and I told her to jump around and really lay into Cannonball with her stick every four or five fences—not every fence because that would just seem like punishment, but once in a while so that he wouldn't know when to expect it. Anne did this, riding jump to jump and every few fences she'd get after him hard to clear any doubt in his mind. We walked back to the ring for her second round. They went clear and redeemed themselves (photo 193).

In the last round of the individual competition, the course was even bigger; so huge, in fact, that some riders were completely overwhelmed. Even riders with very scopey horses had to pull up, tip their hat, and leave the ring. I didn't think Norman Dello Joio's little horse Irish had the scope or heart for that giant course, but Norman gave us all a riding lesson and rode so brilliantly. I recall advising Norman on how to ride the triple combination on Irish, who was a very careful horse but didn't have the biggest scope. He rode it perfectly. Norman jumped the triple, not the horse! It was if Norman threw his heart over the jumps in front of them and Irish was inspired to follow. And for his amazing performance, Norman won an Olympic bronze medal. I was so happy for him. It may not have been the best Olympics for the Americans, but there were some wonderful moments for our riders (photo 194).

I really enjoyed watching the dressage events (as I always do at every Olympics) and I had the pleasure of getting to know Carl Hester in Barcelona, who was the youngest British equestrian to represent his country. I could see Carl was a freak genius on a horse; he was empathetic, soft, and had that special touch in the saddle. I said then that he was Conrad Homfeld on a dressage horse. Now, of course, Carl is a top European trainer and rider and has produced Charlotte Dujardin, the gold-medal winner in the London 2012 Olympics.

In recent decades, I have also watched the three-day eventing at the international championships. After being so discouraged by the injuries and horse deaths in this discipline in the fifties and sixties, the sport became safer and more humane and I gravitated back to it. I personally knew some wonderful

Australian, New Zealand, and British three-day riders from teaching clinics in various countries who were riding in the Barcelona and Seoul Games, like Mark Todd, Blyth Tate, and Vaughn Jefferis.

Kathy Moore, Greg Hall, Chrystine Tauber, and I rented an apartment together for the Olympics and enjoyed the city as well as the Olympic events. You could look out the window of our tenth-floor apartment and see them building the course for the next day down in the ring! Barcelona is a fabulous city—my favorite in Europe nowadays, with its wonderful restaurants and gorgeous beaches. It's like the Brazil of Europe! Robert Dover, Robert Ross, Carl Hester, Emile Faurie (the famous British dressage rider), Greg and I went out to the very well-known beach-resort town called Sitges and had fun checking out the town and hanging out on the beach. I've never experienced an Olympic Games, before or since, where the personal side of my life was such a part of things. I think it had everything to do with Barcelona having such a progressive, colorful, and open culture.

Chrystine Tauber

On Mondays while on tour in Europe, I'd organize a group outing to see something cultural, like a museum. George would always say, "I love traveling with Chrystine—I don't even have to think!" I also had the responsibility of monitoring one of George's biggest weaknesses when I managed European tours or championship teams. At Aachen one year, I noticed George was unusually tired in the evenings and had a hard time rallying to go out to official dinners. I started to keep an eye on him and discovered he was regularly hitting the Toblerone chocolate stand, located conveniently next to the competitors' grandstand area. Every time he went back and forth, he'd buy a chocolate bar. By each evening, he'd have a major sugar low and fall flat on his face. I got on his case and told him he was cut off, but I still had to keep an eye on him because he would try to sneak over there for his chocolate fix!

I rode on the USET for several years when I was younger, and I had the honor of, just like George, being sent back up the stairs by Bert de Némethy for not being dressed appropriately while on tour in Europe. It was the Twiggy era and I had a cute bob hairdo, big fake eyelashes, and a miniskirt, and it certainly did not meet Bert's impeccable standards! The influence of Bert—way beyond our outfit choices—was tremendous on all of us, George Morris and myself certainly included.

Each of us has our calling and I went into the administrative end of the sport, and ultimately to the Presidency of the United States Equestrian

Federation. It's not always easy to make big decisions for horse sports, whether it's for hunter/jumper, dressage, Saddlebreds, or Arabians. Each breed or discipline has its own set of challenges, with both professionals' and amateurs' points of view. I have always found good counsel with George and that's where our friendship has been invaluable.

George has been a tremendous influence on the sport over several decades. He took a strong lead in terms of what he felt needed to be done in America with hunter-seat equitation, the jumpers, and also was the visionary behind the International Hunter Derby. George has helped the United States maintain a position as a world-class nation that is always in contention at international championships. He keeps us at that high standard; he demands nothing less. George has forced us to take a look at the issues in our own sport. He doesn't mince words and you can count on him to be honest and speak up with the goal of improving the sport.

George and I grew up in an era where doing anything for the right reason was paramount. I rode for Sallie Sexton who was a big proponent of drug testing for horses when the AHSA started the very first drug-testing program. We had to have armed guards with us around the clock because of threats that our horses would be poisoned and our property damaged because some other trainers were against drug testing. George has always taken the high road, as I have tried to do. It's ingrained in George and others from that era.

George can be demanding and even occasionally demeaning in lessons and some riders can't take it. My opinion is that if you can't take it, then you won't make it to the top. What I've experienced and observed with George, even at the highest level, is that he has such a strong sense of belief in his teaching and the methodology that he elevates the ability of riders. His riders trust their training so much that they raise their level of riding, right there on the spot at a big international championship.

Back at Hunterdon that following year, my relationship with Greg Hall continued. Greg had a rent-controlled apartment in the city and we would go out fairly often together. Business at Hunterdon was going very well still, and Greg continued to ride and show two or three horses with me in both hunters and jumpers. Despite being a nervous rider who sometimes had difficulty trusting the distance to the jumps, he had great success. Greg won nearly every equitation flat class and always got great ribbons in the under saddles with the hunters (photo 196). Like any adult amateur, he was hit or miss over fences, but when he saw the jumps, the judges always pinned him well. There was drama with Greg in the warm-up ring and at the in-gate, with regular crises of confidence and getting worked up at the horse shows. Greg ended up doing very well in the jumper ring with a wonderful Thoroughbred I bought from Mousie Williams named Turn to Home, eventually riding him in the Intermediate Jumpers.

One afternoon at the Cincinnati show, Greg marched up to me in the schooling ring (after I hadn't seen him all day and wondered what had become of him) with a bundle of fluff in his hands. It was an eight-week-old Beagle puppy and the most adorable dog I'd ever seen! There was a litter of puppies at the show but they were all taken, and Greg loved them so much that he called the breeder and drove to Indiana to pick up a puppy that was so tiny that nobody wanted him. I think Greg paid $50 for him. He was so small and so adorable that we named him Big Dog (photo 197).

Another wonderful dog from the nineties was Mr. Schultz. He was a Dachshund that someone dropped at our vet's Dr. Bower's office to be put down, but he was young and healthy still. We had to save him, and he became a great dog of Hunterdon. Big Dog and Mr. Schultz kept me going through some tough times to come.

Ray Texel had ridden with me for a few years with some good ribbons in big European and North American classes. A working student of sorts, I'd been grooming him to get to the USET and invested quite a lot in his ability and talent. In early '93, Ray walked into my office at Hunterdon to tell me he was leaving with his girlfriend Sunday to open their own business. For me, it was a shock that he was leaving after we had worked so hard together on his development. People come and go and that's just how the sport works, but I was very disappointed to see him go. He had huge potential, and it takes just the right recipe and opportunity for a rider like Ray to get to the top.

In the winter of 1993, after Ray Texel moved on from Hunterdon, I was at a crossroads. The business of running Hunterdon was such a huge commitment. Without an up-and-coming, Grand-Prix-level rider to work with and an assistant at Hunterdon, it all felt less purposeful. There were a few wonderful young professionals who I had spoken with about working with me but most of them had other influences pushing them elsewhere. Rich Fellers, for example, told me he would love to work with me but he and Shelley wanted to raise their family in Oregon.

I sought out Chris Kappler while down in Tampa and made him a proposition. After riding at Hunterdon off and on for periods of time as a pupil and establishing himself as a young professional there, Chris had moved back to Chicago and spent several years running a business. I was frank. I told him

I only wanted to keep Hunterdon open if I had the right rider to work with. Either he was going to come and work with me or Hunterdon may close its doors. Chris' family was very supportive and he accepted my invitation to come back East. He won the Garden State Grand Prix on Ike at his first show back and I was thrilled. In my gut, I knew he was the right man for the job! It was the start of a great partnership (photo 199).

III. THE WORLD CATCHES UP TO THE AMERICANS

Chris Kappler

I remember George came home from Europe, and it was one of the first times I'd been on my own for a while running Hunterdon without him around for support. Running a barn isn't easy; George joked to me once, "If it weren't for clients and staff, it would be an easy business!" That being said, I'd lost a grasp on the grooms and standards had slipped a little. The grooms were maybe a little above themselves and the clients were showing up not quite on time for lessons. When he returned, George was absolutely brutal in the barn, on the grooms and the clients, reasserting his authority over the entire place. The whole staff dug in and worked in a very somber mood in response to George's toughness; this went on for a week or more. Morale got pretty low. Then one day, he brought in a framed sign and propped it up on the front of his desk. It said, "The beatings will continue until morale improves." It was classic George! Just when things were really starting to look like the dark cloud would be there to stay, everyone laughed about the sign and things lightened up a little bit as we went back to work as usual. It was just what was needed. He knew what it took to rein everyone back in, but he also knew when to release the hold and when his point had been made.

We had a great twenty years together, George and I, and we've remained very close ever since. His ability to stay current in the sport is pretty amazing. He stays sharp, brings in new people all the time, and wants to learn from other people's perspectives and disciplines.

The World Cup Finals in 1993 showed the world that the Americans still had a lot of fight! After Ian Millar won the '88 and '89 World Cup Finals and North America had appeared unbeatable with wins every year of that decade, the nineties had started off poorly. John Whitaker won the World Cup Finals

in 1990 and 1991 and the domination of European teams had begun. However, the '93 Finals found us clawing our way back to the top with Michael
Matz finishing third on Rhum IV, Susie Hutchison fourth on Samsung Woodstock, and Beezie Patton fifth on Ping Pong and French Rapture. It was great
to see our American riders back in the top five. I wish I could say it got even
better in the following years, but actually it would be quite some time until
we'd witness it again.

The '94 World Equestrian Games were in The Hague and once again all
seven equestrian disciplines came together. Representing the U.S. Show Jumping Team were Tim Grubb on Elan Denizen, Leslie Burr Lenehan on Charisma,
Susie Hutchison on Samsung Woodstock, and Patty Stovel on Mont Cenis.
Patty rode with me as a junior and was a very hard-working, talented rider
who became a professional. She was second in the Medal Finals in 1975 on
a four-year-old! Initially, Leslie was going to be riding Gem Twist instead of
Charisma, but he came down with an infection in his suspensory that sidelined
him for the better part of a year.

Patty Stovel

For my fifteenth birthday my parents got me lessons with George Morris, and I spent three days down at Hunterdon. After that I occasionally
shipped a horse or two and spent a couple of days riding my horses
there as well as having the chance to lesson on some of George's green
hunters. I was a small-time rider and mostly did the local shows in Connecticut on my equitation horse that was sort of a practice horse. Later,
I got a three-year-old that was big and quiet, and I started bringing him
along to ride in the equitation.

George invited me to go to Florida as a working student, and I
brought my now four-year-old down with me to show. It opened my eyes
considerably to the world of horse showing at that level, and I had the
opportunity to ride some of the other students' hunters during the week
since they would only come down to show on weekends. In Ocala that
winter, I was warming up to ride my green horse in the jumper ring and it
was pouring rain. George put a cooler on an oxer, and my horse spooked
at it. George was trying to help, yelling, "Stick! Spur! You have to MAKE
him do it!" Then, of course, he left the schooling area, and I fell off and
ended up covered head to toe in mud. I scrambled back into the saddle
and walked up to the ring to show in my muddy clothes. It was the most
memorable moment of that winter!

What we saw at The Hague was that the Europeans had become wise and raised their game. The German team captured team gold and Franke Sloothaak, a fabulous rider, won individual gold. It's not as if we weren't in the mix of top countries; the American team sat in fifth place when all was said and done. But after the streak of dominance in the late seventies and eighties, all of us—from the casual fans to those of us in the business—were expecting that to continue. Fifth felt like the basement after all that winning. Now we were the ones scratching our heads!

While I was there, Pierre d'Oriola (who was the only rider to win the individual show jumping Olympic gold medal twice, in '52 and '64) drove from France to watch the WEG. His comment to me was something to the effect of, "They sit down in the saddle too much, the fences are all the same, and therefore all the courses are the same and the spectators get bored. I'm leaving the show." I was surprised to hear someone put it so bluntly, but I couldn't have said it better myself! That was the direction show jumping had been going in for years, and we've continued on that trend every since. For most shows, the arena is very much the same and the fence material is the same. The courses are familiar. The riders, for the most part, are behind their horses, too. The old champion hit the nail on the head over twenty years ago, and we're still facing the same challenge.

The bloom was off the rose and it wasn't anyone's fault; it was just the way the sport had trended. Why, after the United States had held supreme power in show jumping, did we falter in the early nineties? Two key factors contributed. The first was that our American Thoroughbred breeding program had suffered from the lack of attention from the sport-horse perspective. We had completely missed the boat—me included! The horse-racing industry had begun producing more sprinters and fewer distance Thoroughbreds. As a result, that athletic, mid-century, Thoroughbred type that had been plentiful for decades became harder to find. There were still many Thoroughbreds, but not nearly as many that were suited for the show ring. We had taken that lovely show-horse type for granted, thinking that there would be an endless supply of those brave, hot, and well-built Thoroughbreds. It became impractical to weed through all of the Thoroughbreds since too many of them were broken from racing and so many ideal traits had been bred out of them. Sport-horse breeding in Europe was so much more advanced and thus, owners and professionals flocked to Europe to find their next superstar.

The USET had also become distracted and disorganized as a team. Bert de Némethy and his strictly managed program and schedule, with top care and a long-term outlook, had planted seeds that had bloomed during the late seventies and eighties. But being on the USET in the nineties wasn't as straightforward as it had been a couple of decades earlier. The show schedule was grueling, and we were all trying to get that edge back that we had in Los Angeles in '84, but the recipe just wasn't coming out right. To win at that level, over those big and difficult courses (which Bert himself had introduced with his own designs), a disciplined program was critical. Horses and riders had to be razor sharp and no one could maintain that sharpness without time set aside to rest, regroup, and ramp up for the following year. Top riders were wrestling with their own businesses, trying to please owners with prize money, and find a balance between that and representing their country.

There were, of course, other factors too. American horse shows became watered down for the casual hobby rider, with fewer of the big classes at shows. Young American riders weren't getting the same opportunities for challenging jumper classes or Nations Cup format classes that young riders in Europe were exposed to regularly. While our shows declined, the shows in Europe raised their game and got even better. After all, dressage, three-day eventing, and show jumping were born in Western Europe. As accomplished as the rest of the world may be at any given time, I don't believe we will ever take from Europe their mantle of being the center of equestrian sport. Our job is to give them a run for their money! We've done it before and can absolutely do it again.

Susie Hutchison

I grew up riding with Jimmy Williams but would go East as a junior rider in the sixties and watch George teach and ride. I was impressed with him from the very beginning. I took some juniors back for the Medal Finals in the late seventies, and I remember sitting at the in-gate on a hunter at Washington, and George was on a horse nearby, about to ride in the same class. He said he was nervous about riding in the class and I remember thinking, "How on earth can George Morris be nervous about riding a hunter?" But it just goes to show that we all have some nerves once in a while—it's the adrenaline that we have to get pumping through our system to ride the best we possibly can. In 1994, I rode in the WEG and George was really helpful to me then. He knew Jimmy Williams had been my support network and I'd lost that when Jimmy passed away. George stepped in as a mentor.

When Bert de Némethy stepped down as Chef d'Equipe, all the top American riders became very scattered. Bert had everything so structured at Gladstone and as time went on, things changed. Everyone wanted their own trainer and they didn't like the Gladstone concept anymore. When George was chosen to take over as Chef d'Equipe, he helped bring a cohesive group of riders together as a team again. In that gap of Bert to George, everyone was strung out and doing their own thing, and it didn't feel like a team effort even when we converged for the big championships. George's effort to bring that team structure back, however he could, is the reason our success returned, in my opinion. George instilling his belief in our American system back into us is what gave us the bump back up again.

In 1994, Kathy Moore moved on from Hunterdon. Kathy was my "Girl Friday," and she ran my life for almost twenty years and kept many things moving when it came to Hunterdon. Although it felt strange to run the business without her, all good things must come to an end. The following year, the powers that be on the USEF High Performance Committee made a decision that Frank Chapot and I would be co-Chef d'Equipe officially. There was a desire for a more active level of leadership than Frank was sometimes able to provide; he was a fantastic Chef d'Equipe but also had his own business to run. I had been acting in a co-Chef d'Equipe capacity unofficially for many years by being complementary to Frank's role. If he didn't want to go to Europe on a tour or to Calgary, I typically went instead. Being called co-Chefs was a natural transition, and I appreciated having my contribution officially recognized. However, with my business at Hunterdon, serving as Chef d'Equipe was tricky at times—specifically, when I was helping a student who didn't ride for the USET.

One such student was from Mexico, Luis Ximenez. His family had moved to Kentucky and he reached out to me for help in the early nineties. I coached him at some of the big shows here and there, but he was an independent rider and not based at Hunterdon. After a year or two, his family moved back to Mexico, and I visited to teach some clinics and we stayed in touch. Luis had a wonderful sponsor—a wealthy Mexican sport-horse breeder—and in 1995 he emerged from Mexico riding the most beautiful and talented colt that Abdullah ever sired. Luis and the big gray stallion named Airborne Monticello (who looked quite a bit like his sire) had one of those special horse-and-rider relationships where they perfectly understood one another. The pair won the first two Grand Prix classes they ever entered in the United States, and I could see they were going to be a major player at the championships.

I received approval from the High Performance Committee to bring Luis Ximenez with American riders on a European tour. Looking back now, it probably wasn't a good idea because of how it never sat well with some people that I was helping a rider for a non-American team, but there was no policy against it at the time. On the tour, we showed at Hickstead, and Kathy Moore and I thought it would be a great experience for Luis to stay with Dougie Bunn who was the master of Hickstead since the inception of the show in 1961 (and now his children and grandchildren run it). The American team had often stayed with the Bunn family in their huge English manor house over the years. Kathy and I had stayed with Dougie ourselves with our teams in the past and experienced firsthand the late, long nights of socializing with many rounds of pre-dinner cocktails, wine, and after dinner aperitifs. If you left at midnight you would be shamed endlessly and you were still a bad sport if you went to bed at two in the morning! We had learned our lesson and knew better than to think we could keep up with Dougie and still be fresh for the horse show in the morning, so we stayed in a hotel. However, we thought Luis might be up for the challenge—after all, Mexican culture is full of social drinking!

Luis and Airborne had an incredible start to the show and he won the Grand Prix Qualifier class on Thursday. No one had ever heard of Luis in Europe—he came out of nowhere and beat all the world-class riders. The press was enraptured with him and his beautiful gray stallion. He became the odds-on favorite to win the Grand Prix of Hickstead, which is important because they wager on the winners in England. On Thursday morning before the qualifier he told me, "Oh George, I stayed up drinking until four with Dougie Bunn, I'm so tired!" and then each day afterward they stayed up drinking later and later. By Sunday, the day of the big Grand Prix, poor Luis had nothing left! He was a young man and up for drinking and staying out late, but he was ragged as anyone would've been. Unfortunately, he didn't have the best round in the Grand Prix—his hot streak unraveled and everyone was very disappointed.

Frank Chapot decided not to attend the Pan American Games that year, so I acted as Chef d'Equipe for our team in Argentina. It was my first time as acting Chef at an international championship event. Funnily enough, Brigid Colvin, Tori Colvin's mother, was in Buenos Aires grooming Gonzi for Doug Russell. It would be years before Brigid and I met again and that's when I began getting to know Tori after seeing her rise to stardom in the hunter ring. Also named to the team were Debbie Stephens on Blind Date, Nona Garson on Derrek, and D.D. Matz on Tashiling, who joined veterans Norman Dello Joio on S&L Second Honeymoon and Michael Matz on The General. Michael Matz, initially the alternate, stepped in and won individual gold! The U.S. Team won the bronze medal (photo 202).

Michael Matz

In one of the last years I rode on the Pan American Team in Buenos Aires, George was the Chef d'Equipe. Initially, I was going as the alternate, which was fine because I wanted to be there to help my wife D.D. While there, each morning we would meet outside the hotel in the car to head over to the training facility. Well, it seemed like every morning, Nona Garson was about fifteen minutes late, and we'd all be sitting waiting for her while the morning grew warmer with each passing minute. After about the third day, while waiting for her again, I said, "George, would you please tell Nona she needs to try to be down here on time?" George turned around and said, "You tell her, Michael." When Nona came down, I told her, "Look, we're all waiting for you down here. Can you try to come down on time?" And Nona just smiled at me and said, "Michael, look at my hair." Obviously, Nona is a blonde, and instead of yelling, George just looked at me and said, "I told you so." It was so funny the way he handled it—he'd known Nona for so long that I guess he knew it was a losing battle!

George has made a great name from teaching clinics and the success of his students, but I think his commitment to the U.S. Team is his biggest contribution. Whatever he could do, whether he was the official Chef d'Equipe or not, he would help our country field the best possible team. His passion for the team doing well, even from the time he was riding to the time he was the Chef, has always been clear.

Luis Ximenez won the individual bronze medal for Mexico on Airborne Monticello and helped his Mexican team win the silver medal. Since I coached Luis and was helping the competition, his success caused a little kerfuffle. Eyebrows had been raised over the fact that I had helped a rider from another country—and not only helped him but contributed to Mexico winning a medal! I heard the complaints and understood why people felt it was a conflict of interest. It's simply always been my inclination to help good riders who ask me for guidance, no matter what country they're from. However, while in a Chef d'Equipe role, I could see I had to draw a line and be more careful about how I helped riders from other countries. Despite a few eyebrows being raised, overall those Pan American Games were a great success.

Nona Garson had come seemingly out of nowhere as a rookie to qualify for the '95 Pan American Games Team. She had come to ride with me the prior year and won the Gold Coast Grand Prix on her gray horse Derrek, which was the final selection trial. Nona is a lovely rider and I knew her early on because she had been very successful on the East Coast as a junior. Nona had ridden as a girl with her father and Alex Iby, a Hungarian horseman who immigrated to the United States like Bert de Némethy. I began working with Nona, who had been given a disciplined and correct European riding foundation, as a young professional in the early nineties when she began seeing success in the Grand Prix ring.

Nona Garson

I'm a New Jersey girl and grew up around Hunterdon and watched all the great riders come out of that place. I grew up riding with my father because we had our own stable and business, but I always admired what George did at Hunterdon. After my father passed away, I rode with George in some clinics at Hunterdon in the early nineties. Through the years, George had seen me riding here and there at the shows as a successful junior rider, and my first clinic was actually the first chance he had at a closer look. I'll never forget during the clinic when he exclaimed, "You're queen of New Jersey! Now I want to see you be queen of the world!" People say how tough he is—and he can be tough—but I would also call him a great optimist. He's so inspirational in the way he helped me and others take the next step to something bigger. He is so good working around the quirks of great horses and encouraging riders to be their best. If things didn't go well at a show, he was right there too, working through it with you. He has great character that way.

The first horse George helped me with was a horse named Derrek who I rode in the Pan American Games in 1995. He was a great jumper but a very difficult horse to ride. With George's help, we brought out Derrek's talent and had some success. The thing that George always brought to the table was the ability to train horses to be great, even if they weren't necessarily naturally great. If they were green and had quirks or issues, we worked through them with a lot of training as we worked our way up the ranks. We developed green jumpers to become Grand Prix horses. Nowadays you don't see that much anymore. You see fewer horses being developed in America than you used to, with more horses being developed elsewhere and bought already having experience at that level.

My friends in Helsinki advised me to keep an eye on an interesting Russian jumper around 1994. He was a ten-year-old, 15.3-hand Russian Thoroughbred type with Arab blood in him (a breed called Budyonny) and he was scopey, careful, and fast. When I first laid eyes on that horse, he was being ridden in the

Junior Jumper classes by a young Finnish girl. The horse had an interesting story, having been purchased with two other horses from the Russian government stud farm in exchange for a load of washing machines! Then after being a lesson horse in Estonia, the Finnish girl bought him for the Children's Jumpers. He'd been tried by several other top professionals, who thought he was too small and didn't have the scope for international Grand Prix. When Paul Schockemöhle and I watched him win a class easily at Gothenburg, I wasn't sure I agreed with the opinion that he was limited; I became very interested to try him.

It turned out Paul Schockemöhle, who by then reigned as the biggest horse dealer in Europe (and had for quite some time), was also very interested in trying the Finnish girl's horse for John Whitaker. They had beaten me to the punch in speaking with the owners, and I heard they were going to try him at Gothenburg. I was so tempted to watch them try the horse, but for once I was quite clever. I knew if Paul saw me watching them, he would know I was interested and buy him for sure, no matter what the price. So I stayed away from the ring, sat in the stands and pretended I didn't have a care in the world. As it turned out, it worked in our favor! Soon enough, the owners came to me next, giving me the news that Paul and John had passed on him; $300,000 for a junior jumper was very high and they said Paul thought he was too expensive.

I was next in line with an option to try the horse, so I let him go back to Finland and flew out shortly thereafter with Nona to try him. We had an incredible two days with him and Nona loved him just as much as I did. He was a freak and jumped out of his skin! I would put planks at the top of the standards and Nona would gallop him down to the five-foot-six jumps and he wouldn't even breathe on them—of course, we had to snap him up. The fact that he had been traded with two other horses for 150 used washing machines added to his "rags-to-riches" charm. He was called Rhythmical, and he and Nona went on to be legendary together for years afterward.

IV. ATLANTA OLYMPIC GAMES

Robert Dover

George is one of the great communicators of all time, both in person and in print. He is a master of articulation. George and I both learned to ride with military-style training, and we both were very tough on students at times. What I learned later in my career about teaching was that I didn't have to be so hard to get the same thought through. There were times when I was so overworked and very impatient, wanting improvements to happen immediately. I think George and I were both pretty hard on people in those times, but we've both mellowed out a lot over the years.

The way the USET used to function, amateur riders would ride horses that were donated to the team for the purpose of helping the United States have success on the world stage. We had very successful teams and the riders weren't making much money. There's no difference between our disciplines in terms of the evolution in past years and the lack of opportunities for hard-working riders who need financial support. Top horses nowadays are so expensive that professionals want instead to hold onto the money they earn and not risk it all on a top horse. In essence, instead of having poor, successful Olympians like those days past, we now have many professionals who are business people without the same work ethic. You don't have Beezie Maddens around every corner; you have a lot of riders who want to go to the Olympics but they also want to go to the three other shows that month so their Olympic horse gets ridden by other people and he isn't as sharp as he should be. That's where I and others have seen the drop-off in the commitment level. The very very best, however, are still keeping those standards.

The following year, the Olympic Games were in Atlanta, and Frank and I once again shared the Chef d'Equipe responsibilities. Olympic trials were held and the team was chosen from those who placed highest in the trials (photos 203, 204). The weather was brutally hot down in Atlanta. The summer Olympics are always held during the hottest time of the year and often the organizers choose very warm climates to host the Games, which adds an element of concern for the well-being of the horses. The organizers did all they could to help us manage the heat and provided misting fans outside of the rings to help the horses cool down. It was a blessing that the weather was overcast that week, so although it was hot and humid, we were spared the blazing sun.

It was a superb group of riders with lovely horses, and I thought we had a decent chance at the gold medal. It was our best Olympic Show Jumping Team since Los Angeles. Michael Matz on any horse was fabulous and that year he rode a wonderful little bay horse named Rhum IV. Peter Leone and Legato were a very strong team, as were Anne Kursinski and Eros, the little Australian-bred Thoroughbred.

Leslie Burr Howard had a wonderful chestnut mare Extreme owned by Jane Clark. Extreme could be very temperamental, very typical with chestnut mares, but when she was on her game she was an excellent jumper. She also had a funny way of trotting—she threw her shoulder out and winged just a little bit. She wasn't lame, just a slight paddling step that was a result of her conformation. In Atlanta, the ground jury made Leslie jog Extreme over and over, day after day, so they could re-inspect her. Jane Clark was very worried about it, and we would strategize about who should be the one to jog her and which side would better balance her stride to deemphasize her quirk. To be quite honest, it was a nightmare for all of the Games—we were so stressed at the possibility that Extreme might be eliminated altogether! It was a very nerve-wracking experience. In the end, it worked out and the powers that be allowed Leslie to ride Extreme through the Games.

The Germans had a fabulous team once again and they were definitely the team to beat. On the first day of the jumping competition, there was a Nations Cup and the Germans had some issues. Franke Sloothaak had an unusual chip at a spooky jump and Lars Nieberg's chestnut horse For Pleasure stopped out in the schooling ring. As I watched them having these issues, I thought, "Here's our chance to get back in the top spot!" Maybe their bad luck would give us a chance to win gold like '84! Well, I had underestimated Lars Nieberg because he went in and expertly jumped a clear round on For Pleasure. Watching him exit the ring after their clear round, I felt in my gut that we would probably be looking at a silver medal. If Lars' horse had spit it out in the big ring, it would've dampened their scores and given us our chance at gold. Succeeding despite those issues was a testament to the Germans' perseverance and also to their preparation of the horses, which I heard was particularly crafty that year. All things considered, being second to them was nothing to sneeze at. The silver medal was a great result for our home team and I thought it might be a sign of our resurgence as a dominant power in show jumping (photo 205).

Despite the great Atlanta Olympics, the sparse results for the American riders in the World Cup Final returned throughout the rest of the nineties. We didn't have notable finishes in '94, '95, or '96. Anne Kursinski was fifth on Eros in '97 and Richard Spooner was fourth in '98 on Cosino, with Margie Goldstein-Engle and Leslie also tying for sixth that year. We were knocking on the door, but I knew we could get back on top if we could just sharpen our edges a little bit more. With the modern-day culture of the sport having evolved so much in recent years, we were still trying to figure out the right recipe.

Periodically, I would be asked to judge the equitation Finals and I was always honored to do so, whether it was the Maclay, Medal, or USET Finals. Since 1984, I probably have judged them more than anyone else. I never judged the Washington Finals; it's not my favorite judging system to be part of a six-judge panel. I prefer to judge with one or two other judges at most. With my experience as a young rider at Madison Square Garden and all those years taking junior riders to the ring as a teacher, it's always interesting to go back to the world of equitation. Some things never change! At any given time, there are a few top professionals who specialize in equitation and seem to hold the key to helping riders win the big finals. Just like Victor Hugo-Vidal, Ronnie Mutch and me in the sixties and seventies, today's top names bring prestige to the in-gate along with the best young riders in America.

Katie Prudent had a student who was very talented with serious ambition named Alison Firestone (later: Robitaille). Katie had done a fabulous job creating Alison's foundation from a child rider through the equitation and into the jumpers. Katie had taken her to Europe to do the Grand Prix, and she was doing very well on her horse called Major. I had history with Alison's father Bert, who had ridden as an amateur jumper rider with William Steinkraus back in the late fifties, and also knew her mother Diana, who was a daughter of the Johnson & Johnson company founder. Earlier in the year of that World Equestrian Games in Rome, Alison and her parents asked if I would work with her. I welcomed her, as she's a wonderful student and a great rider, and she qualified and rode on the WEG team.

As they had for my entire life, the horses kept me grounded. In 1997, which was that "off year" after the Olympic year, it was time to regroup. I was very focused on Alison Firestone and Nona Garson as clients. Being so committed and obligated to the demands of my business and students, there was always the next goal, and I felt a huge responsibility to keep it all going. It kept me on track; it was a very good thing for me to have this tether to the horses. Even when I relaxed my thirteen-year abstention from alcohol and started having a beer here and there, I kept my focus on the business and on preparing for whatever was coming next on the show schedule.

Alison Robitaille

George always remembers this one class where I left out a stride and made an inside turn to win the class. He might not have agreed with my idea at the time, but he encouraged me to go for it if I thought I could do it. His enthusiasm for the sport and wanting to win is what made him the ideal Chef d'Equipe for so many years.

When we went to look at horses together when I was young, George was very helpful in teaching me about the points of conformation and how they could potentially impact a horse's performance or soundness. I feel very lucky to have worked so closely with someone of his caliber and someone who has seen the evolution of the Thoroughbred and Warmblood show jumpers, too.

In 1997, I was only twenty years old when I went on a tour with Anne Kursinski, Margie Goldstein-Engel, McLain Ward, and Todd Minikus. George put me first to ride on the Nations Cup team in Rome. At the time, it was a huge boost in confidence and probably one of the most important things that he did for me. Having his trust set the tone for an amazing and successful summer.

Outside of the show ring, his sense of humor and love for animals has made for a lasting friendship. We'd talk about our dogs all the time while we were on the road and how much he missed his, in particular, Big Dog.

In 1998, Dublin was initially granted the privilege to host the World Equestrian Games but withdrew from preparation after citing organizational difficulties. Despite the short notice, Rome and Aachen both expressed interest, and in the end the third occurrence of the WEG went to Rome. Returning to that wonderful city where I rode on the Olympic Team in 1960 was particularly meaningful. The show jumping wasn't held in the Piazza di Siena, but instead in an unattractive parking-lot area at the bottom of a large hill. VIP tents were pitched and organizers dropped footing into this lot just a couple of days before the show. After it poured rain the entire week before the WEG events, I was sure we'd have a sloppy situation on our hands. Much to my surprise, it was the best footing I had ever seen! It put to shame some of the best planned footing of other championships. I don't know what it was made of, but someone should have patented it on the spot!

Alison Firestone and Nona Garson (riding Rhythmical) did very well at the WEG that year, along with Anne Kursinski and Eric Hasbrouck. However, unlike the Olympics two years prior, none of the U.S. riders hung on to make the final four. We were still trying to find the right balance and get our edge back as Americans. I did celebrate the success of my old friend Nelson Pessoa's skillful son Rodrigo, who won individual gold at the young age of twenty-five.

Greg and Jeremy were very much alike, in that they were very socially involved with the horse-show scene and easy to bring along while teaching or showing because everyone loved them. However, their social nature also meant they were drawn to the city and became bored out at Hunterdon. After showing with me for many years, Greg eventually became frustrated and discouraged with his limitations on a horse. When that happened, he drifted away and lost interest in the horse-show scene, similar to Jeremy. Even after he wasn't showing himself, Greg traveled with me nearly all of the time until the late nineties. Naturally, he came to Italy for the WEG, but one night in Rome there was an incident that marked the start of our relationship's decline. We met several friends for dinner including a friend I'd met the year before at a show in Spain. The Spanish guy and I definitely had an attraction to one another, which Greg picked up on immediately. After dinner I went back to the hotel and to bed since I had co-Chef d'Equipe duties the next day, and Greg went out with some of the others. To my shock (I had never once seen him have a drink), Greg stumbled into the room at three in the morning blind drunk and sick as a dog. I couldn't believe what I was seeing. After he sobered up, he admitted it was jealousy over the Spanish guy that drove him to drink. That was the beginning of a downward spiral for Greg's struggle with addiction and for our relationship. His friend once told me, "If you ever see Greg with a drink in his hand, knock it out." Now I was finally realizing why.

After the lackluster results in Rome, the pressure was on! The U.S. Show Jumping Team hadn't yet qualified for the Olympic Games and needed a gold or silver medal in the Pan American Games the following year in Winnipeg, Canada, to qualify. Margie Goldstein-Engle rode Hidden Creek's Alvaretto, Alison Firestone rode Arnica de la Barre, Peter Wylde rode Macanudo de Niro, and Leslie Burr Howard rode Clover Leaf. Thankfully, we rebounded with a wonderful result in Winnipeg and won the team silver medal behind Brazil. Peter Wylde rode beautifully and also won the individual silver medal (photo 207).

Greg Hall and I were in the habit of renting a house in Wellington for the winter circuit, and we had about six dogs living with us at any given time. Florida had become so central to the circuit that I decided buying a house there made sense. Renting a house with all those dogs created difficulties, and I had grown tired of renting, anyway. One winter we rented a house in Pinewood East on the extreme northeast side of Wellington, which is the oldest housing development in Wellington. I fell in love with the quiet class, big wooded lots, and unique homes. It was also a decent distance from the horse show, which afforded me some semblance of privacy.

We took a drive through the neighborhood when we got to Wellington in late 1999 and saw a for sale sign on a gorgeous new home. We walked up the driveway and fell in love with the beautiful southern-style of the house with white columns and reddish clay roof. I knocked on the door to ask the owners about it and they let us take a look around. It was absolutely beautiful. From inside, all we saw through the windows was lush foliage and flowers, like our own personal rainforest. We couldn't resist, so we bought it! We even made a deal with the owners that we'd let them stay in the house for three more months, so their children could finish the school year, and they lowered the price $50,000. Still my home today, it's a special place, and there's really nothing else like it in Wellington. Many of the newer developments are cookie-cutter homes with very small lots. I feel so fortunate to have such a beautiful sanctuary away from the world where I can rest and rejuvenate. That winter, with the new millennium upon us, was the first year in my new home in Pinewood East.

Jan Neuharth

I remember when we first invited George Morris to come and teach a clinic at our Paper Chase Farms in Middleburg, Virginia. We'd heard the "George stories," and we were absolutely terrified. We ran around preparing for anything he could possibly want. But when we took George to dinner the night before the clinic I totally fell in love with him. He is a true gentleman and a delight to spend time with. There's a very different George you go to dinner with than the George teaching in the ring. We had wonderful annual dinners with Sallie Sexton and Gail and Jimmy Wofford while George was in town for our clinics. They told amazing stories from "back in the day," and I loved sitting back and listening. I remember a spirited debate over what's more dangerous, foxhunting or three-day eventing.

On the first day of the clinic at Paper Chase, I saw how tough George could be. The stories about him weren't exaggerated! But as the clinic progressed, I saw the transformation in the riders because he knew just how far to push each individual. George pulls no punches. But if you look at how disciplined George is in his own life and career, you begin to see that his desire to see riders succeed is behind his toughness. He's a perfectionist. And he holds others to that same high standard. That's why he teaches the way he does. For example, one girl showed up for a clinic at our farm with her hair dyed bright orange for some Halloween costume. George was brutal to her. At first, I thought maybe George had her pegged from the beginning because of her unconventional hair, but then I realized it was because she just wasn't trying very hard. George had gotten on her horse the first day and had him going beautifully. On the second day, it seemed like the girl was just waiting for George to get back on again and fix things for her. He got after her hard, lecturing her that he knew her type, she'd always had everything done for her— and told her to step up and do something for herself for once! She was embarrassed, upset, and crying, but kept riding and tried harder. You could see it was a turning point for her. At the end of the clinic, I took her aside and asked her if she was okay and, to my great surprise, she said it was the best clinic she'd ever ridden in and that George was right. Riding had come easy for her and that if she ever had a hard time, someone else would swoop in and do it for her. Clearly, she needed a wake-up call, and George's lecture had sunk in. I never saw her again, but I imagine it may have shaken her up enough to change her whole life.

One of the only certainties in life is that things change, and Greg and I parted ways, which was a difficult time. In a way, the birds had come back to the nest for us both. I'd started going out and drinking again in the nineties and getting back to my wild ways. I think for two people like Greg and me, who are tempted by the wild things in life, we held it together and had a good run for many years.

After Greg's drunken night in Rome during the WEG, his life became increasingly out of control. Our lives became more separated as we drifted apart toward the end of the decade. Gravitating toward a new group of friends, Greg befriended a car expert who restored sports cars. Soon afterward, we had a Mercedes, a Porsche, and a Ferrari in the driveway. They weren't brand new cars and he'd gotten deals on them through his friend, but still it was a sizable expense. Supporting Greg's objects of affection over the years when it came to horses and cars was quite a lot for me to bear on its own, but after the drinking and drugs began, it rose to another level. On my birthday in February of 2000, Greg came home drunk and the inside of the Porsche he had driven had been trashed.

After that, I was exhausted with sleepless nights worrying about Greg's recklessness. With my huge business of Hunterdon and high-powered clients like the Firestones, I had to be able to focus on my work. For me, no matter how hard I may have partied in the '60s or '70s, I got myself out of bed and went to work. Maintaining my work routine is what held my life together during those times, even when I let myself get wild.

I knew Greg's problems were not going away without some kind of intervention, but I wasn't in a position to help him change. The stress of Greg's issues on top of my already high-pressure business was killing me, and I had to get someone to help intervene. By pure coincidence, my sister was connected socially through friends to Greg's father, who was remarried and living in Maine. When I reached him on the phone, I appealed to him, explaining that I couldn't care for and cope with Greg's issues. He came down to Florida at once and together, we arranged for Greg to travel to a rehabilitation facility in Tucson, Arizona for about six weeks of treatment.

I knew Greg's recovery would be a long road and I started to get worried that his issues would be a vicious cycle of self-destruction. With a European tour and the Sydney Olympics coming up, I would be on the road nearly every week once Greg came home. Knowing I wasn't in a position to help Greg stay on track when he came back, I called his doctors in Tucson. I explained to them that I had to break off the relationship while he was still there, surrounded by a support network. When Greg heard I was breaking off the relationship, he was very upset. Greg didn't have a professional identity in terms of a job, and his life had, for many years, revolved around mine, which must have made it much more difficult to move forward.

With the help of one of his best friends, a lawyer, Greg filed suit against me for what he felt he was entitled to (which was quite a lot). After all was said and done, it took four years and deep pockets on both sides to resolve the lawsuit. Once it was over, I put it behind me. I carry neither a grudge against Greg nor any bitterness over how our relationship ended. He was a sweet guy and we had a great run together. My life still has very positive elements that Greg brought into it, like Lisa Cole my wonderful bookkeeper and Stan Segal my accountant. They are wonderful people who help keep my life organized, and I owe Greg for finding them both.

Dianne Grod

In the late 1990s, a friend of mine organized a big show in France at Napoleon's estate, and he asked me to find the course designer and be the foreign judge. Robert Ridland designed the course and George brought a team to the show on a developing-rider tour. Vinton Karrasch, Ray Texel, and George were riding. I was judging and George rode in a speed class, and he was absolutely flying around the course when he missed—badly. The horse jumped but carried the top rail a million feet and George ended up in front of the saddle with his legs wrapped around the horse's neck. To complicate things for George, that particular ring's fence was not a real fence; it was only stakes in the ground with ropes like a dressage ring. If the horse had gone through that rope, it could've been a nightmare, and I know this was very clearly on George's mind as he tried to get control of the horse and stay on. Even so, I honestly almost died laughing at the look on his face. He had to circle a couple of times to stop and get control. He stopped and ended up right in front of the judge's box. He looked up and said to us, "What the hell was that?" I hadn't even composed myself yet, I was laughing so hard. My fellow judges barely spoke any English. I never let him forget about it, and we still laugh about it today.

As in past decades, the nineties marked years of personal evolution. At the beginning, my time was split between running my business, teaching, and riding my own Grand Prix jumpers. As the years went by and I no longer had top horses to carry me in the big classes, it was a natural evolution to refocus on Hunterdon and helping young riders achieve their goals of riding on European tours and earning international championship spots on the USET. As my own competitive career wound down, my leadership role officially expanded beyond the interests of my own clients and I was named by the USET as Frank Chapot's co-Chef d'Equipe. This formalization of a role I'd played for many years was an acknowledgement of my contributions in helping prepare, select, and support the American riders at the Olympics, the World Equestrian Games, the Pan American Games, and the World Cup Finals.

Serving not only as a mentor or coach for individual riders but for the entire team, in whatever capacity was needed, came very naturally to me. Having ridden on the team with Bert de Némethy and then after having observed his and Frank Chapot's leadership styles for decades, my own style began taking shape. I wanted to promote cohesiveness among the riders on the championship teams, bring structure and discipline to the day-to-day operations, and find the best ways to complement the established knowledge and success of even the more veteran professional riders. For me, a Chef d'Equipe role was a natural step toward trying to strengthen the sport of international show jumping in America. I was inspired to find ways to adapt the discipline and stability of Bert's structured program to the far-flung network of independent, professional top riders. As my responsibility in my Chef d'Equipe role grew, I was determined to find a way to get the USET back on top with the depth and domination that characterized those unbeatable teams in the eighties.

CHAPTER SEVEN: THE 2000s

A NEW MILLENNIUM

I. DOWN UNDER

The new millennium was upon us and all eyes were focused on the next Olympic Games in Sydney, Australia. Two of my students, Nona Garson and Alison Firestone, were vying for the team, and in order to avoid any potential conflict of interest, Frank Chapot was the exclusive Chef d'Equipe that year. An excellent horseman, Frank was Chef—incredibly—for six Olympic Games, along with many other international championships. As a leader, he was bold and well-loved, and he himself has so much love for the team in return. Frank was involved with the U.S. Show Jumping Team for nearly his entire life, both as a rider under the leadership of Bert de Némethy and as a coach and leader himself. With his natural gift for communicating beautifully with the other countries' Chefs d'Equipe, he was very well respected around the world.

My role as co-Chef d'Equipe in the nineties didn't last long because I simply had too many students who were trying for the championship teams. I was still helping and in regular contact with Frank, but my official role had to fade out with my students being in contention. Olympic selection-trial classes for the Sydney Games were held in California, which was naturally a good stop on the way to Australia, and it was there that the fabulous horse Rhythmical earned his way onto the team. Nona Garson had been winning practically everywhere we went in the world. That horse was a freak, plain and simple! Before we went to the trials, I had worked with Nona on very careful preparation over the water jump, because he was such a sensitive type of horse, with those old Arabian and Thoroughbred lines running through his blood. It paid off; it was the precise preparation of that horse that made him so successful that year in the Olympic trials.

The Olympic Team horses stayed in California under quarantine for several weeks between the end of the trials and traveling to Australia. Nona had struck up a relationship with Anthony d'Ambrosio's brother George some months prior. George is a very nice guy and I had watched his family grow up in the sport (interestingly, his father Tony was one of the first horsemen who had his kids wearing actual riding helmets, not just hunt caps). George played a role in convincing Nona to go out on her own—apparently, I made her more nervous than she would've been otherwise.

Naturally, I was disappointed in Nona's decision to distance herself because I thought she should simply continue to stick with what was clearly working well. Maybe having me on her ass helped her win! I continued to offer my help if she ever needed it and in the meantime, I watched as George took on a coaching role with Nona and Rhythmical in California at the quarantine facility in August. I went back to New Jersey to handle clients at Hunterdon, but before I left I'd given Nona specific instructions for working Rhythmical over the water jump in the sand ring at Gabby Salick's place. While I was away, George and Nona instead took him out to a nearby grass field with an archaic, deep, spooky water jump from the old days. Nobody ever jumped that water anymore! Poor Rhythmical hung up in the air, hit the lip of the water and flipped over, hurting himself badly.

Rhythmical's injury was catastrophic for the Olympic Team and vets from both coasts were consulted. Conference calls were held to keep tabs on his recovery and try to determine whether he would be able go to Sydney or if the alternate, Todd Minikus on his horse Oh Star, should step into their place. We didn't have the luxury that year of having veteran, Olympic-caliber horses to choose from, so the decision was critical. Laura Kraut had Liberty, who was still quite green. Lauren Hough and Clasiko had never even been in a Nations Cup. Margie Goldstein-Engle and Hidden Creek's Perin were great together, but didn't have as much experience as Nona and Rhythmical. Frank and I agreed we must take Rhythmical to Australia if at all possible and monitor his recovery. Thankfully, the vets decided he was sound enough to travel.

The venue in Sydney was top-notch and quite a lot like Atlanta; it was as if they'd picked the stadium up out of Atlanta and plunked it down in Sydney. Walking the cross-country course at the Olympics had by then become a tradition for me, as I often helped three-day riders and was always interested to see the course design. In Sydney, I remember walking the entire course front to back one day, and again back to front a day or so later, to see it from the other direction. Signs on the course read "Beware of serpents," and I trod very carefully, for I knew about the poisonous snakes in Australia from my travels there!

On cross-country day, the Chef d'Equipe of the U.S. Three-Day Team, Mark Phillips, asked me to spot a specific fence and radio him after watching a few horses navigate it, to share with him how best to ride it. The jump in question was in the middle of the course, and I walked out to it and back again. I was no spring chicken, so walking the length of the course three times was pushing it! But I enjoyed watching and helping the team. Nowadays, I'll walk bits and pieces of the course but not the whole thing (photo 208).

Frank had terrible flu during those Olympic Games, but he's such a warhorse that he never missed a beat and watched every horse warm up and show. As the days ticked by, we had to make a decision about Rhythmical. The rules required that the American team officially enter the classes with our four horses and riders the night before the first show-jumping event. Then, in the hour just prior to the class, we had one last chance to make any final changes to the team. Once the first horse jumps the first jump in the first class, the team is set in stone. It was a very difficult decision to make. Todd Minikus had a very good horse in Oh Star, but on that last day before the competition, they didn't look particularly sharp. Nona Garson schooled Rhythmical that day as well and he went very well. Of course, it was hard to predict the risk of Rhythmical's potential for lameness after his injury in California, but he and Nona had been so consistently dominant that it was difficult to resist sending them into the ring. Frank ultimately made the call to take the risk with Rhythmical and Nona, and I was thrilled she'd have the chance to show on the ultimate world's stage.

At each of the Olympic Games I had attended by that time, from Rome in 1960 to Atlanta in '96, the footing was by and large acceptable. Montreal was one exception to that rule, but Mexico City, Munich, Los Angeles, Seoul, Barcelona, and Atlanta all managed to produce safe, quality surfaces for show jumping. That's why it's such a mystery to me why the footing in Sydney was so poorly done. It consisted of loose sand over a hard, concrete-like surface. Horses would try to set themselves at the base of a jump and when they tried to push off, they would slide. The feeling of instability led to the horses jumping defensively and not extending themselves in their take-off. They also couldn't trust the footing on the landing side of the jump and the horses pulled their hind end down more quickly in an effort to get all four feet on the ground. As a result, many more rails came down on course and more faults were incurred. Rhythmical, having already experienced the blow to his confidence with that fall at the big water jump in California, tried gamely to be at his best. But on that awful footing, he dropped into the back rails of the oxers to protect himself. He simply didn't want to fall down. And who could blame him?

Despite Frank having the lead role as Chef d'Equipe, my helping the team in Sydney created unrest, in terms of the selection of Nona for the team. I certainly didn't hold back my opinion when asked, but ultimately, the decision was Frank's to make. Naturally, when Rhythmical had problems with the footing and incurred faults, the choice Frank made to let Nona ride came under more scrutiny than it would have otherwise. Todd Minikus was very disappointed he hadn't been chosen to ride instead, which is understandable. Perhaps we made the wrong choice, but we had to live with the one we'd made. The United States finished out of the medals in sixth place and, at the end of the day, it was another mediocre placing for us against the Europeans. Rhythmical went on to win several more Grand Prix classes after that and the Olympic experience, however lackluster our placing was, absolutely served to benefit Nona's professional education.

Back at Hunterdon, we had six or seven dogs running around in a dog pack with clients' dogs so there could be fifteen dogs there on any given day. For that many, you need a 100-acre place! My tiny little Beagle, Big Dog, that Greg found for me that day in Indiana, had become the love of my life and I was intensely protective of him (photo 210). When I returned to Hunterdon after teaching clinics late that winter, I heard that Big Dog had gone missing while I was away. Although the entire Hunterdon staff searched high and low for Big Dog in the surrounding woods and neighborhoods, he had seemingly vanished.

Jenny Kappler (Chris's wife at that time) decided that desperate times called for desperate measures! Jenny remembered that Anne Kursinski would consult animal psychics about her horses from time to time. She called Anne's psychic, who told her "Big Dog is down at the white bridge." Well, nobody knew of any white bridge anywhere nearby, but when they looked at a map of Pittstown, lo and behold, there was a White Bridge Road three or four miles away.

With cautious hope, they all drove over to White Bridge Road to take a look around. To their dismay, there was no white bridge to be found along the road. But as they were driving along slowly, searching the woods along the side of the road, they passed a little cottage. Suddenly, there he was! Big Dog! He was on the front porch, being fed treats by a little old lady. They pulled in, scooped him up, and brought him back home, much to the disappointment of his new friend. I could hardly believe the story. But ever since then, I don't completely discount the use of psychics. I don't think I would call one myself, but I prick my ears and listen when someone else talks about advice they got from a psychic, because if it hadn't been for one of them, Big Dog might not have ever been found.

Continuing my tradition that began with my childhood trips with my grandmother, I traveled and explored new places. Being out of my long relationship of the nineties, I found myself feeling quite free and looking to travel to open-minded, fun cultures. I returned to Brazil, the country I'd come to love ever since my first trip there in the late seventies. While in Bahia, which is an earthy, beach area in Brazil, I was walking from one place to another and spied a tall, handsome Brazilian guy getting out of a taxi. Afterward, I noticed him across the bar and we met and started talking. Sometimes I just get a feeling about someone and my instinct was right: Leon Ramos and I had an instant connection. After showing me his favorite places and introducing me to his friends and family, I realized I really enjoyed spending time with Leon. When I went home, I invited him to visit me in New Jersey, which he did.

Leon was an "Energizer Bunny" and with him, life was always an adventure (photo 211). I brought him along with me to some nice dinners with Alexander and Lisa Guest and other horse people. He charmed the curls off everyone he met, and women fell in love with Leon left and right. We met Tab Hunter, Dick Clayton (a famous agent of James Dean and other Hollywood stars), and Tommy Ellison for dinner one evening. Leon sat by Dick, who was by then quite elderly, and helped him with his dinner. I think literally Dick thought he had died and gone to heaven!

II. HORSE OF A LIFETIME

In the New Year, we shipped the horses from Hunterdon down to Wellington for the Florida circuit. It was no small operation—between those stabled in our barn and clients who kept their horses elsewhere, we must have had seventy or more horses showing in Florida. By that time, Chris Kappler had become a very high profile rider but hadn't yet competed in a big international championship. For many years, Chris had been committed to riding and developing horses for the Grand Prix ring and worked very hard toward that goal in addition to managing Hunterdon clients and their horses. In Florida one year, we had so many horses that Chris, on his own, rode into the show ring fifty-seven times in a single day; he rode eight horses in a 1.45m division alone!

Jeff Cook and Holly Mitten just kept bringing them up to the ring and Chris hopped from horse to horse.

By 2001, Chris had two good horses but still needed a horse with Olympic scope to lift him to the top. On a trip to Europe searching for just such a horse, Chris called me from Henk Nooren's stable. Henk had a seven-year-old who had been ridden by an amateur but hadn't yet jumped big jumps. I went to Europe and we tested the horse over two days with very difficult lines and fences, assessing his scope and agility. He was 16.3 hands and crooked-legged, with a twisty, hanging style, but despite that was extremely careful with enormous scope. The horse's name was Royal Kaliber. The handsome stallion had an occasional spook that had to be addressed, like for a cut-out wall or Liverpool, but it wasn't a dirty spook. Chris and I both really liked him, despite the Dutch being nervous about his crookedness. I've always been brave when it comes to imperfections with horses. If I really believe in and love the horse, I don't let a flaw scare me away.

Chris Kappler

In '96 and '97, I had great success on European tours with some wonderfully talented horses. After that, I had a few years without a horse that could really compete at that top level beyond the Grand Prix circuit. When we first tried Royal Kaliber, I was over in Europe looking at horses with Henk Nooren in 2001, and the horse seemed a little inconsistent with his form over fences. He hung his legs a little and he had a crooked foot. He was expensive enough that I didn't think anyone would buy him quickly and decided to just wait and told Henk to keep me posted on the horse. That winter afterward, George and I had a couple of weeks between shows, so we flew to Europe to look at horses. I was interested in seeing Royal again, so we went there first and jumped him really big in Henk's indoor that afternoon. The way he could jump big fences was just amazing.

The following day, we set up the oxer-vertical-vertical combination to see how careful he would be, and he felt great. I remember looking at Royal while he was standing still and he was so classy, even in the way he looked through the bridle. He was such a kind, generous-looking stallion. My sponsors, the Kamine family, were wonderful enough to buy him for me to ride and that was the beginning of my time with Royal; he was my horse of a lifetime. And he wasn't just an amazing athlete. He was such a sweetheart in the barn and loved attention. He was a really special stallion and a spectacular partner.

Success is all about good planning. Preparing Royal Kaliber for the 2003 Pan American Games and the 2004 Olympic Games was something we thought a lot about. George helped at every turn. I remember having about a dozen sheets of legal pad paper taped together with notes on every month for a span of about two years (photo 212).

In 2002, the World Equestrian Games were held in Jerez de la Frontera, Spain. Selection trials were held on both the East and West Coasts at various venues and I went to the trials on the West Coast in the midst of my clinic tour schedule. Chris rode Royal Kaliber in the trials, but he had a bad spook in one of the early classes, then later a shoeing problem sidelined Royal for the third trial. After a week off, they were back and won the big Grand Prix, but the time they took to rest Roy was costly, and they didn't make the WEG Team. They were still a bit green so it was all right, but people had noticed how good they were. Despite not making the team, it was an important stepping stone; Chris and Roy had proven themselves as one of the best in the country at that level.

Leon and I went out to Del Mar, California, to one of the WEG trials. I was fortunate, while out there, to spend time with Victor Hugo-Vidal who had moved out West years prior. Victor was ailing from heart problems, but I saw him that entire week, which was so wonderful. Soon after that, he grew gravely ill and passed away. It was hard to lose such an old and dear friend. Victor and I had been on parallel tracks for so many decades of our lives, and the trajectory of my life, especially in my formative years, certainly wouldn't have been the same without him.

Molly Ashe (later: Ashe Cawley), who originally wasn't even planning to try for the team, finished first in the trials with her fantastic mare Kroon Gravin. And European-based Peter Wylde, who you would had to consider a bit of a longshot, was second with Fein Cera. Leslie Burr Howard, a two-time Olympian and WEG veteran who I figured to be a huge asset to the team, wound up third with Priobert de Kalvarie, who had cut quite a swath of wins through Europe. And Nicole Shahinian-Simpson, who missed out on the 2000 Olympics when El Campeon's Circa Z developed an abscess during those trials, hung on to finish fourth. Those four riders traveled to Spain for the WEG.

Frank and I served once again as co-Chefs d'Equipe in Spain. Leon went with me to Spain and was great company, as he was happy either with me at the show or entertaining himself by exploring the city. Peter Wylde, who is an absolutely beautiful example of the correct forward seat, rode excellently on Fein Cera. Fein Cera was a lovely mare. A few years prior to those World

Equestrian Games, Alison Firestone had owned the mare. I jumped her myself and she was very good. Fein Cera's only fault I could see was that she didn't take some jumps seriously because they were so easy for her! I told Peter to really watch out when it came to the plain, insignificant vertical in the corner on course. The mare would be fine with the spooky fences and big oxers, but she wouldn't respect the plain, smaller fences and would have a rail out of boredom. In Spain, the vets were nervous about Fein Cera and thought she wasn't well. Peter came and spoke with me and I told him, "Peter, enter the horse. She's in top form!" So, I pushed Peter to ride the horse despite their concerns and I'm glad I did. In the end, she proved that she was up to the challenge: she was the only horse to jump four clear rounds in the final four, and Peter won the individual bronze medal!

Geoff Teall

I grew up riding in Geneseo, New York, with Mike Kelley. She was a student of Gordon Wright's and would have Gordon out to her farm to give clinics, some of which I was fortunate enough to ride in. Mike Kelley was, in her way, as brilliant as George and Gordon. She taught at a lower level and only out in the country for foxhunting, but she recognized something in me and figured out a way to draw that out. There are so few people at the horse shows now who ever had a chance to foxhunt. Truthfully, every moment I'm on a horse I am frightened. Had I not had the upbringing in foxhunting, I'm not sure I would have carried on in the sport. I have the same system and approach in foxhunting as I do in showing hunters.

Naturally, this beginning led me to George. I worked with Wayne and Frank Carroll at Secor Farms in White Plains, New York, for a year and when I was nineteen years old, I answered an advertisement in *The Chronicle of the Horse* for a groom position at Hunterdon. It was my first real contact with George, but somehow he knew who I was and sent me back a handwritten note. He wrote that the position wasn't suitable for me and recommended I stay where I was and wait for the right opportunity to come along.

Through Mike Kelley, I heard about an opportunity to work for the Jacobs family at Deeridge Farm around 1974. I ended up working exclusively for them for ten years, and they're still my clients forty years later. Shortly after I began, I took the Jacobs family to George's clinic in Buffalo, and George annihilated me in the clinic! It was complete public humiliation in front of my clients and some other professionals. George has always known exactly how to size up a rider in ten seconds flat and understand what each one needs to inspire them to be their best. I think that's George's greatest asset. If people need to be flattered for George to get it out of them, he flatters them. And if shredding them is what it takes, he shreds them! After my annihilation, I took every opportunity to ride or audit George's clinics by essentially following him around the country. If there was any way possible for me to get to any of his clinics, I was there. I made myself available, because I knew that it was where I needed to be for my education. I'm still learning from George today.

Gordon Wright invented the concept of systematically teaching people to ride, step by step. Then George, in turn, labeled that system and taught it in a way that was better understood. When I teach clinics, I start exactly where Gordon started with me and that's how George does it too. At least eighty-five percent of what I know comes from the dozen clinics I rode in with Gordon and George. George has developed a huge group of teachers—myself, Karen Healey, and many others—who carry on that style and system. He is also completely tireless when it comes to the welfare of the sport. Whenever George and I cross paths, wherever we happen to be, he always gives me a job—he'll tell me I need to go speak with someone, or find out what's happening with some organizational board—or he'll simply want to talk about how we need to get better. George teaches standards, drive, discipline, and desire, and he's done it for over fifty years. He knows it's a different world we live in and some of the battles he fights for the sake of the sport are difficult uphill battles. When he feels resistance, he just works harder. And he's still getting through to enough people that it won't ever disappear. Karen Healey and I are devoted to those same standards, to a fault even, in a society that is becoming less and less willing to hear it. We have to do everything we can, at our own expense at times, to maintain and keep these standards alive. I could no more leave the barn without shining my boots with a toothbrush than cut my own head off.

I enjoyed traveling to more exotic locales because as an older, single guy I often found there was more fun to be had in these foreign cities. Honestly, I had been turned off by the American gay scene for some time—it was too over the top, too clichéd for me. When I taught a few clinics in Hungary and went out on the town in Budapest with a friend of mine, I met some interesting friends and characters, including a young bartender named Sergio from Romania. We were immediately impressed with not only his good looks, but how he ran the place with such authoritative, calm leadership.

After I left Hungary, I ended up keeping in touch with Sergio, who lived in the Canary Islands, then went to Madrid, and later to Milan, working for a doctor there. Although the two of us never became very close because of the distance, we had great mutual respect and I was sort of intrigued by him. A few years later he died in a horrible, high speed car wreck and nobody ever knew if he'd been driving that recklessly in joy or in despair. I corresponded with his parents and the doctor he worked with and everyone was devastated. There are people you meet in your life who you feel are destined for great things, whether in the horse world or otherwise—and Sergio was one of those people. His death served to remind me how fragile life can be.

The following year in 2002, my zany artist friend Michael who lived in Provincetown, Massachusetts, invited me with him to Romania. Since I'd had such a good time in Hungary years before, it sounded like fun, and we decided to make a road trip out of it. We began on the western side of Romania, drove across the country to the Black Sea, and then went on to Bucharest. It was beautiful country! In Bucharest, I met Lorenzio, whom I called Larry for short, and we became great friends. Larry and I just clicked right from the start. He's very sweet and laid back and an excellent traveling buddy, especially given that he looks like a bodyguard!

Leading up to the 2003 Pan American Games in the Dominican Republic, Chris and Roy won the American Invitational and the AGA Championship on back-to-back weekends in Florida and established themselves as the darlings of the show world. He was the best horse in the country, and he was talked about all over the world. Frank Chapot asked Chris, "What do I have to do to get you on the team?" and Chris replied jovially, "All you have to do is ask!" Interestingly, when Chris was put on the Pan Am Team that year, he was the first rider subjectively chosen for a U.S. Show Jumping Team since the Dolan's lawsuit over the selection process resulting in complete objectivity in the 1990s. Frank exercised his right to put Chris on the team, and it broke the ice to bring subjectivity back into the selection of the teams. After Frank picked Chris, the pressure was on him to show the sport that subjectivity in selection might sometimes be the right approach.

With great horses like Royal Kaliber, there's always drama. Chris Kappler was very careful about how Roy was cared for and kept fit. But there are always unpredictable moments, especially with stallions. At the Pan American Games that summer, he got loose, jumping over an enormous wall with a drop of ten feet on the far side. Roy proceeded to run at breakneck speed all over the show grounds. By all rights, he should've been injured! He could've slid on the pavement and broken a leg or his neck. By some miracle, Roy was caught and walked away from his tour of the show grounds dead sound, with only a few minor scratches.

Joining Chris on the team for the Pan American Games that year was Margie Goldstein-Engle on Hidden Creek's Perin, Lauren Hough on Windy City, and Beezie Madden on Conquest II. In Santo Domingo, Dominican Republic, the facility was a gorgeous estate about forty minutes outside the city. A welcome barbeque was planned for everyone on the team early in the week so all the USET riders, grooms, and coaches piled on a bus together to drive out to the big estate. After a while, we began to realize our bus driver was completely lost! Not only had he lost his way, he was taking us down narrow, winding roads and he couldn't figure out how to turn around. Everyone began worrying we were seriously lost and possibly even in danger. Frank Chapot and I started freaking out and yelling at the driver, telling him he had to get the bus turned around somehow and get us all out of there. We eventually made it to the barbeque—with our blood pressure through the roof!

The American team did fantastically well at those Pan American Games and took home the gold medal as a team. In the individual competition, Chris and Royal Kaliber were barely edged out by Mark Watring of Puerto Rico. Watring had a career day and was very fast. Chris won the silver and Margie Goldstein-Engle rode fabulously and won the bronze medal. With so many American riders stepping up on the podium, the show-jumping community looked ahead to Athens on the horizon, where we would have another shot against the Europeans at the Olympic Games.

Missy Clark

George's influence in my life has been immeasurable. I have learned so much from him over the years, and to this day I use his philosophies and methods in my teaching. I still keep his *Hunter Seat Equitation* book nearby. George was very fond of my mother, Doris, who was a horsewoman from his era. She taught me to ride at an early age and encouraged me to attend my first clinic with George in Buffalo, New York, at the age of thirteen. Later, George helped me with my jumpers at shows, and I would often go to Hunterdon for lessons.

George was the first horseman to put things into words that made sense for my generation. I have attended many of his teaching clinics, and his system is complete, logical, and easily understood. George's philosophy is based on discipline, a methodical approach to training, and traditional thoughtful horsemanship. Without a doubt, George Morris has been and continues to be one of the most respected and knowledge-able horseman of all time. His influence throughout the United States and across the world has truly been remarkable.

It was costing me about $100,000 a month to run Hunterdon, and the immense overhead didn't feel as worthwhile anymore, when the culture at the barn had become less interesting to me. Most of the riders in my upper barn were hobby riders—amateurs with no great ambition to ride at the upper lev-els. The staff turnover had become difficult to manage as well; we would train young men to work in the barn, then a wealthy rider, often a friend, would offer them three times the salary, and we'd be back to square one.

I realized that my decision to no longer coach the equitation and hunters had come with a downside. Although it was a positive shift in focus to the jumpers and international showing in the eighties, my connections to the most ambitious young riders had weakened over the years. There was some-thing very special about getting promising students when they were eleven or twelve years old and teaching them through the hunters and equitation. Those years created a foundation and skill set that lifted them to the levels of Grand Prix. When I start students young, I help them become champi-ons. But when riders come along when they're older, often times they aren't inspired or don't have the belief that they can get to the top, so they fade and turn into hobby riders.

On occasion, I wonder if it was a disadvantage for the sport in this country that I gave up teaching junior riders on a client basis, rather than primarily in clinics. With my clinic tour I certainly work with more riders overall, but my impact isn't the same without the day-to-day program over time. However, there are wonderful teachers across the nation and around the world, each of whom are committed to the same foundation that I so passionately stand by, and I have passed the torch to them. Still, in recent years, my desire to more deeply impact the education of younger riders has been renewed. With the help of the USEF, I began teaching clinics to riders that go beyond the typical three days. If I can inspire a higher level of ambition in some of those riders, the extra effort absolutely will have been worthwhile.

III. STAR-CROSSED CHAMPION

The United States Show Jumping Team was primed for the Olympics in Athens. Royal Kaliber was in such peak condition that Chris Kappler and I only entered him in seven classes in Wellington that prior winter! Not seven shows—seven *classes*—primarily the Thursday or Saturday Grand Prix. We devised unorthodox plans to prepare Chris for any potential challenge he might face at the Olympics. During those preparation classes, I had him add strides or leave out strides, take angles to certain jumps, and so forth. Our aim wasn't winning those classes, but to get experience. Even so, he easily got seven top ribbons and won two of them outright.

That spring I returned to New York after the Wellington circuit and my nightlife habits started to get a bit out of hand. Although I had long periods of time abstaining and sticking to clean living, I have also at times let the leash out too much. Never in my life had I let it out quite as much as I did that spring though. Late in April, one Tuesday morning, I missed a scheduled lesson with a girl at Hunterdon because I'd been out all night in the city. Although I'd kept up with the business, I also had the self-awareness to realize things had simply gone too far. Jenny, Chris, and Robi Greenberg (one of my longest customers at Hunterdon) rounded me up and took me to West Palm Beach, Florida, to a rehab clinic called Hanley-Hazelden. Very few people ever knew I even went, but I was glad for the support of my friends. I spent the month of May there getting back on track and walked out hating rehab and ready to focus on helping Chris at the Olympic Games.

The rules that year stated only one horse-and-rider combination was allowed to receive a "bye" and be excused from the trials—and it was Chris and Roy who earned it! After six rounds of selection-trial classes at Del Mar and San Capistrano, California, the usual suspects were at the top of the list: Beezie Madden and Authentic were in first (a great finish after her leading mount came up lame), Peter Wylde and Fein Cera were second, and McLain Ward and Sapphire were third. Sapphire, McLain's big chestnut Belgian mare, had competed in her very first Grand Prix class just a year before, so a third place finish against all the top riders was quite an achievement. McLain, who took over his father Barney Ward's business, quickly rose to the top of the rankings with Sapphire.

While in Florida that year, Margie Goldstein-Engle was kicked and broke her femur, which meant no showing for her for most or all of 2004. Margie and Hidden Creek's Perin were a fabulous pair and had great results the prior year.

However, with her injury we couldn't consider her a shoo-in in case they'd lost their edge a bit. In the end, Chris, Beezie, Peter, and McLain were our chosen team for Athens. Alison Firestone earned the alternate spot.

That summer, Mark Phillips invited me to teach a clinic in Middleburg, Virginia, with the Olympic three-day eventers. While driving back to the hotel one night after the clinic, Chris Kappler called from Hachenburg, Germany. Leading up to the Olympics, the team went to Europe for a couple of shows to stay sharp before flying to Athens. Chris told me Royal Kaliber had slipped in a roll-back turn in the jump-off during the Grand Prix and tweaked a hind tendon. He was a little bit off and both Chris and his veterinarian, Tim Ober, were concerned it may jeopardize Roy's ability to go in the Olympics in less than two months. When Chris told me they were considering bringing him back home to the States, I told them it would only be over my dead body! I made it crystal clear that Royal Kaliber—the best horse in the country, mind you—was *not* getting on an airplane. One must always get a second opinion before a decision that monumental! I told them to get Peter Cronau, the wonderful German vet, over to the farm for a second opinion. Peter went to see him and said his opinion was that he just tweaked something and needed a week or two of light work and was okay to go to the show in Aachen.

In the few weeks off between Hachenburg and Aachen, Chris moved Roy to a beautiful nearby stable to give him the best care possible. The tendon was treated with laser therapy and Roy got a little light exercise to keep him conditioned. Then Chris rode him in a couple of speed classes at a smaller, local show and gave him a really good school the week before Aachen. In the end, Roy was sound and ready to go—and a little bit fresh, too! Just like my horse Game Cock back in '52 who had time off before the indoors due to my hurt knee—a fresh horse can be an advantage.

Authentic, another fantastic horse, also had a scare leading up to Athens (photo 213). He started to colic and John Madden turned him out in a sand ring and he came out of it. Thankfully, Authentic got through it; we dodged two bullets with our Athens team that year. With a great horse and a big competition, I tend to be bold when it comes to going for it when there's a borderline issue. What can I say? I'm a horse show man; when it comes to being competitive, I'm an animal!

Aachen was the last stop on the way to Athens, and I flew there to meet the team, including Chris and his recovered Royal Kaliber. Aachen has always been a special place to show. The fanfare for the Nations Cup and the Grand Prix is unimaginably wonderful, with 60,000 fans in the stands, stomping, and cheering. The Grand Prix of Aachen is one of the oldest, most prestigious classes in the history of show jumping, and it's always been a fitting warm-up for each Olympic Games.

There are two built-in Liverpools in the Aachen ring that I jumped back in 1958 on my first European tour. Everyone jumped them back then, but people got a bit soft and started complaining about them being too difficult! This is fairly common nowadays, that the challenging obstacles built into older European show rings are rarely incorporated into the courses. That day at Aachen, those old Liverpools were part of the Grand Prix course, which I loved to see. Ludger Beerbaum, whom I have always liked and admired, was also riding in the Grand Prix that day. Ludger and I have had our disagreements over the years, but I have immense respect for him as a horseman and a rider. He's a tough son of a gun and also has a very sweet side. Ludger walked the course with Chris that day and told him exactly how to ride those old double Liverpools. I was impressed with Ludger's show of sportsmanship.

Posting the fastest clear round gives you the best position in terms of riding last in the jump-off, which allows you to watch the others, plan your strategy, and be aware of exactly the time you need to beat in order to win. Chris had the fastest clear round and was positioned perfectly, riding last—just after Ludger. By the time Ludger walked into the ring, there were already a couple of double clear rounds and so the winner had to also be clear and even faster than his predecessors. I helped Chris and Roy get warmed up, looking over my shoulder at the ring where Ludger was riding.

With the German crowd going ballistic, Ludger went clear in the jump-off and was very fast, securing the top spot. Chris walked in on Royal Kaliber with the pressure on to dethrone Ludger! In my opinion, Roy was the better and faster horse but I think that boisterous German crowd got into Chris's head. I remember feeling much the same way showing in Europe at times. Riding is a mental game. It's difficult not to let the pressure or distractions affect your riding at times, especially in a sport where split-second reactions and adjustments make the difference between winning and losing. During his jump-off, Chris lost his way and weaved around a jump, losing precious time. It was as good as over; at that point, it was impossible to catch up and beat Ludger. And just like that, Chris just missed winning the Grand Prix of Aachen. I was disappointed for him, because I knew they were good enough to have won.

All Olympic Games are wonderful and so special, and Athens was no exception (photo 214). The equestrian facility was outside the city and near the beach and promontories. This was definitely a good thing, because Athens itself has poor air quality and is difficult to navigate as a foreigner. The care of the horses in yet another stiflingly hot climate was made a priority once again. A huge, lovely house had been rented for everyone involved with the equestrian disciplines, but it was like a boarding house with all the riders, grooms, and vets staying together. I stayed with my friend Sara Cavanagh instead, as she was a very old friend of mine and had rented a place. My friend Larry accompanied me. I remember we went to dinner one night on the beach and everyone was ordering these small, delicious lobsters. There were no prices on the menu, which was common there, and Larry, a bodybuilder with a large appetite, ordered three or four lobsters for himself. Little did we know that those lobsters cost $100 each—we learned our lesson fast about the price of lobster in Athens!

Olaf Petersen designed a fabulous Olympic course; it was beautiful and creative and not the huge, simplistic, throw-back fences that we saw in the nineties. Olaf struck a nice balance with his design, testing smart, agile riding as well as bravery and scope. The water jump was placed on the diagonal with the striding between the water and related fences being just far enough to make it difficult to relate the distance. Like Sydney, there was a disastrous footing issue in Athens, but instead of all-weather footing causing issues, this time it was turf. Just as we had discussed at Hickstead years earlier and warned organizers, turf is very problematic. Despite their efforts to avoid issues seen in the past, the turf was like a carpet with a hard, slippery base. When the horses landed on the far side of the jump, it was like a rug had been pulled out from under them.

As part of the decorations on the course, Olaf had placed papier-mâché rocks in the ring. In the jump-off, there was a line from a vertical to a very big oxer that was split by these foot-high decorative rocks, and at first glance, the natural path was to ride around them from jump to jump. McLain Ward, who is a very sharp guy, studied the course and walked the distance between the pile of rocks and a big oxer. When it came time for the jump-off and we saw that turn from vertical to oxer, McLain knew it was three strides from the rocks to the oxer. Chris Kappler hadn't walked it himself and was worried about riding something he hadn't personally walked, but McLain pointed it out from the fence line and Chris trusted him on it. They both hopped the rocks on the way to the oxer, saved valuable seconds, and the U.S. Team beat the Swedes and took the silver medal (photos 215, 216)!

Drug testing played a big role in the Olympics that year; Meredith Michaels-Beerbaum had a positive result in a random drug test on Shutterfly earlier that year at the World Cup Finals in Milan, which eliminated her from competing at the Olympics and helped our chances against the very competitive German team. Even without Meredith, the Germans came out on top with a gold medal in the team competition. However, they were dropped down to the bronze medal (moving the United States to the gold) because a post-hoc drug test of Ludger Beerbaum's horse Goldfever was positive for betamethasone and his score was eliminated. Ludger explained that the substance was in an ointment used to treat a skin irritation and despite the FEI Judicial Committee's assessment that the substance did not enhance Goldfever's performance, the rules had to be followed and he was disqualified.

The individual competition was next and I had high hopes for our American riders. The horses were starting to show signs of fatigue, which was no surprise given that some of them had already jumped three rounds in the Nations Cup. Nowadays, they spread out the rounds over additional days, a very good revision to the schedule. In Athens, there were still two individual rounds over a huge course and the horses' tiredness showed itself in the lack of clear rounds. When you consider that fifty of the best horse-and-rider combinations in the world jumped that course, but only one pair jumped clear in each round, their edge has worn off a bit. Cian O'Connor rode brilliantly for Ireland and captured individual gold, but was later eliminated due to his horse testing positive for several banned substances. Similar to Ludger Beerbaum, the FEI committee accepted that the substances were not intentionally given to enhance performance, but nevertheless he was eliminated.

When Chris Kappler earned four faults in the second round on Royal Kaliber, he naturally figured he was done for the day, but rider after rider had multiple rails down. Suddenly, Chris was summoning me and racing to get Royal Kaliber tacked up again! A tie-breaker was required because Chris was tied for the silver medal with Rodrigo Pessoa. How often do you jump off with four faults? Once in a blue moon at best!

Chris and Roy were such an incredible team. Roy was a fabulous horse, and Chris rode and managed him perfectly. They were one of the greatest horse-and-rider combinations I ever had the pleasure to work with, and as I stood by the ring at Athens that day, I appreciated how far Chris had come since his third place at the Medal Finals at Harrisburg. It was surreal that, only weeks before, Roy had been gazing out of his big stall window and looking out over my back yard in the Pittstown countryside. Now he was walking into the ring in Athens, Greece, jumping off for an Olympic medal! It's truly a thrill to have a horse you love as a pet compete at that level.

Rodrigo was fast in the jump-off but had a rail, so he opened the door for Chris and Roy, who walked into the ring and started the jump-off course at a decent clip. As I watched I knew they were faster and could beat Rodrigo—they could have a rail and still win! Two fences to go, they were still clean and fast. As they galloped across the ring to a double in-and-out of planks on flat cups, I stood at the in-gate wondering if a horse going that fast could get through that in-and-out cleanly. Just at that very moment, Chris suddenly pulled up and jumped off Roy's back. Later, Chris said on the landing side of that fence that he felt two bad steps and knew Roy was done. He had simply broken down. It was a combination of the incredible stress of all that jumping on those crooked legs over that awful turf. If even one of those three disadvantages hadn't been a factor for Roy, I believe he would've held up through it. It was heartbreaking to think how just a couple fences later, Roy would've been rested for weeks.

Even in great horses, tests like the Olympics bring out little weaknesses. If the horse stops once in five hundred jumps, he'll stop at the Olympics. If the horse drifts way to the side when he jumps a big Swedish oxer, he'll drift. If a horse has issues respecting the water jump, it'll come out. No matter what you do, at the end of the day, the horse always tells the truth. No matter what training, what bits you use, what horse-care program, the horse always tells the truth. The concussion from jumping isn't evenly distributed on a horse with crooked legs like Roy, and it puts undue stress on tendons and joints. Even his ample heart couldn't overcome the obstacles that day in Athens (photo 217).

Tim Ober is a fabulous vet and he rushed into the arena to attend to Roy. A trailer pulled straight into the ring and a team of people carefully loaded him and took him to the equine hospital. He had very badly bowed a tendon, with significant separation from the bone. Jenny Kappler Banks loved Roy—he was like her baby—and she stayed with him and kept watch over him during his treatment. Despite pulling up before the jump-off was finished, Chris held onto his third place finish behind Cian O'Connor and Rodrigo Pessoa, which was upgraded to the silver medal after Cian's horse's test results disqualified him. We didn't realize it at the time, but Chris and Rodrigo were jumping off for the gold medal.

Timothy Ober, DVM

It was an incredibly sad situation. Three or four other horses at those Games had similar injuries to Royal Kaliber's. We learned later that there were a couple of specific areas on the course where horses were having particular problems because the footing was not holding up to the landing pressure on the far side of the jumps.

196. Greg Hall riding Clown, a horse I bought from Australian, Matt Ryan, the 1992 Olympic Three-Day Champion.

197. Big Dog, the tiny Beagle puppy Greg surprised me with.

198. Giggle, a dachshund that Kathy Moore and I got from Mrs. Barnes, a breeder and the well-known, back-ring announcer at Hickstead.

199. With my new partner in Hunterdon, Chris Kappler. © Bob Langrish

200. With Jane Clark, one of the leading sponsors of the USET. © The Book LLC

201. *With Orlando Izzo and Greg Hall at Piazza Donegani in Milan, Italy, honoring my one-sixteenth Italian blood!*

202. *The bronze-winning, 1995 Pan American Games Team (left to right): Michael Matz, D. D. Matz, Debbie Stephens, and Nona Garson.* © Tricia Booker

203. *At the in-gate with Hap Hansen and Anne Kursinski at the Old Salem Olympic Trials, 1996.*

204. With Katie Monahan Prudent at the Old Salem Olympic Trials, 1996.

205. The silver-medal team at the 1996 Atlanta Olympic Games (left to right): Anne Kursinski, Leslie Burr Howard, Michael Matz, Peter Leone, and Frank Chapot.

206. Nona Garson and Rhythmical became legendary together at CHIO Aachen, 1999. © Peter Llewellyn

207. 1999 Pan American team, Winnipeg (left to right): Margie Goldstein Engle, Frank Chapot, Sally Ike, Leslie Burr Howard, Alison Firestone, Peter Wylde, and Francie Steinwedell-Carvin.

208. I'm working with the U.S. Three-Day Eventing Team at the 2004 Olympic Games in Athens (from second left): Kim Severson, John Williams, Julie Richards, Amy Tryon, and Darren Chiacchia. © Charles Mann

209. Lauren Hough on Clasiko at the 2000 Sydney Olympic Games. © Diana De Rosa

210. *With Big Dog.*

211. *In Brazil with Leon Ramos, the "Energizer Bunny."*

212. *Chris Kappler and Royal Kaliber. The pair were so dialed in after the Pan Am Games in 2003 that he was only ridden in seven classes in Wellington all winter.*
© Randi Muster

213. *Beezie Madden and Authentic at the Olympic Games in Athens, 2004.*
© The Chronicle of the Horse/Molly Sorge Photo

214. With McLain Ward and Chris Kappler in Athens.

215. The silver-medal team at the Athens Olympic Games in 2004 (left to right): Chris Kappler, Peter Wylde, Beezie Madden, and McLain Ward. © Diana De Rosa

216. *A bittersweet moment for Chris as he joins Rodrigo Pessoa and Cian O'Connor on the podium for the individual Olympic show jumping medal ceremony in Athens.*
© INPHO/Patrick Bolger

217. *Royal Kaliber made up for his flaws with ample heart.*
Painting by Jan Lukens

218. Nations Cup winners in La Boule, France, 2005 (left to right): Georgina Bloomberg, Laura Kraut, Beezie Madden, and Schuyler Riley.

219. (Left to right) Jeffrey Welles, Lauren Hough, McLain Ward, and Laura Kraut: the Super-League-winning team in 2005.

220. *My last time in the show ring, riding Laci Marrone's Ulysses Van De Krekebeke in a 1.35m jumper class in the de Némethy ring at the Palm Beach Equestrian Center, 2005. My riding style is virtually the same as decades before.*
© The Book LLC

221. With other Chefs d'Equipe in Calgary, 2003, discussing the predicament of bad weather interfering with the Nations Cup.

222. *With one of my oldest and best friends and pupils, Melanie Smith Taylor, at the Show Jumping Hall of Fame induction ceremony when I presented her with Calypso's award, 2003.* © Randi Muster

223. *Meredith Michaels-Beerbaum and Shutterfly, fierce competitors.* © The Horse Magazine Australia

224. *McLain Ward and Sapphire at the World Equestrian Games in Aachen, 2006.*
© *Ken Braddick/dressage-news.com*

225. *With my World Equestrian Games silver-medal team (left to right): McLain Ward,*
Margie Goldstein Engle, Beezie Madden, and Laura Kraut. © *Bob Langrish*

We immediately tried to manage Roy's pain and make him comfortable. Roy didn't go home on the first plane; there just wasn't enough time to get him comfortable before leaving Athens. We stayed with him twenty-four hours a day for about a week and took our turns sleeping in the barn to keep a close eye on him. He was doing well and comfortable enough that we were ready to get him on a plane to go to Holland, I went back to the hotel to pack my bag and check out. I was only gone a short time, but when I got back, he had started to show symptoms of colic. Looking back on it, it's extraordinary that we were even able to get him out of Athens, given everything we were facing.

Once in Holland, Roy held steady for a while. While things weren't going in a bad direction, they weren't going in the right direction, either. After a couple of weeks, we decided to do exploratory surgery, which identified and fixed the problem. After that, he improved so much that he was able to go to another farm in Holland and be turned out. He was doing well there and we were all breathing easier, but then he colicked a second time and the nature of that colic was severe. We did all the proactive things we could and even won some battles in his recovery, but unfortunately in the end we couldn't win the war.

Roy had a lot of heart and ability, without question. Sure, his conformation probably played a role, but he had jumped a lot of rounds with that same conformation and managed successfully for many, many years. The footing really tipped the scales against us in Athens—it was substandard. Something positive did emerge from the Athens Olympics injuries in that the FEI established standards for footing quality, including the publication of the "Equine Surfaces White Paper" written by a number of academics and sponsored by the FEI and other organizations. There is now an elaborate method of assessment of footing that gives me a decent degree of confidence.

Royal Kaliber's second colic, which occurs sometimes when horses are immobilized for serious injuries, was terribly tragic. It was devastating for the Kapplers and for the Kamine family who owned him and loved him so dearly. Roy was a great horse but he was also in a Greek tragedy. He was brilliant, but born under the wrong star. Throughout his training, we always knew he was balancing on a tightrope between champion of the world and a pasture ornament. It was a terrible hurt for Chris to lose Roy, and I don't think he really ever got over it. It can be very hard when you're that close to a horse and lose him before his time.

Holly Mitten

I miss the Hunterdon days. I helped care for Royal Kaliber and slept upstairs in the apartment in the barn above his stall. He would start banging down there in the middle of the night, and I would go running down the stairs to check on him at all hours. I remember how glad I was when he shipped out to the Olympics so I could just get a night's sleep. But after everything that happened with him, I missed hearing that banging downstairs.

A true horseman, course designer Olaf Petersen never stops working; he'll go anywhere and build any course. The week after the Olympics, I drove to Culpeper, Virginia, to meet some clients and teach at a show, and there was Olaf, building a two-foot-six course. I had to shake my head at the two of us, both back to our humble business after being on the world stage in Athens. The word, of course, had spread about Roy's injury. Kenny Wheeler and Bucky Reynolds, top Virginia horsemen whom I've known since the fifties were there as well. They told me, "George you can't be too upset. You did pretty well with that crooked son of a bitch!" They were trying to buck me up—and they were right! With Roy's legs, some would say he didn't have the license to do as well as he did. The stallion had a huge heart and was such a wonderful jumper; it's incredible what he achieved! History won't ever forget him. It's comforting to know they bred him a little and he has offspring with Royal Kaliber blood out there somewhere.

IV. FOR THE GOOD OF THE SPORT

Diane Carney

After years of comments circulating among professionals about how the hunters had become a dead end and that the classes were boring and predictable, George decided something had to be done. On the Sunday evening after his clinic in Chicago in 2006, he pointed his finger at me, and said, "Diane, you have to fix the hunters." I protested at first. I said, "Me? I have to fix the hunters? They don't want to be fixed! Those people don't even like me!" but he said, "They are ruining things for us at the Olympic level. YOU have to fix the hunters. I will give you the map and I will get the support we need, but you have to do the legwork."

George and I assembled a team and decided we had to come up with the kind of hunter class that we wanted to see and host it ourselves. When I recruited help from friends, they looked at me like I had three heads! I told them we all had to be "all-in" at least through the first class. We realized we had to be willing to do it totally on our own. If that's what it took, we would host an unrecognized, stand-alone event at someone's farm, potentially without the support of any of the horse show associations. As the planning came together, word got around. In the end, we ran our own class in Chicago in 2007 and the response overall was wonderful. We also met with some resistance and criticism at first, with the naysayers claiming hunter riders didn't want to jump that high or that the money wasn't going to support it. George made a lot of calls and, in the end, we gathered the powers that be at a big dinner and gave the United States Hunter Jumper Association the option to come on board with us, which they did. After that, it took off! We called the class a Hunter Derby, and Jenny Sutton wanted to sponsor it at her Wrenwood Farm in Naples, which is an absolutely beautiful place.

I took a management team down to Wrenwood in the fall of 2007 to plan it all out for the following April. My contribution was designing and building all the jumps. I started by using the Regular Working Hunter classes in Calgary as a model for how I wanted them to look. They weren't going to be the ordinary four-foot to four-foot-three course of plain jumps on level ground. It was the hunter version of a Grand Prix! I wanted gorgeous, challenging courses with all the pomp and circumstance you could imagine. Jenny Sutton told us to build the course exactly how George had imagined it, which we did. We built two of every jump in case one was damaged during the show.

With Jenny's team at Wrenwood working on the landscaping in the months leading up to the event, it was positively bursting with green and flowers when we arrived in April! It was the most gorgeous show grounds I had ever seen. When George arrived before the show, he looked around and then walked up to me, put his arm around me and said, "It's Aachen for hunters." There was no greater compliment than that! The Hunter Derbies of today came about because of George and are a result of his desire to go back to the future, to put the sport back in the hunters, and to fuel the quality of the hunters to create better riders and horsemen that funnel up to the American show jumping teams.

The creation of Hunter Derbies helped the hunters, and I was grateful to Diane Carney and the others who helped to get them started. However, despite all of our best intentions, the derby classes haven't completely lived up to the spirit in which they were intended. The courses must test the horses appropriately and require boldness and brilliance even more than they do now, in my view. When the derby classes became more common across the country, competitors complained about the banks or the table jumps. In response to the pressure, show organizers first gave options on course so riders could avoid them and then, in some cases, removed them altogether. We all have a responsibility to keep the Hunter Derbies challenging and thrilling to watch. Watering down the courses means that the focus goes back to judging on the most perfect round, instead of judging the most talented hunter horse.

My good friend Andrew Lustig was inspired to bring hunter classes to the rest of the world after the Hunter Derby classes began, which was a very intriguing idea. Finally, with the Hunter Derbies bringing the guts back to the hunters, those classes might be more welcomed at European shows. It would be a new side of the sport for them and with all of the European sport-horse breeding, it's only practical that some of their horses would be better suited to hunters than jumpers. Perhaps an international hunter-class option in Europe would provide a market for those very horses, or a starting place for developing green jumpers as it has been in North America for many years. Andrew helped plan a demonstration hunter class in Kentucky during the 2010 World Equestrian Games to help encourage international interest. Unfortunately, the horse community doesn't seem quite ready for that leap yet.

Andrew Lustig

I never rode with George when I was young, but we are all students of George's, aren't we? There's a well-known saying that there are some people that can stand on the shoulders of their predecessors and see even farther down the road. George is one of those people. He took classical riding and made it neo-classical. From a historical perspective, George carried our sport through an evolutionary process and ushered riding to a whole different level.

I became friends with George after I had already become a professional. The first time I worked with him was when Susie Humes was teaching Alexandra Thornton, the daughter of an executive at Goldman Sachs. At the time I was helping Susie and she brought George in. I became a student by proxy, watching George work up close for the first time. I had been to clinics, but I'd never watched him work day to day and in detail, the way he does it from the ground up—from teaching

Alexandra how to adjust her stirrups to coaching her in the high junior jumpers, and everything in between.

Being a teacher myself, seeing how George really worked with one student over many months was such a privilege. How he verbalizes concepts as a teacher is incredible! With him, a rider will become very good very quickly. A simple example of his eloquence, but one I'll never forget, was at Capital Challenge when George was teaching Alexandra in the schooling area. Susie Humes, Geoff Teall, and I were all standing by the jump. Every trainer says, "Close your fingers," but George will say, "Your thumb holds the rein to your first finger." It's just a lovely way to verbalize a very common, simple concept so that you understand it more completely than just closing your fingers. We were listening to George teach as Alexandra jumped back and forth over the schooling fence and Geoff turned to me and said, "This is so depressing. George is such a genius—none of us even come close!" Which is true, none of us do! I agreed and laughed, and Geoff smiled and said, "Well the only thing we have going for us is that at least we know how lacking we are! Others don't even know!"

After the Athens Olympic Games, it was understood that Frank Chapot was retiring as Chef d'Equipe. However, some months later when the application process began for new candidates, Frank entered the interview process himself. The Selection Committee agreed that it was important for the new Chef to be willing to travel to Europe for tours outside of the big championships, and over the years Frank had shown less interest in those trips. It was no secret that Frank preferred to travel abroad only for the big championships: the World Cup Finals, the Olympics, and the Pan American and World Equestrian Games. For many years, I, and others like Joe Fargis and Conrad Homfeld, had taken teams on European tours to help fill that gap.

As part of the Selection Committee to find the new Chef d'Equipe, I considered the list of candidates. In my opinion, the best candidates for the job were oddly enough not from the United States. I am a patriot when it comes to the success of the U.S. Team and for me, it's just not as ideal to have a foreign Chef d'Equipe. That was the point at which I wondered if it was time for me to throw my hat in the ring. There were some stipulations if I had serious intentions for applying for the position. First and foremost, I would have to step down from the Selection Committee and submit an application. Second, I would absolutely have to sell Hunterdon. The conflicts of interest that had arisen in the past, when I taught pupils trying to make the teams, would of course need to cease.

After some lengthy consideration, I accepted these stipulations. Deep down, as much as I loved Hunterdon, I was ready to part ways with it. The overhead of running that stable was so immense, and it wasn't producing riders with eyes on international show jumping any longer. Chris Kappler and his performance at Athens was, in a sense, the final product of that Hunterdon heyday of the seventies. With the U.S. Team getting the gold medal and Chris getting the individual silver, it was a wonderful way to wrap up the Hunterdon jumper stable when all was said and done. I stepped down from the committee, submitted an application, and went to the interviews in Florida. There were eight applicants altogether and in the end, they chose me.

As with Bert de Némethy before him, there was some bitterness for Frank during this passing of the torch. It was a touchy situation; after all, no one enjoys feeling they are no longer welcome. Both Bert and Frank are such tremendous horsemen and I hate even the thought of them feeling disrespected in any way. Of course, it was not anyone's intention to create this feeling, but naturally a departure of the Chef d'Equipe usually follows some recognition by the showing community that a change would be beneficial. I myself, in the year or so at the end of my reign as Chef, had similar moments of feeling I was unjustly criticized. There seems to always be a little bitterness that goes with the territory.

Once the decision was made and I was chosen, I found myself very eager to move into a new phase in my career. We had a big auction to sell off all my furniture, antiques, and horse memorabilia that my Wellington home simply couldn't house. Oddly enough, my beautiful antiques sold for very little. My horse memorabilia went for much more by comparison! While the Hunterdon property waited for the right buyer to come along, I gifted the business itself to Chris Kappler who still runs his business out of the upper barn today. Eventually, Steve and Lori Racioppo, very lovely people who seemingly fell out of the sky, purchased the farm and continued renting to Chris.

I remember driving out of Hunterdon for the last time at the end of 2005 and heading to Florida. Nostalgia struck me hard with so many fabulous memories, but leaving it behind in capable hands was also a relief. I don't miss the burden of the business for a second and never looked back! On the way to Wellington, I stopped at Patty Heuckeroth's home in Southern Pines, North Carolina, as I often did, to break up the drive. Patty and I have been lifelong friends, going all the way back to riding together at the Ox Ridge Hunt Club, so it was a fitting time to visit her and talk of the past and the future.

It felt very much like a natural progression into my new annual schedule. I taught a busy clinic circuit around my Chef d'Equipe responsibilities and enjoyed a greater focus on more meaningful activities without the distraction of running a business. In that first year as Chef, I worked very closely with Sally Ike at Gladstone to look ahead and plan for the future. In later years, Lizzy Chesson stepped into that role and helped run the tours and organize the schedule and events. Both Sally and Lizzy were invaluable to me during these years.

Sally Ike

I first met George in 1965. My aunt had married a racehorse trainer and breeder in New Jersey, and the first horses I ever had were young horses my uncle didn't want to train for the track. I showed hunters before becoming an eventing rider and one year while wintering in Aiken, South Carolina, we went to a show in Savannah, and George happened to be the judge. He noticed me and my horse and we met and talked a little bit. Our paths didn't cross for a long time after that first meeting. That same year a director of the USET who wintered in Aiken asked me to take my horse up to Gladstone and have Bert de Némethy look at him. I'll never forget as I watched my five-year-old Thoroughbred become absolutely transformed under Bert's riding. I got on afterward and was inspired to learn how to do it on my own.

It's so important that George is focusing so much on young riders today. Before he was Chef d'Equipe for the United States Show Jumping Team, we did the earliest versions of the young-rider clinics at Gladstone. The Regional Training Sessions we have for USHJA's Emerging Athletes Program are modeled after them. Even in those earlier years, George stressed the importance of having a stable management component, which is so critical. I babysat an EAP clinic last year at Sweet Briar College. Cynthia Hankins was the riding panelist, and she was one of the last to have ridden with Bert de Némethy. We talked all weekend about the basics and stressed how there are no shortcuts.

George has had an amazing influence on so many people because of the importance he places on the basics—both on the horse and in the stables. Back when I was working a lot in the office at Gladstone but still trying to fit in rides, I would call up Hunterdon and ask if there were any horses to ride. I became quite familiar with Hunterdon and the system there. For starters, there was not a pair of draw reins on the property. Today, we have too many pretty riders and not enough who truly understand and implement the principles that have guided George for so long. It really worries me that those basic principles will be lost if someone doesn't teach them. My hope is that EAP will be able to fill some of those gaps.

I started 2005 as Chef d'Equipe by taking a team to Europe for the summer months for the Samsung Super League, which is a series of eight Nations Cup classes across Europe that began in 2003. Various horse-and-rider pairs were scheduled to ride for the United States at each of the eight Nations Cups. This was in the early days of the Super League, and we had an excellent season. The last of the shows was in Barcelona, and we held on to beat the Germans! The Barcelona team was Jeffrey Welles on Armani, Lauren Hough on Casadora, McLain Ward on Oasis, and Laura Kraut on Anthem. The Super League series win was a huge feather in our collective caps, and 2005 was the first and last time the Americans ever won it, although we have come in a close second place in other years (photos 218, 219).

Hunterdon was not without its continuing antics even after my departure. One day Frederick, a friendly, handsome young Swedish man whom I had met and traveled with in Sweden in years past, showed up at Hunterdon with seven pieces of luggage and a terrier with five newborn puppies. Frederick was a little bit on the eccentric side—he would charm the leaves off the trees but was so emotionally complicated that he was a burden on everyone who took him in. He was straight some days, gay some days—and definitely confused all of the time! I was no longer there when he showed up at Hunterdon, but he told Chris Kappler I had offered him a job, which I hadn't, so Chris sent him packing. Then Frederick called me down in Wellington to ask what he should do and I sent him to stay at my friend Marilyn's. Marilyn worked at Gladstone and is a lovely, classy girl, but when Frederick arrived at her doorstep, she was a little afraid of him!

Frederick was a lost soul—like other Swedes I've met, he was very elegant but always searching for his identity. Marilyn tolerated him and his pack of dogs for a while, then he moved on once again. Frederick showed up at Washington during the indoor shows and was picked up by some guy there who he stayed with for a few weeks. That guy hosting Frederick called me on the phone toward the end of his stay, telling me he couldn't handle him any longer and couldn't get him to leave. As it turned out, he had picked up Frederick hoping for some action, but Frederick just dragged him all over town with no reward! Days later, Frederick showed up on Marilyn's doorstep again, and *she* called me freaking out, saying she was afraid he was going to take advantage of her. He eventually retreated back to Sweden, but the tale of Frederick the Swede lingers still today.

Georgina Bloomberg

I was the youngest rider on the team in 2005 when we went on the European tour. To ride on a team with George was very intimidating. I was terrified of him initially and had to earn his respect, which I think is a good thing. I learned so much from him. Eventually I learned that he has a funny, devilish side. Recently he brought up one of the worst times when I got in trouble with him and we were laughing together about it. I was so mortified at the time, but I learned a big lesson, just like I always did when I got in trouble with George!

It's interesting even now that I'm not riding under him, how much those lessons he taught me are still drilled into me. Today, even when I spot him at a horse show, I sit up straighter and check to be sure my hair is tidy under my helmet and my boots are shined. I notice it with other riders too—there's a little added pressure when he's watching. Even though he's my friend now, too, just knowing he's watching gives me a little bit of an edge. It's the immense respect I have for him, and I think that it's a sign of a lesson well-taught. There are so many of his lessons that I want to teach my kids. I hope the next generation in our sport has an opportunity to have someone that they respect as much as we all respect George.

My favorite George story is when he was giving me love advice. I respect him so much more that he has had a wonderful life outside of horses. I love talking to him and hearing all of his stories. I had just got out of a relationship or was having some man trouble and he said, "Georgina, just remember that men are just like distances—never take the first one you see, because a better one will come along!"

V. HANKY PANKY

Kenneth Braddick

I've been in the news business my whole life, and I have always found George to be wonderfully candid with an incredible sense of humor, which I very much appreciate. In addition to the Super League, I covered the Olympics and the Pan American Games. George's stature among the other Chefs d'Equipe was so apparent in how they would address him with such reverence and respect. George treated them the same way, but he had a very special effect on the others.

At the Nations Cup in Calgary in 2005, one of only three Nations Cup classes in North America in those days, I witnessed a rare occurrence. There was a torrential downpour in very cold September weather that created very icy conditions. It was absolutely miserable at the horse show, and the conditions on the course were so poor that a group of riders rebelled and refused to ride in the second round of the Nations Cup, citing dangerous conditions from the bad weather. This group of riders from various countries asked George to be their spokesman. After a somewhat colorful and heated debate between the riders and the organizers about whether the second round would proceed, George handled the situation with noticeable aplomb. George looked surprised to hear some of the language coming from the mouths of some of these people, but he took it all in stride. He was polite to the organizers, yet firm. After that meeting, he very respectfully came into the press room and held a news conference, explaining that the welfare of the horses must come first. It was a huge event and a dramatic scene. All these years later, they still remember it up in Canada. The Southern family had put together this amazing show at an unbelievable venue with a lot of deep-pocketed sponsors, and it was unthinkable that any riders would refuse to ride. And there stood George, representing them as their sacrificial lamb. It was top sport and a very heavy-duty situation. If you want anyone to have your back, it's George!

Sometimes you have to make the hard choice to fight for the horses and stand up for what you believe is right, even when it's unpopular with some people (photo 221). Being a good Chef d'Equipe means standing up and representing your team (and sometimes riders and horses on all the teams), however uncomfortable it might be. This sport involves a lot of money and interests, and it can be easy for people to lose perspective about what's important.

When I became Chef d'Equipe, I constructed a selection procedure for choosing our championship teams. The process had three stages of evaluating and choosing the horses and riders most likely to be successful. First, certain horse-and-rider combinations were granted byes and were excused from selection-trial classes because their consistent success was so well established. Second, as in the past, selection-trial classes were held and the top-placed riders from those classes were short-listed. Third, while it still existed, ten riders were selected to travel to Europe for the Super League. If you did well at the trials but missed the Super League, you risked sacrificing a top spot because the European experience translated so well to the environment of the big championships. Riders who had earned byes already held spots on the short list, so the competition for the remaining spots would be—and was, in fact—quite fierce. After those three stages, the team was chosen completely subjectively—it was not based on numeric placing from classes, but on a horse and rider's performance at all of the competitions in previous months, in the context of who we felt was the most likely to win at the championship level.

The selection trials and the Super League tour kept everyone working hard to earn a spot on the team for the Aachen World Equestrian Games in 2006. Miss Independent was a very nice horse for Laura Kraut but she was no Cedric; Laura simply *made it happen* in Europe and jumped clear in mud and rain. Those two really showed their colors and earned their way on to the team. Margie Goldstein-Engle did the same, expertly guiding Quervo Gold (who wasn't always the most careful) to top rounds in show after show. McLain Ward on Sapphire, and Beezie Madden aboard Authentic rounded out our team of four.

Lauren Hough

The first time I ever rode with George, I was probably around thirteen years old. My father had gotten me some lessons with him over the summer. I was terrified of him, but he's always been a huge mentor to me. I remember when he became Chef d'Equipe, I had been riding on the USET at the end of the Frank Chapot era and immediately noticed George's attention to detail. You always had to be dressed properly for the course walk, and your horse always had to be braided for the Nations Cup and the Grand Prix. There was a practice jog and a team meeting and everyone had to be present, no excuses. When George told you that you had to be present, you were going to be there! He commanded a high level of respect—every detail was important to him—not just the showing and trying to win, but the management of your horse and yourself were of the utmost importance.

One funny story: I think it was in 2010 in Rotterdam and we were an all-girls team. At the beginning of the week he was annoyed at us as a whole. Each of us had done something a little bit off and were in the dog house with George. Then we ended up winning the Nations Cup on no faults! We were so thrilled and happy. After the win, Lizzy Chesson came up and said there was a team meeting at the barn in twenty minutes and not to miss it. We all were thinking, "We just won! What do we need to have a meeting about?" and at the meeting George said sternly, "Congratulations, it was a great day today. But all of you need to shape up! What you all did at the beginning of the week was unacceptable and don't let it happen again." Of course, he was really proud of us, but he wanted to be sure we knew those small things still mattered!

The Aachen show organizers did a wonderful job hosting the WEG; it was the best WEG I'd ever seen. I had wondered how they would find a suitable location for a cross-country course, but they did and it was fantastic. As anyone who has ever worked with me or ridden with me knows, I get very intense and aggressive during a big competition. I'm always very highly strung at shows because it takes a lot of focus and energy to operate at that level.

My former student Meredith Michaels-Beerbaum was starting to do very well for the German team on her Shutterfly. The day before the WEG, I was out in the warm-up ring and riders were schooling. I noticed that Meredith hopped off Shutterfly and got on another horse of hers named Checkmate. Shutterfly and Checkmate were both brown and with the cold and rain, most of the horses were bundled up in rain sheets and perhaps many people wouldn't have looked twice. I recognized Checkmate and a red flag immediately went up for me. It was very clear in the rules that each rider could only have one horse on the WEG grounds. The alternate and his or her horse were the only option beyond the four riders and each of their horses on each team. It simply wasn't fair, if for no other reason than the simple fact that riding an extra horse helps you stay sharper and stronger. Take Margie Goldstein-Engle, for instance. Theoretically, a rider like her is used to riding twenty-five horses a day and only riding Quervo Gold is an uncomfortable change. I would have loved to have her hack a second horse.

As it turned out, Checkmate was on the show grounds for a legitimate reason, to receive a sort of award. But it still struck me as improper. Even if it gave Meredith the teeniest advantage, however insignificant her team considered it, it was simply not right, regardless of the legitimacy of Checkmate's presence. I went to the Chef d'Equipe meeting and threw an absolute fit about it. I was screaming and Markus Beerbaum was yelling right back at me—it was high drama! The other Chefs and the show organizers couldn't argue with the fact that it was against the rules. It was quite the *cause célèbre* for that WEG. They shipped Checkmate off the grounds immediately. Historically, I was always on the warpath to keep up the sharpness of our U.S. Show Jumping Team against the Europeans. They are so tough and competitive, and they will walk all over someone if you let them. I irritated the Europeans something fierce at times like that, but they respected me for it, too! I always speak up if something seems fishy. Even the smallest details matter and I stand up for my team—and for the rules to be followed—no matter how minute an issue.

After all the drama, the United States had a wonderful World Equestrian Games. Our team won the silver medal in the team phase, behind the Dutch. We hadn't medaled in a WEG since 1986, which was also at Aachen, and it was wonderful to experience as the sole, official Chef d'Equipe. Margie Goldstein-Engle did an incredible job with her very scopey but difficult to ride Quervo Gold. Laura Kraut was fabulous on Miss Independent and both Beezie Madden and McLain Ward were no longer rookies—they had each settled into their peak years as partners to top horses.

In the individual competition, Beezie seemed unbeatable after the first round and was securely in the top spot going into the final four. However, once the final phase begins in the WEG, all scores reset to zero. It was down to Beezie, Meredith Michaels-Beerbaum, Jos Lansink of Belgium, and Edwina Alexander from Australia. Only one of the four—longshot Edwina Alexander—had a rail down in any of her four rounds (on Shutterfly) and it was enough to land her in fourth. Since neither Meredith, Jos, or Beezie had any faults at all, it was necessary to go to an additional jump-off between the three of them.

Although it makes for an exciting finish for the fans to watch, we all groaned a little at the horses having to jump again after so many rounds. Those horses jumped *so many fences* at that WEG—something like sixty fences after five days of competing. William Steinkraus never liked the riders changing horses at the end of the World Championship and the World Equestrian Games because although it's a good show, the change of horse and rider round doesn't really reflect who the world champion is.

Each of the three riders got back on his or her own horse and was allowed just two warm-up jumps before heading back into the ring to jump the same course once again. This being the fifth time jumping that sequence of jumps, the horses knew exactly where they were going. Naturally, a horse that jumps the same course so many times presents a risk of getting a bit dull or thinking ahead of its rider. Going first, Jos was fast and clear on his white stallion, Cavalor Cumano. Meredith dropped a rail with Shutterfly, who suddenly seemed nervous about the crowd noise prior to going back into the ring. Now it was up to Beezie! The last of the four to ride Authentic had been Edwina Alexander. Despite her clear round, her deep driving seat hadn't gone over well with Authentic's fiery Thoroughbred-like personality, and she was run away with a bit. Beezie, as unflappable as always, steadied Authentic back down as they jumped the course.

Beezie was fast and way ahead of Jos's time as they galloped down to the very last fence, a Rolex oxer toward home, where Edwina had left out a stride on Authentic. It was an awkward spot to jump into because the roped-off staging area where the grooms held the horses forced riders to turn hard right after the oxer. Coming down to that oxer, Authentic got fired up all over again and roared over it, just barely tipping the back rail off the cups. The crowd erupted! Jos celebrated. So close! Cavalor Cumano displaced Authentic as the Best Horse, even though Beezie had led for the entire WEG up until that last tie-breaker. Even so, I was ecstatic. The silver medals were an excellent finish for Beezie and for our American team, and we went home happy (photo 225).

Beezie Madden

George always had a four-year plan for us as Chef d'Equipe and started planning ahead in a very detailed way. He's set the bar to what it means to have a vision. George began as coach during an era when we had shifted mostly to objective selection of teams. During his period as Chef, it shifted more to subjectivity for selection of teams and I think that's been a positive thing. Back in the eighties when the USET was so successful, it was a subjective process as well.

What George is so great at is teaching others to teach and teaching people how to create a system. I rode as a demonstrator with Katie Prudent in George's clinics. Part of the reason I always enjoy watching his clinics or helping with them is that there's always either something new or something worth rehearsing. To hear the repetition and be reminded of the things you need to focus on is so valuable.

George has always been a cheerleader of mine. I remember when Mike Henaghan took me to have my first lesson with George out in the big field at Hunterdon. The central part of the field was mowed and there was a border area that wasn't. A jump was set on an angle where a straight approach to it would take you into the long grass. George asked me to start my course with that jump, and I figured I should stay in the mowed area, so I didn't have the best approach to the fence. He yelled at me for doing that, for thinking I was so good I didn't need to have a decent approach to the first fence. Now that I know George, I think maybe there was no right answer. Perhaps if I'd ridden in the long grass I would've got into trouble instead for not being brave enough to try the harder turn. Either way, it got my attention. Part of the way he teaches is about establishing command. I think that's important in your teaching. Above all, students need to believe in your strength of leadership and they need to trust that you're going to be there. That's one of George's big strengths.

Thrilled with our great results in 2005 and 2006, I was certain that my excitement about the great medals and the depth on our American team would be echoed by the masses. I expected a groundswell of positive energy in the horse show community. Our success was a sign that a new era of domination for America in show jumping had begun. However, I discovered it was not to be as time went by and nothing changed. I suppose I'm naïve when it comes to the gumption of this country—I assumed that my own desire to win would be equaled by those around me. It's hard for me to fathom feeling any other way!

The Pan American Games coinciding with the Super League series in 2007 was the first indication that we were spreading ourselves too thin with all of our commitments. We had to have two separate teams—one for the Pan American Games in Rio de Janeiro, and the other for Europe, with World Cup horses available as well. Not only that, but there were big shows with ever-increasing Grand Prix prize money tempting owners and riders elsewhere. I was starting to realize it was going to be very difficult to have riders and horses to represent the United States at all the events. Adding pressure was the need to get a quality team to the Super League to avoid placing last or second to last and being relegated out of the League for the following year. Of course, I wanted to do well in the Pan Am Games, but it wasn't as a high a priority that particular year, because the U.S. had already qualified for the 2008 Olympics with the great World Equestrian Games results finish.

The 2007 World Cup results were a parade of Swiss and German riders who captured the top eight spots, with McLain Ward tying Marco Kutscher for eighth place. Since that previous streak in the eighties when every single year saw a North American rider take first place, there had only been a smattering of American riders with good ribbons in about half of the fifteen World Cup Finals since. I knew we could get back on top, but I had to find a way to balance all of the demands on our team's schedule, which seemed more challenging than ever.

The 2007 Pan American Games were held outside of Rio de Janeiro at The Deodoro Military Club. We stayed in nearby Barra, in a hotel near the beach about fifteen to twenty minutes south of Rio. The Club, a wonderful facility for the equestrian events, was inland, and we were transported there in minivans with security details because of safety concerns driving through the edge of the favelas. The chosen team, our "B Team" after those showing in the Super League in Europe, consisted of Lauren Hough on Casadora, Cara Raether on Ublesco, Laura Chapot on Little Big Man, and Todd Minikus on Pavarotti. Frank Chapot was there to help his daughter Laura, which was wonderful; Frank and I always worked so well together and seeing his pride in Laura was special (photo 226). After all, I had known Frank and Mary since the fifties and had watched Laura grow up and earn her way on the team. Everyone rode well and the team won the bronze medal behind Brazil and Canada. Cara Raether was the highest placing individual American rider with eighth place on Ublesco. It was a fair finish. I knew we were capable of a better result, but we didn't have our most veteran horses and riders competing.

VI. HONG KONG HIJINKS

Will Simpson

I went to George's before I went to Medal Finals to take what I thought would be equitation lessons. Before that, I'd only seen him at the shows and witnessed his larger-than-life persona from a distance. I got to Hunterdon and I was set to ride one of George's horses. The equitation lessons quickly turned into jumping banks and natural obstacles that were in the field. Riding a green five-year-old, I rode up to the table jump and jumped it, but George said I needed to get much deeper. So I really rode him to the base of the jump the next time and George said, "No, no, you need to get him there much deeper than that." So I galloped up to it again, to a spot that I thought I was much too deep, and the horse hit the table on the way up, tripped, and fell down onto the top. So there I was, taking this "equitation" lesson, and the horse I had borrowed was lying down on the table, and I was standing there next to him holding the reins. I was petrified, thinking I had broken George's nice horse, and I stood there frozen, not sure what to do. Then George broke the spell by screaming, "THE CLOCK IS RUNNING! THE CLOCK IS RUNNING!" By now I was completely freaked out, but I jumped back on the horse, kicked him to stand up, and we jumped down off the table. This was my first introduction to George. In one sense the experience seemed crazy and at the same time, it was so matter of fact. You were in the middle of jumping a course and something went wrong—you need to just keep doing what you're doing! Don't stand there in bewilderment; get back to the exercise! It was incredible how his straightforward approach to getting the job done sunk into my eighteen-year-old mind.

In 2007, I had a couple of horses at Spruce Meadows Masters and George was there. I had a tough first day. I had a rail down with the first horse, but with the second horse, I was clear and had made it to the jump-off. In the jump-off, there was a sharp turn to the right after a particular jump, and my plan was to come in on the right-hand turn and jump the fence dead straight and then turn right again. I realized when I got into the ring that there was this big shadow cutting across the middle of the fence, which I really didn't like the look of. So I changed my plan. I decided to come in on a right-to-left angle to the fence and then continue right. As I got to the fence, the horse left a full stride out and crashed through the fence—it was a complete disaster.

I was thinking of all these excuses after my plan had failed: the sun was in my eyes, plus the shadow created a false ground line, which made the horse leave long. I had all these excuses in my mind and as I walked up into the stands I saw George. I asked him if he saw what happened and he said, "Will, what were you thinking? You have to get straight. You have to go right after the fence and you were jumping going left! You were going the wrong way!" I started protesting about the sun and the shadow across the jump, and he said without a beat, "It doesn't matter, Will, you were going the WRONG WAY! What were you thinking?" He put it so matter of fact. It reminded me that I needed to stop overthinking things and just get the job done. No more excuses.

The next day, with George's words taken to heart, I won both of my classes. Getting my butt kicked into gear that day by George was the start of some important changes in attitude. I had been showing in Europe and even though my horses were doing really well, the idea of making it to the Olympics was not even yet fully formed. It was George who reminded me to knock it off with the excuses, to focus, and get the job done, and in following his advice and seeing the difference it made, it lit my ambition on fire. With this newfound confidence and motivation, I decided I should try for the Olympic Team. Both of my impactful encounters with George, even though they happened so many years apart, undoubtedly were the catalysts that led to me riding in the Olympics. The rest, as they say, is history!

The year 2008 started off with a heartening performance by Rich Fellers at the World Cup Finals in Gothenburg, Sweden. Rich had just a little bad luck with a tick at the very last fence that dropped him into second place. Little did Rich know that he'd have a chance at vindication four years later!

Another Olympic year was upon us, and Beezie Madden on Authentic and McLain Ward on Sapphire earned byes from the trials yet again. Will Simpson, riding Carlsson vom Dach, had three clear rounds on the series of trial classes on his tour and had missed the last day of the trials because his horse had a neck injury. It was a smart play by Will—even if his horse could've managed to jump, he had everything to lose and realistically, not much to gain by jumping again. I would have sat out the last day too, if I were Will.

Laura Kraut ran the board at the selection trials with her fabulous new horse named Cedric. Cedric was still green and would have the occasional spook or bunny hop a jump, but Laura put on a brilliant show of riding when she won the trials. She just clicked with the gray from the beginning and he had confidence in her.

After the trials, all the candidates headed to Europe for the Super League show series in order to demonstrate their ability to succeed on the international stage before we finalized the Olympic Team. By mid-summer, I had four wild-card horse-and-rider combinations in my mind facing off for the two remaining spots. All the horses in the running for the team stabled at Johan Heins's place in Holland that summer, which is north of Amsterdam and in a beautiful, quiet location. Johan has been a partner of John Madden's and a wonderful host to the American team for many years. We moved from Johan's to a farm down the street to avoid a horse that may have been sick. The new farm was a lovely, quiet place behind cornfields, and we were hosted by the wonderful Koopman family.

Aachen was the last show in late summer before the Olympics, and we were considered a heavy favorite for the Nations Cup. Anne Kursinski had a very successful show on her horse Champ 163. Laura Kraut came to me and suggested we not push Cedric and enter him in the smaller of the Grand Prix classes on Saturday. I agreed with her judgment, and it was the right choice for the horse, but it raised some eyebrows. Some people think you should always push and go for it, but in an Olympic year, you have to carefully manage not just your horses' health and fitness, but also confidence in the months leading up to the Games. We were short a horse for the Nations Cup, and Will Simpson took one for the team and brought in Carlsson vom Dach in case we needed him.

Selecting that Beijing Olympic Team, as it is with all selection procedures, was filled with the anxiety and pressure of having to disappoint so many riders. After Aachen, I arrived home and took one look at the sweet, aged Big Dog, and knew it was time. He'd been battling cancer bravely for some years and had deteriorated so significantly that it was all I could do to wait until the next morning so that I could take him to the vet and put him down. I never thought

I could feel such urgency to do something like that to an animal I loved so much, but I knew in my heart it was overdue. That same day I had to pick the Olympic Team—it was the week from hell!

In the end, we chose Beezie Madden, McLain Ward, Will Simpson, and Laura Kraut with Anne Kursinski as the alternate. Their riding power was equal to the '84 Los Angeles Team, but it wasn't quite the same horsepower with a few of our horses being green. Choosing Laura Kraut and Cedric was a risk; although Laura was a veteran, he was green and could've gotten spooky, but when he went well, he was very careful (photo 229). Anne rode Champ brilliantly, but she had to ride him so specifically to hold him together to avoid having rails down; in the end, with such a difficult decision to be made, this fact relegated her to the alternate spot. Both Laura and Will were such careful, clever riders, and I thought they were both well worth the gamble despite their greener elements.

When it was time to fly from Amsterdam to Hong Kong where the equestrian events were being held for the Beijing Olympic Games, the weather became a concern. Just as we were about to fly out of Schiphol, we heard about a typhoon hitting Hong Kong, and I started to worry. Our flight was going to hold precious cargo—not only our entire team, our grooms, staff and dozens of other passengers, but also our horses. We had a choice: risk landing in Hong Kong during a typhoon, or if a detour was necessary, landing in Taiwan, unloading, and having a very complicated quarantine for the horses. I didn't want to ship the horses by boat from Taiwan either; there were too many health risks for the horses. The question arose whether to leave the horses behind at the airport in Amsterdam and delay their transport to Hong Kong until after the storm was over. But there was a catch—the airline officials insisted that only one groom could stay at Schiphol with all five of the horses. I explained that leaving one groom was totally unacceptable! All grooms must stay with their horse no matter what. In the end, they relented and we left the horses—and their grooms—behind.

Once we were airborne and hours had passed, the co-pilot came back into the cabin and asked who the coach of the United States Team was. I stepped forward and he explained that it was time to decide whether to risk landing in Hong Kong with the bad weather or divert to the airport in Taipei. To my astonishment, he asked *me* to decide! This wasn't just our Olympic Team's fate we were talking about here; the plane was full of people. To have their fate in my hands was a very heavy responsibility indeed. I sat and thought about it for a while. I knew that going to Taiwan and dealing with customs would be

lengthy and tiring for all involved. I made the decision to risk the stormy landing. Once I made it, I sat in my seat and worried myself sick. In the end, it was
a good decision. The typhoon was minor and the rain and wind weren't very
severe. We made it and the horses arrived the following day.

At every Olympics there are hijinks and Hong Kong was no exception.
Just looking at the way the venue was laid out on the first day, I knew it would
be open season on hanky panky! Tight security to keep an eye on everyone
had become very important and the show grounds in Hong Kong were enormous. It was reminiscent of the Los Angeles Games at the Santa Anita racetrack,
which was a similarly huge venue. Barcelona, Atlanta, and Sydney were also
very hard to police because there was so much space to cover. In Seoul, for
example, poling devices were found, and there were rumors of stall switching.
In Hong Kong, we were on a racetrack exactly like Seoul, and it had lots of
trees and foliage.

On cross-country day, Mark Phillips asked the show jumpers to help spot
fences, and as always, we agreed and went out to support the Three-Day Eventing Team. McLain Ward stayed behind to work Sapphire, but the rest of us
went off to help. At the Games, the schedule and locations for warming up or
working horses was very organized and strictly monitored. When McLain saw
another country's jumping team hacking their horses together in the big arena
with the dressage horses, he brought Sapphire in too and let her take a look
around. When we returned from helping the Three-Day Team and McLain
told me others had ridden outside of their posted time, I immediately called a
Chefs d'Equipe meeting.

Working their horses outside of the schedule is against the rules, but some
people know they can fly under the radar! Certain European teams are at the
center of the sport and in most cases at the big events, they fill roles that run the
operational side. They aren't shy about getting on committees that afford them
some control. The stewards and heads of the ground juries for each discipline
in Hong Kong were all European. In the past, I've heard firsthand from riders
who were given an early look at a course or heard details about it from the
course builder or technical delegate. So, as you can see, I have reason to prick
my ears about them working horses outside of the posted schedule! It was simply against the protocol. At the spontaneous Chefs' meeting, we reestablished
rules on the hours of exercising.

I was still concerned, however, about the infield of the track. The track area
was as big as Belmont Park and wooded with trees and bushes. The track and
infield remained open until eleven at night due to the cooler temperatures after

sunset, and it was impossible for stewards to police the whole area, especially with all the foliage concealing certain parts. The next day toward dusk, some European riders started to ride their horses out to the racetrack's infield. Clark Shipley and Lee McEver, who were the caretakers of Authentic and Sapphire, saw them riding that direction and decided to tail them by hand-walking the horses out to graze. The three riders walked around trying to evade Clark and Lee and eventually gave up and went in, but to me it was clear that those riders weren't out there just to hack!

Now, I grew up with poling and learned a kinder, minimal way of using that strategy to sharpen up a jumper. Of course, FEI rules strictly forbid any kind of poling, and while many of us grew up with it being used openly at horse shows, the practice is all but nonexistent—and most certainly in public settings. Anyone with half a brain knows that risking injury to a valuable horse with a lot of heart, as these horses at the Olympic level were, would be the epitome of foolishness. But in their hunger for a good performance in the ring, some might be tempted to think that a quick tap behind some bushes the day before the big class might plant a seed in that horse's mind that he'd like to avoid another tap. In a game of millimeters, riders are sometimes tempted to find such an advantage. In my opinion, those riders likely went out at dusk to the infield to sharpen their horses up and it was our vigilance that prevented it.

Hong Kong had a new test for capsaicin that was present in topical creams and liniments. Several horses were eliminated due to capsaicin (one each from Norway, Germany, Brazil, and Ireland). There are always new products to give riders an edge. After the new gimmicks appear, science catches up and the powers that be derive a test for it to eliminate that edge and bring back the level playing field. It's a cat and mouse game, always in sports, since the days of Rome!

Almost daily there were suspicious issues that came up in Hong Kong. We had at least three extra Chefs d'Equipe meetings in Hong Kong to discuss issues like these. Besides the meetings to confirm the exercise schedules and the allowance for evening riding in the infield, there was also a meeting to talk about the issue with John Whitaker's horse Peppermill. John is one of my idols, and I admire him very much. In the first round of the Nations Cup, John rode into the ring and then rode right back out. Something had happened to Peppermill: John said he couldn't even trot; he was either lame or otherwise unwell. Sometime after this, the Swiss Chef d'Equipe called and told me he'd heard that John's horse was fine and could start in the second round of the Nations Cup. He supported John being allowed to jump in the second round and I admit that at first, I said, "Well okay, we're talking about John here, and he's a straight shooter, so I'm all right with it." But afterward, the Dutch Chef d'Equipe made an excellent point. He said, "We'd like to let John jump, but we can't. It's plainly against the rules."

The Dutch Chef d'Equipe was exactly right. Withdrawing from the first round and riding in the second round is strictly against the rules. It gives John an unfair advantage to go in with a fresh horse and there's only one instance when that scenario is acceptable: when there are three clear rounds for a country, the team's fourth rider can opt out to save the horse since the score cannot be improved upon (lowest score is dropped). Greg Best, who was the Chef d'Equipe for the New Zealand team, was wonderful and very supportive during the discussions; the English riders got very angry at the other teams for not letting John and Peppermill jump, but we did what we had to do, no matter how sportsmanlike it seemed in this instance to let John jump in the second round.

My description of these events isn't to lecture that sharpening practices in themselves are wrong, but rather that the playing field simply *must* be level at the Olympic Games. The rules have to be followed by everyone and no team should have any undue advantage—if it does, the integrity of the competition is sacrificed. It's the same with any top sport: whether it's steroid use, corked bats, or underinflated footballs, policing a sport for unfair advantages is part of upholding its integrity. Show jumping is no different. I'm sure that, at every Olympic Games, someone gets away with something, however minor. And then, of course, there are those who have been caught red-handed, which is proof that some continue to try. In Hong Kong, I took it upon myself—as did our entire team—to help the stewards police the rules of the game. And in hindsight, I think we helped prevent some of that hanky panky.

The first Olympic event for our team was a qualifier for the last day's individual medal class. Beginning with approximately seventy-five horses, the qualifier class weeds out the weaker riders at the start of the show jumping events, which results in about thirty-five top riders for the individual final round. All qualifiers start the individual final competition with a clean slate, so there's a strategy in that if you're a top rider, you don't need to pull out all the stops. Typically, everyone over twelve faults is basically out of the individual competition after that qualifier. Of course, you try to be as careful and clean as you can be, but you can get a rail or two down or some time faults and still qualify for the individual with a clean slate.

When it came to the riding itself, Hong Kong was an unbelievably fabulous Olympic Games for the American team. All four riders had wonderful rounds and very few faults. Uncharacteristically, the German team unraveled.

The Americans won the team gold medal with Will Simpson putting in the final clear round in the jump-off to clinch it! At the conclusion of the individual event, Eric Lamaze of Canada riding Hickstead and Rolf-Göran Bengtsson from Sweden riding Ninja La Silla jumped off for the gold medal. Eric, the talented student of my seventies Hunterdon disciple Diane Dubuc, won the gold for Canada. Then, Beezie and Authentic prevailed in a five-horse bronze medal jump-off (that included McLain and Meredith Michaels-Beerbaum). It was an excellent showing by the Americans with particularly good performances by our greener horses (photo 231).

Eric Lamaze

George is the best teacher in our industry, not only because of the way he teaches, but also because of his fundamental belief in his system of classical, forward riding. Even as the sport has changed, with new styles of riding coming into fashion and new training tools being introduced, George has always stuck to his basic principles of simplicity and has continued to advocate forward riding. He has never changed his ways throughout the years and always stayed true to his method. George was able to bring the U.S. Team to the highest level of the sport while still maintaining simplicity and being true to his system. He's such an important voice in our sport and is so highly respected. Not only the riders who have trained with him, but anyone who has ever had the privilege of walking a course or being in the warm-up ring with him has benefited from his knowledge.

As Chef d'Equipe, one always operates in four-year blocks, with the Olympics being the finale in each four-year quadrenium. When Melanie Smith Taylor called to congratulate me, she said, "Oh George, you can retire with this wonderful win!" Having considered it, I didn't think it would look right for me to retire just after such a successful Olympics—it would be like winning at marbles and running home! I decided I wasn't ready to retire just yet; leaving on a high note didn't seem fair to the country. If this sport were all blue ribbons and bright lights, I would've quit a long time ago. I decided that I would rather continue working for the good of the sport as long as I could, even if I go out without a bang!

VII. POLITICAL THRILLER

Laura Kraut

We were in La Boule in 2005 for a Nations Cup in the Super League series. It was an all-girl team of Beezie Madden, Schuyler Riley, Georgina Bloomberg, and me. Right before the class, as Schuyler Riley was about to walk into the ring, George said to her, "Schuyler, if you jump a double clear, I will kiss your feet!" Well, she jumped a double clear on her horse Ilian and we won the Nations Cup that day. That night, we were in the bar at the hotel gathering to get ready to go to dinner. George walked into the bar and across to us and said, "Oh Schuyler—all right, go ahead, give me your foot." And he kissed her foot! It was so funny. He could've definitely got away with not doing it, but he's a man of his word. I know Schuyler will never forget that and neither will I.

It's hard to describe how much George has meant to me, even more so because I didn't grow up riding with him. When he became Chef d'Equipe and I had a chance to ride with him on the teams, I considered it such an opportunity to be able to learn from him. For whatever reason, we always seemed to connect and get along very well. He gave me a lot of direction and all of his wisdom, but at the same time made me feel free to make my own decisions. George was just so very devoted—most days he was there before anyone else in the morning and the last to leave at the end of the day. He would watch every class and study everything.

At the World Equestrian Games at Aachen, I went to look at a horse before the second day of the competition began and got lost on the way back. Nearly having a heart attack about running late, I ran to the ring and got there just at the moment they were opening the gate to let everyone into the ring for the course walk. I didn't have time to change into my white breeches and still had my schooling breeches on, but at least I had made it in time. We all walked the course as a team and gathered around George to talk through the whole course again. He turned to me and said, "Don't you ever, EVER walk a course in those breeches again." I was two inches tall when he finished with me, and he was right. I felt really bad about it. But then later on, when I saw George before the class, it was like it had never happened. He talked to me just like he always did. I appreciated that straightforwardness. George says what he has to say and makes his point, but then he moves on. I really appreciate the discipline he instilled in all of us, even those of us who were older and had been in the sport for so many years—we still had to toe the line. The horses had to be presented a certain way and we had to be dressed a certain way and we had to be there on time and that was that. There was never any wavering, which was great. Sometimes teams from other countries would poke fun at how regimented we were, but I loved it. It created a comradery between us that really worked.

At the Nations Cup in Rotterdam, when George retired as Chef d'Equipe, for weeks and weeks afterward I would get teary-eyed thinking about it. Robert has done a magnificent job and I give him so much credit for following George in that position. But it was really sad the last year, just thinking we wouldn't have George there with us anymore. It was the highlight of our day, seeing him. Never, ever, ever did he make me feel like I couldn't do something, even when I probably couldn't! He was never that kind of a Chef d'Equipe. He wasn't a cheerleader, either. He was just matter-of-fact about everything. We all had instant credibility if we were with George when it came to the international stage. It was magical. I hope the kids who are coming up in the sport will be inspired to be part of international teams just like I was.

As I've mentioned, the year after the Olympic Games tends to be quieter because there's no Pan American Games, no World Equestrian Games, and no Olympics for which to prepare. In 2009, we did have the Super League series serving as our summertime European tour, which was a good opportunity to keep tabs on our horses and riders and watch other teams ride. After the success in Aachen at the WEG and in Hong Kong, I was full of hope that everyone would be inspired to a greater standard. I imagined it would jump-start our ambition and wealthy owners would line up to buy great horses for our most talented home-grown riders. I envisioned the smaller trainers dreaming of bigger things and seeing the fruits of those dreams in the years to follow! People will be motivated to ride better, emulate that American style we saw being so successful, and also care for their horses better. I suppose that's a reflection of who I am—when I do well, it inspires me to dig in and work harder. But America doesn't react like that. When we're against the wall, we do better—and when we're successful, everyone relaxes! I was shocked to see the level of complacency in our sport that set in after 2008. I did see, however, a young California girl showing in Calgary that year and was really impressed with her riding. It was Ashlee Bond. Suddenly I found myself considering her for a team I was putting together for a Nations Cup that November in Argentina.

Ashlee Bond

While showing at Spruce Meadows in 2009, I had just jumped clear in the $75,000 Sun Life Financial Grand Prix on Cadett 7, which I ended up winning. George Morris asked to speak with me at the back gate. I was standing there with my dad and George said, "Ashlee, I have three questions for you." I said, "Okay." He said, "One, how far do you want to go in this sport?" I said, "All the way to the top!" He said, "Two, can you put your hair up in your helmet?" I laughed and said, "Yes, of course I can!" (I went home after Spruce and got my extensions taken out and voilà, hair in helmet!) Then George said, "Just one more question. Can you braid your horse's mane?" I replied, "No, but I can learn!" He said, "Okay, then I'd like to put you on the Four-Star Team for CSIO Buenos Aires."

The following summer, I was showing in Europe with Richard Spooner, Laura Kraut, and Christine McCrea on the team. We had just found out we were tied with Germany and had to go into a jump-off to win the Nations Cup in St. Gallen. Obviously, I was the rookie with the least amount of experience but my horse and I had jumped three consecutive double-clear rounds in all the Grands Prix so far. We had been so consistent that George asked me to do the jump-off, but I was not as sure of myself. Whoever was going to jump for our team had to go head to head against Marcus Ehning, who is a legend. I said that I thought it would be best to have Richard jump with Cristallo. After going back and forth about it, George said, "Well, how about we just flip a coin and see who jumps off for us?" I called heads and Spooner jumped! I was relieved, to say the least! Richard ended up having one rail down but was really fast. Marcus went for the careful clear on Plot Blue and ticked the last jump, so we won! It was an incredible moment—to have won that Nations Cup after also winning in Rome.

As I've said before, it's common for younger riders to be a little shaky when they're new to Europe and it's important for them to get experience. Ashlee came along on a Super League tour in Europe in 2009 and rode in La Boule, Rome, and St. Gallen in Switzerland. At the first show in La Boule, she was double clear in the Nations Cup and rode fabulously in the Grand Prix, too—she would've won it except her horse slipped! I thought it *had* to be beginner's luck. In Rome, incredibly, Ashlee went double clear in the Nations Cup again and got a good ribbon in the Grand Prix.

As I began wondering what kind of phenom I had on my hands, I watched her have another great show with clear rounds in St. Gallen. I told Ashlee that I was going to keep her in Europe. "You're going to Aachen," I told her. She replied, "Oh, I've heard of that show! What country is that in? Spain?" and I said, "No it's in Germany." When we got to Aachen, Ashlee was the talk of the show. Wednesday has the second biggest individual class at Aachen, called the Grand Prix of Europe. Ashlee rode very early in the order and went clear. Fourteen made the jump-off and all of the biggest, famous riders were in it. With all those riders going in the jump-off, we knew it was going to be fast. Ashlee went in either first or second in the jump-off and that girl rode California junior-jumper, belly-to-the-ground fast and clear. Those veteran riders going behind her—Ludger Beerbaum, Jos Lansink, John Whitaker, and Meredith Michaels-Beerbaum among them—didn't even know what to do! If they tried to beat Ashlee, they would have a fence down. If they rode to go clear, there's no chance they'd be fast enough. I stood with Ashlee near the ring watching the rest of the jump-off and I started jinxing every rider. A French rider rode into the ring and I told her, "The French are so fast, this one will surely beat you." But the Frenchman didn't beat her. "Oh Ashlee, the British can turn on a dime, you're in trouble now. Here come the Germans, it's Ludger. Oh no, here we go." Horse after horse went in, and I jinxed every horse, and she won!

Coincidentally, Ashlee is from the same California hometown as Meredith Michaels-Beerbaum. As she rode into the ring to accept her prize, she dropped the reins, took two bouquets of flowers, and waved to the crowd in all directions. I thought perhaps she was stealing the crown from Meredith as the new California girl conquering Germany. That weekend, if she hadn't just relaxed just a little bit at the last jump, she would've won the Grand Prix of Aachen, too.

John Whitaker

George Morris is one of the great characters in the sport of show jumping. He is not only a renowned trainer and team manager, he is a real horseman. Over the years I and many others have learned a lot from watching him both ride and train. George has inspired his teams and riders with his will to win and has had a massive influence in the sport all over the world.

I was deeply honored that year to be presented with the Golden Whip and the title of Horseman of Honor from the Cadre Noir of Saumur, the French National Equitation School. It was only the fourth time the award had ever been presented and naturally, I was very moved to have been chosen to receive it. It was not only a nod to my achievement, but also an acknowledgment of the impact that America has had on the sport as a whole. For an American to receive a sparingly given, storied award from such a European institution demonstrates the grand evolution of the sport since my coming of age in the fifties.

One afternoon I was in Wellington at the show grounds watching a Jumping Derby and I saw a fellow spectator that looked like Matt Lauer standing with Jeffery Welles. I watch Matt Lauer on the news all the time, but I'd seen this look-alike at the shows before and not for a moment did I believe it was really the news anchor. A bit later, I walked over to say hello to Jeffery and he introduced me to the man who was indeed Matt Lauer. Matt's wife Annette is Dutch and not only a beauty but a very good horsewoman. We got to talking; I admitted I was starstruck meeting them both, Annette laughed and said she was starstruck meeting me! The following summer, they wanted to have a little dinner party for me at their house on Long Island during the show at Southampton. Well, what I thought would be a small affair turned out to be a fifty-person guest-list straight out of a New York celebrity black book. Mayor Bloomberg was there, along with Kelly Ripa, Bruce Springsteen and Patti Scialfa, Robert Duvall, Howard Stern, Anjelica Huston, and the heads of NBC and Warner Brothers. Being the guest of honor, all of them were saying hello and congratulating me left and right, but most of them had no idea who I was! It was a night I'll never forget.

McLain Ward

George and his teams had a lot of great success together during his tenure as Chef d'Equipe; it was an incredible time with Sapphire and also with Beezie Madden and Authentic in those years. We developed a friendship that will last a lifetime. I have gained so much from his knowledge, experience, and professionalism. I hope in some small way, he has gained a little in return from my youth and ambition.

First and foremost, George is a horseman and a horse lover, and for him, horse sports are his life's pursuit. That's the kind of person I want to be in the trenches with, and in my view, it is a key to George's success and to his popularity—not just among the masses, but among the top athletes. George is not just preaching from the sidelines; he is someone who lives and breathes horses, day in and day out. As a boy, I knew who George was and even though I wasn't one of his students he absolutely influenced me. George set the tone for what the modern teaching system was in the United States and around the world. I've always taken it as a great compliment that even though I wasn't one of George's students, others feel I have embodied and followed his system. George's dedication to excellence and striving to improve and to win is something you only see in a handful of people in the sport. Riders like Beezie and myself take that philosophy to heart. In our sport, where methods are constantly evolving, George's approach of staying true to classical horsemanship while being open-minded with a desire to learn and continue to improve is one I emulate. There's a balance—you have to be open-minded to evolution and improvements while appreciating the classical base of correct riding and horsemanship.

The most critical focus with George is how you do your job. The winning and losing is important, but upholding the principles of his system is the key. I've ridden and watched many jumper classes over the years where the winning riders think they were great, but in reality they got lucky and barely won by the skin of their teeth. And by the same token, someone might have a fantastic performance and still have a rail down. You have to recognize that and make it about the performance itself and not just the result, because the performance is really more connected to how well you're doing your job.

The following year, in 2010, the World Cup Finals were held in Geneva in the enormous indoor ring at the Palexpo in Le Grand-Saconnex. We had a fantastic group of riders qualify for the Finals that year including Mario Deslauriers, Michelle Spadone, Hillary Dobbs, Lauren Hough, Ken Berkley, Todd Minikus, Rich Fellers, Joie Gatlin, Richard Spooner, and McLain Ward. McLain and Sapphire had really hit their stride; he handled her so well and refused to over-show her. Their partnership was so fine-tuned in those days that they seemed positively invincible.

My friend Larry, whom I'd had a fun long-distance relationship with for some time, came to the Finals with me, but he had a reaction to the very rich food in Western Europe. Experiencing terrible chest pains, poor Larry thought he was having a heart attack, but the diagnosis turned out to be severe acid reflux. I simply couldn't stay up all night with him at the hospital and be on my game as Chef d'Equipe the next day, so Larry nobly took a taxi to the hospital and spent the night there. On Friday, he still wasn't well. We were both worried and he decided he should fly home to Romania and see his doctor at home. These personal things sometimes happen at big championships and they can be quite a distraction. It was plenty of drama for one World Cup Finals! Little did I know, the real drama was just beginning.

For the first time in years, we were having a fabulous World Cup with great rides by many American riders. Hillary Dobbs, Lou Dobbs's daughter, won the speed classes at the beginning of the week. Mario Deslauriers and McLain

Ward were sitting first and second after Thursday night's first leg of the Finals: a speed class (a Table A course run under Table C rules, with faults converted to seconds). We were off to a great start!

Lizzy Chesson

I started working at USEF in 2006 under Sally Ike, and my role has evolved over the years, eventually to Managing Director of Show Jumping. My first event overseas was in Gothenburg in 2008, and that's when I worked with George for the first time. I'll never forget the pep talk he gave me about being sure to dress appropriately.

On a more serious note, I felt very fortunate to be in the position to work with him. A day did not go by where I did not learn something from George. Of course, there was much to glean from the horsemanship perspective, however, I would say what I learned most from George was about people. He has a wonderful way of combining his value of discipline with his charisma in order to push people to be the most successful they can possibly be. It was an honor to work with someone who was so deeply respected by all of the riders—and not just our own athletes but those around the world. At a show you could barely get from one place to another because everyone would stop to say hello to George. It was, and still is, quite something!

There were many moments throughout the "George Years" that were challenging and awe-inspiring, but it was the everyday moments that still put a smile on my face: his addiction to Coca-Cola and chocolate; his idea of being on time being fifteen minutes early; and the devilish smile that comes across his face when he is about to tell me something I do not want to hear! Putting all that aside, George's love for the United States Team is clear above all else—even today he still calls me to talk about how things are going!

Friday's second round of the World Cup Finals is the traditional format with an initial round and a timed jump-off. The whole American contingent was up at the ring to watch and support one another. In the middle of everything, someone ran up and told me that Sapphire was being tested for hypersensitivity back at the barn. I wasn't unduly concerned hearing about it, because it's very common at shows. The FEI routinely selects random horses to be tested at all such events and our team vet is always there to help take the blood sample or assist in whatever was needed. I couldn't go back to the barn myself at that point, because I was needed at the ring and the stalls were some distance away.

Ten American riders were in the class and scattered throughout the order of go, with one riding every few trips. McLain finished second and Mario Deslauriers was third, but after those first two rounds, McLain was in first overall by a wide margin. We were still in a great position and I was very pleased.

Most of the American team stayed that evening for the driving competition, which is always wonderful to watch, and it was quite late at night when we left. Lizzy Chesson and I had eaten dinner together at the horse show during the driving and we got back late to the hotel, around midnight. I was just under the bed covers and turning off the light, feeling very tired indeed, when the phone rang. It was Lizzy and our vet, Tim Ober, and they told me I had to get back over to the show immediately. Officials were retesting Sapphire for hypersensitivity, and they wanted to eliminate her from the rest of the World Cup. I was stunned! On my way out of the hotel, I ran into a good friend of McLain's, Rodrigo Pessoa. Rodrigo, who was head of the rider's club, had also heard about the testing, and we decided to go over to the show together and see what it was all about. We arrived back at the Palexpo and marched up to the crowd around Sapphire's stall. The president of the FEI was there, Princess Haya, along with the head of the horse show and the ground jury. The testing committee, a small team consisting of a special English vet, the show vet, and the head of the ground jury, had prodded that mare fifty-odd times on each pastern and coronary band with a small blunt instrument about the size of a pen. The newly implemented hypersensitivity test was meant to locate any sensitivity or soreness in a particular area that would indicate the horse shouldn't be competing. From Sapphire's reaction to the poking and prodding, the committee had determined that she was showing signs of hypersensitivity on a spot on her left front leg and should be eliminated. I immediately distrusted the findings. It just didn't make sense—what person or animal wouldn't show sensitivity when being poked over and over like that? For half the night, we had meetings protesting the decision, but it was hopeless—they eliminated her. Exhausted and upset, I stumbled back into bed around three that morning (photo 234).

A couple short hours later, I was up and back at the show early. Saturday was a day off between rounds two and three of the Finals. McLain was hand-walking Sapphire in the warm-up ring, as the press and spectators looked on. I went over to her, squatted down and felt her legs. To this day, I assure you, I never saw any reaction to pressure anywhere on that leg. She trotted perfectly sound and in my view, she was ready to jump in the final round on Sunday. It was utterly heartbreaking to all of us that she was eliminated. The stars had aligned for our first United States World Cup win since 1987, but the powers that be pulled the rug right out from under us! The third and final round of the Finals on Sunday is a two-round competition and the longer distances would have suited Sapphire's big stride—everyone felt she and McLain were practically a shoo-in! I was furious and frustrated, as was McLain.

A Swedish horseman and friend of mine who was a spectator at the Finals came over to speak with me on Sunday. He had quite a story. On the Wednesday previous, while dining at a restaurant in town, he'd overheard a German and Swede discussing with one another that Sapphire would be eliminated. This was well before the testing process began on Sapphire. Some Europeans hate it when a North American rider does well, and they knew McLain and Sapphire were the ones to beat. It's very hard indeed to not think the entire charade was politically concocted. I saw the handwriting on the wall—they simply got rid of them! I was deeply embittered by the entire experience. Marcus Ehning ended up taking home the top spot for Germany, and I went home with a fire in my belly.

Timothy Ober, DVM

This is what I can tell you: I was there for the whole thing, for the entire process. I saw the horse. In my opinion, she was a normal horse—the same Sapphire I had known for years. It's important to understand that at that time, it was the implementation of a very subjective test on an aspect of a horse's health. It was simply done incorrectly. There was absolutely nothing correct about the way the test was implemented and it was unbelievable to me that they could stand there and make the decision that they did and look any of us in the eye. It was too hard to reconcile what I was seeing with what I was hearing. I didn't feel it was right. At the end of the day, McLain is a class act and a total professional. He put it behind him and went back to work. I think he let it go before I did and that shows what a professional he is. The approach to sensitivity testing these days is extremely different, because it was absolutely necessary to change what they were doing. It was a sad chapter in our team history and a sad day for the sport.

There was outrage across the show-jumping community and I give McLain credit for handling the situation as a complete gentleman. Arbitration was held afterward with the FEI, but the USEF was in a vulnerable position in arguing our case with the World Equestrian Games being held in Lexington, Kentucky, that fall, just a few months later—naturally the Federation didn't want to damage its relationship with the FEI before such a huge event. Our cause

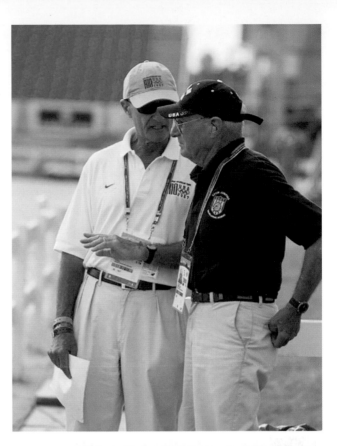

226. *With Frank Chapot at the 2007 Pan American Games in Rio de Janeiro.*
© PhelpsSports.com

227. *Through my years as the official Chef d'Equipe of the U.S. Show Jumping Team, I continued my clinic circuit with dozens of stops each year.* © Sharleen Knox

228. *With the 2008 Beijing Olympic Games (held in Hong Kong) Show Jumping Team (left to right): Tim Ober, Will Simpson, Laura Kraut, Beezie Madden, Anne Kursinski, Sally Ike, and McLain Ward.*

229. *Laura Kraut rode fabulously on her green horse Cedric in Hong Kong.* © Bob Langrish

230. *In Rome, with the brothers Raimondo and Piero d'Inzeo, my dear friends and excellent horsemen, who together won twelve Olympic medals in show jumping.*

231. *Will Simpson, Laura Kraut, Beezie Madden, and McLain Ward with me looking on: our gold-medal Olympic team, 2008. Beezie won individual bronze.* © Bob Langrish

232. *Escorting the U.S. flag bearer at the Nations Cup in Wellington, 2008, which the U.S. Team won.* © Debra Jamroz

233. *My office at my very private home in Wellington, which is surrounded by my own personal jungle.* © Karen Robertson Terry

234. *Sapphire was unfairly eliminated after taking the lead in the 2010 World Cup Finals.*
© Amy Dragoo

235. *McLain Ward, a class act, speaking with the press after Sapphire was eliminated from the World Cup Finals based on results of a hypersensitivity test.* © scoopdyga.com

236. *I'm demonstrating proper, balanced collection with elevated hands and no stirrups at a Florida clinic.* © The Chronicle of the Horse/Molly Sorge Photo

237. *With the 2010 WEG Team (left to right): McLain Ward, Mario Deslauriers, Lauren Hough, Laura Kraut, and Candice King.* © Lesley Ward

238. *With my dear friend, Nelson Pessoa.*

239. *Coaching Georgina Bloomberg, a wonderful rider and friend, with Jimmy Doyle.*

240. *Demonstrating at a clinic in Middleburg—and looking directly through the window at Betsee Parker!*

241. *Celebrating the 2011 Pan Am Games gold medal with (left to right) Kent Farrington, Christine McCrea, Beezie Madden, and McLain Ward.*

© *Shannon Brinkman*

242. *Rich Fellers and Flexible, World Cup Finals winners in 2012.*   © *Kit Houghton*

243. *With the 2012 London Olympic Team (left to right): Beezie Madden, Rich Fellers, Reed Kessler, McLain Ward, and Charlie Jayne.* © Shannon Brinkman

244. *Rich Fellers jogging Flexible after sprinting across half the city of London to make it on time!* © Joanie Morris

245. *It's a family affair! I'm with Shelley, Savannah, Christopher, and Rich Fellers.*
© Karen Robertson Terry

246. Coaching Reed Kessler
in London. © NoelleFloyd.com

247. *Beezie Madden and Coral Reef Via Volo at the American Gold Cup at Devon, 2013.* © PhelpsSports.com

248. *At home in Wellington.* © GeorgeKamper.com

249. *With John and Beezie Madden and Robert Ridland at the London Olympic Games.* © Diana De Rosa

250. *Robert Ridland is a fabulous Chef d'Equipe and the teams are in very capable hands.* © PhelpsSports.com

251. *I love this girl! Coaching Athina Onassis at a show in 2013.* © *NoelleFloyd.com*

252. *Teaching the Horsemastership Clinic in Wellington, Florida.* © *USEF Archives*

253. *With Mark Cassells and Diane Carney acting as judges during a mock FEI jog at a Young Riders clinic.* © *Chicago Equestrian*

254. *Victoria Colvin and Cafino winning the $25,000 Suncast 1.50m Classic in 2015.*
© *Sportfot*

255. *With Victoria Colvin and Andre Dignelli.*

was somewhat vindicated when the FEI released a statement shortly afterward admitting that Sapphire had been "incorrectly eliminated" from the final round at the Finals. Sadly, there is no reparation for the fact that our sport's history—and McLain and Sapphire's record—was forever altered by this undeserved turn of events (photo 235).

I continued my trips to Brazil a couple of times a year to teach a clinic or two and enjoy the wonderful culture. There's a well-developed horse community and a big international show held at the club in Rio de Janeiro where I originally rode back in 1977. I always loved Brazil; it is filled with people who have next to nothing in terms of money or material things, but their lives are full of family and joy and warmth. They are grateful for all that life gives them and live in this wonderfully appreciative way without the material greed you see in the States. I wasn't always fully comfortable in either very straight or very gay social situations outside of the horse world. That's why I like Brazil. The gay culture there is very different from the way it is in Europe or America in that it's not segregated from the straight social world and is very relaxed and flexible. There aren't those stereotypical effeminate or gossipy elements either, which never suited me. It's simply a comfortable and welcoming culture, and I feel very much at home there.

On one such trip, a few years ago, to teach and have some time off, I was out at a watering hole in Rio de Janeiro with a good friend Marcus and a big group of friends. We would often go out with this roving group of guys, which was a lot of fun. We would meet others along the way and that night I met Raphael Torres. Raphael is a very astute guy from a modest family and an easy talker. As it turns out, he makes friends with everyone wherever he goes, but he also has a mischievous side, which makes him even more attractive. Since he's a model, DJ, and dancer at clubs in Europe, he's a total gym addict and so we have a common interest in fitness. After getting to know Rafa, I invited him to meet me in Chile, which is a great stop coming back from Australia. We stayed in a fabulous resort hotel and had a great time together. He's got a sweet side, but is still bad enough to keep my interest! We've had a long-distance relationship for over five years and it works wonderfully. He's a very straight-looking and -acting man, but he's definitely gay and not simply dabbling on the side like some men are known to do. He's the opposite of me in terms of the organized quality of his life, but we have great chemistry, and he has no hang ups about the age difference. In Brazilian culture, it's far less unusual for older and younger people to have relationships with one another. The young appreciate the wisdom and experience of the older generations.

Rafa will meet me at shows in Europe and we've traveled together to Israel, Australia, and New Zealand. He's not dependent or a distraction from my work, but he's a wonderful person to relax with and take a break from the horse world. Although we are in touch daily, Rafa generally doesn't spend a lot of time with me at clinics or horse shows because he would get bored and restless. I started him riding a little bit, and he had talent for it and a great eye for distances, but it wasn't something he's focused on. Rafa is very Brazilian in that his attention and thoughts wander; his focus isn't steady on a particular pursuit outside of his social life and his career with dancing, about which he's very steadfast.

VIII. UNEASY LIES THE HEAD THAT WEARS THE CROWN

The World Equestrian Games were upon us once again and this time, we were hosting it in Lexington, Kentucky. In the year leading up to the WEG, the three-phase selection process went into effect to choose the WEG Team. After the completion of the selection-trial classes, the selection committee approved fifteen horse-and-rider combinations for the WEG long list. The top nine were listed according to their rank after the trials. Then, six additional pairs were chosen by the committee subjectively, which included three that had already been given byes (McLain Ward and Sapphire, Laura Kraut and Cedric, and Lauren Hough on Quick Study). The top fifteen pairs were divided into three teams to cover the summer's Super League series in Europe.

Our experience with the disqualification of Sapphire at the World Cup Finals had shaken me more than any other political issues I'd encountered in the sport. It was a terrible thing to feel like my hands were tied when I had tried to change the course of the injustice. However, to my delight, McLain and our team enacted sweet revenge in the shows that summer. In La Baule, France, we won the Nations Cup and after that, McLain won two huge Grand Prix classes on Sapphire. In Rotterdam, we won the Nations Cup again with our all-women team, which was fabulous. After Dublin, the Selection Committee assembled and chose our WEG Team (photo 237).

Being Chef d'Equipe is no cakewalk! Everyone on the Selection Committee feels the weight of responsibility to the sport and to our country. The reality is that every time we chose a team, no matter how exciting it was to bring a team to the big event, we had a couple of dozen people upset with us for not selecting them. It's difficult being the target of such criticism, but I also know that people get Olympic fever. It's hard to have your hopes dashed. I had that experience myself when the 1956 Olympic Team was chosen and I wasn't on it! But we must choose who we feel gives our team the very best opportunity to bring home medals for our country.

As one example, Richard Spooner was very disappointed about not being selected for the WEG Team that year. I thought initially he and Cristallo were going to make it, but a couple of things dropped them down on the list. In La Baule, he had a couple of rails, decided to use the round as a schooling opportunity, and ended up with twenty-four faults. There is a time and place for schooling and a Super League class is not it, as it's considered one of the selection trials. Cristallo also wasn't the most consistent horse. In Rome, he came out very fresh and Richard worked him hard until he was overly soft, and he ended up stopping out in the Nations Cup. With those two marks against him on paper, my hands were tied. Believing in a horse and rider isn't enough; their record must support my vote.

The only people who aren't upset with us in the end are the four who ride into the ring! In the case of the 2010 WEG, those four were McLain Ward with Sapphire, Laura Kraut with Cedric, Lauren Hough with Quick Study, and Mario Deslauriers with Urico, with Candice King as the alternate. Candice was very impressive at Rotterdam but her horse was still quite green; even so, her brilliance earned her that alternate spot. Mario earned his place on the team with the highest placing at the World Cup that year and had consistently done well in the trials and in Europe.

The Kentucky Horse Park is a beautiful venue with lots of spacious country to host all the equestrian disciplines. It has become, in some ways, the geographical center of our sport in the United States. Mario Deslauriers and McLain Ward were first and second in the speed leg, giving our team a very comfortable lead. The Germans were right behind us! On the second night, which was the first round of the Nations Cup, Lauren and Quick Study had the misfortune of going first, which always adds an element of difficulty, not seeing how the course rides for anyone else. After all was said and done, none of the American riders had clean rounds that day and there were some significant riding mistakes that contributed. Even so, we were definitely still in the running because we'd ridden so well on the first night.

In the second round of the Nations Cup the following day, the wheels fell off the wagon. Whatever could go wrong did go wrong. Lauren and Mario both had a very difficult time; Quick Study switched off in the schooling ring and was uncharacteristically stopping out at the jumps. He was always a bold, brave jumper but something really got under his skin that day. A few years before, I had seen Quick Study react that way, but he'd been so consistent for so many years that I never expected to see it again. Lauren had to over-ride him to keep him from stopping and, as a result, he had rails down. Mario had very tough rounds both nights of the Nations Cup on his Urico. Cedric freaked out about some carriages he saw on the first night and it took a while for Laura to get his mind back on business. Even Sapphire, normally so reliably brilliant, seemed to have lost her peak form just a bit by the WEG, which can happen sometimes in the autumn months after a long show season.

Everyone had some good moments in the ring on certain days in Kentucky, but there were disastrous ones too and they really brought down the team. We went from clearly the winner after the start to landing in tenth place. Oddly enough, not only were we first and second after the first night in the speed class, but on the last day McLain and Sapphire tied for first in the second round of individual competition. So in the end, even though we won the top spot in two out of the four events, we landed in the basement as a team.

As a result of our disappointing finish at the WEG, we hadn't yet qualified for the Olympic Games. That fact really shook up the country. Only the top five teams from the WEG earn a spot, then the other spots are determined by the Pan American Games and the European Championships. Historically, it wasn't unprecedented—this had happened to Frank during his tenure when the team didn't qualify for the Athens Olympics on WEG results. After the debacle with Sapphire at the World Cup and the lackluster finish in Kentucky, I was no longer infallible as a Chef d'Equipe. While it bothered me that these poor results in some sense damaged my leadership credibility, I still had a lot of confidence in my ability to make good decisions. The wonderful success we'd had all summer in Europe was proof that we had the riders, the horses, and the leadership needed to win.

Every year there's a CSIO Nations Cup in Wellington at the end of the winter circuit. It's an important competition, but I didn't like asking some of our best veteran horses to jump in a Nations Cup in early March. Horses like Sapphire, Authentic, and eventually Cedric when he got older, needed to be saved for bigger things later in the year. The younger horses would all be in the mix, and we would still have very good home team representation. There were others, though, who didn't like this decision and I was the subject of criticism for taking away our best chances for a win by the home team—and also the owners' chances at the prize money. If we didn't have the Super League to contend with all summer long, I might have looked at it differently. But looking back now, I would've made the very same call.

All of my decisions as Chef d'Equipe come from a horsemanship or teaching perspective. Good horse people know that a horse only has so many jumps in him. Those top horses had all year to jump huge fences. Just a few months earlier, I had witnessed Sapphire getting a little past her peak performance window in Kentucky. We needed to plan better and preserve her stamina so that she could sustain her peak performance through the late summer. Jumping in a Nations Cup in March meant starting preparation even earlier in the winter, which cut into her recovery time between seasons. Less time off and longer, harder seasons for the horses is not good horse management! Bert de Némethy would've certainly put his foot down; he had a cycle of giving horses time off in the winter, then slowly bringing them back into form. That program helped keep top horses healthy and competitive.

We began preparing for the Pan American 2011 Games in Guadalajara, Mexico. With the poor result at the WEG, there was great pressure to finish in the top three teams at the Mexican Pan Ams in order to secure our spot in the 2012 London Olympics. Counting in our favor was the fact that Canada and Mexico had already earned Olympic berths from WEG standings. Teams who had already qualified aren't counted in the Pan Am Games' Olympic-qualification spots. Therefore, we simply had to be among the top three country teams outside of Canada and Mexico. Our chances were very good, but still, anything can happen at a horse show. The pressure was on!

Fielding our best team in Guadalajara for the Pan American team meant that sending a "B team" to that year's Super League series (that conflicted with the Pan Am games on the schedule) would be unavoidable. The Super League, as successful as it was for us in 2005, turned out to be difficult in later years for reasons like the conflict with the Pan Ams. It was such a big commitment to keep with all the other demands of the show schedule. Each year it became harder for me to get riders to commit to riding in the Super League shows. The 2011 Super League classes directly competed with rich Grand Prix classes like Calgary and the Rider's Tour, another European show series. Trying to field teams at the Super League Nations Cup classes, while also sending the top riders to Calgary and other top shows, led to exhausted horses. The owners and riders couldn't digest it, and they started to break away and go on their own planned tours.

Our immediate mission was doing well at the Pan American Games and securing our spot in the London Olympics. We had a wonderful team assembled for the Games in Guadalajara, Mexico: Christine McCrae on Romantovich

Take One, Beezie Madden on Coral Reef Via Volo, Kent Farrington on Uceko, and McLain Ward on Antares F. It was a beautiful Pan Am Games, with the hotel within walking distance of the club. Each venue was absolutely gorgeous. It was one of, if not the nicest Pan Am Games ever held. The police struck some sort of deal with the drug cartels so that there wouldn't be any trouble for the tourists, and we all felt quite safe.

The courses were also wonderful, although the footing was tan bark and wood chips, which can ride a little bit loose and slippery. The team rode excellently and we got the boost we sorely needed! Chrissy McCrea won individual gold on Romantovich Take One, Beezie Madden won individual silver on Coral Reef Via Volo, and the U.S. Team won the gold medal (photo 241). Our domination reminded me a little of the Pan Am Games in 1975, as it was certainly the most successful since then. In fact, the American dressage, three-day eventing, and show jumping teams all won gold medals, so it was a wonderful result across all the disciplines. I was thrilled and relieved we had qualified for the Olympic Games, and we turned our eyes to London.

IX. THE LAST QUADRENNIAL

Kent Farrington

I grew up in Chicago and was riding for Nancy Whitehead who told me to get into the George Morris clinic when I was a junior. After the clinic, I was standing with my mom and George walked up. He told us that he thought I could really be something in the sport and that he'd like to help me. George said I needed to take a chance, break out of the Midwest circuit, and go down to show in Wellington at a higher level. He invited me to Hunterdon to train with him, and a bunch of people at home helped me get horses together to take there. George also gave me three of his own horses to ride, which was an amazing opportunity. That whole experience was a big boost and it got me to a higher level. I made great contacts in Wellington afterward and my career grew from there.

Later, when I started having a lot of success in the Grands Prix, George once again pushed me onward. He said to me, "Great job, but now you need to win in Europe." George is such a competitor. When we're with George on a team, we are there to win. He encouraged me to take that next step and has always been a quiet influence in my career, from that early leg up he gave me. I started my own business when I was really young and he has always been very supportive. There are professionals all over the country whose businesses are run the way they are because of George, and mine is no exception. That's the kind of legacy you leave behind when you have the influence that George has had—and continues to have—on the sport.

To populate Super League teams in 2011 while handling all the competing priorities elsewhere, I recruited some young or amateur riders. Many of them rose to the challenge and did a great job, like Lucy Davis. We were simply up against the best Europe had to offer and although the riders stepped up and rode well, we came in sixth at the end of the Super League show series. To have a chance at winning the entire Super League, realistically you must have at least three or four of your "A team" horse-and-rider combinations showing. As a consequence, we were low enough in the placing that we were relegated from the Super League. On one hand, I was devastated I'd allowed it to happen, but at the same time my relief was just as strong.

It was a blessing in disguise, as it turned out, because without the obligation of the Super League in 2012, we were in a better position to have fresh horses for the Olympics. We did have one drawback, in that we had to supplement with shows in North America to replace selection-trial opportunities for choosing the team. However, we were better able to focus on getting qualified for London and preparing without stressing our best horses. It felt fitting that Calgary was my last North American show before the Olympics as Chef d'Equipe. It was also in some ways a relief for me to have it behind us.

Selecting the London Olympic Team then became the focus. McLain Ward had a great record on Antares F and they had won the Grand Prix of Dublin, but he broke his leg in a fall off another horse before the selection trials. I proposed we grant him a bye from the trials and he was approved, along with Laura Kraut on Cedric and Beezie Madden on Coral Reef Via Volo. McLain was added to the Olympic Team long list riding either Antares F or Sapphire. The byes we gave Laura, Beezie, and McLain didn't mean they had made the Olympics. It was simply a pass from the selection-trial shows. They would still be evaluated on the short list at the qualifying Super League replacement shows, in Del Mar, Kentucky, Devon, and Calgary.

At the trials, Margie Goldstein-Engle on Indigo and Reed Kessler on Cylana both jumped magnificently and tied for first place. They decided to share first place rather than jump their horses again for the tiebreaker. Afterward, Margie didn't have as great a summer with Indigo in Europe. He'd lost his confidence showing on wet grass footing and started banking the oxers, similar to how Rhythmical jumped in Sydney. He wasn't paddling, but he was jumping in a defensive posture and pushing off the front rail with his back feet. It didn't happen in the trials, but I'd seen it happen at previous Nations Cup classes before the trials. Indigo also ducked out in a big class and pitched Margie off. My predecessors Bert de Némethy and Frank Chapot taught me that you pick championship teams based on a horse and rider's worst day, not their best day. So even though Margie won the trials, Indigo was at his best in that comfortable home-field ring. I worried that Indigo wouldn't hold up under pressure in a big unfamiliar Olympic setting.

During the process, McLain Ward and other riders asked for the Selection Committee to rank the riders as we went along. After the trials, we ranked the riders and horses, including those three that had byes on the short list. It was a tricky exercise, because what's on paper only tells you one side of the story. A rider getting four faults tells me next to nothing. What kind of four faults was it? A tiny tick on a rail resulting in a knock down is very different than banking the oxer and almost falling down or having a stop! That's why you have selectors and some element of subjectivity. If you just go on the numbers on paper, you may pick a team less likely to have success in the Olympics.

The World Cup Finals in 's-Hertogenbosch, Holland that year resulted in another feather in our home team's cap leading up to London. Rich Fellers, whom I have taught in clinics since he was sixteen out in the Pacific Northwest, won the World Cup on his wonderful chestnut stallion Flexible. It was a huge win for him and for the country—our first U.S. World Cup Finals winner since 1987! Rich is such a caring and committed professional in the sport. I am still so proud of his win because he has been my student for so long. You could tell some of the European spectators were tittering in the stands watching Rich gallop to the jumps in his classic American forward seat. The Dutch seat is very upright and deep, not forward like ours. Each night of the World Cup, Rich rode better and better and the tittering got quieter and quieter. It was a great shot in the arm for our home team (photo 242)!

Luca Moneta

I met George four years ago when he was coaching the American team, and I was showing as an individual. I asked him if I could stay close to him to learn because I wanted to watch him teaching his team. George was so kind and welcomed me, taking the time to explain things. At another horse show a few months afterward in Falsterbo, Sweden, where I was again showing as an individual, George was there coaching and saw my round. He came up to me and gave me some suggestions. It was then I told him that although I didn't have much money, I would love to learn from him. He invited me to a clinic later that year in California to assist him and ride some of the horses that were difficult for the students. Also, George said perhaps he could find me a horse to ride in the clinic and incredibly, that I could ride in the clinic free of charge. And he did! It was an incredible opportunity and it really helped me. After the clinic, George asked me if I was going to show in Florida for the winter circuit and I thought, "Why not!" If George sees you have a passion and you are motivated to learn, he is happy to teach you and help you. George used to complain to me, "I don't understand why you come to learn from me. After all, I learned so much of what I know from the Italians! Why should I now be teaching an Italian rider?" And I replied, "Because we forgot, George! We forgot."

I went in for my usual annual physical in the spring of 2012 at the Good Samaritan Hospital in West Palm Beach. I enroll in a program there annually and have access to a team of doctors all located in one building. It's a great system for me, because I can see specialists for anything I might need all in the same building in a network of doctors. That year, my routine exam showed that my prostate-specific antigen (PSA) level had risen substantially and the urologist Dr. Brown scheduled me for a prostate biopsy. After the World Cup Finals, I had the biopsy and the results showed twelve very aggressive points of cancer in the prostate.

Men forty and older should be so vigilant about their health and I'd recommend they get their PSA levels checked annually (and later, twice a year) because it's a marker for prostate cancer. A great friend of mine Barney Ward passed away due to prostate cancer and I learned about the seriousness of the condition. I've never been one to let anything slide when it comes to health. The majority of men will have some form of prostate cancer in their lifetime, but of course the severity varies greatly.

When I was diagnosed, I had three options for treatment, since watchful waiting was not a viable option for me due to the aggressive nature of my cancer. Therefore, it would be surgery, radiation, and/or chemotherapy. I had several consultations with doctors, including a radiologist and a surgeon. The radiation/chemotherapy involved months of drawn-out therapy, going once a day for weeks on end. That form of treatment didn't appeal to me at all. The surgery carried its own risks, like any surgery does, but was a much faster treatment option. All of the doctors agreed that the best course of action was to have the prostate surgically removed.

My doctors told me it would be a bad idea to wait until after the Olympics at the end of August that year, so we scheduled the surgery immediately and I had it done shortly after the World Cup. I notified the Olympic Team and committee and we all agreed my Chef d'Equipe responsibilities could be done successfully around the surgery because of the short recovery period. I was only in the hospital a few days and it was an easy procedure.

After the World Cup, the riders on the short list rode in the chosen observation shows in North America. For the observation shows in Kentucky, Del Mar, and Devon in early June, I reviewed the shows on tape or watched them live online whenever possible while I recuperated. The Selection Committee met by phone, and I did make it to the Calgary observation show in person. Although I was still getting my strength back, Lizzy Chesson was very helpful to me in making sure I could watch the key horses and riders. Lizzy and I became wonderful friends during my Chef d'Equipe years and she did (and still does) a superior job managing the team. She's a bright, attractive overachiever and we had a lot of fun together. Afterward, the Selection Committee chose the team for London. It worked out, but I'll admit it didn't feel the same. I was concerned the national process didn't put those riders at the same level of preparation as the Super League shows had done for past teams. Rich Fellers just kept on winning after his victory at the World Cup and had earned a very clear spot on the Olympic Team. Beezie Madden and Via Volo rode in two out of the four shows and they were clear in both and earned their way on the team. Laura Kraut also had a bye, but she had a tough round in Devon, made a big mistake, and Cedric didn't make it through the triple. He hit the water and had twelve faults. Unfortunately, incurring twelve faults doesn't get you on Olympic Teams. McLain won the Grand Prix at Devon on Antares F and he was clear in both his shows, which was critical because he had been recovering from the broken leg and really needed to prove that he was sharp and able to compete at that level after the injury.

Reed Kessler had tied with Margie Goldstein-Engle for first place in Palm Beach and her horse went very, very well. Margie's horse had that weak link of banking off the oxers. Reed was very young, but she had great consistent rounds in Kentucky and Devon. Charlie Jayne had a great, veteran horse named Chill R Z who'd been sick, which forced them to miss the trials, but then he rode brilliantly in his first two observation shows. Not only that, he went the extra mile and rode in a third observation show in Calgary and had a great show there too. He really put himself in front of the selectors and earned his way onto the team as our alternate.

Reed Kessler

George has been one of the greatest influences on my riding career. He is so much more than a technically great rider—he has a mastery of the mental qualities one needs to be successful. He taught me that talent is meaningless without twice as much determination and hard work to back it up. I feel so incredibly lucky that I got to work with him at the very end of his tenure as Chef d'Equipe. He was willing to spend all day on someone who was hungry to learn. I can't put into words how thankful I am for the time he spent with me.

We chose the team in mid-June: Rich Fellers on Flexible, Beezie Madden on Via Volo, Reed Kessler on Cylana, McLain Ward on Antares F, and Charlie Jayne and Chill R Z were the alternates (photo 243). The venue and courses were beautiful, and as Great Britain is one of the oldest equestrian cultures, they lived up to their reputation and provided top-notch facilities. One of the most dramatic events at the London Olympics was not riding related, but during one of the jogs.

There's a rule at the Olympics that the jog must occur in the exact listed order, team by team in alphabetical order, and riders must jog their own horses. Naturally, the United States Team was one of the very last to jog. Rich's horse was first of our five horses to jog and if you miss your turn, you are completely disqualified from the Olympic Games. There are absolutely no exceptions. The only way you can miss a jog is if you have an official letter from a doctor that is approved in advance by the ground jury explaining why you're physically unable to jog your horse.

Rich & Shelley Fellers

Rich: I grew up in a tiny town in Oregon and I was hauling in to ride with Joan Kerron Curtin once in a while, growing up. I was about fourteen or fifteen years old when Joan hosted a George Morris clinic and suggested I ride in it, and that was the first time I'd heard about George; I wasn't much of a reader and we were far away from Hunterdon. I remember George being very complimentary of my riding. Thinking back, Joan probably warned him I was a backyard kid and a little rough around the edges but had some talent. George had the effect on me that he has on everyone—he really inspired me to work harder and helped me believe I could succeed. I've ridden in his clinic nearly every single year since then.

Shelley: I rode with George in my very first clinic in 1986, and I even broke my hand on the last day—it didn't matter because I loved it. It's amazing how he gives you confidence. You'll try anything he tells you to try. He's not interested in seeing you do the stuff you're already good at, which is why he challenges you. George pushes you out of your comfort zone, but with confidence, to do things you haven't done before. He pushes you to get better. I always jump at every chance I have to ride with him.

Rich: We see him once a year and he never disappoints with the stuff he sets in the ring. Backward triple bars and big waters. If Shelley set it or I set it, we'd look at each other and say, "Why did you set that? I'm not jumping that!" But when it's George, you don't question it. If he says do it, you don't think, "Oh I can't do that!" Instead, you immediately start thinking about how you'll get it done. Everyone has so much respect for George and when you respect someone that much, you want to please him so badly. That's what brings the teams together when George is Chef d'Equipe and also what inspires our students who ride in his clinics. You want to give him your best.

Shelley: There is no one more respected all over the world in our sport. As Chef d'Equipe, George is very into the details and the discipline. The program we run here at home is modeled after George's program. In 1989, George invited us to come to Florida and ride and help out. He mentored us, trained us, and had me go through the barn with his barn manager to find out how they fed, how they cared for the horses. He did all that and he didn't charge us a penny. He wanted to "up our game," plain and simple. George's system is so good and it has been a huge factor on our whole business and our careers. If you believe in it and you use it, it works. It just makes sense.

Rich: If you're disciplined enough and you're detailed enough to understand it and put his system into action, you will see it work for yourself.

There's one particular story I'll never forget. In London at the Olympics, the jog was in the evening early in the week. Lizzy, our team manager, let us know we would be due up very late in the jog. I was there with Shelley and we had a large clan of family, friends, and a few customers all in London with us. I had worked Flexible earlier that day and there was nothing else to do at the barn, so we talked to Lizzy about timing and knew our team was one of the very last to jog. We decided to walk back to the flat we rented and have a barbecue with the whole clan. I asked Lizzy to text me when it was getting close or if anything changed, so I could get back for the jog.

We walked back to the flat, and we were just settling in and hadn't even started getting the food out and I got a text saying that we were next in the jog. It was about a twenty-minute walk back to the stadium and I had taken my riding boots off and left them in the tack room back at the barn. When I got the text, I just took off running! It was a warm evening and I went running through the streets of London. About half-way there, I got a call from George, who was livid. "RICH, WHERE ARE YOU? Get here NOW!" I ran all the way to the entrance and had to pass through security, which is like an airport security line. I finally made it through, took off running, and all these Olympic pins I had collected flew out of my backpack all over the ground and people were shouting to warn me they had fallen out. I scrambled, picked a few up and then kept sprinting toward the stadium.

I skipped going to the barn for my boots and went straight to the stadium in my breeches and tennis shoes. When I came into the corner of the big Olympic stadium, I had entered on the opposite side from where the jog was being held. George saw me all the way on the other side. It was like he had his voice personally piped into the loudspeakers of the whole stadium as he screamed, "RICH, GET OVER HERE NOWWWW!" I leaped over some ropes and gates and made it just in time to take Flexible's reins for the jog. I had never seen George so upset and I felt horrible. We had a team meeting after the jog and he unloaded on me. I was demoted from anchor rider, but mostly I just hated disappointing George. There's nothing worse. It's funny now when we tell the story, but it definitely wasn't funny then!

One thing I've thought about many times over the years is that George's principles and approach to his program—they apply not just to the sport of show jumping, they apply to life. Like Shelley said, you work on the things you're not good at, you strive to improve yourself. You can't be afraid to fall on your face; you have to keep at it. If you focus on improving the things you don't do as well, you're going to be a better person and be more successful in life.

I almost had a stroke waiting for Rich to show up for that jog. I remember thinking what utter heartbreak it would be if he were to lose his chance to ride in the Olympics. Those fifteen minutes waiting for him were excruciating! At the exact moment the ground jury called for Flexible to be jogged, there was

Rich across the arena, looking around desperately like a bleating sheep. In his breeches, socks, and sneakers, he sprinted across the arena like Usain Bolt himself. He grabbed the bridle and the day was saved by the skin of his teeth. Our relief was unbelievable (photo 244).

The team you bring to the Olympics must have not only seasoned, veteran, great riders but also those rare superstar horses. If you don't have both, you don't have a chance to win a medal—not just gold but *any* medal. In Kentucky at the WEG in 2010, we had rider mistakes even though we had great horses. In London in 2012, it turned out to be the opposite: we had great riders who knew how to win, but we didn't quite have the seasoned horses like we'd had in Athens, Hong Kong, and Barcelona—and it showed. Everybody rode very well but little things kept us out of the medals. McLain got the best out of Antares but the horse wasn't quite as good as we needed him to be. Cylana had a shoeing issue leading up to the games that shortened her stride and put her and Reed off their game a little, as well. And Rich and Flexible were a heartbeat away—just some unlucky rails fell despite them being at the absolute top of their game.

As a team, we placed sixth in London and that's right about where we should've been, given the team we had. Considering that the French and the Germans didn't even get to return for the second round, we didn't fare too badly. Not that sixth was great, but with what we had, a bronze medal would've been all we had a chance for, even if we had a stellar day and everyone outperformed my expectations. Everyone rode well and we earned that sixth place finish.

X. COMING FULL CIRCLE

Ready to return to a role that showcased the work closest to my heart—riding, teaching, and training—I retired as Chef d'Equipe. Even though I would've preferred to end on a more positive note with some Olympic medals in London, I still feel I had a good run! My identity is not tied to the verisimilitude of show jumping results, but rather is represented by my life's work and my efforts in helping all riders, not only the championship teams. What we had with Bert de Némethy with the USET and the early Gladstone years was a different era. The great advantages of having everyone coordinated, stabled, and training together in a cavalry atmosphere is so appealing to me, even while I personally had my ups and downs when I rode with Bert myself as a young man. Rules, discipline, regimentation, and consistent long-term planning were simply how I was brought up with horses. While we have certainly gained some advantages and improvements on the old system, I do think something has been lost with all the change in our sport.

Across the board in this country, professionals are very wrapped up in their local scene and are too specialized. Most professionals today don't have the vision to connect their business on a local level to our country's bigger goals in the sport. They try to earn the little bit of profit that is possible to make in their business, and I realize how difficult it is to punch out of the local scene and take clients up to a national and international level.

After Hong Kong, I had hoped our success was going to inject the country with ambition and work ethic. As the years ticked by, I started to become disillusioned with what the country could bring to the party. Half of the big horse owners here choose to own horses for riders outside of the United States, and frankly, I can understand the attraction. Those riders hustle and they will ride anything; they earn their owners' support with their ambition!

There is a void in this country waiting to be filled with ambitious riders. The United States should have the ability to field three medal-quality teams for every big championship. We will continue to have great moments; after all, we have a great system and foundation of horsemanship in this nation. Wonderful teachers grew up, as I did, with quality American horsemanship and those teachers will produce some fabulous riders who will have an opportunity to form special partnerships with truly great horses. As Americans, I know we're already on the path to have moments of brilliance. However, if we continue as we are now, we'll always be part of the crowd. To achieve a streak of dominance again won't be easy now that nations with vast riches have entered the arena. With some of the unlimited budgets we now see, those owners can practically buy their medals! For the more prudent American investors, buying a horse has to make sense: they can't take the risk and pay $10 million for a horse.

We had a short window of absolute domination with the U.S. Show Jumping Team but it's not easy to keep up with Europe, with their wealth of historic sport-horse breeding and incredibly wonderful horse shows. After all, they invented the sport! To match or exceed their results, we as a country must have a perfect recipe of investment and hard work and talent. It's heartbreaking for me to see how much the standards have fallen in our sport in recent years. I see it in how riders are turned out, how they jump their horses, how they use gimmicks to take shortcuts. We all must take responsibility to raise these standards because it's only perseverance and attention to those details, every day, that will result in another era of dominance for our show jumping team.

It is absolutely possible to achieve—after all, we have done it before—and we gave the Europeans a kick in the pants in the eighties when they were forced to raise their game! I wholly believe that even with the changes in our sport since then, we are capable of being that dominant again. It won't be done by thinking about it or talking about it. Enough horsemen and -women in our industry must strain to reach that level and devote themselves with a renewed fervor for it to come to fruition.

I was delighted to pass the torch to Robert Ridland because he has a wonderful homegrown background. Not only does he have a fantastic personable nature, but he's a great teacher and a fabulous rider. Riding as a junior with Jimmy Williams, Robert received that same wonderful foundation of classical horsemanship that I grew up with. As a young man, he also experienced the leadership and teaching of Bert de Némethy on the USET. He's one of the last lucky people to experience Bert's era at Gladstone and Frank Chapot's tenure, in addition to my own. That experience gives him invaluable perspective on the old guard of the USET and the roots of our sport's history in this country. Robert has contributed on FEI committees, managed big championship shows, and built great courses over the years—it was a beautiful transition and Robert hit the ground running, having marvelous success with Beezie Madden winning the World Cup in Gothenberg, Sweden in 2013. He's also realized how difficult it can be to stay on top, when in Barcelona the American team didn't make the cut for the top eight. Like all Chefs d'Equipe, he'll have ups and downs, but I have so much confidence in Robert and he's great for our sport and our country (photo 250).

Robert Ridland

I was so fortunate to be able to look over George's shoulder during the year of the London Olympics. I went with George to the selection trials and the Olympics themselves and he was so unbelievably supportive during the transition. Perspective is absolutely an asset when you're Chef d'Equipe and I've been fortunate to be in the sport long enough to experience the old guard of the USET in the 1970s. I learned the fundamentals from Jimmy Williams and was fortunate to be the youngest rider on the European USET squads with Bill Steinkraus, Frank Chapot, Kathy Kusner, and Neal Shapiro. I was the youngest by far at nineteen years old and the reserve rider in '72 in Munich, which was an invaluable experience. I had been riding at Gladstone for three years and had learned from Bert de Némethy and those fellow team riders. Back then, the whole structure was different, and it was the very end of the amateur era. Owners would donate or loan horses to the team and send them to Gladstone, the riders were selected separately, and Bert would match up riders and horses. There was a hierarchy, too. I was the rookie, so when we got to Europe, I drove the VW bus and carried the suitcases. It was unbelievable to be able to learn from them and experience that system. A few short years later, the professional era began and we all had owners. It was amazing how it changed in the period of four years. That kickstarted the unbelievable decade of the eighties when a group of our riders completely dominated—winning so many World Cup Finals and the Olympic gold in '84.

George is the greatest teacher worldwide in our sport, ever. He's been able to span decades of evolution and in many cases, he has led the changes. And this is not history—George is out there, right now, still educating. What he's doing with riders all over the country is exactly what he's always done. George brings with him, through the decades of the sport evolving, those same classical concepts from Gordon Wright and Bert de Némethy and makes them relevant. Those concepts are the foundation of everything we do. We heard about the flatwork from Jimmy and Bert, but somehow, George has always made it more relevant to students, and that's what great teachers do. If you have talent in any sport, there are always ways to shortcut the basics. But if you have a teacher who makes it so relevant that it becomes apparent why you *shouldn't* take those shortcuts, you're going to learn a lot more—simple as that. Great teachers like George are able to use the perspective of the student, more so than the perspective of the teacher. I would venture to say that George is more at the top of his game than ever before and just keeps getting better.

What George did in that decade of total dominance was he connected with those kids in the seventies and got through to them and that helped feed that dominant 1980s group of riders. We all witnessed how great that generation was, and they were so strong that they stayed at the top for many years afterward, which eventually left a void. In subsequent years, the nineties in particular, those same riders were monopolizing the top horses provided by the big owners. That happens in any sport; it's hard to break up a team when things are going well. But at some point, you end up with a lot of aging athletes. As coach, I want to make sure we never do that again. The next generation needs to be brought along just as our current generation is on top. It's a natural flipside of success. When things are going well, you have to remember to play for the future or you'll fall behind. The British team fell into the same trap; there was a group of them who dominated the sport for a long time and then all of a sudden, they realized they were behind and had to make a conscious effort to recover. They did so and have had the revival we've seen them have in the sport.

There is a way to win with your top teams and still give the next generation the experience they need. George is very aware of this need to prioritize balancing the next generation with wanting to win now. We are partners in this effort, with George working hard to educate young, talented riders and I stand ready to help provide opportunities for the next generation to get experience. The goal is to give as many riders as we can the opportunity to ride on Nations Cup teams while maintaining great results and not compromising our chances.

In the first year of my new teaching schedule, I kept up my tradition of traveling to Australia and New Zealand for the month of January to break up the slower winter season. I simply couldn't sit in Wellington with the circuit going on for the entire winter with no stable of my own to manage. When I returned in early 2013, I was sought out by a few different owners or riders who asked for help. One was Jane Clark, who after searching for some time for the right rider, asked Ben Maher to ride her horses. Since I had ridden Jane's horses, she asked me to work with Ben to oversee some of their operations.

Christine McCrae, who has always been a beautiful rider, asked for some help as well. I was only too happy to give it. Doda de Miranda and his wife Athina Onassis also approached me for some coaching and guidance, for Athina in particular, who wanted some regular lessons (photo 251). Suddenly I found myself helping four world-class Grand Prix riders. Friends were happy to see me back in a teaching role at the shows and it felt great to be there. All three of them had a fantastic Florida circuit that year; Chrissy won class after big class and Ben had an incredibly successful circuit. When all was said and done, the final Grand Prix of the circuit resulted in Doda first, Ben second, and Athina third—not bad!

I had great fun and success with those four riders. But I learned a good lesson from the experience of teaching them, which is that I have a hard time being in a lesser "consultant" role with the older, more established riders. I could sense in some cases that they didn't welcome or feel they would benefit from my training. They have their own system worked out and they don't want rigid, classical flat lessons. That's not always the case with the riders I know:

Beezie Madden and Rich Fellers, for example, are both very receptive to getting basic flatwork and gymnastic instruction from me.

Andrew Ramsay

I first met George when I was about ten years old, and he was teaching a clinic at Sutton Place in Morgan Hill, California. I can remember few details of the lessons with the exception of the complete attention, focus, and effort given by his students. Recently, some twenty years after our first meeting, I have been fortunate to work closely with him. I feel as though I have come to understand why he constantly receives that focus and effort: George is a remarkable human being and horseman. His knowledge and experience is matched by his ambition. At an age when many would be well into their retirement, he continues to pursue his passion without falter, teaching and working to make a difference in individual horsemen and the equestrian community as a whole.

As a teacher, it's not enough for me to be limited to being only a coach and going to the ring with a rider. I want to be involved in a holistic way and give everything I'm able to. When I went to Europe to help some clients at shows, I was relegated to simply walking the course and giving a few words of support at the in-gate. As kindly as I was treated, it seemed a waste to put me on a pedestal in the corner. In frustration, I left and came home early. Being limited to being a ground man and a sounding board is just not what I'm interested in. If I'm going to help someone show, I want to be involved in everything—with the day-to-day training, the horses, the management, the flatwork, the vet and farrier. It doesn't mean I make those decisions for them, but simply being brought into the loop, to assess the whole picture with the perspective I have and figure out where I can help. When you experience a system that works for so many years, just being a ground man at the shows feels like painting a picture with only one color.

From time to time at clinics, I spot young riders who pique my interest and I keep an eye on them. If I see rare young talents with the ambition to match, I will occasionally try to put them in a better position to be successful. Some could use a lot of help, and others might just benefit from a little. I saw a boy ride in Buffalo named Oakley Clark; he's from Vermont and despite his rough-and-tumble turnout, Jennifer Alfano and I both saw something special in how he rides. I immediately invited him to be my demonstrator in my next clinic in Providence, Rhode Island. He drove down and rode ten or twelve horses in that clinic, each one better than the last. I could see how all the spectators and girls loved him! You know, it's not just about riding talent and the picture you make. It's about your personality and your ability to withstand the pressure of show jumping. He has charisma and owners like him and want to support him. I have a feeling he just might be able to go the distance.

Of course, you never know for sure. It's just like horses. I never thought Melanie Smith Taylor and Norman Dello Joio would reach the heights that they did. With Conrad Homfeld and Buddy Brown, I knew it all along. With Oakley, if I see that he's ambitious and committed as I am, then he'll have my support. Tori Colvin is perhaps the most exciting young rider to watch in America right now. Even though I met her mother Brigid back at the 1995 Pan American Games, I've had the great pleasure of getting to know the Colvins and helping Tori a little bit in recent years. I owe it to my old Studio 54 partner in crime Betsee Parker, who had the wisdom to recommend to Scott Stewart that I help Tori prepare for the equitation. I give Betsee all the credit for insisting on bringing me in on a supplementary teacher basis.

I have never—in all my years—seen a young rider with such natural, soft ability. Her sympathetic and intelligent ride on any horse is incredible to watch. On course, Tori's horses melt into any distance that shows up; her skill and softness always make it look beautiful. The level of empathy in her ability is staggering—she's part horse! It's a gift from God, like it always is with riders like Tori. But even those natural talents need education. Coming from a horse family background, she has been supported by wonderful teachers and owners along the way—there's no doubt Tori will exit her junior years as the most successful young rider our country has ever seen (photos 254, 255).

Victoria Colvin

The first time I crossed paths with George was actually a very funny experience. It was at Boston Market and George was standing in line in front of my mom and me. He turned around to say hello and said to me, "I know you—and not just because you win blue ribbons. I've heard a lot about you." It made my day to hear that he'd watched me ride and noticed me. My mom was floored. After that meeting, we set up some riding lessons.

George is a very unique trainer and nothing ever goes unnoticed. He doesn't miss anything. If your outside heel isn't all the way down, he would notice—he must have X-ray vision! He goes back to basics and has taught me so much about flatwork that I feel like I could even compete in dressage someday. When George rides your horse for you, it is amazing to watch what he does and how he reacts with your horse. I ride a horse named Clearway in the equitation and his lead changes were not the best. Since I had some lessons on him with George, they've improved drastically, and I now know the proper way to ask for changes.

When I had my first lesson with George, my mother and everyone at the barn was freaking before he got there. For me, I didn't really know better. When he came in, he greeted everyone warmly with hugs or kisses on the cheek, but when he came up to me I didn't want a hug. Not to be rude, but I just didn't personally know him yet. My mother was kind of horrified that I'd snubbed George Morris! But I loved his response that day. He said, "In due time, you'll learn to respect and love me." And he was right. Now I can hug him because it means something. I even give him kisses on the cheek!

Education has always been my passion and it was a natural transition after my retirement from Chef d'Equipe to turn my attention to teaching. I remained closely involved with the Federation on the Young Rider program and special clinics like the Horsemastership Clinic around Christmastime. I never get tired of riding or teaching, even after all these years. My voice sometimes tires, but my mind never does. Picking up additional clinics to fill in the gaps was more attractive to me than putting my feet up at home. I'm always happier working, staying current with the sport, and doing what I can to help those ambitious, talented young riders who seek my help. A life on the road can be tiring, but at nearly every place I teach, I also renew old friendships and meet the next generation of great riders.

One of the things I most enjoy is meeting young people in the sport who have the desire to learn and the patience to develop a correct system without shortcuts. If I see someone who is ready to work and learn, I will always try to share my time and knowledge. I only recently met a young professional by chance at a clinic, but was impressed by his enthusiasm and invited him to demonstrate at clinics for me. Noel Clark, based in Alberta, Canada, was on the long list for the Canadian three-day eventing team in 2006 and has the kind of thoughtful, ambitious attitude that catches my attention.

Noel Clark

Many have asked how I was fortunate enough to have the opportunity to be a demonstration rider for George. The answer is that I was in the right place at the right time and that I stuck my neck out! George was a guest instructor at the 2013 Mane Event in Red Deer, Alberta. As he always does, he was going to ride a horse in one of his sessions and needed a leg up. I jumped out of the stands and offered my assistance. Apparently, I gave a good leg up, because he turned and asked what I charge. I, somewhat jokingly, replied, "Let me be your official leg-up guy." He replied, "That's what I hoped you would say." In return, he gave me an incredible leg up of his own and asked me to join him on a clinic tour.

I would have to say that the most significant message I will take away from the experience is to always stay committed to doing what is best for the horse—to always ensure that how I'm riding, what I'm asking of the horse, and what method I use to train always has the horse's welfare as the first priority. This doesn't mean always being soft but rather knowing when to be hard, and more importantly, knowing when to be soft. Being certain that I understand why I'm doing something with a horse and how it affects him mentally and physically to achieve my goals. I can't count how many times I heard George say that this is based on true classical principals and true classical riding. I walked away from my time with George being committed to furthering my knowledge and understanding of the horse, applying these methods as best I can, and passing on what I have learned to as many others as I can.

My life with horses has come full circle. I got into this sport for riding and it will always be my first love. Teaching, on the other hand, is like walking a familiar road with many stops along the way, where new things can always be discovered. I've been teaching clinics since 1962 and thoroughly enjoy my clinic tour each year, but since retiring as Chef d'Equipe, I'm also working with a few select clients. This revival of one-on-one work with riders is a throwback to my Hunterdon days, and it's exciting to bring riders to the in-gate. I'm doing what I've always done—it's back to the future! With all the decades of horses behind me, from the Ox Ridge Hunt Club to ringside at a Winter Equestrian Festival Grand Prix, I'm still reading and learning about horsemanship. If only I had seventy more years ahead of me to learn twice what I know now! My understanding of the depth and intricacy of the relationship between horse and rider is always growing, as is my awareness of my own self.

APPENDICES

What follows are chronological lists of the AHSA Hunt Seat Medal and ASPCA Maclay Champions (1950–1980), as well as the individuals and teams that represented the United States in show jumping at the four major international championships: the Olympic Games, the World Championships/World Equestrian Games, the Pan American Games, and the FEI World Cup Finals (dates included up to the time of writing).

AHSA MEDAL & ASPCA MACLAY
CHAMPIONS (1950–1980)

AHSA (USEF) Medal Finals	ASPCA Maclay Finals
1950 Ronnie Mutch[1]	1950 Mary Gay Huffard
1951 Victor Hugo-Vidal	1951 G. Baker Schroeder, Jr.
1952 George H. Morris	**1952 George H. Morris**
1953 Cynthia A. Stone	1953 Glenna Lee Maduro
1954 Margaret McGinn	1954 Ronnie Martini
1955 Wilson Dennehy	1955 Wilson Dennehy
1956 Michael Page	1956 Barbara Friedemann
1957 Michael Del Balso	1957 J. Michael Plumb
1958 Susan White	1958 Wendy Hanson
1959 Wendy Hanson	1959 Hank Minchin
1960 Mary Mairs	1960 Mary Mairs
1961 Bernie Traurig	1961 Bernie Traurig
1962 Carol Altman	1962 Carol Altman
1963 Stephanie Steck	1963 Wendy Mairs
1964 Jimmy Kohn	1964 Lane Shultz
1965 Chrystine Jones	1965 Chrystine Jones
1966 Rita Timpanaro[2]	1966 Debbie Wilson-Jenkins
1967 Conrad Homfeld[3]	**1967 Conrad Homfeld**
1968 Brooke Hodgson[4]	**1968 Brooke Hodgson**
1969 Fred Bauer	**1969 Katie Monahan**
1970 James Hulick	**1970 Fred Bauer**
1971 Joy Slater	**1971 Anna Jane White**
1972 Katie Monahan	**1972 Leslie Burr**
1973 Buddy Brown	1973 Michael Patrick
1974 Robin Ann Rost	1974 Alex Dunaif
1975 Cynthia Hankins	**1975 Katharine Burdsall**
1976 Frances Steinwedell	**1976 Colette Lozins**
1977 Elizabeth Sheehan	**1977 Frances Steinwedell**
1978 Hugh Mutch	**1978 Michael Sasso**
1979 Mark Leone	**1979 Gary Young**
1980 Joan Scharffenberger	1980 Laura Tidball

Note: Names in **bold face** type indicate students of George H. Morris

[1] 1950: AHSA Medal Finals held at Madison Square Garden for the first time.
[2] 1966: AHSA Medal Finals held in Washington, D.C.
[3] 1967: AHSA Medals Finals held in Bloomfield Hills, Michigan.
[4] 1968: AHSA Medal Finals held in Harrisburg, Pennsylvania for the first time.

OLYMPIC GAMES
U.S. SHOW JUMPING MEDALISTS (1956–2012)

	Individual Results	Team Results
1956 Melbourne, Australia Chef d'Equipe: Bertalan de Némethy	No U.S. Medals	**5th Place:** Hugh Wiley on *Trail Guide* William Steinkraus on *Night Owl* Frank Chapot on *Belair*
1960 Rome, Italy Chef d'Equipe: Bertalan de Némethy	No U.S. Medals **4th Place:** George H. Morris on *Sinjon*	**Silver Medal:** George H. Morris on *Sinjon* Hugh Wiley on *Master William* Frank Chapot on *Trail Guide* William Steinkraus on *Riviera Wonder/Ksar d'Esprit*
1964 Tokyo, Japan Chef d'Equipe: Bertalan de Némethy	No U.S. Medals	**6th Place:** Frank Chapot on *San Lucas* Kathy Kusner on *Untouchable* Mary Mairs on *Tomboy*
1968 Mexico City, Mexico Chef d'Equipe: Bertalan de Némethy	**Gold Medal:** William Steinkraus on *Snowbound*	**4th Place:** William Steinkraus on *Snowbound* Frank Chapot on *San Lucas* Kathy Kusner on *Untouchable* Mary (Mairs) Chapot on *White Lightning*
1972 Munich, Germany Chef d'Equipe: Bertalan de Némethy	**Bronze Medal:** Neal Shapiro on *Sloopy*	**Silver Medal:** Neal Shapiro on *Sloopy* Kathy Kusner on *Fleet Apple* William Steinkraus on *Snowbound/Main Spring* Frank Chapot on *White Lightning*
1976 Montreal, Canada Chef d'Equipe: Bertalan de Némethy	No U.S. Medals	**4th Place:** Frank Chapot on *Viscount* Dennis Murphy on *Do Right* Buddy Brown on *A Little Bit/Sandsablaze* Robert Ridland on *South Side* Michael Matz on *Grande*
1980 Rotterdam, The Netherlands *(Alternate Olympics)* Chef d'Equipe: Bertalan de Némethy	**Bronze Medal:** Melanie Smith on *Calypso*	**5th Place:** Melanie Smith on *Calypso* Terry Rudd on *Semi Tough* Norman Dello Joio on *Allegro* Katie Monahan on *Silver Exchange*
1984 Los Angeles, U.S. Chef d'Equipe: Frank Chapot	**Gold Medal:** Joe Fargis on *Touch of Class* **Silver Medal:** Conrad Homfeld on *Abdullah*	**Gold Medal:** Joe Fargis on *Touch of Class* Conrad Homfeld on *Abdullah* Melanie Smith on *Calypso* Leslie Burr on *Albany*
1988 Seoul, South Korea Chef d'Equipe: Frank Chapot	**Silver Medal:** Greg Best on *Gem Twist*	**Silver Medal:** Greg Best on *Gem Twist* Anne Kursinski on *Starman* Joe Fargis on *Mill Pearl* Lisa Jacquin on *For the Moment*
1992 Barcelona, Spain Chef d'Equipe: Frank Chapot	**Bronze Medal:** Norman Dello Joio on *Irish*	**5th Place:** Norman Dello Joio on *Irish* Lisa Jacquin on *For the Moment* Anne Kursinski on *Cannonball* Michael Matz on *Heisman*
1996 Atlanta, United States Chefs d'Equipe: Frank Chapot & George H. Morris	No U.S. Medals	**Silver Medal:** Peter Leone on *Legato* Leslie Burr Howard on *Extreme* Anne Kursinski on *Eros* Michael Matz on *Rhum IV*
2000 Sydney, Australia Chefs d'Equipe: Frank Chapot & George H. Morris	No U.S. Medals	**6th Place:** Laura Kraut on *Liberty* Lauren Hough on *Clasiko* Nona Garson on *Rhythmical* Margie Goldstein-Engle on *Hidden Creek's Perin*
2004 Athens, Greece Chef d'Equipe: Frank Chapot	**Silver Medal:** Chris Kappler on *Royal Kaliber*	**Silver Medal:** Chris Kappler on *Royal Kaliber* Beezie Madden on *Authentic* Peter Wylde on *Fein Cera* McLain Ward on *Sapphire*

		Individual Results	Team Results
2008	**Beijing, China** **Chef d'Equipe:** George H. Morris	**Bronze Medal:** Beezie Madden on *Authentic*	**Gold Medal:** Laura Kraut on *Cedric* Beezie Madden on *Authentic* Will Simpson on *Carlsson Vom Dach* McLain Ward on *Sapphire*
2012	**London, England** **Chef d'Equipe:** George H. Morris	No U.S. Medals	**6th Place:** Rich Fellers on *Flexible* Beezie Madden on *Via Volo* Reed Kessler on *Cylana* McLain Ward on *Antares F*

WORLD CHAMPIONSHIPS/WORLD EQUESTRIAN GAMES U.S. SHOW JUMPING MEDALISTS (1956–2014)

		Individual Results	Team Results
1956	**Aachen, Germany**	No U.S. Medals **5th Place:** William Steinkraus on *Night Owl and First Boy*	Team scoring began in 1978
1960	**Venice, Italy**	No U.S. Medals **4th Place:** William Steinkraus on *Ksar d'Esprit* **10th Place:** George H. Morris on *Sinjon*	
1966	**Buenos Aires, Argentina**	No U.S. Medals	
1970	**La Baule, France**	No U.S. Medals	
1974	**Hickstead, England**	**Bronze Medal:** Frank Chapot on *Main Spring*	
1978	**Aachen, Germany**	**Bronze Medal:** Michael Matz on *Jet Run*	**Bronze Medal:** Conrad Homfeld on *Balbuco* Denis Murphy on *Tuscaloosa* Buddy Brown on *Viscount* Michael Matz on *Jet Run*
1982	**Dublin, Ireland**	No U.S. Medals	**4th Place:** Peter Leone on *Ardennes* Melanie Smith Taylor on *Calypso* Michael Matz on *Jet Run* Bernie Traurig on *Eaden Vale*
1986	**Aachen, Germany**	**Silver Medal:** Conrad Homfeld on *Abdullah*	**Gold Medal:** Michael Matz on *Chef* Conrad Homfeld on *Abdullah* Katie Monahan on *Amadia* Katharine Burdsall on *The Natural*
1990	**Stockholm, Sweden**	**4th Place:** Greg Best on *Gem Twist*	**4th Place:** Greg Best on *Gem Twist* Joe Fargis on *Mill Pearl* Anne Kursinski on *Starman* Joan Scharffenberger on *Victor*
1994	**The Hague, The Netherlands**	No U.S. Medals	**5th Place:** Tim Grubb on *Elan Denizen* Leslie Howard on *Charisma* Susan Hutchison on *Samsung Woodstock* Patti Stovel on *Mont Cenis*
1998	**Rome, Italy**	No U.S. Medals	**9th Place:** Alison Firestone on *Major* Nona Garson on *Rhythmical* Eric Hasbrouck on *Freestyle* Anne Kursinski on *Eros*

Continued

WORLD CHAMPIONSHIPS/WORLD EQUESTRIAN GAMES
U.S. SHOW JUMPING MEDALISTS (1956–2014)

		Individual Results	Team Results
2002	Jerez de la Frontera, Spain	**Bronze Medal:** Peter Wylde on *Fein Cera*	**6th Place:** Leslie Howard on *Priobert de Kalvarie* Beezie Madden on *Judgement* Nicole Simpson on *El Campeon's Cirka Z* Peter Wylde on *Fein Cera*
2006	Aachen, Germany	**Silver Medal:** Beezie Madden on *Authentic*	**Silver Medal:** Margie Goldstein-Engle on *Quervo Gold* Laura Kraut on *Miss Independent* McLain Ward on *Sapphire* Beezie Madden on *Authentic*
2010	Kentucky, United States	No U.S. Medals	**10th Place:** Laura Kraut on *Cedric* Lauren Hough on *Quick Study* Mario Deslauriers on *Urico* McLain Ward on *Sapphire*
2014	Normandy, France	**Bronze Medal:** Beezie Madden on *Cortes 'C'*	**Bronze Medal:** McLain Ward on *Rothchild* Kent Farrington on *Voyeur* Lucy Davis on *Barron* Beezie Madden on *Cortes 'C'*

PAN AMERICAN GAMES
U.S. SHOW JUMPING MEDALISTS (1959–2015)

		Individual Results	Team Results
1959	Chicago, United States	No Individual Scoring in 1959	**Gold Medal:** George H. Morris on *Night Owl* Frank Chapot on *Diamant* Hugh Wiley on *Nautical* William Steinkraus on *Riviera Wonder*
1963	Sao Paulo, Brazil	**Gold Medal:** Mary Mairs on *Tomboy* **4th Place:** Frank Chapot on *San Lucas*	**Gold Medal:** Mary Mairs on *Tomboy* Frank Chapot on *San Lucas* Kathy Kusner on *Unusual* William Steinkraus on *Sinjon*
1967	Winnipeg, Canada	No U.S. Medals **5th Place:** Kathy Kusner on *Untouchable*	**Silver Medal:** Kathy Kusner on *Untouchable* Mary Chapot on *White Lightning* Frank Chapot on *San Lucas* William Steinkraus on *Sinjon*
1971	Cali, Colombia	U.S. Team did not compete due to Venezuelan Equine Encephalitis	
1975	Mexico City, Mexico	**Gold Medal:** Buddy Brown on *A Little Bit* **Silver Medal:** Michael Matz on *Grande*	**Gold Medal:** Michael Matz on *Grande* Denis Murphy on *Do Right* Joe Fargis on *Caesar* Buddy Brown on *A Little Bit / Sandsablaze*
1979	San Juan, Puerto Rico	**Gold Medal:** Michael Matz on *Jet Run*	**Gold Medal:** Norman Dello Joio on *Allegro* Buddy Brown on *Sandsablaze* Michael Matz on *Jet Run* Melanie Smith on *Val de Loire*
1983	Caracas, Venezuela	**Gold Medal:** Anne Kursinski on *Livius* **Bronze Medal:** Michael Matz on *Chef*	**Gold Medal:** Michael Matz on *Chef* Leslie Burr Howard on *Boing* Donald Cheska on *Southside* Anne Kursinski on *Livius*
1987	Indianapolis, U.S.	**Silver Medal:** Rodney Jenkins on *Czar*	**Silver Medal:** Greg Best on *Gem Twist* Rodney Jenkins on *Czar* Lisa Jacquin on *For the Moment* Katharine Burdsall on *The Natural*

		Individual Results	Team Results
1991	Havana, Cuba	No U.S. Medals	**Bronze Medal:** Debbie Shaffner on *Poor Richard* Andre Dignelli on *Gaelic* D.D. Alexander on *Bon Retour* Richard Fellers on *El Mirasol*
1995	Buenos Aires, Argentina	**Gold Medal:** Michael Matz on *The General* ★	**Bronze Medal:** Michael Matz on *The General* D.D. Alexander-Matz on *Tashiling* Nona Garson on *Derrek* Debbie Stephens on *Blind Date*
1999	Winnipeg, Canada	**Silver Medal:** Peter Wylde on *Macanudo De Niro*	**Silver Medal:** Alison Firestone on *Arnica de la Barre* Leslie Burr Howard on *Clover Leaf* Margie Goldstein-Engle on *Hidden Creek's Alvaretto* Peter Wylde on *Macanudo De Niro*

2003	Santo Domingo, Dominican Republic	**Silver Medal:**
		Chris Kappler on *Royal Kaliber*
		Bronze Medal:
		Margie Goldstein-Engle
		  on *Hidden Creek's Perin*
			Gold Medal:
			Margie Goldstein-Engle
			  on *Hidden Creek's Perin*
			Lauren Hough on *Windy City*
			Beezie Madden on *Conquest II*
			Chris Kappler on *Royal Kaliber*

2007	Rio de Janeiro, Brazil	No U.S. Medals	**Bronze Medal:** Lauren Hough on *Casadora* Laura Chapot on *Little Big Man* Cara Raether on *Ublesco* Todd Minikus on *Pavarotti*

2011	Guadalajara, Mexico	**Gold Medal:**
		Christine McCrae
		  on *Romantovich Take One*
		Silver Medal:
		Beezie Madden
		  on *Coral Reef Via Volo*
			Gold Medal:
			Christine McCrae on *Romantovich Take One*
			Beezie Madden on *Coral Reef Via Volo*
			McLain Ward on *Antares F*
			Kent Farrington on *Uceko*

2015	Toronto, Canada	**Gold Medal:** McLain Ward on *Rothchild* **Bronze Medal:** Lauren Hough on *Ohlala*	**Gold Medal:** Georgina Bloomberg on *Lilli* Kent Farrington on *Gazelle* Lauren Hough on *Ohlala* McLain Ward on *Rothchild*

★ *Bronze Medal: Luis Ximenez of Mexico, a student of George H. Morris*

FEI WORLD CUP FINALS: TOP RESULTS FOR NORTH AMERICAN SHOW JUMPING (1979–2015)

		North American Individual Placings
1979	Gothenburg, Sweden	2. Katie Monahan on *The Jones Boy* 3. (tie) Norman Dello Joio on *Allegro*
1980	Baltimore, United States	1. Conrad Homfeld on *Balbuco* 2. Melanie Smith on *Calypso*
1981	Birmingham, England	1. Michael Matz on *Jet Run* 2. Donald Cheska on *Southside*
1982	Gothenburg, Sweden	1. Melanie Smith on *Calypso*
1983	Vienna, Austria	1. Norman Dello Joio on *I Love You* 3. Melanie Smith on *Calypso*
1984	Gothenburg, Sweden	1. Mario Deslauriers on *Aramis*★ 2. (tie) Norman Dello Joio on *I Love You*
1985	Berlin, Germany	1. Conrad Homfeld on *Abdullah*
1986	Gothenburg, Sweden	1. Leslie Burr Lenehan on *McLain* 2. Ian Millar on *Big Ben*★ 3. Conrad Homfeld on *Maybe*

Continued

FEI WORLD CUP FINALS: TOP RESULTS FOR
NORTH AMERICAN SHOW JUMPING (1979–2015)

		North American Individual Placings
1987	Paris, France	1. Katharine Burdsall on *The Natural* 3. Lisa Jacquin on *For the Moment*
1988	Gothenburg, Sweden	1. Ian Millar on *Big Ben*★
1989	Tampa, United States	1. Ian Millar on *Big Ben*★ 3. George Lindemann on *Jupiter*
1990	Dortmund, Germany	None
1991	Gothenburg, Sweden	None
1992	Del Mar, United States	5. Bernie Traurig on *Maybe Forever*
1993	Gothenburg, Sweden	3. Michael Matz on *Rhum IV* 4. Susan Hutchison on *Samsung Woodstock* 5. Beezie Patton on *Ping Pong / French Rapture*
1994	's-Hertogenbosch, The Netherlands	None
1995	Gothenburg, Sweden	None
1996	Geneva, Switzerland	None
1997	Gothenburg, Sweden	5. Anne Kursinski on *Eros*
1998	Helsinki, Finland	4. Richard Spooner on *Cosino* 6. (tie) Margie Goldstein-Engle on *Hidden Creek's Alvaretto* 6. (tie) Leslie Burr Howard on *S'Blieft*
1999	Gothenburg, Sweden	None
2000	Las Vegas, United States	None
2001	Gothenburg, Sweden	5. Candice King on *John Em* 6. (tie) Leslie Burr Howard on *Priobert de Kalvarie* 6. (tie) Peter Wylde on *Fein Cera*
2002	Leipzig, Germany	4. (tie) McLain Ward on *Viktor* 4. (tie) Leslie Burr Howard on *Priobert de Kalvarie*
2003	Las Vegas, United States	5. (tie) Laura Kraut on *Anthem*
2004	Milan, Italy	None
2005	Las Vegas, United States	5. Kimberly Frey on *Marlou*
2006	Kuala Lampur, Malaysia	None
2007	Las Vegas, United States	8. (tie) McLain Ward on *Sapphire*
2008	Gothenburg, Sweden	2. Rich Fellers on *Flexible* 7. (tie) Peter Wylde on *Esplanade*
2009	Las Vegas, United States	2. McLain Ward on *Sapphire*
2010	Le Grand-Saconnex, Switzerland	None
2011	Leipzig, Germany	2. Eric Lamaze on *Hickstead*★ 4. (tie) Beezie Madden on *Danny Boy / Coral Reef Via Volo* 10. McLain Ward on *Rothchild & Antares F*
2012	's-Hertogenbosch, The Netherlands	1. Rich Fellers on *Flexible*
2013	Gothenburg, Sweden	1. Beezie Madden on *Simon* 5. McLain Ward on *Super Trooper de Ness* 10. Reed Kessler on *Cylana*
2014	Lyon, France	7. (tie) Beezie Madden on *Simon* 9. McLain Ward on *HH Carlos Z / Rothchild* 10. Charlie Jayne on *Chill RZ*
2015	Las Vegas, United States	4. Beezie Madden on *Simon* 9. Lucy Davis on *Barron*

Note: North American results beyond 3rd place noted beginning with 1992 World Cup Finals

★ *Represented Canada*

INDEX

Page numbers in **bold** indicate commentary passages written by the named individual. Numbers for photo plates, noted in *italics*, correspond to image numbers in the photo insert pages.

Morris Rattl[e]
During Ethe[l]

Tomorrow

$\forall$ hm
and a w
my love
hope
Hammer.
love,
Geor

OLDS HORSEMANSHIP CLINIC. George Morris, of New Canaan, [mem]ber of the [Unit]ed States Olympic equestrian team, gives instructions to Eilleen Gilmore, [stude]nt, yester[day] at the Tyrrell Park Riding Ring, in connection with a two-weeks clinic on horsemanship con[duct]ed by himself at the Tyrrell Park Riding Club. Above, Miss Gilmore is negotiating a jump on [her] mount, Hootch, which is owned by the Tyrrell Park stables. (Enterprise Photo by Bob Ward)

Horsemanship Clinic
Conducted at Tyrrell

A clinic for [junior] ho[rseman]ship is [being conduc]ted [at] the Tyrrel[l] [Club unde]r, G[eorge]

national honors, including the

Morris Horse Show Veteran at 20

New York Journal-American ★ ★ Thurs, Nov. 6, 1958-31